The First Steps in Seeing

The First Steps in Seeing

R. W. Rodieck

Bishop Professor
The University of Washington

Sinauer Associates, Inc. • Publishers
Sunderland, Massachusetts

Cover foreground photograph: © A. & M. Shah/Animals Animals
Cover background photograph: courtesy of Dennis M. Dacey

The First Steps in Seeing

Library of Congress Cataloging-in-Publication Data

Rodieck, Robert W.
        The first steps in seeing / Robert W. Rodieck.
                p.   cm.
        Includes bibliographical references and index.
        ISBN 0-87893-757-9 (cloth)
        1. Vision,   2. Eye—Physiology.   I. Title.
QP475.R49 1998
612.8'4—dc21   98-3963
                                                CIP

Printed in U.S.A.

9 8 7 6 5 4 3 2 1

Brief Contents

Contents

Preface

This book is about the eyes—how they capture an image and convert it to neural messages that ultimately result in visual experience. An appreciation of how the eyes work is rooted in diverse areas of science—optics, photochemistry, biochemistry, cellular biology, neurobiology, molecular biology, psychophysics, psychology, and evolutionary biology. This gives the study of vision a rich mixture of breadth and depth.

The findings related to vision from any one of these fields are not difficult to understand in themselves, but in order to be clear and precise, each discipline has developed its own set of words and conceptual relations—in effect its own language—and for those wanting a broad introduction to vision, these separate languages can present more of an impediment to understanding than an aid. Yet what lies beneath the words usually has a beautiful simplicity.

My aim in this book is to describe how we see in a manner understandable to all. I've attempted to restrict the number of technical terms, to associate the terms that are used with a picture or icon that visually express what they mean, and to develop conceptual relations according to arrangements of these icons, or by other graphical means. Experimental findings have been recast in the natural world whenever possible, and broad themes attempt to bring together different lines of thought that are usually treated separately.

The main chapters provide a thin thread that can be read without reference to other books. They are followed by some additional topics that explore certain areas in greater depth, and by notes that link the chapters and topics to the broader literature.

My intent is to provide you with a framework for understanding what is known about the first steps in seeing by building upon what you already know.

Acknowledgments

I am deeply grateful to the E. K. Bishop Foundation, both for their support of my research efforts over almost 20 years, and for their continuing support during the writing of this book. Both activities were carried out in the Department of Ophthalmology of The University of Washington, and I would like to thank Robert E. Kalina, former chair of the department, for his support. The assistance of Toni Haun for most of this period has been invaluable, and this book has greatly benefited from her efforts.

David J. Calkins read every chapter more than once. He had a clear grasp of what and whom I was aiming for, and guided his comments toward improving that end. Clyde W. Oyster read about half the chapters, provided many useful comments, and suggested a major reorganization of the material in the chapter on eye movements. Krzysztof Palczewski read the material on phototransduction, patiently answered my many questions, and helped me refine the molecular icons used to describe this process. Edward N. Pugh, Jr., read and contributed to early drafts of the material on phototransduction, and provided a number of key insights into the biochemical cascade, as discussed in the notes to that topic.

Many others contributed to this book by reading drafts, responding to queries, and providing original data and illustrations. I would like to express my appreciation to Meredithe L. Applebury, Peter W. Atkins, Denis A. Baylor, Joseph C. Besharse, Robert R. Birge, Brian B. Boycott, Elaine L. Chuang, Dennis M. Dacey, Julie Epelboim, Norval E. Fortson, Chris R. S. Kaneko, Heidi E. Hamm, Stewart H. Hendry, Jonathan C. Horton, Robert E. Kalina, Eileen Kowler, Michael F. Land, Barry Lia, Donald I. A. MacLeod, Steven C. Massey, William W. Parson, Dianna A. Redburn, John C. Saari, Julie M. Schnapf, Stanley J. Schein, David M. Schneeweis, Max D. Snodderly, Robert M. Steinman, Andrew Stockman, Lubert Stryer, Edward R. Tufte, David I. Vaney, Heinz Wässle, and William Zagotta.

The watch

Was the Eye contrived without Skill in Opticks . . . ?

Isaac Newton, 1718

The contrivances of nature surpass the contrivances of art, in the complexity, subtilty, and curiosity of the mechanism; and still more, if possible, do they go beyond them in number and variety. . . . I know no better method of introducing so large a subject, than that of comparing a single thing with a single thing: an eye, for example, with a telescope.

William Paley, 1802

The eye to this day gives me a cold shudder . . .

Charles Darwin, 1859

Vision is a precious gift that deeply enriches our lives, for it allows us to see the order and beauty of this world. So immediate and powerful is seeing that our language gives this word additional connotations: to imagine, to comprehend, to regard, to perceive, to know from first-hand experience, to foresee. Furthermore, vision is the primary medium of literature, art, and dance.

But what is it for, and how did it come to be?

Three giants of our intellectual heritage, Isaac Newton (1642–1727), William Paley (1743–1805), and Charles Darwin (1809–1882), became preoccupied with these questions. As it happened, all three attended Cambridge University: Newton at Trinity, and Paley and Darwin at Christ's College. Although their lives did not overlap, their thoughts did, and came to shape the way in which we have come to see the world.

Some historians mark the start of the Enlightenment with the publication of Isaac Newton's *Mathematical Principles of Natural Philosophy* in 1687. In this book he laid out the law of gravity, which governs everything from earthly events, such as the falling of apples and the motions of tides, to the orbits of planets and comets around the sun. Newton's *Opticks*, published in 1704, revolutionized the understanding of the laws that governed light; most of his insights on the physical and physiological nature of color remain valid today. Newton's synthesis of previous work with his own discoveries presented the dawn of the Enlightenment with a harmonious universe, an enormous clockwork, governed by laws that found their expression in mathematics.

Newton was a private man with two consuming passions. The nature of the physical world was his passion of youth; with age came a desire to discern the nature, existence, and glory of its creator—God. The first editions of *Principles* and *Opticks* didn't mention theology, but their very contents raised some disturbing questions that were to reverberate throughout the coming age and well into the next.

If the laws of mechanics and of gravity governed the motions of everything but light, and the laws of optics took care of that, then what was left for God to do? Newton's first writings on this topic appear in four letters written to Richard Bentley during 1692 and 1693. Robert Boyle's will had provided funds for a series of lectures "in illustration of the evidences of Christianity, and in opposition to the principles of infidelity." Bentley was asked to give the first series of lectures, and had written to Newton, seeking his advice on the evidences to be found in nature. That Boyle, a scientist, should fund such a series of lectures, and that Bentley, the young chaplain to the Bishop of Worcester, should seek evidences in science are both emblematic of Enlightenment values. Newton replied that the world cannot be reduced to mechanics, and that some divine agent is needed to explain the universe. For example, mechanics may describe the orbit of Mars around the Sun once it is set into motion, but it cannot explain why Mars has the size or mass it has, its average distance from the Sun, or why the Sun is lucent but Mars is not. There is a specific *design* to nature, the planets, Earth with its mountains and streams; the designer of both the laws and the things upon which they operate was God.

The thoughts contained in these letters were published in later editions of *Principles* and *Opticks*. In the *Queries* that first appeared in the third edition of *Opticks*, Newton worked backward from the design that was apparent to him in the universe to invoke the necessity of a designer, or cause:

> Whence is it that Nature doth nothing in vain; and whence arises all that Order and Beauty which we see in the world? . . . How came the Bodies of Animals to be contrived with so much Art, and for what ends were their several Parts? Was the Eye contrived without Skill in Opticks, and the Ear without Knowledge of Sounds? How do the Motions of the Body follow from the Will: and whence is the Instinct in Animals? . . . does it not appear from Phænomena, that there is a Being incorporeal, living, intelligent, omnipresent, who in infinite Space, as it were in his Sensory, sees the things themselves intimately, and throughly perceives them, and comprehends them wholly by their immediate presence to himself: Of which things the Images only carried through the Organs of Sense into our little Sensoriums, are there seen and beheld by that which in us perceives and thinks.

Newton was the first to put forward a modern and scientifically based version of what is known as the *design argument* for the existence of God. The essence of the argument is that if there is design, there must be a designer. As historian Robert Hurlbutt (1963) noted:

> Arguments for the existence and attributes of God are, of course, legion; and the major ones have names as famous as philosophy itself: there are ontological, cosmological, moral arguments; there are arguments from faith, from scriptures, from revelation, and from authority. There are others. But when the theological chips are down, and when all other means of subduing the skeptic have failed, the devotee will always, as does Cleanthes in Hume's *Dialogues*, remonstrate impatiently ". . . but look round the world . . . ," and deal out the design argument.

William Paley was an influential figure during the latter part of the Enlightenment, and wrote a series of books on the relations between Man, Law, the State, and God that were widely read and went through many printings. Perhaps more than anyone else of his time, Paley spoke for the English Enlightenment. He was a persuasive writer, and never more eloquent than in his development of the design argument. This is how his book *Natural Theology* (1802) begins:

> In crossing a heath, suppose I pitched my foot against a stone, and were asked how the stone came to be there: I might possibly answer, that, for any thing I knew to the contrary, it had lain there for ever; nor would it perhaps be very easy to show the absurdity of this answer. But suppose I had found a watch upon the ground, and it should be inquired how the watch happened to be in that place; I should hardly think of the answer which I had before given,— that, for any thing I knew, the watch might have always been there. Yet why should not this answer serve for the watch as well as for the stone; why is it not as admissible in the second case as in the first? For this reason, and for no other, namely, that when we come to inspect the watch, we perceive—what we could not discover in the stone—that its several parts are framed and put together for a purpose, e.g., that they are so formed and adjusted as to produce motion, and that motion so regulated as to point out the hour of the day . . .
>
>   . . . the inference we think is inevitable, that the watch must have had a maker: that there must have existed, at some time, and at some place or other, an artificer or artificers who formed it for the purpose which we find it actually to answer, who comprehended its construction, and designed its use.

Paley then turned to nature, where he found endless examples of structures that reflected purpose. He used as his prime example the eye, which he described in detail, and pointed out that its optical properties compared favorably with the best telescopes then produced. One could conceive of how nature alone might produce a rock, but when it comes to a watch or an eye, one is forced to concede that some presence other than nature is required. Later editions of this book often began with diagrams of the eye.

Early in 1828, Charles Darwin entered Christ's College, where he planned to obtain a degree and eventually be ordained as a clergyman of the Church of England. Cambridge offered a broad education that included both natural philosophy (science) and moral philosophy. Every undergraduate was required to read books by William Paley—a policy that continued into the twentieth century—and Darwin was both impressed and charmed by the power of Paley's reasoning.

Darwin's plans for joining the clergy didn't pan out; instead, he became a diligent and dedicated naturalist. His great insight was that only a fraction of one generation gives rise to the next. In order to do so, each individual of this fraction must live long enough to procreate. There is always variation among individuals, even those in the same brood. So, just as a breeder of domestic animals shapes the breed by selecting which animals shall reproduce, the competition to survive, acting over many generations, shapes each species. Could this process, and it alone, result in the evolution of species? If so, then there is no watchmaker; design results not from the existence and plan of some conscious agent, but emerges as a by-product of the struggle for survival within each generation of a species, applied over countless generations.

During the Enlightenment there was a cozy relationship between science and theology, and Paley wrote not to convince the skeptic, but to fortify the belief of the faithful. His line of argument, based mainly on induction and analogy, is not accorded much importance in contemporary Christian theology. But it was the conventional wisdom when Darwin came to write *The Origin of Species* (1859), and he was faced with the painful task of separating issues of nature from issues of theology. Although he did not refer to Paley directly, Darwin attempted to deal with Paley's arguments point by point. In a chapter titled *Difficulties with the Theory*, Darwin dealt extensively with the eye. Asa Gray, a botanist at Harvard and a frequent and supportive correspondent with Darwin, received an early copy of the book and wrote to Darwin that the weakest part dealt with the eye. Darwin replied:

> About the weak points I agree. The eye to this day gives me a cold shudder, but when I think of the fine known gradations, my reason tells me I ought to conquer the cold shudder.

Today, issues of science and theology are better separated; evolution has become the cornerstone of biology, and only a few of the faithful seem challenged by it. Thus the biological answer to "What is vision for?" is "To enhance survival."

In the following pages you will encounter a system that undoubtedly works very well, and is exquisitely complex. But because evolution is not engineering—rather more like tinkering—it is not design. So there are no real answers to structural questions such as "Why do we have two eyes rather than three?" nor to functional questions such as "Why is the focusing mechanism in our eyes 'inferior' to that found in other vertebrates?" For each evolutionary stress (something that imperils survival) there are usually evolutionary strains (a variety of potential adaptations that can reduce stress), and there is an element of chance as to which adaptation emerges from the random variation of properties—recognized today as genes—that are found within the species. The visual system never had an opportunity to be designed—or redesigned—from scratch; instead, both form and function reflect its long, particular, and capricious history. Ironically, it is from this perspective that we can best understand the appeal of Paley's argument, despite its logical weaknesses, for whether put there by evolution, by God, or by a combination of both, the minds we are born with seem naturally to search for pattern and design, order and beauty, in the world that we see about us.

A. & M. Shah / Animals Animals

1

The chase

Vision is a precious gift, but in our sheltered lives, we have lost much of our appreciation of the rigors of nature that confronted our ancestors and over countless generations shaped our eyes and the portions of the brain that allow us to see. So it is perhaps appropriate that we begin with an enriched visual experience, where the issues of survival and selection are given full opportunity to come into play.

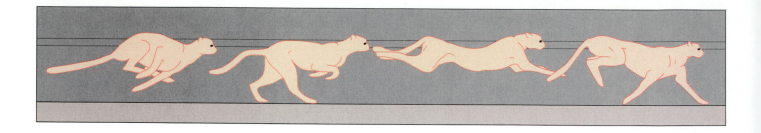

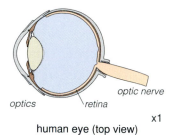

optics   *retina*

optic nerve

x1

human eye (top view)

Vision is dynamic

Few scenes in nature are as dramatic as a cheetah chasing a gazelle. Both animals move at great speed, eyes darting, the machinery of the body reacting to what each sees before it. During the chase, each animal's view of the external world rapidly changes as it covers ground and turns its body, head, and eyes.

Seeing begins when the optical portions of the eye form an image of the external world upon the back of the eye. Imagine that either animal has a miniature video camera strapped to the top of its head, and you are attempting to follow the chase on a video monitor. The picture on the monitor would shift about in a jerky and unpredictable manner, and you wouldn't be able to make much out of the confusion. But such jerky images are not what either animal is seeing, nor are they what you would be seeing if you were part of the chase. What we see depends upon two factors: the direction of the head, and the direction of the eyes with respect to the head. Within limits, we can *change* our direction of gaze by moving either the head or the eyes. More important, we can *preserve* our direction of gaze in the presence of head movements by moving the eyes in the opposite direction.

The image at the back of the eye is formed in the same general way that the lenses of a camera form an image on film. But instead of film, the eye is lined with a thin sheet of interconnected nerve cells **(neurons)** called the **retina**. The portion of the *external world* that is imaged on the retina depends upon the direction in which the eyes are pointed; that portion is termed the

nerve cell, neuron

From the Indo-European root *snéu-* = sinew or tendon; thus this root fails to distinguish between tendons and nerves, both of which are long and white. The Greek word *neuron*, which is based upon this Indo-European root, was likewise used to refer to both. Today *neuron* means a single cell of the nervous system. Some of these cells have long extensions, termed *axons*, which are used for sending messages from one part of the nervous system to another. *Nerves* are bundles of *axons*, bound by supporting cells. The cell bodies of many neurons give rise to a branching arbor of processes, termed *dendrites*, which receive from the axonal processes of other neurons.

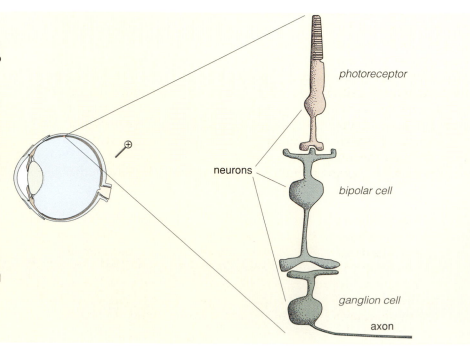

photoreceptor

neurons

bipolar cell

ganglion cell

axon

after Hildebrand, 1959, 1961

visual world. Some of the light of the image is captured by retinal neurons termed **photoreceptors**; other neurons connected to the photoreceptors both *compare* the rates at which different photoreceptors capture light and *convey* this information to the brain via the optic nerve.

Eye movements catch images and hold them steady on the retina

The video camera fixed to the head of the animal records what the eyes would see if they could not move within the head. But of course the eyes do move; each rotates within its orbit of the skull, driven by muscles that turn the eyes toward something of interest. There is a certain portion of the retina that is most sensitive to detail; in most vertebrates, including cheetahs and gazelles, it is termed the **area centralis**. We humans have a specialized area centralis that is termed a **fovea**. When we **gaze** at something, we direct our eyes so that its image falls on the center of the fovea.

Eye movements direct gaze and, because of changing circumstance, are often sophisticated; nevertheless, they have but two aims. The first is to quickly direct the center of gaze to some new target in the external world, and thereby bring the image of that target onto the area centralis; in effect, these eye movements visually **catch** some target in the visual world. The second aim is to **hold** the image steady long enough for the photoreceptors to capture some of the light, and for the rest of the visual system to interpret this pattern.

As the gazelle dashes across the plain, its head turns and changes position. The image seen by the video camera fixed to its head rotates as the head turns. But the gazelle, whose eyes are not fixed to the skull, has two options. It can hold the retinal image of some target, such as a footfall, roughly stabilized on the retina by turning its eyes in the direction *opposite* to the head motion. Alternatively, the gazelle can catch a new target, first seen out of the corner of an eye, by means of a combination of eye and head movements, in which both eyes and head initially turn in the *same* direction. The situation is more complicated for the cheetah, whose intent is not so much to stabilize the image of some portion of the visual world, but to pursue a gazelle that is moving rapidly and unpredictably. Thus what the cheetah is attempting to catch and hold onto involves the motions of both animals.

When the gazelle dashes in a straight line, and the cheetah is in direct pursuit, their heads bob only slightly. As shown in the illustration at the top of these pages, like dancers, they stabilize the height and orientation of their heads by a combination of body and neck motions that aid in stabilizing the image on the retina. Ordinarily, we tend to think of the visual system as limited to the eyes and the portions of the brain directly concerned with vision. But these reflex motions of the entire animal that help to stabilize gaze remind us of our integrated nature.

retina
The term *retina* comes indirectly from Greek to Latin, through Arabic, back to (Medieval) Latin *réte* = net. The original Greek term referred to a "cobweb tunic"; the glistening appearance of the retinal surface in the opened eye may have suggested a cobweb covered in dew. The tunic portion, however, suggested something thrown around, as a thrown net is used to catch fish; after multiple translations, this is what stuck.

During the chase, the cycle of catching and holding repeats itself three to four times a second. The direction of gaze of each eye is determined by the activity of six eye muscles, which work together to determine the direction and orientation of the eye. So it is really the muscles of the eyes of the cheetah and the gazelle, as well as the muscles that control their heads and limbs, that are so busy at this time. All of these muscles are in turn driven by nerves activated by the brain.

Saccadic and smooth eye movements are used to catch and hold images

The general catch-and-hold pattern is common to the vision of all animals, but different species achieve this pattern in different ways. Long-necked birds hold the image by means of head movements rather than eye movements, and winged insects hold the image by orienting the entire body. Gazelles are alarmed by this *catch-and-hold* terminology. They prefer the specific terms that describe the two forms of eye movements used by most mammals: saccadic and smooth.

The only eye movement we can ordinarily make voluntarily is a quick rotation termed a **saccadic eye movement**, or simply a **saccade**. By this means, the cheetah or gazelle can quickly move its eyes to *catch* a new image—a possible site for a future footfall, an upcoming tree trunk, the flanks of its prey. It does so by means of a brief but powerful activation of the eye muscles that *flings* the eye to a new position. The time that the eye is rotating within its orbit is too brief for the animal to attempt to correct or refine the movement. Making a saccadic eye movement is thus like throwing a rock at a target—all of the aiming has to be done before you release the rock.

Smooth eye movements are used for holding, so as to keep the image of some portion of the visual world located within a small region of the retina. The object viewed may be moving, and the eyes themselves are typically in motion as a result of head movements. Either form of motion will shift the image of the object on the retina. The task of smooth eye movements is to turn the eyes in the direction opposite to the difference between object and head motion. For ordinary viewing, about 95% of the movement of the image relative to the retina is removed by means of such compensatory smooth eye movements. Move your finger slowly across this page, and follow it with your eyes. Your eyes moved smoothly, tracking your finger. Now look at one letter on this page, and slowly turn your head from left to right, while continuing to look at the letter. Again, your eyes moved smoothly, compensating for your head movements by moving in the opposite direction. You can also move your head in some pattern (e.g., left to right), and your finger in some other pattern (up and down), while still following the tip of your finger by means of the same smooth eye movements. This is a sedate version of the movements of the cheetah's eyes as it chases the gazelle.

In order to make smooth eye movements, it is necessary to have something to track. You can demonstrate this by asking someone else to track the horizontal movement of your finger. You will observe that their eyes move smoothly. Now put your hand down and ask them to move their eyes in the same way as before. You will now observe jerky eye movements, characteristic of a sequence of saccades. Although you choose what to track, the tracking process itself occurs outside your conscious awareness.

Surprisingly, gazing at a *stationary* object also involves smooth eye movements. This is because your head is always in slight motion as the

---

saccade

The word *saccade* is of French origin, and means pulling sharply on the reins of a horse, so as to check it. The origin of this term is odd, for it appears to have been coined to describe *holding* rather than *catching* movements. In 1887, Javal reported that the pattern of eye movements during reading contained an unexpected feature. He had arranged letters on a pane of glass and viewed the eyes of a reader from the other side. Instead of scanning each line in a regular manner, the reader's eyes repeatedly stopped. The term *saccade* was presumably suggested by this halting, although Javal may have had the entire jerky pattern in mind.

Javal may have thought that words were acquired as the eyes rapidly moved over a portion of the text and digested during the pause, although this is speculation. In fact, vision is effectively inactivated during the quick movement that came to be termed a *saccade*.

muscles of your body and neck attempt to maintain your posture. Thus when you look as steadily as possible at some small stationary object, such as a pebble on the ground, your slight head movements cause the image of the pebble to move on your retina. This motion gives you something to track, and smooth eye movements compensate for your head movements so as to keep your gaze on the pebble. Looking at a pebble is thus not a passive act, but an active one. From a narrow perspective, the only difference between gazing at a pebble and gazing at an ant is the added motion of the ant. From a broader perspective, when you look at a pebble, the *background* is also stabilized—except for those swarming ants. From an even broader perspective, you can choose to look at the *swarm*. This is easy to do, although you may no longer see any particular ant or pebble. Often we are tracking the entire visual world, in order to compensate for our head and body movements. We do this every time we walk. If we track something in the visual world that has motion of its own, then that motion is combined with our own so as to stabilize its image on the retina.

Thus whatever we choose to track, the motion of its image is mainly canceled by smooth eye movements in the opposite direction. The qualifier *mainly* proves to be quite important, for, as we are about to see, eye movements never fully compensate for head movements.

The image of the visual world is always moving on the retina

This diagram shows typical changes in the direction of gaze for one eye of a subject who sat as still as possible and directed his gaze toward a small and distant target. In order to provide a sense of the extent of these movements, I've replaced the target with the letter **E** of an eye chart, 6 meters away from the subject. The path of the angular movements of the eye is drawn on this chart as if traced by a laser beam emanating from that eye.

During the 30-second interval in which the subject was attempting to hold his gaze as steady as possible, the changes in the direction of his gaze were considerably greater than the size of the letters to be identified on the line for normal vision. The angular changes in head position, due to slight head rotations, were much larger than the change in gaze shown in this diagram. Smooth eye movements removed most, but not all, of the image motion caused by these head rotations. Nevertheless, the residual changes in the direction of gaze are significant, and give some indication of the degree to which the image of the visual world is in constant motion with respect to the retina.

path of eye on chart

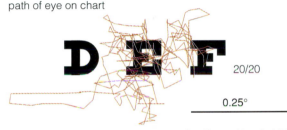

20/20

0.25°

after Skavenski et al., 1979

Image motion elicits smooth pursuit

Although the circumstances may vary, choosing *what we track*, however accomplished, is a straightforward matter, readily grasped. By comparison, the mechanism that underlies *how we track* is counterintuitive, and is something of a surprise in that we are generally unaware of it. Using the ant as an example, you might suppose that when the ant moves to a new position, its image falls on a different portion of the retina, and we turn our eyes to return its image to our center of gaze. Put in mechanistic terms, the brain detects a change in the position of the ant, and generates eye movements that recenter it. But it is not the change in the *position of the image* of the ant that initiates the smooth eye movement; rather, it is the *velocity of this image* that does so.

At first sight, this difference between a mechanism driven by a change in image position over time and one driven by image velocity might seem like no difference at all, since we understand *velocity* to mean a change in position with time. The difference can be seen if you imagine driving along a road parallel to a railroad track. A train is traveling in the same direction, and you are attempting to follow it either by its position relative to you or by its velocity relative to you. In the first case, you are aware of the position of some part of the train, and you adjust the accelerator accordingly. You thereby end up traveling at the same velocity as the train. In the second case, it is the relative movement of the train, gradually pulling ahead with respect to your car, that prompts you to adjust the accelerator, and you unavoidably lose ground with respect to the train.

The fact that smooth eye movements depend upon image velocity rather than image position has important consequences for understanding how we see. If they accurately tracked changes in position, then we could view what is presented to the retina as a sequence of static images, one following each saccade—like a shutterbug taking a series of pictures. But tracking by means of velocity means that the image is never static, so that what is presented to the retina is always a moving image. Here the metaphor of the eye as a camera breaks down.

This requirement for a movement within at least some portion of the visual world has an interesting corollary: *we cannot voluntarily make smooth eye movements in the absence of something to follow*. This is surprising, because it seems to us that we make them all the time. But the left-to-right movement of your eyes as you read this sentence consists entirely of a sequence of *saccades*.

It is possible, by experimental means, to hold the image stationary on the retinal surface. When this is done, *our perception of the image disappears in a fraction of a second*. The visual system thus *requires* movement of the image in order to work, and this is another unexpected and counterintuitive aspect of vision. We don't know why vision requires image motion, but the reason does not appear to lie within the eye, as most of the neurons that send information to the brain about the differences in the light catch of the photoreceptors continue to do so when the image is stabilized. In any case, because smooth eye movements require image motion, they can never fully stabilize the image on the retina.

We are surprised to learn of this constant movement of the image, mainly because we are unaware of it. If you touch a nearby stationary object, you can check with your hand that it is stationary. When you look at it with "fixed" gaze, it likewise appears to be stationary. Touch and vision thus agree, and this makes sense. There is no evolutionary need for us to be aware of the internal workings of the visual system. What is less clear is whether evolution has played an active role in creating compensatory neural mechanisms that remove this motion from our conscious awareness.

What we see doesn't move when we move our eyes

The previous discussion of eye movements makes it clear that our thought experiment in which a miniature video camera was strapped to the head of a moving animal wasn't going to work. We saw the external world in the direction of the animal's head, whereas the animal saw it in the direction of its eyes.

We could mount the camera on a set of gimbals, so as to allow it to rotate through the same range of angles over which the eyes are able to move. Furthermore, we might be able to somehow monitor the smooth and saccadic movements of one of the eyes, and use this information to drive a system of motors attached to the gimbals that could both smoothly turn and suddenly fling the camera about. A miniature inertial detection system, mounted on the head, could provide the motor system with information about head movement, and could potentially improve the performance of the whole contraption by overcoming limitations in the eye-monitoring apparatus. Aside from the fact that the camera would be a bit higher, and centered on the head, the image it would record would then be close to the image falling on one of the animal's retinas. Now we can connect the output of the camera to a monitor and sit back and watch the chase.

Our view would be much improved, for it would consist for the most part of episodes of smooth holding movements interrupted by saccades. But are we now seeing what the animal sees? No, not at all. The differences reveal two striking features of how we see.

First, as mentioned earlier, the smooth eye movements used to stabilize the image do not fully compensate for head motion. The image is thus in continual motion during the period between two saccades, when the features of the image are being extracted by the retina and sent to the brain. As you watched the monitor, you would see the image moving about. Yet we are wholly unaware of these *smooth* movements of the image across our own retinas, and so too, presumably, is the animal.

Second, look up and move your eyes; notice that the visual world remains stationary. Since all voluntary eye movements are saccadic, the image on the retina suddenly shifts with each saccade. If you had the video camera strapped to your head so as to track your eye position, anyone viewing the monitor connected to it would have seen the image jump about on the monitor. But you see little or no such movement of the world around you—which is amazing!

The perception of a stable external world is experienced from such an early age that we take it for granted. If we wanted the person watching the monitor to see things more like we do, we would have to mount the monitor on a mechanical apparatus that quickly moved the monitor as our eyes moved, so as to keep objects on the screen in the same place in the viewing room. Better yet would be a large screen corresponding to the stationary external world upon which would be written the images caught by the moving eyes. Each image would persist until overwritten.

Now someone might say: "You are making too much of the notion that what we see appears stationary when we attempt to hold our gaze steady, or to look about. After all, we know that rocks and trees don't move when we move our eyes. Thus, whenever our eyes do move, or when we see everything in the visual world moving as a whole, we have simply learned to assume that what we see is really stationary. There is nothing more to it than that!"

A simple experiment refutes this argument. Close your left eye, bring your right index finger up to the side of your right eye, and gently tap your upper lid. The visual world moves! Why does it do so when you use your *finger muscles* to move your eye, but not when you use your *eye muscles* to move it? It is possible to detect a slight amount of motion when looking about by mentally attending to eye movements while simultaneously attempting to ignore the context of the visual world. But this subtlety only demonstrates a technique for partially overcoming the ordinary impression. Why the world appears stationary as our eyes move and the image shifts across the retina remains a mystery, one that lies outside the scope of this book, but enough is known to be fairly certain that it involves built-in neural machinery in parts of the brain that appear to be specialized for this purpose. However accomplished, the advantage of possessing a visual world within the mind's eye that correlates with what is going on in the external world is obvious.

Orientation and transition

The visual system of every animal is an integrated machine, created and shaped by evolution. Neural mechanisms enable an image to be stabilized on the retina in a rough manner, however hectic the circumstances. Other mechanisms, partly under voluntary control, quickly fling the eyes to a new position. Still others use the brief snapshots taken during eye stability to compose a stable perception of the locations of objects and surfaces in the external world.

A perspective critical to our understanding of vision comes from considering the conditions under which it enhances the probability of survival. The forces that shaped the visual system were not so much the common or general features of the external world, but rather those aspects of it that, for whatever reason, had the greatest influence on survival. Much of our common visual experience appears to be a by-product of this process, so we shouldn't make too much of the role the more ordinary features of the world have had in shaping our visual system.

Understanding vision is not ultimately a matter of learning how the retina processes the image that falls upon it, how various brain centers process messages from the retina, and so on. A deeper, though poorly grasped, understanding is based upon the recognition of those critical visual experiences of life that have shaped the visual system over hundreds of millions of years to the end of improving our survival, at least for a while. Knowledge of the evolutionary pathways of the genes that form and maintain the visual system should enable a comparative synthesis that will reveal in broad outline when various traits were acquired and how they were modified. But the complex and subtle interactions of this world, and permanent ignorance of many details of the past, will limit our understanding of just how and why these traits were selected.

It is our internal representation of the world that the messages from our eyes, ears, skin, muscle sensors, and memory all contribute to and modify. This is all done by neural machinery, but, as the gazelle and cheetah would attest, it seems very real—and of course it is. Whether the situation is desperate or not, the first steps in seeing begin with the retina, to which we now turn.

The neural substrate

The retina is a sheet of neural tissue that is about 0.4 millimeters thick, or about half the thickness of a credit card. It lines the interior of the back surface of the eye, and extends forward toward the optical portion of the eye, which consists of the cornea, the iris, and the lens (left). To a first approximation, the retina is composed of five **classes** of neurons (top of facing page). As their name suggests, **photoreceptors** are stimulated by light. The simplest common pathway from the eye to the brain is from photoreceptors to **bipolar cells** to **ganglion cells**. Each ganglion cell has an axon that passes across the surface of the retina to the optic disc, where it enters the optic nerve. **Horizontal cells** and **amacrine cells** serve in a variety of ways that greatly enrich the performance of the retina.

The retina contains about 100 million photoreceptors, 10 million or so horizontal, bipolar, and amacrine cells, and about 1.25 million ganglion

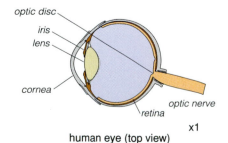

optic disc
iris
lens
cornea
retina
optic nerve
x1
human eye (top view)

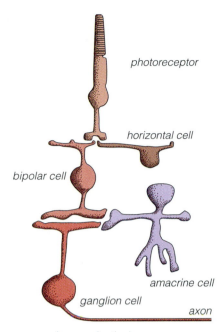

classes of retinal neurons

cells. Information about the visual world, received by the retina as the rates at which the photoreceptors are catching light, is delivered to the brain, via the optic nerve, by the axons of the ganglion cells. The optic nerve is thus a bottleneck through which all of the information about the visual world must pass. This restriction is interesting from a conceptual point of view, but as we will see, when all of the various factors at stake are considered, this bottleneck proves to have few, if any, practical consequences.

Each of the cell classes illustrated above is found all across the retina, and cells of each class occupy particular layers within the retinal thickness. The photoreceptors lie in the **outer** portion of the retina, at the very back of the eye; consequently, light must pass through almost the entire thickness of the retina in order to reach the **outer segment** of each photoreceptor, which contains **visual pigment molecules** specialized to catch the light (right).

Among vertebrates there are two general forms of photoreceptors, termed **rods** and **cones**. Rods are able to convey variations in light intensity in dim conditions, but in bright light they lose this ability. Cones are slightly less sensitive then rods, but they are well suited to work in the bright light of a sunny day. Cones are found throughout the human retina, but are concentrated in the foveal region. As noted earlier (page 9), when we gaze at something, we turn our eyes so that its image falls upon this portion of the retina. In the peripheral retina, the outer segments of the cones are slightly conical, whereas those of the rods are always cylindrical, and the names of these two photoreceptor groups are based on this difference.

The fovea lies about 5 mm from the center of the optic disc, as shown in the diagram of the back surface of the eye (shown on the next page), which is termed the **fundus**. This is a schematic version of what an ophthalmologist sees when she looks into an eye with an ophthalmoscope; also shown are some of the blood vessels that nourish the retina and some bundles of ganglion cell axons.

As you read this text, successive portions of it are brought to the foveal region of each of your retinas by means of saccadic eye movements. Ganglion cells are also concentrated in this region, and thus the optic nerve contains a relatively large number of axons arising from ganglion cells located near the center of the fovea.

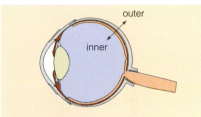

inner, outer
The terms *inner* and *outer* mean closer to and farther away from the center of the hemispherical retina; *lateral* means parallel to its curved surface.

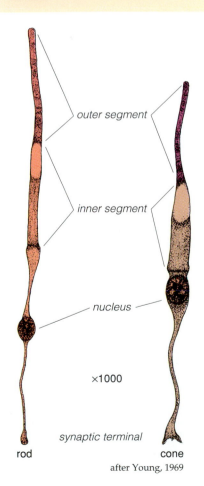

×1000

rod   cone

after Young, 1969

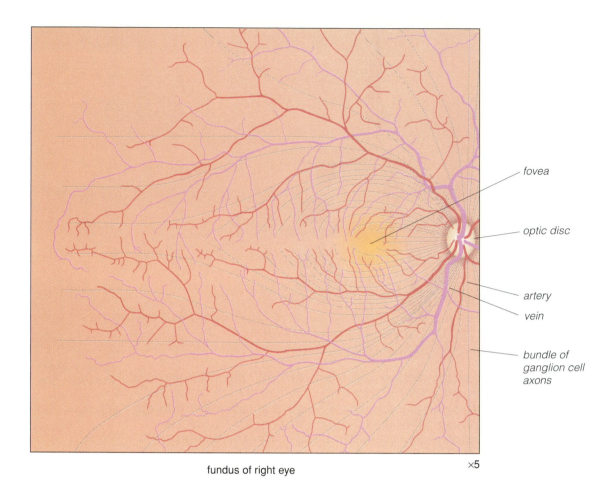

fundus of right eye   ×5

fovea

optic disc

artery

vein

bundle of
ganglion cell
axons

Orientation and transition

The retina is a highly ordered structure composed of different types of neurons. The properties of each type, and the manner of their interconnections, were forged over eons by evolution. We can say little about these evolutionary steps, but we can say quite a bit about what they have realized.

Now that we know something of the moving image and something of the structure of the retina, we turn to a common visual experience, and trace the sequence of events from the object viewed to the eye, and then to the brain.

Camping

Take yourself camping; go beyond city lights. The morning is cool and clear as you ascend toward the forested high point where you plan to spend the night. There has been much to see. Earlier, in crossing a meadow, you came across an odd-shaped rock, so different from all the others that you picked it up, wondering how it came to be there. It is late afternoon by the time you reach your destination, and a light rain is falling on your face, each droplet barely perceptible to your skin. By the time you have strung your hammock between two trees, the rain has ceased, and in the quietness of twilight, you slide into your sleeping

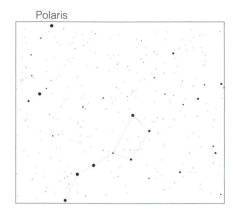

Polaris

bag, pull aside the hammock's rain cover, settle down, and idly view the darkening sky. With dusk, the border between the tops of the trees and the overcast sky gradually becomes less distinct. Later, the clouds pass away, and the stars appear. You are facing north, and can see enough of the Big Dipper to sight from it to the North Star, Polaris.

Catching the light

Both the Sun and the stars shower Earth's surface with a rain of **photons,** which we call light. Now, a photon is not a measure of something—like a bushel, a centimeter, or a gram. It's a particle—just one—you can't cut it in two. Polaris gives off photons that other objects, such as your eye, eventually catch.

As you look toward Polaris, some of its photons pass through your pupil and are concentrated into a small spot on your foveal cones. Some of the photons will be caught by the visual pigment molecules of the cones' outer segments. Over an 0.1-second "shutter time," the spatial distribution of photons from Polaris might look something like this diagram:

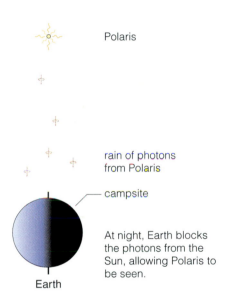

Polaris

rain of photons from Polaris

campsite

Earth

At night, Earth blocks the photons from the Sun, allowing Polaris to be seen.

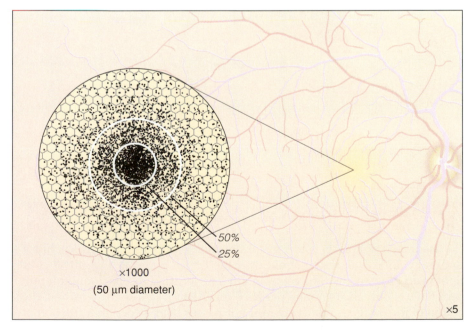

50%

25%

×1000
(50 µm diameter)

×5

The small spot on your fovea is magnified by a factor of 1000 at the left portion of this diagram, where the array of cones is represented by the hexagonal shapes visible in the background, and the photons are represented as black dots. Half of all of the photons from the star that strike the retina fall within the larger white circle, and 25% of the total fall within the small white circle, where they are densely concentrated. The image of Polaris marked by the inner white circle falls on about 30 cones (right).

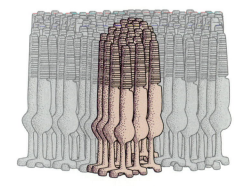

cluster of 30 cones

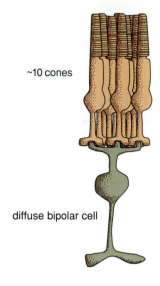

~10 cones

diffuse bipolar cell

Cones contact a number of different types of bipolar cells. We will concentrate here on a type of bipolar cell referred to as **diffuse**, because the processes of these cells spread out laterally so as to receive from about 10 cones (left). These diffuse bipolar cells, in turn, contact a number of different types of ganglion cells. We will follow the path from the diffuse bipolar cells to a group of what are known as **parasol** ganglion cells. Each parasol ganglion cell receives from 5 or 6 diffuse bipolar cells, which collectively receive from 20–25 cones (below left).

The cones stimulate the diffuse bipolar cells according to the rate at which they are catching photons, and the diffuse bipolar cells stimulate the parasol cell according to the degree to which they are stimulated. Like all ganglion cells, the parasol cell has an axon that passes across the surface of the retina to the optic disc. The axon of the parasol cell then passes within the optic nerve to a region of the brain termed the **lateral geniculate nucleus (LGN)**. There the terminal of the axon stimulates the cell body of a single neuron. The axon of this neuron passes out of the LGN to a region at the back of the brain called the **striate portion of the visual cortex**, where it branches so as to stimulate a number of other neurons. Neurons in the visual cortex are thus stimulated by this LGN neuron in a manner that depends upon the rate at which a small patch of 20–25 cones is catching photons. This description is oversimplified, but it captures the first things to know about this pathway:

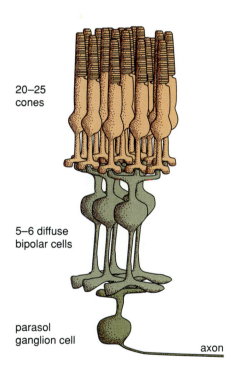

20–25 cones

5–6 diffuse bipolar cells

parasol ganglion cell

axon

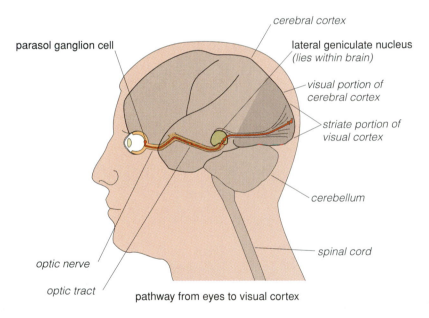

parasol ganglion cell

cerebral cortex

lateral geniculate nucleus
(lies within brain)

visual portion of cerebral cortex

striate portion of visual cortex

cerebellum

spinal cord

optic nerve

optic tract

pathway from eyes to visual cortex

The image of Polaris is in constant motion on the retinal surface, like a small rain cloud wandering about over the foveal plain, as a result of your slight head movements. The cones in any one location receive a photon rain from Polaris only as its image passes over them. At these dimensions, the motion of the image is relatively rapid; it passes over a cone in a fraction of a second. So from the perspective of one cone, there is drought, a sudden and brief shower, and a return to drought. As previously noted, each parasol ganglion cell receives signals arising from about 20–25 cones, which is about the same number as are covered at any one time by the densest rain of photons from Polaris. But the moving image may cover only a portion of this patch of cones, and thus only partially stimulate the parasol cell. In any case, the stimulation of the parasol cell will be brief.

A different perspective emerges if we change our focus from this particular parasol cell to the *array* of parasol cells and the *array* of cones in the retina. The retina as a whole is receiving a continuous shower of photons, as you might water the lawn with a hose and spray nozzle. At any instant there is always a patch of cones receiving this photon rain, at least two stimulated parasol cells that are receiving signals via diffuse bipolar cells, at least two stimulated cells in the LGN, and a group of stimulated neurons in the visual cortex. It is in this changing activity from cell to cell that the retina presents Polaris to the brain.

When you look at Polaris, a number of ganglion cells—parasols and others—are simultaneously activated. Their activity, conveyed to the visual cortex, leads to your conscious awareness of the star. How does such cell-by-cell activity lead to this experience? We have not the slightest idea. Although a great deal is known about the structure and function of the visual cortex, there remains a basic ignorance about such simple matters. It is not even clear how to frame the issues. Thus the gap between the retinal cell activity initiated by photons from Polaris and the conscious visual experience it elicits remains too big to bridge with the concepts we now have. This encourages speculation, which is healthy—but appreciating our ignorance comes first.

This doesn't mean that nothing meaningful can be said about the conscious visual experience, or that we are forbidden to speak of it. But in order to really understand the innards of the experience, we need to build upon inferences sufficiently simple and secure that we can rely upon them. One of the things we can be sure about is that interruptions in this chain of events, produced by disease or injury, can take that experience away.

Orientation and transition

This chapter has spun the thinnest of threads, and it's time to go back and thicken it. This is done in the remaining 13 *chapters*. Additional information may also be found in a number of *topics*. Each is linked to chapters and other topics by means of icons that appear in the margin, and look like this:

 Biochemical cascade *371*

The page number associated with the nearby icon indicates either the start of this topic, or some portion of it.

Each of the chapters presents values and statements of fact without attribution; associated with each are notes, found at the back of the book, that indicate where this information comes from and link it to the scientific literature. In order to thicken the thread, we will return to the eye and retina, and take a closer look at their structure.

Robber fly (*Neoaratus hercules*)

Male mayfly (*Chloeon dipterum*)

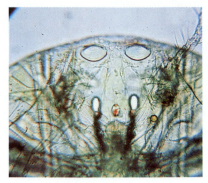

Copepod (*Sapphirina*)

Squid (*Histioteuthis*)

Ogre-faced spider (*Dinopis subrufa*)

Scallop (*Pecten maximus*)

Invertebrate eyes show great diversity. Counterclockwise from top right: *Sapphirina* has one set of lenses near the front surface and another set below, which form a "telescope" for light-catching cells. The back lenses and receptors move to and fro a few times per second to scan the visual world. The male mayfly also has two sets of eyes, and uses the large eyes on top of its head to detect the dark shapes of females hovering above against the darkening twilight sky of their late-summer mating season. The robber fly has high acuity at the front of its eyes to help it catch other insects on the wing. *Histioteuthis* has a large eye that points upward, and a small eye. The ogre-faced spider preys on cockroaches in dark forests; its large (1.3 mm diameter) eyes are adapted for catching light rather than for fine resolution. In the scallop, the image is formed not by lenses, but by a concave reflecting layer (tapetum) at the back of each eye. Photographs courtesy of Michael F. Land.

2

Eyes

This book focuses on how we see, so we will be taking a close look at the structure and function of our own eyes and retinas. However, there are some features of our eyes that are common to all animals that detect light, and it will help our broader understanding to be aware of what they are. Other features of our eyes are common to other vertebrates, or—with increasing restriction—other mammals, other primates, or other members of our own species (e.g., eye color). There are also aspects of our eyes that reflect adaptations to our more recent environment rather than our line of descent. It is this mix of various factors that produced the eyes we were born with.

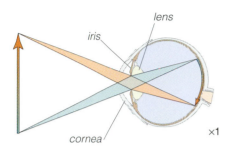

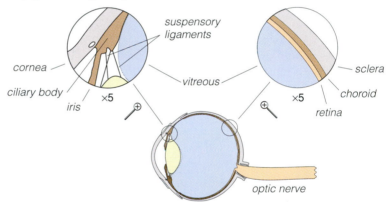

The eyes of all vertebrates show a common structural plan

Virtually all animals have vision, but—as you know—the eyes of insects, spiders, and most other invertebrates are very different from our own. We are vertebrates, animals with backbones, the group that includes fishes, amphibians, reptiles, birds, and mammals. The eyes of all vertebrates are based upon a common structural plan, similar to that of a pinhole camera, in which light passing through the pupil forms an inverted image on the retina. The **pupil** is the hole in the **iris**; it is larger than a pinhole, and the light passing through different portions of it is brought to focus on the retina by the **cornea** and the **lens** (left).

Much of the surface of the eyeball consists of tough but flexible fibrous tissue, termed the **sclera**, which corresponds to the white of the eye. Just within the sclera lies a dense meshwork of blood vessels and other tissue termed the **choroid**, and the retina forms the inner surface over the back portion of the eye. The lens is supported by thin fibrous strands called the **suspensory ligaments**; behind the lens lies a gelatinous body termed the **vitreous.** The shape of the eye is maintained by pressure within the eye generated by cells of the **ciliary body**. These cells secrete fluid into the eye, which is forced to flow out of the eye via narrow, tortuous channels, thereby producing the pressure:

Also common to all vertebrates are some of the types of neurons found in the retina, their interconnections, and the places in the brain that receive their axon terminals. It is not known how these common features of the vertebrate eye or visual system came to be. Partly because the eye is soft tissue, it has not been possible to detect successive stages of its evolutionary development in the fossil record, nor are major stages evident among living species. Most or all of the common features of vertebrate eyes appear to have been present in the *proto-vertebrate* (Greek *protos* = first). At a still earlier stage of evolution, there appears to have been a common origin for vision in all animals. These issues are discussed in more detail in the Box *SIMILARITIES AND DIFFERENCES*.

The interior of the eye can be viewed with the aid of a simple optical device

Light passes into the eye through the pupil, and continues through its mainly transparent interior to reach the retina. The portion of the light that is not caught by the photoreceptors is either absorbed or scattered in all directions by the underlying tissues. Some of the scattered light passes back through the pupil and out of the eye. But when we look into another per-

sclera
The term *sclera* is New Latin from Greek *skleros* = hard. In fact, the sclera is tough but pliable; the hardness of the eye is due to the intraocular pressure.

choroid
Choroid comes from a scribal error for the Greek word *khorioeides* = resembling the *chorion* (Greek: *khorion*), which is the embryonic portion of the placenta that becomes the afterbirth.

vitreous
Vitreous is a shortened form of *vitreous body* (anatomical extent), which contains *vitreous humor* (watery gel). The term comes from Latin *vitreus* = glasslike.

ciliary body
Ciliary is an early term apparently derived from Latin *ciliaris* = resembling an eyelid or eyelash; it may come from the radial striations that can be seen when viewing the interior of the front of the eye.

Similarities and differences

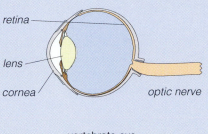

vertebrate eye
(human)

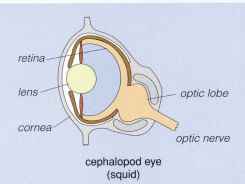

cephalopod eye
(squid)

Of the many varieties of eyes found among invertebrates, those of cephalopods (squids, octopuses, and cuttlefishes) have the same optical plan as is found in vertebrates. The way they develop in the embryo is, however, quite different, and this suggests that different evolutionary routes converged on a similar optical plan. By contrast, the eyes of other invertebrates, such as arthropods (e.g., flies), have very different optics and neural pathways.

Nevertheless, as we will see, the specialized protein molecules used to catch light in the eyes of every animal, known as **visual pigment molecules**, are all descended from the same remote ancestor—they are *homologous as light-catching proteins.* Other protein molecules, found only in the eye and specialized for some aspect of vision, also appear to be homologous among all animals. Furthermore, one of the vertebrate genes concerned with the formation of the eye has proved to be homologous with one of the genes concerned with the development of the fly's eye. These correspondences are fascinating, for they strongly suggest that, despite their differences, the eyes of all animals have a common origin. Vertebrates did not invent or reinvent vision, they inherited it. The great differences among the eyes and developmental plans of

cephalopods, arthropods, and vertebrates suggest, however, that the eyes of their common ancestor had a relatively simple plan.

There are so many aspects of vision that most vertebrates share that it is useful to consider the vertebrates as a group when discussing their retinas. Within this context, the *differences* among the retinas of vertebrate species can enhance our understanding of our own eyes, because these differences often reflect adaptations to the particular environment of the species.

These comparisons need to be viewed with caution, however, because they lie outside the domain of strong inference, which allows one to devise experiments to rigorously test between multiple hypotheses. Nevertheless, from a psychological perspective, comparisons *are* useful in that the observations they provide form thin strands of association that add to the fabric of our mental picture. The creative aspect of mind, searching for pattern, weaves in some strands of its own. Finally, the rational aspect of the mind explores this domain, evaluating and picking up what is needed to apply its methodology. The mental pictures may be those of an individual, or those of the field as a whole, as reflected in its paradigms.

son's pupil, the back of the eye, or **fundus**, appears black. This is because the optical pathway of the light that *enters* the eye and falls on a given region of the fundus is the same as that of the light scattered from that region, which *leaves* the eye through the pupil. In effect, in order to see the interior of the eye under ordinary conditions, one has to place one's head into this common pathway of the light.

A brilliant young clinician, Hermann von Helmholtz (1821–1894), grasped this issue, and realized that all he needed to do to see the interior of another person's eye was to devise an optical device by which he could get both his head and the light into the pathway. He did so by placing a piece of glass between his eye and the patient's and angling the glass so that it partially reflected the light from a lamp into the patient's eye, as shown on the next page. The piece of glass and the lamp formed a device termed an **ophthalmoscope** (Greek *opthalmos* = eye + *skopion*, from *skopein* = to see). Modern ophthalmoscopes have a built-in light source, colored filters to

fundus

The word *fundus* is an anatomical term, meaning the back surface of an organ farthest away from the opening, as in the eye or the uterus. Its origin is remotely Latin (= bottom). The formal name for the fundus of the eye is the *ocular fundus;* this term is rarely used, however, because there is little chance of confusion.

Hermann von Helmholtz

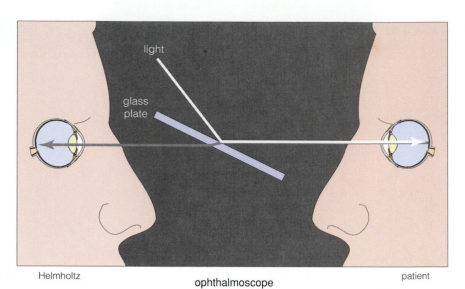

Helmholtz   ophthalmoscope   patient

emphasize some aspect of the view, and lenses to correct for any error in the optics of the clinician or the patient (i.e., lenses of the same power that they might use in spectacles).

With his ophthalmoscope, Helmholtz could view the fundus—and there was a lot to see. The optic disc is not only where the axons of ganglion

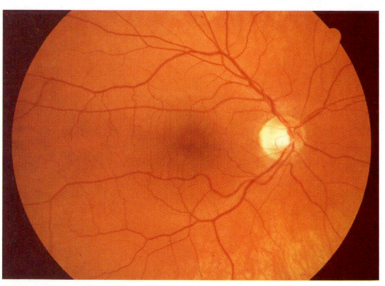

fundus of the human eye   ×5

cells come together to enter the optic nerve, but is also where the arteries and veins that nourish the inner portion of the retina enter the interior of the eye. The fundus is the one place in the body where small arteries and veins are directly visible. These vessels branch successively as they spread across the retina, the arterial tree sending blood to the venous tree via a fine meshwork of capillaries. These capillaries, however, stop short of the center of the fovea, and instead surround it in a ring (facing page). The absence of blood vessels in this region of the retina specialized for sharpest vision gives an image uncorrupted by the passage of red blood cells through the capillaries. In this central region of the fovea, the inner cells of the retina are displaced radially away from the center of the fovea so as to produce a shallow pit. This brings them closer to the ring of capillaries so as to meet their nutritional needs. It may also produce a small improvement in the quality

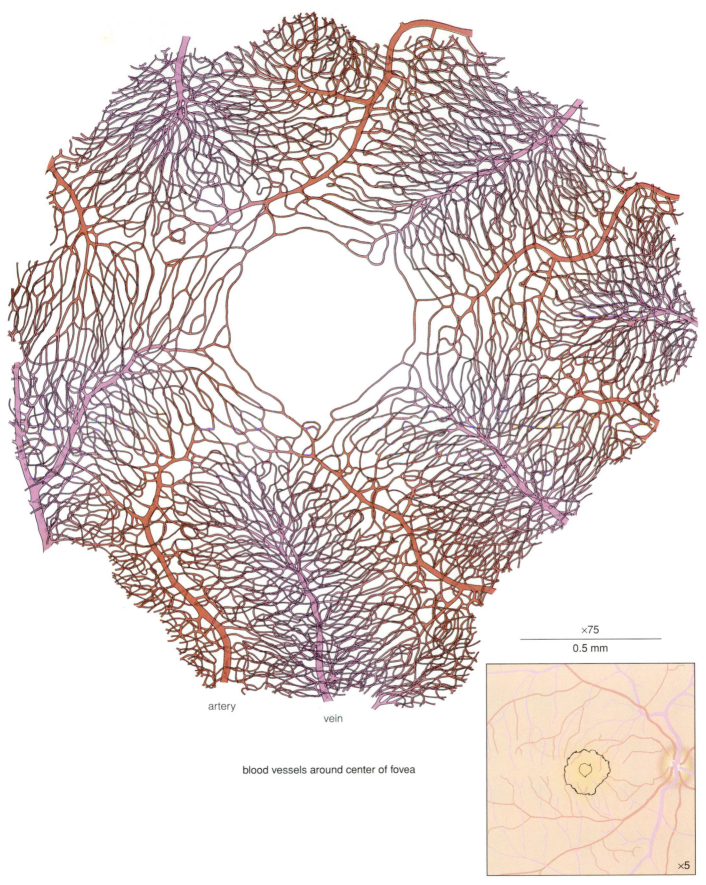

artery

vein

blood vessels around center of fovea

×75

0.5 mm

×5

after Snodderly et al., 1992

ophthalmology

From Greek *opthalmos* = eye + *logos* = word or speech, but in this context meaning "the study of." Ophthalmologists are clinicians trained in ocular disease and surgery. *Optometrists* (Greek *optos* = visible) treat certain visual defects by means of corrective lenses or other methods that do not require license as a physician. *Opticians* make lenses for spectacles.

of the optical image in the central region by making the inner retina thinner and thus reducing the scattering of light passing through it. Many diseases, not all of them unique to the eye, alter the appearance of the fundus. For clinical specialists in the medical aspects of the eye, known as **ophthalmologists**, a view of the fundus is a most useful diagnostic tool (see the Box *RETINITIS PIGMENTOSA*).

The retinal region around the fovea contains a light-absorbing pigment that screens the photoreceptors' outer segments from much of the blue light that falls on them. This pigment gives this portion of the fundus a yellow tinge, and thus this region is termed the **macula lutea** (Latin *macula* = spot + *lutea* = yellow). This tinge is quite noticeable when the retina is removed from an eye, but in the fundal view, it is difficult to see when illuminated with ordinary light, as in the photograph on page 24. It can be made more visible by using a bluish light.

The appearance of the rest of the fundus is relatively uniform in normal eyes. What one sees is based on the overlap of different layers. The back surface of the human retina consists of a single layer of melanin-containing epithelial cells, termed the **retinal pigment epithelium**. This non-neural layer serves some of the metabolic needs of the photoreceptors and acts as a barrier to ions and most molecules. Its cells contain melanin molecules, packaged in pigment granules, that strongly absorb light throughout the visible spectrum; consequently, most of the light that is not caught by the photoreceptors' outer segments is absorbed by this layer, which makes the fundus appear dark. In some other species, the epithelial layer in the upper portion of the fundus lacks pigment granules, and the generic term **retinal epithelium** is used instead.

Just behind the retinal epithelium is a rich meshwork of large capillaries and associated blood vessels, termed the **choriocapillaris**, that supplies oxygen and nutrients to the retinal epithelium and thereby indirectly nourishes the outer portion of the retina. In the human retina, these blood vessels can be vaguely seen as an irregular pattern through the retinal pigment epithelium. (See the Box *THE RETINA IS NOURISHED ON BOTH SIDES* for more information on the retinal epithelium and the choriocapillaris.)

Most eyes are specialized to view either a point, or the visual horizon, or a mixture of both

As noted earlier, most vertebrates have some region of the retina that has a high concentration of ganglion cells, cones, and cone bipolar cells. These regions take two general forms: an **area centralis** (central area), which is roughly circular, and a **visual streak**, which is a horizontal elongation. The spatial density of ganglion cells across the retina is a good indicator of the degree to which an eye shows either of these specializations, or—most often—some mixture of both. This semi-schematic diagram shows the general distribution of ganglion cells for each specialization; the darker the color, the greater the density of ganglion cells:

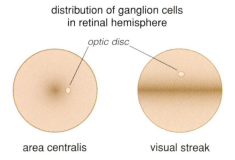

distribution of ganglion cells
in retinal hemisphere

optic disc

area centralis   visual streak

Retinitis pigmentosa

There are many ways in which retinal function may be directly impaired as a result of disease. One of the most common is a condition known as glaucoma, in which an increase in the pressure within the eye damages the optic nerve where it enters the eye at the optic disc. Other conditions, such as diabetes, damage the smaller blood vessels throughout the body and thereby affect retinal function, particularly near the fovea. This box describes a relatively common disease condition known as retinitis pigmentosa.

The term *retinitis pigmentosa* is used to describe a number of different diseases, all of which lead to a degeneration of the photoreceptors and of the adjacent retinal pigment epithelium. These are all hereditary diseases, and collectively they affect about 1 person in 4000 throughout the world (about 70,000 people in the United States). The name itself is a misnomer, since *retinitis* means an inflammation of the retina, yet no inflammation is present; *pigmentosa* refers to the spillage of pigment granules from the degenerating retinal pigment epithelium into the inner retina late in the course of the disease. Generally both eyes are involved. The first signs, which usually appear by the age of 20, are a slowed ability to adapt to dim light conditions ("night blindness") and a loss of peripheral vision. At this stage the fundus may appear normal, and foveal vision may be unaffected. But as the disease progresses, pigment granules from the retinal pigment epithelium leak into the retina, where they form coarse clumps, or "bone spicules," in the inner retina, as seen in this image of the fundus. Foveal visual acuity is often preserved until the end stages of the disease, when all photoreceptors are lost. Although all forms of retinitis pigmentosa are progressive, the rate of progression varies among genetic types. There is as yet no cure for this condition, but treatment for related complications, such as cataracts, and the use of various optical aids can make best use of what vision remains.

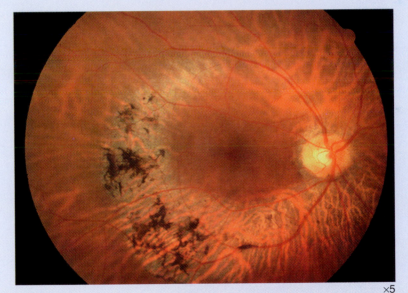

×5

fundus of patient with retinitis pigmentosa

An area centralis is specialized for best vision at some point in visual space. When an animal with an area centralis looks at something, it orients its eyes via head and eye movements so that the image of the target is centered on this region of the retina. Likewise, smooth pursuit movements act to keep the target roughly stabilized on the area centralis. In the diagram on page 30, the line connecting the center of the area centralis with the target corresponds to the direction of gaze.

The human fovea is a specialized version of an area centralis. You can sense that it sends more axons to the brain than other portions of the retina by means of the following experiment. Look directly at two or three of your upraised fingers, viewed at arm's length. Judge what detail you can discern. Now, without changing the direction of your gaze, swing your outstretched

The retina is nourished on both sides

For the same mass of tissue, the metabolic needs of the retina are about seven times those of the brain, and the highest of any tissue in the body. The blood supply to the eye and retina reflects this fact. There are two separate circulations, **retinal** and **choroidal**.

The larger arteries and veins of the *retinal circulation* can be readily seen when the fundus is viewed with an ophthalmoscope (see the photograph on page 24 and schematic diagram on page 16). They can be seen in greater detail if a fluorescent dye is injected into a vein and the fundus photographed with blue light, which causes the dye to fluoresce green (right). This is a standard clinical test for detecting leakage and other abnormalities in the arteries and veins, since the dye can be seen spilling out at these sites.

Just as in the rest of the body, the arteries and veins of the retinal circulation branch and thin until they interconnect via a dense meshwork of capillaries. The capillaries extend through the inner half of the retina. Capillaries are thin tubes made of cells, so thin that blood cells must pass through them single file. A general rule for mammals is that a metabolically active cell anywhere in the body is never more than about a tenth of a millimeter (100 μm) from a capillary, so that substances can be exchanged between the blood and the tissue via diffusion.

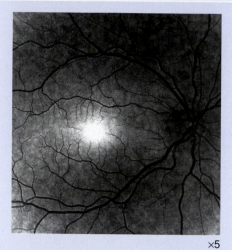

×5

retinal blood vessels visualized by means of fluorescein angiography

Throughout most of the body, capillaries are rather leaky. Their cells confine the red blood cells, but allow large molecules, and even some other cells carried in the blood, to pass between them. But in the capillaries of the retinal circulation, the cells are connected in such a way that nothing can pass between them. These cellular specializations are termed **tight junctions**, and consist of multiple strands of protein molecules that bind the capillary cells together. Because of these tight junctions, anything that goes into or out of the capillary must pass *through* the cells that form its walls. Each of these cells has a membrane with one face toward the blood within the capillary and another face toward the extracellular fluid outside the capillary. Thus whatever goes between the blood and the extracellular fluid must pass through both membrane faces. Water and small molecules such as glucose readily do so, as do dissolved gases, such as oxygen and carbon dioxide. But other cells and large molecules, such as proteins, that are circulating within the blood do not. The retinal capillaries thereby form part of the **blood–retinal barrier**, limiting what can enter or leave the environment of the neural cells of the retina. Similar capillaries are found in the brain, where they contribute to the **blood–brain barrier**.

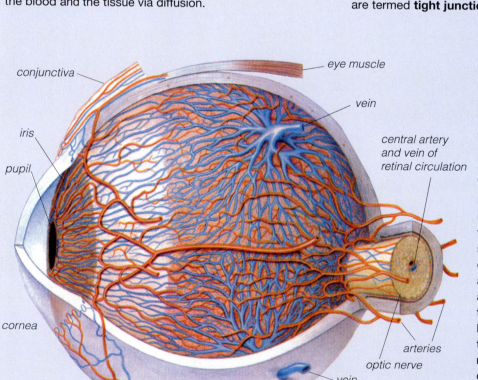

conjunctiva

eye muscle

iris

vein

pupil

central artery and vein of retinal circulation

cornea

arteries

optic nerve

vein

source: Hogan et al., 1971

The *choroidal circulation* provides a second means of nourishing the retina. The **choroid** consists of pigmented tissue that supports a dense meshwork of blood vessels that nourishes the outer retina. It is part of a system of blood vessels termed the **uveal circulation**, which also nourishes the iris and the ciliary body. Whereas the retinal circulation springs from a retinal artery and vein that pass through the optic nerve and emerge from the center of the optic disc, the arteries and veins of the uveal circulation pass through the sclera (bottom of facing page). The choroidal arteries and veins branch and pass inward until they suddenly break into a stellate meshwork of very large capillaries, termed the **choriocapillaris**, as shown schematically in the diagram to the right. Because these capillaries are very large, and the path from artery to vein is short, the rate at which blood passes through them is very high; this keeps the concentration of oxygen high and that of carbon dioxide low. Furthermore, heat from the focused rays of the sun can be quickly removed.

On the side of the capillary facing the retinal epithelium, the cells are thinned in spots to form a **fenestrated capillary bed** (Latin *fenestratus* = with windows or openings), which are shown in the schematic illustration at the lower right. The fenestrae further promote exchange across the wall of the capillary. Unlike the cells of the retinal capillaries, those of the choriocapillaris are not interconnected by means of tight junctions. Thus substances can pass through these cells, between them, or directly through the fenestrations. The blood–retinal barrier is thus not maintained by the choriocapillaris. Instead, the cells of the retinal epithelium itself are interconnected by means of tight junctions so as to form this outer portion of the blood–retinal barrier.

The photoreceptor layer lacks blood vessels, and its metabolic needs are met mainly by the choroidal circulation. Considering the rich vasculature of the choroidal circulation compared with that of the retinal circulation, one might surmise that the metabolic needs of the photoreceptors are higher than those of the cells of the inner retina. But measurements of oxygen consumption indicate that both the retinal and the choroidal circulations supply oxygen at about the same rate. Thus the rich vasculature of the choroidal circulation appears to provide a means of compensating for the restriction that anything it provides or receives from the retina must pass through both the inner and outer membranes of the cells of the retinal epithelium and also diffuse through the photoreceptor layer.

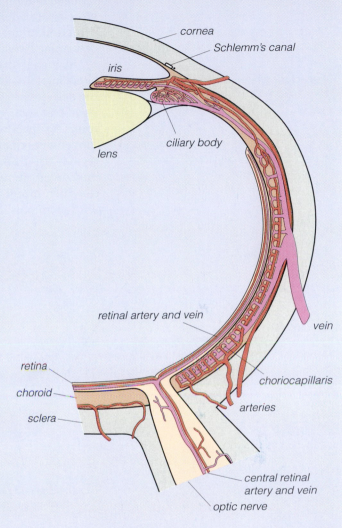

after Leber, 1865

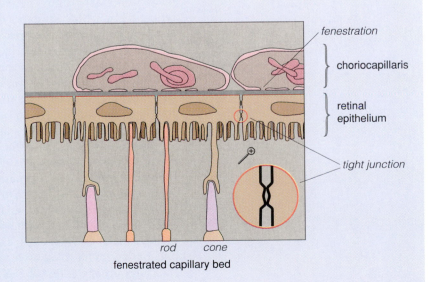

fenestrated capillary bed

arm toward your side, so that it forms an angle of about 45° with respect to your direction of gaze. The detail you will be able to discern will be much reduced, although you will probably be able to count the number of fingers. Now rotate your outstretched arm so that it is almost perpendicular to your direction of gaze, with the fingers still in view. Is there enough detail to determine how many fingers are raised?

A visual streak, by comparison, is specialized for best vision along a horizontal line in the visual field. If you had a visual streak, and performed the above experiment, you would detect a relatively small loss in detail as your arm swung to your side (some loss is expected because of optical factors). Animals with a visual streak tend to show different patterns of eye movements than those with an area centralis. For example, rabbits, whose retinas are dominated by a visual streak, do not show smooth pursuit movements in response to targets moving horizontally. Likewise, the extent to which rabbits move their eyes in any direction is limited as compared with mammals that have an area centralis.

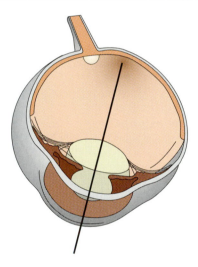 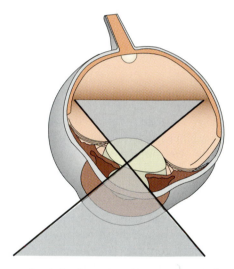

an area centralis receives from a small circular region in visual space

a visual streak receives from an elongated horizontal region in visual space

Which form of regional specialization is found in a given species depends more upon the habitat to which the species is adapted than upon its evolutionary origins per se. Animals that live in trees or in thick forests, where there is little or no horizon, typically have eyes that are dominated by an area centralis. In most primates and many reptiles and birds, the central area becomes so specialized for sharp vision that the inner retina is thinned over the central portion of this region; it is this specialization that warrants the name **fovea centralis**, or simply *fovea* (New Latin from Latin—and possibly Etruscan—*fovea* = small pit). The region within 2.5 millimeters of the center of the human fovea occupies only 2% of the total retinal area, but about *one-third* of all of the ganglion cells are found in this small region.

Mammals that live on the open plains generally have a visual streak. A visual streak is always associated with some form of *visible horizon* in the habitat of the species. For land animals, this horizon is the apparent intersection of earth and sky. Among aquatic animals, visual streaks occur in both bottom feeders and surface feeders, as both the top and bottom surfaces of a body of water create their own horizons.

Cheetahs and gazelles, as well as domestic cats and dogs, hedge their bets by having both an area centralis and a visual streak, as is evident from the diagram at the top of the facing page showing the density of ganglion

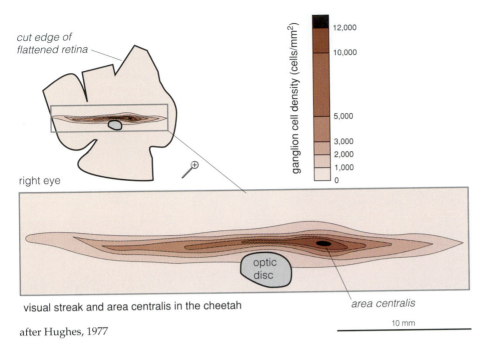

ganglion cell density (cells/mm²)

12,000
10,000
5,000
3,000
2,000
1,000
0

cut edge of flattened retina

right eye

optic disc

visual streak and area centralis in the cheetah   *area centralis*

10 mm

after Hughes, 1977

cells in a cheetah retina. The black lines within the retinal border are **iso-density lines**, meaning that along each line, the spatial density of ganglion cells is the same; these lines are similar to the isobars of a weather map, along which atmospheric pressure is constant. Even animals with a well-developed visual streak, such as rabbits, have a region along the visual streak that has a higher concentration of ganglion cells than the rest of the streak. See the Box *FUNDI OF CHEETAHS AND GAZELLES* for more on this topic.

Turtles also have a well-developed visual streak. If you tilt a turtle left or right, or fore and aft, its head and eyes automatically turn in the opposite direction so that the streak continues to view the horizon. These movements are automatic and occur even in complete darkness, and can be seen in these photographs, in which the shaded line indicates the position of the turtle's pupil, a horizontal slit:

after Brown, 1969

The left brain views the right visual field

In every vertebrate, what is to the right passes to the left side of the brain, and vice versa. For example, the signals from touch or pain receptors on the right side of your body pass to the left side of your brain. Likewise, it is the left side of your brain that controls the muscles on the right side of your body. There appears to be no obvious advantage to this arrangement, whose evolutionary origins are remote and uncertain. But it is such a fundamental topological pattern that, however arrived at, no vertebrate has since violated it.

Fundi of cheetahs and gazelles

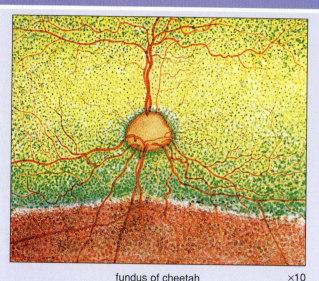

fundus of cheetah   ×10

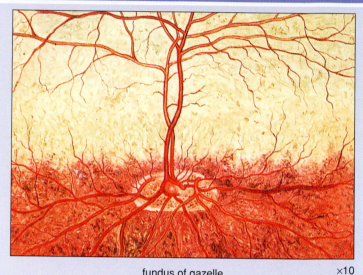

fundus of gazelle   ×10

from Johnson, 1968

In humans, the cones, ganglion cells, and other neural cell types are clustered around the fovea. The form of this concentration is reflected in the pattern of the retinal blood vessels, which ramify and narrow into a circular bed of capillaries as they approach the center of the fovea (page 25). The cheetah (*Acinonyx jubatus*) has both a visual streak and an area centralis (page 30), which are also reflected in the pattern of blood vessels. As shown in the photograph above, made with an ophthalmoscope by Lindsey Johnson, the cheetah visual streak lies above the optic disc, and the blood vessels approach it from above and below. The finer blood vessels to the upper right of the optic disc indicate the location of the area centralis.

Well below the optic disc, the cheetah fundus, like that of humans, appears dark because of pigment granules in the retinal epithelium. Near and above the optic disc, however, pigment granules are absent from the cells of the retinal epithelium, and within the choroid lie layers of cells that reflect the light that passes through the retina without being absorbed, giving the photoreceptors a second opportunity to catch these photons. This reflecting layer, also found in the eyes of cats and dogs, is termed a **tapetum**, and is the basis of the greenish eyeshine found in these animals. The term *tapetum* refers generally to a thin layer or covering, and comes from the Greek *tapes* = tapestry; in the eye, it refers only to this reflecting layer.

The fundus of the gazelle (*Gazella dorcas*) was also observed by Lindsey Johnson. Gazelles also have a visual streak, and, as seen above, the pattern of fundal blood vessels is similar to that in the cheetah. Gazelles also have a tapetum, but unlike that of the cheetah, it is composed of a matrix of collagen fibers, and consequently appears paler.

The enhancement of light sensitivity provided by a tapetum comes at the expense of spatial acuity because the reflected light is partly scattered. Because the eye is spherical, every portion of the retina has an unobstructed view of every other portion. Consequently, this scattered light can fall on other retinal regions, producing glare. So most tapeta are found only in the upper portion of the retina, which views the ground, and not in the lower portion, which views the sky.

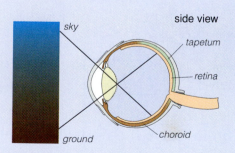

Vision also follows this pattern. In animals with laterally directed eyes, such as most fishes, the right eye views the right visual field and the left eye the left visual field, with little or no binocular overlap of the two fields directly in front of the animal or behind it. The optic nerve from the right eye crosses over the midline of the body to enter the left side of the brain,

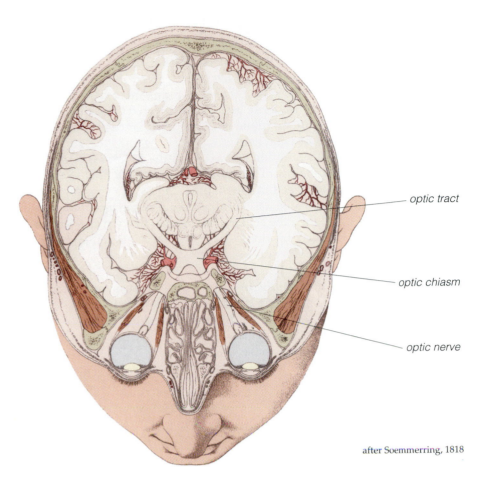

optic tract

optic chiasm

optic nerve

after Soemmerring, 1818

and vice versa. This is the simplest, and presumably the earliest, means by which what is visually to the right is passed to the left side of the brain.

In other species, including most predators, the eyes are directed forward. This arrangement allows the slight differences in the views from the two eyes to be used to judge depth. But it also forces a neural rearrangement, since both eyes now view much of both the left and the right visual field. In mammals, instead of the two optic nerves crossing over one another, they come together at a juncture termed the **optic chiasm**:

optic chiasm
The term *chiasm* is based upon Greek *khiasma* = a cross, which comes in turn from another word, meaning to mark with the Greek letter chi (χ).

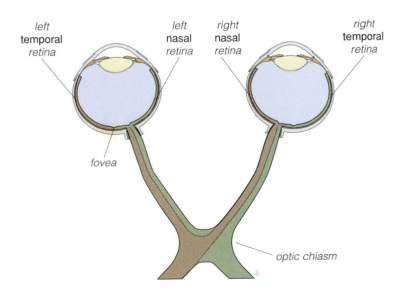

left temporal retina

left nasal retina

right nasal retina

right temporal retina

fovea

optic chiasm

ipsilateral, contralateral

More succinct expression of whether two parts of the body are on the same side or opposite sides can be achieved by using the anatomical terms *ipsilateral* (Latin *ipse* = same + *lateralis* = side) and *contralateral* (Latin *contra* = opposite). Thus the visual cortex on one side of the brain receives from the contralateral visual field; ganglion cells in the nasal retina always project contralaterally.

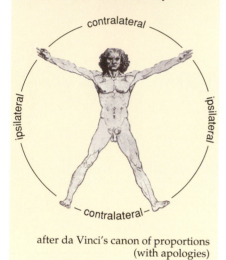

after da Vinci's canon of proportions
(with apologies)

Rather than continuing to speak of *left . . . goes to right . . . and vice versa*, let us introduce some terms that will be useful when dealing with forward-directed eyes. The portion of the retina nearest the *nose* is termed the **nasal retina**, and the portion nearest the *temple* is termed the **temporal retina**. Thus the axons of ganglion cells in the nasal retina must cross to the opposite side of the head, just like those in laterally directed eyes. But axons from ganglion cells in the temporal retina *must not* cross, since they are receiving an image of the opposite visual field.

In primates, all the ganglion cell axons in the temporal retina project ipsilaterally. The overall flow of information from visual field to visual cortex in humans is summarized in the diagram below. As you might expect, the dividing line between the nasal and temporal retina lies at the center of the area centralis, and thus the center of the fovea. Even in species that lack an obvious area centralis, this division of the image into left and right portions of the visual world still applies.

We have had a look at what surrounds the retina, and have learned something about the distribution of ganglion cells across the retina and the disposition of their axons within the brain. The stage is now set for returning to the different classes of neural cell introduced in THE CHASE, and having a closer look at the various neural cell types that compose each class and the interconnections that they make.

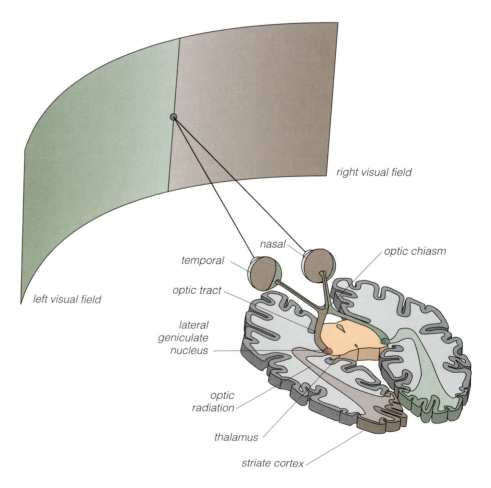

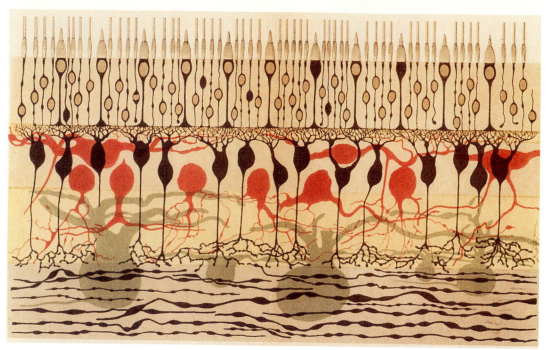

from Tartuferi, 1887

3

Retinas

The vertebrates form a highly diverse group of animals that are found in almost every environment this world offers. As we saw in the last chapter, their eyes show many conserved features that reflect their common origins, but they also show liberal amounts of variation that reflect adaptations to either their present or their ancestral environments. The same holds true when we consider the internal structure of their retinas, in which certain features, such as cell classes and certain cell functions, are highly conserved; but within these classes, vertebrates have liberal variations in both the number of cell types and the relative numbers of cells within each type. The following description is based primarily upon the conserved features, and is illustrated mainly by our own retinas.

Retinal structure

The retina is layered

In every vertebrate retina, the cell bodies of the neurons are grouped into three distinct layers, separated by two layers that are virtually empty of cell bodies but are rich in sites of contact between neurons. This photomicrograph shows a thin transverse section of the human retina about 1.25 mm from the fovea, which lies to the right, beyond the border of this micrograph. This section is oriented so that the interior of the eye is at the bottom; thus the light that impinges upon the retina is coming from below. This is the convention used in visual science; clinicians, on the other hand, usually show the photoreceptors at the bottom, rather than the top.

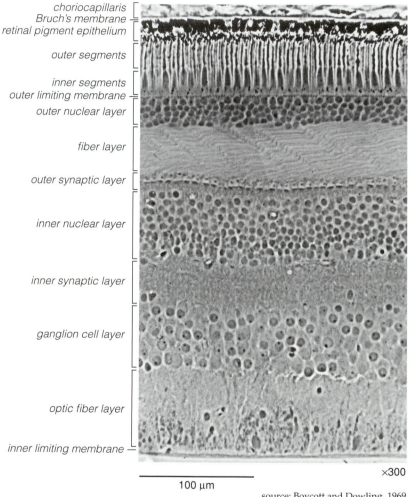

choriocapillaris
Bruch's membrane
retinal pigment epithelium

outer segments

inner segments
outer limiting membrane
outer nuclear layer

fiber layer

outer synaptic layer

inner nuclear layer

inner synaptic layer

ganglion cell layer

optic fiber layer

inner limiting membrane

×300

100 µm

source: Boycott and Dowling, 1969

The retina is essentially transparent; this section has been stained and illuminated so as to highlight its various layers. You can't make out individual cells, but each cell has a dark-staining **nucleus**. The nuclei are clustered in three zones, termed **nuclear layers**. Between the nuclear layers lie two zones in which the neurons make functional contacts with one another, termed **synapses** (Greek *syn-* = with or together + *haptein* = to clasp). The cellular processes that make these contacts are too fine to be seen with the light microscope using conventional staining methods. Because of this, these zones were termed **plexiform layers** by nineteenth-century microscopists (Latin *plexus* = a braid). This term is still used, but we will use the alternative term, **synaptic layers,** because it better reflects our current understanding.

The retina is a neural circuit composed of different cell classes

This diagram shows the main classes of neurons found in the retina, which were introduced in THE CHASE. It is highly schematic; in particular, the synaptic terminals of the photoreceptors are greatly enlarged in order to show the contacts they make with other cells.

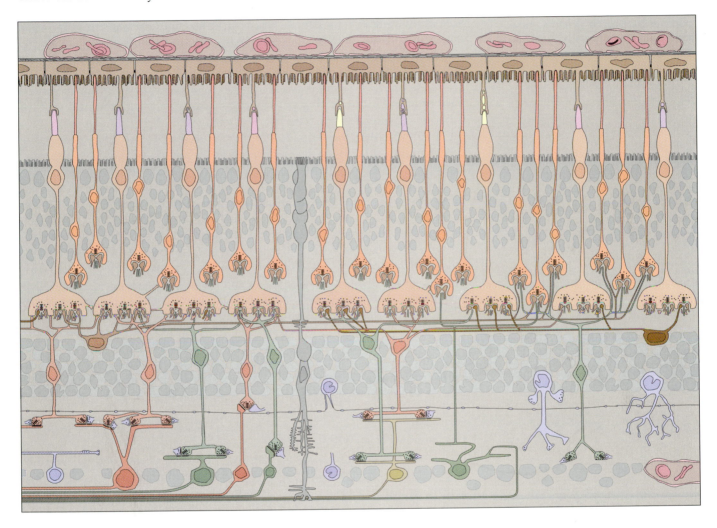

The photoreceptors lie farthest from the incoming light, and moreover, detect it with their outermost portions. Consequently, the light must pass through the other cells of the retina, and travel most of the length of the photoreceptors themselves, in order to be captured. On the face of it, placing the light-catching portion of the retina farthest from the light appears to be a rather strange way to go about things. It may be a secondary consequence of the infoldings of neural tissue from which the retina is derived. But it has the advantage that the outer portions of the photoreceptors, which are metabolically very active, lie close to the retinal epithelium and choriocapillaris, which supply the photoreceptors with oxygen and nutrients (see EYES: *THE RETINA IS NOURISHED ON BOTH SIDES*, page 28).

As described in THE CHASE, each photoreceptor converts the photons it captures into a neural signal, which it relays to a number of bipolar cells. The bipolar cells in turn convey these signals to the ganglion cells, and thus to the brain. At the synapse between the photoreceptor terminals and the bipolar cell processes, there are also processes from **horizontal cells,** so named because their processes extend laterally across the retina; they are colored

neural circuit
The term *circuit* comes from Latin *circumire* = to go around. The original use of this term in electronics referred to a single closed path formed by electrical components around which a current flowed, or could flow. Later it became generalized to refer to any pattern of interconnections of electrical components. Neurobiologists then took this generalized meaning to refer to any pattern of connections between nerve cells.

brown in the schematic diagram. The horizontal cells both receive from and act upon the photoreceptors they contact. These interactions cause the neural signals received by the bipolar cells to emphasize spatial differences in light intensity at the expense of the average light level, as discussed below.

Perhaps the most interesting cells of the retina, from the point of view of **neural circuitry** at least, are the **amacrine cells,** which are colored blue in the schematic diagram. They are so named because they appeared to lack an axon (Greek *a-* = lacking, + *makros* = long + *inos* = fiber). In fact, some amacrine cells do have one or more axons, although these axons are wholly confined to the retina. Their processes lie in the inner synaptic layer and make synaptic contacts with bipolar cells, ganglion cells, and one another. There are many different types of amacrine cells, and they appear to serve a variety of roles; but at present we have a reasonable understanding of the functions of only a single type.

To summarize, the retina is a highly layered structure, with zones composed mainly of cell bodies separated by zones dominated by neuronal processes and their synaptic contacts. The synapses in the retina are primarily found in two zones, the **outer synaptic layer,** where photoreceptors make synaptic contacts with bipolar and horizontal cells, and the thicker **inner synaptic layer,** where bipolar cells, ganglion cells, and other cell classes make synaptic contacts. Some synapses occur within the nuclear layers, and a few cell bodies occur in the inner synaptic layer. Nevertheless, the degree of segregation between cell bodies and neuronal processes that is found in the retina is virtually unique in the nervous systems of vertebrates. In the brain and spinal cord, neuronal processes make extensive synaptic contacts with both the cell bodies and the processes of other neurons, so that both processes and cell bodies are mainly intermixed. The evolutionary factors that resulted in this retinal segregation are not clear. It could possibly reduce light scatter by bringing together the nuclei, which have a higher index of refraction than does the less dense cytoplasm found in the processes, but the magnitude of such a reduction has not been estimated.

The retina detects and compares

The vertebrate retina has two functions. The first, performed by the photoreceptors, is to act as a *transducer,* converting absorbed photons into neural signals. The second, performed by the neural circuitry between the photoreceptors and the ganglion cells, is to *compare* levels of neural activity in different cells.

Comparisons are fundamental to visual function. The level of activity of the photoreceptors is not important in itself, because there is considerable change in the ambient level of light intensity throughout the day. Most objects in the natural world give off no light of their own, and can be distinguished only in the differing ways in which they reflect light, and thus the differing ways in which they activate the photoreceptors. Thus distinguishing objects is a matter of responding to *differences* in light intensity across the retinal image of the visual world. Under optimal conditions, we can detect changes in light intensity over the photoreceptor array as small as one part in 500.

The signals generated by photoreceptors and bipolar cells consist of graded changes in the voltage across their cell membranes; the greater the signal, the greater the change in voltage. By contrast, the signal generated by a ganglion cell consists of a sequence of electrical pulses, termed **action potentials**, which enable the signal to propagate along the ganglion cell's axon to the brain. As we will see, neural signals based upon electrical pulses are inherently less reliable than those based upon graded changes. There is

action potential
The cell bodies of ganglion cells generate brief changes in the voltage across their cell membranes, termed *action potentials*. The action potentials generated by the ganglion cell body are conveyed to the brain along its axon. The action potentials conveyed by the axons are always identical, but they can vary in the rate at which they occur (see page 95).

thus an advantage in using graded potentials to make visual comparisons, and most of these comparisons are made in the retina. It is this factor, more than any other, that gives the retina its complexity and accounts for the great diversity of cell types found within it.

Rods and cones are found in every vertebrate retina. As noted in THE CHASE, rods are adapted to operate in dim light, whereas cones are adapted to operate in the brighter conditions of daylight. For the moment, we will concentrate on the differences between rods and cones; later, we will consider the differences between the three cone types found in our retinas.

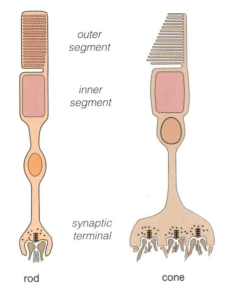

Rod outer segments contain a set of membranous discs, derived from the surface membrane of the cell but no longer continuous with the surface membrane or with each other. They resemble a stack of coins.

outer segment

inner segment

Cone outer segments are composed mainly of infoldings of the surface membrane of the cell. Outside the foveal region, these outer segments taper slightly, and this gives the cones their name.

The rod synaptic terminal is termed a **spherule** (Latin *spherula* = small sphere). It contains a single **invagination** of the cell membrane, termed a synaptic cleft; within this invagination lie the processes of two horizontal cells and two to five rod bipolar cells.

synaptic terminal

rod   cone

The cone synaptic terminal is termed a **pedicle** (Latin *pedicellus* = small foot). It contains a number of invaginations. Each invagination contains the processes of two horizontal cells and the processes of two or more bipolar cells. Additional bipolar cell processes lie near the invaginations or at the base of the terminal.

The outer segments of both rods and cones contain **visual pigment,** which catches the light of the retinal image. Visual pigment consists of molecules composed of two portions: a protein portion and a light-catching portion termed the **chromophore**. Variations in the protein portion of the molecule determine its sensitivity to different portions of the visible spectrum of light, just as variations in the proteins of a hair determine its color. Each primate photoreceptor contains only one type of visual pigment molecule. Visual pigment molecules are synthesized in the inner segment of the photoreceptor and transported to the outer segment, where they are incorporated into membranes that take up about half of the volume of the outer segment. The core of the inner segment is denser than its surroundings, and this causes the light passing through it to be funneled into the outer segment. To a first approximation, the *outer* segment contains all of the components necessary for the conversion of light into an electrical signal, whereas the *inner* segment contains all of the components necessary for the metabolism of the cell.

Because the outer segments of the photoreceptors are aligned across the retina, they collectively approximate a uniform layer of pigment molecules,

pigment layer

with a thickness of about one-fortieth of a millimeter (25 μm) (left). Away from the fovea, the cone inner segments become thicker than the outer segments, which disrupts the notion of a uniform layer of pigment molecules. But since the inner segments funnel the light into the outer segments, the efficiency in catching light is about the same as if there had been a uniform layer.

invaginate, invagination
To turn within, or introvert; also, to enclose in a sheath. Latin *in* = in + *vagina* = sheath. In photoreceptors, the pockets at the base of the synaptic terminal that partly enclose the processes of bipolar and horizontal cells are termed *invaginations*.

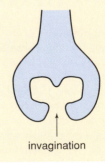

invagination

chromophore
Greek *khroma* = color + *phoros* = producing. This term is applied to the light-catching portion of any molecule.

Cones concentrate in the fovea

This diagram shows the distribution of cones along a horizontal strip of retina that includes the fovea and the optic disc. The region around the center of the fovea contains only cones. Toward the center of the fovea, the inner and outer segments of the cones are thinner than elsewhere, and the spatial density of cones rises to a sharp peak. Away from the center of the fovea, the spatial density of cones drops rapidly, and beyond 3 mm, levels off to a value of about 7000 cones/mm^2:

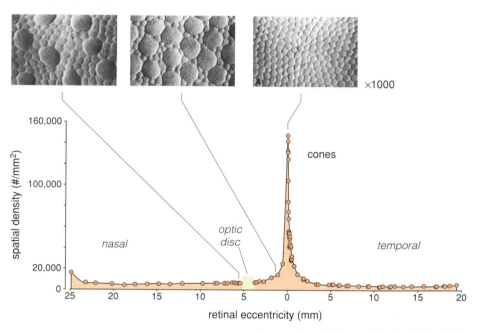

after Østerberg, 1935; as modified by Rodieck 1988;
micrographs from Curcio et al., 1990

The micrographs above the diagram show horizontal sections of the photoreceptor layer, with the plane of focus of the microscope at the level of the inner segments. The micrograph on the right shows the center of the fovea, where only cones are found. The middle micrograph shows the cone array at a **retinal eccentricity** of 1.35 mm at the same magnification. The cone inner segments (large profiles) are much thicker than those at the center of the fovea, and form an irregular hexagonal array, between which rods (small profiles) can be seen. The micrograph at the left illustrates the pattern seen in the peripheral retina. The cone inner segments are slightly thicker than at 1.35 mm, and the cone density has decreased; there is thus more space between the cones, which is filled by the rods. In the peripheral retina there are many more rods than cones, but because the diameter of the cone inner segments increases, they still cover between 20% and 25% of the area.

The contour map at the top of the next page has been shaded according to the spatial density of cones across the entire surface of the retina. The cones show a peak spatial density at the center of the fovea. The overall density of cones in the central region of the fovea is approximately constant from person to person, but the peak density varies. For some people, the peak is sharp like the Matterhorn; for others, it is more blunted. The spatial density of cones in the peripheral retina is irregular and also shows individual variation, but typically has a horizontal elongation, particularly in nasal retina.

retinal eccentricity
The distance from the center of the fovea or area centralis, usually expressed in millimeters. For species with a visual streak, this term refers to the distance above or below the streak. For more information, see VISUAL ANGLE AND RETINAL ECCENTRICITY in THE RAIN OF PHOTONS ONTO RODS (page 125).

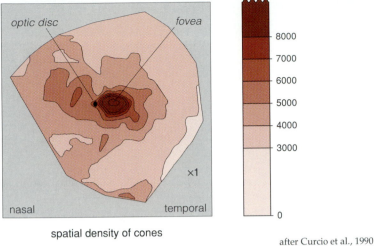

optic disc   fovea

×1

nasal   temporal

spatial density of cones

after Curcio et al., 1990

This diagram shows the spatial density of rods superimposed upon that of cones:

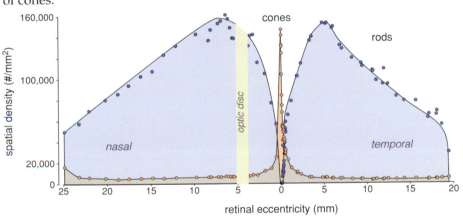

cones

rods

spatial density (#/mm^2)

optic disc

nasal

temporal

retinal eccentricity (mm)

after Østerberg, 1935; as modified by Rodieck, 1988

The spatial density of rods is zero in the center of the fovea, but rises quickly to reach a peak at an eccentricity between 5 and 7 mm, beyond which it steadily declines. There is a compensating increase in the thickness of the rod inner and outer segments, however, so that the photoreceptors continue to intercept almost all the light that falls on the retina.

The contour map to the right has been shaded according to the spatial density of rods across the entire surface of the retina. A rod-free area can be seen at the center of the fovea. The highest rod densities form a rough ring around the fovea with a radius of about 5 millimeters. The rod density is a bit lower along a horizontal strip through the fovea, as a consequence of the higher cone density in this region. There is usually a peak or "hot spot" of rod density above the fovea, as seen here, or beneath it as an indirect consequence of the reduced rod density along the horizontal strip through the fovea. The curve of rod density along a horizontal strip through the fovea, from the previous diagram, is shown below the contour map.

A brief functional walk through the retina

In THE CHASE, we traced a pathway through the retina that involved 20 or so cones, 5 or 6 bipolar cells, and a single ganglion cell (see the Box *VISUALIZING SINGLE NEURONS*). We now retrace our steps, taking both a broader view and a closer look as we go along.

spatial density of rods

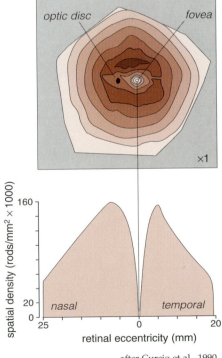

optic disc   fovea

×1

spatial density (rods/mm^2 × 1000)

160

20

0

nasal   temporal

25   0   20

retinal eccentricity (mm)

after Curcio et al., 1990

Visualizing single neurons

Neurons are densely packed in both the retina and the brain. Special techniques are needed to visualize single neurons; otherwise, it is a matter of not being able to see the trees for the forest. Late in the nineteenth century, two such techniques were discovered, which revolutionized our understanding of the nervous system.

Camillo Golgi chanced upon a method of preparing tissue for microscopic examination that caused crystals of silver to form and grow within a single cell, thereby revealing the shape of that cell. The illustration at the beginning of this chapter is from a student of Golgi, Ferruccio Tartuferi, who used the dispositions and arrangements of cells that had taken up silver to construct the semi-schematic diagram shown. It is the first drawing to show the basic wiring plan of the retina.

The second method, discovered by Philip Ehrlich, is based upon adding a dye named methylene blue to living neural tissue. This dye also selectively—although capriciously—stains single neurons; an example of ganglion cells of the same type stained by this method is shown on page 199.

Most modern methods for revealing the structure of a single neuron start by placing a fresh retina, or a portion of the back half of the eye, in a small chamber. The chamber is placed on a microscope stage, and the tissue is nourished by an oxygenated medium, similar to blood plasma, that flows across it. A single cell is identified by some means and penetrated with a microelectrode under direct visual observation. The microelectrode contains a staining substance that is injected into the cell by passing a weak current through it. The substance may be a fluorescent dye that diffuses throughout the cell.

An enhancement of this technique is to inject an additional substance that may not be visible at the time of the injection, but can serve as a substrate for chemical reactions that lead to the concentration of a dye when the tissue is later fixed and processed. Most of the individual cells shown in this book were stained by variants of this approach. A refinement of this technique allows the responses of the retinal neurons to be recorded when the retina is stimulated by light.

We start with a retina presumed to consist only of photoreceptors. We then add horizontal cells to this retina, see how they are attached to the photoreceptors, and briefly consider what they do. Bipolar cells are added next, followed by amacrine cells, then ganglion cells. Of course, much will have to be left out of this sketch, but it will help us to get the lay of the retinal land.

Photoreceptors

Primates, like other mammals, possess a single rod type. But primates also have three different cone types, whereas most mammals have only two. These three cone types, termed **L**, **M**, and **S**, are distinguished mainly by the portion of the spectrum of light to which each is most sensitive. These sensitivities will be described in the next chapter. But it is useful at this point to know that each photon of light has a **frequency** that remains essentially unchanged during its lifetime. Over the visible range, L cones are most sensitive to **l**ow-frequency photons, M cones to **m**iddle-frequency photons, and S cones to **s**upra-frequency photons. The three sensitivities are not equally spaced across the visible spectrum; instead, the spectral sensitivities of the L and M cones lie relatively close together toward the low-frequency end of the visible spectrum, and that of the S cones lies at the high-frequency end, as shown in the diagram at left.

The spatial distribution of S cones across the retina differs from that of L and M cones in a number of respects: S cones constitute only about 10% of the cone population, and are absent from the center of the fovea. There are 2–4 times as many L cones as M cones; otherwise these two types show similar spatial distributions, and appear to be randomly intermixed.

All vertebrate photoreceptors use the same mechanism for converting absorbed photons into a neural signal. This is a detailed process, taken up step by step in the next three chapters. For the moment let us put this matter aside, presume that they do so, and have a broad look at the layer of photoreceptors. Including rods, there are four photoreceptor types, each with its

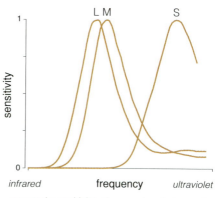

spectral sensitivity of cone visual pigments

own spatial distribution across the retina. Each photoreceptor of each of the four distributions receives the light from a different portion of the image, and responds according to the rate at which it catches photons. In this sense, the image has been converted into the activation of four different arrays of photoreceptors. But there is an odd complication, because, as we will see, the arrays are not really functionally independent of one another.

Processes from cone pedicles spread out to contact other cone pedicles, as well as rod spherules. At each such contact there is a low-resistance junction, termed a **gap junction**, that provides a partial electrical coupling between the two cells, and allows small molecules to pass between them:

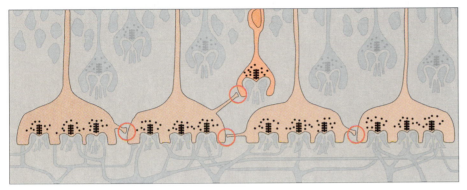

interphotoreceptor contacts

The role of these **interphotoreceptor contacts** remains unclear. This may be part of a broader problem in cell biology, since there are gap junctions between many cells of the body—including cells that do not produce an electrical response—whose functional roles are likewise a mystery. Our immediate concern is whether these contacts have any significant influence on the dynamic processing of the image as it moves across the retina. As discussed in the next chapter, it may be that the dynamics of the moving image sufficiently outpace the spread of electrical changes via interphotoreceptor contacts, and that these contacts play no significant role in the dynamic aspects of visual processing.

Just above each invagination in a pedicle or spherule lies a specialized structure termed a **synaptic ribbon**, which, as we'll see in A CONE PATHWAY, plays an important role in the transmission of signals from a photoreceptor to the horizontal and bipolar cells it contacts (right).

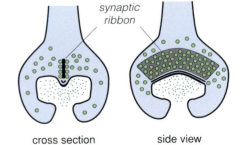

synaptic ribbon

cross section   side view

Horizontal cells

We now attach the horizontal cells to the photoreceptor arrays. Whether in rods or cones, each invagination contains two horizontal cell processes, each from a different horizontal cell. These two processes lie deep in the invagination, one on each side of the synaptic ribbon:

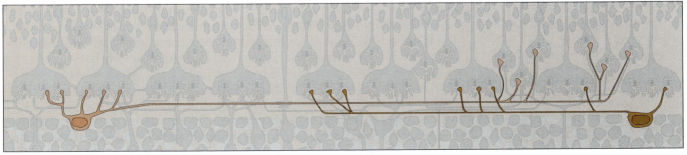

HI   horizontal cells   HII

There are two types of horizontal cells, termed HI ("H one") and HII ("H two"). Cells of each type are found throughout the retina:

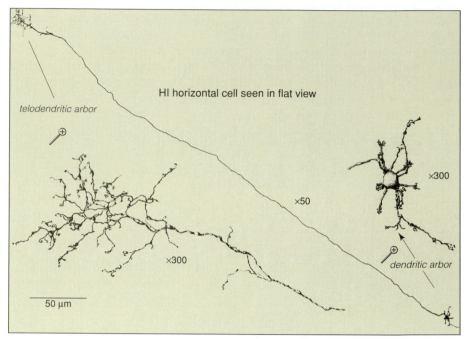

HI horizontal cell seen in flat view

telodendritic arbor

×300

×50

×300

dendritic arbor

50 μm

after Rodieck, 1988

Both types have a small dendritic arbor about the cell body; in addition, each HI horizontal cell has an axon that extends a millimeter or more across the retina, at which point it repeatedly branches to form a **telodendritic arbor**. This arbor is extensive, covering a region that contains about 700 rods. Each rod synaptic terminal contacts two lateral telodendritic arbor processes, each from a different HI horizontal cell. The axon of the horizontal cell does not generate action potentials, and is sufficiently long that the graded electrical activity taking place in the telodendritic arbor is isolated from that of the dendritic arbor. The axon thus serves to isolate two functionally distinct portions of the same cell. How this evolutionary path came to be taken is unknown, and clear instances of intermediate forms in other mammals have yet to be observed.

Each of the terminals of the HI telodendritic arbor is stimulated by the rod spherule it contacts according to the rate at which the rods are catching photons. As discussed in THE RAIN OF PHOTONS ONTO RODS, the arbor then acts on the rods it receives from according to the degree that it has been stimulated by those rods.

Each rod synaptic terminal also contains two to five processes that belong to a corresponding number of **rod bipolar cells**, one of which is shown schematically in the diagram shown at the top of the next page. Each rod bipolar cell contacts between 30 and 50 rods in this manner, and is activated by those rods. However, the magnitude of this activation is modulated by the activity of the horizontal cells. In particular, *the greater the stimulation of the telodendritic arbors of the horizontal cells by rods, the smaller the effect of each rod on the rod bipolar cells it contacts.* In effect, the influence of each rod is reduced by an amount that depends upon the combined activity of the surrounding rods.

This is an example of a very common form of neural circuitry, whose function is given the generic term **lateral inhibition**. Here, the effect of the overall level of light intensity on the rods, and hence on the HI telodendritic arbors, causes the activation of the rod bipolar cells to depend more on *dif-*

rod synaptic terminals

HI horizontal cell

rod bipolar cell

ferences in light intensity within the image, such as at a border, than on the overall level of light intensity. Because each rod contacts two HI telodendritic arbors, the overlapping arbors tend to act as a single functional entity, in which the borders of any one arbor are of no particular importance.

We now turn to the other end of the HI axon, which provides another example of lateral inhibition, this time involving cones rather than rods. The dendrites of adjacent HI cells are strongly coupled together by means of gap junctions. This can be demonstrated by injecting dye into the cell body of one HI cell, which spreads to the other HI cells by means of the gap junctions:

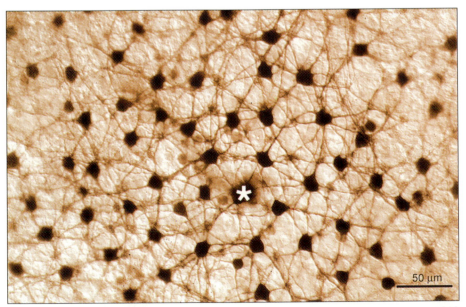

50 μm

×300

HI horizontal cells labeled following injection of one HI cell (∗)

after Dacey, Lee, and Stafford, 1996

However, HI horizontal cells are coupled only to one another, never to HII horizontal cells, and the selective manner in which they contact the cones is striking.

The dendritic terminals of HI cells receive from both L and M cones, *but never from S cones*. In this diagram, the ovals represent the cone pedicles viewed end on:

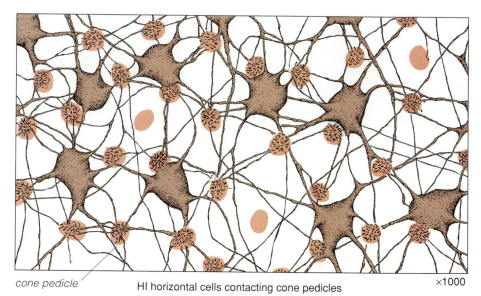

cone pedicle

HI horizontal cells contacting cone pedicles

×1000

after Dacey, Lee, and Stafford, 1996

A few cones are seen to make no contacts with the HI dendrites; they are S cones. Almost all of the lateral processes in the invaginations of the remaining cones come from HI horizontal cells. Each invagination contains two lateral processes, each from a different HI cell. The functional relation between the HI dendrites, the cone pedicles, and the cone bipolar cells appears to be basically the same as that between the HI telodendritic arbors, the rod spherules, and the rod bipolar cells. Although this neural circuitry is different, it too acts to reduce the effect of the overall level of light intensity on the cone bipolar cells, and thereby produces a relative enhancement of their response to differences in light intensity. Note, however, that unlike the rod circuitry, the HI dendritic arbor receives from two different cone types, L and M, and it is their combined contribution to the HI array that acts on each cone so as to reduce the cone's effect on the bipolar cells it contacts.

We now turn to a third form of lateral inhibition, this one involving HII horizontal cells, S cones, and the cone bipolar cells that receive from them:

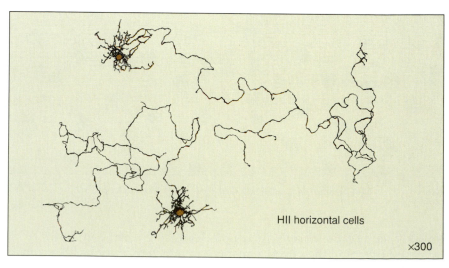

HII horizontal cells

×300

source: Rodieck, 1988

HII horizontal cells lack a long axon, but do have a shorter process from which arises a few short dendritic branches. HII horizontal cells are also strongly coupled to one another via gap junctions, and a dye injected into one cell spreads extensively into other HII horizontal cells over a wide region:

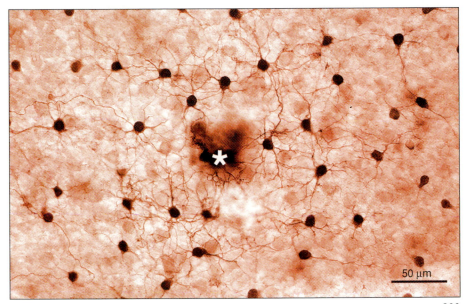

HII horizontal cells labeled following injection of one HII cell (∗)   ×300

after Dacey, Lee, and Stafford, 1996

All of the lateral processes in the invaginations of S cones are dendritic terminals of HII horizontal cells. About an equal number of dendritic terminals from HII horizontal cells contact M and L cones. But since there are about nine times as many M and L cones as S cones, each M or L cone receives only a minor influence from HII cells as compared with HI cells. Although the L and M cones do not appear to be strongly influenced by HII cell circuitry, the S cones obviously are. By means of this pattern of contacts, the array of HII cells is activated in about equal measure by S cones on the

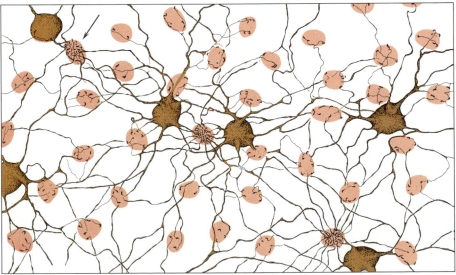

HII horizontal cells contacting cone pedicles   ×1000

after Dacey, Lee, and Stafford, 1996

one hand and a mixture of M and L cones on the other. This combined input influences the bipolar cells that receive from S cones. Later we will consider the functional roles played by this circuitry, and that of the HI dendritic system, on color vision.

To summarize, horizontal cells provide lateral inhibition, which acts to enhance spatial differences in photoreceptor activation at the level of the bipolar cells. There are three forms of lateral inhibition. One is exclusive to the rods and rod bipolar cells and is mediated by the telodendritic arbors of HI horizontal cells; the spatial effect comes from the large sizes of the overlapping telodendritic arbors. The second involves the dendrites of HI cells, L and M cones, and the cone bipolar cells that receive from them; here the spatial effect results from gap junctions between HI cells. The third form of lateral inhibition involves HII cells, all cone types, and the bipolar cells that receive from the S cones, with the spatial effect due mainly to gap junctions between HII cells.

Bipolar cells

Now we add the bipolar cells to the retina. Drawings of primate bipolar cells impregnated with silver granules show that they can take a variety of forms (below). Each bipolar cell has some dendritic processes in the outer synaptic layer, a cell nucleus in the inner nuclear layer, and some axon terminals in the inner synaptic layer (the occasional swellings seen between the cell nucleus and the axon terminals do not occur in living tissue, but are artifacts of the procedures used to prepare the tissue).

Several types of bipolar cells are shown schematically in the diagram at the top of the next page. The dendritic processes of a bipolar cell receive either from cones or from rods, never from both. Thus we can distinguish **rod bipolar cells** (those that receive from rods) from **cone bipolar cells**. The cone pedicles all lie at the same level in the retina, and the rod spherules lie

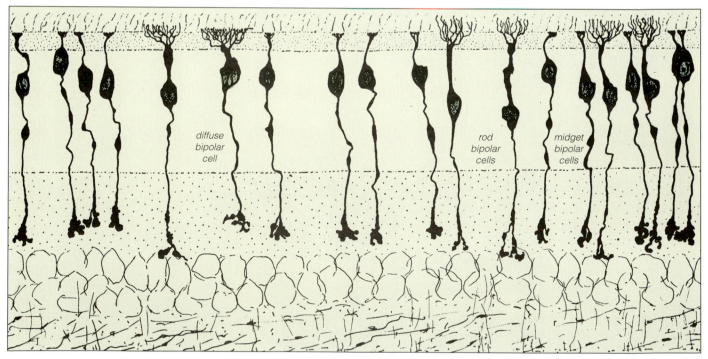

diffuse
bipolar
cell

rod
bipolar
cells

midget
bipolar
cells

×300

after Polyak, 1941

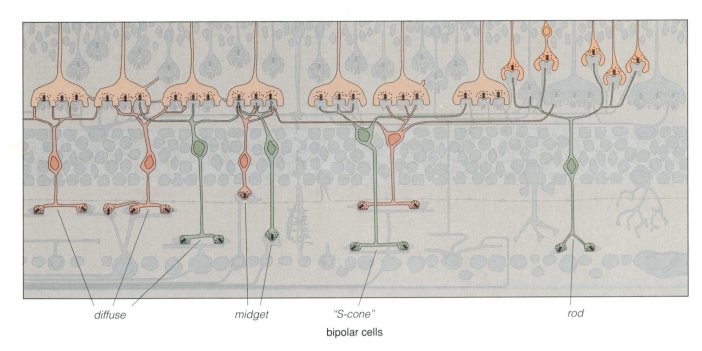

diffuse   midget   "S-cone"   rod

bipolar cells

backed up behind them. The dendritic processes of the rod bipolar cells must thus pass between the cone pedicles in order to reach the rods, and thus lie at different levels, whereas the dendrites of the cone bipolar cells all necessarily lie at the same level. Each rod contacts between 2 and 5 rod bipolar cells, and as noted earlier, each rod bipolar cell receives from 30–50 different rods (right).

The other types of bipolar cells receive only from cones, and there is an extravagant variety of them. Some thirteen different types are currently recognized, which can be arbitrarily grouped as follows:

Bipolar cell group	Number of types
Midget	5
Diffuse	6
"S-cone"	1
Giant	1

The schematic diagram above includes some of these different cone bipolar cell types. Only one "giant" type is listed in this table, but there are probably more.

The term **cell type** has a particular meaning, and because it will be used a lot from this point on, it is worth making its meaning clear. In general, each *class* of retinal cells (photoreceptors, bipolar cells, etc.) consists of a number of cell *types*. These individual types are real; they have an objective reality that can be demonstrated by an absence of intermediate forms between them. By contrast, the grouping of types into *classes* is part biology and part definition. It could have been otherwise, but the members of each retinal cell type show very similar properties. For example, they release the same transmitter substance, make the same connections to other cell types, and generally have the same **morphology**. It is as if every member of a cell type, in the process of differentiating, had chosen the same items from a menu of properties that characterizes cells of that type.

Among the members of any one cell type, the greatest variation one observes generally follows the change in the spatial density of cells of this type across the retina. For example, in moving from the foveal region to the

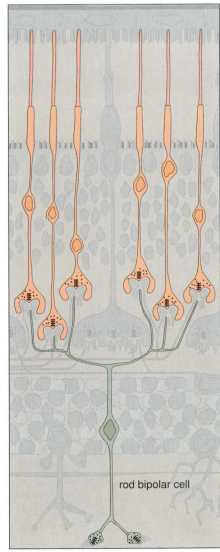

rod bipolar cell

parasol ganglion cells

acacia trees in Djibuti

after Polyak, 1941

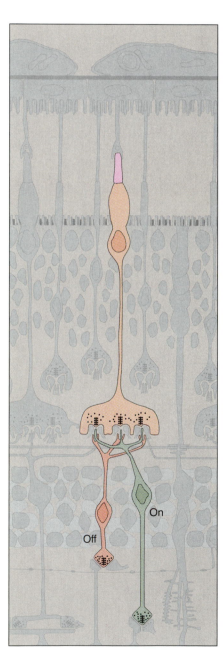

off- and on-midget bipolars

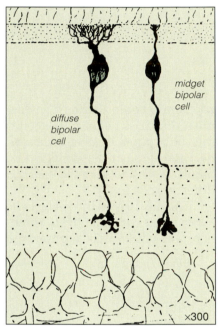

midget bipolar cell

diffuse bipolar cell

×300

after Polyak, 1941

periphery, the spatial density of most (but not all) cell types decreases, and the lateral extent of the cell's processes increases. These changes are similar to those between forest and meadow trees of the same species.

Returning to the thirteen different types of cone bipolar cells in the primate retina, three important differences among them are these:

1. *Number of cones that contact the bipolar cell.* A midget bipolar cell, for example, receives from a single cone, whereas a diffuse bipolar cell near the fovea receives from 5–10 cones (right).

2. *Type of contacts made.* Each M or L cone in the fovea contacts two midget bipolar cells of differing types (left). The midget bipolar cell whose dendritic processes project into the center of the cone invaginations is activated by an *increase* in the photon catch of the cone. It is termed an **on-midget bipolar cell**. The other midget bipolar cell has processes that lie near the invagination; it is activated by a *decrease* in the photon catch of the cone, and is termed an **off-midget bipolar cell**. Thus, from bipolar cells onward, some visual neurons respond to an increase in light, whereas others respond to a decrease. As you might expect, this is a critical feature of the visual system, and one that we will return to many times. (In the schematic diagrams, "on" bipolar cells are shown in green, and "off" bipolar cells are colored red.) By the way, the terms "on" and "off" come from the idea of turning a light on or off; but it is better to see through this terminology and think in terms of increases or decreases in the photons captured by the photoreceptors.

3. *Type(s) of cones that contact the bipolar cell.* For example, there are two *types* of on-midget bipolar cells, termed an **L-on-midget bipolar cell** (receives from an L cone) and an **M-on-midget bipolar cell**. These two types differ not only in the cone type they receive from, but also in the

number of contacts each makes in the inner synaptic layer with the processes of amacrine cells. As its name suggests, the **S-on bipolar cell** is a type that receives from S cones and is activated by an increase in the photon catch; it can receive from one or a few S cones.

As you might anticipate, a lot more could be said about the different types of bipolar cells, but enough has been presented here to give something of a feel for the richness and diversity of bipolar cell types and the nature and specificity of the contacts they make. Each bipolar cell conveys its changing level of activation to the inner synaptic layer, where it contacts the processes of both amacrine and ganglion cells.

Amacrine cells

Now we add the amacrine cells to the retina. There are many different types of amacrine cells, which vary greatly in size, morphology, and function. The

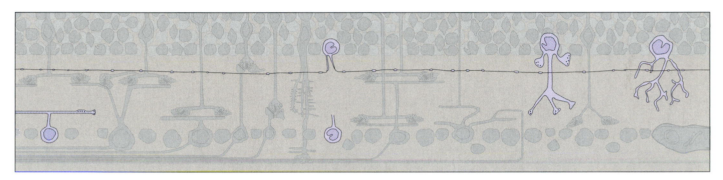

amacrine cells

number of types is uncertain, but there are no fewer than 20; my guess would be closer to 40. This view of the inner surface of a monkey retina shows a variety of different types of amacrine cells:

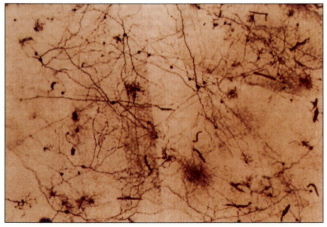

x100

amacrine cells of monkey retina, seen in flat view

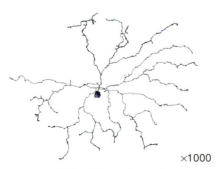

×1000

starburst amacrine cell

source: Rodieck, 1989

Most types, like the "starburst" amacrine cell shown in greater detail at right, have a characteristic and distinctive morphology.

Amacrine cells receive from bipolar cells and other amacrine cells. In turn, they send their messages to bipolar cells, other amacrine cells, and ganglion cells. All this suggests that amacrine cells play a variety of roles in retinal function, but with few exceptions, their specific roles remain unknown.

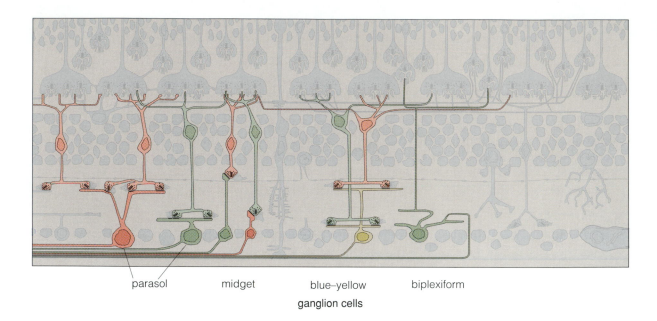

parasol   midget   blue–yellow   biplexiform

ganglion cells

Ganglion cells

Finally we add the ganglion cells (above) to the retina. Each ganglion cell sends a message to the brain in the form of the rate at which it generates action potentials. This rate is influenced by the activity of the different amacrine and bipolar cells that the ganglion cell receives from. As a general rule that has possible exceptions, the activity of bipolar cells tends to increase the firing rate of the ganglion cell, and the activity of amacrine cells tends to decrease it. Ganglion cells of a given type make stereotypic connections with bipolar and amacrine cells. For example, on- and off-midget ganglion cells receive from on- and off-midget bipolar cells, respectively, as shown on the next page.

Unlike the other cell classes we have discussed, ganglion cells send their messages out of the eye, rather than to other retinal cells. Most ganglion cell types respond in specialized ways. For example, some respond to the movement of a border in one direction, but not to movement in the opposite direction. This directional selectivity is probably a property of some of the amacrine cells these ganglion cells receive from, rather than a property somehow created by the ganglion cell from the signals it receives from amacrine and bipolar cells. In this sense, the response properties of the ganglion cell have more to do with the extent and grain (density of processes) of its dendritic field, and with the cell types that it receives from, than with any particular features of the ganglion cell itself.

The number of different ganglion cell types in the primate retina is uncertain. There is a minimum of 22 distinct types; a better guess, based upon differences in morphology, might be closer to 30. Each ganglion cell type is specialized for coding some particular aspect of the visual world (e.g., contrast, color, movement). Thus the brain receives a wide variety of different messages from the retina. As we will see, the axons of different types of ganglion cells go to six different regions within the primate brain. Each region is adapted to subserve a different type of visual function, and the ganglion cells that go to a region are likewise adapted to provide the specific information about the visual world needed for that function.

The basic circuitry throughout the retina is the same

The retina contains a fixed number of cell types that make the same kinds of connections again and again. The relative numbers of each cell type, and thus the convergence of the signals of cells of one type onto those of another, may change with location in the retina. There may also be a few other changes that have to do not so much with convergence as with the greater spread of processes needed to achieve this convergence. But such differences are details; if we could know how one square millimeter of the retina works, then we would know all but the details.

This is a broad sketch of some of the general patterns of interaction found in the vertebrate retina. Later we will see specific examples of retinal circuitry adapted to convey specific aspects of the visual world and our interaction with it.

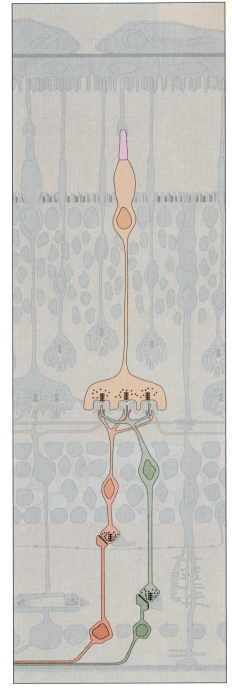

off- and on-midget pathways

INTERLUDE

Size

In the coming chapters we will encounter a large range of distances, times, and intensities. Most of the magnitudes and all of the units will be expressed in scientific notation or SI units. If you are unfamiliar with these means of representing physical quantities, you should read the "Numbers and units" section of this Interlude.

You may have noticed that each diagram of an object includes a magnification factor. These are provided throughout this book, using a limited set of magnifications. This is a less common method of indicating size than a scale bar, and doesn't work for projectors and slides. But it has the advantage of conveying relative size in a consistent way. This is useful because different aspects of the physical world come into play at different magnifications. "Matters of scale" describes this approach, and illustrates it by means of different magnifications of the retina. Most readers should find this section useful.

Many of the diagrams that follow will contain logarithmic scales, and you may wish to read the section of this Interlude that reviews this means of plotting data as well.

Numbers and units

Scientific notation

In this book we will encounter some very large numbers, such as the frequency of light from the blue portion of the spectrum, which, in cycles per second, is about

$$667,000,000,000,000$$

A more compact way of representing this number is to consider it the product of a number equal to or greater than 1.0 but less than 10.0, multiplied by some product of 10s:

$$6.67 \times 100,000,000,000,000$$

Scientific notation concatenates the second factor into a power of 10:

$$6.67 \times 10^{14}$$

The superscript to the 10 is termed the **exponent** (Latin *exponere* = to expound, in this case meaning something to be laid out or expanded). The progression is simple:

10	10^1	
100	10^2	
1,000	10^3	thousand
10,000	10^4	
100,000	10^5	
1,000,000	10^6	million

and so on.

In this book we will also encounter very small numbers, such as the time it takes for a photon of this frequency to exert its effect on a visual pigment molecule within a photoreceptor, which, in seconds, is about

$$0.000,000,000,000,003$$

The way in which numbers smaller than 1 can be represented in scientific notation can be seen by extending the previous table *upward:*

. . .		
0.001	10^{-3}	thousandth
0.01	10^{-2}	
0.1	10^{-1}	
1	10^0	
10	10^1	
100	10^2	
1,000	10^3	thousand
. . .		

The notion that 1 is equal to 10^0 may seem odd, but that is the sequence of the exponents as one divides or multiplies by 10. Notice that for numbers less than 1, the number of zeros after the decimal point is one less than the magnitude (i.e., the value not including the sign) of the exponent. Thus for one-thousandth, in the left column above, the number of zeros to the right of the decimal point is 2, and in the right column, the magnitude of the exponent is 3. Applying this rule to

$$0.000,000,000,000,003$$

we get

$$3 \times 10^{-15}$$

Scientific notation simplifies the calculation of the product of two numbers of any magnitude. For example, the large number above multiplied by the small one,

$$667,000,000,000,000 \times 0.000,000,000,000,003$$

converts to:

$$6.67 \times 10^{14} \times 3 \times 10^{-15}$$

or

$$20.01 \times 10^{-1}$$

The 0.01 portion is an outcome of the calculation, but suggests precision that is not intended. Rounding gives:

2

This calculation provides the useful information that light exerts its effect on a photoreceptor within two cycles of the light's oscillation (see *PHOTONS ARE PARTICLES OF LIGHT* page 72 for a discussion of *frequency* and *oscillation*). Division is equally easy, with the exponent of the denominator being *subtracted* from that of the numerator, as you may easily verify.

Examples of scientific notation can be found in the Appendix STANDARD OBSERVER. This collection of quite different things with quite different magnitudes is an example of the sorts of situations in which scientific notation is most useful. But scientific notation has its drawbacks. In particular, the most important aspect of the magnitude, the exponent, is, by convention, printed using the smallest font size. Also, compare the following two numbers:

$$9.370 \times 10^{13}$$

$$1.126 \times 10^{14}$$

The second number is larger than the first, but in a column of values of similar things, that fact is easy to miss. Here it is better to break the rule of always using numbers greater than 1.0 in the first factor:

$$0.937 \times 10^{14}$$

$$1.126 \times 10^{14}$$

The SI system, discussed in the next section, takes a slightly different tack. It is the other method used in this book, and throughout science generally, to describe quantities.

SI units

The metric system, first proposed in 1670 and first adopted, in France, in 1795, is now universal in science. But until recently, there was a good deal of inconsistency in how it was applied. Some physical quantities were expressed in centimeters, grams, and seconds; others in meters, kilograms, and seconds. A consistent system, known as the International System of Units (*SI units*), was introduced in 1964, and is formally summarized in an Appendix to this book. Here we describe some of its flavor.

The frequency of a blue light is represented in SI units as:

667 THz

This notation consists of three parts:

667 THz

value multiplier unit

The SI unit for frequency is *Hertz* (Hz, from Heinrich Hertz, 1857–1895, who investigated the propagation of electromagnetic energy). The multiplier associated with this unit, T, is pronounced *tera*, and represents a trillion, or 10^{12} (Greek *teras* = monster). The frequency of this blue light is thus *six hundred and sixty-seven terahertz*.

In SI units, multipliers are, in general, multiples of 1000 (i.e., the exponent is a multiple of 3), rather than multiples of 10, as in scientific notation. That is why the value is given as 667, rather than 6.67×10^{14}, as in scientific notation.

The time it takes for a bit of blue light (or any light) to exert its effect on a photoreceptor, expressed in SI units, is

$$3 \text{ fs}$$

The units are seconds (s). The multiplier, f, represents 10^{-15}, and is pronounced *femto* (Danish or Norwegian *femten* = fifteen).

The etymology of the various multiplier prefixes is interesting. The multipliers larger than one all have Greek roots, the first three smaller than one come from Latin, and the remaining three in the table, which are of more recent origin as prefixes, come from other European languages.

Multiplier	Prefix	Symbol	Origin
10^{12}	tera	T	Greek *teras* = monster
10^{9}	giga	G	Greek *gigas* = giant
10^{6}	mega	M	Greek *megas* = large
10^{3}	kilo	k	Greek *khilioi* = thousand
10^{0}	—	—	—
10^{-3}	milli	m	Latin *milli-* from *mille* = thousand
10^{-6}	micro	μ	Latin *micro* = small
10^{-9}	nano	n	Latin *nanus* = dwarf
10^{-12}	pico	p	Spanish *pico* = small amount
10^{-15}	femto	f	Danish or Norwegian *femten* = fifteen
10^{-18}	atto	a	Danish or Norwegian *atten* = eighteen

Units can be multiplied together just as numerals can; for example, 1 meter × 1 meter = 1 square meter, which is written 1 m^2. Likewise, 1 square millimeter is written as 1 mm^2. The exponent 2 applies to both the basic unit and its multiplier, as if it were written 1 (mm)^2. In effect, when you combine a multiplier with a basic unit, you create a new unit with a new name.

In the section "Matters of scale" below, I've used a number of alternative forms of expressing magnifications and scales in order to provide examples of scientific notation and SI units.

Any true understanding of retinal function requires an appreciation of magnitudes, particularly relative magnitudes. It is thus useful to develop rough measures, easy to calculate, that allow magnitudes to be expressed in familiar quantities. For example, the population of the United States is roughly 250 million. A billion dollars (which in SI units would be G$, or *gigadollars*, although there is no $ unit in SI) is thus about 4 $ per person (I've placed the $ after the number to make it look like an SI unit). Although 250×10^6 is a huge number of people, and 10^9 $ is an unimaginable amount of money, 4 $/person is easy to grasp. A budget *deficit* of 300 G$ is thus about 1200 $/person. The U.S. *national debt* is currently 5.5 *trillion* dollars (5.5 T$ = 5500 G$), which comes to 22,000 $/person—graspable, but *monstrous*.

Matters of scale

The range of sizes one comes across in considering retinal function extends from the size of the eye to atomic dimensions, which are about 100,000,000

(10^8) times smaller. It is useful to keep the relative sizes of objects in mind. Therefore, all of the illustrations of organs, structures, cells, cellular components, molecules, and atomic components will be shown using a limited set of magnifications. Here is an overview of these magnifications, starting with the eye and increasing the magnification step by step until the atomic component that catches a photon of light is reached.

Magnification = 1

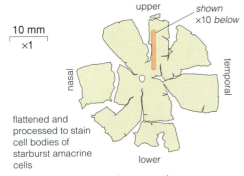

10 mm
×1

upper

shown ×10 *below*

nasal

temporal

flattened and processed to stain cell bodies of starburst amacrine cells

lower

human eye

human retina

Ten times magnification

1 mm
×10

upper

lower

labeled cell bodies of starburst amacrine cells in 1 mm wide strip of human retina

after Rodieck and Marshak, 1992

One hundred times magnification

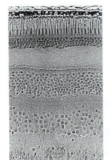

100 μm
×100

photomicrograph of a thin transverse section of the retina stained to show cell bodies, which are just visible at this magnification

Three hundred times magnification

At a magnification of 300 much of the dendritic morphology of stained neurons can be seen.

100 μm
×300

parasol ganglion cells

after Polyak, 1941

One thousand times magnification

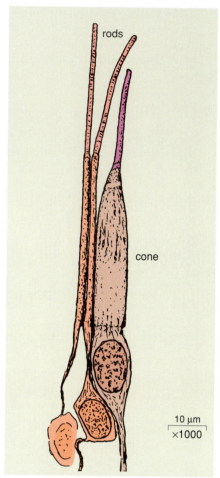

macaque photoreceptors

after Polyak, 1941

Ten thousand times magnification

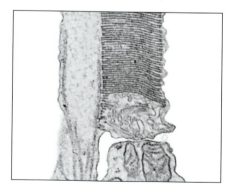

macaque cone outer segment

after Young, 1971

Photomicrographs from a light microscope can show detail only up to a magnification of about 1000. This limitation arises from the wavelength of light. This micrograph was made using an electron microscope, which has a much higher resolution. The tissue has been stained with metal ions, which cause cell membranes to appear dark. At this magnification, the outer segments of the photoreceptors can be seen to be filled with cell membranes.

One hundred thousand times magnification

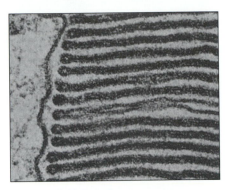

macaque rod outer segment

At a magnification of 100,000 the membranes within the outer segment can be seen to form flattened discs.

100 nm
×100,000

from Dowling, 1967

One million times magnification

The shapes of large molecules become visible at this magnification, although the images obtained from an electron microscope—or any magnification device—are blurry. Molecular models or stylized icons of about the same magnified size are often used instead:

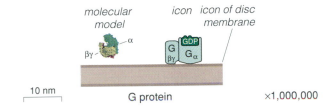

molecular model   *icon*   *icon of disc membrane*

10 nm

G protein

×1,000,000

In the **macroscopic** world of our everyday experience, we are familiar with *temperatures* and *pressures*, and at first sight, it might seem plausible that these properties would extend to the microscopic world of molecules as well.

But as we focus on this **microscopic** level, temperature and atmospheric pressure fade from view and are replaced by the motions of individual molecules or particles. These motions include flying about in the air, tumbling about in fluids, and vibrating back and forth in solids.

Temperature is a good example of an *emergent property*. The rules of heat are based upon the average behavior of enormous numbers of microscopic objects such as molecules and atoms. The whole is not greater than the sum of its parts, but it shows properties not manifestly evident in, although predicatable from, the behavior of its parts.

macroscopic, microscopic
Greek *macro-* = large + *-skopion* = to see; colloquially, "the big view." Greek *micro* = small.

reduction, emergence
These terms are used here in an informal way. *Reduction* refers to some model within the broader domain of science that forms an underpinning to the topic at hand. *Emergence* refers to the same relationship, but points in the opposite direction. If a step toward reduction leads to a set of rules, then emergence is the step in the other direction that explores or reflects the consequences of those rules, not all of which are obvious or, in some cases, even predictable.

Biological evolution provides boundless examples of the sorts of emergence that gave Darwin a shudder because of the seemingly endless number of steps required. But the physical world is also filled with emergent phenomena, as in the relation between atomic mechanics and temperature or pressure. The subtleties that can result from the application of simple rules are well illustrated by the Oriental game of Go. So emergence is not so much a consequence of physics or biology per se; rather, it is the rich domain of possibilities that results from the application of a limited set of rules.

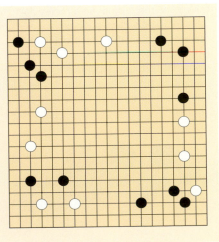

Ten million times magnification

This small light-catching molecule combines with a larger protein molecule to form the visual pigment molecules found in rods and cones.

This molecule is released by photoreceptors and bipolar cells. At this magnification, molecules begin to be seen as particular arrangements of atoms.

×10,000,000

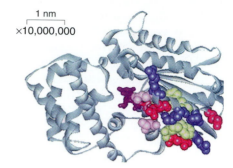

11-*cis* retinal

glutamate molecule

α subunit of G-protein molecule

after Hamm, 1998

Thirty million times magnification

At this magnification, the individual atoms of a molecule come into view, as seen in these atomic models of small molecules.

Illustrations such as these are useful for showing the arrangement of the atoms that compose a molecule. But atoms do not have a sharply defined extent, as the hard surfaces in these illustrations suggest.

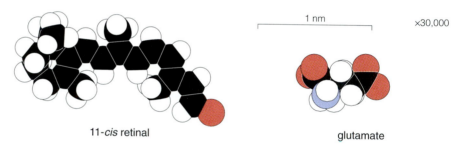

1 nm   ×30,000

11-*cis* retinal

glutamate

The elegant drawings of David Goodsell, such as this rendering of 11-*cis* retinal, better illustrate this aspect of molecular structure. The molecule is shown from a slightly different perspective, which foreshortens its apparent width compared with the previous illustration.

1 nm
×30,000,000

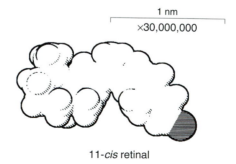

11-*cis* retinal

from Goodsell, 1993

atomic model
A common means of representing the atoms that compose a molecule is by simple shapes, such as spheres, that fill the space occupied by the approximate shape of the molecule. Here, these shapes are colored according to the nature of the atomic element.

hydrogen carbon nitrogen oxygen phosphorus

×30,000,000

A magnification of about one million or so represents a practical limit to imaging microscopic things. One can, of course, print images at any magnification, but they will show an intrinsic fuzziness. It is possible to resort to molecular models, derived from measurements of crystals of the molecule.

But they *are* models, and are able to represent only a few features of the real thing. At even higher magnifications, the representation becomes abstract, and the icons used to represent the smallest things, such as photons and electrons, can no longer reflect structure; they can only suggest something of the manners in which these particles interact with the world. On reflection, this is what we should expect of the smallest things, for if they were little spheres, then we should be able to chop them up and see what sort of stuff *they* are made of.

Summary

This section has considered only the representation of objects, or parts thereof, shown at different magnifications. It is worthwhile to keep in mind that the higher the magnification, the less the microscopic world looks and acts like the macroscopic world we are used to and are adapted for.

It is worthwhile to keep the magnification in mind when viewing some bit of the retina, both to compare and contrast the sizes of different things, and to get a feel for the pace of things and the relative importance of the physical forces that act upon them.

With increasing magnification, not only does the appearance of the world change, but the way it works changes as well. We saw the first indication of this at a magnification of about 1,000,000, where temperature and pressure, which reflect the average properties of many things, are superseded by the mechanical motions of a few things. The physical laws don't change, but their relative importance does.

Logarithmic scales

"Matters of scale" presented several views of the retina at different magnifications. This diagram shows portions of these illustrations at magnifications that are multiples of 10. These multiples are equally spaced across the page, as indicated by the scale below them. One step to the right *increases* the magnification by a factor of 10; likewise, one step to the left *decreases* it by the same factor.

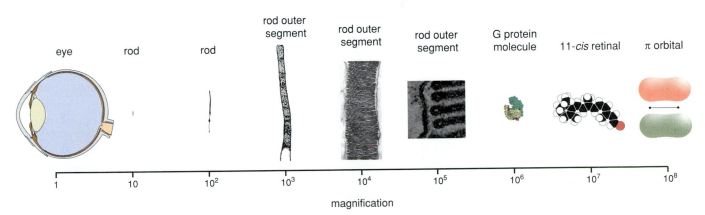

This type of scale is termed **logarithmic** (Greek *logos* = ratio + *arithmos* = number) because the ratio of the values from one step to the next is always the same. The tick marks on the scale are separated by a factor of ten. But this choice is arbitrary; had a ratio of two been chosen for the tick marks and numbers, then this same logarithmic scale would be marked as in the lower portion of the following diagram. With these markings, a step to the right doubles the value of the previous step, whereas a step to the left halves it:

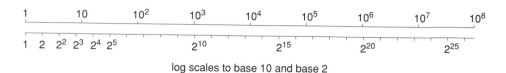

log scales to base 10 and base 2

The logarithmic scale is the same in either case, and equalizes ratio steps of any fixed value. If one plots any particular magnification on this scale, it still falls in the same position. For example, a magnification of 1000 (10^3) is slightly smaller than a magnification of 1024 (2^{10}).

The ratio used to mark the scale is thus rather arbitrary. Whatever ratio is chosen is termed the **base** of the logarithmic scale. The most commonly used base, and the one used in this book, is ten; this convention is termed a **common logarithmic scale**.

Everyone is familiar with an *arithmetic scale* (Greek *arithmos* = number):

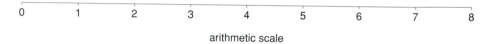

arithmetic scale

One step to the right *increases* the value by 1; likewise, one step to the left *decreases* the value by 1. Notice that in an arithmetic scale, the step is *added* to the previous value in going from left to right, whereas in a logarithmic scale, the step is *multiplied* by the previous value.

If we had chosen a step size of 0.5, the arithmetic scale would be drawn like this:

arithmetic scale

Of course, a value of, say, 3.7 plots to the same point on the arithmetic scale, whichever step size is used. The step size is arbitrary, just as it is for a logarithmic scale.

A logarithmic scale is useful when one is attempting to show a large range of values, as illustrated above for magnification, but it has other uses as well. In particular, a logarithmic scale is the natural choice when we are concerned with relative values (i.e., the ratio of two values). For example, a 10% change often has more meaning than a specific value (10% off!; a 15% tip). We often think in terms of ratios—when following a recipe, we may halve or double each of the items. The rate of inflation is expressed in terms of a certain percentage per year. Earnings from compound interest move to the right along a logarithmic scale at a regular rate determined by the interest rate.

All things considered, thinking in terms of ratios (twice as much wood) is a concept at least as old as, if not older than, thinking in terms of numbers (17 goats). Even bean counters need a logarithmic scale when the numbers get large. The decimal system is a compact way of arranging digits so that each digit has a multiplier 10 times greater than the one to its right (i.e., 342 = $3 \times 10^2 + 4 \times 10^1 + 2$). So even the conventional way in which we represent numbers is based upon an implicit logarithmic scale.

But both arithmetic and logarithmic scales have their uses, and we go back and forth between them. Consider the time intervals of our lives:

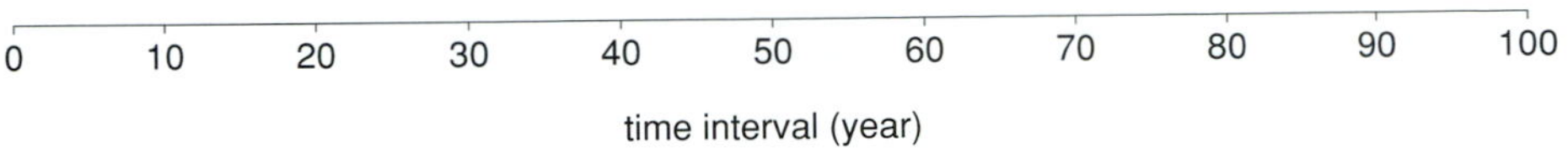

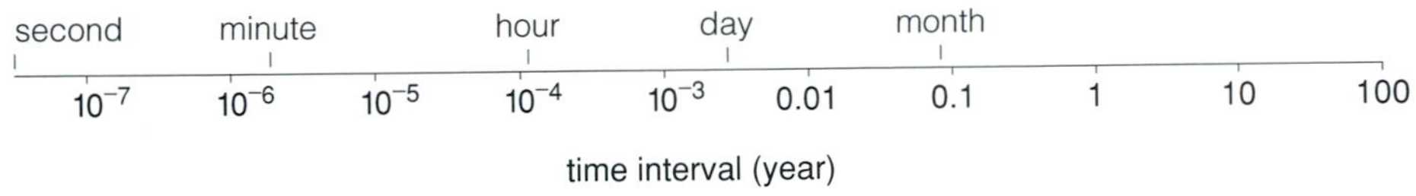

```
0     10    20    30    40    50    60    70    80    90    100
```

time interval (year)

```
second        minute        hour      day       month
    10⁻⁷    10⁻⁶    10⁻⁵    10⁻⁴    10⁻³   0.01      0.1      1      10      100
```

time interval (year)

stars that can be seen via cones

4

The rain of photons onto cones

THE CHASE *briefly described the sequence of events that occurred when you went camping and looked at a star. This chapter retells part of that story in greater detail, starting with the light from the star and ending with the activation of visual pigment molecules within the cones that view the star. This retelling will be concluded in* A CONE PATHWAY, *which describes the responses of cones to the photons they catch, and one pathway from the cones to the brain.*

We see a star when its photons activate our neurons

Almost all photons come from stars, including our nearest star, the Sun. Stars convert matter to energy and dissipate that energy as photons. Polaris is so far away that the photons it emits take about 6.5 years to reach Earth. Nevertheless, it showers Earth's surface with a steady rain of photons.

About 18,000 photons from Polaris arrive every second on each square millimeter of Earth that faces this star. Formally, we can say that the **flux density** of photons from Polaris is 18,000 photon/s/mm²:

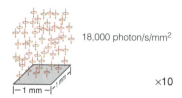

flux density of photons from Polaris

The term *flux* refers to the total amount of light (18,000 photons per second), and the term *density* refers to their concentration (per square millimeter).

On the sunny side of Earth, there is a torrential rain of photons from the Sun. They flood Earth's sky and surface, and we cannot discriminate the photons from Polaris in this downpour:

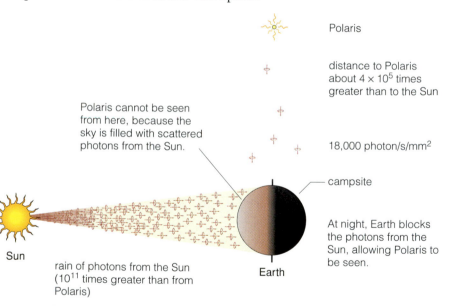

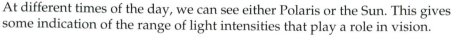

photon

Photons are fundamental particles of physics and as such have no adequate representation in the macroscopic world of our senses. This photon icon used in this book serves only to remind us of some of the properties that photons possess.

At different times of the day, we can see either Polaris or the Sun. This gives some indication of the range of light intensities that play a role in vision.

Heated bodies radiate photons over a range of frequencies

Photons differ from one another in two independent ways: each has a **frequency** of oscillation, which we will consider here, and each has a **polarization**, which we will ignore for the time being. Like any heated body, Polaris radiates photons into space. These photons have a wide range of frequencies, extending from near zero to over 1000 THz (see the Box *PHOTONS ARE PARTICLES OF LIGHT*, page 72).

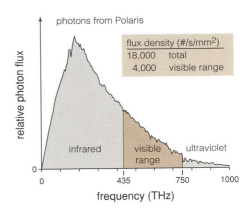

flux density (#/s/mm²)
18,000   total
4,000   visible range

photons from Polaris

The diagram at right shows the approximate distribution of the frequencies of the photons that reach Earth's outer atmosphere from Polaris. The distribution for Polaris has not actually been determined over the full frequency range shown, so the distribution shown is that of photons from the Sun, which is similar. (See the Box *LOOKING AT SPECTRAL DENSITY CURVES* on page 74 for more information about spectral distribution diagrams like this one. If you are familiar with spectral distributions described in terms of wavelengths and energies, then see WAVELENGTH AND ENERGY for a discussion of why frequencies and photons are used here.)

Most of the photons from the Sun or stars have frequencies in the infrared portion of the spectrum. They warm us when they are absorbed by our skin, but we can't see with them. The frequencies at which our photoreceptors have some chance of catching a photon extend from about 435 THz to about 750 THz. At each of these ends of the scale, our sensitivity to photons falls to about 1% of our peak sensitivity. Photons between these limits are said to lie in the **visible range**.

Before the photons in the visible range can reach our eyes, they must pass through Earth's atmosphere. Some are absorbed by ozone molecules, water droplets, and other particles in the air. Still others are scattered by the atmosphere so that when they reach Earth, they do so from a different direction than that from which they entered the atmosphere. We can never say with certainty that a given photon will be absorbed or scattered, because these events have only probabilities of occurring. But if we consider a large enough flux of photons—as in this case—then the fraction of this population that will be absorbed or scattered will be reasonably constant from moment to moment. This fraction depends upon a variety of atmospheric factors. It also depends upon how much atmosphere the photons have to pass through in order to reach our eyes; when we look toward the horizon, the path is longer than when we look directly overhead. Thus the lower the latitude, the longer the path through the atmosphere from Polaris to our eyes (see the diagram at right).

The following diagram shows the fate of photons as they pass through a clear sky in the temperate zone of the Northern Hemisphere. The diagram shows only the visible portion of the spectrum. The upper curve is taken from the previous spectral diagram, and shows the spectral distribution of the rain of photons that reaches Earth's atmosphere. Ignoring the small irregularities, there is a continuous decline in the relative number of photons from lower to higher frequencies.

Wavelength & Energy *513*

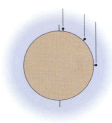

Polaris

Earth

path through atmosphere depends upon direction of gaze

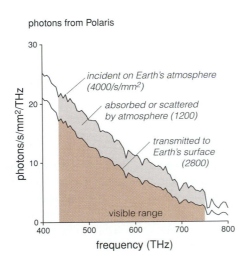

photons from Polaris

incident on Earth's atmosphere (4000/s/mm²)

absorbed or scattered by atmosphere (1200)

transmitted to Earth's surface (2800)

visible range

frequency (THz)

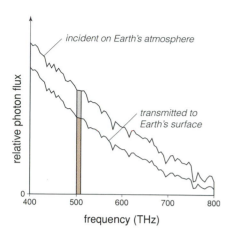

incident on Earth's atmosphere

transmitted to Earth's surface

relative photon flux

frequency (THz)

The total flux density over this portion of the spectrum is 4000 photon/s/mm², or about 22% of the rain of photons of all frequencies from Polaris. Of these, 1200 are scattered or absorbed by the atmosphere, leaving 2800 photon/s/mm² to reach Earth's surface.

In interpreting these diagrams, it is important to know that when a photon interacts with matter, its frequency does not change. Thus photons with frequencies in the range from, say, 500 to 510 THz have the same frequencies at Earth's surface that they had above Earth's surface (left). Any photons in this spectral band that do not reach Earth directly must have been either absorbed or scattered. As will soon become apparent, loss of photons by absorption and scattering is a recurring theme.

Of course, this rain of photons need not fall on the ground, for as you gaze at Polaris, some portion of them will fall on your face, and a smaller fraction will fall on your eyes. We will track the photons that encounter the cornea of one of your eyes, and consider their fate on the journey toward your retina. As it happens, about the same fraction of photons will be scattered or

Photons are particles of light

You may have heard that light is made of "waves," or of "rays." These terms come from models that are used to explain how light can form images, and are properly used in that context. But photoreceptors catch photons, not waves, and in order to appreciate how photoreceptors work, it is necessary to understand a few of the properties that photons possess.

From our perspective, the most important property of a photon is the frequency at which it oscillates. The power company sends us *electrons* that oscillate at a rate of 60 times per second (60 Hz). Radio stations send us *photons* whose frequency of oscillation ranges from 550 to 1600 kHz in the AM spectral band, and from 88 to 108 MHz in the FM band. The Sun sends us photons that lie mostly in the infrared region of the spectrum, but a quarter of them lie in the visible spectral range, from 430 to 750 THz. The difference in these frequency ranges is so great that it is necessary to use a logarithmic scale to distinguish them:

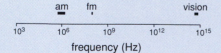

am   fm   vision

10^3 10^6 10^9 10^{12} 10^{15}

frequency (Hz)

When sunlight is passed through a prism, the photons of higher frequencies are bent more than those of lower frequencies; a rainbow is produced by raindrops in a similar manner. We see a spectrum of colors over the visible range, which looks something like the image at the top of the next column. One might be led to believe that photons come in different colors, but as Isaac Newton recognized, this is a conceptual mistake; the photons are not colored.

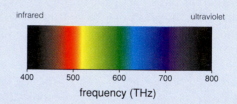

infrared   ultraviolet

400   500   600   700   800

frequency (THz)

As we will see, we have evolved cones with different spectral sensitivities, as well as neural mechanisms that compare the outputs of these cones. These neural mechanisms allow us to distinguish lights of different spectral composition, which we perceive as color differences. So the purpose of this diagram is only to provide a rough relation between the frequency of a photon and the sensation that is produced when we see a light composed of photons of that frequency.

Frequency is important because each photon has a certain amount of *energy* that is directly proportional to its frequency:

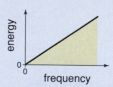

energy

0

frequency

The photons that radiate from the sun have different frequencies, and thus different energies—lower toward the infrared and higher toward the ultraviolet. With reference to the logarithmic scale above, we see that a photon in the visible range has about a million times more energy than a

absorbed in passing through your eye as were lost in passing through the atmosphere. Furthermore, for some frequency interval the fraction lost in your eye is greater at higher frequencies, just as in the atmosphere. What is useful to keep in mind is not photon flux per se, but where the losses occur, since the fractional loss for any given frequency interval is the same whether the light is from Polaris, from the Sun, or from anything else that we see.

Some photons are lost in passing through the eye

When you look up at Polaris, the cornea of each eye intercepts a little of the star's photon rain. A small fraction of these photons (about 2.5%) are reflected from the surface of the cornea. The interior of the cornea absorbs or scatters about 9% more, and the remainder ($\approx$2,350 photon/s/mm^2) reach the pupil. The pupil is larger in dim conditions than in bright ones; at night, it has an area of about 40 mm^2, so about 94,000 photons in the visible range reach the lens of your eye every second.

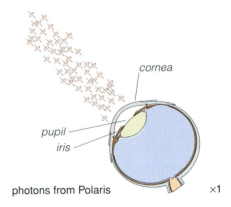

cornea

pupil

iris

photons from Polaris   ×1

photon broadcast by an FM radio station. At the microscopic level, water molecules and other molecules of your body are in constant motion, and this motion gives them a certain amount of energy, which rapidly fluctuates as each molecule exchanges energy with others as they collide with one another. The average energy of any of these molecules is proportional to the temperature. The energy of a photon in the visible portion of the spectrum is about 100 times greater than the average energy of a molecule in your body, and, as we will see, this large ratio is critical to our ability to see in dim light.

A photon is created when it is emitted by an electron; it moves with the speed of light until it is absorbed by another electron. For all practical purposes, each photon keeps the same energy, and thus the same frequency, from the time that it is emitted by an electron until the time that it is absorbed, although during that period the photon may have been reflected or otherwise deflected a number of times.

We have seen that a photon oscillates at a certain frequency, but not what it is that oscillates. Physicists use different terms for what oscillates. When speaking mechanically, they refer to it as **angular momentum,** or spin; this is represented in the icon for the photon as a circular arrow:

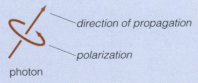

direction of propagation

polarization

photon

When speaking optically, physicists describe the oscillation as a **state of polarization.** Although the frequency of the

photon is fixed, its state of polarization changes each time it interacts with matter but is not absorbed. Because polarization plays only a minor role in our vision, and takes some time to explain, only two aspects of it are mentioned here. First, photons can differ in only two independent ways: in their frequencies and in their states of polarization. Second, just as we have evolved different photoreceptor types and neural circuitry that allows us to make discriminations on the basis of the frequencies of photons, other species have evolved different photoreceptor types and neural circuitry that allows them to discriminate on the basis of the states of polarization of photons.

The way in which a photon goes from place to place follows simple rules that describe everything known in optics. A useful rule to keep in mind is that *photons never interact with other photons;* in other words, they go about as if other photons did not exist. The phenomena of interference and diffraction are produced by a photon interacting with *itself* in different physical configurations. Since we are mainly concerned with the retina, and less with the optics of the eye, we will ignore the complexities of how photons really go from place to place.

Wave optics uses a simplifying assumption in which waves are replaced by rays, yielding *geometrical* optics. Here, we make an equivalent simplifying assumption that photons travel along a straight line unless deflected by a refracting surface—in effect, along the paths of the rays of geometrical optics. That simplification, and the notion that photons are little packets of energy, with a frequency proportional to that energy, is all that we will need for a while.

Looking at spectral density curves

A spectral distribution is a quantitative means of describing how light from some source is spread across the spectrum. The spectrum is plotted on the horizontal axis, and the amount of light per unit interval of the spectrum is plotted on the vertical axis.

The following diagram shows the spectral distribution of light within a heated chamber at a temperature of 5762 K (degrees Kelvin). At this temperature, the spectral distribution approximates that of light from the sun, at least over the visible range. Chambers at a fixed temperature are termed *blackbody radiators,* and their spectral distribution is characterized entirely by the temperature, independently of other factors, such as the shape of the chamber or the

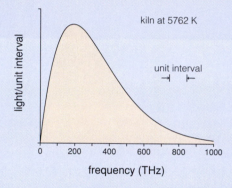

nature of its walls. The actual spectral distribution of the Sun is somewhat irregular, and for reasons that will become apparent, it is useful here to consider only smooth distributions.

Blackbody Radiation *401*

In this book, the spectrum is always plotted as frequency, and the density of light is expressed as photons per Hz or THz. Mainly for historical reasons, the spectrum is usually plotted in units of wavelength, and the density is plotted in units of energy. WAVELENGTH AND ENERGY describes how to convert between photon/frequency units and energy/wavelength units.

A heated body, such as Polaris or the Sun, throws off photons of different frequencies. Let's assume

Wavelength & Energy *513*

that we could capture 10 photons from the blackbody radiator we are considering and measure the frequency of each. A list of the resulting values, measured in terahertz, in the order obtained, might look something like this: 116.559, 241.941, 184.609, 314.939, 438.102, 24.029, 185.289, 211.670, 765.946, 51.275.

We can plot the frequency of each photon (shown by arrows in the diagram at the top of the next column) along a frequency axis. Notice that the frequencies of the photons are clustered at the lower end of the scale.

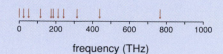

Another way to plot these data is to count the number of photons in each 100 THz interval (or "bin"), as indicated by the tick marks on the scale. Two of the 10 photons have frequencies between 0 and 100 THz, three between 100 and 200 THz, and so on:

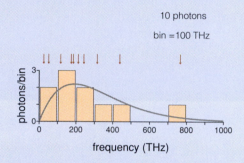

A plot in this form is termed a **histogram.** The sum of the heights of all of the bins is, of course, equal to the total number of photons.

The lack of smoothness in our histogram is due to our small sample size. If we now collect 1000 photons and do the same thing, the histogram becomes more regular:

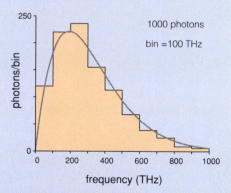

Again, the sum of the heights of the bins is equal to the total number of photons. (For reference, the first bin contains 120 photons.)

The irregular form of the profile is due to two factors. One is that all of the photons with frequencies between 0 and 100 THz are lumped together in the first bin, all those between 100 and 200 in the second bin, and so on. Thus we have lost precise information about the frequency of each photon; all we can say is that it was somewhere within the frequency interval encompassed by the bin. The other factor has to do with variations in sampling. If we collected a second set of 1000 photons, measured their frequencies, grouped them into bins, and plotted the histogram, that histogram would probably look similar to the one in the previous diagram, but the heights of the bins would differ. Thus there is an uncertainty in the horizontal direction because of the bins, and an uncertainty in the vertical direction because of the sampling variation in the number of photons in each bin. If we attempt to reduce the uncertainty in one direction, we will end up increasing the uncertainty in the opposite direction. For example, if we reduce the uncertainty in frequency by narrowing the bin width, we will lower the average number of photons in each of the bins, and thereby increase the relative uncertainty of the average number in each bin because of the smaller sample size.

A handy rule is to choose a bin width that approximates the *cube root* of the number of items sampled. Then the uncertainty in the horizontal direction is roughly equal to that in the vertical direction. This is true for the above histogram, and it is also true in the following histogram, in which the bin width has been reduced to 10 THz and the number of photons sampled has been increased to one million:

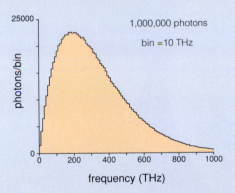

Notice that the vertical and horizontal uncertainties are roughly equal. That is why it was useful to base this discussion on a smooth distribution.

There is a problem with expressing the vertical scale as photons/bin, in that the vertical scale changes when the bin width is changed. It is more convenient to express the vertical scale as the number of photons over some *fixed frequency interval*, such as 1 THz, independent of what bin size is chosen. The plots for samples of 10^3 and 10^6 photons now look like the top two diagrams at right. In the distribution on the top, the bin width is 100 THz, but the vertical scale is expressed in photons/THz. The amplitude of the first bin is 1.2 photons/THz. Since the bin width is 100 THz, the *area* of the first bin corresponds to 1.2 photons/THz × 100 THz, or 120 photons, which is the same value as when the vertical scale was expressed as photons/bin. Thus when the vertical scale is expressed as photons/THz (or per any chosen frequency interval), the amount of light corresponds to the *area* of the profile. In this case, the area in the diagram on the top is equal to

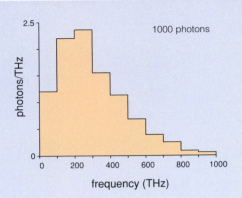

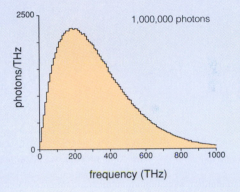

991 photons (9 photons had frequencies greater than 1000 THz, and are thus off the horizontal scale). The vertical scale for the bottom diagram has values 1000 times greater than the one on the top, simply because the sample plotted contained 1000 times more photons.

Of course, counting photons is rather arbitrary. What we are often interested in is the *flux density of photons*. As discussed in this chapter, this quantity is expressed as number of photons per unit of area over a unit of time (e.g., photons/s/mm²). In the case of sunlight, we have:

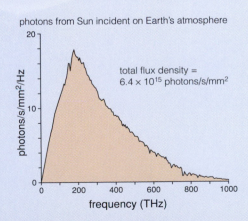

The sunlight falling on the Earth is so intense that the spectral unit used in the vertical scale is 1 Hz rather than 1 THz.

A second is a long time in the visual system, and in THE CHASE, we made use of a shorter time interval of 0.1 s. This value is not arbitrary: it is about the duration of the response of a cone to a single photon or a brief flash of photons. It is also a value that comes up in rod vision, in responses to rapid changes in the intensity of light. Finally, it is about the shortest time between successive saccadic eye movements. For these reasons, this time interval will be termed the **shutter time** of the retina. A case can be made for referring to it as the shutter time of the *visual system*, but this association is more speculative. During the shutter time, 9400 photons from Polaris enter your eye (see the Box PHOTONS ARRIVE ONE BY ONE).

To visualize the photon flux that enters your pupil, imagine an "ideal" photographic film placed just inside it. "Ideal" means that the film absorbs, and thereby marks the location of, *every* photon that falls on it. Exposed over the shutter time, the developed film would look something like the diagram below. The images of the photons would be distributed over the film in a random manner, like raindrops on pavement.

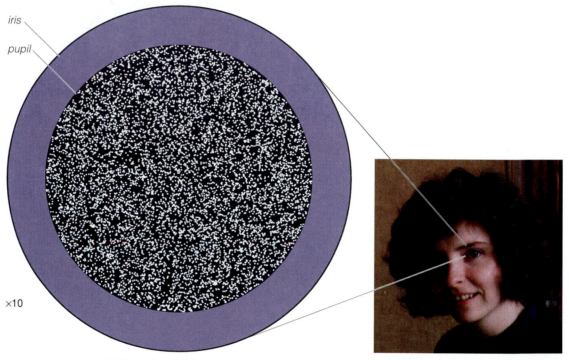

iris

pupil

×10

9,400 photons in plane of pupil

The 9400 photons that pass though your pupil next encounter the **lens** and **vitreous**. Within the eye, much of the scattering and absorption of photons is due to the cornea and the lens. The lens contains pigment molecules

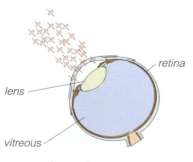

retina

lens

vitreous

photons from Polaris   ×1

that absorb all photons with frequencies in the ultraviolet region of the spectrum, and most of those in the violet region; it also scatters some photons with frequencies throughout the visible spectrum. The vitreous, discussed in EYES, is the watery gel that fills most of the interior of the eye; only a small fraction of the photons that pass through it are scattered or absorbed.

Photons arrive one by one

Photons travel at a velocity of 300,000 km/s, and thus travel 30,000 km—about twice the diameter of the Earth—in the 0.1 s shutter time. So you can imagine a thin column of 9400 photons from Polaris, 30,000 km long, with a diameter equal to that of your pupil. The average distance between the photons in this column is about 3 km. Thus the photons from Polaris enter the eye one by one, and the probability of two of them being within the eye at the same time is very small (≈0.001%). Put another way, the retina catches photons one by one. Each caught photon, however, produces a relatively long-lasting response (≈shutter time), and this allows the responses to a number of photons to be superimposed.

Our bookkeeping on the spectral distribution of photons between the cornea and the retinal surface now looks like the diagram at right. Once again, photons of all frequencies have been scattered, reflected, or absorbed, but absorption by the lens is particularly strong at the higher frequencies, and it removes virtually all photons with frequencies above 750 THz.

When you look directly at Polaris, its image falls on the center of the fovea. As you will recall, this portion of the retina, contains the macular pigment, which absorbs photons in the blue–violet region of the spectrum (page 26). The macular portion of the retina thus cuts further into the spectral distribution of photons before the light can reach the outer segments of the photoreceptors. The density of the macular pigment varies from person to person; on average, it absorbs about half of the photons in the blue–violet portion of the spectrum, as shown in the lower diagram at right.

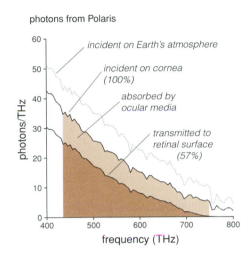

Why the lens and macula contain light-absorbing pigments

The pigments in the lens and macula appear to serve no other function than to reduce the fraction of higher-frequency photons that reach the photoreceptors. In so doing they appear to improve vision in two ways. First, the interior of the eye is mainly composed of water, and one property of an optical system based upon water is that it focuses higher-frequency photons in front of the other photons that lie within the visible spectrum. In optical terms, higher-frequency photons in rays that pass from air to water are bent (refracted) more than those of lower frequencies. This difference in the paths taken by photons of different frequencies is termed **chromatic aberration**; as a consequence of this aberration, the image (which can be thought of as a collection of photon paths) will be out of focus when it falls on the photoreceptors. Therefore the removal of higher-frequency photons serves to sharpen the image.

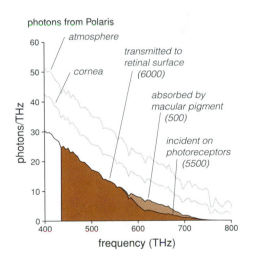

The second means by which the pigments of the lens and macula aid vision comes from the potential damage that high-frequency photons can do. The energy of a photon is proportional to its frequency (see the Box *PHOTONS ARE PARTICLES OF LIGHT*). When a photon is absorbed by a molecule, all of its energy is transferred to the molecule. In visual pigment molecules, some of this energy is used to change the shape of the molecule and thereby activate it. But all of this energy must be dissipated by some means, and the higher the energy of a photon, the greater the probability that the molecule will be broken or otherwise damaged by this encounter. Thus too many high-frequency photons can damage the retina, and their absorption by the lens and macula offers some protection to the photoreceptors. For the chemical nature of the macula pigment, see page 512.

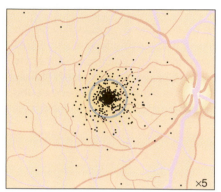

5500 photons from Polaris

The image of a point of light is spread over many cones

The optics of the eye cause the 5500 photons that were not scattered or absorbed by the cornea, lens, or macula to come to focus at the level of the photoreceptors, and thereby form an image of Polaris. The spatial distribution of these photons across the fovea looks something like the diagram at left. The photons concentrate at the center of the fovea, but because of scattering, they are distributed over a region that is millimeters across. Some 2% of the photons lie farther than a millimeter from the foveal center, as indicated by the gray circle. These photons were strongly scattered by close encounters with molecules as they passed through the ocular media. When we are dazzled by the glare of a small but intense source of light, it is these strongly scattered photons that constitute the glare.

When the magnification is increased by a factor of 100 to give a total magnification of 1000, the distribution of the photons collected during the 0.1 s shutter time looks like the diagram below. Thanks to the optics of the eye, the region shown, only 50 µm in diameter, contains 72% of all of the photons that reach the photoreceptors. Half of the total number of photons lie within 12 µm of the center of the image; the border of this region is indicated by the brown circle.

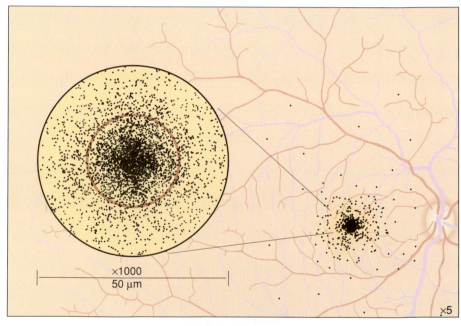

×1000
50 µm

5500 photons from Polaris

If we superimpose this distribution of photons on the array of cone outer segments at the center of the fovea, it looks something like the diagram at left. The cone outer segments are tightly packed together to form a rough hexagonal array, here represented as a hexagonal lattice. The zone containing 50% of all photons is again represented by a brown circle. The inner white circle has a diameter of 10.4 µm, and contains 25% of the 5500 photons of the image.

The image of a point of light characterizes the optical properties of the eye

The spread of the distribution of photons has nothing to do with the diameter of Polaris, or with its distance from us. Even the nearest stars are so far

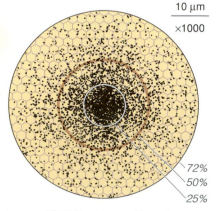

10 µm
×1000

72%
50%
25%

image of Polaris on array of foveal cones

away that they appear to our eyes—or for that matter, our best imaging telescopes—as points of light. But because of optical factors, the image of a point of light is not itself a point, but a hill spread across the retina. The image of a nearby star has exactly the same relative shape as that of a star farther away; the only difference lies in the rate of arrival of photons, and thus how bright the star appears.

At night the pupil is fully open, and the spread of photons is due mainly to the optical imperfections of the eye; the effects of these imperfections increase rapidly with pupil size. The other factor that contributes to the spread of photons is intrinsic to the nature of how photons go from place to place, and is termed *diffraction*. This factor is not significant here, but in daylight, when the pupil is small, the spread of photons in the retinal image is due mainly to diffraction.

A magnification of 1000 is still too small to show the distribution of photons at the center of the image, but it can be resolved if the magnification is increased to 4000, as in the diagram below. The 25% region contains some 1452 photons, which overlie about 20 cones. Remember, however, that both the locations of the photons and their exact number will change with successive shutter times. Like any image, that of Polaris is in continual motion across the retina (see THE CHASE). If we assume an image drift of 0.2°/s, then the center of the image passes over about 23 foveal cones each second, or about two cones in the 0.1 s shutter time we have been considering. Thus the static relation between the image and the cone array in the illustration below fails to convey a true sense of the dynamics involved, but it is the best we can do here.

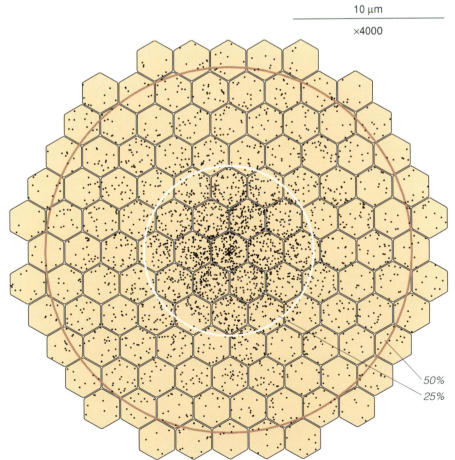

10 μm

×4000

50%
25%

distribution of photons from Polaris on array of foveal cones

The peak of the image approximates the size of a single cone

For convenience, let us place the center of the image of Polaris at the center of one of the cones, so that there are more photons falling on this cone than on any of those nearby. This diagram shows the number of photons falling on each cone during the shutter time, again ignoring the dynamics of the moving image:

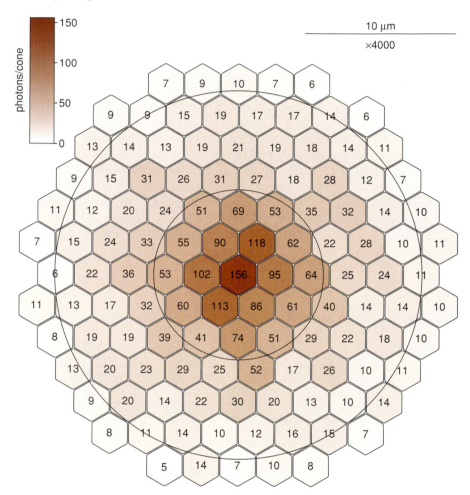

number of photons falling on each cone during shutter time

The central cone receives 156 photons, which is some three times more than are received two cones away. If we think of the effective size of the image as the distance over which the received photons have dropped to half the peak value, the effective width of the image is a little more than three foveal cones.

In the three-dimensional diagram at the top of the next page, each cone is represented by a vertical column whose height is proportional to the number of photonsfalling on it. Just as for the previous diagram, each column is shaded according to the number of photons the column represents. The scale to the left refers to the color at the top of the column. This representation provides a convenient means of visualizing the dynamic image of Polaris. As the image moves across the retina, the array of cones remains fixed, but the height of each cone column rises or falls according to the path of the image and the spatial distribution of photons—like something moving under a rug printed with a hexagonal pattern.

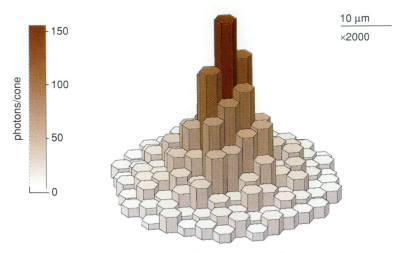

photons from Polaris on array of foveal cones

The shape of this moving "hill of photons" is best seen when it is viewed from the side:

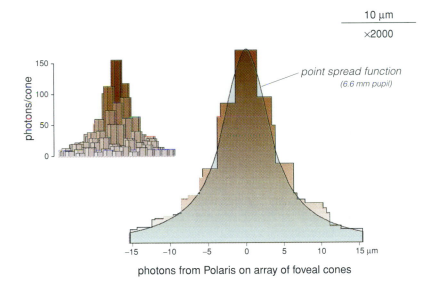

photons from Polaris on array of foveal cones

If the image were stable, and we waited a long time to collect photons, the fluctuations in the distribution of photons would be smoothed out, resulting in the green shape at the center of the diagram. This curve is termed the **point spread function**, and it provides a useful means of characterizing the optics of the eye. (It was in fact used to generate the distribution of photons used in the previous illustrations.)

As noted earlier, the spread of photons across the retina is determined by the optics of the eye, not by Polaris. The shape of the point spread function varies with pupil diameter, and its central portion is narrowest when the pupil has a diameter of about 3 mm, which is roughly its value during daylight. Because of chromatic aberration, it also varies with the frequencies of the photons, but this complexity has a relatively minor effect for natural viewing and is ignored here.

Real eyes have quite irregular point spread functions that contain a number of bumps, as shown in the illustration at right. Although the resolution in this diagram is too coarse to show them, the point spread function also contains many thin radiate lines that extend well beyond the bumps.

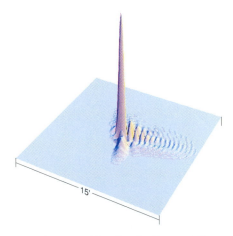

point spread function for 5 mm pupil
after Liang, Williams, and Miller, 1997

The photons that fell outside the foveal region in previous illustrations came from these lines. You can observe the point spread function of one of your own eyes whenever you see a radial pattern caused by sunlight reflected from a small bright object. If you tilt your head to the side, the radiate pattern rotates as well, demonstrating that this phenomenon is due to the optics of the eye. Every eye shows these effects, which are due to the arrangement of cells within the lens. But, like fingerprints, every eye differs in its exact pattern. Hence the point spread function used here is a necessarily idealized version of the real thing.

The size of the cone outer segments, and thus the peak spatial density of cones, also varies from person to person. Diffraction and cone spacing act to limit spatial resolution, whatever the performance of the rest of the visual system. However, the situation is more complicated than it might first appear, since we can resolve spatial differences much smaller than the diameter of a single cone, and thus much smaller than the point spread function. The critical factor is the *sequential activation* of the cones as an image moves across the cone array. To the degree that we can discriminate differences in the *times* at which the cones are successively activated, we can discriminate spatial differences, even when differences in image intensity are narrower than a single cone.

To summarize, the image of Polaris that falls on the retina is sufficiently sharp that a single cone can encounter significantly more photons than an adjacent one. About one-quarter of the photons fall within a region that contains about 20 cones. Beyond that region, the flanks of the point spread function flatten out and show a variety of irregularities.

Until now we have considered the *arrival* of photons at the cones. Some of these photons will be absorbed by the cones; others will not. Of course, we see only by means of the photons that are absorbed. So we now turn our consideration to the factors that determine which of the arriving photons will be absorbed by the cones.

The capture of photons by cones depends upon their direction and frequency

Just as for photons absorbed by the atmosphere or the ocular media, we cannot predict that a particular photon will be absorbed by a cone. We can only assign a probability that this will happen. This probability depends upon three factors, which, in temporal order, are:

the direction of arrival of the photon;

the frequency of the photon;

the type of the cone.

The first factor is important because a cone is sensitive to the *direction of arrival* of photons with respect to its long axis. For optical reasons, which will be discussed later, the inner segment of a cone helps to *guide* incoming photons into the outer segment and thus to the visual pigment molecules contained there. But this funneling depends upon the direction of arrival of the photon, and is most efficient when this direction is parallel to the long axis of the cone. In our simplified model of how a photon goes from place to place (see the Box PHOTONS ARE PARTICLES OF LIGHT), a photon is viewed as traveling along a narrow path, or *ray*. Photons arrive at the cone inner segment from different directions because they pass through different points in the plane of the pupil (see the diagram at the top of the next page).

Since foveal cones are aligned toward the center of the pupil, they are most sensitive to photons that travel through its center. By comparison, the

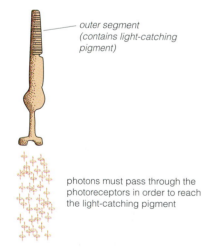

outer segment
(contains light-catching pigment)

photons must pass through the photoreceptors in order to reach the light-catching pigment

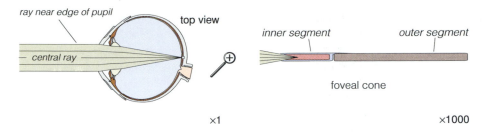

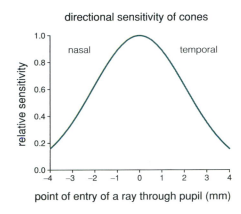

photons arrive at photoreceptors from different directions

sensitivity of these cones to photons entering near the edge of the pupil is reduced to about 20% of the peak value. The diagram at right shows the relative sensitivity of cones to rays entering at *different distances from the center of the pupil*. This optical effect is termed **directional sensitivity**. It is as if the cones were looking through a smaller pupil. Since photons passing through the center of the pupil produce the sharpest optical image (i.e., the narrowest point spread function), this effect acts to sharpen the portion of the image that enters the cone outer segments, and thus narrows the effective width of the distribution of photons that can be absorbed. For the same reason, the cones are also less sensitive to stray light caused by scattering within the eye. Rods show little, if any, directional sensitivity, and are thus equally sensitive to all entering photons, whatever their path through the pupil.

To a first approximation, the directional sensitivity of the cones does not depend upon the frequency of the photons, so we can treat all of our 5500 arriving photons in the same way. Their points of passage through the pupil will be randomly distributed in the plane of the pupil, just as before, but this time we will divide the pupil into different zones, corresponding to different ranges of relative sensitivity. The upper portion of the diagram at right replots the curve for directional sensitivity. This curve may be viewed as a horizontal slice through the center of the pupil, as shown in the lower portion. For points within 1.4 mm of the center, the relative sensitivity lies between 0.8 and 1. This portion is shown darkest in both parts of the diagram. It covers 16% of the area of the pupil and thus includes 16% of the incident photons. About 90% of the photons that enter this zone of the pupil and reach a cone inner segment will thus be funneled into the outer segment. Near the edge of the pupil, the relative sensitivity drops to between 0.2 and 0.4. This ring occupies 36% of the area of the pupil, and thus includes 36% of the incident photons. Only about 30% of these photons will be funneled into cone outer segments. Overall, 54% of the photons (≈2,900) will be funneled into cone outer segments, where they can be absorbed by the visual pigment molecules.

In the peripheral retina, the long axes of the cones are not directed toward the center of the eyeball. Instead, their long axes are aligned with the direction of the arriving rays (see next page).

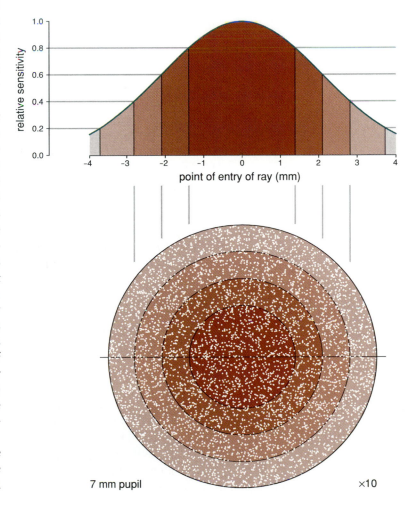

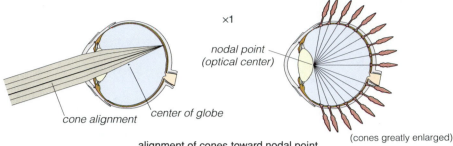

×1

nodal point
(optical center)

cone alignment   center of globe

(cones greatly enlarged)

alignment of cones toward nodal point

The long axes of cones in different locations in the retina are all directed toward an imaginary point located near the back surface of the lens, which is termed the **nodal point**. As discussed in THE RAIN OF PHOTONS ONTO RODS (page 125), the nodal point is effectively the optical center of the eye, and is the reference point for measuring the angular size of viewed objects.

In summary, cones capture photons best when the path of the photons is parallel to the long axis of the cone. At any location in the retina, the cones are aligned toward the direction of the incoming photons, which has the effect of maximizing their photon catch.

The remaining two factors—photon frequency and cone type—need to be considered together, because the cone types differ in their sensitivities to photons of different frequencies. As discussed in the previous chapter (page 44), there are three types of cones, each containing a different type of visual

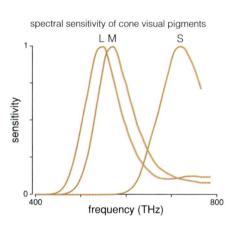

spectral sensitivity of cone visual pigments

pigment molecule (left). Each of these curves shows the sensitivity of one type of visual pigment molecule to different photon frequencies over the visible portion of the spectrum. Each type has a different **peak sensitivity**, meaning the frequency at which its sensitivity is greatest. Except at their high-frequency ends, each of the three curves has about the same shape.

As discussed in the previous chapter, the different cone types are named by the letters **L** (low-frequency), **M** (medium-frequency), and **S** (supra-frequency). We will use the same letters to distinguish the visual pigment each contains. The S pigment has a peak sensitivity at about 719 THz. However, as we have seen, almost all the photons that have frequencies near this value are absorbed by the lens or the macula lutea. This filtering gives the fovea the sharpest image, but leaves little role for S cones, which are absent from the center of the fovea. When we are looking directly at Polaris, its image will thus fall only on L or M cones.

As shown in the diagram above, the L and M pigments differ only slightly in their peak spectral sensitivities, and thus differ only slightly in the photons they are able to absorb from Polaris. Doing the bookkeeping on both types would add an unnecessary complication to our exercise, so we will make the simplifying assumption that all the cones viewing Polaris have the spectral sensitivity of the L cones, which are the predominant type (left). The vertical axis in this diagram shows the probability that an arriving photon of some particular frequency will be absorbed by a foveal cone. Even at the frequency to which an L cone is most sensitive, only 68% of the

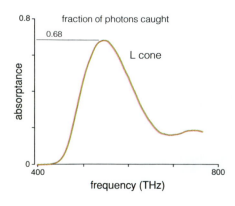

fraction of photons caught

photons are absorbed. As we move toward the lower limit of the visible range, this percentage drops smoothly toward zero. The photons that are not absorbed by visual pigment molecules pass through the outer segments, and almost all are then absorbed by the pigment granules in the retinal epithelium.

The spectral density curve for the photons from Polaris that reach the outer segments can be placed below the spectral sensitivity curve of the L cones so that the two may be compared, as seen in the upper portion of the diagram at right. As discussed earlier in the chapter in the Box *LOOKING AT SPECTRAL DENSITY CURVES*, the area of the curve for the spectral distribution of photons, shown shaded, corresponds to the total number of photons. These are the 2900 or so photons from Polaris in the visible range that, in our 0.1-second shutter time, have passed through space, through Earth's atmosphere, and through the interior of the eye to reach the cone outer segments.

Consider the photons that have frequencies in the range from 500 to 510 THz, which are highlighted in the diagram at right. The area of this highlighted portion of the spectral density curve is 6% of the total area, which corresponds to 170 photons. The L cones absorb about 50% of the photons that have frequencies in this range, and thus absorb some 85 of these 170 photons, as shown in the lower plot. In a similar manner, we can calculate the number of photons that are absorbed in each frequency interval. The total number of photons absorbed can then be found by adding up the number absorbed over all of the frequency intervals (lower panel). Few photons at low frequencies are absorbed because the visual pigment molecules in the L cones are insensitive to them, and few photons at high frequencies are absorbed because few are available to be absorbed. Most of the photons absorbed are in the middle range of frequencies, where photons are available and the L cones are sensitive to them. We now consider what happens to these absorbed photons.

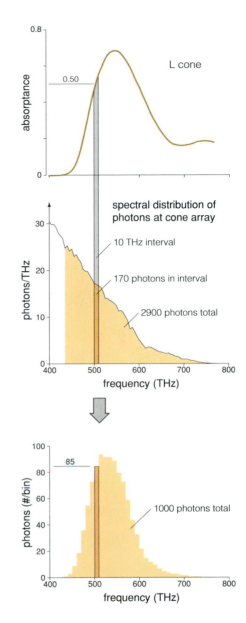

An absorbed photon must activate a visual pigment molecule

About half the volume of a cone outer segment consists of infoldings of the cell membrane, which contains many protein molecules, most of which are visual pigments (below).

As mentioned in the previous chapter, each visual pigment molecule has a portion specialized for catching light, termed a *chromophore*. Until a photon is absorbed, the chromophore has a bent form. As I'll discuss in

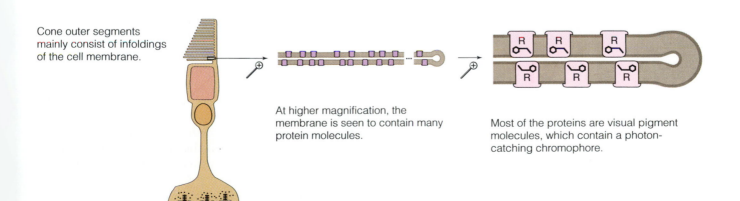

Cone outer segments mainly consist of infoldings of the cell membrane.

At higher magnification, the membrane is seen to contain many protein molecules.

Most of the proteins are visual pigment molecules, which contain a photon-catching chromophore.

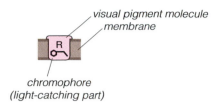

visual pigment molecule
membrane

chromophore
(light-catching part)

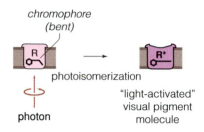

chromophore
(bent)

photoisomerization

photon

"light-activated"
visual pigment
molecule

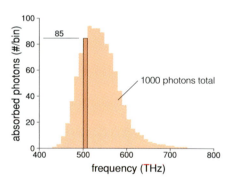

85

1000 photons total

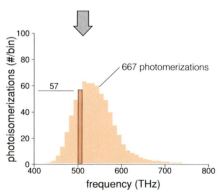

667 photomerizations

57

greater detail in HOW PHOTORECEPTORS WORK, the only visual action of a photon of light is to change the shape of the chromophore so as to straighten out the bend. This change in shape is the critical event in vision, as it leads to the activation of the visual pigment molecule, and subsequently to the activation of the photoreceptor as a whole.

Two molecules that differ only in shape are termed **isomers**. A change in the shape of a portion of a molecule is termed an **isomerization**, and a change brought about by the absorption of a photon is termed a **photoisomerization**. Thus a photon must not only be absorbed by a visual pigment molecule, it must also **photoisomerize** that molecule in order to contribute to vision.

Somewhat surprisingly, only about two out of three absorbed photons photoisomerize a visual pigment molecule. This fraction is termed the **quantum efficiency factor**, and has a value of about 0.67, whatever the frequency of the absorbed photon. The energy of the photons that fail to produce a photoisomerization is dissipated as heat. From a visual perspective, this failure of one in three photons seems unfortunate, but from the perspective of photochemistry, given the potential for alternative fates, the success of two-thirds of them is impressive.

So, in considering how we see Polaris, we are not so much concerned with the rate at which photons are absorbed as with the rate at which they photoisomerize—and thereby activate—visual pigment molecules. For brevity, the terms **effective catch** or **effective capture** will be used to refer to absorption followed by photoisomerization. More often, the abbreviated forms **catch** or **capture** will be used. Thus any time these terms appear in a discussion of photoreceptors, you can assume that they refer to the activation of visual pigment molecules by photons.

Over the spectral band from 500 to 510 THz, we saw that the cones received some 170 photons from Polaris during the shutter time, and absorbed 85 of them. Now we know that two-thirds, or some 57, of the photons in this spectral band photoisomerized a visual pigment molecule. Applying the same quantum efficiency factor to all of the spectral bands gives a total of about 700 photons caught (photoisomerized) over the 0.1 s shutter time. This is about 0.6% of the total number of photons in the visible range that encountered the cornea as you viewed Polaris (left).

The principle of univariance captures what photoreceptors respond to

We have come to an important principle, known as the **principle of univariance**: Each photon that photoisomerizes a visual pigment molecule has the same effect as any other photon that does so.

As discussed above, photons differ in only two independent ways: they can have different frequencies, and they can have different polarizations. Each of these properties has an important influence on whether a particular photon will photoisomerize a particular visual pigment molecule. But if the photon does so, then its effect upon the visual pigment molecule is the same as that of any other photon that photoisomerizes any other visual pigment molecule, whatever the frequency or state of polarization of the second photon. Consequently, a photoreceptor has no means of distinguishing the properties of the photons that photoisomerize its visual pigment molecules; they could have been from an intense photon rain near one of the limits of the visible range, or from a weaker rain nearer the middle of the visible range. In effect, a photoreceptor can convey to the brain only a measure of the number or rate of photons it catches. This rather ordinary fact has many ramifications, and it is because of them that it is given a special name.

So we can now put behind us all of the various factors that produce photoisomerizations and consider only their rate. During the shutter period, some 700 photons from Polaris were photoisomerized, but only half of them fell within 25 μm of the center of the retinal image. The distribution of these 350 or so photoisomerizations might look something like the diagram below. The seven central cones each caught 10 to 15 photons in each 0.1 s period; this is about the same number each would catch when looking at more extensive objects under moderate daylight conditions (e.g., a gray rock or bird, lit by daylight rather than direct sunlight, and observed during the morning).

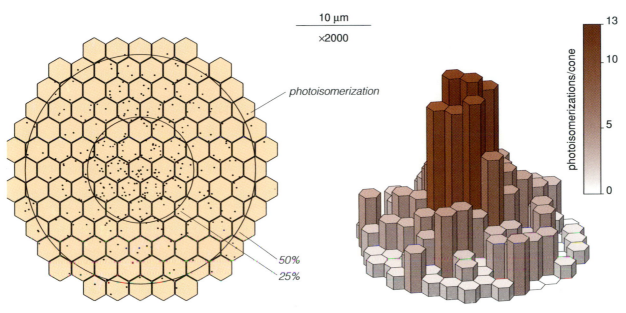

photoisomerization of cone visual pigment molecules by photons from Polaris

To summarize, when we gaze directly at Polaris, some of the photons it sends to Earth are brought to focus on the array of cones found at the center of the fovea. Some of these photons photoisomerize the visual pigment molecules of the cones that lie within the image of this star. Since all such photons have the same effect on a photoreceptor, we can sum their number over the shutter time of the photoreceptor (about 0.1 s) to determine the effect of Polaris on each of the cones that catch the image. A cone can signal nothing of the frequencies or polarizations of the photons that photoisomerize its visual pigment molecules.

This brief description includes all of the factors that have any significant effect upon the photons that reach the eye and are caught by photoreceptors. A CONE PATHWAY continues this story of our camping trip, when we gazed at a star; it describes how the cones respond to the photons they have just caught, and traces a pathway from them to the brain.

Neurons

This is an elementary description of how neurons work, which introduces the terminology associated with neurons that is used in the following chapters.

Much of basic neurobiology deals with the movements of ions into and out of cells. The movement of these charged particles across the membrane of a cell produces a change in the voltage across the membrane which spreads to other portions of the cell. Neurons use the change in voltage produced by ion movement as a signal to control cellular mechanisms that lie elsewhere in the cell. Because of the importance of ions, we begin by considering their environment.

Water molecules are polar

A water molecule has no net electrical charge, but its oxygen atom pulls on the electrons of its two hydrogen atoms, and this results in a separation of charge within the molecule:

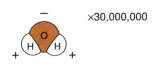

water molecules are polar

Molecules that show such a separation of charge are termed **polar molecules**. Water molecules are in constant motion, but because they are strongly polar, they tend to briefly stick to one another, so that at any instant they form a quasi-ordered pattern produced by the mutual attraction between their positive and negative charges:

water molecules tend to stick together

This adhesion is what gives water a strong surface tension, allowing some insects to "skate" upon ponds.

Many salts, when dissolved in water, dissociate into **ions**. An ion is an atom or molecule that carries a net electrical charge as a result of gaining or losing one or more electrons. For example, a crystal of table salt, NaCl, dissociates into a negatively charged chloride ion (Cl^-) and a positively charged sodium ion (Na^+). Negatively charged ions are termed **anions**, and are colored blue in this book; positively charged ions are termed **cations**, and are colored red. The net charge of any ion is considerably stronger than the small charge displacement found in a water molecule. As a result, water molecules tend to cluster around an ion, producing patterns like those shown here, again produced by the attraction between positive and negative charges:

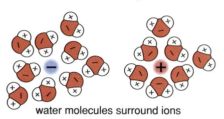

water molecules surround ions

Because all molecules and ions in solution are in constant and rapid motion, the local environment changes from moment to moment; nevertheless, the water molecules surrounding an ion at any instant can limit the ion's ability to pass through a narrow channel. All charged molecules or atoms are said to be **hydrophilic** ("water loving") because of the attractive forces between them and the polar water molecules.

Cell membranes block the movement of polar molecules

Every living cell has a surface membrane, termed the **plasma membrane,** that separates the **intracellular** environment from the **extracellular** environment. Within the cell are other membranes, such as the surface membrane of the nucleus. All of these membranes are primarily composed of a double layer of **lipid** molecules. Each of these molecules consists of a *head group* and two *hydrocarbon tails*. The head group contains charged oxygen atoms, and is thus hydrophilic. The hydrocarbon tails are nonpolar. Nonpolar molecules, or portions thereof, are referred to as **hydrophobic** ("water fearing"); this is really a misnomer, since they tend neither to bind to one another nor to repulse water.

Membranes have a tendency to form spontaneously, with the head groups of the lipid molecules aligned at a water interface, and the nonpolar hydrocarbon tails forming the core (see the diagram at the top of the next page). In essence, the water molecules are pulled away because of their own mutual attraction, leaving the lipid molecules to arrange themselves with respect to the water that borders them. The resulting **lipid bilayer** has a fluidity about equal to that of olive oil, and individual lipid molecules can rapidly diffuse about within the plane of the bilayer. The reason water molecules, as well as other polar molecules, are excluded from the core of a lipid bilayer is that they are normally attracted to other polar molecules. Put another way, the stability of a lipid bilayer is due primarily to the attractive forces of the water molecules on either side of it.

The lipid molecules of a membrane don't engage in chemical reactions; instead, they diffuse about within the nonpolar environment of the membrane. Compared with other molecules we will consider, these lipid molecules are rather passive; consequently, there is no need to represent individual lipid molecules here. Instead, the membrane is graphically represented in this book as a "hydrophobic" core, formed by the hydrocarbon

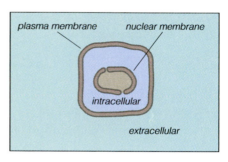

plasma membrane   *nuclear membrane*

intracellular

extracellular

every cell is bounded by a membrane

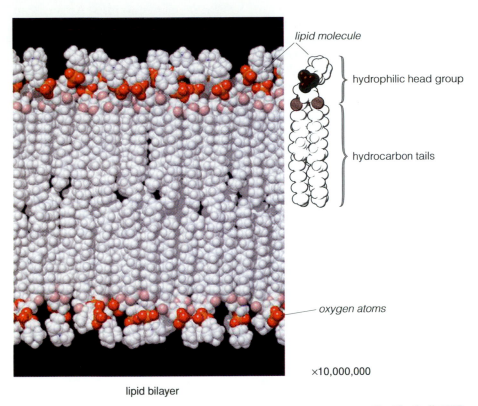

lipid molecule

hydrophilic head group

hydrocarbon tails

oxygen atoms

×10,000,000

lipid bilayer

after Goodsell, 1993

tails, with hydrophilic borders on each side, formed by the heads of the lipid molecules:

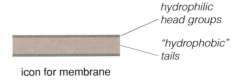

hydrophilic head groups

"hydrophobic" tails

icon for membrane

The critical feature of a membrane composed only of a lipid bilayer is that it acts as an impermeable barrier to ions. However, as we will see, the plasma membrane of every cell contains aqueous pores, made from protein molecules, that selectively allow certain ionic species to pass from one side of the membrane to the other. But before describing how ions can pass across the membrane, we consider the consequences of their general inability to do so.

Separation of charge across the cell membrane produces a voltage

Every cell in the body has a small separation of electrical charge across its surface membrane, such that the interior of the cell is negative with respect to the outside of the cell (right). In a metal, charge is carried by electrons, but in an aqueous environment there are no free electrons, and the charge is carried by ions.

Charges of different signs attract one another, with the result that they are normally pulled together so as to minimize charge separation. But in this case they are prevented from doing so by the plasma membrane, which acts as a barrier to the movement of ions. This small separation of charge is

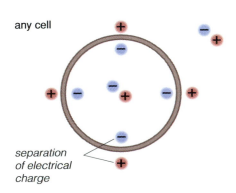

any cell

separation of electrical charge

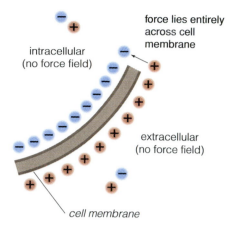

intracellular
(no force field)

force lies entirely
across cell
membrane

extracellular
(no force field)

cell membrane

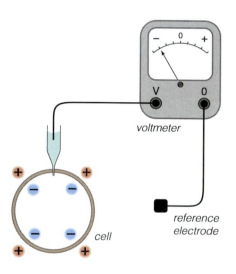

voltmeter

*reference
electrode*

cell

needed in order to maintain the integrity of the cell, for reasons that do not immediately concern us.

The separation of charge produces a net **electric force field** across the membrane. Under the conditions shown in the diagram at left, the entire force field lies within the membrane. Every charged particle in this field will have a force applied to it, and the direction of this force depends upon the sign of the charge. So every ion will move in response to this force, if it can do so. **Voltage,** or **electric potential,** is a measure of the energy required to move a charge some distance against the force of the electric field.

The voltage across the entire thickness of the membrane is termed the **transmembrane potential.** This voltage can be measured with a voltmeter by placing one terminal outside the cell and connecting the other to its interior by means of a fine-tipped electrode made of pulled glass or quartz that contains a conducting solution (below left). By convention, transmembrane potential is measured with reference to the outside of the cell, and typically has a value of about –0.05 to –0.08 V (volts). Instead of expressing the transmembrane potential as a decimal fraction of a volt, however, the convention is to use thousandths of a volt (millivolts, abbreviated mV). Thus the transmembrane potential of a cell is about –50 to –80 mV; by comparison, a common flashlight battery has a potential across its terminals of about 1500 mV.

Charge separation tends to be distributed uniformly across the cell membrane

Just as gravity causes spilled water to spread across the floor, the repulsion between electrical charges of the same kind causes the charge separation on either side of the plasma membrane to spread uniformly across it, so as to eliminate any electric fields within the conductive interior of the cell. Consequently, the transmembrane potential of at least a small cell is ordinarily the same across whichever part of the membrane is measured.

If there is a sudden change in the separation of charge in one portion of the cell's membrane, then the charge separation within and without the cell will quickly redistribute itself so that it is again uniformly distributed over the inner and outer surfaces of the membrane. This redistribution of charge is virtually instantaneous, taking about 100 ps (picoseconds), or 10^{-10} s.

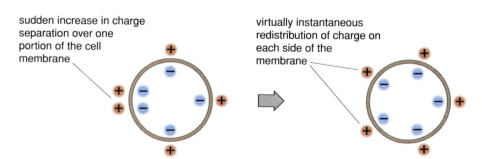

sudden increase in charge
separation over one
portion of the cell
membrane

virtually instantaneous
redistribution of charge on
each side of the
membrane

In the example shown above, the amount of charge separation was somehow instantaneously increased, and thus the magnitude of the voltage measured across the membrane must have instantaneously increased as well. The voltmeter will now show a more negative transmembrane potential with respect to the outside, and we say that the cell has become **hyperpolarized** (Greek *hyper* = over, above or exceeding). Had the charge separation decreased, we would say that the cell had become **depolarized.**

A change in the transmembrane potential is termed either a **hyperpolarization** or a **depolarization**, as indicated in this diagram:

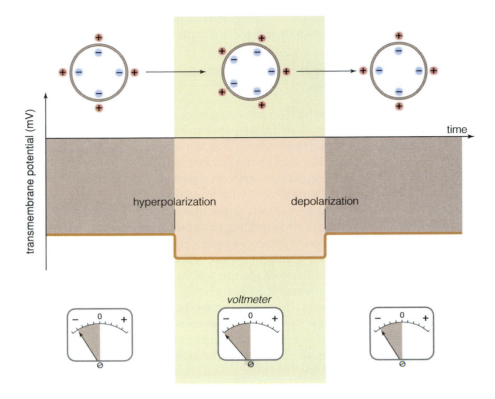

This redistribution of charge, termed **electrotonic spread,** is a purely physical phenomenon, which results from the redistribution of charges of like sign on either side of the membrane due to their mutual repulsion. This same sequence of events would therefore occur if the cell had a different shape, or even if the cell were dead, provided the membrane was intact.

In the undisturbed state, the charge separation is uniformly distributed across the surface membrane of this cell. → The charge separation is suddenly increased over one portion of the membrane. → The change in charge separation is immediately redistributed throughout the surface membrane of the cell.

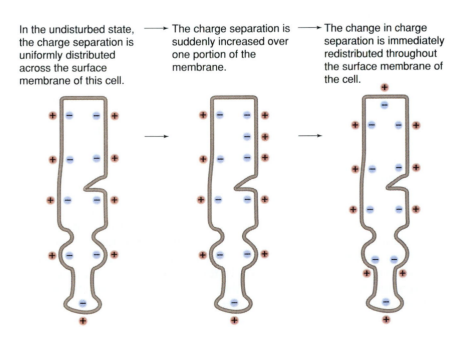

Neurons exploit electrotonic spread to convey information from one portion of the cell, where a change in the local charge separation is initiated, to another portion of the cell, where the resulting change in transmembrane potential can be detected. They create the change in charge separation by allowing ions to pass through their plasma membranes.

Ions can pass through aqueous pores in the cell membrane

There are three ways in which an ion can pass into or out of a cell, each of which depends upon specialized protein molecules that lie embedded within the membrane and extend from one side to the other. These molecules are termed **pumps**, **exchangers**, and **channels**. Pumps and exchangers are discussed on page 96; since most ions are conveyed across the membrane by means of **ionic channels**, we will deal with them first.

Channels are formed by protein molecules arranged in the form of a donut. The hole in the donut forms an **aqueous pore** in the membrane, through which certain ionic species can pass. Specialized portions of the channel proteins determine whether the pore will be open or closed. The size of the pore, and the distribution of charge within it, determine which ionic species can pass through it when it is open.

The charge displacement across the membrane produces an electric field, which extends through the aqueous pore. Because the interior of the cell is negative, this electric field tends to pull cations into the cell and pull anions out of it, and this movement of charge is termed a **current**. The net movement of a given ionic species, however, depends upon both the electric field and the relative concentrations of ions on each side of the membrane. For example, the electric field tends to pull potassium ions (K^+) into a cell. Partly as a consequence of this, the concentration of potassium ions inside a cell is much higher than that in the extracellular fluid. But this also means that more potassium ions will encounter the aqueous channel from inside the cell, and some of them will have a sufficient velocity to overcome the electric field and pass out of the cell. In effect, the net direction of movement of a given ionic species through an ionic channel is determined by a combination of the strength of the electric field—and thus the transmembrane potential—and the ratio of the concentrations of these ions on each side of the membrane.

Each type of channel can be characterized according to the set of ionic species that can pass through it (e.g., sodium ions and calcium ions), and what conditions act to open or close it (e.g., some special molecule that attaches to the channel, mechanical pressure, a change in the transmembrane potential). Most of the functional properties of nerve cells are a consequence of the nature and distribution of different types of ionic channels, pumps, and exchangers over their plasma membranes.

Ions move randomly about in solution, and it takes time for one of them to encounter an open channel and pass through it. This limits the rate at which ions can pass through the channel, and thus the rate at which the charge separation across the membrane can be altered. Consequently, the time it takes for a change in circumstance, such as the opening of channels, to be felt throughout the cell is on the order of milliseconds rather than picoseconds. Some channels in the membrane are always open, and they slowly pass ions one way or the other so as to hold the transmembrane potential near its resting value. In long, thin neurons, these channels act to limit the distance of electrotonic spread to a millimeter or so.

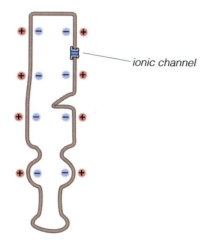

ionic channel

current

An electrical current consists of a net movement of positive charge, and thus to cations moving in the direction of the charge, or anions moving in the opposite direction. The macroscopic measure of charge is the **coulomb** (C), which is equal to 6.242×10^{18} unit charges. The macroscopic measure of current is the **ampere** (A), which is specified in coulombs of charge per second (in SI units, for reasons that are irrelevant here, the ampere is the basic measure, and the coulomb is the derived measure). At the microscopic level of ionic channels, currents are typically specified in picoamperes (pA) or femtoamperes (fA). One femtoampere corresponds to about 6,000 unit charges per second.

Neural communication depends upon voltage-gated ionic channels

As noted above, a redistribution of charge initiated in one part of the cell spreads electrotonically to other portions. Those portions of the cell may contain **voltage-gated ionic channels,** which are adapted to sense a change in the electric field across the channel and to open or close in response to this change.

An **action potential** is a brief change in the transmembrane potential of a neuron that propagates along its axon (right). By this means a neuron can send a message over longer distances than electrotonic spread allows. Action potentials are produced by two types of voltage-gated ionic channels, both of which open briefly in response to *depolarization* of the cell membrane. One voltage-gated channel type is selective mainly for *sodium ions*. When the depolarization is sufficient to open these channels, sodium ions pass into the axon, driven inward by the electric field, and do so in significant numbers because of their relatively large concentration outside the cell. This inward movement of positive charge reduces the charge separation across the membrane, and thus further depolarizes it.

The transmembrane potential is almost immediately pulled back down by the other voltage-gated ionic channels, which open more slowly and allow *potassium ions* within the cell to pass out of it. The combined effect of both types of channels is to generate an action potential: a brief positive swing in the transmembrane potential, which lasts for a millisecond or so. The action potential propagates down the axon because the initial inward current carried by the sodium ions spreads electrotonically farther down the axon, depolarizing the transmembrane potential, and thereby causes the voltage-gated sodium channels farther along the axon to open.

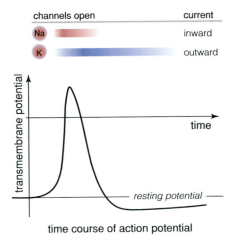

time course of action potential

Toward the trailing edge of the action potential, depolarization eventually results in the opening of K⁺ selective channels, and the exit of these cations from the axon results in a repolarization of the transmembrane potential.

At the leading edge of the action potential, depolarization causes Na⁺ channels to open, and the entry of these cations into the axon results in a depolarization that spreads further along the axon.

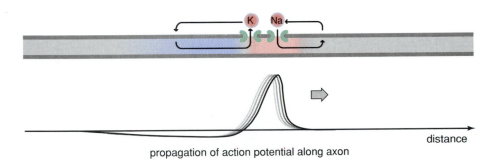

propagation of action potential along axon

It is by means of action potentials that ganglion cells send messages along their axons from the retina to the brain. Most of the other cell types in the retina do not produce action potentials, because the electronic spread of charge is sufficient to cause a change in transmembrane potential throughout the cell. The importance of voltage-gated ionic channels can hardly be exaggerated, for by providing a means by which information can be conveyed rapidly from one portion of an organism to another, they allow animals larger than a millimeter or so to join in the struggle for survival.

A third important type of voltage-gated ionic channel allows one neuron to send a message to another. These channels, which also open in response to *depolarization*, are adapted to pass calcium ions. In the interior of cells, there are virtually no free calcium ions. When these channels open, calcium ions move into the cell from the extracellular environment, and this causes the nearby region of the cell membrane to release molecules of a certain type, the consequences of which we will take up in a moment.

To summarize, neurons have exploited the speed and distance over which a change in the charge distribution across some portion of their plasma membrane can spread. Ionic channels are common to all cells, but in neurons, they are adapted to detect and respond to changes in the transmembrane potential. Depolarization of the transmembrane potential is the critical event for both the production of action potentials and the release of chemical substances.

Pumps use metabolic energy to move ions up energy gradients

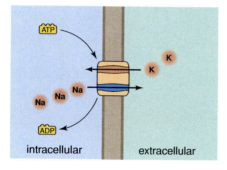

Na/K pump

As we saw in the previous section, if an ionic channel able to pass sodium ions is open, then these ions will enter the cell, because there is both an electrical gradient and a concentration gradient across the cell's membrane that favor their entry. This movement is spontaneous, like water running downhill. However, just as it takes energy to pump water back uphill, it takes energy to move the sodium ions back out of the cell. The sodium ions are removed by means of molecular pumps that span the membrane. They are termed Na/K pumps because they simultaneously move potassium ions *into* the cell, against a smaller energy gradient.

The energy required to drive Na/K pumps is supplied by the conversion of high-energy ATP molecules to lower-energy ADP molecules. When we are at rest, about a third of our metabolic needs come from these pumps, which are found in every cell in the body.

Exchangers use the energy gradients of some ions to move other ions up their energy gradients

Biochemical cascade *371*

An exchanger is another molecular machine that spans the membrane and can move ions *up* an energy gradient; the energy it uses to do so comes from the movement of other ions, typically sodium, *down* their energy gradients. This diagram shows the icon for an exchanger that is used to pump calcium ions out of photoreceptor outer segments (see BIOCHEMICAL CASCADE):

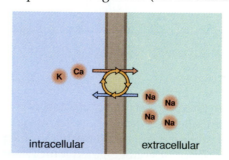

Na/Ca, K exchanger

The sodium ions that drive this exchanger must ultimately be moved out of the cell via the Na/K pump. Unlike pumps, exchangers can run in either direction, depending upon the concentrations of the various ions on each side of the membrane, although in normal circumstances, conditions are such that they go in only one direction.

Synapses are sites of communication between neurons

The primary way in which nerve cells communicate with one another is by means of **synapses**. There are a number of different types of synapses found in the nervous system, most, if not all, of which are found in the retina.

Chemical synapses involve the release and detection of a neurotransmitter

Many cell types in the retina, including photoreceptors, signal other neurons by means of a change in their rate of release of certain molecules. Neurons throughout the animal kingdom do this in a highly stylized and conserved manner. Each type of molecule released by a neuron that affects some other cell is termed a **transmitter substance** or a **neurotransmitter**. Synapses at which one or more types of neurotransmitter are released are termed **chemical synapses**.

The release of neurotransmitters is always initiated by a depolarization of the cell membrane at the release site, which results in the entry of calcium ions, as just described. The calcium ions trigger the release of neurotransmitters, although the amount and duration of this release can be influenced by other factors. The neurotransmitter molecules are packaged within small **synaptic vesicles**, about 10,000 molecules per vesicle. The entry of calcium ions initiates a sequence of events that causes the membrane of the vesicle to fuse with the cell membrane, thereby releasing the neurotransmitter molecules into the synaptic cleft:

vesicle
An anatomical term meaning a small bladder or sac, from Latin *vesica* = bladder, blister.

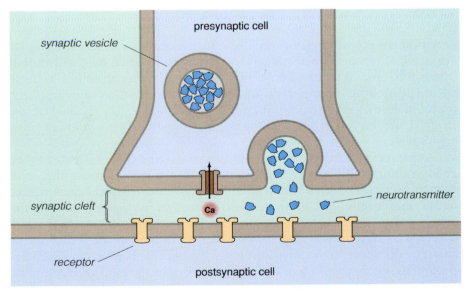

chemical synapse

The membranes of nearby neurons, or their processes, may also contain **receptor molecules**, which are adapted to detect particular neurotransmitters. Each receptor molecule contains a "pocket" on its extracellular face into which a portion of a particular type of transmitter molecule can fit. Weak electrical forces briefly hold the transmitter molecule within the pocket and thereby activate the receptor molecule; the transmitter molecule is said to **bind** to the receptor molecule, even though the event is usually momentary. The cell that releases the neurotransmitter is referred to as the **presynaptic** cell, and the cell that contains receptors to the neurotransmitter is termed the **postsynaptic** cell.

The release of transmitter substances always depends on depolarization of the presynaptic membrane, regardless of whether this depolarization is the result of a propagated action potential or passive electrotonic spread. There appears to be no reason why a hyperpolarization could not cause transmitter release, but this has never been reported; thus the relation between depolarization and transmitter release appears to be an example of evolutionary conservatism.

There may be different types of receptor molecules that span the surface membrane of the postsynaptic cell, and these receptor types determine how the cell will respond to the transmitter molecules released by the presynaptic cell. Each receptor spans the plasma membrane of the postsynaptic cell, and consists primarily of a number of protein subunits.

Some receptors possess an ionic channel that opens when one or more neurotransmitter molecules bind to some other portion of the receptor molecule; they are termed **ionotropic:**

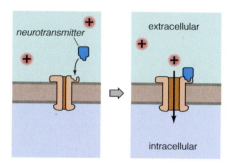

ionotropic receptor

A typical ionotropic receptor contains one or more sites on its extracellular surface that recognize a specific neurotransmitter, and a mechanism that opens the ionic channel when neurotransmitter molecules bind to these sites. The binding is temporary, so when the concentration of neurotransmitter molecules in the extracellular medium decreases, the channel closes. In effect, the fraction of time that the channel is open depends upon the concentration of the neurotransmitter.

Other receptor molecules do not possess an ionic channel; instead they change their shape when they bind neurotransmitter molecules, and thereby become **activated. (**Activation is represented in the diagram below, and in subsequent ones, by an increase in the saturation of the color of the icon representing the activated molecule.) The receptor's change in shape is detected by other molecules, termed **G protein molecules,** which move about by diffusion on the inner surface of the plasma membrane. When a G protein molecule encounters an activated receptor molecule it recognizes, then it too becomes activated:

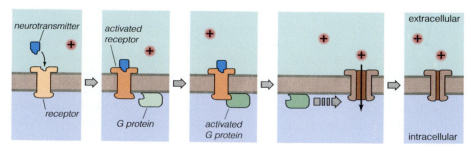

metabotropic receptor

Each activated G protein molecule acts upon other molecules, not discussed here, to open or close ionic channels on the membrane; this indirect influence of an activated G protein molecule on an ionic channel is indicated in the last diagram by the dashed arrow. The metabotropic receptors in the retina cause ionic channels to close, as shown in the last panel of the diagram.

The opening of ionic channels in the postsynaptic cell may result in a depolarization, a hyperpolarization, or a "clamping" of the transmembrane potential to its current value. Synaptic activation that results in depolarization is termed **excitatory** because both neurotransmitter release and initiation of action potentials require depolarization. Such synapses are termed **sign-conserving** because depolarization of the presynaptic cell results in depolarization of the postsynaptic cell:

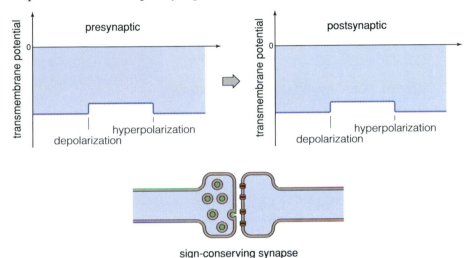

sign-conserving synapse

Synapses in which neurotransmitter release results in hyperpolarization of the postsynaptic membrane are termed **sign-inverting**:

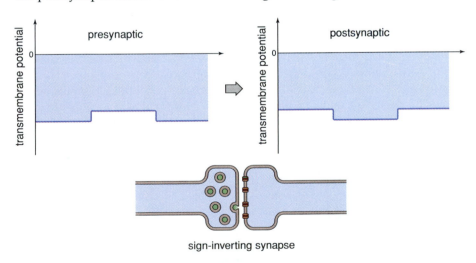

sign-inverting synapse

Gap junctions provide sites of intracellular continuity between cells

A quite different type of communication occurs at an **electrical synapse**, in which two cells are electrically coupled together at specific sites on the membrane surface, which are termed **gap junctions** (right). A gap junction

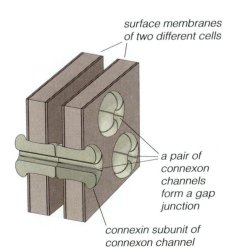

surface membranes of two different cells

a pair of connexon channels form a gap junction

connexin subunit of connexon channel

consists of a number of channels, sometimes hundreds, that allow ions and small molecules to pass from one cell to the other. Each channel consists of two subchannels, termed **connexons**, one from each cell, which lie in register so as to form the intercellular channel. Each connexon, in turn, consists of six protein subunits, termed *connexins,* as shown on the preceding page. There are a number of different types of subunits, and a variety of factors influence whether their configuration will open or close the subchannel.

By their nature, gap junctions are always sign-conserving, but they can differ in the number of channels and in the types of connexons that compose them:

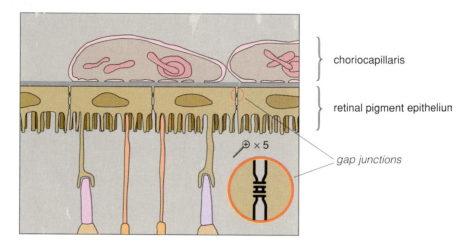

Gap junctions are common in non-neural cells as well as in neurons. For example, as mentioned above, the cells that compose the retinal epithelium are all interconnected by means of gap junctions.

Ribbon synapses occur at sites of continuous neurotransmitter release

Some presynaptic terminals contain a ribbonlike structure that appears dark when viewed with an electron microscope (it is said to be **electron dense**). This **synaptic ribbon** is surrounded by a halo of synaptic vesicles that are lightly attached to it, and it usually lies parallel to a bend in the presynaptic membrane, termed the **synaptic ridge**. Between the synaptic ribbon and the synaptic ridge lies a troughlike, electron-dense structure termed the **arciform density** (having the from of an arc, Latin *arci* from *arcus* = bow). Both the presynaptic and postsynaptic membranes possess this structure.

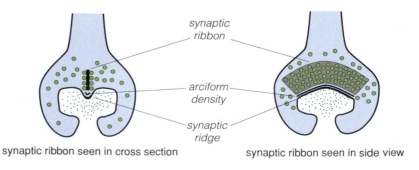

synaptic ribbon seen in cross section   synaptic ribbon seen in side view

Ribbon synapses are found throughout the animal kingdom, and have thus far been found only in neurons that do not generate action potentials. In the retina, they are found in both photoreceptor and bipolar cells. The function of synaptic ribbons is not known for certain, but it seems likely that they have a weak affinity for synaptic vesicles, and thereby corral them from the (three-dimensional) volume of the cytoplasm to the (two-dimensional) surface of the ribbon. This concentration of vesicles, moving rapidly by diffusion on the ribbon surface, provides the release sites on or near the synaptic ridge with a ready supply of synaptic vesicles for neurotransmitter release.

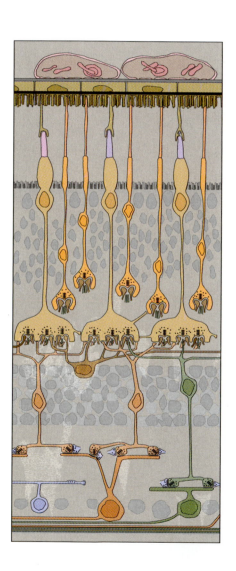

5

A cone pathway

THE RAIN OF PHOTONS ONTO CONES *retold the first part of the story of our camping trip, when we looked at a star; it ended with the capture of photons by some of our foveal cones. Here, we consider how cones respond to the photons they have just caught, and trace a pathway from the cones to the brain.*

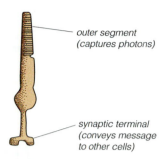

outer segment
(captures photons)

synaptic terminal
(conveys message
to other cells)

hyperpolarization, depolarization, electrotonic spread
See NEURONS (page 89) for the definitions of these terms and a general description of the broader aspects of neural function that are relevant to this section.

A change in photon capture causes a change in neurotransmitter release

When the outer segment of a photoreceptor catches photons—or increases the rate at which it is catching them—a sequence of events occurs that leads to a **hyperpolarization** of its **transmembrane potential.** This change in potential is graded; the greater the increase in photon catch, the greater the hyperpolarization. The hyperpolarization spreads **electrotonically** throughout the plasma membrane of the entire cell, and it is this process that allows events within the outer segment to influence events within the synaptic terminal:

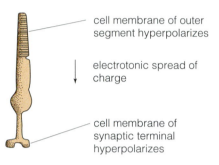

cell membrane of outer
segment hyperpolarizes

electrotonic spread of
charge

cell membrane of
synaptic terminal
hyperpolarizes

Within the synaptic terminals of photoreceptors, there are many small membrane-bound **synaptic vesicles,** each containing about 10,000 **glutamate** molecules. Some of these vesicles are temporarily attached to a membranous structure above the invagination, termed the **synaptic ribbon.** This diagram of the rod synaptic terminal shows the synaptic ribbon in cross section:

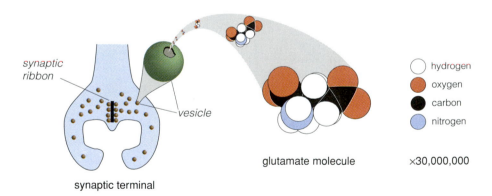

synaptic
ribbon

vesicle

synaptic terminal

hydrogen
oxygen
carbon
nitrogen

glutamate molecule   ×30,000,000

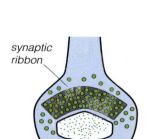

synaptic
ribbon

synaptic ribbon seen in side view

In side view, the synaptic ribbon can be seen to curve around the invagination, and thus partially envelops the processes of other cells that lie within it (diagram at left).

The synaptic vesicles near the base of the synaptic ribbon are continuously fusing with the cell membrane, so as to release the glutamate molecules they contain into the invagination. The rate of this merging and release depends upon the transmembrane potential at the synaptic terminal. A depolarization causes an increase in the rate of release of glutamate molecules, whereas a hyperpolarization causes a decrease. This pattern appears to be a general rule for all neurons in all species: *depolarization increases the rate of transmitter release, and hyperpolarization decreases it.* Since an increase in the rate of photon catch results in a hyperpolarization, the effect of light is to *reduce* the rate of release of glutamate molecules at the synaptic terminal (see the diagram on the next page). Thus the maximum rate of release of glutamate molecules occurs in the dark, and the action of light is to reduce this rate of release.

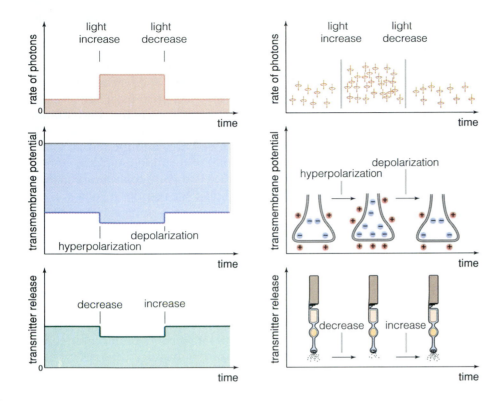

It may seem strange that an increase in photons causes a decrease in transmitter release, and vice versa, but that's the way it is; there is no obvious reason why. Evolution is a matter of tinkering, rather than designing, so the paths it takes are sometimes tortuous, and it is generally more useful to consider how well a mechanism works (e.g., how sensitive, noisy, or reliable it is) than to wonder about how it came to be (a difficult question, which we will cautiously consider later).

As discussed in RETINAS (page 45), cones make interphotoreceptor contacts with other cones. The transmembrane potential at a cone's synaptic terminal is thus influenced both directly, via the change in potential in its outer segment, and indirectly, via interphotoreceptor contacts with other cones. In normal viewing, in which the image is always moving, the indirect contributions made by these contacts may be rather minor, since the image may be moving across the cone array faster than the rate at which electrical currents flowing between different cones can alter their transmembrane potentials.

We have seen that, however accomplished internally, the external behavior of a photoreceptor is rather simple: a change in photon catch results in a change in the rate of glutamate release. The glutamate molecules released into the invaginations can bind to glutamate receptors located in the terminal processes of the postsynaptic horizontal cells and bipolar cells. Glutamate molecules are also continuously being removed from the extracellular space within the invagination, partly by **uptake mechanisms** within the synaptic terminal. The moment-to-moment concentration of glutamate molecules within the invagination is thus a balance between the rate of release, the degree of binding to the glutamate receptors, and the rate of uptake. For example, a flash of light can produce a hyperpolarization sufficient to briefly block the release of glutamate molecules. The uptake mechanisms continue to remove glutamate molecules from the region of the invagination, causing the glutamate concentration to fall. Conversely, darkness results in a rise in the rate of release of glutamate molecules that exceeds their rate of removal, causing the concentration of glutamate molecules to rise until a balance is reached.

We now come to a critical point: so far as we know, *the only actions of a photoreceptor that directly affect the horizontal and bipolar cells are its release of glutamate molecules into the invagination and its removal of them via uptake mechanisms.* Just as photoreceptors are adapted to detect photons of light, bipolar cells and horizontal cells are adapted to detect changes in the concentration of glutamate.

In RETINAS, we took a brief functional walk through the retina, which provided an overview of the functional roles of the different *classes* of neurons that compose the retina. We now retrace that path, concentrating on an overview of the roles of the specific neural *types* we use to see Polaris.

Pathways from cones to ganglion cells

When we look directly at Polaris, all the foveal cones along the path of its moving image are involved in our perception of the star. But this perception probably depends upon only two types of ganglion cells, out of the twenty-two or so that are present in our retinas. The other ganglion cell types are either concerned with other aspects of the image, or are not directly involved in visual perception, or do not operate reliably under these conditions. Likewise, no more than about half of the thirteen different types of bipolar cells (see RETINAS, page 51) appear to be involved in this perception.

Yet there are common functional themes shared by all bipolar cells—so too for all ganglion cells and all amacrine cells. This section describes these general patterns of functional organization. Following it, we conclude our extended discussion of viewing Polaris by tracing the particular pathways involved from the cones to the visual cortex.

Each cone contacts a few hundred processes of bipolar and horizontal cells

Whereas a rod has a single synaptic ribbon and contacts no more than seven or so processes from horizontal or bipolar cells, each cone contains many synaptic ribbons and contacts hundreds of processes. In *transverse* section, each cone pedicle can be seen to contain a number of invaginations, each associated with a synaptic ribbon (see diagram at left). A pair of horizontal cell processes occupies much of the volume of each invagination and lies closest to the synaptic ribbon. This association of a pair of horizontal cell processes with a synaptic ribbon is termed a **triad,** and appears to be the basic synaptic subunit of a cone pedicle. Each cone pedicle also contacts many bipolar cell processes. The most distinctive of these are the ones directly below the synaptic ribbon; these are termed **invaginating,** or **central,** processes. Other bipolar cell processes branch on either side of the invaginating processes, so as to surround them; these are termed **triad-associated** or **semi-invaginating** processes. The remaining bipolar cell processes abut the base of the pedicle, and are termed **non-triad-associated** or **flat** processes.

Transverse sections are useful for revealing the different types of processes that can receive from a cone pedicle, but they do not show much of the spatial arrangement of these processes, nor do they reveal the number of processes involved. These properties are best revealed by making thin horizontal sections through the cone pedicle. Such a section through a peripheral cone pedicle at the level of the synaptic ribbons reveals that, in the

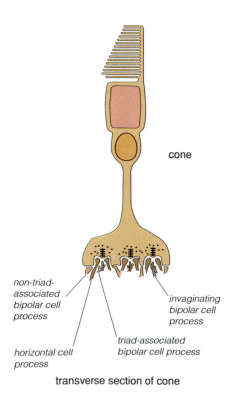

cone

non-triad-
associated
bipolar cell
process

invaginating
bipolar cell
process

horizontal cell
process

triad-associated
bipolar cell process

transverse section of cone

peripheral retina, each cone pedicle has about 40 synaptic ribbons. The ends of the ribbons tend to group together, forming a rough pattern:

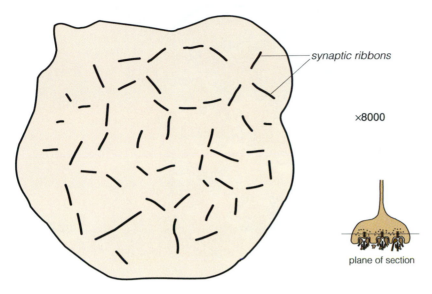

synaptic ribbons

×8000

plane of section

horizontal section of cone pedicle

after Chun et al., 1996

A section closer to the base of the cone pedicle reveals that each ribbon is flanked by the terminal processes of horizontal cells:

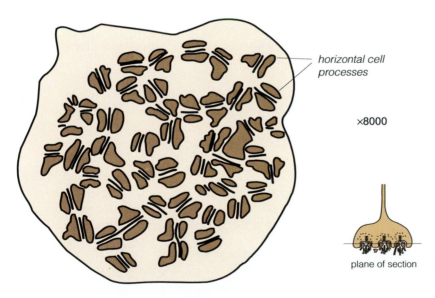

horizontal cell processes

×8000

plane of section

horizontal section of cone pedicle

after Chun et al., 1996

The typical pattern is for each ribbon to lie between a pair of horizontal cell processes, so as to form a triad. However, the two longer ribbons visible near the bottom of the diagram are each associated with *two* pairs of horizontal cell processes; thus a single ribbon can contribute to more than one triad. There are 46 triads in this cone pedicle, which thus contains 92 horizontal cell processes.

In a section closer to the base of the cone pedicle, the invaginating processes appear, lying directly below the synaptic ribbons:

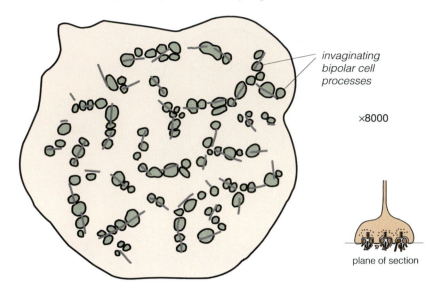

invaginating
bipolar cell
processes

×8000

plane of section

horizontal section of cone pedicle

after Chun et al., 1996

The synaptic ribbons lie above the invaginating processes, and are shown here only for reference; for simplicity, the cross sections of the horizontal cell processes are omitted. As shown, the invaginating processes sometimes lie between ribbons, so it is not always possible to associate each process with a particular triad. In this pedicle there are 104 invaginating processes, or about two such processes per triad. Some 24 of these processes are thicker than the others; they probably come from a single on-midget bipolar cell. The other processes probably arise from a number of diffuse bipolar cells of different types.

A horizontal section just below the base of the cone pedicle shows about 470 different processes, arising from both horizontal and bipolar cells:

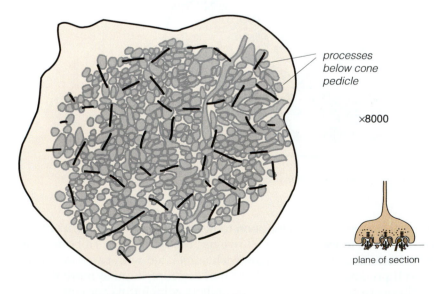

processes
below cone
pedicle

×8000

plane of section

horizontal section of cone pedicle

after Chun et al., 1996

As noted above, 92 of these processes arise from horizontal cells, and 104 of them come from bipolar cells with invaginating processes. The remainder come from bipolar cells that make either triad-associated or non-triad-associated contacts. It has not yet been possible to distinguish triad-associated and non-triad-associated processes in horizontal sections, so their arrangements are not known.

The above description is based upon the pedicles of cones in the peripheral retina. The pedicles of foveal cones are smaller, with about half the cross-sectional area and about half the number of synaptic ribbons. They contain only 18 or so invaginating processes, most of which are thick and arise from a single on-midget bipolar cell.

To summarize, cones make contact with the processes of both horizontal cells and bipolar cells. The processes of horizontal cells make invaginating contacts and form the lateral elements in each triad. The processes of bipolar cells are of three types: *invaginating* processes, which lie directly below the synaptic ribbon; *triad-associated* processes, which are aligned on each side of the overlying synaptic ribbon; and *non-triad-associated* processes, which abut the base of the cone pedicle.

Horizontal cells antagonize cones

Cones are presynaptic to horizontal cells in a **sign-conserving** manner: when cones hyperpolarize in response to light, they cause horizontal cells to hyperpolarize as well. Presumably receptors in the lateral processes of the horizontal cells respond to the fall in the concentration of glutamate molecules, but this has not yet been demonstrated. The sign-conserving synapse from a cone to a horizontal cell is represented schematically in the diagram (top right).

Critical to the function of horizontal cells is the fact that *they* are presynaptic to cones in a *sign-inverting* manner (right). The mechanism that underlies this synaptic action is not known, but there is tentative evidence that horizontal cells modify the voltage sensitivity of the calcium channels on the cone membrane that regulate transmitter release. The functional consequences of these sign-inverting synapses become clear when we recall that horizontal cells of the same type are electrically coupled together by means of gap junctions. (The precise cellular locations of the gap junctions between horizontal cells of the same type are not known. At bottom right they are arbitrarily shown between the horizontal cell icons.)

Each cone makes a sign-conserving synapse onto all of the horizontal cell processes that contact it. In the case of L and M cones, these processes come mainly from HI horizontal cells. Hyperpolarization of a cone produces a hyperpolarization of the HI horizontal cells it directly contacts. This postsynaptic hyperpolarization then spreads electrotonically to nearby HI horizontal cells via the gap junctions. We can thus view each cone as making a separate sign-conserving contribution to the array of nearby HI horizontal cells. Each cone makes only a small contribution, but collectively, they can produce a significant change in the transmembrane potential of the interconnected horizontal cells.

It is this combined hyperpolarization of HI horizontal cells that acts in a sign-inverting manner back upon each of the cones that contributed to it. For example, a spatially uniform light will hyperpolarize cones over a wide area of retina. The sign-conserving synapses of these cones onto HI cells will cause all of those HI cells to hyperpolarize. The hyperpolarization of the HI array acts in turn in a sign-inverting manner on the same set of

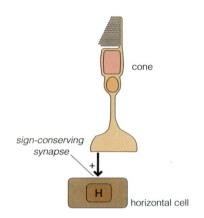

cone

sign-conserving synapse

horizontal cell

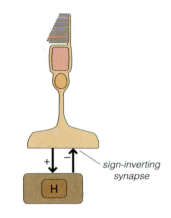

sign-inverting synapse

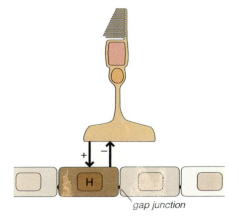

gap junction

cones, so as to antagonize the effect of the hyperpolarization of the cones produced by the steady light.

One possible function of horizontal cells is to reduce the influence of light intensity per se. Between sunrise and sunset, the ambient light intensity of the natural world changes greatly, and a mechanism that acts on cones to reduce the effect of this large variation in light intensity would obviously provide some benefit. However, we lack a quantitative and detailed description of how mammalian horizontal cells act upon the photoreceptors, so it is not possible to say much more without engaging in speculation. Another possible function of horizontal cells, mentioned in passing, is to enhance spatial or color contrast by acting in a subtractive manner, as if their contribution were equivalent to a negative light. These possibilities, also somewhat speculative, are explored in CELL TYPES (page 232).

The response of a bipolar cell depends upon the types of contacts it makes

The cell membrane at the tip of each bipolar cell process that receives from a cone contains receptors for glutamate. As discussed in NEURONS, there are two general classes of receptors, *ionotropic* and *metabotropic*. All *invaginating* bipolar cell processes appear to have *metabotropic* glutamate receptors. In response to glutamate, they act to *close* ionic channels in the plasma membrane and thereby *hyperpolarize* the bipolar cell. The synapse between a photoreceptor and a bipolar cell with invaginating contacts is thus *sign-inverting*. As a consequence, an *increase* in the rate of photon absorption by a cone will decrease the concentration of glutamate molecules released by the cone pedicle and thereby *depolarize* the bipolar cell, as shown in the diagram below. A bipolar cell that is activated (*depolarized*) in response to an *increase* in photon catch (*on*) is termed an **on-bipolar cell.**

By contrast, other bipolar cells have processes that contain *ionotropic* glutamate receptors at their synapses with cones. Glutamate molecules *open* these ionic channels, and thereby allow sodium ions to flow into the bipolar cell, so as to depolarize it. Thus the synapse between a cone and a bipolar cell process that contains ionotropic receptors is *sign-conserving*, since a *depolarization* of the cone leads to a *depolarization* of the bipolar cell. A bipolar cell that is activated in response to a *decrease* in photon catch (*off*) is termed an **off-bipolar cell** (see diagram at top of next page).

This on/off classification of bipolar cell types is arbitrary, but it is useful in that it focuses our attention on whether a bipolar cell is activated as a result of an increase in photon catch or a decrease. As we have seen, the difference between on- and

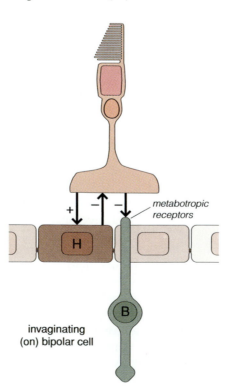

metabotropic receptors

invaginating
(on) bipolar cell

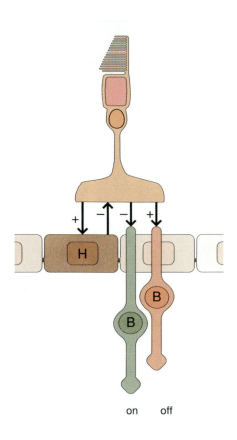

on   off

off-bipolar cells is based upon the types of glutamate receptors each contains. Nevertheless, the on/off terminology does not refer to a property of the bipolar cell per se, but rather to the outcome of a sequence of events that starts with photon capture and leads to hyperpolarization of the photoreceptor terminal, a decrease in glutamate release, and a fall in glutamate concentration. It is their response to this fall in glutamate concentration that distinguishes on- and off-bipolar cells.

Although all of the bipolar cell types that make invaginating contacts appear to be on-bipolar cells that make sign-inverting contacts with cones, no general rule appears to hold for the other types of contacts made by bipolar cells. Thus triad-associated contacts may be either sign-conserving or sign-inverting. It seems likely that the glutamate receptors on the processes of the other bipolar cell types that make sign-inverting contacts are metabotropic, and those that make sign-conserving contacts are ionotropic, but this has not been shown. It may be that non-triad-associated contacts are all sign-conserving, but this is likewise uncertain.

There is, however, one anatomical feature that strongly correlates with whether any bipolar cell is of the on or the off type. Surprisingly, this feature has nothing to do with the dendritic processes of a bipolar cell, or with anything in the outer synaptic layer. Instead, it has to do with the level at which the bipolar axon arborizes in the inner synaptic layer. On-bipolar cells arborize in the inner half of this layer, whereas off-bipolar cells arborize in the outer half, as seen in the diagram at right. This rule appears to hold for most, if not all, of the different types of bipolar cells. The coloring of the cells and sublayers in the schematic diagrams reflects this on–off dichotomy. Cells that depolarize in response to an *increase* in light, and sublayers rich in their processes, are greenish (on = "go"); those that depolarize in response to a *decrease* in light are orange or red (off = "stop"). This coloring has nothing to do with the neural mechanisms of color vision. Rather, it reflects a fundamental segregation of the neural interconnections of the inner retina on the basis of a distinction established in the outer retina.

Bipolar cells are presynaptic to both amacrine and ganglion cells

Both on- and off-bipolar cells make the same kinds of contacts in the inner synaptic layers. The terminals of bipolar cells contain synaptic ribbons, just as cone pedicles do, and all of the contacts bipolar cells make with postsynaptic cell processes are at sites that contain a synaptic ribbon. There are almost always two postsynaptic processes at these ribbon synapses; this

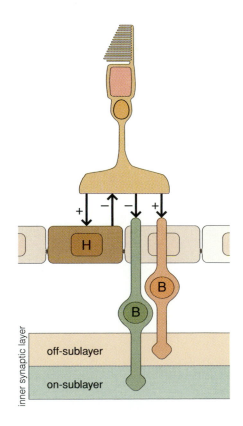

inner synaptic layer

off-sublayer

on-sublayer

triad, dyad

The names for these terms are confusing, for they mean less than they suggest. It used to be thought that each invagination within a cone pedicle contained just three processes: two from horizontal cells and one from a bipolar cell, as this arrangement was typical of what one saw in thin transverse sections of a cone pedicle. It was on the basis of this impression that the term *triad* was introduced. Recently, horizontal sections of cone pedicles and three-dimensional reconstructions of them have shown that the cone invaginations can contain a number of bipolar cell processes, as previously illustrated (page 108), and thus are similar to the single invagination of the rod spherule. This prompted a redefinition of *triad*, based on the two horizontal cell processes and the synaptic ribbon; but this in turn compromised the meaning of the term *dyad*. Such terminological confusions inevitably occur in all fields, so it is useful to think of the terms used as *identifiers* rather than *descriptors*. Mr. Green is not green, and it doesn't much bother us that he isn't. In the same spirit, *triad* refers to an invagination in a cone pedicle, and *dyad* refers to the synaptic arrangement about a ribbon in a bipolar cell terminal, and that's all there is to it.

arrangement is termed a **dyad.** Usually one of these postsynaptic processes belongs to an amacrine cell and the other to a ganglion cell (see diagram at right).

Like photoreceptors, all bipolar cells appear to release glutamate as their neurotransmitter. On the postsynaptic side, the membrane of the amacrine or ganglion cell process contains receptors for glutamate. So far as is known, the receptor molecules on the ganglion cell processes are all ionotropic and sign-conserving. Thus on-ganglion cells receive from on-bipolar cells, and off-ganglion cells receive from off-bipolar cells (below). Whereas on- and off-bipolar cells differ in the glutamate receptors of their dendritic terminals, on- and off-ganglion cells differ according to whether they receive from on- or off-bipolar cells. This notion that the response properties of a neuron are partly due to its own properties and partly due to those of the neurons it receives from is a recurring theme in vision. The synapses of bipolar cells onto amacrine cells also appear to be sign-conserving, although this has not been demonstrated.

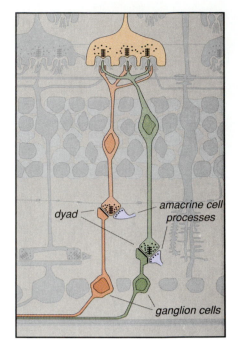

Amacrine cells provide feedback and thus complexity

The manner in which amacrine cells make chemical synapses onto other cells is uncertain; nevertheless, the most common neurotransmitters used by amacrine cells, **glycine** and **GABA** (see top of next page), are usually associated with sign-inverting synapses in which receptors for these neurotransmitters cause ionic currents to flow that either tend to hyperpolarize the postsynaptic membrane or to hold it at a steady value, thereby limiting the effects of other sign-conserving synapses.

Ganglion cells receive many synaptic contacts from amacrine cells. There are many types of ganglion cells and many different

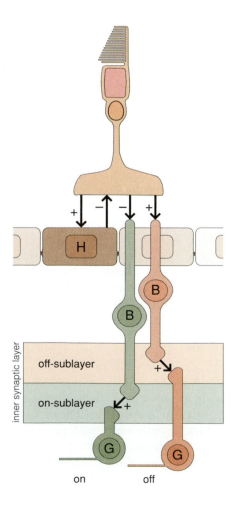

×30,000,000

glycine   GABA

types of amacrine cells, as well as a number of neurotransmitters other than those I've mentioned, so it is difficult to generalize about these contacts. However, to a first approximation, amacrine cells make sign-inverting synapses onto ganglion cells, as summarized in this diagram:

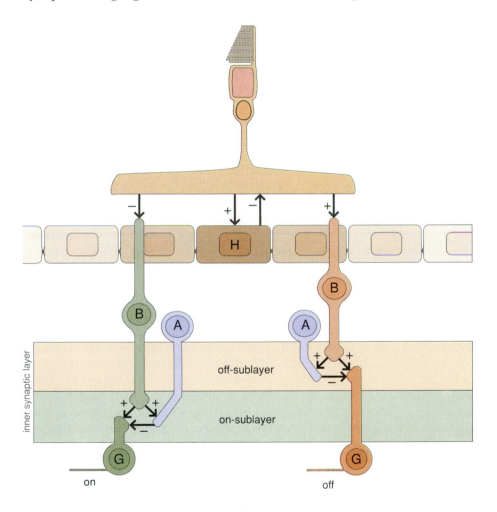

If we view the arrows in the diagram as one-way bridges, they show only two routes from a bipolar cell to a ganglion cell: the direct (sign-conserving) path and the indirect (sign-inverting) path via the amacrine cell. Of course, a ganglion cell can receive from a number of bipolar cells and a number of amacrine cells, but as shown there are never more than two synapses between a bipolar cell and a ganglion cell. Some neural processing clearly could be done with such limited pathways, although the possibilities for complex interactions would be severely limited. For example, some amacrine cells might receive from many bipolar cells, and act on ganglion cells so as to hyperpolarize them. These amacrine cells would thus influence ganglion cells in a manner similar to that in which horizontal cells influence bipolar cells.

But some ganglion cell types produce responses more complex than can be readily accounted for by the limited pathways summarized above. For example, some respond if an image is moving from right to left, but not if the movement is in the opposite direction. The manner in which this is accomplished is still not clear, but it seems almost certain that it involves additional synaptic contacts made by amacrine cells that are not included in the above diagram.

Amacrine cells are not only presynaptic to ganglion cells, they are also presynaptic to bipolar cells, as well as to other amacrine cells. The contact onto a bipolar cell dyad is shown schematically in the diagram to the left. These contacts are common to both on- and off-bipolar cells, so the bipolar cell and the ganglion cell shown are colored gray. The diagram at left shows that at a dyad, a bipolar cell can be presynaptic to an amacrine cell, and that amacrine cell can be presynaptic to the same dyad, forming a reciprocal synapse. What it fails to show is that the same amacrine cell may have a number of processes that make reciprocal synapses with other bipolar cells. It seems likely that most, if not all, of the synapses of amacrine cells onto bipolar cells are sign-inverting, but this has not been shown.

Again, consider the arrows to represent one-way streets, and consider the possible pathways from a bipolar cell to a ganglion cell. Because the arrows from many amacrine cells loop back, the potential pathways are unlimited. Each loop is termed a **feedback pathway,** since the signal produced by one of the neurons in the loop can be returned to the cell itself so as to modify its output. These feedback pathways may involve a number of bipolar cells and amacrine cells, but end at the ganglion cells, since they are not presynaptic to any other retinal cell, as we will see in the next section. The synaptic contacts of horizontal cells back onto cones provide another example of this sort of interaction, which ends at the bipolar cells.

Feedback pathways occur throughout all levels of biology, and it is their prominence that most distinguishes biology from the other basic sciences. Like any biological tissue, the retina contains many different feedback pathways, both within cells and among them. The feedback pathways provided by amacrine cells almost certainly play significant roles in the regulation of retinal function; however, although there are many different types of amacrine cells, we currently have a good understanding of the neural pathways of only one of them, which will be described in the next chapter. There are also gap junctions between cells in the inner half of the retina, just as there are in the outer half. They play an important role in the retinal pathways arising from rods, and are also discussed in the next chapter.

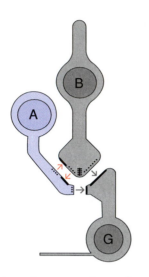

reciprocal synapses of amacrine cells

Ganglion cell dendrites are always postsynaptic

In mammals, the synaptic contacts made by the dendritic processes of ganglion cells are always postsynaptic. These dendritic processes thus lack synaptic vesicles as well as the membrane specializations that are characteristic of a presynaptic site.

The basic function of ganglion cells is to collect signals from bipolar and amacrine cells and send a signal to the brain in the form of a sequence of action potentials. The signals a ganglion cell receives are in the form of neurotransmitter concentrations, which are detected by different types of receptor molecules at postsynaptic sites on its dendrites. The effect of these receptor molecules is to open or close ionic channels, so as to alter the ganglion cell's transmembrane potential.

In most ganglion cells, the length of the dendritic processes is sufficiently small, and they are sufficiently thick, that the locations of the synaptic contacts are either irrelevant or exert only a minor influence. In effect, the postsynaptic ionic currents, mediated by the different receptors on the ganglion cell membrane, combine to influence the net charge separation across the membrane and thus the transmembrane potential. Action potentials are initiated at a region termed the **axon hillock,** located where the axon joins the cell body. The cell membrane at this site contains a high concentration of voltage-gated channels selective for Na$^+$ ions. The generation of action potentials appears to depend only on the degree of depolarization of transmembrane potential at the axon hillock. Thus the ganglion cell has little opportunity to do much more than combine the signals it receives and convey the result to the brain. There may be exceptions to this generalization, but they have not been reported.

To summarize, each cone pedicle connects to many cone bipolar cells. There are thirteen or so different types of cone bipolar cells, which can be arbitrarily grouped according to whether they depolarize in response to light increase (on-bipolar cells) or light decrease (off-bipolar cells). These two groups of cell types can also be distinguished by the level at which their axons arborize in the inner synaptic layer; the off group arborizes in the outer sublayer, and the on group in the inner sublayer.

Most bipolar cell synaptic contacts occur at a dyad; each bipolar cell process contains a synaptic ribbon and lies in apposition to two other processes, commonly one from a ganglion cell and the other from an amacrine cell. The bipolar cell is presynaptic to both processes, and the amacrine cell process is typically presynaptic to the bipolar cell. The feedback pathways between amacrine and bipolar cells allow for complex neural processing to take place at the retinal level.

Ganglion cell dendrites are always postsynaptic; this implies that the response properties of ganglion cells are primarily a result of the combined response properties of the amacrine and bipolar cells presynaptic to them.

We see a star when its photons activate our neurons—concluded

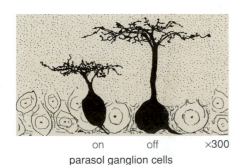

on   off   ×300
parasol ganglion cells

after Polyak, 1941

As you might suspect by now, there are *two* retinal pathways by which we see Polaris when we gaze directly at it. One consists of foveal cones, bipolar cells that receive from a number of cones, termed *on-diffuse bipolar cells*, and a ganglion cell type termed an **on-parasol.** This is the pathway that was introduced in the first chapter. The other consists of the same foveal cones, *off-diffuse bipolar cells*, and **off-parasol** ganglion cells (right). The "on" property of an on-parasol ganglion cell is a consequence of the connections it makes with on-bipolar cells, and ultimately, with the metabotropic receptors those bipolar cells possess, which track the concentration of glutamate at the cone–bipolar synapses. Corresponding relations link off-parasol ganglion cells, off-bipolar cells, and the ionotropic receptors at the contacts they make with the same group of cones. Amacrine cells are involved in both pathways, but our knowledge of their types, connections,

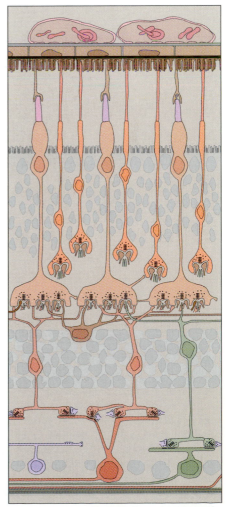

off-parasol   on-parasol

and influences on the ganglion cells is poor, so it is not possible to say much about them.

As described in the first chapter, on-parasol ganglion cells near the fovea receive from 5 or 6 diffuse bipolar cells, which collectively receive from 20 to 25 cones. Off-parasol ganglion cells show a similar pattern of connections. Either parasol cell type may also make a few contacts with **midget** bipolar cells, each of which usually receives from a single cone; the minor contribution of these synapses will be ignored for the time being. We have seen that the response properties of on-parasol and off-parasol ganglion cells are a consequence of the response properties of the other cell types involved—cones, bipolar cells, and amacrine cells—as well as the extent and nature of the patterns of connections among them. Although parasol cells constitute only about 4–10% of the ganglion cells in our retinas, they may be the most important group with respect to our conscious visual experience; SEEING discusses their role in vision in greater detail.

As mentioned earlier (page 40), the axons of ganglion cells convey information to the brain via propagated action potentials, which are generated at the axon hillock, where the axon connects to the cell body. It is worth noting that, compared with graded potentials, propagated action potentials provide a rather poor means of communication between nerve cells. But only action potentials can traverse the relatively long distance between eye and brain. Each action potential lasts for about one millisecond (1 ms) and propagates along the axon at a velocity of about 20 meters per second (20 m/s). Another way of expressing this velocity is 20 millimeters/millisecond (20 mm/ms); since the duration of an action potential is 1 ms, this implies that an action potential extends for about 20 mm along the length of the axon.

Neural messages depend upon an increase in firing rate

All action potentials are alike in size and shape, so the information they convey is contained entirely in the time pattern of these brief electrical pulses. Parasol cells generate a continuous stream of action potentials, even in the absence of retinal stimulation. This ongoing or **maintained activity** is illustrated in the diagram, which represents a recording of the electrical activity of a single parasol cell:

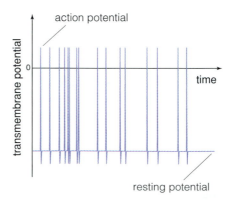

maintained activity of parasol ganglion cell

firing rate
When a neurobiologist records the electrical activity of a neuron that is producing action potentials, he or she usually connects the recording amplifier to a loudspeaker so that the activity can be heard. The sound of the sequence of pulses (similar to the sound of a Geiger counter) may have suggested this terminology.

Notice that the sequence of action potentials is irregular; the period between successive action potentials may be short or long, without evident order. The rate at which a neuron produces action potentials is usually referred to as the **firing rate**. Most ganglion cells have a maintained firing rate, which is always irregular.

The relation between the firing rate of a parasol cell and the transmembrane potential of one of the diffuse bipolar cells that synapses with it is shown schematically in the diagram at right. The stimulus is a small spot of light whose intensity is changed for a period of 250 ms. This duration was chosen because it corresponds to a typical interval between successive saccades during ordinary visual activities, such as reading (see LOOKING, page 310). Bipolar cells do not generate action potentials, only graded potentials. During the stimulus the bipolar cell depolarizes, which leads to a depolarization of the ganglion cell. In response to this depolarization, the ganglion cell produces an increase in the rate at which it generates action potentials. *Note that the diagram does not indicate whether the spot of light increased or decreased in intensity during the 250 ms period.* An increase would imply an on-diffuse bipolar cell and an on-parasol cell; likewise, a decrease would imply an off-diffuse bipolar cell and an off-parasol cell. But it makes no difference, since this description applies to both possibilities.

Almost immediately after the depolarization of the bipolar cell, the ganglion cell produces a burst of action potentials lasting 50 to 100 ms. Fifty milliseconds is about the minimum duration of the burst, even for a very brief flash of light. Although the bipolar cells initiate this transient increase in firing rate, the subsequent time course of their direct effects on the parasol cell may be due in part to the activity of some of the amacrine cells that are also activated by these bipolar cells. After the burst, the firing rate decays to a value somewhat greater than the maintained rate. At the end of the 250 ms period, when the bipolar cells hyperpolarize, there is a brief period in which the generation of action potentials is blocked, followed by a return to the maintained rate of firing. This brief block is not evident in this diagram (or in most actual recordings), since it is shorter than the average period between action potentials during maintained activity, but it can be revealed if many responses are averaged. This brief cessation in firing is presumably the result of a transient hyperpolarization of the transmembrane potential of the parasol cell below its resting level, possibly due to amacrine cells.

The response shown in the diagram is prototypical of the behavior of either type of parasol cell, and a number of inferences can be drawn from it. What the brain receives from each parasol cell is a sequence of action potentials that are essentially indistinguishable from one another. The maintained firing rate continues even in complete darkness, or in the presence of a uniform white field. A brief burst of activity can be readily distinguished from the maintained activity because the maintained rate, although irregular, rarely, if ever, produces so many action potentials in so short a period. By comparison, a brief cessation of action potentials is generally indistinguishable from the maintained rate, since equally long intervals without action potentials are quite common in the maintained rate.

With these inferences in mind, it is useful to distinguish the actual sequence of action potentials sent by a parasol cell to the brain from the **message** this sequence contains. In order to sharpen this distinction, imagine some visual stimulus that causes a parasol cell to produce a sequence of action potentials that is statistically indistinguishable from the maintained activity. Because there is no means of distinguishing this response from the maintained activity, *there is no message.* Conversely, in order for there to be a message, the firing pattern must differ in some way from that of the maintained activity. As a rough quantification, we can think of a pattern of action potentials that differs only slightly from the maintained activity as a **weak message**; conversely, a pattern of action potentials never seen in the maintained activity is a **strong message.**

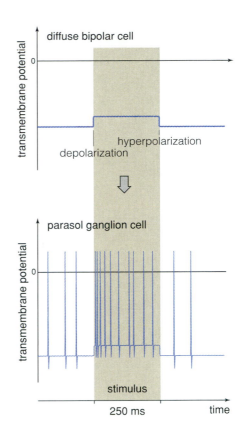

As illustrated by the firing pattern in response to a change in light intensity, *the only message that a single parasol cell can convey is in the form of an increase in firing rate*. If the change in light intensity is small, then the message may be weak; in this case the brain may have the opportunity of comparing the cell's activity with that of nearby parasol cells of the same type, provided they are also responding to the spot.

The foregoing discussion has ignored the difference between on-parasol cells and off-parasol cells, since it applies equally to either type. When we now *compare* on- and off-parasol cells, their distinctive roles become clear. An *increase* in light intensity would cause an *on-parasol cell* to generate a strong message (a high firing rate), whereas an off-parasol cell would generate a message (a brief cessation of action potentials) so weak as to be nonexistent. Conversely, *off-parasol cells* are adapted to send messages about *decreases* in light intensity.

Each type of parasol cell tiles the retina

Having considered the properties of individual parasol cells of each type, we are now in a position to consider how arrays of these two distinct ganglion cell types respond when we gaze at Polaris.

The retinal region over which a ganglion cell's dendrites extend is termed its **dendritic field**. The dendritic fields of both types of parasol cell **tile** the retina. This means that any point on the retina lies within the dendritic field of at least one on-parasol cell and at least one off-parasol cell. The two tilings are separate, so that some point might lie at the center of the dendritic field of an on-parasol cell, but near the periphery of the dendritic field of the off-parasol cell that includes that point. Many cell types tile the retina; this property is discussed in greater detail in RETINAL ORGANIZATION.

We see Polaris by means of messages conveyed by arrays of parasol cells

THE CHASE summarized the role of parasol ganglion cells in viewing Polaris:

The image of Polaris is in constant motion on the retinal surface, like a small rain cloud wandering about over the foveal plain, as a result of your slight head movements. The cones in any one location receive a photon rain from Polaris only as its image passes over them. At these dimensions, the motion of the image is relatively rapid; it passes over a cone in a fraction of a second. So from the perspective of one cone, there is drought, a sudden and brief shower, and a return to drought. As previously noted, each parasol ganglion cell receives signals arising from about 20–25 cones, which is about the same number as are covered at any one time by the densest rain of photons from Polaris. But the moving image may cover only a portion of this patch of cones, and thus only partially stimulate the parasol cell. In any case, the stimulation of the parasol cells will be brief.

A different perspective emerges if we change our focus from this particular parasol cell to the array *of parasol cells and the* array *of cones in the retina. The retina as a whole is receiving a continuous shower of photons, as you might water the lawn with a hose and spray nozzle. At any instant there is always a patch of cones receiving this photon rain, at least two stimulated parasol cells that are receiving signals via diffuse bipolar cells, at least two stimulated cells in the LGN, and a group of stimulated neurons in the visual cortex. It is in this changing activity from cell to cell that the retina presents Polaris to the brain.*

Now that arrays of both on-parasol and off-parasol cells have been introduced, this picture can be extended in a manner that clarifies the roles of both ganglion cell types. Imagine a large display composed of arrays of many lights that can be turned on and off, like the ones used in a sports stadium. Imagine that each light corresponds to a parasol cell, and that its brightness reflects the rate at which that parasol cell is producing action potentials. On-parasol cells are represented by green lights and off-parasol cells by orange lights.

The image of Polaris moves about over the foveal region as a result of slight head movements. As the image moves over the array of on-parasol cells, a sequence of green lights can be seen to trace a path, like a little green worm, as each activated on-parasol cell responds by producing a burst of action potentials. The length of the worm depends upon both the duration of each burst and the rate at which the image is activating successive on-parasol cells. The head of the green worm follows the *leading* edge of the image as it moves over the cone array. Close behind the head of the green worm is an orange worm, whose head follows the *trailing* edge of the image of Polaris. Depending upon the velocity of the image across the retina, the orange worm may overlap the green worm. But the heads of the two worms remain separated by the width of the image of Polaris, together with any difference in the speed of transmission between the on- and off-pathways.

To summarize, the image of Polaris that falls on the foveal cones is conveyed to the brain in the form of messages from two separate arrays of ganglion cells: the array of on-parasol cells provides a sequence of messages about the leading edge of the image, while the array of off-parasol cells provides a sequence of messages about the trailing edge of the image. Based upon the two sequences of messages, the brain can gain information about the image itself—this is how seeing begins.

The axons of parasol cells go to the magnocellular portion of the LGN

As briefly described in THE CHASE (page 18), each parasol cell sends its axon through the optic disc and within the optic tract to a nucleus in the middle of the brain termed the lateral geniculate nucleus (LGN). The upper, or dorsal, portion of the LGN contains neurons with relatively small cell bodies, and is termed the **parvocellular** (Latin *parvus* = small) portion. This region receives from a number of different types of ganglion cells. Most of them belong to a group of small-bodied ganglion cells known as **midget ganglion cells,** which have already been mentioned but will be described in detail later. So far as we know, the ganglion cell axons that go to the parvocellular portion of the LGN do not branch to go to any other region of the brain. Each parvocellular neuron generates an action potential only when it receives one from the axon of a retinal ganglion cell. The axons of the parvocellular neurons terminate in a specific layer of the striate portion of the visual cortex (right).

The lower, or ventral, portion of the LGN contains neurons with large cell bodies and is termed the **magnocellular** (Latin *magnus* = great) portion. Both types of parasol cells send their axons to the magnocellular portion of the LGN (a small fraction of them branch and terminate in another region of the brain, termed the pretectum). Parasol cells also have large cell bodies, apparently because they have thick axons, which constitute about 97% of the total volume of the cell. The velocity with which an axon conducts action potentials is proportional to its diameter, and parasol cells have the thickest axons of any ganglion cell type. Each parasol cell axon makes a

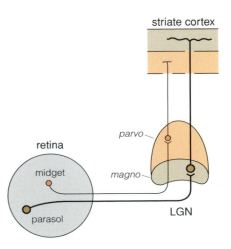

strong synaptic contact with one of the large-bodied neurons of the magno-cellular layer. The axon of the magnocellular neuron is also thick, and passes to a different layer of the striate visual cortex than do the axons of cells from the parvocellular layers. Like the cells of the parvocellular LGN, each magnocellular neuron generates an action potential only when it receives one from the axon of a parasol cell. Thus, to a first approximation, the magnocellular neuron simply relays the pattern of action potentials generated by the parasol cell to the striate cortex.

The LGN *receives* many more axons from the striate cortex than it does from the retina. The function of these cortical axons is unknown, but it is possible that their synaptic contacts somehow act as selective gates, controlling which ganglion cell axon potentials are relayed to the striate cortex.

There is a good deal more to be said about parasol cells, and the roles they play in vision, so we will return to them later. The next chapter, THE RAIN OF PHOTONS ONTO RODS, discusses how we see Polaris when we do not gaze directly at it and its image falls onto a region containing both rods and cones.

stars that can be seen via rods

6

The rain of photons onto rods

Let us look again at Polaris, but this time with our peripheral retina, where its image will fall on a retinal region containing mostly rods. We will follow the signals of individual rods through the retina in much the same way that we followed the signals of cones in the previous chapter. Part of the rod pathway is piggybacked upon the cone pathways at the level of the cone bipolar cells. By this and other means, parasol cells convey the signals of rods, as well as cones, to the visual cortex.

Camping

Take yourself camping; go beyond city lights and wait for dawn. You are lying in a small open space, and you have been looking directly at Polaris. Idly, your gaze wanders off in the direction of the bowl of the Big Dipper. Polaris is suddenly brighter! You again look directly at Polaris, and it dims; you look away in any direction, and it again brightens!

Away from the fovea, the retina is dominated by rods

When you look directly at Polaris, its image falls on the center of your fovea, which contains only cones. When you look away by about 15°, the image falls on a region of your retina that has about the same spatial density of photoreceptors—but they are mostly rods (see diagram at left). At this retinal eccentricity, the spatial density of the rods is close to its peak value, and rods outnumber cones by a ratio of about 30:1 (see below). But the cones are considerably thicker than the rods, and take up 20–25% of the cross-sectional area of the retina at the level of the photoreceptor inner segments. The cones thus intercept 20–25% of the incident photons. This fraction is approximately constant throughout the peripheral retina. The image of Polaris at this location is about 50% wider than the foveal image because of off-axis aberrations of an eye with a wide pupil. As we have seen, the

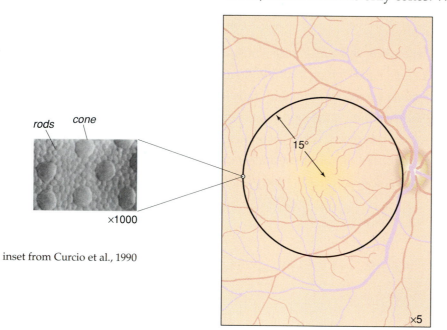

rods   *cone*

×1000

inset from Curcio et al., 1990

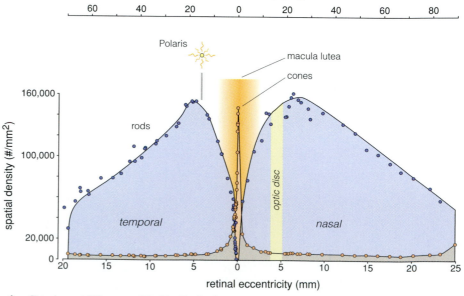

after Østerberg, 1935; as modified by Rodieck, 1988

Visual angle and retinal eccentricity

An ordinary angle is measured with respect to some point, termed the **apex:**

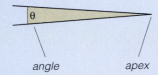

angle   *apex*

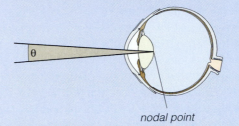

nodal point

A **visual angle** is simply the angle formed by some dimension of an object when the apex corresponds to the eye:

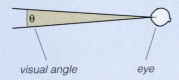

visual angle   *eye*

Visual angles are always expressed in **degrees**. Some useful "rules of thumb": at arm's length, the visual angle of the width of your index finger is 2°; the width of your outstretched hand is about 20°.

The notion of a visual angle is useful because objects with the same visual angle have the same size on the retina, whatever their spatial extent in the visual world (see below). If the object is far away, then the position of the apex is unimportant. But when an object is close to the eye, it is necessary to specify the location of the apex with greater precision, in order that objects that subtend the same visual angle still have the same size on the retina. Simple optical theory identifies a point within the optical system, termed the **nodal point,** at which to place the apex (as shown at top right). For most eyes, the nodal point lies about 7 mm behind the cornea, a point in the eye that happens to lie near the back surface of the lens.

In common English, *eccentric* connotes departing or deviating from the conventional or the norm. It arises from the Greek word *ekkentros* (*ex* = out or away from + *kentron* = center or point). Its usage in the terminology of machinery

reflects this origin. In vision, *eccentricity* refers to the distance away from some reference point or line on the retina. In general, that reference is the region of the retina that contains the greatest concentration of ganglion cells, where vision is sharpest. In humans, retinal eccentricity is the distance from the center of the fovea. In rabbits, which have a pronounced visual streak, retinal eccentricity is the perpendicular (vertical) distance from the streak.

Eccentricity can be expressed either as a distance on the retinal surface, measured in millimeters, or as the visual angle between some point on the retina and the center of the fovea:

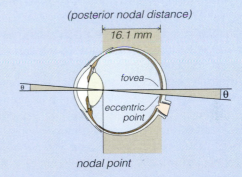

(posterior nodal distance)

16.1 mm

fovea

eccentric. point

nodal point

If one knows the distance from the nodal point to the retina, which is termed the **posterior nodal distance,** then it is simple to convert between visual angle and retinal eccentricity. For adult humans, the posterior nodal distance is about 17 mm.

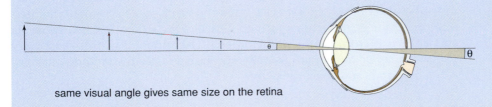

same visual angle gives same size on the retina

optical quality of the eye is highest at or near the fovea, where the point spread function is narrowest; it falls gradually with increasing retinal eccentricity up to 20°, beyond which the loss in quality becomes severe. The number of photons effectively caught in the retinal shutter time is about the same for rods in the periphery (about 1040) as for foveal cones (about 1100); the various factors involved are discussed in the Box *CALCULATING THE ROD PHOTON CATCH*.

Calculating the rod photon catch

Calculation of the number of photons effectively caught by rods closely follows that for cones, as described in THE RAIN OF PHOTONS ONTO CONES. Rods and cones catch about the same fraction of the photons passing through their outer segments; both catch about 70% of the photons whose frequency corresponds to that for which they are most sensitive. There are, however, four factors that result in a difference in photon catch between rods and cones.

First, rods are most sensitive to photons with frequencies of about 600 THz, whereas the peak in foveal cone sensitivity lies at about 540 THz (see illustration at right). The upper diagram shows the density of photons of different frequencies over the visible range; their relative numbers decrease smoothly toward higher frequencies. The lower diagram shows how the sensitivity of foveal cones (L and M) and of rods varies with frequency. The frequency scale is common to both diagrams. Because rods prefer photons of higher frequency than those preferred by foveal cones, they catch fewer incident photons from Polaris (only about 60% as many).

The second factor has to do with a difference in the directional sensitivity of cones and rods (see page 83). Whereas the efficiency of cones in capturing photons declines strongly for photons not entering through the center of the pupil, rods are almost equally efficient in capturing photons regardless of where they enter the pupil. This allows rods to capture about 60% more of the photons that enter the dilated pupil than do cones, and balances the decrease caused by the higher peak frequency of rods.

The third factor is that the macular pigment extends only to a retinal eccentricity of about 2.5 mm (9°). The rod photon catch rate is thereby increased by about 10%, com-

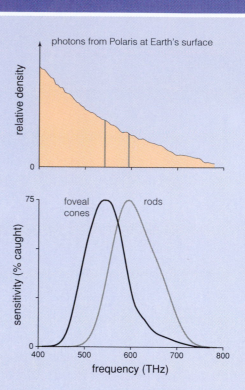

pared with what it would be in the presence of the macular pigment.

The final factor is that the cross-sectional area of a rod inner segment at this retinal eccentricity is only about 80% of that of a foveal cone, and is thus able to intercept only about 80% of the incident photons. Combining these factors gives the rods a total photon catch of about 1040 in the 0.1 s shutter time, compared with some 1100 for foveal cones.

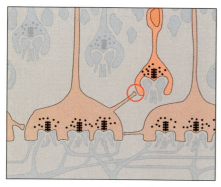

cone–rod gap junction

The synaptic terminal of a rod is pear-shaped, and much of its interior is infolded to form a single invagination that is larger than those of a cone pedicle. The primary synaptic pathway is formed by contacts between the rod spherule and rod bipolar cells, but a rod can also send signals via interphotoreceptor gap junctions formed between the side of the rod spherule and a process from a cone pedicle (left). The function of this secondary pathway may be to route rod signals through a faster-responding pathway when both rods and cones are active.

Rods contact a single type of bipolar cell

The synaptic contacts of the rod spherule are relatively simple: its single invagination contains two lateral processes from horizontal cells and two to four processes from rod bipolar cells. These connections are summarized in the diagram at the top of the next page. Two horizontal cell processes are shown; each is supplied by the axonal arbor of a different HI horizontal cell. Each arbor both receives from and acts on about 700 rods, and each rod contacts two different arbors.

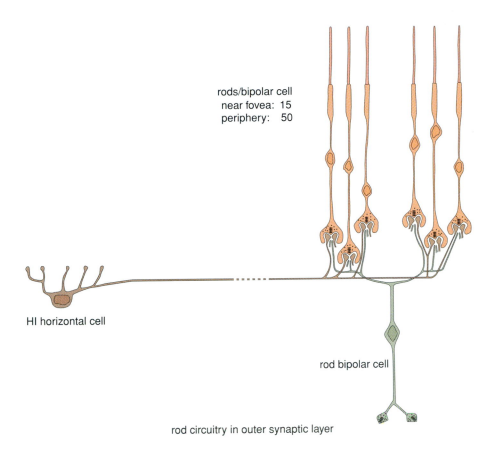

rods/bipolar cell
near fovea: 15
periphery: 50

HI horizontal cell

rod bipolar cell

rod circuitry in outer synaptic layer

The drawing below shows the axonal arbor of one horizontal cell, seen in flat view. The swellings, seen mainly at the branch points, are artifacts that arose when the tissue was processed. The axon of an HI horizontal cell does not conduct action potentials, and it is sufficiently long that the axonal arbor is electrically isolated from the dendritic arbor. The axonal arbor probably interacts with rods in the same way that the dendritic arbor interacts with M and L cones (see page 48), but this has not been directly demonstrated.

The dendritic terminals of rod bipolar cells contain metabotropic receptors to glutamate molecules, which cause these cells to *depolarize* in response to a *decrease* in the concentration of glutamate. They are thus on-bipolar cells. In transverse section, the dendritic processes of rod bipolar cells can be seen to pass between the feet of the cone pedicles to reach the rod spherules; at higher

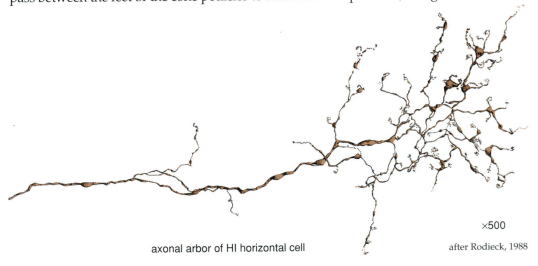

×500

axonal arbor of HI horizontal cell

after Rodieck, 1988

magnification, they can be seen to form the central processes within the synaptic terminals of the rods (right). Near the fovea, each rod spherule contains three or four central invaginating processes; in the peripheral retina, there are two or three. So far as is known, each of these processes arises from a different rod bipolar cell. Each rod bipolar cell contacts between 15 and 50 rods, the number increasing with retinal eccentricity. The drawings below show the dendrites and cell bodies of rod bipolar cells at different eccentricities.

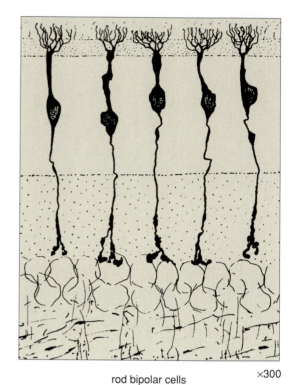

rod bipolar cells   ×300

after Polyak, 1941

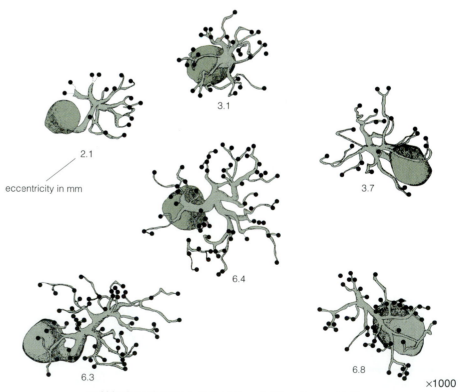

eccentricity in mm

rod bipolar cell body and dendrites at different eccentricities

×1000

after Grünert and Martin, 1991

Rod bipolar cell axons make contacts in the innermost portion of the inner synaptic layer

The axons of the rod bipolar cells pass though most of the inner synaptic layer to terminate in a few swellings (also called **terminal lobes** or **varicosities**):

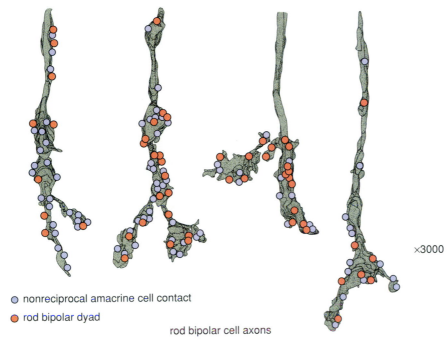

×3000

○ nonreciprocal amacrine cell contact
● rod bipolar dyad

rod bipolar cell axons

after Grünert and Martin, 1991

These swellings extend as far as the ganglion cell layer, but make no direct contact with ganglion cells. Three-dimensional reconstructions of rod bipolar axonal endings from a series of thin sections show that synaptic contacts occur mainly in the inner half of the inner synaptic layer, particularly on the swellings. Most, if not all, of these contacts are with amacrine cells. Reciprocal contacts are common at dyads; in addition, there are nonreciprocal contacts at other portions of the axon. Seen in horizontal section, the terminal swellings of an array of rod bipolar cells form a quasi-regular pattern at the inner border of the inner synaptic layer (right). This arrangement, by which rod bipolar cells terminate in the innermost portion of the inner synaptic layer, whereas cone bipolar cells terminate in the remaining portion in the on- or off-sublayers, is common to all mammals, and forms an additional subdivision of the inner synaptic layer:

rabbit   ×300

rod bipolar axon terminals

after Young and Vaney, 1991

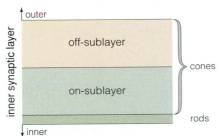

All amacrine cells convey the rod signal to cone bipolar cells

The main synaptic contacts made by the axon terminals of rod bipolar cells are onto an amacrine cell type with a small dendritic field known as an **AII** amacrine ("A-two"). These amacrine cells are **bistratified,** with thick, rounded endings in the outer portion of the inner synaptic layer, termed **lobular appendages,** and thinner dendritic processes in the inner portion:

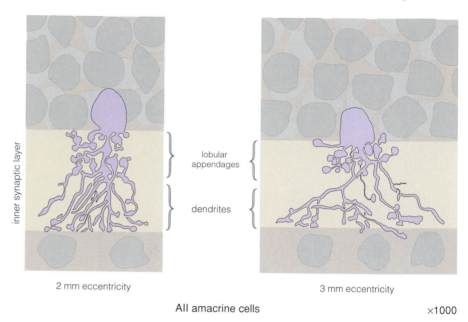

lobular appendages

dendrites

inner synaptic layer

2 mm eccentricity

3 mm eccentricity

AII amacrine cells   ×1000

after Grünert and Martin, 1991

AII amacrine cells are coupled together by means of gap junctions between their dendrites; they thus form a pool of activity much like that of horizontal cells. If a small molecule, such as Neurobiotin, is experimentally injected into one cell, it spreads to the others via the intercellular paths provided by the gap junctions. The following pair of photographs shows a patch of AII amacrine cells so labeled:

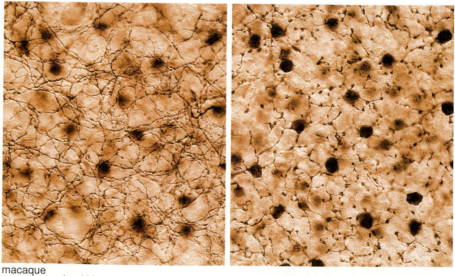

macaque

dendritic processes   lobular appendages and cell bodies

AII amacrine cells

courtesy of Dennis M. Dacey

At the left, the plane of focus of the microscope lies near the inner border of the inner synaptic layer, so as to show the dendritic processes. At the right, the plane of focus lies near the outer border, where the lobular appendages and the inner portions of the cell bodies lie. The processes in both strata are disposed in a quasi-regular manner, so as to provide more or less uniform coverage.

AII amacrine cells are the most common amacrine cell type in the retina, and they play a critical role in linking the rod bipolar cells to the ganglion cells. Their major connections are summarized in this schematic diagram:

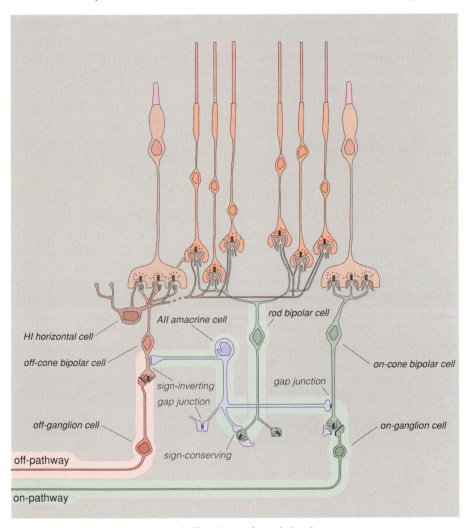

on- and off-pathways for rod signals

Rod bipolar cells make sign-conserving synapses onto the dendrites of AII amacrine cells. Thus, when the rod bipolar cells depolarize in response to an increase in light intensity, so too do the AII amacrine cells. These amacrine cells contact on-cone bipolar cells via gap junctions. The depolarization of the AII amacrine cells thus spreads into the on-cone bipolar cells, thereby activating the on-ganglion cells that they contact. In effect, the signals of rods and cones add together at the level of some of the on-cone bipolar cells.

The AII amacrine cells also make chemical synapses onto off-cone bipolar cells, via the lobular appendages, at which they release glycine molecules. These synapses are sign-inverting and thus inhibitory. There are thus two sign-inverting synapses between the rods and the off-cone bipolar cells, the first at the rod–rod bipolar cell synapse and the second between the AII amacrine cells and the off-cone bipolar cells. Thus a light decrease will ultimately depolarize the off-cone bipolar cells via the rod pathway by reduc-

glycine   ×30,000,000

ing the inhibitory effect of the AII amacrine cells. By this means a light decrease causes rods to activate off-ganglion cells.

Thus both on- and off-cone bipolar cells are able to combine rod and cone signals in an additive manner. Whereas the distinction between on- and off-cone signals arises in the outer synaptic layer, and involves a difference in the postsynaptic receptors of different cone bipolar cells, the distinction between on- and off-rod signals arises in the inner synaptic layer as a result of circuitry that involves an additional cell type.

To summarize, AII amacrine cells provide a means by which the signals from rods can be "piggybacked" onto the neural circuitry that connects cones to ganglion cells in both the on- and the off-pathways. The schematic diagram on the preceding page is oversimplified; other amacrine cell types make reciprocal synaptic contacts with rod bipolar cells and with the AII amacrine cells. These other amacrine cells have not been as well characterized as the AII amacrine cells, and their functions may be more involved in modulating or regulating levels of activity than in conveying the rod signal per se.

Viewing Polaris with your rod pathway

As noted at the outset, a star viewed at an eccentricity of 15° or so appears considerably brighter than one viewed with the fovea. This is because in dim conditions, rods and their circuitry produce a greater response at the level of the ganglion cells than do the foveal cones and their circuitry. As a consequence, when the image of the night sky falls on our rods, we are, under the best conditions, able to see stars with magnitudes up to about 6, whereas when the image falls on our cones, we can see stars only up to a magnitude of about 3.5 (see the Box STELLAR MAGNITUDES). Since each step in stellar magnitude corresponds to a factor of 2.5, this difference in magnitude corresponds to an intensity ratio of about 10. Under experimental conditions, where the light of the night sky can be excluded, the ratio of the sensitivity of rod vision to that of cone vision for a point of light is closer to 100.

The next chapter takes up the issues involved in rod and cone sensitivities from a broad perspective that focuses on the range of light intensities encountered in the natural world.

Stellar magnitudes

The Greek astronomer Hipparchus (190–127 B.C.) devised a star catalog in which the apparent brightness of each star was listed as a **magnitude** ranging from 1 (brightest) to 6 (dimmest). In the nineteenth century, quantitative measurements by William Hershel and others indicated that an increase in magnitude by 1 corresponded to a decrease in intensity by a factor of about 2.5. In effect, Hipparchus had devised a logarithmic scale of magnitudes, using 2.5 as the base.

Stellar magnitudes can be converted to radiometric units of **total irradiance** above Earth's atmosphere via the following equation:

$$E_n = E_{n0} \times 10^{-0.4m} \, (\text{photon/s/m}^2)$$

Radiometry *499*

where m is the magnitude, E_n is the irradiance, and E_{n0}—the irradiance of a star of 0 magnitude—is equal to 1.15×10^{11} photon/s/m². For example, Polaris has a magnitude of 2.02, which gives it a total irradiance above Earth's atmosphere of 1.8×10^{10} photon/s/m².

Magnitudes can be converted to photometric units of **illuminance** above Earth's atmosphere via the following equation:

$$E_v = E_{v0} \times 10^{-0.4m}$$

where E_v is the illuminance of the star, m is its magnitude, and E_{v0}—the illuminance of a star of 0 magnitude—is equal to 2.54×10^{-6} lm/m².

Photometry *453*

border between an overcast sky and the tops of trees

7

Night and day

Between night and day, light intensity can change by a factor of about forty billion. The pupil is smaller in bright light, so that the change in light intensity at the retina is not as great, but it is still about three billion. Yet rods and cones can each respond to differences in light intensity over a dynamic range of only about 100. This chapter discusses how rods and cones manage to allow us to see over the much greater range of light intensities that we encounter daily. An understanding of how they collectively pull off this feat leads to a better appreciation of why the retinas of virtually all species contains these two classes of photoreceptors.

Rods reliably signal the capture of single photons

Rods have an astonishing ability to signal the capture of even a single photon. Viewing the just detectable border between the overcast night sky and the trees demonstrates this ability in a striking way, because at that time the rate at which each of your rods is catching photons is about once every *85 minutes*. The next chapter, HOW PHOTORECEPTORS WORK, describes how rods manage to accomplish this feat, which seems ever more amazing the better one understands it. Here we accept this ability as fact, and consider some of its implications.

The advantage of a reliable response to a single photon is enormous

Consider two hypothetical animals, A and B, identical but for one fact: Animal A has photoreceptors able to respond to one absorbed photon, whereas animal B has photoreceptors that require two. We want to test the visual ability of these two animals in very dim light. We adjust the light intensity to the point at which animal A is just able to perform a visual test. Now we test animal B, and find the intensity at which it is just able to perform the same test. How much brighter does the light have to be for B to pass the test? Twice as bright? The answer may surprise you.

In order for the responses of two photons to add together to make a bigger signal, the two photons cannot be separated in time by much more than the shutter time, which is about 0.1 s. Thus the rods of animal B need to catch two photons in this time interval to generate a signal. The photoreceptors of animal A can respond to every caught photon, even if the average rate of capture per photoreceptor is only once every 85 minutes (5100 s). Of course, the photons neither arrive nor are absorbed in a clockwork manner; instead, their arrival and absorption are random, and thus entirely unpredictable. When raindrops fall on the ground, a drop hitting the ground at some location may almost immediately be followed by a second drop falling at about the same location. The lighter the rain, the less frequent this event will be; so too for photons on the rods of animal B.

The French mathematician Siméon Poisson (1781–1840) developed an equation that allows one to calculate the average rate at which some combination of random events will occur. If the average rate of photon capture is once every 5100 s, then the rate at which a particular rod will capture two photons in 0.1 s is once *every 16 years*. Thus animal B couldn't see a thing at this light intensity.

How much brighter would the scene have to be in order to enable animal B to just make out the border between the overcast sky and the trees? As discussed in POISSON DISTRIBUTION, the relation is:

$$\text{intensity factor} = \frac{2 \times \text{time to capture one photon by animal A}}{\text{shutter time}}$$

$$= \frac{2 \times 5100 \text{ s}}{0.1 \text{ s}} = 102{,}000$$

catch, capture
As discussed in THE RAIN OF PHOTONS ONTO CONES (page 86), the term *catch* or *capture* is used here to refer to the absorption of a photon by a visual pigment molecule and the photoisomerization of its chromophore, resulting in the activation of the molecule.

shutter time
The term *shutter time* is discussed in THE RAIN OF PHOTONS ONTO CONES (page 76). It refers to a time period of about 0.1 s, which, from a number of different perspectives, captures the effective duration over which photons have influence.

Poisson distribution *485*

Thus in order for animal B to have as many rods responding as animal A, it would be necessary to raise the light intensity not by a factor of two, but by a factor of about 100,000!

The advantage of having photoreceptors that can reliably respond to a single photon, as compared with photoreceptors that require more, or are less reliable, is enormous. Photoreceptors able to produce reliable responses to the capture of a single photon are common to all vertebrates, and to every invertebrate thus far tested. Given the competition among species for survival, we should not be surprised at the universality of this ability, which probably arose long before there were vertebrates.

Dim lights are noisy

Under bright conditions, when photoreceptors are catching hundreds or thousands of photons per second, we can ignore photons and treat light as continuous. But in the natural world, we spend more than half our time in light sufficiently dim that photoreceptors must respond to photons one by one. Under these conditions, the random nature of the arrival of photons becomes a significant factor in how we see.

Photons act independently of one another; this allows the properties of a population of photons to be calculated from the properties of a single photon. The property of a photon that we are interested in here is its ability to photoisomerize the chromophore of a visual pigment molecule, but this event is never a certainty, only a probability. We saw something of this uncertainty in THE RAIN OF PHOTONS ONTO CONES, first in the distribution of all the photons in the visible range that constituted the retinal image of Polaris (page 80), and then in the photons of this image that were caught by the photoreceptors (page 87). These diagrams also showed that the smaller the number of photons, the greater the fluctuations in their number relative to the average number.

This randomness can also be seen in the image of the border between the overcast sky and the tops of the trees, as shown in the simulation at right. The lower portion of this diagram simulates the image on the retina; it has been inverted by the optics of the eye, so that the darker trees appear at the top. The width of the image is 60°, which is about the same as the

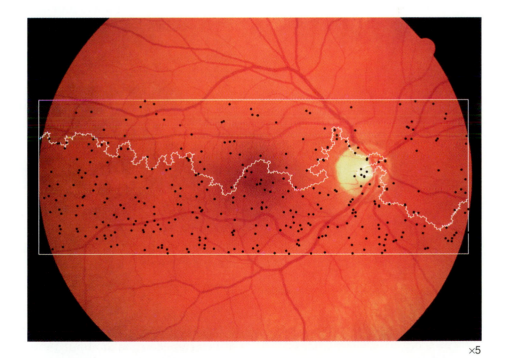

×5

|————————————————— 60° —————————————————|

image of border between an overcast sky and the tops of trees

chapter-opening illustration when viewed at reading distance. The upper portion of the diagram on page 137 shows a hypothetical photon catch from this image by the retina over the 0.1 s shuttertime. For reference, the border between the trees and the sky is shown in both panels as a thin line. The rate at which any single rod catches photons is very low, but the image covers a lot of rods. The rods receiving from the sky portion of the image caught 280 photons, and the rods receiving from the tree portion caught 83 photons.

Camping

The clouds disappear, the stars return, and the border between the night sky and the trees becomes easy to see. Even on this moonless night, and ignoring the visible stars, the clear night sky is much brighter than the overcast one was.

At this time, each of your rods, viewing the diffuse light of the night sky, is catching a photon about once every 30 seconds.

About one-third of the light of the night sky that illuminates Earth is due to stars. The remaining two-thirds consists of a more or less uniform background. This diffuse light comes from three sources: chemical reactions in Earth's upper atmosphere, zodiacal light (sunlight scattered from interplanetary dust), and—to a lesser extent—galactic light (stars and galaxies too dim to be seen individually, combined with starlight scattered from interstellar dust).

Camping

In the high mountain air, above the dust and other particles of the lower atmosphere, there are many stars to be seen. The dimmer stars disappear when you look directly at them. You search for the dimmest star you can detect, picking one out of the corner of your eye.

Dim stars disappear from your direct gaze because their rain of photons is insufficient to be reliably conveyed by the foveal cones. Consider a square millimeter of retina at about 15° eccentricity receiving the image of a dim star, which has a magnitude of 5 (see STELLAR MAGNITUDES, page 132). Over the 0.1 s shutter time, the distribution of captured photons from both the dim star and the diffuse light of the night sky might look something like the diagram at the top of the next page. For simplicity, let us assume that only one star occupies the portion of the sky imaged on this patch of retina. Its image consists of a cluster of caught photons toward the upper right of the diagram. This image is similar to the image of Polaris, described in the previous two chapters, except that the intensity of this star is only 6% that of Polaris, and the pile of photons that represents the image is correspondingly smaller.

The diffuse light from the rest of the night sky results in an average rate of 1 photon caught per rod every 30 seconds. With 160,000 rods in the 1 mm^2 patch, an average of 500 photons will be caught in the shutter time of 0.1 s. Of course there is no reason for these caught photons to form a spatial pattern, because each photon acts independently of the others. Instead, they

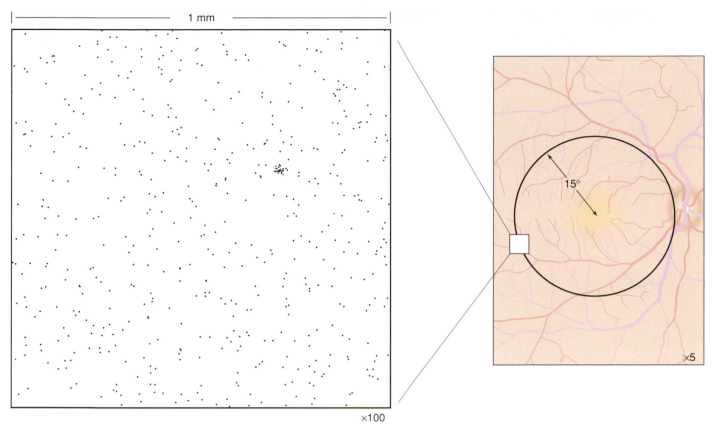

×100

photon catch from image of a star and the light of the night sky

are randomly distributed within the square, just as they were in the image of the sky and trees in the previous diagram. Their spatial distribution seems sparse in some parts of the square and concentrated in others. This is not a consequence of variations in the light intensity of the corresponding portion of the night sky; rather, it is the ordinary variation expected for randomly distributed points in a plane. The spatial distribution of raindrops on a square of sidewalk shows similar variations.

Returning to the image of the dim star, the average number of photoisomerizations in 0.1 s is about 28. The distribution of caught photons from the star alone is shown here at left:

one sample, 28 photons caught

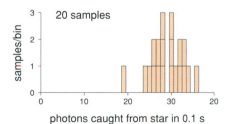

photons caught from star in 0.1 s

We assume that 28 photons were in fact caught; only 25 are shown in this diagram, because three were strongly scattered in passing through the eye, and fell well outside the bounds of this rectangle. The histogram at the right of the diagram shows the number of photons from the star that were caught in 20 sample shutter times. This number varied from a low of 19 to a high of 36 (see the Box *ESTIMATING VARIATION*).

Estimating variation

There is a simple geometric way of getting a feel for the amount of variation to be expected in certain phenomena. Take the average number of events (in this case, photoisomerizations, but it doesn't make any difference what kind) and arrange them in rows and columns to form a square as best you can. Thus 28 photoisomerizations can be arranged to form a 5 × 5 square with three left over:

Now subtract the number of rows from the average number (28 − 5 = 23), and add it to the average number (28 + 5 = 33). About two-thirds of the samples will have values that lie within this range (23 to 33), and the remainder will have values either below or above this range.

Often we are concerned with the *relative* variation, meaning the ratio of the variation (±5) to the average value (28). This fractional variation is equal to 1 divided by the number of rows, or about 20% on either side of the average value.

This rule of thumb is general, and has nothing to do with photons or stars. It applies when the probability of each event is independent of that of the others. This relation (mathematically expressed: variance = mean) summarizes one property of a POISSON DISTRIBUTION; such distributions characterize the properties of randomly distributed things, and arise frequently when we consider retinal events (e.g., the number of ionic channels that are open any moment).

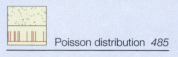

Poisson distribution *485*

Camping

The intensity of the dim star, viewed out of the corner of your eye, seems to fluctuate from moment to moment. So too does the background light of the night sky, which seems to scintillate. You settle in and close your eyes. But instead of a uniform darkness, there is a dimmer but more noticeable scintillation, which is not blocked when you put your hand over your eyes.

Rods are noisy

As described in the next chapter, rods in total darkness generate electrical events that cannot be distinguished from their responses to a caught photon. Electrical recordings from individual rods show such events occurring about once every 160 seconds. It is as if an additional light were present, with an intensity equal to about 20% of the diffuse light of the night sky. This phenomenon is what causes most, if not all, of the scintillation just described.

Long before electrical recordings from rods were made, measures of the limitations of human vision when viewing dim test spots before dim backgrounds suggested that these limitations could be accounted for if one assumed that a false or "dark" light was falling on the retina. This equivalent light was termed the **eigengrau** (German: *eigen* = one's own + *grau* = to grow gray, dawn—thus one's own dim light). These psychophysical studies showed that the intensity of the eigengrau was equivalent to 1000 photons caught per second for each square millimeter of retina. At a retinal eccentricity of 15°, where the density of rods is about 160,000/mm², this corresponds to one photon per rod every 160 seconds. Thus, the eigengrau found in these experiments is most likely due to spontaneous photon-like events produced by rods in total darkness.

The cause of these spontaneous events in the rods is uncertain, but they are known to be dependent on temperature, which suggests that they are due to the isomerization of visual pigment chromophores as a result of molecular agitation. Regardless of their actual cause, the rate of these observed events sets an upper bound on the rate at which a visual pigment molecule in the rod outer segment can *incorrectly* report the effective absorption of a photon. Each rod outer segment contains about 1.4×10^8 visual pigment molecules, and presumably any one of them could produce a spontaneous event. Let N = number of visual pigment molecules = 1.4×10^8; R_{rod} = the rate at which rods produce spontaneous events = $1/160$ s = $6 \times 10^{-3}\,s^{-1}$; and R_{vp} = the rate at which visual pigment molecules produce spontaneous events. Then the rate at which a rod produces spontaneous events is the rate at which each of its visual pigment molecules is producing these events times the number of visual pigment molecules:

$$R_{vp} \times N = R_{rod}$$

Solving for R_{vp}:

$$R_{vp} = \frac{R_{rod}}{N} = \frac{6 \times 10^{-3}\,s^{-1}}{1.4 \times 10^8} = 4.3 \times 10^{-11}\,s^{-1}$$

This is a very slow rate, best appreciated by taking its reciprocal, which gives the average time it takes a visual pigment molecule to produce a spontaneous event:

$$\frac{1}{R_{vp}} = \frac{1}{4.3 \times 10^{-11}\,s^{-1}} = 2.3 \times 10^{10}\,s = 710 \text{ years}$$

Whether or not the cause of the eigengrau actually lies within the visual pigment molecules, their stability is impressive.

The diagram on page 139, which showed the spatial distribution of photons from a star and the night sky, failed to include the effect of the eigengrau. The diagram at right includes this effect. The photons and photon-like events are colored so that the contributions of each can be distinguished. The coloring, is of course, artificial; the rods make no such distinction, nor can they.

When viewing the night sky, we cannot detect stars whose magnitude is greater than 6 at high elevations or greater than 5 at Earth's surface. In 1901, Heber Curtis, an astronomer at the Lick observatory, attempted to determine the dimmest stars that could be seen in the *absence* of the diffuse light of the night sky. He viewed the sky through a small hole in a blackened screen in order to exclude this extraneous light and was thereby able to

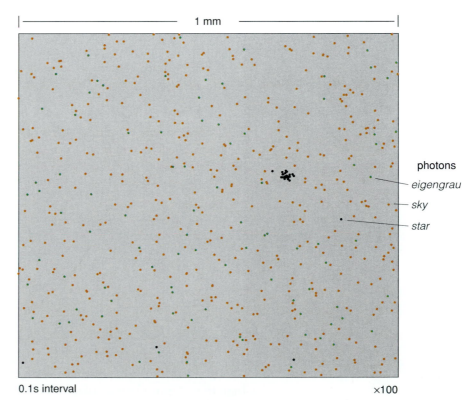

1 mm

photons
eigengrau
sky
star

0.1s interval   ×100

photon catch from image of a star and the light of the night sky

detect stars with magnitudes as great as 8.5. Thus the principal limit to the detection of dim stars is the diffuse light of the night sky, which, as noted earlier, is about five times brighter than the eigengrau.

For a star of magnitude 8.5, the average number of photons caught in 0.1 s is 3.3. Here is a snapshot of what such a star might look like in the **presence** of the diffuse light of the night sky and the eigengrau (below left). Photons from the star contribute to the image, but there are so few of them that it is not possible to locate the star. It is not clear which, if any, of the clusters of 2, 3, or 4 photons in this 0.1 s snapshot corresponds to a star. Even a one-second snapshot of the image is ambiguous (below right):

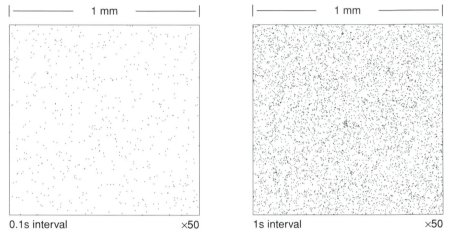

photons from night sky, eigengrau, and 8.5 magnitude star

But in the absence of the diffuse light of the night sky, the 8.5 magnitude star, at the middle of the diagram, is almost detectable in a 0.1 s snapshot (below left) and becomes obvious if the duration of the snapshot is extended to 1 second (below right):

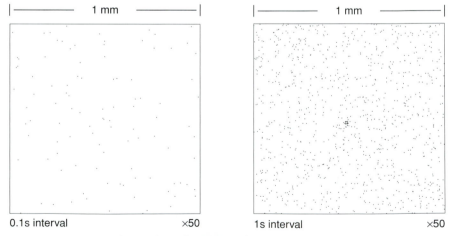

photons from eigengrau and 8.5 magnitude star

Although much of our vision appears to involve a shutter time of about 0.1 s, we can see dimmer things when they are presented for a period longer than this; it is as if we mentally average over time in a search for recurrence of pattern. This is apparently what we do when we detect the border between the trees and the overcast sky, where the eigengrau is significantly more intense than the overcast sky.

Camping

The hours pass, and the sky to the east begins to lighten, obliterating first the 6th magnitude stars, then the 5th magnitude stars, and so on, until they are gone. In the early dawn, you putter around camp, with enough light to see by. The intensity of the reflected light from different objects has grown to about one photon per rod every 5 seconds. Compared with when you could just make out the border between the overcast sky and the trees, the intensity of the light has increased by a factor of 1000. You begin to notice the colors of objects, and thereby become aware of the signals from the remaining 5% of your photoreceptors, the cones. By morning, the Sun has risen, and the rods are now catching about 100 photons per second, an increase in light intensity by a factor of 500 since early dawn.

Rods saturate

By this time, your rods have begun to **saturate,** meaning that the response of a rod to each additional increase in light intensity becomes smaller and smaller. A little later, every rod is catching about 500 photons per second and is within 1% of full saturation. The light may increase further, thereby increasing the photon catch of a rod, but the response of a rod will not significantly increase further.

In natural viewing, we need to distinguish between the ambient or background light intensity, which rises with the sun, and the variations in the light reflected from the objects around us, which allow these objects to be distinguished. A rod has only a limited range of response to light intensity. Thus, as the ambient level of light intensity rises, it activates the rods to a certain degree, and thereby reduces their ability to respond to further increases in light intensity. This is illustrated in the diagram at right, in which an increase in the response to the background light intensity (shown in gray) progressively cuts into the range (colored area) over which a further increase in light intensity can alter the response of a rod. For example, when the ambient light is producing an average catch rate of about 100 photon/s, it has already used up about 60% of the response range of the rods, limiting their response to additional increases in light intensity to about 40% of their full response range in the dark. When the ambient light level rises to 400–500 photoisomerizations per rod per second, the rods essentially lose their ability to response to further increases in light intensity.

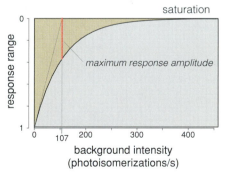

after Baylor, Nunn, and Schnapf, 1984

Rods have a limited dynamic range

The sensitivity of rod vision is a wonder of nature, but the range of light intensities over which any one rod will respond is limited. The term **dynamic range** refers to the ratio of the largest to the smallest signal to which some mechanism will respond; smallest means just detectable, largest means saturation.

We need to distinguish between the dynamic range for a continuous *rate* and for a brief *flash*. Both are relevant for natural viewing. Ignoring lightning, much of the visual world consists of either steady light or fluctuations about some mean level, favoring the consideration of a dynamic range based upon responses to different *rates* of photon capture. But the light falling on a photoreceptor depends not only upon the visual world, but upon our interaction with it, particularly eye movements that stabilize gaze upon one portion of the scene and then quickly jump to another. These sudden changes in gaze can produce large changes in photoreceptor illumination, and thus favor a dynamic range based upon responses to different *flash* intensities.

Consider first a dynamic range based upon rate. The effective responses to single photons begin to overlap when they are closer in time than about 0.1 s. Thus a reasonable lower bound for a dynamic range based upon rate is about 10/s. Placing the upper bound at saturation (500/s) gives an effective dynamic range of about 50. A dynamic range based upon flash intensity has, of course, a lower bound of one caught photon. The response of a rod to a flash saturates when the flash intensity exceeds about 100 absorbed photons when the flash duration is of the order of 0.1 s or less. Thus the dynamic range of rods, however considered, is about 50–100.

The site at which rod saturation occurs lies in the outer segment. It certainly does not happen because the visual pigment molecules are exhausted, for, as we have seen, there are millions of such molecules in each rod, yet a rate of 500 caught photon/s, or a flash of 100, is sufficient for saturation. Instead, saturation involves the mechanism that relays the signal from the outer segment to the synaptic terminal, which is described in the next chapter.

This diagram shows the dynamic range of rod vision plotted on a logarithmic scale:

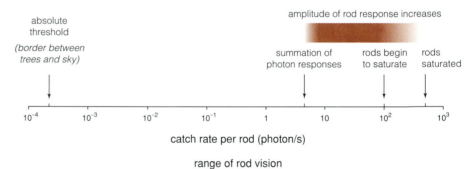

range of rod vision

The dynamic range of rod vision is slightly greater than six log units, or an intensity ratio of about two million. Over most of this range, rods respond on a photon-by-photon basis; this part of the range encompasses all of night vision and most of dawn and twilight vision. The range of rod vision over which rods are summing the responses of photons is about 2 log units (colored bar) and overlaps the dynamic range of cone vision for most natural viewing.

Rod bipolar cells receive a compressed rod input

An interesting problem occurs when we consider how rod signals converge on rod bipolar cells (see the diagram at left). To be specific, let us assume that a rod bipolar cell is receiving from 15 rods; recall from the last chapter (page 128) that this amount of convergence is typical of rod bipolar cells near the fovea. When you could just see the border between the trees and the sky, each rod was receiving a photon once every 85 minutes, so each of these rod bipolar cells was receiving a rod response to one of these photons about once every 6 minutes. Clearly, a rod bipolar cell must be able to respond reliably to a single rod activated by a single photon. But rod vision

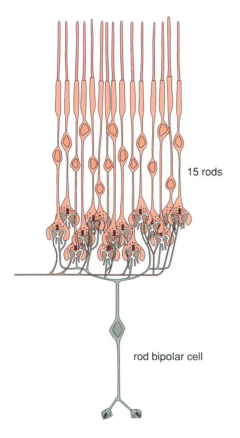

15 rods

rod bipolar cell

can follow changes in light intensity right up to rod saturation, which begins when each rod is catching 100 photons per second, and the rod bipolar cell is thus receiving the summed responses to 1500 such events per second. Yet the response of rod bipolar cells, like that of rods, is also limited to a dynamic range of about 100.

The issue at stake here is not particular to rod bipolar cells, but applies wherever there is neural convergence. The rod bipolar cell must be able to reliably convey the response of any of the rods to a photon. But it must also be able to change its output when all of the rods it contacts increase their photon catch from, say, 100 to 200 photons per second. It is here that the axonal arbor of the HI horizontal cell plays a critical role. Each axonal arbor contacts a pool of a few hundred rods, and appears to interact with them in the same general way that the dendrites of the horizontal cells interact with cones. If only a few rods are receiving photons, the rod signals pass to the rod bipolar cells unaltered. But as the photon catch rises, the axonal arbor becomes activated, and acts so as to attenuate the effect of each rod on the rod bipolar cell. Thus one can draw a general parallel between the action of the axonal arbor of the HI cell on the rod pathway and the action of its dendrites on the cone pathway. Nevertheless, convergence appears to be a primary factor for the rod pathway, whereas regulation along the cone pathway involves higher light levels, different types of photoreceptors, and different types of bipolar cells. Thus the specific mechanisms may well be different.

×300

axonal arbor of HI horizontal cell

Camping

In the early dawn, you were puttering around camp with just enough light to see by. When the light intensity rose to the point that your cones were catching about 10 or more photons per second, you began to notice the colors of objects.

By mid-morning, your rods were saturated, and you were seeing only with your cones.

By noon, the sun is beating down. You climb higher, and reach a field of snow more brilliant than the sky behind it. There is a sharpness to the visual world about you. As you look at a patch of snow, each of your foveal cones is catching about 300,000 photons per second.

Cones are adapted for daylight vision

Other than reflections from the sun, snow in sunlight at high elevations is about the brightest thing we see when viewing the natural world, and forms a practical upper limit for natural viewing, for reasons that will become clear in the following discussion. Nevertheless, under steady light conditions, cones can continue to respond to a photon catch rate as high as 1,000,000 per second. The diagram on the next page shows the lower and the upper limits of cone photon catch on a logarithmic scale. As discussed in the next chapter, the duration of a cone's response to one photon is about 50 ms, or one-twentieth of a second. Assuming that cone responses are summed when their photon catch exceeds 20 per second, the dynamic range of the response of individual cones to steady light is about 50,000. This is considerably greater than the dynamic range of rods to steady light, which, as noted above, is only about 50. This difference between rods and cones has to do with features of the upper end of the cone dynamic range, which will be discussed after we consider the lower end.

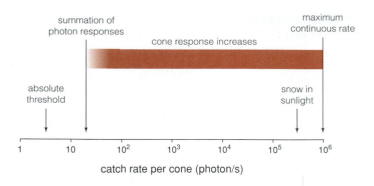

Cones can signal the capture of single photons, but are noisier than rods

As discussed in the next chapter, the lower threshold for cone vision occurs when each cone is catching about 3 photons per second, or, on average, one photon every 300 ms. Since the duration of the response to one photon is only about 50 ms, the response to one photon is usually over before the next photon is caught by the cone. This means that individual cones are able to respond to photons on a one-by-one basis, just like individual rods. But if we shift our focus from individual photoreceptors to their populations, a different picture emerges, since the threshold for rod vision can be as much as 15,000 times lower than that for cone vision (one photon per 5000 s vs. 3 photon/s).

What links these seemingly disparate perspectives is the concept of *reliability*. In rods, each caught photon produces a relatively large electrical response and, to judge from the behavior of the rod bipolar cells, a decisive reduction in the rate of transmitter release. In this sense, rods act like the idealized photoreceptors possessed by hypothetical animal A, described at the beginning of this chapter. Consequently, the light intensity limit for rod vision is set mainly by the eigengrau.

By comparison, cones respond to a single photon with an electrical response that has an amplitude only about 5% of that of rods. This and others factors appear to limit the sensitivity of cones. It is not that individual cones fail to respond to single photons, only that this relatively weak response is "buried in the noise" produced by other activities. Only by combining a number of individual responses can a reliable signal be produced. In this sense, cone vision is more like that of hypothetical animal B. Other than their weaker electrical responses, the factors that make cones more "noisy" than rods—giving them a larger eigengrau—are not known. However, there is some evidence to suggest that cone visual pigment molecules are less stable than those of rods.

To summarize, seemingly small differences in the properties of single photoreceptors can become large differences in the properties of their populations and pathways—as animals A and B will attest.

Cones do not saturate to steady light levels

In response to *flashes* of light of increasing intensity, cones saturate just as rods do; under these conditions, both rods and cones have a dynamic range of about 100, as described in HOW PHOTORECEPTORS WORK. But if the *level* of light intensity gradually rises, changes take place in the cones that allow them to operate at any light intensity, no matter how bright.

Two quite different mechanisms come into play to accomplish this. The first mechanism reduces the effect of each caught photon according to the

noise
The term *noise* refers to an abstract measure intended to reflect the combined effects of a number of different irregular or random physical processes. An example already considered is the notion of an eigengrau, by which spontaneous thermal isomerizations are converted into a measure of light. This "effective" light can then be added to the diffuse light of the night sky so as to produce a measure of the "noise" that limits the detection of dim stars.

Biochemical cascade *371*

degree to which the cone hyperpolarizes in response to illumination. This mechanism lies within the outer segment and involves a rather complicated biochemical pathway, which is summarized in BIOCHEMICAL CASCADE. By means of this mechanism, cones are able to operate at levels of light intensity high enough to allow the second mechanism to exert its effect.

The second mechanism acts at steady light levels to limit the photoisomerization rate to a maximum of about 1,000,000 per second by reducing the number of functional visual pigment molecules. This mechanism is something of a side consequence of the need to *regenerate* visual pigment molecules after they have been photoisomerized. As we have seen, visual pigment molecules contain a light-catching portion, termed a chromophore, which normally has a bent form. An absorbed photon converts the chromophore to a straightened form, which causes the visual pigment molecule to become activated. In order for the visual pigment molecule to be restored to its original form, the straightened chromophore must be removed and replaced with a bent one. This can occur immediately, but on average it takes about two minutes. During this period, the remaining portion of the visual pigment molecule either fails to respond to absorbed photons (straightened chromophore) or is unable to absorb them at all (chromophore removed). As the level of light intensity rises, more of the visual pigment molecules will be in these inactive states, and thus fewer of the remaining molecules will be able to catch photons and respond to them. This normal process of regeneration thus limits the maximum rate at which outer segments can catch photons under steady light conditions. This maximum rate is about 1,000,000 photon/s. If the light intensity increases further, then the number of available visual pigment molecules will decrease until the photoisomerization rate falls to this maximum value. In principle, the light level can increase until the cones cook.

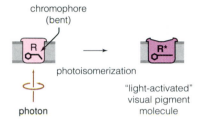

chromophore
(bent)

photoisomerization

photon

"light-activated" visual pigment molecule

Why rods and cones?

"Why rods and cones? Why should there not be a single kind of receptor with two different nerve organizations? Why, best of all, should there not be a single type of receptor and a single convertible nerve organization?" I cannot answer these questions. But not to know the answer is not to understand something fundamental in the evolution and performance of the retina.

W. A. H. Rushton (1962)

William Rushton recognized that the difference between rods and cones posed a deeper question than why the outer segments of rods are rod-shaped while those of extrafoveal cones are slightly cone-shaped. As we have seen, the great range of light levels over which the vertebrate retina can operate is due to the presence of both photoreceptors able to respond reliably to single-photon events and photoreceptors that never saturate to ambient light levels. Any single photoreceptor that possessed both these properties would thus be able to cover the entire range. But, as I will discuss in HOW PHOTORECEPTORS WORK, factors that improve performance with regard to one of these properties tend to degrade performance with regard to the other. No cones of any vertebrate species are known to saturate to a steady background light; all individual rods thus far tested do so.

It thus appears that for most, if not all, vertebrate species, nature has not been able to devise a photoreceptor both able to reliably detect single-photon events and able to continue to respond to the intense rain of photons encountered during the day. In order to respond to the range of light intensities encountered through night and day, at least two classes of photoreceptors are therefore required—one to provide the extension to low light levels, the other to provide the extension to high light levels—and these appear to require quantitatively different biochemical machinery and different morphology. Other factors that distinguish rods from cones, such as the shape and size of the synaptic terminal, the presence of voltage-gated channels, and infoldings of the outer segment membrane, appear to be secondary reflections of the range of ambient light levels over which rods and cones are able to operate.

Plotting light intensity

*This section presents a graphical means of relating the enormous range of
light intensities encountered in the natural world to the dynamic ranges
and photon catch rates of rods and cones. It is not necessary to understand,
but you may find it helpful.*

Physics considers all photons, not just those in the visible range. Physical
measurements of the number or rate of incident photons over different frequency intervals belong to a system of measurement termed **radiometry.** A
derived system of measurement, termed **photometry,** deals with light in the
visible range.

Radiometry *499*

The ideas behind photometry were introduced at the beginning of THE
RAIN OF PHOTONS ONTO CONES, when we saw that the photoreceptors caught
only a small fraction of the rain of photons from Polaris. To review, the light
entering the eye is composed of photons of differing frequencies. A form of
bookkeeping can be done on the photons in each small interval of the frequency spectrum, recording how many were lost or scattered by various
factors, until we are left with the number of photons that were caught by
the photoreceptors. In effect, a spectral distribution *curve* is converted to a
single *value*. This is the basic idea behind photometry: combine the radiometric spectral distribution of the light coming to the eye, the spectral sensitivity of the photoreceptors, and other factors so as to arrive at a value that
reflects photon catch.

There are two forms of photometry, **scotopic** (New Latin back to Greek
skotos = darkness) and **photopic** (Greek *phot-* = light). As its name suggests,
scotopic photometry deals with rod vision, and weights the spectral distribution of the light arriving at the rod outer segments according to the spectral sensitivity of the visual pigment molecules they contain. Photopic
photometry is based upon a spectral sensitivity function that combines the
sensitivities of the M and L cones; the reasons for doing so are discussed in
PHOTOMETRY.

Photometry *453*

In THE RAIN OF PHOTONS ONTO CONES, photons came to the eye from a star,
and thus from a **point source.** But in the natural world, we are generally
interested in light that comes from **extended sources,** such as a portion of a
leaf or a uniform patch of snow or sky. The relevant photometric measure of
the amount of visible light coming to the eye from an object or other
extended source is termed **luminance.** The designated unit of luminance is
termed a **nit;** perhaps because this sounds a bit silly, the equivalent unit of

candelas per square meter (cd/m^2) is more commonly used. The terms *scotopic* and *photopic* are used as modifiers of photometric measure in order to distinguish which form of photometry is involved (e.g., scotopic luminance).

The range of light intensities in the environment is enormous

The dimmest things that we can see were represented in the last chapter by the border between the trees and the overcast night sky. The brightest object in the natural world is the Sun. The following diagram shows both of these extremes, plotted on a logarithmic scale of light intensity:

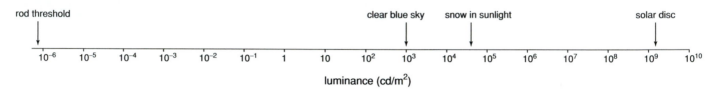

The intensity ratio between the rod threshold and the sun is about 2×10^{15}. This ratio is equivalent to the distance between Earth and the Sun divided by the length of a rod. It is dangerous to stare directly at the solar disc, although everyone has looked at it briefly. But even if we restrict our consideration to things on Earth, the intensity ratio between snow in sunlight and the rod threshold is still about 4×10^{10} (forty billion). Different factors come into play over this dynamic range of light intensity, and the purpose of this section is to bring them together within a common framework.

When we see an object, some of the light reflected from it enters each eye to form an image on the retina. The intensity of this image, termed the **retinal illuminance,** is proportional to the luminance of the object. But this is not the only factor at stake, since the amount of light from the object that can enter the eye is also proportional to the area of the pupil. In order for the retinal illuminance to be proportional to both of these factors, it must be proportional to their product:

$$\text{retinal illuminance} \sim \text{object luminance} \times \text{pupil area}$$

where "~" means "is proportional to." In visual science, a special unit of measure termed a **troland** (td) is used to quantify retinal illuminance. It is defined as the luminance of the object, expressed in candelas per square meter (cd/m^2), multiplied by the pupil area, expressed in square *millimeters* (mm^2):

$$\text{retinal illuminance (td)} = \text{object luminance (cd/m}^2) \times \text{pupil area (mm}^2)$$

The intensity of the image also depends upon other factors, such as the length of the eye, which varies slightly among individuals. But these factors are difficult to measure and vary little, so they are left out of this definition.

The diameter of the pupil varies from a maximum of 8 mm to a minimum of about 2 mm. The pupil diameter thus varies by a factor of 4, which corresponds to a factor of 16 for the pupil area. This factor of 16 is thus the maximum variation in retinal illumination that can be produced by a change in pupil size.

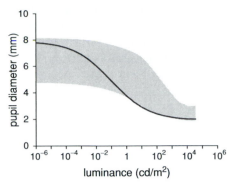

based upon Wyszecki and Stiles, 1982

A variety of factors influence pupil size, including age and emotional state. Nevertheless, the pupil tends to be large in the dark and small in bright light. The curve in the diagram at left shows one estimate of the average pupil diameter as a function of the average luminance. The light gray region shows the extent of individual variation among twelve subjects. Because of this variation, the curve indicates only a trend: the pupil is large in the dark, small in bright sunlight, and has a variable size in between. But for the practical purpose of converting object luminance to retinal illuminance, we will assume that this curve characterizes the relation between ambient luminance and pupil size. Furthermore, we will assume that the luminance of an object viewed in this environment is the same as the ambient luminance—some objects will be brighter and some will be darker.

The relation between luminance and pupil size over the range from rod threshold to snow in sunlight is reproduced in this diagram:

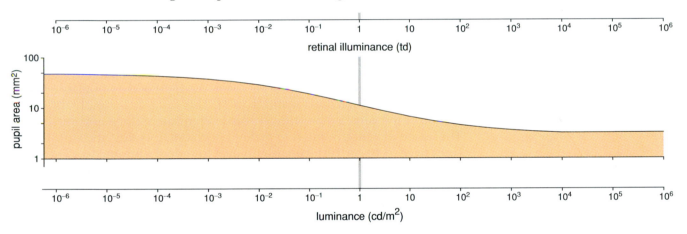

The vertical scale has been converted to pupil area, and is plotted on a logarithmic axis with the same unit size as for the luminance axis. The reason for plotting pupil area in this way will become clear in a moment.

Above the plot of pupil size is an axis showing retinal illuminance, also plotted on a logarithmic scale. The two horizontal scales are in alignment, so that a retinal illuminance value of 1 troland lies directly above a luminance value of 1 candela/m², as indicated by the vertical gray line. Since retinal illuminance is defined as the product of object luminance and pupil area, these two values would correspond if the pupil area were equal to 1 mm². The pupil is rarely, if ever, this small. But consider a pupil area of 10 mm². Then a luminance value of 1 cd/m² would produce a retinal illuminance value of 10 td. Likewise, a luminance of 1000 cd/m² would produce a retinal illuminance of 10,000 td, and so on. In general, the value on the logarithmic scale of retinal illuminance is shifted to the right relative to the logarithmic scale of luminance by the logarithm of the pupil area. This is why the pupil size was expressed as an area and plotted on a logarithmic scale. A slide rule generates the product of two values in just this way.

A simple geometric construction ties together object luminance, pupil size, and retinal illuminance, as shown here:

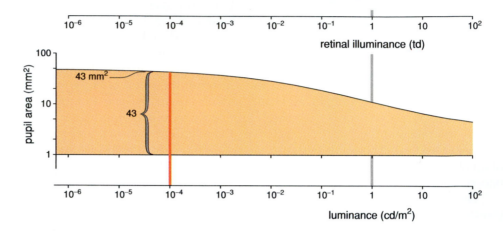

Starting from some chosen luminance value, we draw a vertical line through the plot of pupil area; in this case, the chosen luminance value is 10^{-4} cd/m^2, which gives a pupil area of 43 mm^2. By definition, the retinal illuminance is equal to the product of these two values, or 4.3×10^{-3} td. This point on the retinal luminance scale lies to the right of the luminance value by a distance equal to the logarithm of 43. This distance is simply the intersection of the vertical line with the shaded portion of the pupil area curve. This same distance, rotated to make it horizontal, is thus the shift to the right needed to convert from luminance to retinal illuminance. Since the vertical and horizontal distances are equal, they combine to form a square, as shown in this diagram:

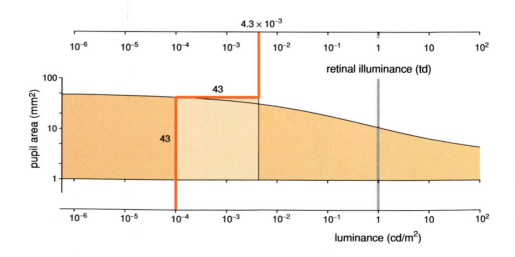

By construction, the right side of this square marks the product of the luminance and the pupil area; its upward extension thus marks the corresponding point on the axis for retinal illuminance.

Rod photon catch

Retinal illuminance is the starting point for calculating the photon catch of the photoreceptors. A number of factors, which were introduced in THE RAIN OF PHOTONS ONTO CONES and are discussed quantitatively in PHOTON CATCH RATE, are involved in calculating scotopic photon catch. For rods at a retinal eccentricity of 10–15°, these calculations yield a value for each rod of 4.6 photons caught per second for each troland of retinal illuminance. This value sets the horizontal position of the logarithmic scale of rod photon catch, as shown in this diagram:

Photon catch rate *471*

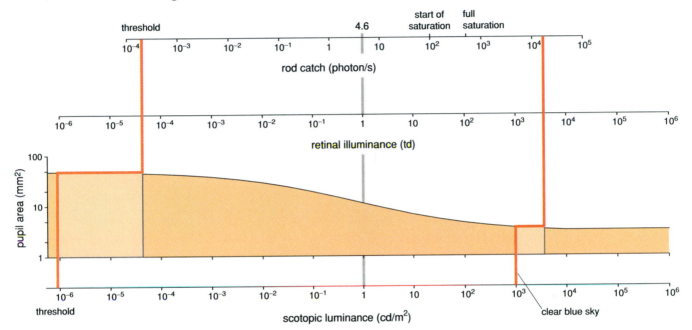

At the left, the diagram shows the luminance at which the border between the treetops and the overcast night sky is just visible. The resulting scotopic photon catch rate (2×10^{-4} photons/s) corresponds to one photon per rod every 85 minutes. At the right, a clear blue sky (luminance = 1000 cd/m^2) is the starting point, and gives a catch rate of about 20,000 photons/s, an intensity at which a rod is saturated.

Cone photon catch

As noted earlier, photopic photometry is based upon a weighting function that combines the spectral sensitivities of the M and L cones. The spectral sensitivities of these two cone types are similar. Thus, to a first approximation at least, we can consider that the calculated value for photon catch applies to either cone type. The scale shown for photon catch is based upon foveal cones. Cones in the periphery have wider inner segments, and thus catch more photons per troland than do foveal cones.

Two additional factors need to be taken into account. The first deals with the reduction of visual pigment molecules at high light levels, which is discussed in HOW PHOTORECEPTORS WORK. The second has to do with the directional sensitivity of the cones (page 83); it is called the **Stiles–Crawford effect,** after the investigators who first described it. Both factors act to reduce the photon catch of cones, and each is shown below its reference axis in the diagram on the following page.

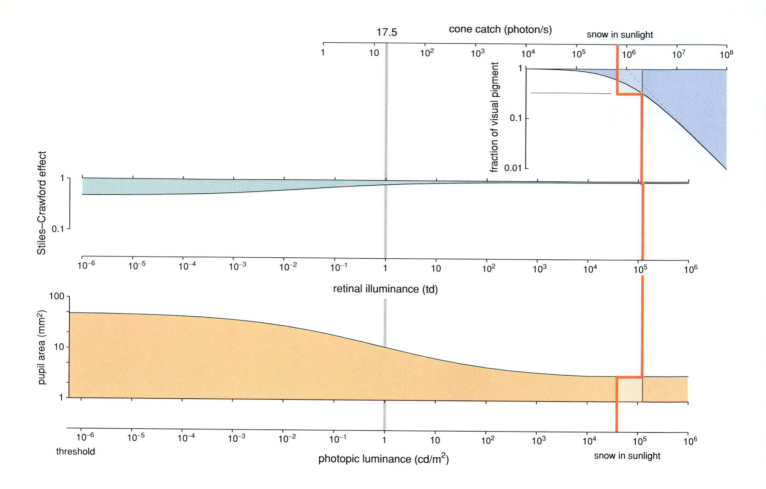

Consider first the effect of the decrease in intact visual pigment molecules produced by intense steady background light (shown shaded blue). The fraction of molecules that are intact depends upon the retinal illuminance. For example, snow in sunlight produces a retinal illuminance of about 1.2×10^5 photopic trolands, as shown. A line extended vertically from this point shows that the fraction of intact visual pigment molecules has dropped by about half a log unit, which corresponds to about one-third of the total number. Thus the photon catch rate has been reduced by half a log unit, and the resulting photon catch is obtained by constructing a square in the same general manner as for pupil size. You can experiment with such geometric constructions using different values for the steady retinal illuminance. No matter what value you choose, the resulting cone photon catch never exceeds 10^6 photon/s, because this value corresponds to the maximum rate at which the visual pigment molecules can regenerate, as discussed earlier. (All of this applies only to steady viewing; if you look briefly at the Sun, the photon catch rate can greatly exceed this value.)

The curve for the Stiles–Crawford effect is based upon pupil size. The photon catch of cones is not proportional to pupil area, because photons passing near the edge of a large pupil have a lower probability of entering a cone outer segment than do pupils passing through the center of the pupil, as discussed earlier (page 83). It is possible to calculate the fractional loss in the catch rate due to this effect, and the resulting curve is shown in the diagram on the next page in green. Again, the vertical axis is plotted on a log scale, and the same geometric construction can be applied to calculate the reduction in photon catch due to this effect.

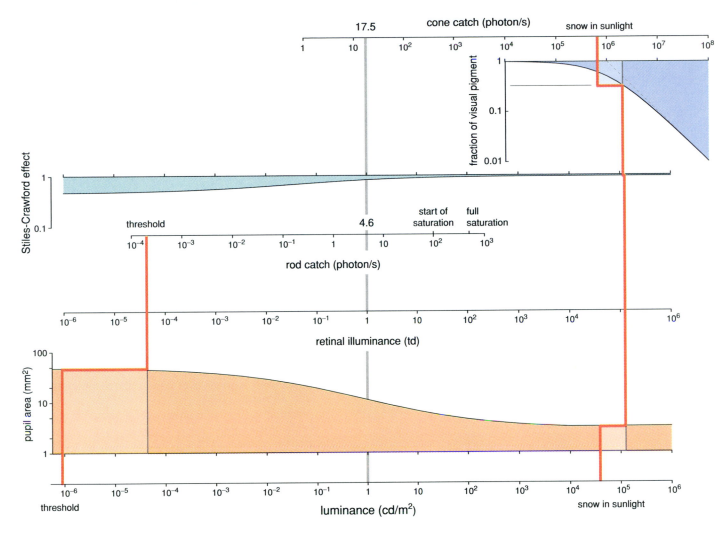

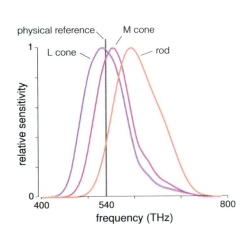

As noted earlier, the threshold for cone vision corresponds to a catch rate per cone of about 3 photons per second. Under daylight conditions, the pupil tends to be small, and the fractional loss due to the Stiles–Crawford effect is small enough to be ignored. Likewise, under the nighttime conditions that produce a large pupil, much of what is seen is so dim that it is below the cone threshold, so here too this effect can be ignored. But when you gazed directly at Polaris with your foveal cones, the pupil was large, due to the dim surroundings. Under these conditions, as well as a few others, the Stiles–Crawford effect can be significant.

With a bit of caution, the relation between light intensities and the photon catches of both rods and cones can be combined into a single diagram as shown above. There is an ambiguity to this diagram in that it does not indicate whether the luminance values are scotopic or photopic. However, a geometric construction that leads from the luminance axis to the axis for rod photon catch obviously implies scotopic luminance and scotopic trolands. One troland yields a photon catch rate of 4.6 for rods and 17.5 for cones. This difference has nothing to do with the relative photon catches of rods and cones, but rather is a consequence of the physical standard of light upon which both forms of photometry are based. This standard consists of photons with a frequency of 540 THz, which is much closer to the peak sensitivities of the M and L cones than to that of the rods (right). Based on the frequency for which each is most sensitive, peripheral rods and foveal cones appear to have about the same PHOTON CATCH RATE.

Photon catch rate *471*

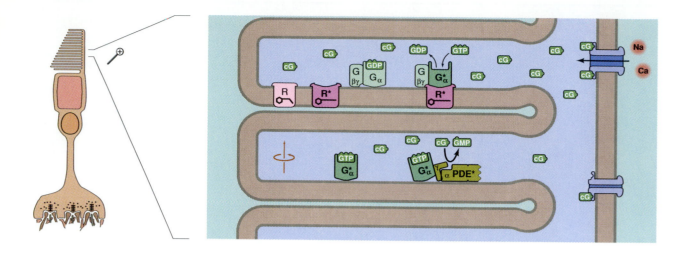

8

How photoreceptors work

The last three chapters described rods and cones from the outside, the light presented to them, and the effect of the resulting decrease in transmitter release on the other cells of the retina. Perhaps the most significant feature of photoreceptors to emerge from this description is the overwhelming importance of the ability of rods to reliably detect the capture of a single photon. This chapter begins with a detailed description of how rods accomplish this extraordinary feat. As it turns out, the manner in which rods respond to the capture of many photons involves little more than the sum of the rod responses to single photons. Essentially the same process occurs in cones, except that their response to single photons is smaller. What most distinguishes cones from rods is the ability of cones to operate under daylight conditions when hundreds of thousands of photons are captured every second, and this chapter also describes the factors that allow them to do so.

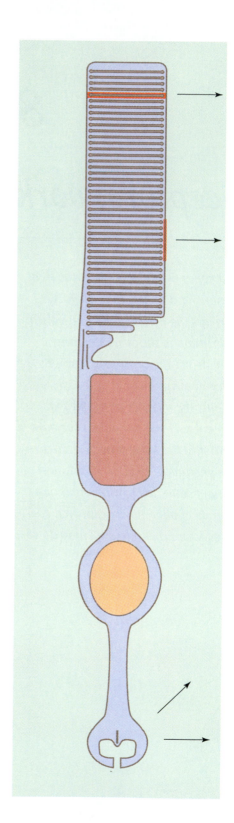

Both rods and cones operate in the same general manner, as summarized in the following diagram, based on a rod:

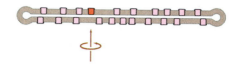

Photoactivation:

A photon is absorbed by a visual pigment molecule lying in one of the membranous discs contained in the outer segment.

↓

Biochemical cascade:

In the dark there is a steady movement of positively charged ions (cations) into the outer segment, via ionic channels. The visual pigment molecule, activated by the photon, initiates a cascade of events that ultimately closes these channels.

↓

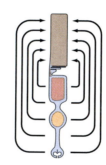

Electrotonic spread:

Normally, the movement of cations into the outer segment is balanced by the outward movement of cations, mainly through the inner segment. The decrease in inward current creates a net outward current, which makes the interior of the cell even more negative. This hyperpolarization of the cell membrane spreads throughout the cell. This is how the information about light absorption spreads to the synaptic terminal.

↓

channel

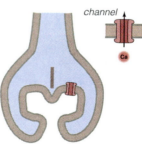

Synaptic deactivation:

At the synaptic terminal there are calcium channels that open when the voltage across the cell membrane depolarizes and close when it hyperpolarizes. Thus the hyperpolarization of the cell membrane leads to a decrease in the rate of entry of calcium ions. Free calcium ions are continuously being removed from the cell interior, so a decrease in the rate of entry of calcium leads to a decrease in the internal concentration of free calcium ion.

↓

glutamate molecule

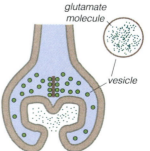

vesicle

Decrease in glutamate release:

The synaptic terminal contains vesicles that in turn contain glutamate molecules. In the presence of calcium ions, they are continuously released into the synaptic cleft. Thus a decrease in the internal concentration of calcium ions leads to a decrease in the rate of release of glutamate molecules.

This chapter takes a deeper look at each of the steps in this process, focusing on what happens when a single photon is absorbed by a rod. When only the rod pathway is active, each rod is absorbing photons at a rate of less than one per second, and each rod is thus responding to photons on a one-by-one basis. An understanding of the response to a single photon is thus a description of how rods work over most of their operating range. Responses of rods and cones to brighter conditions are then considered and compared. As it happens, the response of a rod or a cone to a single photon can be used to predict how it will respond to higher light levels.

A great deal is known about how photoreceptors work—too much to discuss fully in this chapter, which has two limited aims. The first is to introduce a common framework for discussing the various aspects of photoreceptor function in greater detail. The second is to provide an overview of photoreceptor function that can serve as a basis for understanding the subsequent events in vision.

catch, capture
As discussed in THE RAIN OF PHOTONS ONTO CONES (page 86), the term *catch* or *capture* is used here to refer to the absorption of a photon by a visual pigment molecule and the photoisomerization of its chromophore, resulting in the activation of the molecule.

How a rod responds to a single photon

When you were just able to see the border between the trees and the overcast night sky, each of your rods was catching a photon about once every 85 minutes. Assuming that the scene near the border represents 5% of your visual field, the corresponding region of the retinal image includes about 5 million rods. We will now focus in on just one of these rods as it is just about to capture a photon, and sketch out the sequence of events that takes place. Fortunately, there is a lot we can ignore. Of the 1000 or so discs in the rod outer segment, we will consider only *the disc* that is about to capture a photon, and ignore the rest. Of the two sides of the disc, we will consider only *the membrane* that will capture the photon, and ignore the other side. Of the 80,000 or so visual pigment molecules contained in that membrane, we will consider only *the molecule* whose chromophore is about to photoisomerize in response to the absorbed photon, and ignore all the others.

Photoactivation

The chromophore of visual pigment molecules in both rods and cones is based upon a molecule termed **11-*cis* retinal,** which consists of a head portion coupled to a hinged tail. The 11-*cis* prefix refers to the particular **geometric isomer** of the retinal group. A visual pigment molecule that uses 11-*cis* retinal as its chromophore is termed a **rhodopsin.** All mammalian visual pigments are rhodopsins; thus there is rod rhodopsin, S-cone rhodopsin, and so on. The protein portion of a rhodopsin molecule is termed **opsin.** The chromophore lies embedded within the opsin and is attached to it. The diagram on the next page shows a rhodopsin molecule

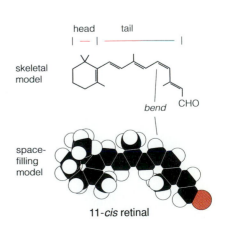

chromophore
The term chromophore (Greek *chromo-* = color or pigment + *-phore* = producer) is applied to the light-catching portion of any molecule.

geometric isomers
Geometric isomers are molecules that differ from one another only because of a structural asymmetry about a double bond (Greek *isomeres* = *iso-* = same + *meros* = part).

rhodopsin
Greek *rhodo-* = rose or rose-red, as in rhododendron, + *opsin* = sight. Named for the color of the rod visual pigment, which dominates most retinas. In this book, all visual pigments that use 11-*cis* retinal as their chromophore are referred to as rhodopsins.

lying within the disc membrane, which is shown in green, whereas the chromophore is shown in purple. Above the rhodopsin molecule lies another molecule, termed a G protein, which is discussed below.

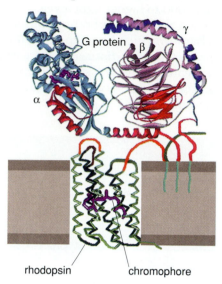

rhodopsin   chromophore

It only takes about 3 femtoseconds (fs) for a photon to be absorbed and impart its energy to a visual pigment molecule. The fundamental action of an absorbed photon is to straighten the tail of the chromophore, converting it to a rigid form so as to yield an isomer termed **all-*trans* retinal**:

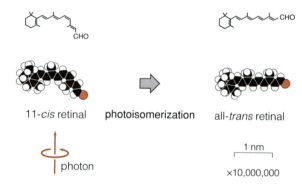

11-*cis* retinal   photoisomerization   all-*trans* retinal

photon   1 nm
                                           ×10,000,000

This **photoisomerization** of the chromophore constitutes the first step in photoactivation, and takes about 200 fs, a time significantly longer than that for absorption.

Most of the photon's energy is required for the photoisomerization to occur. This requirement is important, and it is worth explaining the reason for it. A chromophore is always taking up and throwing off small amounts of energy as a result of molecular collisions. If only a small amount of energy were required to convert the chromophore to the all-*trans* form, then a fortuitously well placed and vigorous molecular collision could flip the 11-*cis* isomer to the all-*trans* form, and thereby activate the rhodopsin molecule. Rods and cones would then be unreliable because they would not distinguish light from heat. The energy of a photon is proportional to its frequency (page 72), and it takes the energy of a photon in the visible range of the spectrum or above to isomerize the chromophore. Most of the energy of the photon is taken up by the chromophore and then imparted to the entire rhodopsin molecule. This allows the rhodopsin molecule to be boosted to an activated form, and later return to its normal inactive form, without needing any additional energy.

Within the rhodopsin molecule, the straight, rigid tail of the chromophore thrusts against the enveloping walls of the opsin that surround it, thereby changing the shape of the molecule and making it slightly larger. This alteration takes about 0.25 to 0.5 ms, or about a billion times longer than the photoisomerization step, and completes the photoactivation of the rhodopsin molecule. The fine details of how the rhodopsin molecule changes shape are not fully understood, but this change causes the molecule to become **activated** in a manner discussed in the following section. An inactive rhodopsin molecule is represented by the letter **R,** and a photoactivated rhodopsin molecule by **R*** ("R star"). Symbolically, photoactivation can thus be summarized as:

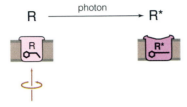

Biochemical cascade

This section introduces most of the various molecules that are involved in the biochemical cascade of photoreceptor activation, and briefly describes the landscape of their little world. Each large molecule can be likened to a machine, built by evolution to perform a specific function in a reliable and efficient manner. These various molecular machines operate in concert in the factory of the outer segment. Our first concern is not how each machine is built of atomic nuts and bolts, but what each of them does. Like the rhodopsin molecule, each molecular species will be represented by a distinctive icon.

The biochemical cascade begins when a rhodopsin molecule in a disc membrane is activated, and ends when the ionic channels in the outer segment plasma membrane close. In the dark, these channels maintain an inward electrical current, which is carried by sodium and calcium ions. Because the concentrations of both Na and Ca cations are lower within the outer segment than outside it, and because the interior of the cell is electrically negative with respect to the outside, the net movement of both of these cations through an open channel is from the outside to the inside, as shown in the diagram on page 160. It is this current, discussed in greater detail below, that the biochemical cascade will ultimately act upon in response to light.

In order to see where we are going, it is useful to consider what regulates these channels. In the dark, an outer segment contains small molecules called **guanosine 3′,5′ cyclic monophosphate,** which is abbreviated as **cG.** cG is one of four related molecules involved in phototransduction, including **GMP, GDP,** and **GTP,** whose properties are summarized in *NUCLEO-TIDES.* As a result of random molecular collisions, each cG molecule moves rapidly about within the cytoplasm of the outer segment. This process is known as **Brownian motion** or **diffusion.** It would take only about a second for a cG molecule to traverse the length of a water-filled outer segment, but about half of the interior of a rod outer segment consists of the membranous discs, which act as partial barriers to the diffusion of ions and molecules within the cytoplasm. For the moment, we will ignore this complexity and show only the disc that contains the rhodopsin molecule that will become activated. The cG molecules will be presumed to be diffusing about

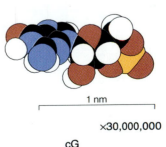

1 nm

×30,000,000

cG

Nucleotides

Nucleotides are small molecules that are found in every living cell. They are the building blocks of DNA, and serve in a variety of additional roles. Each consists of three parts: a nitrogen-containing ring compound termed a **base**, a sugar, and a chain of one to three phosphate groups:

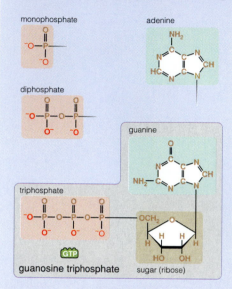

monophosphate

adenine

diphosphate

guanine

triphosphate

GTP

guanosine triphosphate   sugar (ribose)

nucleotides

Our direct concerns lie with nucleotides derived from the bases **guanine** and **adenine**. All of the nucleotides directly involved in phototransduction are derived from guanine, and are termed **guanosines**. The nucleotides based upon adenine are termed **adenosines**;

in the outer segment they are used as fuel for ionic pumps and other energy-requiring processes. Combining these two bases with the three phosphate groups yields the six nucleotides.

	mono-	di-	tri-	
adenine	AMP	ADP	ATP	phosphate
guanosine	GMP	GDP	GTP	

cG   cyclic guanosine monophosphate

The bumps on top of the icons correspond to the number of phosphate groups.

cG differs from GMP by the presence of an additional bond between the phosphate group and the sugar, thereby creating an additional ring. Consistent with the abbreviations for the other nucleotides, this molecule is also known as cyclic GMP, or cGMP. The abbreviation cG is used here because it yields the smallest icon.

cyclic guanosine monophosphate (cG)   breakage   guanosine monophosphate (GMP)

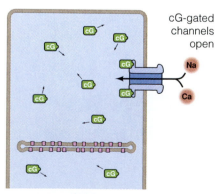

cG-gated channels open

Na

Ca

dark

as if the other discs did not exist, except that their effective rate of diffusion will be lowered by about half in order to compensate for the absence of the other discs (left).

The concentration of cG molecules in the outer segment plays a critical role in vision. In a nutshell, the activated rhodopsin molecule, **R***, initiates a sequence of events that causes the concentration of cG molecules to fall, and this fall is detected by the ionic channels on the plasma membrane, which close. In effect, the change in cG concentration is an *intracellular message*, sent by events on the disc surface and delivered to ionic channels on the plasma membrane. This is an example of a common form of intracellular communication in which some event that acts on a cell (the "first messenger") is detected and signaled within the cell by means of a change in the concentration of some small molecule, which is termed the **second messenger.**

As already noted, when open, the ionic channels on the plasma membrane allow Na and Ca cations to pass through them, maintaining an inward electrical current. But in order to remain open, each of these channels must have cG molecules bound to specialized sites on the channel; thus they are dubbed **cG-gated channels.** The cG molecules are not tightly bound to a channel site; instead, they attach and detach at a rapid rate as a result of random molecular collisions. The rate at which they attach to free sites on the channels is proportional to their concentration in the cytoplasm, as you might expect. The rate at which they are knocked off the sites by molecular collisions is more or less fixed. Thus the average number of cG molecules attached to these channels at any moment depends on the intra-cellular concentration of cG molecules; in essence, a *decrease* in cG concentration within the cytoplasm causes a decrease in the number attached, and this reduces the number of open channels.

Our reference point is the concentration of cG molecules in the dark, which is about 4 μM. At this concentration, only a small percentage of the cG-gated channels are open at any instant. This might seem surprising, considering the earlier statement that the effect of an absorbed photon is to close some of the channels that are open. But there are so *many* channels in the plasma membrane of each outer segment that roughly 10,000 are open in the dark at any given time. This arrangement proves to be efficient for a number of reasons, which are discussed in cG-GATED CHANNELS.

cG-gated channels *405*

Turning now to the disc membrane, it is about 2 μm in diameter and contains a number of protein molecules, most of which are rhodopsin molecules. All of these proteins are diffusing about within the oily layers of lipid molecules and bumping into one another, again as a result of random molecular collisions. A photon of light now converts one of the rhodopsin molecules on one of the disc surfaces to the activated form, **R*** (right). The **R*** molecule continues to diffuse within the disc membrane. But when it encounters other molecules, known as **G protein molecules,** that are diffusing about on the surface of the membrane, it activates them. These molecules are most often referred to as *G proteins,* but for consistency of terminology I'll refer to them as *G molecules.*

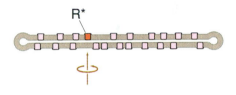

As described in the next section, the activated G molecules cause the disc surface to become a trap for cG molecules. The rapid movement of the cG molecules within the outer segment brings many of them into contact with the disc surface, where they are removed by conversion to a different molecular species (GMP). Although these events take place at the surface of a single disc, the rapid diffusion of cG molecules causes their concentration to fall over a region encompassing many discs. This decrease in the concentration of cG molecules causes the cG-gated channels in this region of the outer segment to close:

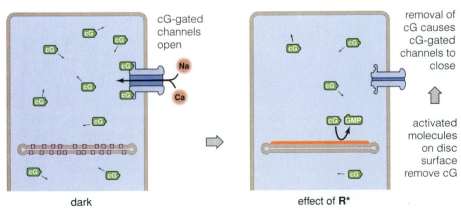

This closure of ionic channels in the plasma membrane reduces the current passing into the cell, and thereby causes the cell's transmembrane potential to hyperpolarize by about 1 mV for a period of about 200 ms. We will now consider each of these steps in greater detail.

R* activates many G molecules

Shortly after the rod outer segment catches a photon, there is one **R*** molecule on a disc membrane, there are some open cG-gated channels on the plasma membrane, and there is a relatively high concentration of cG molecules in the cytoplasm:

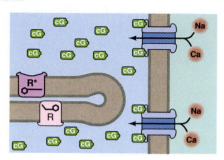

For simplicity, only the cG-gated channels that are open are shown.

Many cellular processes make use of G molecules. For example, the action of the metabotropic glutamate receptors of the on-bipolar cells, discussed earlier (page 110), is mediated by G molecules. G molecules are so named because they bind to either of two guanine-based nucleotides, GDP and GTP; and are always bound to one or the other. Each G molecule consists of three subunits: G_α, which binds the nucleotide, together with G_β and G_γ, which are shown combined in the icon at left. Each G molecule can freely diffuse across the surface of the disc membrane, just as rhodopsin molecules are able to diffuse within it. The icon shows the inactive form of the G molecule, with GDP bound to it. This is the usual state of the G molecule—diffusing about and bumping into other protein molecules. In the dark, these encounters are without effect.

The activation of a G molecule by **R*** is initiated when the two molecules encounter one another and orient themselves in a such a manner as to bring into apposition *epitopes* (Greek *epi* = on + *topos* = location or site) on each molecule—sites that are mutually attracting. The epitopes come together so as to temporarily bind the **R*** molecule to the G molecule. In less than 0.1 ms, a sequence of events occurs in which GTP replaces GDP on the G_α subunit, which then separates from the $G_{\beta\gamma}$ subunit and the **R*** to become an activated G protein subunit, $\mathbf{G^*_\alpha}$ ("G star alpha"):

G protein

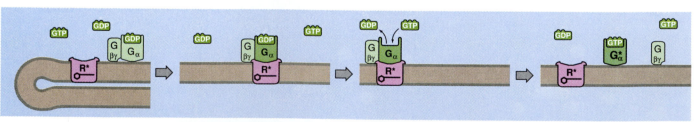

By means of diffusion, **R*** encounters an inactive G molecule.

The G_α part of the G molecule comes to lie over the exposed surface of the activated rhodopsin molecule.

As a result of interacting with **R***, the GDP molecule held by the G_α portion is replaced by a GTP molecule, which converts this subunit to an activated form.

Activation of the G_α subunit, now $\mathbf{G^*_\alpha}$, causes it to separate from both the rhodopsin molecule and the $G_{\beta\gamma}$ portion of the G molecule.

R* remains activated, and is thus free to continue to diffuse through the membrane, encountering and activating other G molecules that it meets.

Looking onto the surface of the disc membrane, the initial events following the creation of **R*** are suggested in the schematic diagram at the top of the next page. Diffusion acts very quickly over small distances, and

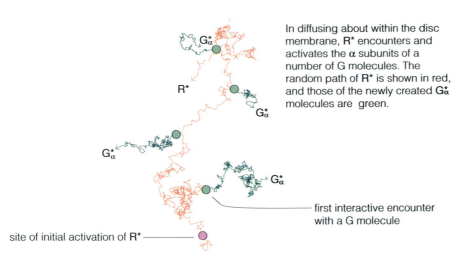

In diffusing about within the disc membrane, **R*** encounters and activates the α subunits of a number of G molecules. The random path of **R*** is shown in red, and those of the newly created G_α^* molecules are green.

first interactive encounter with a G molecule

site of initial activation of **R***

within about 100 ms, a single **R*** molecule will have created about 700 G_α^* subunits. **R*** thus activates about 8% of the G molecules on the disc surface. *This is the primary activation step in the biochemical cascade.* The schematic diagram of the portion of the outer segment that we have been considering now looks like this:

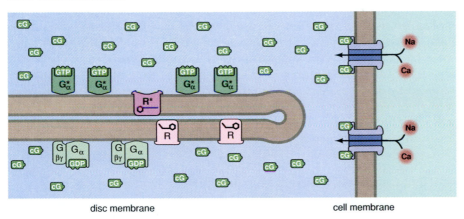

disc membrane　　　　　　　　　　　　cell membrane

The four G_α^* subunits in the diagram represent the hundreds that have been activated. The diffusion of these membrane proteins is confined to one surface of the disc. **R*** can activate only those G molecules that lie on the same surface; during the 0.1 s period we have been considering, it activates about 8% of the G molecules on the surface.

The next step is for each G_α^* molecule to bind to a molecule named cG phosphodiesterase, abbreviated as **PDE**, whose icon looks like this:

The PDE molecule contains two almost symmetrical portions. Each portion has a **catalytic site** that can act on cG molecules. This site is normally blocked by another subunit, dubbed PDE_γ, and represented as ⌐ in the icon. A G_α^* subunit can bind to either of the two portions so as to displace the PDE_γ subunit, and expose the catalytic site.

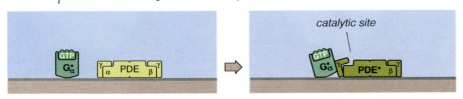

catalytic site

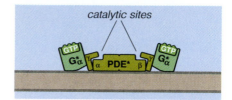

catalytic sites

The two portions of the PDE molecule appear to act independently, so the second portion may also be activated by another G_α^* molecule (left). So, conceptually, we can view the PDE molecule as consisting of two independent subunits, either of which can be activated:

PDE subunit

When activated, a **PDE*** ("PDE star") subunit can break a specific bond in a cG molecule, converting it into a GMP molecule:

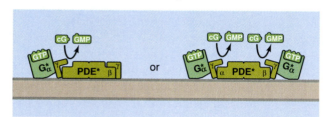

If G_α^* molecules attach to both ends of a PDE molecule, then two catalytic sites will be activated.

During the activation phase of the rod, which lasts for about 200 ms, each catalytic site rapidly converts a number of cG molecules into GMP. GMP molecules are relatively inert and are unable to attach to the cG-gated channels; thus the real effect of this conversion is the removal of cG molecules from the cytoplasm. At the peak of the activation phase, a single **R*** molecule has caused the number of cG molecules in the outer segment to be reduced by about 1400, a value that we will term **disc amplification.** (This term may seem strange, since it refers to a *decline* in the number of cG molecules, but the important thing is that the **R*** molecule has caused a *change* in the number of cG molecules by this amount.)

Channel amplification results from multiple binding sites for cG

Each cG-gated channel is composed of four protein subunits, which combine to form a symmetrical structure with a pore at its center through which cations can pass:

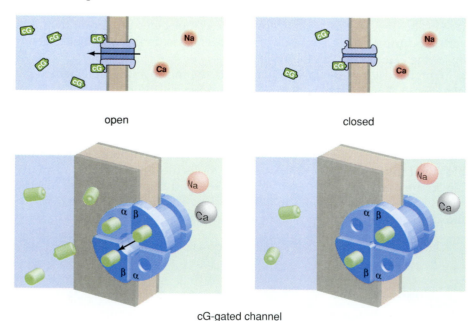

open   closed

cG-gated channel

Each subunit contains a **binding site** for cG at its intracellular surface, so that each channel has four potential binding sites. The detailed structure of these channels is not known; consequently, the icons used to represent them are simple.

To a first approximation, a channel is either open or closed, but it can change between these two states very quickly. In order for the channel to be open at any moment, *at least three of the four binding sites must have a cG molecule bound to it.* Thus a channel that has three cG molecules bound to it will be open, but if it loses any one of the three, it will close. As a consequence, the fraction of channels that are open is not proportional to the concentration of cG, but varies as the *cube* of this concentration. Thus a 1% change in cG concentration causes a 3% change in the fraction of channels that are open, and a reduction of the inward current by a similar percentage. We can refer to this relation as **channel amplification.**

At the peak of the activation phase, a single **R*** molecule reduces the number of cG molecules in the outer segment by about 1400, which is equivalent to a decrease in their concentration of about 0.7%. The inward current passing through the cG-gated channels is thus reduced by three times this value, or about 2%.

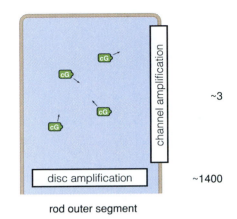

rod outer segment

The effect of R* extends over 20% of the length of the outer segment

The previous description focused on the molecular players in the biochemical cascade of photoreceptor activation. It is useful at this point to take a step back and consider these events with respect to the disc membrane that contains **R*** and the channels that are distributed over the entire plasma membrane of the outer segment.

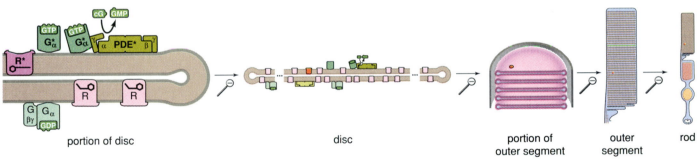

| portion of disc | disc | portion of outer segment | outer segment | rod |

As described in the last section, **R***, like other molecules of the disc membrane, is in continuous random motion as a result of thermal agitation. The molecules that compose each disc membrane, including **R***, are confined to it, but are free to move laterally via diffusion (this type of movement is known as *translation*) and to jiggle about in the direction perpendicular to the plane of the disc (*rotation*):

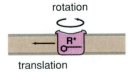

rotation

translation

Our focus remains on **R***, the one molecule in all of this chaos that has been directly affected by a photon. This diagram of one surface of a disc membrane shows a typical migration path that **R***, or any rhodopsin molecule, might take over a period of 0.1 s (right). This period was chosen because it is approximately equal to the effective lifetime of **R***, as discussed

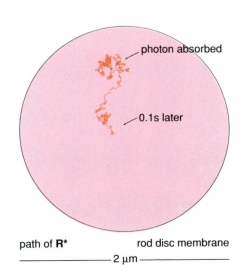

path of **R***   rod disc membrane
———————— 2 μm ————————

below. During this period, the average distance that **R*** will migrate from its starting position is about 0.8 μm, which is only slightly less than the radius of the disc. The average migration distances for any of the G molecules or PDE molecules attached to the disc membrane are similar. Each G molecule moves about with its own Brownian motion across the membrane surface, taking a path similar to that shown above for **R*.**

During this 100 ms period, **R*** activates about 700 G molecules, or about 8% of those on the surface of the disc membrane. If each of these G_α^* molecules were represented by a dot, their distribution at the end of the 0.1s period might look something like the diagram at left. The path of **R*,** now shown in black, is included only for reference. Notice that at this point, the G_α^* molecules are not randomly distributed across the disc surface, but tend to cluster near the path of **R*,** where they were created. On average, the earlier they were created, the farther they will have migrated.

As G_α^* molecules bind to PDE subunits and activate their catalytic sites, cG molecules are rapidly converted to GMP molecules, thereby lowering the concentration of cG. The diffusion of cG molecules within the cytoplasm of the outer segment is sufficiently rapid to bring them to the disc surface containing the **PDE*** subunits while they remain activated. Therefore, the cG concentration was lowered not only in the immediate area of the disc, but over a portion of the outer segment above and below it that includes many other discs.

Let us assume that the photon was absorbed in a disc lying midway along the length of the outer segment. The spatial distribution of the concentration of cG molecules along the outer segment then looks something like this 0.1 s after the absorption of the photon:

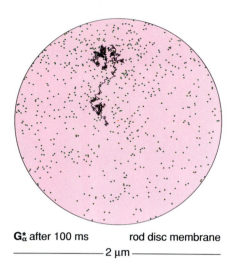

G_α^* after 100 ms   rod disc membrane

——————— 2 μm ———————

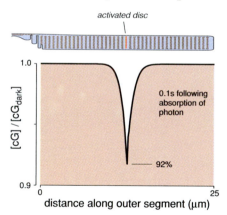

activated disc

0.1s following absorption of photon

92%

$[cG] / [cG_{dark}]$

distance along outer segment (μm)

based upon calculations by E. N. Pugh Jr.

Near the activated disc, the cG concentration drops to about 92% of what it would be in the dark; to a lesser degree, some decrease occurs over about 20% of the length of the outer segment, equivalent to a region containing about 200 discs.

The interaction of cG molecules with the cG-gated channels is sufficiently fast that the fraction of these channels open at any moment faithfully follows the change in cG concentration. The maximum resulting change in the inward *current* carried by Na^+ and Ca^{2+} ions is about 0.7 picoamps (pA), which corresponds to the net closure of about 230 cG-gated channels, or about 2% of all of the channels in the entire outer segment that are open in the dark. Yet the plasma membrane nearest the disc with **R*** contains only about 10 open channels. Thus the channels that do close have to extend over a much greater area of the outer segment membrane. They can do so because the decrease in the concentration of cG molecules extends over many discs, even though the site of their reduction lies on only one side of one disc.

BIOCHEMICAL CASCADE takes a broader and deeper look at each step in this cascade. CG-GATED CHANNELS discusses the structure of these channels and their dependence on cG in greater detail. Here, we will continue to follow the sequence of events that leads to the reduction in the rate of glutamate molecules at the synaptic terminal, starting with the decrease in the inward current produced by the biochemical cascade.

The electrical response to an absorbed photon is a photocurrent

In the dark, a current of about 34 pA, termed the **dark current,** flows *into* the outer segment. By convention, a current that flows *out of* a cell is *positive*, giving the dark current a value of –34 pA. Sign conventions can be confusing, and the following illustration is intended to serve as a reference for currents:

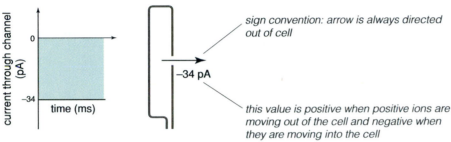

sign convention: arrow is always directed out of cell

this value is positive when positive ions are moving out of the cell and negative when they are moving into the cell

Because currents and voltages are conventionally measured from the interior of the cell to the extracellular fluid, a current is positive if it passes out of the cell and thus negative if it passes into the cell. Hence the dark current has a negative value.

When a single visual pigment molecule is photoisomerized, there is a 2% decrease in current at the peak of the response. The *change* in the dark current caused by the absorption of one or more photons is termed the **photocurrent.**

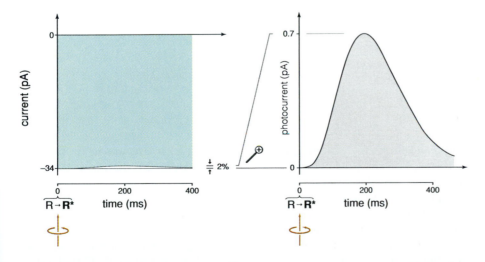

Before a photon is absorbed, the *inward movement* of positive charge, in the form of Na and Ca cations, into the outer segment is balanced by an *outward movement* of charge, carried by K cations via K-selective channels located in the inner segment.

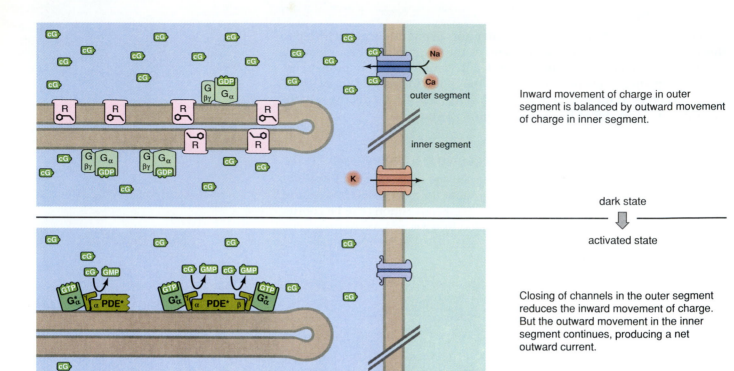

Inward movement of charge in outer segment is balanced by outward movement of charge in inner segment.

dark state

activated state

Closing of channels in the outer segment reduces the inward movement of charge. But the outward movement in the inner segment continues, producing a net outward current.

When the cG-gated channels close, the inward movement of Na$^+$ and Ca^{2+} ions is reduced by about 1 pA, but the outward movement of K$^+$ ions continues. Thus there is a net loss of positive charge within the rod, and its transmembrane potential hyperpolarizes by about 1 mV:

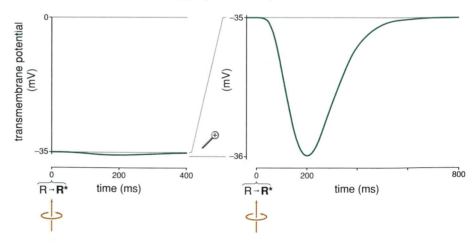

The *change* in the transmembrane potential caused by the absorption of one or more photons is termed the **photovoltage,** just as the change in the dark current is termed the photocurrent.

The peak of the photovoltage occurs about 200 ms after the photoisomerization of a rhodopsin molecule. The photovoltage returns to its dark value more slowly, dropping to within 10% of its peak value in about 450 ms. This *deactivation phase* is the consequence of the deactivation of both **R*** and the **G$_\alpha^*$–PDE*** complex, and restores the concentration of cG molecules to the dark value. As the concentration of cG molecules is restored, the number of cG-gated channels that are open at any moment increases, the rates of inflow of Na and Ca cations are returned to their previous values, and the resting state of the outer segment is thereby restored.

This brief description of the inactivation phase leaves out a lot, but to discuss it in greater detail here would require bringing in a number of other factors that are not needed for this overview of the activation phase. It is more fully described in BIOCHEMICAL CASCADE.

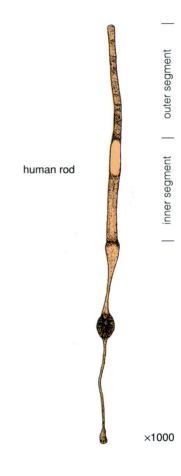

Biochemical cascade *371*

Electrotonic spread

Rods are long and thin (right) and *electrotonic spread* provides the means by which a change in the transmembrane potential, generated in the outer segment, spreads to the synaptic terminal. This is a physical process, described in NEURONS (page 93). The transmembrane potential of any cell results from a slight excess of negative charge on the inside surface of the plasma membrane and an equal slight excess of positive charge on the outside surface. The two layers of charge attract one another, but are prevented from coming together by the membrane, which acts as a barrier between them. This slight excess of charge on either side of the membrane is termed the **charge displacement.** By physical factors alone, the charge displacement tends to redistribute itself across the entire plasma membrane so as to equalize the transmembrane potential across every portion of the membrane. Thus a change in the charge displacement in one region of a cell spreads rapidly across the membrane so as to equalize the transmembrane potential throughout.

human rod

×1000

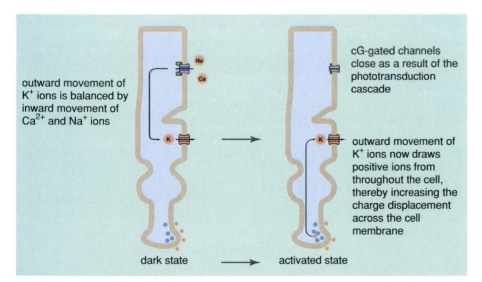

outward movement of K$^+$ ions is balanced by inward movement of Ca^{2+} and Na$^+$ ions

cG-gated channels close as a result of the phototransduction cascade

outward movement of K$^+$ ions now draws positive ions from throughout the cell, thereby increasing the charge displacement across the cell membrane

dark state ⟶ activated state

The left portion of this diagram shows the dark state of a rod. Positive charge is flowing into the cell via the cG-gated channels, and out of the cell via K$^+$-selective channels. The rate at which positive charges leave the cell is equal to the rate at which they enter. The charge displacement neither increases nor decreases, and consequently, neither does the transmembrane potential.

It is worth noting here what we are *not* considering. First, the ionic species that carry the charge across the membrane are irrelevant. A calcium ion conveys two charges; sodium and potassium ions only one. But we are not doing our bookkeeping on ions, only on charges. Second, we are not concerned here with the locations of the ionic channels. The channels conveying the inward current are located on the membrane of the outer segment, whereas those conveying the outward current are located on the inner segment. But, to a first approximation, this is also irrelevant. Our bookkeeping on charge displacement deals with the net movement of charge into or out of the cell, not where it moved in or out.

The right portion of the diagram shows the cG-gated channels closed. The outward movement of K⁺ ions now removes positive charge from throughout the interior of the cell, thereby decreasing the charge displacement. The path of current shown in this diagram is included to make the point that some of this charge comes from the region of the synaptic terminal, but it comes from everywhere, including the outer segment.

And that is just about all there is. A change in the transmembrane potential at one end of a cell shows up at the other end. A more detailed analysis might consider the overall geometry of a photoreceptor and the ease with which ions can move along the length of it, or within the extracellular space, in order to redistribute the charge displacement. It turns out that the resistance of the extracellular space to current flow is so small it can be ignored. Within the cell, the only significant constriction of the intracellular volume occurs at the ciliary stalk connecting the outer and inner segments. Because the discs almost fill the cross section of the outer segment, they may also impede the longitudinal flow of current. To the degree that either of these factors is significant, there is an advantage to placing the K⁺ channels on the plasma membrane of the inner segment rather than that of the outer segment, since the intracellular voltage drop between the inner segment and the synaptic terminal is minimized.

Thinking more deeply about current flow

If you were able to view the interior of a rod at an atomic resolution, you would not see a stream of positive ions heading toward the inner segment and passing through the channels like water through a hose. Instead, all you would see would be the random chaotic motion of ions and molecules within the cell. Only by making many measurements and looking at the average would you be able to discern a slight tendency for positive ions to take a small step toward the inner segment, or if within it, toward a channel. Thus the paths of current flow, such as those shown in the schematic diagrams, do not describe the movement of one charge going the whole distance, but rather the movements of many charges, each going a small distance—as in response to the command, "Everyone take one step to the right."

We can take another perspective on this process by keeping an eye on one of the K⁺ ions that has passed through the channel and out of the cell. Tracing its movement backward in time for 10 ms or so might give a path something like the diagram at left. This K⁺ ion happened to encounter a channel through which it could pass, and happened to have sufficient

kinetic energy to carry it up the electrical potential gradient across the channel. Whatever minute intracellular electrical field may have existed between its initial location and the ionic channel had virtually no effect upon the subsequent path of this ion.

What, then, is the significance of the current paths shown in the earlier diagrams? These current paths are only a *model* of what is going on, one that deals with *populations* of charged particles. The model leaves out all the factors that prove to be irrelevant, including microscopic factors such as the one highlighted here. It is this sophisticated simplification that provides a model upon which insight and understanding can be built.

What, then, is the relation of the path of the K⁺ ion to our model of current flow? As discussed above, a minute electrical field within the cell has virtually no effect upon the path of any particular ion. But this minute field acts on *every* ion, and that is what proves to be important. We are unaware of the gravitational fields of the Sun and Moon as we move about in the world along our own paths. But those gravitational fields act upon every water molecule and thereby create tides.

It is useful to be aware of the nature of the more reductional levels of explanation; it is also useful to be aware that the deeper levels may provide *less* understanding of the phenomena that concern us. That is why we need to see the dichotomy of reduction and emergence as a two-way street, to be traveled in both directions as it suits our needs.

Synaptic deactivation

As described in NEURONS, page 97, the voltage-controlled release of neuro-transmitters includes a common sequence of events that is found through-out the animal kingdom. The critical link is a voltage-gated ionic channel that allows calcium ions to pass into the presynaptic terminal when the transmembrane potential is depolarized. There are very few free calcium ions within a cell; their concentration is a thousand or more times lower than in the extracellular space. This low concentration is brought about by two mechanisms: first, calcium ions are actively removed from cells by means of pumps or exchangers (page 96); second, calcium ions that enter a cell are almost immediately bound to protein molecules. Thus, unlike sodium and potassium ions, which diffuse more or less freely within cells, free calcium ions tend to be found only near their sites of entry. This is described more fully in the Box *CALCIUM ENTRY*.

In photoreceptors, neurotransmitter release occurs at specialized mem-brane sites located just below the synaptic ribbon. The calcium channels appear to be located at or near these sites (because of graphical restrictions, the schematic diagrams show them more to the side). The synaptic ribbon has a slight binding affinity for synaptic vesicles, concentrating them from the three-dimensional volume of the synaptic terminal cytoplasm onto the two-dimensional surfaces of the ribbon. Thus the edge of the ribbon nearest the release site on the plasma membrane provides a relatively constant and concentrated supply of synaptic vesicles. Put simply, the ribbon guides the vesicles to their site of release.

The release of glutamate molecules from vesicles into the invagination of the photoreceptor terminal is regulated by the concentration of calcium ions near the release sites. This concentration depends upon the rate of entry of calcium ions, and thus the degree to which the calcium channels are open. In the dark, the transmembrane potential is depolarized by the entry of sodium and calcium ions into the outer segment via the cG-gated channels. The hyperpolarization produced by a decrease in the number of open cG-gated channels acts upon the voltage-gated calcium channels in the synaptic terminal, which tend to close, thereby lowering the internal cal-cium concentration and reducing transmitter release.

The mechanism by which the calcium channels sense the transmem-brane potential is not understood. In particular, it is not known whether the functional relation between this voltage and the degree of opening is fixed, or can be modulated by other factors. In fishes, there is preliminary evi-dence that the hyperpolarization of horizontal cells somehow acts on the voltage-sensitive mechanism of these channels so as to cause them to require a greater amount of hyperpolarization in order to close, and it is possible that this is true for mammals as well.

Calcium entry

It is interesting to note that the closure of the cG-gated channels decreases the calcium concentration within the outer segment—by decreasing calcium entry—and within the synaptic terminal—by hyperpolarization. In mammals, the outer segment and synaptic terminal are sufficiently far apart that the synaptic terminal is unaffected by the decrease in outer segment calcium; but in some cold-blooded vertebrates, where the distance between the outer segment and the synaptic terminal is smaller and the pho-toreceptors wider, outer segment calcium may play a more direct role in transmitter release. As discussed in BIOCHEMI-CAL CASCADE, the fall in outer segment calcium concentration plays a regulatory role in outer segments, but one wonders whether this role evolved more recently than the possibly more ancient effect of a decrease in outer segment calcium on transmitter release.

Decrease in glutamate concentration

Thus far we have considered only variations in the rate at which glutamate molecules are released into the extracellular space within the invaginations of photoreceptors. But there must also be a comparable *removal* of glutamate molecules from this space in order to maintain long-term equilibrium. Most of this removal appears to be due to an uptake mechanism within the synaptic terminal of the photoreceptor, which is not discussed here. Some of the adjacent cells may also take up glutamate molecules, and some of them may simply diffuse away. The removal of glutamate is a complicated process, poorly understood, with many detailed factors in play.

However it is accomplished, the decrease in glutamate concentration must be both fast and decisive. This is perhaps best seen by considering the time when you looked at the border between the treetops and the overcast night sky, when each rod was capturing a photon about once every 5000 seconds. With a shutter time of 0.1 second, it would take 50,000 rods for there to be one event at any instant within this large population of cells. Imagine a stadium filled with 50,000 sports fans, each of them yelling as loud as they can. One of them falls silent, and that silence is the event. Compare this situation with a hushed stadium in which one member of the crowd suddenly yells out. Evolution is not engineering, and this contrast provides a striking example of this fact.

So perhaps the most remarkable feature of the reliable response to a single photon lies not at the outer segment, but at the synaptic terminal. It is at this terminal that a 1 mV change in transmembrane potential must cause an immediate and decisive decrease in the *rate* of glutamate release. Bipolar cells do not directly detect a change in rate; rather, they detect a change in glutamate *concentration*. This change can occur only if there is an equally immediate and decisive removal of glutamate molecules from the extracellular space within the invagination. The uptake mechanisms that do this must operate continuously, and at a high rate.

Seen in this way, it is the uptake mechanism that lowers the concentration of glutamate molecules in the extracellular environment around the metabotropic receptors on the terminals of the on-bipolar cells, thereby activating them. But a powerful and continuous uptake mechanism must be matched by an equally powerful and often continuous release mechanism. Put another way, one of the prices that needs to be paid to make the whole thing work is a very large rate of turnover of glutamate molecules between the intra- and extracellular environments.

Summary of the rod response to a single photon

The primary task of a rod is to reliably convey to the rod bipolar cells that receive from it the message that the rod has caught a photon. The bipolar cells respond to a reduction in the concentration of glutamate molecules at their terminals. This reduction is brought about by a hyperpolarization of the transmembrane potential of the rod cell, combined with the continual removal of glutamate molecules from the synaptic cleft via uptake mechanisms. The hyperpolarization results from the closure of ionic channels on the plasma membrane of the rod outer segment. These channels close when the internal concentration of cG molecules is reduced. The concentration of cG molecules is reduced by PDE molecules bound to activated G molecules. Many G molecules are activated by a single rhodopsin molecule, and the rhodopsin molecule, in turn, is activated by the capture of a photon.

Wait for dawn . . .

    The hours pass, and the sky to the east begins to lighten, obliterating first the 6th magnitude stars, then the 5th magnitude stars, and so on, until they are gone. In the early dawn, you putter around camp, with enough light to see by. The intensity of the reflected light from different objects has grown to about one photon per rod every 5 seconds. Compared with when you could just make out the border between the overcast night sky and the trees, the intensity of the light has increased by a factor of 1000. It is at this level of light intensity that you begin to be aware of signals from your cones, because objects begin to appear colored.

How rods and cones respond to many photons

When considering the response of a rod to many photons, we can ignore the large dynamic range of vision during which only the rod system is active. The photon catch over this entire range is so low that rods respond on a photon-by-photon basis. We are concerned here with higher levels of light intensity, at which the responses to single photons overlap.

The photocurrent response to a flash is predictable from the single-photon response

Perhaps the first question to ask is to what degree the response to many photons can be accounted for by the response to a single photon that we have just considered. One means of addressing this question experimentally is to present brief flashes of light of different intensity to a rod, and record the amplitude of the change in the inward current and transmembrane voltage produced by each:

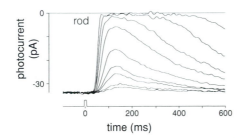

source: Baylor, 1987

Nine traces are shown here, some of which are averages of a number of responses in order to reduce noise. For the smallest response, the intensity of the flash is about 3 photoisomerizations. The time course of this response is indistinguishable from that of the response to a single photon, as one would expect. The intensity flash for the largest response is about 560 photoisomerizations. The time courses of the responses in between show a characteristic change in shape, and flatten out for the brightest two flash intensities. This flattening occurs because the inward current has dropped to zero, indicating that all of the cG-gated channels have closed.

    It is also evident that the heights of the response curves become compressed with higher flash intensities. This can be better seen by plotting the relative amplitude of the response as a function of the flash intensity:

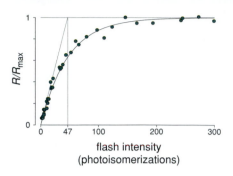

after Baylor et al., 1984

The vertical axis in this graph plots the amplitude of the response (R) relative to the maximum amplitude (R_{max}) observed with the brightest flashes. The data were collected from five rods, and this normalization simplifies their comparisons.

For dim flashes, the amplitude of the response is proportional to the average number of photoisomerizations. This is indicated by the data points that lie along the straight gray line that arises from a flash intensity of zero. This relation holds true for flash intensities up to about 10 photoisomerizations per rod, and can be accounted for by the simple summation of the individual responses to those photoisomerizations. Above this value, the peak of the response grows more slowly, and the rods saturate at about 200 photoisomerizations. The curve shown is an *exponential* with an intensity constant of 47 photoisomerizations. Since this constant sets the initial slope of the exponential, this value is simply the dark current (34 pA) divided by the peak photocurrent response to a single photoisomerization (0.7 pA).

At first sight, it might seem that what we learned about the response to a single photoisomerization allows us to account for flash intensities only up to about 10 photoisomerizations. But as mentioned earlier, there is more to the biochemical cascade than a simple reduction of the current flowing into the outer segment. As it happens, a more detailed and quantitative description of the biochemical cascade leads directly to the exponential observed. In qualitative terms, it results from a decrease in the catalytic rate of the **PDE*** subunits when many are active, because of the fall they produce in the concentration of free cG.

Put simply, a **PDE*** subunit can act only on the cG molecules that encounter it. When the concentration of cG falls because of the combined actions of many such subunits, the rate at which cG molecules encounter a given **PDE*** molecule also falls, thereby lowering the rate at which each activated PDE molecule can convert cG to GMP. When this factor is taken into account, *the mechanism that underlies the response to a single photoisomerization fully accounts for the response to a flash of any intensity that is presented in the dark.*

Exponentials *439*

Cones are similar to rods

In cones, the protein molecules of the biochemical cascade are similar to those of rods. However, they occur for the most part on infoldings of the plasma membrane, rather than on discs (as shown in the diagram at the top of the next page). The cone's rhodopsin molecules, and probably the other membrane proteins as well, are able to diffuse from infolding to infolding. This expands the number of G molecules an **R*** molecule can encounter, and

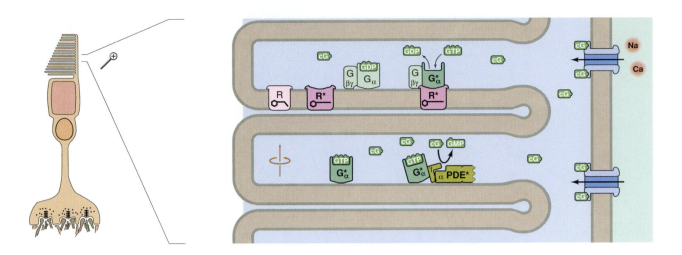

the number of PDE molecules a G_α^* molecule can encounter. At low photoisomerization rates, the availability of G and PDE molecules is not a problem, as discussed in the previous section. What happens at higher rates is uncertain, but it is possible that a decrease in their concentrations provides one of the means by which cones avoid saturation.

The response of a cone to a flash of light in the dark looks quite different from the rod response:

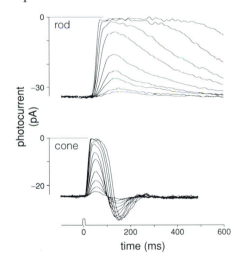

source: Baylor, 1987

The most notable difference is that the cone response is **biphasic:** the falling phase does not approach the equilibrium level gradually, but undershoots it. A more detailed description of the biochemical cascade provides a plausible explanation for this phenomenon. Briefly, the concentration of cG in the outer segment is maintained by means of an enzyme named **guanylate cyclase,** which synthesizes it from GTP. A fall in the concentration of cG indirectly causes this enzyme to become activated. The resulting increase in cG concentration opens some of the cG-gated channels, and thereby counteracts a fraction of the channel closings due to the light. This mechanism is common to both rods and cones, but it is sufficiently strong and fast in cones to produce a biphasic response by means of a temporary overproduction of cG molecules. The difference between rods and cones thus appears to be primarily quantitative rather than qualitative. In effect, both rods and cones use the same biochemical plan, but differ in quantitative measures such as relative concentrations of molecules and relative rates of reaction.

Biochemical cascade *371*

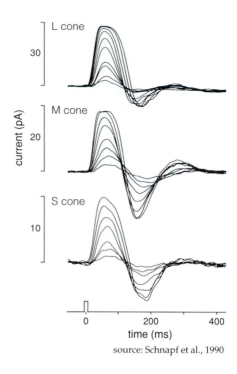

current (pA)

L cone

30

M cone

20

S cone

10

0   200   400
time (ms)

source: Schnapf et al., 1990

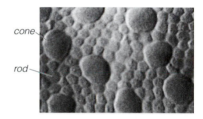

cone

rod

array of rod and cone outer segments
in peripheral retina

source: Curcio et al., 1990

The responses of all three cone types shown at left, are similar. The variations in the amplitudes of the responses in this graph (note the vertical scales) have more to do with the recording conditions than with any differences between the cone types. Here we will ignore the inactivation phase and consider only the activation, or rising, phase. In this diagram, the range of flash intensities to which cones respond is considerably higher than for rods, ranging from 190 to 36,000 photoisomerizations, because cones are less sensitive than rods. Whereas the peak photocurrent response to a single photoisomerization for a rod is about 700 fA (= 0.7 pA; see Appendix A), it is about 33 fA for a cone. Thus the peak photocurrent per photoisomerization in rods is about 20 times greater than that in cones.

But this is not the whole story.

Cones can convey the absorption of a single photon

Human subjects can detect light with their cones when there are about 3 photoisomerizations per cone per second. However, as we saw above, the duration of the cone photocurrent is only about 0.1 s. In effect, at this rate, the responses are occurring one by one. The argument that a cone requires two or more nearly simultaneous photons to produce a response is made improbable by the linear nature of a cone's response at low flash intensities, which is discussed below. Thus, like a rod, a cone can convey the absorption of a single photon to the bipolar cells it contacts.

In the peripheral retina, the effective cross-sectional area of a cone inner segment (left) is about 13 times greater than that of a rod. All else being equal, this means that the photon catch rate of a cone will be about 13 times greater than that of a rod. Thus, at the threshold of cone vision, the effective photon catch of a rod is about 3/13, or about 1 photon every 4 seconds—as in the early morning when you were puttering around the campsite. One photoisomerization per rod gives a peak photocurrent of 700 fA. At this same flash intensity, a cone in the same retinal location catches about 13 photons, and thus generates a peak photocurrent of 13×33 fA, or 430 fA. This is not greatly different from the photocurrent of a rod.

It may be that the critical factor for transmitter release at the synaptic terminal is not the *peak* in the transmembrane potential, but its *rate of rise*. The time to the peak is about 200 ms for rods and about 50 ms for cones—a ratio of about 4. This factor is more than enough to give the cones a rate of rise of the photocurrent at least as great as that of the rods.

When differences between the parameters that characterize the responses of rods and cones become as small as this, further quantitative attempts to compare the abilities of rods and cones become somewhat irrelevant, because what differences there are remain uncertain and because each of the numbers used to make these calculations has some uncertainty associated with it. Furthermore, we don't know the details of the differences in synaptic machinery between rods and cones. The data on the cone thresholds of human subjects are reliable, at least to a factor of 2 or so either way. So the conclusion that a cone can convey a single photoisomerization event seems unavoidable. From the perspective of how cones work, there appears to be nothing known that would prevent them from doing so.

As discussed in NIGHT AND DAY, we can see at much lower light levels with our rods than we can with our cones. This difference comes about because rods can convey the capture of photons to their bipolar cells in a more reliable manner than cones can. It seems likely that the reliability of cones is degraded not because they fail to convey the capture of each photon, but because their responses are smaller and cannot be reliably distinguished from the influences of other factors on synaptic transmission.

Voltage-gated channels shape the response

Although the *photocurrent* shows no qualitatively new features with increasing flash intensity, the *time course* of the change in transmembrane potential produced by this current does. The diagram at top right shows the change in transmembrane potential, or photovoltage, of a rod in response to flashes of different intensities, ranging from 5 to 2300 photoisomerizations. For low-intensity flashes, the time course of the photovoltage follows that of the photocurrent. But when the amplitude of the response reaches half the maximum or more, a new phenomenon appears. The response rises quickly to its peak, but then quickly decays. This sudden fall appears to be due to voltage-gated channels located on the plasma membrane of the inner segment of the rod. These channels open shortly after the photovoltage reaches about −10 mV. They carry an inward current, thus partly compensating for the loss of inward current that results from the closure of the cG-gated channels. The overall effect is for the photovoltage response to emphasize *changes* in light intensity. This mechanism operates only at higher light intensities, and it is not clear what role it plays in the normal function of rods. A similar effect is seen for cones when the photovoltage exceeds about −8 mV, as shown at right.

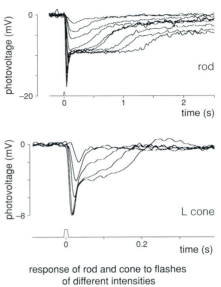

response of rod and cone to flashes
of different intensities

after Schneeweis and Schnapf, 1995

The flash response predicts the response to other light intensity changes

A flash of light is as rare as lightning in the natural world, but it does provide a useful means of investigating the responses of photoreceptors. This is particularly true when the flash intensity is low enough that the response to a number of photons is simply the sum of the responses to each one. This range of intensities is termed the **linear range.** Within it, the response to an impulse (flash) or to a step change, such as when a light is suddenly turned on or off, can be used to calculate the response to any variation in light intensity that lies within the linear range. In the dark, the linear range for both rods and cones extends up to about one-third of the total dark current. For rods, this corresponds to about 16 photoisomerizations; for cones, about 380.

The diagram at right shows the response of an M cone to both a flash and a step change. Each trace shows the averaged response to 46 alternating presentations of the flash and the 1 s step change. The circles in the lower diagram show the expected response to the step change, based upon the flash response. This is calculated by assuming that the step change consists of a temporal sequence of flashes and summing the sequence of responses produced. The agreement between the calculated and the measured responses is reasonably good, and thus serves to demonstrate the approximately linear behavior of these cones. The voltage-gated channels that shape the photovoltage do not "kick in" until the photocurrent has exceeded half its maximum value. Hence, over the linear range, the time course of the photovoltage mirrors that of the photocurrent. The firing rates of some ganglion cell types show a similar time course of response to a step change (SEEING, page 339).

To summarize, in the dark, the response to a flash of any intensity is based upon the same mechanism that underlies the response to a single photon. When the amplitude of the photoresponse is less than about one-third of its maximum value, the response is approximately linear. When the response exceeds about half of its maximum value, voltage-gated channels open, pulling the net inward current to a lower value. The effect is to produce a more transient change in the transmembrane potential, and thus to emphasize changes in the photocurrent, and thus changes in the photon catch rate.

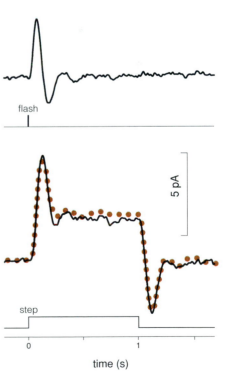

source: Schnapf et al., 1990

How rods and cones respond at different light levels

In the natural world, the most common experience is of scenes viewed at different levels of ambient light over the course of the day. However, because of eye movements, the photoreceptors receive many changes in light intensity. These changes are always sudden during a saccade, and may be sudden during smooth eye movements as borders within the image sweep across the retina.

In an illuminated scene, what we see depends upon the spectral reflectance of objects and the level of ambient light that falls upon them. Each photoreceptor type will capture some *fraction* of the light reflected from the scene. The amount of light caught will vary as the direction of gaze changes. For any one photoreceptor, the photon catch rate over time might look something like this:

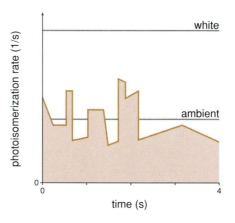

Assuming that the surfaces in the scene scatter photons rather than reflect them, a white surface defines an upper bound of light intensity. The level of *ambient* or *background* light in the scene is somewhat arbitrary, for it depends upon the visual interests of the observer, and thus changes over time. Nevertheless, for the sake of simplicity, it is indicated here by a horizontal line. This is an approximation and simplification of a real situation, but it is still somewhat complicated. For analysis, let us consider a flash presented against a steady background light:

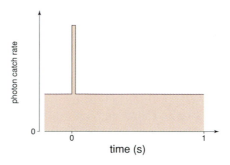

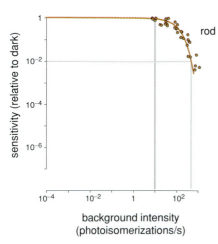

after Baylor, 1987

Because the range of background light intensity is very large, it is useful to plot the photon catch rate on a log scale. For other reasons, it is also useful to plot the amplitude of the rod response on a log scale, normalized to the amplitude in the dark (left). Up to a background light intensity of about 10 photoisomerizations per rod per second (vertical gray line), the amplitude of the rod response is uninfluenced by the background light intensity. But by 500 photoisomerizations/s, the amplitude of the response to the flash drops to about 1% of the dark value (horizontal gray line).

What is happening appears to be simple. The steady background light reduces the photocurrent carried by the cG-gated channels, as expected. But in doing so, it lowers the remaining photocurrent available to be reduced by the flash. The curve plots the amplitude of the rod response predicted from the expected decrease in photocurrent caused by the background light. Actual observations (represented by circles) correspond to these predictions. These results are consistent with viewing responses to both flash and background as the summed effects of the photoisomerizations they produce upon the cG-gated channels. No other mechanisms appear to be required. The same appears to hold for the cones, except that they do not saturate, as discussed below.

Camping

The sky to the east begins to lighten, obliterating first the 6th magnitude stars, then the 5th magnitude stars, and so on, until they are gone.

The sensitivity of rod vision is much lower than that of individual rods

This diagram shows the sensitivity of rod vision as measured by psychophysical means. A subject viewed a steady background, 20° in diameter, upon the center of which was flashed a test spot, 10° in diameter. The subject adjusted the intensity of the test flash until it could just be seen. When the intensity of the background light was equal to or less than 1 photoisomerization per 1000 seconds, the threshold intensity of the test flash was the same as when the steady background light was not present. In other words, these background intensities had no effect on the minimum light intensity needed to see the test flash. But when the background light intensity rose to 1 photoisomerization per rod per 100 seconds, the subject had to increase the intensity of the test flash by a factor of about 2 (0.3 on the log scale), as indicated by the dark gray line, in order to see it.

This is a striking result; clearly the steady background light could not be exerting a direct effect on the rods that caught the photons from the test flash, since during the test flash, few if any of these rods would also catch a photon from the background light. It is easy to show that this dim background light exerts no long-term effect on the rods, since the subject's threshold drops to the dark level as soon as the background light is turned off.

When the intensity of the background light has risen to a catch rate of 1 photon per second per rod, it is necessary for the subject to increase the intensity of the test flash by a factor of 100 (sensitivity relative to dark of 10^{-2}), as indicated by the pale gray line. Recordings from retinal ganglion cells show the same pattern that is seen psychophysically. Thus, somewhere between the rods and the ganglion cells, there has been an enormous loss of sensitivity that has nothing to do with the responses of individual photoreceptors.

Since the earlier diagram of rod sensitivity had the same vertical scale (sensitivity relative to dark value, and the same horizontal scale (photon catch rate per rod) as the psychophysical diagram, we can combine the two diagrams so as to compare the sensitivity of single rods to test lights with the sensitivity of subjects to test lights (right). For background light intensities from 10 to 100 photoisomerizations per second, the sensitivity of a single rod was only slightly reduced, yet the subject had to increase the intensity of the test flash by a factor of between 1000 and 10,000 in order for it to be seen!

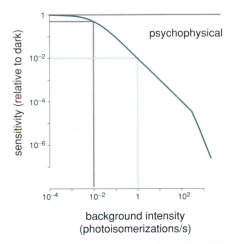

after Baylor, 1987

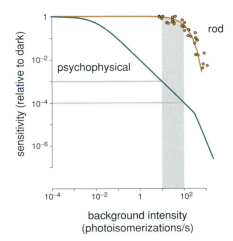

after Baylor, 1987

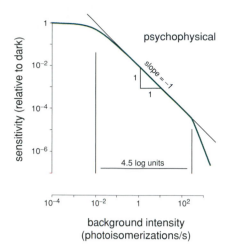

psychophysical

slope = –1

4.5 log units

background intensity
(photoisomerizations/s)

after Baylor, 1987

At first this might seem bizarre, particularly after considering the mechanisms by which both rods and cones are able to convey single-photon events. A brief explanation is that the retina acts to code contrast rather than light intensity per se. Cheetahs are more interested in gazelles than in light. The *amount* of light coming from a gazelle increases as the sun rises. But the *ratio* of light from different portions of the gazelle, or between the gazelle and the backdrop does not change as the general level of daylight increases. Put another way, if sensitivity is *halved* when background intensity is *doubled*, then *the response to some difference in spectral reflectance will be independent of the ambient level of light intensity.* In effect, what we see won't change much as the level of light intensity varies.

A relation in which one parameter varies inversely with respect to another plots as a straight line with a slope of –1 on a graph in which both axes are logarithmic. The psychophysical relation between the sensitivity of rod vision as a function of background light intensity shows this relation over about 4.5 log units, which corresponds to a dynamic range of about 30,000. As noted, this relation is not a property of rods, but of the neural circuitry of the retina.

Notice that although we have considered individual rods to saturate at a capture rate of 400–500 photoisomerizations/s, the psychophysical data show that flashes can still be seen at even higher background levels. However, there is no real conflict between the two sets of data, rather, there is simply a difference in the criteria used to define saturation.

Camping

By noon, the sun is beating down. You climb higher, and reach a field of snow more brilliant than the sky behind it. There is a sharpness to the visual world about you, even though only 5% of your photoreceptors are still signaling. As you look at a patch of snow, each of your cones is now catching almost 300,000 photons per second.

Rods saturate at bright light levels but cones do not

As seen in the previous two diagrams, rods begin to saturate when the photoisomerization rate exceeds about 400 photoisomerizations/s. As discussed earlier, this is primarily due to the reduction in the dark current that is produced by steady background light. The details are a bit more complicated than described here, and are taken up again in BIOCHEMICAL CASCADE.

Here we concentrate on why cones do not saturate at steady background light levels of *any* intensity. At first sight this seems quite surprising, for just about everything that we are familiar with seems to saturate at some level. As discussed in NIGHT AND DAY (page 146), the essential reason that cones don't saturate is that there is a maximum possible photoisomerization rate that cannot be exceeded by any steady background light. This rate corresponds to the maximum *regeneration* rate of the rhodopsin molecules. After a rhodopsin molecule has been photoisomerized and deactivated, a sequence of events, discussed in VISUAL PIGMENT REGENERATION, replaces the photoisomerized chromophore (all-*trans* retinal) with the dark form (11-*cis* retinal). This is a biochemical process that for cones has an *exponential* time constant, τ, of about 120 s. Put another way, if all of the visual pigment molecules were suddenly photoisomerized by a powerful flash, the concentration of rhodopsin molecules would recover in an exponential manner with this time constant (see diagram at right).

The number of rhodopsin molecules in a foveal cone outer segment is comparable to that in a rod, which is about 140 million:

$$R_{\mathrm{dark}} = 1.4 \times 10^8$$

The rate of regeneration is the total number of unregenerated rhodopsin molecules divided by the time constant of regeneration. The largest value occurs when all the molecules, R_{dark}, are in the unregenerated state. The fastest rate at which rhodopsin molecules in cones could ever be regenerated is thus R_{dark}/τ, or about 1.2×10^6 molecules/s. Clearly no light, however bright, could be *continuously* absorbed by the rhodopsin molecules of a cone at a higher rate than this. The best the photons could do would be for one of them to be absorbed by a rhodopsin molecule as soon as the molecule was regenerated. Since the rate of regeneration is limited to 1.2×10^6 molecules/s, this is also the maximum rate of continuous absorption. The maximum rate of continuous photoisomerizations is two-thirds of that value, or about 0.8×10^6 photoisomerizations per second. The numbers used to make this calculation are approximate, and for convenience, we round this value up to 10^6.

During the day, as the light intensity increases, more photons are absorbed and the fraction of regenerated rhodopsin molecules decreases. It is this decrease in rhodopsin molecules that serves to limit the maximum continuous rate of photoisomerizations. Of course, sudden increases in light intensity, as when you look briefly into the sun, will cause the rate of photoisomerization to exceed 10^6/s, but it cannot remain at this level for very long, because the higher photoisomerization rate reduces the number of rhodopsin molecules toward zero.

Clearly, *if* a cone can continue to operate when the photoisomerization rate is as high as the maximum rate at which it can regenerate visual pigment, then it will never saturate to any steady ambient light level, no matter how bright. The fact that cones do not saturate to steady light levels indicates that they are able to deal with photoisomerization rates as high as this.

A rate of 10^6 photoisomerizations/s is about 100 times greater than the photoisomerization rate at which rods saturate, as discussed above. But for cones, the *amplitude* of the photocurrent response to each photoisomerization is about 20 times smaller than for rods (33 fA vs. 700 fA). Furthermore, the *duration* of the cone photocurrent is about four times shorter than for rods (100 ms vs. 400 ms). Thus these factors alone account for a factor of about 80 that should be included when cones and rods are compared. An additional factor of about 10 would allow the cones to function normally at the maximum photoisomerization rate.

As mentioned earlier (page 179) when describing the "undershoot" of the cone responses, there is a mechanism for the restoration of cG that is common to both rods and cones. This mechanism causes the rate of synthesis of new cG molecules to depend upon the fraction of cG-gated channels that remain open. In essence, a fall in the concentration of cG molecules causes cG-gated channels to close, which indirectly leads to an increase in the synthesis of new cG molecules, thereby opening the channels. This mechanism is described in detail in BIOCHEMICAL CASCADE. It is this additional mechanism that, over their normal operating range, is strong in cones and weak to absent in rods. This mechanism supplies an additional factor that can help cones operate at any light level.

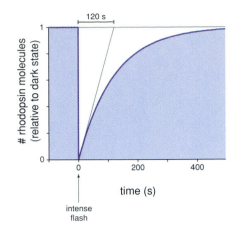

120 s

rhodopsin molecules
(relative to dark state)

1

0

0   200   400

time (s)

intense flash

Visual pigment regeneration *509*

Exponentials *439*

Biochemical cascade *371*

Photoreceptors generate spontaneous photonlike events

In complete darkness, rods occasionally generate electrical events that cannot be distinguished from the effect of a photoisomerization produced by an absorbed photon:

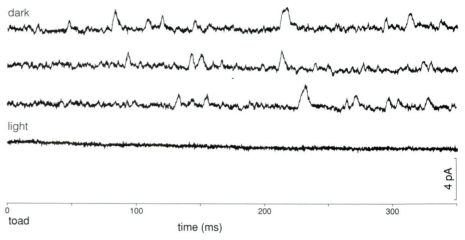

from Baylor et al., 1980

These dark events were first demonstrated in the rods of toads, where they have a mean rate of about one event every 50 s. This rate increases with temperature in a manner that suggests that they are due to photoisomerization of the chromophore of a rhodopsin molecule as a result of thermal agitation. So fortuitously well placed and vigorous molecular collisions apparently *can* occasionally flip the 11-*cis* isomer to the all-*trans* form—which brings home the notion that high-energy photons, thrown off by the Sun, supply Earth not only with energy that can be used to fuel this world, but with information (rare energy values) that can be used to see it.

In primate rods, these dark events have not been directly observed or recorded because of experimental limitations. By indirect means, they have been estimated to occur at an average rate of 1 event per rod every 160 s. This value is close to the psychophysically determined limit of visual performance, which, as discussed in NIGHT AND DAY, is termed the eigengrau.

The protein portion of visual pigment molecules consists of a single chain of amino acids, which forms seven coils, termed α helices. The helices span the membrane of the disc, and surround the chromophore, as shown in this cutaway view. The helices are linked together by loops in the rest of the chain; although these loops are shown spread out, they probably form more compact structures on either side of the membrane.

In this two-dimensional representation, the seven helices are arranged in a line so as to show the sequence of amino acids that lie along the chain. Proteins are made from 20 different amino acids; each amino acid is represented by a circle containing a letter that represents it, as shown in the key.

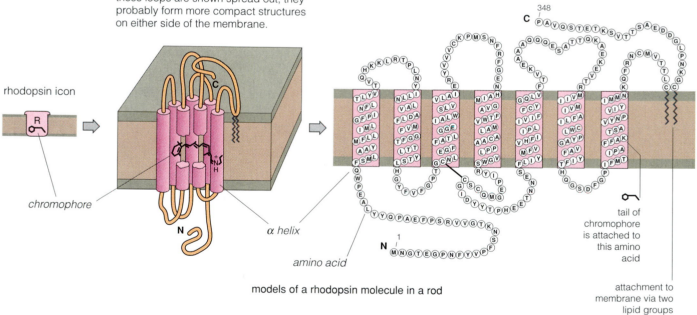

rhodopsin icon

chromophore

α helix

amino acid

tail of chromophore is attached to this amino acid

attachment to membrane via two lipid groups

models of a rhodopsin molecule in a rod

Rhodopsins

This interlude takes a closer look at the internal structure of the rhodopsin molecule. It describes the approximate manner in which the single amino acid sequence of this molecule folds so as to allow it to lie within the membrane, and the manner in which it attaches to and envelopes the chromophore. The rhodopsins of all animal species originated from a single ancient common ancestor; this is illustrated by comparing the amino acid sequence of our rhodopsin with those of other species. Mutations of our rhodopsins can lead to blindness, and this is illustrated by discussing the mutations that cause retinitis pigmentosa.

Key

- (A) alanine
- (C) cysteine
- (D) aspartic acid
- (E) glutamic acid
- (F) phenylalanine
- (G) glycine
- (H) histidine
- (I) isoleucine
- (K) lysine
- (L) leucine
- (M) methionine
- (N) asparagine
- (P) proline
- (Q) glutamine
- (R) arginine
- (S) serine
- (T) threonine
- (V) valine
- (W) tryptophan
- (Y) tyrosine

- ○ nonpolar
- ○ polar or ambiguous
- ● charged

Rhodopsin molecules, in every type of photoreceptor in every species, consist of a single chain of amino acids (see diagram on facing page). In most species, including humans, all photoreceptors of the same type contain the same type of rhodopsin molecule. This proves to be equivalent to saying that they all have the same sequence of amino acids along the chain. Conversely, rhodopsin molecules differ according to their amino acid sequences. For example, humans have four different photoreceptor types, each with a different sequence, as discussed in PHOTORECEPTOR ATTRIBUTES.

Although the sequence of amino acids along each rhodopsin chain is known, the precise manner in which the chain is folded upon itself to form a functional molecule is not. So we currently lack a detailed understanding of the structure of any rhodopsin molecule. Nevertheless, it is possible to devise and refine a model of this structure, based in part upon the properties of the amino acids along the chain. A particularly useful property is the way in which each type of amino acid interacts with water—in particular, whether it is nonpolar ("hydrophobic") or charged. As discussed in NEURONS (page 89), charged molecules or ions are strongly attracted to water because of its polar nature. As a consequence of these mutual attractions, nonpolar molecules, or portions thereof, tend to be excluded from the aqueous environment, and thereby form their own domains.

Most *soluble* proteins are folded so that they have a central core of nonpolar amino acids; this core is surrounded by polar or charged amino acids that face the surrounding aqueous environment. As you might expect, membrane proteins use nonpolar amino acids to span the nonpolar interior of a membrane. The following diagram shows the locations of all of the nonpolar amino acids of human rod rhodopsin:

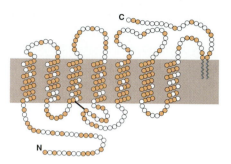

nonpolar amino acids of rod rhodopsin

Seven α helices span the disc membrane in roughly the manner shown. The α helices contain a high fraction of nonpolar amino acids, as one would expect. The loops on either side of the membrane contain some nonpolar amino acids as well; they presumably cause the loops to form compact structures whose form remains unknown.

By comparison, the membranous portion of the molecular chain contains only four charged amino acids (left). The two pale-colored amino acids toward the middle left of this diagram are glutamic acid. They are shown this way because in an aqueous environment, glutamic acid is negatively charged by the loss of a proton; but within the membrane portion of this molecule, the proton is present, so they are actually uncharged. This leaves only two charged amino acids, aspartic acid at the left and lysine at the right.

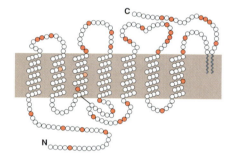

charged amino acids of rod rhodopsin

As shown schematically in this diagram, the tail of the chromophore is attached to the charged lysine, and a net positive charge results from the nature of this attachment:

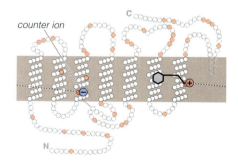

charge distribution about the chromophore

The isolated chromophore, 11-*cis* retinal, can absorb photons only in the ultraviolet portion of the spectrum. This particular attachment of the chromophore to the amino acid chain, termed a protonated Schiff base, shifts its spectral sensitivity into the visible range. The net positive charge produced by this attachment is balanced by the negative charge of the aspartic acid shown to the left, which is termed the counter ion. In this and the other two-dimensional illustrations, the amino acid is shown unwrapped from the chromophore. But when the α helices are wrapped around the chromophore, as in the middle portion of the chapter-opening diagram of this Interlude, the protonated Schiff base and the counter ion are brought much closer together, as suggested by the dashed line above. The spectral sensitivity of the molecule is also influenced by the counter ion, as well as by nearby polar molecules in the chain.

Although this discussion has focused on human rod rhodopsin, other rhodopsins, whether from rods or cones, are similar. The human M and L cone pigments, however, have sixteen additional amino acids attached to the N terminal of the chain (right). Additional similarities and differences between the rhodopsins of human photoreceptors are discussed in the next chapter.

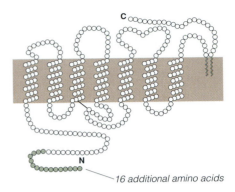

16 additional amino acids

M and L cone rhodopsins

Rhodopsins are ancient

Most of what we know about the properties of rod rhodopsins comes from rod rhodopsin extracted from cow (bovine) eyes, since they can be readily obtained from a slaughterhouse. Bovine rod rhodopsin is very similar to human rod rhodopsin. The protein portion of each consists of a single chain of 348 amino acids that form seven transmembrane helices. They can thus be compared according to their amino acid sequences. As the following diagram shows, the two sequences differ at only 23 of the amino acid positions:

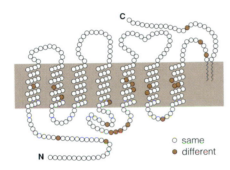

○ same
● different

human and bovine rod rhodopsins

Within protein chains, some amino acids show similar biochemical properties. For example, except in special circumstances, glutamic acid (E) can be substituted for aspartic acid (D) without altering the functional properties of a protein. There are six such groups of amino acids in which any amino acid within the group can be substituted for any other member of the same group. If a genetic mutation replaces one amino acid with a similar one that does not alter the function of a protein, then there is no evolutionary pressure to weed that mutation out of the population via selection. If amino acids within these groups are considered to be equivalent, then the number of differences between human and bovine rod rhodopsin is reduced from 23 to 8.

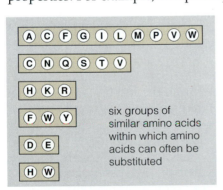

A C F G I L M P V W
C N Q S T V
H K R
F W Y
D E
H W

six groups of similar amino acids within which amino acids can often be substituted

All life appears to have originated a few billion years ago from a single ancestor. Thus at some point in the past, any two living species shared the same ancestor. (The last common ancestor of humans and cows, for example, lived about 120 million years ago.) Many vertebrate rod rhodopsins have been sequenced, and all show the same seven transmembrane helices. The difference in sequence between any two species more or less reflects the amount of time since their last common ancestor (right).

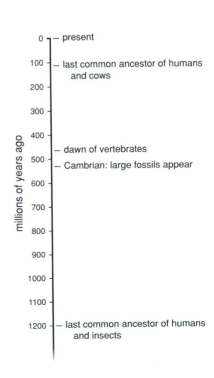

millions of years ago

0 — present

100 — last common ancestor of humans and cows

200

300

400

500 — dawn of vertebrates
— Cambrian: large fossils appear

600

700

800

900

1000

1100

1200 — last common ancestor of humans and insects

The fruit fly *Drosophila* has a compound eye, whose optical plan and neural circuitry seem totally unlike our own. Our last common ancestor with *Drosophila* lived about 1200 million years ago. Yet *Drosophila* has two types of rhodopsin, each with seven transmembrane helices. Each of these rhodopsins has an amino acid sequence similar to that of human rod rhodopsin, as illustrated by the following comparison with one of them:

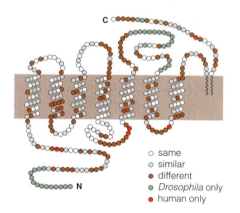

○ same
◎ similar
● different
● *Drosophila* only
● human only

human rod and *Drosophila* rhodopsins

The difference is comparable to that between our own rod and S cone rhodopsins (page 221), suggesting that the origin of the differences between the genes that code for these two rhodopsin types is also ancient.

Point mutations in rod rhodopsin can lead to retinitis pigmentosa

As discussed earlier (page 27), *retinitis pigmentosa* is a collection of genetically inherited diseases whose first signs are night blindness and a loss of peripheral vision. These diseases are progressive and lead to a degeneration of the photoreceptors and the adjacent retinal pigment epithelium. Some of these diseases are due to an inherited mutation in the gene that codes for the protein sequence of rod rhodopsin.

The cells of the human body contain 23 pairs of **autosomal** (nonsex) chromosomes; one of the pair is inherited from the mother and the other from the father. Each pair has been assigned a number; the gene for rod rhodopsin is located on chromosome 8. Because autosomal chromosomes come in pairs, there are two genes that code for rod rhodopsin. Only rod cells activate this pair of genes, and each is used by the cellular machinery to manufacture rhodopsin molecules. Because the two genes are normally identical, the rhodopsin molecules produced by transcribing the maternal gene are the same as those produced via the paternal gene.

If there is a mutation in either gene that results in an altered sequence of amino acids along the chain, then about half the rhodopsin molecules manufactured will be altered. Many types of mutations are possible, including deletions or additions of one or more amino acids. The most common type of mutation associated with retinitis pigmentosa is a substitution of one amino acid for another along the chain, which is referred to as a **point mutation**. Within the population there are probably a number of such point mutations in which an amino acid has been replaced by a similar one with-

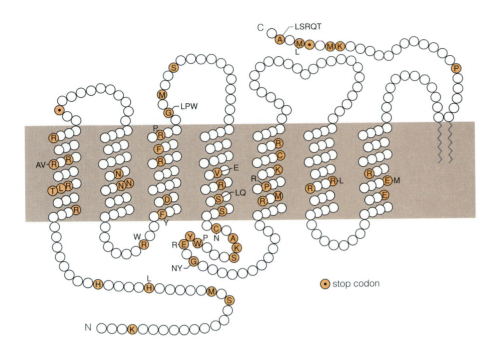

point mutations of rod rhodopsin that lead to retinitis pigmentosa

out producing any noticeable effects. But other substitutions in one of the two genes can lead to retinitis pigmentosa and eventual blindness.

The first report of a link between a point mutation in rod rhodopsin and retinitis pigmentosa was published in 1990. As of this writing, some 88 different point mutations have been linked to retinitis pigmentosa. These mutations are summarized in the diagram at the top of the page. Each colored circle identifies a site along the chain at which an amino acid substitution has been found. The letter within the circle identifies the substituted amino acid. At some of these sites, two or more different substitutions can produce retinitis pigmentosa; these are indicated by the letter or letters placed to the side. Two of the sites—marked with the symbol "●" and labeled **stop codon**—indicate mutations that cause the transcription of the gene for the amino acid chain to be prematurely terminated. In addition to these mutations, nine different deletions and/or insertions of amino acids along the chain have thus far been linked to retinitis pigmentosa.

It is not at all clear why any of these mutations should lead to the destruction of the rods and the adjacent retinal pigment epithelium. After all, half of the rhodopsin molecules in each rod are normal. Somehow, in ways that are still not understood, the mutant rhodopsin molecules have a toxic effect upon the rods. In a sense, our ignorance of these mechanisms is not surprising, because while the main events in phototransduction are now known, the maintenance and regulatory aspects of photoreceptor function remain poorly understood.

There is preliminary evidence that mutations in some of the other proteins that are involved in the biochemical cascade can result in retinitis pigmentosa, and it is clear that there is much more to be learned about the causes of these diseases. Some of this knowledge may come from a seemingly unlikely source. Mutations to some of the amino acid sites in *Drosophila* that correspond to those in humans that cause retinitis pigmentosa likewise lead to age-dependent degeneration of the photoreceptors of this fly.

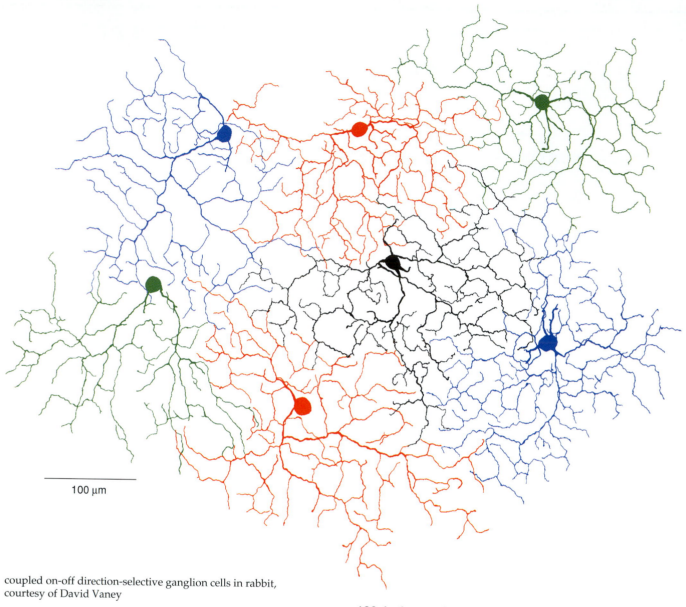

coupled on-off direction-selective ganglion cells in rabbit,
courtesy of David Vaney

9

Retinal organization

This chapter takes a closer look at some of the general features of retinal organization. It begins with a discussion of what constitutes a description of retinal organization. Chemical substances (neuromodulators) that modify this organization are then discussed.

In addition to electrical coupling between horizontal cells of the same type, there are a variety of other couplings within the retina; some are between cells of the same type, but there are other couplings between different neural types. In all vertebrates there is a decline in the spatial densities of most cell types with increasing retinal eccentricity, and this is particularly true for mammals. This decline is more or less matched by an increase in the sizes of the dendritic fields of these cells, and these variations appear primarily to be due to differential retinal growth during development. The development of the fovea shows a more complex developmental sequence.

The inner synaptic layer shows at least three different forms of anatomical stratification that reflect broad functional differences in the types of ganglion cells whose dendrites ramify within the different strata.

Is there a theory of retinal structure and function?

The rate at which new findings about the structure and function of the retina are revealed has been increasing for some time, and one can't help but wonder where all of this is heading. There will come a time, possibly not too distant, when all the cell types in the retina and their connections will be known. At that point, the investigation of the functional properties of this circuitry will have entered a new stage of refinement. Many other aspects of the retina, such as its development and the various roles played by different regulatory genes within each cell type, may still not be well understood. But we will no longer be able to avoid the question of what constitutes an understanding of the retina and how it can best be explained. When all the details are put aside, what key features of retinal structure and function will emerge as most significant to this understanding?

In her book *Neurophilosophy* (1986), Patricia Churchland, in discussing theories of brain function, asks:

> What is available by way of theory? Are there theories that have real explanatory power, are testable, and begin to make sense of how the molar effects result from the known neuronal structure? Less demandingly, are there theoretical approaches that look as though they will lead to fully fledged theories? . . .
>
> . . . flowcharts describing projection paths in vertebrate nervous systems are sometimes characterized as theories. Insofar as they are theories, they are typically theories of anatomical connections, sometimes with a highly schematic complement of physiological connections. Although they may suggest a rough description of what happens at each stage, they do not really explain the processes such that from a given kind of input, a given kind of output results. For example, the circuit diagram for the cerebellum is sometimes taught as though it were a theory of how the cerebellum coordinates movement, but in reality it is no such thing. . . .
>
> . . . Circuit diagrams often represent a huge experimental investment, and they are absolutely essential in coming to understand the brain's functional properties, but theories of brain function they are not.

She has a point. No matter how detailed and complete our emerging description of retinal circuitry becomes, this description is not in itself a theory. A theory is a system of rules and assumptions that accounts for current findings and predicts others. Is there a theory of the retina that awaits discovery? I think not, and I question the utility of all-encompassing notions of this sort.

Over the last 20 years, Sydney Brenner and colleagues have described the entire nervous system of a 1 mm long nematode roundworm named *Caenorhabditis elegans*. Unlike vertebrates, this animal develops according to a fixed plan that produces an adult with a fixed number of cells—exactly 959—including neurons that have a fixed set of connections. *C. elegans* contains 302 nerve cells that are linked together by some 8000 connections. The investigators also traced the development of this organism from embryo to adult on a cell-by-cell basis. In the process, they determined the *entire cell lineage sequence of cell division* that generates all of the neurons. Thus we now have the entire wiring diagram for a complete nervous system and a complete developmental map of the cells that compose it. This information does not constitute a complete reductional description of the animal; for example, the functional properties of the synapses remain poorly understood. But we have enough information to ask what generalizations can be made, what unifying principles emerge. If a theory in neuroscience is worth anything, it should be able to simplify the description of a neural circuit. But, as Brenner put it, "There appears to be no simpler description of the lineage map or the neural circuit than the thing itself."

The interaction of any species with its environment is complex, diverse, and multifaceted, and so is the interaction of its visual system and retina with this environment. At this level of analysis, we can make broad generalizations about the function of a particular feature ("it improves survival"), but a robust and falsifiable theory seems most unlikely. In order to get anywhere, it is thus necessary to narrow our focus. If we do so, then the standard scientific method of devising, discriminating, and testing between multiple hypotheses would seem to be the most fruitful approach. The process of gaining an understanding of the retina seems a lot like learning about history, computers, gardening, wood, people, or biology in general: incremental, with a few broad and tenuous themes, a mass of detail, and a variety of exceptions that prove each rule.

Neural interactions

One neuron can influence another either by releasing a chemical substance or by means of intracellular communication via gap junctions. The rudiments of these interactions were summarized in NEURONS (page 99). Having considered specific examples of each in previous chapters, we are in a position to take a broader look, beginning with the molecules released by one neuron that influence another.

Chemical messengers

Consider the chemical synapse between a photoreceptor and a bipolar cell. A decrease in the rate of photon catch depolarizes the transmembrane potential of the photoreceptor, and this causes an increase in the rate of glutamate release. The effect of this increase depends upon the nature of the bipolar cell. Off-bipolar cells have ionotropic glutamate receptors that cause them to depolarize in response to this increase in glutamate concentration, whereas on-bipolar cells have metabotropic receptors that cause them to hyperpolarize. It is only a slight abstraction to view the role of glutamate as that of a **chemical messenger**. Since the two bipolar cell types respond in opposite ways, it is clear that the message is not a directive to the postsynaptic cell (depolarize!); rather, it is information about some change that has taken place in the presynaptic cell. The message is not glutamate molecules per se; rather, it is the *change* in glutamate concentration.

The nervous system contains a variety of chemical messengers. Some of them, such as glycine, GABA, and acetylcholine, act at chemical synapses in a manner similar to glutamate: a change in their rate of release by the presynaptic cell directly or indirectly opens or closes ionic channels in the postsynaptic cell and thereby causes its transmembrane potential to change. The term **neurotransmitter** is reserved for these chemical substances, which are concentrated in synaptic vesicles. Neurons can also contain larger **secretory vesicles**, which concentrate small proteins known as **neuropeptides**. Whereas synaptic vesicles appear to concentrate only a single type of neurotransmitter, secretory vesicles may contain different neuropeptides. A number of different neuropeptides have been found in the retina, but their roles in the retina are unknown, so they are not further considered here.

Some neurons are not presynaptic to any other particular neuron. Instead, they release chemical substances that diffuse within the extracellular space between neurons, so as to reach all of the neurons within the region of diffusion. These chemical messengers, termed **neuromodulators,** tend to be longer-lived and produce longer-term changes in cells that have receptors to them. Two of them, **dopamine** and **serotonin**, are found within certain amacrine cells in the retina. The functional role of the serotonergic amacrine cells is not known. The dopaminergic amacrine cells are described later in CELL TYPES.

Cell coupling

Thus far, we have seen two forms of cell coupling within the retina. Horizontal cells of the same type are electrically coupled by means of gap junctions; such coupling by cells of the same type is termed **homotypic** (Greek *homos* = same + *tupos* = impression). The coupling between cones and rods (page 45) and the coupling between AII amacrine cells and on-cone bipolar cells (page 131) are examples of **heterotypic** coupling (Greek *heteros* = other). This terminology does not easily encompass interphotoreceptor coupling between cone types, in that the coupling is heterotypic at the level of photoreceptor type but homotypic at the level of cones as a group.

Until recently, these were the only known examples of cell coupling within the retina (see the Box *CONTINUITY AND CONTIGUITY*). But the use of small tracer molecules able to pass through gap junctions with pores smaller than those between horizontal cells has revealed a variety of couplings between retinal cells, both homotypic and heterotypic, as discussed later. The only couplings for which we have any understanding of their functional role are homotypic couplings of horizontal cells and heterotypic coupling of AII amacrine cells. Their functional roles depend upon electrical coupling between cells. But to the degree that small molecules can pass between certain cells, there exists the possibility of chemical interactions within a cell type or between specific cell types.

Disposition of cells

To a first approximation, all retinal cell types are found throughout the spatial extent of the primate retina. The only known exceptions occur at the center of the fovea, which lacks rods and S cones as well as the other cell types (e.g., rod and S cone bipolar cells) that are specific to the pathways of those photoreceptor types. Immediately outside the central fovea, the spatial density of each cell type falls with increasing retinal eccentricity. The rods are the major exceptions, since their spatial density doesn't peak until an eccentricity of about 6 mm (left). Beyond this distance, which corresponds to a visual angle of about 20°, the changes in photoreceptor densities are less pronounced. (If you spread your fingers apart, and hold your hand at arm's length, the distance between the tips of your thumb and little finger

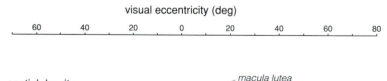

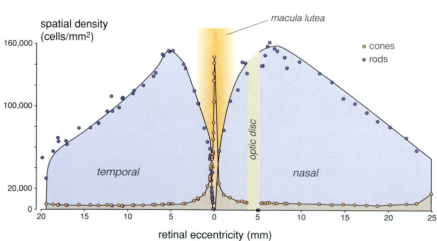

after Østerberg, 1935, as modified by Rodieck, 1988

Continuity and contiguity

About a hundred years ago there was a great debate as to how neurons were interconnected. Was it by means of *continuity*—direct intercellular connections that allow intracellular material to flow (or at least diffuse) between the cells—or was it by means of close contacts that somehow allowed signals to pass between cells at their sites of *contiguity*? This was an important debate within neurobiology in the late nineteenth century, for it had a strong influence on how one thought about the way the nervous system might work.

Those who held for continuity, known as *reticularists*, looked for evidence to support their view, and found it in the retina. A German anatomist, Philip Ehrlich, had found that a dye known as methylene blue, when applied to living tissue, selectively and capriciously stained certain neurons, allowing their morphology to be revealed. It is still not understood how this stain acts. Alexander Dogiel, working in Tomsk, Siberia, successfully applied this stain to human retinas, remarking, somewhat chillingly, that "a

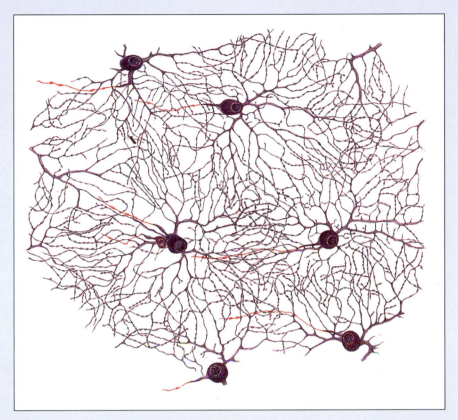

human parasol ganglion cells

from Dogiel, 1891

large number of adequately fresh human retinas were recently placed at my disposal." As this drawing of parasol ganglion cells shows, the stain revealed that the tips of some dendritic processes of some neurons merge with those of others, creating a continuous network. Dogiel stressed that cells of the same type had processes that ramified at the same level in the retina, allowing such contacts to form. These findings seemed to support the reticularists' position.

Those who held for contiguity had as their champion a Spaniard named Santiago Ramón y Cajal. Looking for evidence to support his view, Cajal likewise seemed to find it in the retina. He used another selective stain, which had been discovered by the Italian anatomist Camillo Golgi, to describe the different retinal cell types in fishes, amphibians, reptiles, birds, and mammals. In 1893 he published his findings as a monograph, in which he concluded that all retinal cells are discrete and that "the transmission of neural signals takes place by means of articulations of contacts between the processes of the different retinal cells." A generalized version of this statement became known as the *neuron doctrine*.

Today we know that both forms of neural interactions are present in most neural tissue, including the retina. Whereas gap junctions are necessarily sign-conserving, chemical synapses can be of either type; furthermore, chemical synapses are unidirectional and can *amplify* in the sense that the change in transmembrane potential in the postsynaptic cell can be larger than that in the presynaptic cell. One could build a computer with parts that showed the properties of chemical synapses, but would be hard pressed if the parts could show only the properties of gap junctions. Still, under the appropriate conditions, gap junctions provide a means of neural communication that can be fast and has no specific metabolic requirements. In addition, gap junctions can be opened or closed by neuromodulators, as discussed in CELL TYPES.

is about 20°.) For most of the other cell classes, the decrease in spatial density is partly or wholly compensated for by an increase in the sizes of their dendritic fields.

Coverage

The larger the dendritic field of a cell, the more cells of other types it can potentially receive from, directly or indirectly. If the dendritic fields of cells of the same type overlap, then more than one of them can receive from the same presynaptic cell. The quantitative aspects of retinal circuitry are constrained by these factors.

While it is obvious that some cells have larger dendritic fields than others, it is difficult to devise a good measure to quantify this fact. A common means of quantifying a dendritic field is to connect the tips of the distal dendrites together so as to form a convex polygon:

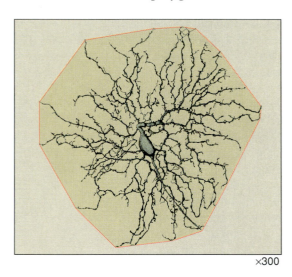

×300

parasol ganglion cell circumscribed by convex polygon

after Watanabe and Rodieck, 1989

One measure of the size of the dendritic field is the area of this enclosing polygon. Notice that for this measure to be consistent, the polygon must be convex, because there is no effective end point to including the tips of the interior dendrites, and the area shrinks as each is added. If you have an interest in geometry, you will recognize that the underlying problem with any such measure has to do with estimating the two-dimensional size of something composed of a finite number of one-dimensional parts.

There is a useful quantity associated with measures based upon area that is termed the **coverage factor**. Assume that the area of the dendritic field of a certain cell is measured in square millimeters, and that the spatial density of the surrounding cells of this type is measured in the number per square millimeter. If the area of some feature of the cell (e.g., the dendritic field; the cross section of a photoreceptor inner segment) is multiplied by the spatial density, then the square millimeters cancel out, leaving a dimensionless number, which is the coverage factor:

$$\text{coverage factor} = \text{area} \times \text{spatial density}$$

What this means is best seen by example. Assume that a certain cell type extends over a square area 0.1 mm on each side, and that nine of these cells are distributed across the retina, as shown at left. The area of each cell is 0.01 mm^2, and the portion of the retina considered has an area of 0.81 mm^2, giving a spatial density of 11.1/mm^2 and a coverage factor of 0.111 (i.e., 1/9).

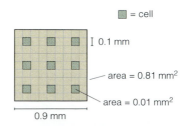

☐ = cell

0.1 mm

area = 0.81 mm^2

area = 0.01 mm^2

0.9 mm

$$\text{spatial density} = \frac{9}{0.81 \ \text{mm}^2} = 11.1/\text{mm}^2$$

$$\text{coverage} = 11.1/\text{mm}^2 \times 0.01 \ \text{mm}^2 = 0.111$$

schematic coverage of retina by cell type

As discussed below, there is great variation in the value of the coverage factor among different cell types at a given point in the retina, ranging from less than 0.1 (e.g., S cones) to over 700 (A1 amacrine cells). By comparison, the variation in coverage factor as a function of retinal eccentricity for a given cell type is typically small because a decrease in spatial density is partly balanced by an increase in dendritic field size. A coverage factor of less than 1 indicates incomplete coverage, a coverage factor between 1 and 3 *may* indicate overlap, and larger coverage factors generally guarantee overlap. It is often useful to estimate the average number of cells of some type that are found within the dendritic field of *another* group of cells, such as the number of cones within the dendritic field of a bipolar cell. This can be done in the same manner, as shown in the diagram at right.

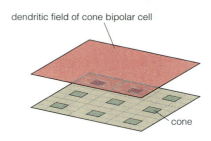

coverage = cone spatial density × dendritic field area

coverage of cones by dendritic field

Another measure of dendritic field size is diameter. This is usually determined by calculating the diameter of a circle whose area equals that of the convex polygon:

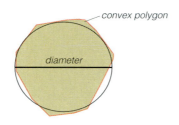

dendritic field diameter

This measure is useful when attempting to relate dendritic field size to different forms of visual acuity as determined psychophysically, and is the one mainly used in this book.

Tiling and territorial domains

When it is possible to stain the dendrites of all the cells of a certain type, one often finds that the population **tiles** the entire retina in an irregular manner and without significant overlap. This gives each cell a **territorial domain** within the retina with respect to others of the same type.

A good example of how cells of the same type combine to produce a uniform pattern of dendritic arbors comes from a study of the rabbit retina, as is seen in the illustration of eight bistratified ganglion cells, distinguished by color (shown on the next page). The dendritic field of each cell ramifies at two different levels in the inner synaptic layer. The processes that ramify in the on-sublayer are shown in the upper portion of the illustration, and the processes that ramify in the off-sublayer are shown below. These ganglion cells all belong to a single cell type within a group known as on-off direction-selective cells. As discussed in LOOKING, they play a role in the control of eye movements, but that is not our immediate concern. Cells of this type are interconnected by means of gap junctions, just as horizontal cells are, forming an interconnected array that extends throughout the retina.

The cell drawn in red received an injection of a tracer substance, which spread to many other cells in the array. The seven other cells shown were sufficiently well labeled that their entire dendritic arbors could be drawn. Notice the large variability in the dendritic morphologies of the individual cells. In particular, the cell drawn in red shows a single field in the on-sublayer, but four separate domains in the off-sublayer. In the absence of the

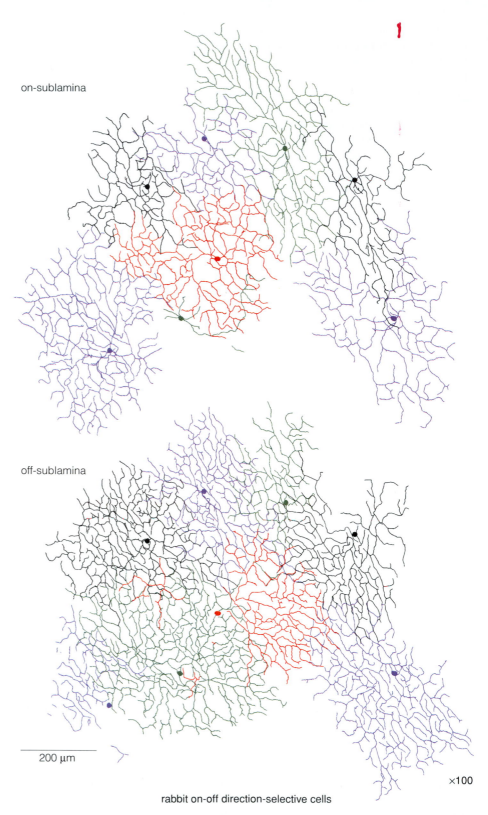

on-sublamina

off-sublamina

200 µm

×100

rabbit on-off direction-selective cells

source: Vaney, 1994a

other drawn cells, one might be tempted to speculate as to the functional implications of such a peculiar pattern. Likewise, the green cell to the lower left shows broad stratification in the off-sublayer, but hardly any in the on-sublayer.

But if we ignore the colors and the cell bodies and focus on the dendritic processes in either sublayer, we see that they cover that sublayer in a uniform manner, with relatively little overlap. In this manner, the array of dendritic processes of all the cells of this type shows far more uniformity than do the dendritic processes of any individual cell.

The *effective* coverage factor of the dendritic processes in either sublayer is close to 1. However, the *calculated* coverage factor, based upon the processes of any one cell, would be larger (e.g., consider a convex polygon drawn about the processes of the red cell in the off-sublayer). There is thus an inherent bias in this method that tends to overestimate calculated coverage factors based upon the areas of single labeled cells, which has proved to be difficult to eliminate. An effective coverage factor near 1 observed in the array may result in calculated coverage factors of 2 or even 3 based upon the fields of single cells.

The nasal quadrant of the retina has a higher density of cells

As shown in the diagram below, the spatial density of retinal cells is not radially distributed around the fovea. Outside the foveal region, the spatial density of cells is higher in the nasal quadrant than in other regions at the same retinal eccentricity. This feature has been found in all primates thus far investigated, as well as in many other mammals. Thus a region of visual space to the right of your direction of gaze is coded by more ganglion cells in the nasal portion of your right retina than in the corresponding temporal portion of your left retina:

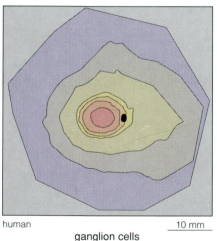

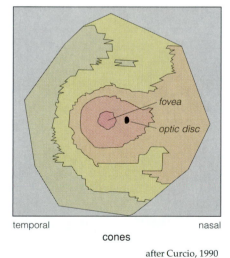

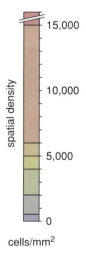

human   10 mm   temporal   nasal
ganglion cells   cones   cells/mm²

after Curcio, 1990

The reason, if any, for this asymmetry is not understood, but it has some practical consequences, since the sizes of the dendritic fields of cells of a given type depend not so much upon their retinal eccentricity per se as upon their spatial density. This is illustrated in the scatter diagram on the next page, in which midget and parasol ganglion cells from the nasal quadrant are distinguished from others. Away from the fovea, the dendritic fields of midget ganglion cells in the nasal quadrant are smaller than those of cells in the other quadrants, because the spatial density of midget ganglion cells is higher in the nasal quadrant. One means of dealing with this

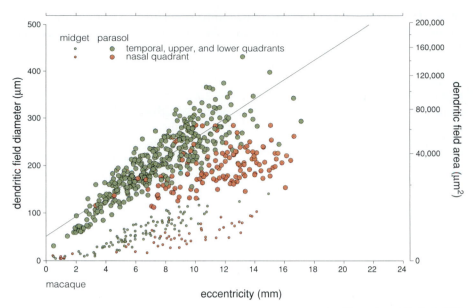

after Watanabe and Rodieck, 1989

complication is to use an alternative measure of eccentricity, termed **equivalent eccentricity**, which plots cells in regions with the same spatial density at the same position along the horizontal axis (see the Box *EQUIVALENT ECCENTRICITY* for more information). When the data points in the above diagram are replotted using this measure, the nasal cluster and the cluster from the rest of the retina coincide:

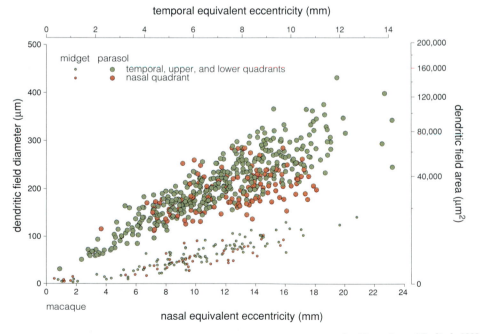

after Watanabe and Rodieck, 1989

Differential retinal growth and cell birth dates shape spatial density

As we have seen, the spatial density of cells can vary considerably in moving from the center of the retina to the periphery. For example, the spatial density of all ganglion cells taken together varies by a factor of 30. By comparison, the spatial density of all photoreceptor types is relatively constant.

Equivalent eccentricity

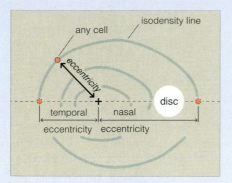

equivalent eccentricity

after Watanabe and Rodieck, 1989

The *retinal eccentricity* of a cell is the distance between it and the center of the fovea. An *isodensity line* can be drawn around the fovea along which the density of similar cells is constant. To the degree that the dendritic field sizes of cells of the same type depend upon the local spatial density of cells of that type, all such cells on or near this isodensity line should have about the same size dendritic fields, and thereby form the tightest cluster in a scatter diagram.

A horizontal dashed line drawn through the center of the fovea intersects an isodensity line at two points. The nasal equivalent eccentricity of any cell on that isodensity line is the horizontal distance from the fovea to the point on the right; likewise, the temporal equivalent eccentricity is the distance from the fovea to the point on the left at which the isodensity line intersects the horizontal line through the fovea. Either of these equivalent eccentricities can be used when plotting the effective distances of cells from the fovea (as can any straight line from the fovea). In macaque retinas, the pattern of isodensity lines is such that the ratio of the temporal to the nasal distance is approximately constant, with a value of 0.61. This allows both nasal and temporal eccentricities to be plotted on the same diagram.

Ideally, the isodensity lines should be based upon the spatial densities of cells of the same type. In practice, the densities that are available (e.g., all ganglion cells) often have to suffice.

Much of this variation in spatial density appears to be due to differential retinal growth. During development, different cell types are *born* at different times. Let us assume for the moment that all of the cells of a given type are born at the same time, and are uniformly distributed across the retina, as shown schematically in this illustration:

uniform distribution of some cell type at birth

For simplicity, the retina is represented as a flat disc rather than as a hemisphere, but it is useful to think of it as covering half the surface of a balloon. If the retina grows uniformly until it has doubled in width, then the number of cells will still be the same, and they will still be uniformly distributed, although their spatial density will have decreased by a factor of 4 (top right). But if the peripheral portion of the retina grows faster than the central portion, the cells will no longer be uniformly distributed (bottom right).

It is the latter growth pattern that actually occurs in primates. In monkeys, the distance between the fovea and the optic disc is 3.8 mm in both the two-month embryo and the adult, although the area of the adult retina is some twelve times greater than that of the embryonic retina at this stage. If the retina first grows in the horizontal direction, certain cells are then born, and differential growth resumes in the vertical direction, a visual streak

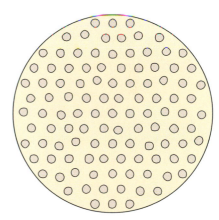

cell distribution after uniform growth

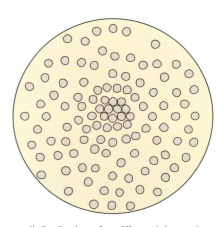

cell distribution after differential growth

results. Cells that are born late, such as rods, tend to be the most uniformly distributed:

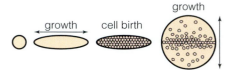

formation of visual streak by differential growth

This description leaves out a lot of detail and complexities in order to illustrate how differential retinal growth, coupled with different birth dates for different cell types, can sculpt the spatial density of each cell type across the retina. Other mechanisms may also play a role in creating these patterns.

Formation of the fovea produces radial displacement in cell connections

This schematic diagram shows the layers of the retina around the fovea in cross section, together with an indication of the connections between cones, bipolar cells, and ganglion cells:

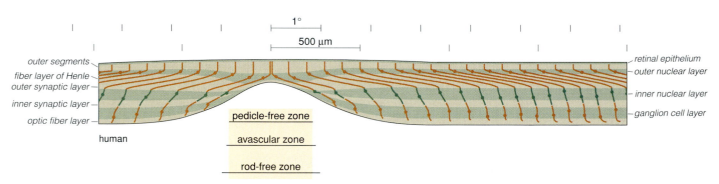

retinal layers and pedicle-free zone after Polyak, 1941;
pedicle and ganglion cell displacements after Schein, 1988

This pattern is formed by a complex sequence of cellular migrations during development; this sequence concentrates the cone inner and outer segments and causes a radial migration of the cone pedicles as well as the cells of the inner retina. The result is a circular zone termed the **foveola** ("little fovea"), which is about 400 μm in diameter and free of overlying blood vessels (avascular zone). This distance corresponds to a visual angle of 1.4°, which is about the width of the tip of your little finger viewed at arm's length. The foveola contains about 15,000 cones with a peak spatial density of about $200,000/mm^2$, which drops to about $80,000/mm^2$ at the edge. These are average values; there is considerable variation between individuals.

If you look steadily at a uniform bright area, you will be able to see bright moving points of light that appear suddenly, move across your field of view for a degree or so, and then disappear. They tend to follow each other along the same paths, but are never observed within about 0.8° of the center of the fovea. Capillaries are only wide enough to permit a single row of blood cells to pass through them; the bright spots are due to either a break in a row of red blood cells or a circulating white blood cell. The absence of retinal capillaries within the foveola presumably serves to avoid this distraction.

There are no cone pedicles within the foveola, perhaps because of the absence of blood vessels there. Bird retinas lack retinal capillaries, and their foveas show no displacement of cone pedicles or other retinal cells. The pedicles of the central cones are radially displaced by about 250 μm in humans, and by about 150 μm in macaques. The following graph shows the radial displacement of the pedicle of a cone in macaques with respect to the cone's inner segment, plotted as a function of the retinal eccentricity of the inner segment:

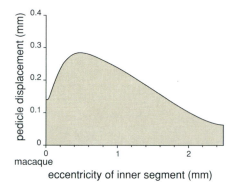

source: Schein, 1988

Notice that the radial displacement of the pedicle grows with increasing retinal eccentricity, reaches a peak, and then more slowly declines. The cross section on page 206 shows the corresponding radial displacement for human cones.

This displacement is the result of an interesting packing problem. The inner segments of the foveal cones have diameters as thin as 2.4 μm, but the minimum diameter of a cone pedicle is about 7.4 μm. Since the arrays of inner segments and of pedicles each form a single packed layer, each successive ring of cone inner segments requires a wider ring of cone pedicles, as suggested in the schematic diagram at right. The increase in radial displacement continues until cone density falls sufficiently to allow space for the pedicles.

The thickened zone of cone processes below the layer of cone nuclei is called the **fiber layer of Henle**, and extends for 3 or 4 millimeters around the center of the fovea. There is an additional but smaller displacement of bipolar cells and their connections, as seen in the human cross section and the following graph for the macaque where the bipolar cell displacement corresponds to the pedicle to ganglion cell displacement:

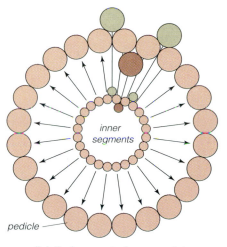

radial displacement of cone pedicles

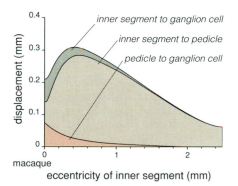

source: Schein, 1988

The main practical consequence of these special features of the fovea is that the locations and spatial densities of cells in the inner portion of the retina need to be corrected for their radial displacements if they are to be compared with the array of cone inner segments.

The inner synaptic layer
shows different forms of stratification

This diagram shows some generalizations about functional stratification within the inner synaptic layer that appear to apply to all vertebrate classes:

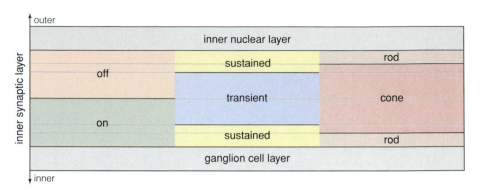

The left portion of the diagram shows the division of the inner synaptic layer into the on-sublayer and the off-sublayer, and reflects the connections made by different types of bipolars, as previously described. The right portion of the diagram reflects the fact that the synaptic contacts of cone bipolar cells lie mainly in the middle of the inner synaptic layer, rod bipolar cells are presynaptic to AII amacrine cells in the innermost portion of this layer, and the presynaptic contacts made by AII amacrine onto off-cone bipolar cells lie mainly in the outermost portion. The middle portion of this diagram refers to the properties of ganglion cells. In response to a light turned on or turned off, some ganglion cells—such as parasol ganglion cells—respond mainly to the *change* in light intensity, and are said to respond *transiently*; their dendritic fields lie mainly in the middle portion of the inner synaptic layer. Other ganglion cells—such as midget ganglion cells—respond by means of a sustained change in their maintained firing rate; their dendritic fields lie either in the innermost portion of the inner synaptic layer, or the outermost portion. For example, the dendrites of on-parasol ganglion cells ramify in the region of overlap between the *on* portion and the *transient* portion (left and middle panels). There these parasol cells connect to a subgroup of diffuse cone bipolar cells, whose dendrites ramify over most of the central portion of the inner synaptic layer (right panel). The rod input to these cone bipolar cells comes from the axonal arbors of rod bipolar cells, which ramify in the inner rod zone (right panel). These processes are presynaptic to AII amacrine cells, whose lobular appendages ramify in the outer rod zone (see diagram on page 131).

The relative positions of the boundaries between these layers vary across species, and within particular animal groups there are both further refinements and exceptions. In any case, these generalizations give us a reasonable place to start.

Synapses between retinal cells may follow simple rules

There is a hypothesis about retinal organization that does not appear to be in conflict with any known finding, but which considerably simplifies the question of the manner in which the retina is synaptically organized. It states that any given type of retinal cell makes synapses only with certain types of retinal cells, but does not distinguish among the processes of cells of the same type. The wiring of the retina would thus depend entirely on the disposition of the dendritic and axonal processes of these cells and on the general rules by which they form synaptic contacts. These rules may include spatial attributes of the cell itself: for example, only certain contacts may be allowed on the cell body or on certain regions of dendrites.

There appear to be a few exceptions to this rule. For example, a midget ganglion cell type in the foveal region appears to receive from only a single midget bipolar cell, yet the processes of different midget bipolar cells in adults tend to lie close together, and presumably did so as well during development when these contacts were formed. But to the degree that this rule is true, it serves to draw attention to the exceptions.

Retinal organization has a number of other general features, and most of them will come up at some point in the remainder of this book. But we are now well poised to take a closer look at some of the different cell types of the retina, starting with the photoreceptors.

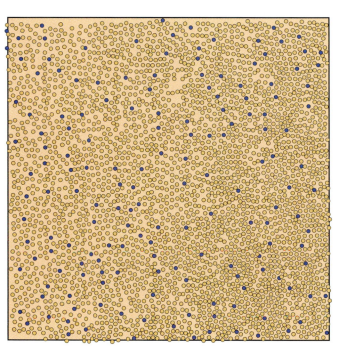

distribution of S cones just temporal to the center of the fovea

after Curcio et al., 1991

10

Photoreceptor attributes

Photoreceptors are highly specialized sensory neurons in which the different cellular components are stratified along the length of the cell. New rhodopsin molecules are created and incorporated into discs at the base of the rod outer segments under the control of a biological clock contained within the photoreceptor. S cones, common to almost all mammals, show a number of special features, most of which are a consequence of the chromatic aberration of the eye at high frequencies. The other mammalian cone type (LM) diverged in Old World primates, to produce L and M cones; red–green color vision is based upon a neural comparison of the photon catches of these two cone types. In some New World monkeys this form of color vision is based upon a different plan, and suggests a number of possibilities as to how our ancestors may have evolved this trait.

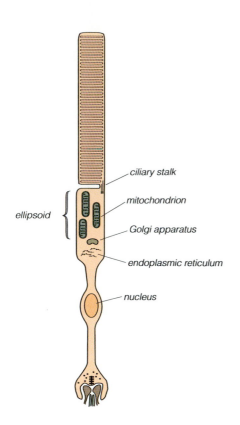

ciliary stalk

mitochondrion

ellipsoid

Golgi apparatus

endoplasmic reticulum

nucleus

components of the inner segment

Photoreceptor inner segments contain the metabolic machinery

Whereas the outer segment of a photoreceptor contains all of the components necessary for the conversion of light into an electrical signal, the inner segment contains all of the components necessary for the metabolism of the cell (see diagram at left). The outer portion of the inner segment is packed with mitochondria, which form a dense mass termed the **ellipsoid**. This dense packing of membranes gives the ellipsoid a higher optical index of refraction than the surrounding cytoplasm, and thereby provides the means by which the inner segment funnels arriving photons into the outer segment. As in all cells, the mitochondria supply the high-energy ATP molecules (see *NUCLEOTIDES*, page 164) that fuel many of the energy-requiring processes that take place in the photoreceptors. The major energy demands come from the removal of Na ions from the cytoplasm and the synthesis of new rhodopsin molecules. The Na ions are removed by ionic pumps located on the plasma membrane of the inner segment. The energy supplied by one ATP molecule is sufficient to pump three Na ions out of a cell, and two K ions in:

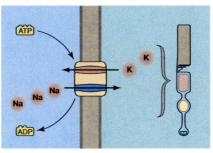

Na/K pump

The inner portion of the inner segment contains the **Golgi apparatus** and the **endoplasmic reticulum**, where proteins are synthesized. Each rhodopsin molecule is composed of 348 amino acids that are linked together in a single long chain. The creation of each link in the chain requires the energy supplied by one ATP molecule.

Photoreceptor outer segments are continually renewed

Most of the components of metabolically active cells are continually being created and destroyed. The specialized nature of rod outer segments allows this process to be observed by means of radioactive labeling techniques that distinguish newly synthesized proteins. The following description deals with the creation and fate of rhodopsin molecules, but applies to other proteins found on the disc as well.

The gene for the rhodopsin molecule is transcribed to messenger RNA in the nucleus of the photoreceptor. The RNA migrates to the endoplasmic reticulum, located at the base of the inner segment, as shown at the top left of the next page. There the genetic code for rhodopsin is translated into a chain of amino acids to form the protein portion of the rhodopsin molecules, which are represented as black dots. The endoplasmic reticulum and the Golgi apparatus incorporate the rhodopsin molecules into the membranes of small vesicles, which migrate to the ciliary stalk between the inner and outer segment, as seen in the second photoreceptor in the diagram

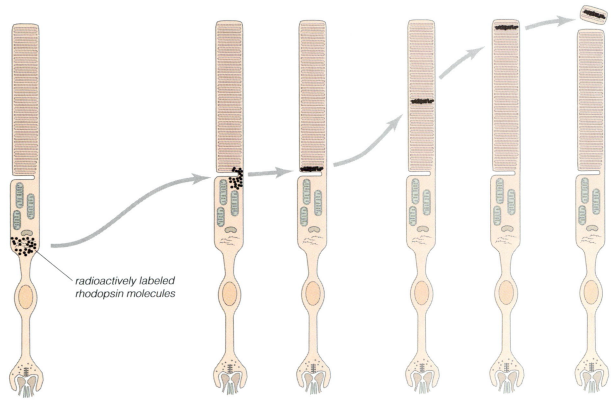

radioactively labeled rhodopsin molecules

after Young, 1970

shown above. The vesicles pass into the outer segment and merge with the plasma membrane of the cell (third drawing above). As new discs are created at the base of the outer segment, the discs containing the group of labeled rhodopsin molecules are displaced outward until they reach the tip of the outer segment. Packets of discs shed from the outer segment are taken up as phagosomes by the cells of the retinal epithelium, where they are digested.

The formation of new discs from the expanding plasma membrane is a complicated topological maneuver, as summarized schematically in the illustration at right. The drawings in the left column present a surface view. Those on the right present a cross section; the plane of section is indicated by the dotted lines in the left column. Briefly, new membrane is added to the plasma membrane to form an *evagination*. This is followed by the incorporation of new membrane into the sides formed by successive evaginations, which progressively move around the perimeter of the rod until they meet at a point opposite the ciliary stalk so as to create an invagination. There they join together, pinching off the flattened invagination, which becomes an internalized disc. The discs undergo no further change in form, and their progressive displacement creates the cylindrical form of the rod outer segment.

The creation of new discs at the base of the outer segment is balanced by the removal of discs at its distal tip. Packets of 8 to 30 discs at a time are shed from the outer segment. Normally there is a region of free cytoplasm above the endmost discs into which the packet destined for removal curls or folds up (see top left on the next page). The free cytoplasm moves downward, and the plasma membrane proximal to the packet constricts about it, dissecting the discs and the surrounding plasma membrane from the outer segment. The packet is then enveloped by the apical processes of the retinal epithelium, drawn into its cytoplasm via a phagosome, and digested.

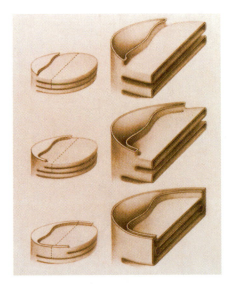

formation of rod discs

source: Steinberg et al., 1980

macaque ×26,000

disc shedding at tip of rod outer segment

source: Young 1971

The lifetime of a disc is about two weeks. Since an outer segment contains about 140 million rhodopsin molecules, each rod must synthesize about 10 million new rhodopsin molecules every day. In rods, synthesis of new rhodopsin molecules occurs just before dawn, and disc shedding occurs in the morning, after vision has shifted from rods to cones.

A similar sequence of events occurs in cones, but because the cone outer segment membrane is not compartmentalized in discs, newly synthesized membrane proteins can diffuse throughout the outer segment. In cones, synthesis of new rhodopsin molecules occurs in the late afternoon, before dusk; membrane is shed from the tips of the outer segments at about the time that vision comes to depend upon rods. Thus both rods and cones continually make rhodopsin molecules, which are eventually removed from the tips of their outer segments and digested by the retinal epithelium. Cones maintain their conical shape by means of additional infoldings along the length of the outer segment, which increase length at the expense of width, a phenomenon not seen in rod outer segments.

It is not known why there is such a rapid turnover of the membrane proteins of photoreceptor outer segments. It may be that outer segments are fragile as a result of their extreme specialization, and their renewal provides a means of preserving vision throughout life. However, this possibility does not explain why the renewal is so rapid. Alternatively, it may be that some rhodopsin molecules eventually denature in a manner that causes them to continuously activate G molecules. For rod vision, even a few such molecules per rod would result in a significant loss of sensitivity.

Photoreceptors contain a circadian clock

As we have just seen, there is a daily cycle of rhodopsin synthesis and shedding in both rods and cones. In rods, we know that this rhythm cannot be caused by the **diurnal** rhythm of light and dark, since it can continue in complete darkness. Such independent, or free-running, biological clocks are common in all forms of life and are termed **circadian** (Latin *circa* = about + *dies* = day) rhythms. By one means or another, these clocks are synchronized to the diurnal rhythm. An important feature of a clock is that it can keep time and thereby anticipate events. For example, in rods, the synthesis of new rhodopsin molecules occurs *before* dusk.

As discussed in INFORMING THE BRAIN, vertebrates have a small pair of nuclei just above the optic chiasm that generate a circadian rhythm. This rhythm affects our sleep-wakefulness cycle, temperature, hormone levels, and a number of other aspects of our physiology. This global clock is synchronized to the diurnal rhythm by means of axons of certain retinal ganglion cells that enter the nuclei via the optic chiasm and terminate within them.

The influence of circadian rhythms on rhodopsin synthesis and disc shedding in rods was originally thought to be a consequence of this global clock, perhaps through changes in hormone levels. But it turns out that vertebrate photoreceptors contain their own circadian clocks that are synchronized by light. These clocks regulate the production of an enzyme needed for the synthesis of a hormone called **melatonin**, and as a result photoreceptors synthesize and release melatonin in the dark. The synthesis of melatonin is inhibited by dopamine; conversely, the synthesis of this neuromodulator is blocked by melatonin. These interactions are discussed in CELL TYPES in the context of dopaminergic amacrine cells (page 247).

The influence of circadian rhythms on cones does not appear to have been studied yet. The shedding of discs by rods is affected both by the pho-

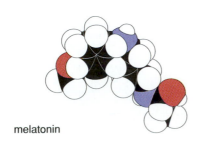

melatonin

1 nm ×30,000,000

toreceptor circadian rhythm, possibly through melatonin, and by light and darkness. Shedding by rods is blocked in continuous light, but can be induced by two hours of darkness.

The circadian clock whose mechanism is best understood is that of the fruit fly *Drosophila* (see the Box *FRUIT FLY CLOCKS*), which is also blocked by continuous light. This mechanism involves two genes, and a close homolog of one of them *(per)* has recently been identified in the human genome, suggesting that both fruit flies and humans have inherited at least some of their clock mechanisms from an ancient common ancestor.

Fruit fly clocks

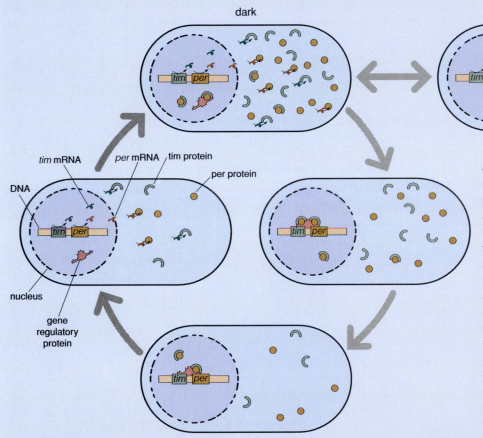

Photoreceptor cells in the eyes of fruit flies, as well as certain other fruit fly cells, contain a circadian clock. This clock has a period that is slightly longer than a day, and continues to cycle in complete darkness. Its mechanism involves two proteins named **period** (per) and **timeless** (tim) whose concentrations cycle up and down together on a daily basis. The normal sequence of events is summarized in the diagram above. (A convention adopted here is to use lowercase italics for a gene [*per*] and roman type for its protein product [per]).

Consider first the cycle on the left, which can continue in darkness. It shows four stages within a single cell. Starting with the stage shown to the left, the genes for these two proteins are both active; each gene is transcribed to pro-duce a messenger RNA (mRNA) that moves from the nucleus to the cytoplasm where it is used to synthesize one of the two proteins, per or tim. Neither of these proteins can enter the nucleus on its own. But as they accumulate in the cytoplasm (top), per and tim molecules combine with one another so as to form a per–tim complex. These complexes *can* enter the nucleus, where they bind to a gene regulatory protein so as to activate it. This activated protein then binds to the *per* and *tim* genes so as to block further production of their mRNAs (lower right). The messenger RNAs are short-lived so their concentration in the cytoplasm rapidly falls. The per–tim protein complexes are somewhat more stable, but are nevertheless short-lived, and their concentration falls over a period of hours. This reduction in the number of per-tim complexes causes them to move off of the gene regulatory protein, which is no longer able to bind to the *per* and *tim* genes (bottom). The synthesis of the per and tim mRNA is restored, and a new cycle begins (left).

The action of light, shown at the upper right, is to destroy tim proteins. By doing so, light prevents the accumulation of per–tim complexes, and thus both genes continue to be active. But when darkness comes, tim proteins accumulate, per–tim complexes are formed, which enter the nucleus, and the free-running dark cycle becomes synchronized to the diurnal rhythm of night and day.

Most studies of circadian rhythms in vertebrates have been done on frogs, fishes, or birds, mainly for methodological reasons, and it is not yet clear to what degree these findings apply to mammals generally, or to primates. On the other hand, a mammalian clock gene (*clock*) has recently been cloned in mice, circadian rhythms in melatonin synthesis can be demonstrated in cultured hamster retina, and primate cones have receptors for dopamine. Thus mammalian photoreceptors show at least some of the properties demonstrated in other vertebrates.

S cones differ from M and L cones in a number of ways

As mentioned in RETINAS (page 44), S cones constitute only about 10% of the cone population, and are absent from the center of the fovea. S cones are most sensitive to photons with frequencies at the high end of the visible spectrum. But when the eye is in focus to the frequencies to which M and L cones are most sensitive, the image is out of focus for the S cones, as a result of **chromatic aberration**.

The lower portion of the diagram at left combines data from two different studies (distinguished by the color of their data points) that show the chromatic aberration of the eye. The vertical scale shows the strength of the lens that would be needed to correct for chromatic aberration when the eye is accommodated to frequencies near the peak sensitivities of the M and L cones. Near the frequencies to which the S cones are most sensitive, a lens of about −1.3 **diopters** would be required to correct for chromatic aberration.

As Helmholtz first noted in 1866, much of the chromatic aberration of the eye can be accounted for by the **dispersion** of water. The blue curve in this diagram shows the expected chromatic aberration of the eye if it were made entirely of water:

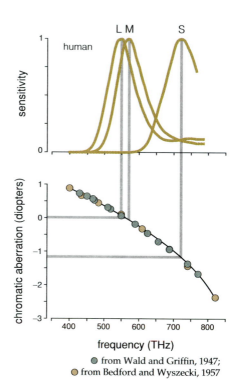

● from Wald and Griffin, 1947;
○ from Bedford and Wyszecki, 1957

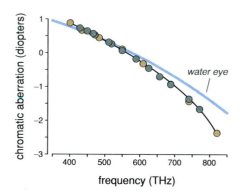

The data show a greater amount of dispersion than this, probably due to an additional contribution from proteins in the lens. The fact that photons become increasingly out of focus toward the violet end of the spectrum has a number of consequences. Each of these photons has a relatively high energy, and all of the photoreceptors are sensitive to them. As we saw in THE RAIN OF PHOTONS ONTO CONES (page 76), the pigments within the lens absorb virtually all photons in the ultraviolet portion of the spectrum, and the macular pigment absorbs most of those in the blue-violet portion.

The adaptations of the S cone population arise because the image they are sensitive to is blurred. S cone inner segments are absent from the center of the fovea, quickly rise to a peak spatial density of about 2000/mm^2, and fall to half that value within a millimeter (as shown in the diagram on the

refractive index
The power of a transparent material to bend the path of photons incident on its surface toward the perpendicular.

dispersion
A change in the refractive index of photons as a function of their frequency.

diopter
The power of a curved transparent surface to focus photons.

chromatic aberration
The change in focus produced by dispersion.

left). Expressed as a percentage of all cones, S cones are rare in the fovea, and rise to about 8% in the periphery (diagram below right):

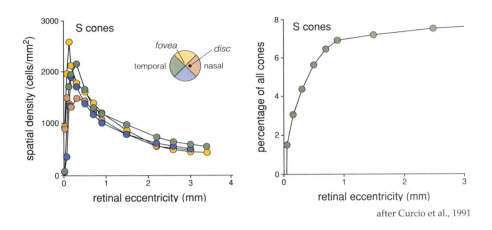

after Curcio et al., 1991

Near the fovea, S cones are distributed in a quasi-regular array that shows a relatively small increase in spatial density at smaller eccentricities compared with that of M and L cones:

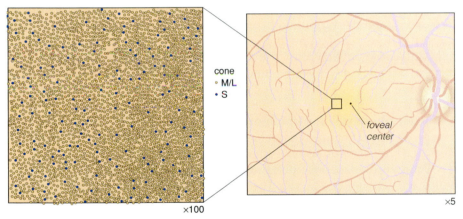

distribution of S cones just temporal to the center of the fovea

after Curcio et al., 1991

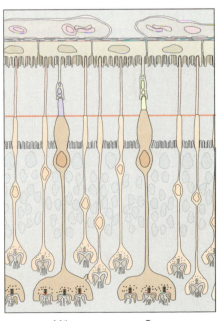

M/L   S

S cones are never seen to lie adjacent to one another, as some would if they were distributed in a random (Poisson) manner. The basis of the quasi-regular nature of their distribution is not known.

There are a few other minor morphological differences between S cones and M or L cones, the main one being that the inner segment of S cones is a little longer, as indicated by the red horizontal line in the diagram at right.

Most mammals are dichromats

Except for primates, most mammals have only two cone types, S cones and a type we will refer to as "LM cones." (In this context, "LM" refers to the cone type involved in intensity discriminations, as discussed in PHOTOMETRY.) Chickens have a gene similar to that for the S cone pigment and another similar to that for the LM cone pigment. Thus the common ancestor of birds and mammals appears to have possessed both cone types.

 Photometry *453*

Light absorption *443*

This diagram compares the typical pattern of spectral sensitivity in non-primate mammals with that in Old World primates (the group that includes humans). The curves show the *absorbance* of the visual pigments (see LIGHT ABSORPTION, page 444), as this measure depends only on the pigment, not on the length of the photoreceptors or the transmission properties of the ocular media, both of which are species-dependent.

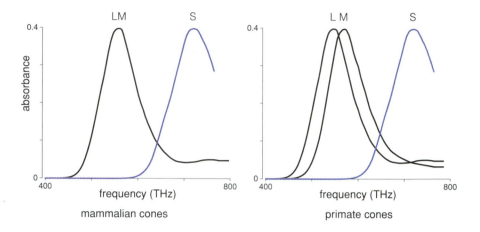

As we have seen, mammals need cones to see in sunlight, because their rods saturate under bright light conditions. Mammals that have developed sharp daylight vision show high spatial densities of cones, cone bipolar cells, and cone ganglion cells. The presence of two cone types with different spectral sensitivities allows mammals to compare the responses of the two types of cones and thereby obtain additional information about the contents of the visual world. Light that contains a relatively large number of high-frequency photons will stimulate the S cones more strongly than the LM cones—and vice versa—whatever the intensity of the light. This is neural basis of a type of color vision we term *yellow–blue*.

Color vision depends upon the number of spectrally distinct cone types within a given region of retina. The terminology is based upon this number.

Cone types	Designation
1	Monochromat
2	Dichromat
3	Trichromat

These terms are somewhat misleading, as *chroma-* comes from Greek *khroma* = color. They may be partly responsible for the common misconception that each cone type codes a different color (L cones for red, M cones for green, and S cones for blue). This misconception may be the basis for an even greater one, namely, that the primary function of cones is to discriminate color rather than intensity.

Monochromats are color-blind, since the minimum number of cone types necessary to make a comparison is two. The rainbow appears to them as a bright arc. Human cone monochromats exist, but are very rare, so much so that it has been difficult to estimate the fraction of the population that shows this condition.

Dichromats can distinguish whether a signal based upon the photon catches of S cones is greater than that from LM cones, or vice versa. Most, if not all, nonprimate mammals in nature fall into this category. Humans that lack functional L cones or M cones are also dichromats. Rare human dichromats have this deficit in only one eye. To that eye, a rainbow appears blue in the inner portion of the arc, fades to colorless toward the center, and progresses to yellow toward the outer edge of the rainbow.

Humans, of course, have trichromatic vision. This doesn't mean that we can see only three colors, for we can see many—only that we possess three cone types with differing spectral sensitivities. But if the ancestral protomammal had only two spectrally distinct cone types, how did we end up with three? The remainder of this chapter focuses on this question.

The genes for M and L cone rhodopsins lie together on the X chromosome

As we saw in RHODOPSINS (page 192), the gene for *rod* rhodopsin lies on chromosome 8. Each cell contains two such chromosomes, one from each parent, and each can be transcribed to manufacture the rod visual pigment. The gene for S cone rhodopsin lies on chromosome 7, which is also autosomal (nonsex). But the genes for M cone and L cone rhodopsins both lie on the X chromosome, and this has a number of consequences.

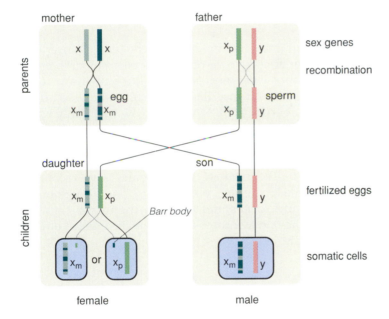

The cells of females contain two X chromosomes, one from each parent, whereas the cells of males contain a single X chromosome inherited from the mother and a single Y chromosome inherited from the father. Thus females possess two chromosomes that contain the genes for the visual pigments of L and M cones, whereas males possess only one such chromosome. During embryonic development, one of the two female X chromosomes in each cell becomes inactivated, for reasons still not understood, and this inactivation is inherited as cell division continues. Consequently, every female is a *mosaic*, consisting of patches of cells containing an active maternal X chromosome and an equal number of patches containing an active paternal X chromosome. In particular, a female retina consists of a mosaic of such patches, whereas all the cells in a male retina contain the maternal X chromosome.

Each X chromosome contains a single gene for the L cone pigment. Interestingly, the human population contains two alleles (varieties) of this gene. The difference between them is based upon a single amino acid sub-

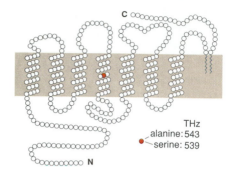

two alleles of the L cone pigment

stitution, which results in a small difference of 6 THz in the spectral sensitivities of the resulting pigments (left). Males possess one or the other of these alleles; females may possess both, and express one or the other in different patches of their retinal mosaic.

A fascinating feature of the X chromosome is that it can contain a variable number of genes coding for the visual pigment contained within the M cones. The diagram below shows three different arrangements of L and M cone genes found on human X chromosomes. Each gene is represented by

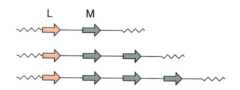

L and M genes on X chromosome

an arrow, which indicates the direction in which it is transcribed. The gene for the L cone pigment is followed by a variable number of genes for the M cone pigment, two being the most common, but only the M cone gene nearest to the L cone gene is transcribed in M cones. Between these genes lie introns (noncoding portions of DNA) that are highly homologous. There are a number of other arrangements within the human population, but the three shown are the most common.

The duplication of the M genes presumably occurred at some stage in evolution when a mother's two X chromosomes were recombined (mixed together) to form the X chromosome of an egg. The strong homologies, both between the M and L genes and between the introns, suggest that the recombination of the two X chromosomes may have fallen out of register, as shown in this diagram:

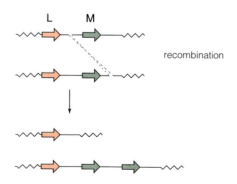

duplication of M gene on X chromosome

One of the resulting X chromosomes gained a second gene for M cone rhodopsin, which initially had little or no effect on the males or females that inherited it. The other X chromosome that resulted from this ancestral crossing-over lost the gene that codes for the M cone rhodopsin. Males that inherit a chromosome of this form lack the ability to synthesize M cone rhodopsin and are thus functional dichromats. Females that do so are generally not much affected, presumably because their retinal mosaic contains patches from their other X chromosome, and cone comparisons can be made at the border between patches, but little is known about this area.

The difference between M and L cones is recent

Like those of rod rhodopsins (page 190), the amino acid sequences of S cone rhodopsins from different mammals are very similar, strongly suggesting that they are all homologous at the level of cone types. In addition, there is strong sequence homology among mammalian LM cones and between them and primate M or L cones. But the greatest similarity of all is between primate M and L cones, which in humans differ in only 15 of the 364 amino acids (shown at right). Just three of these differences account for almost the entire difference between the spectral sensitivities of the M and L cones. Primates are thought to have emerged about 80 million years ago; based on their sequence similarities, the gene duplication that produced the difference between M and L cones may have occurred only about 30 million years ago. By comparison, there are many differences between the amino acid sequence of human S cones and that of human M or L cones, and many differences between the amino acid sequences of any human cone rhodopsin and human rod rhodopsin:

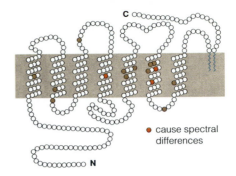

● cause spectral differences

M and L cone differences

source: Nathans et al., 1986

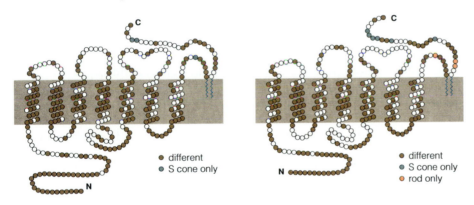

M and S cone differences

● different
● S cone only

S cone and rod differences

● different
● S cone only
● rod only

source: Nathans, Thomas, and Hogness, 1986

This phylogenetic tree of vertebrate visual pigments is based upon the similarities of their amino acid sequences:

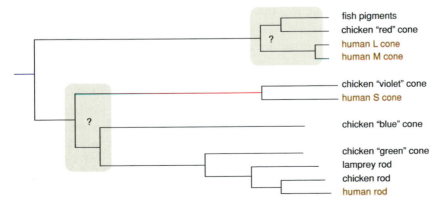

fish pigments
chicken "red" cone
human L cone
human M cone
chicken "violet" cone
human S cone
chicken "blue" cone
chicken "green" cone
lamprey rod
chicken rod
human rod

similarity tree of visual pigment amino acid sequences

after Okano et al., 1992

So far as possible, all of the pigments are arranged vertically according to the frequency of their peak sensitivity. The horizontal distances are proportional to the differences between sequences (note, for example, the short distances between the human M and L cone pigments). The branch node between them is presumed to represent the last ancestral pigment common to both. One would like to assume that such distances reflect in some way the time since that ancestor, but this is less certain, since the tree is based upon differences between single genes, rather than many. Without further information, it is not possible to tell whether the ancestral pigment more closely resembled the M or the L cone pigment. Thus the vertical displacement between these pigments, and the location of the node on the line connecting them, are arbitrary. Many such trees are possible, and the one shown is the most parsimonious. However, certain other arrangements of portions of this tree produce nearly as good a fit; these portions are highlighted with a dull yellow background.

The human M and L cone pigments are well separated from the S cone pigment; in fact, these two groups are closer to those of other vertebrates than they are to each other. This separation provides additional evidence that the differences between them are ancient. On the other hand, the distances between rod visual pigments in different species are relatively short. Only the human rod rhodopsin is shown because those of other mammals are very similar to it. Furthermore, the rod rhodopsin branch is connected to a portion of the cone tree. This suggests that rods followed cones in evolution, although it is hard to say at what time or at what point on the phylogenetic tree of species. The ability of a rod to reliably convey the capture of a single photon is a remarkable specialization that depends upon the optimization of many factors, and it is difficult to imagine that the first photoreceptor possessed this ability. Earlier (page 131), we saw that the rod circuitry is piggybacked onto the cone circuitry, and this too is consistent with the idea that a progenitor of vertebrate rods evolved from a progenitor of vertebrate cones.

Some New World monkeys show a form of color vision based upon different alleles of the same LM gene, as discussed in the following section, which suggests a possible means by which the neural circuitry for making use of a difference between two "LM" cones may have come about even before gene duplication.

In some New World monkeys only females are trichromats

New World monkeys diverged from humans, macaques, and apes some 30–40 million years ago. Just like Old World primates, and mammals generally, they have a gene for S cone rhodopsin. But unlike most Old World primates, New World squirrel monkeys and marmosets have only a single gene for a cone rhodopsin on the X chromosome. In this respect they are like other mammals. As a consequence, male squirrel monkeys and marmosets can express only two distinct cone pigments, and are thus dichromats.

Although there is only a single gene site on the X chromosome for a cone pigment gene, there are three different alleles within the population that can occupy that site. This diagram summarizes the situation:

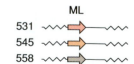

alleles of "ML" gene in squirrel monkey

The number at the left is the frequency (in THz) of the peak sensitivity of the expressed rhodopsin. The differences within the alleles of the squirrel monkey or within the alleles of marmosets are small compared with differences between these two genera, which suggests that each set of alleles diverged independently. Squirrel monkeys and marmosets diverged about 18 million years ago. On the basis of the genetic drift between these two species over this period, it has been estimated that the three alleles of squirrel monkeys diverged about 5 million years ago, and those of marmosets about 10 million years ago.

Whereas all male squirrel monkeys and all male marmosets are dichromats, most females of either species are trichromats in the sense that they can make color discriminations in the red–green range of the spectrum, where S cones catch virtually no photons. Each female has two X chromosomes, and thus two genes for their "LM" cones. The mosaic of their retina thus contains patches that express the gene in the maternal X chromosomes as well as patches that express the gene in the paternal X chromosome. If each of these chromosomes contains a different allele, the patches will contain LM cones with two different spectral sensitivities, making some form of discrimination possible. However, at least a third of the females will inherit the same allele from both parents, and will thus be dichromats. Here we see an advantage of having three alleles over having only two, for in the latter case no fewer than half of the females would be dichromats. On the other hand, having a larger spectrum of alleles would not be much of an improvement, since random draws would still yield females with only a small difference between the spectral sensitivities of their two alleles. The degree to which these New World species have developed specific neural mechanisms able to reliably convey these differences to the brain, and to exploit them within the visual cortex, is not known.

In striking contrast to squirrel monkeys and marmosets, howler monkeys have two rhodopsin genes on their X chromosome and show normal primate trichromatic color vision with good color discrimination. Sequence analysis indicates that it is unlikely that New World monkeys had two genes for cone visual pigments on their X chromosome at the time they diverged from Old World primates and that an ancestor of spider monkeys, marmosets, and some other New World genera then lost one of them. Instead, howler monkeys appear to have acquired their second pigment via gene duplication, just as did an ancestral Old World primate.

Did ancestral howler monkeys—or for that matter, Old World primates—pass through an evolutionary stage in which there were different alleles for the LM cone rhodopsin gene? If so, then any neural mechanisms that evolved to exploit the spectrally distinct cone types those alleles produced might readily be adapted to a gene duplication mutation that would have provided trichromatic color vision for all males and females. Whether true or false, this possibility provides at least a potential means of solving the conundrum of how red–green color vision, which requires both a spectrally distinct pair of cones over this portion of the spectrum and a neural mechanism to exploit the difference in their photon catches, may have evolved.

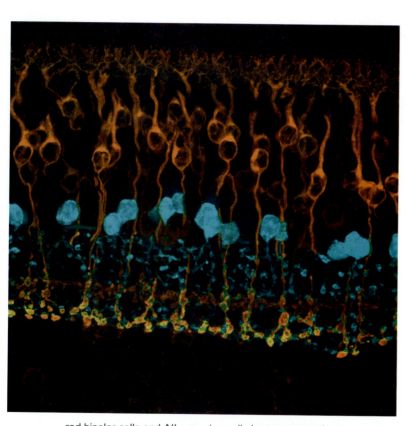

rod bipolar cells and AII amacrine cells in macaque retina

courtesy of Steven C. Massey

11

Cell types

This chapter takes a closer look at the properties of some of the different cell types in the retina. It approaches the border of what we know about some of these cell types, where there is much uncertainty, and there are more questions than answers. Even so, more is known about different retinal cell types than is practical to summarize here. Instead, the aim of this chapter is to provide an introduction to this very broad topic.

Cell types can be distinguished by the lack of intermediate forms

One of the factors that has strongly influenced our developing understanding of visual function has been the *discovery* and *demonstration* of various cell types within the retina. Discovery is often a creative act to which many factors may contribute, not all of them entirely logical or readily expressed; it is not further considered here. Unlike discovery, which is typically an event, demonstration is more like a process. A claim that a certain cell grouping constitutes a distinct type may be initially tentative and weak, but may gain strength with further investigation. The process of demonstration may go on for some time, and many investigators may contribute to it.

Because of our strong human ability to detect patterns, it is often easier to recognize differences than it is to objectify or to communicate them. Our ability to recognize faces, and our difficulty in expressing how we do so, provides a common example. Those researchers who have been faced with the task of communicating a neural discharge pattern or morphological form that they instantly recognize are familiar with this problem.

Initially, at least, a cell type may be characterized in rather qualitative terms, by illustrating typical members of the type and noting similarities to and differences from other types. The claim for a new type may rest initially on little more than the implied assertion that if readers were to study comparable data for a comparable period of time, then they too would agree that a certain cell group constitutes a distinguishable type. While many of the currently accepted cell types were first described in this way, it is also true that the literature contains a greater number of cell groupings no longer accepted, and this fact, if nothing else, justifies a certain degree of initial skepticism regarding such claims. This skepticism can be overcome by various demonstrations of the ways in which a certain cell grouping is distinguishable. Likewise, the only satisfactory means of resolving conflicting claims is by demonstration.

What constitutes a demonstration depends upon how one approaches the notion of "cell type." As used here, this term refers to categorical distinctions that exist in nature, and thus have a reality that is independent of their investigation. Here is an example of how such natural distinctions can become recognized.

If one views a flat-mounted primate retina that contains a number of labeled ganglion cells, some of them will be seen to have a relatively compact dendritic field, with processes that repeatedly branch to form a thick, "bushy" arbor. The general form of their dendritic trees can be readily distinguished from those of other ganglion cells, in the same way that we have no difficulty distinguishing between a dogwood and a cherry tree. Everyone will agree that the cells in what I will temporarily call the "bushy" group can be readily distinguished, and thus a labored attempt to define "bushy ganglion cells" would be as pointless as an attempt to define "dogwood trees." The term "bushy" is just a name I've chosen for this group, not a description or means of identification; I could just as well have named it the "foo" group.

Two "bushy" ganglion cells, observed at about the same retinal eccentricity, are shown in the diagram at the top of the next page. It is obvious that the dendritic fields of these two ganglion cells differ greatly in size. In itself, this doesn't necessarily mean much. But within the local region, the other "bushy" ganglion cells have dendritic fields that may be either small or large, but none has a middle-sized field. Nearer the fovea, where the dendritic fields of all ganglion cells tend to be smaller, the same pattern persists: some are large, others small, but few if any lie in between.

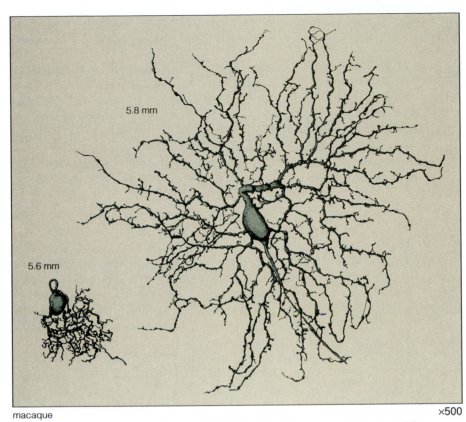

macaque   ×500

ganglion cells with "bushy" dendritic fields at about the same retinal eccentricity

after Watanabe and Rodieck, 1989

This impression can be confirmed by plotting the size of the dendritic field of each "bushy" ganglion cell as a function of its retinal eccentricity:

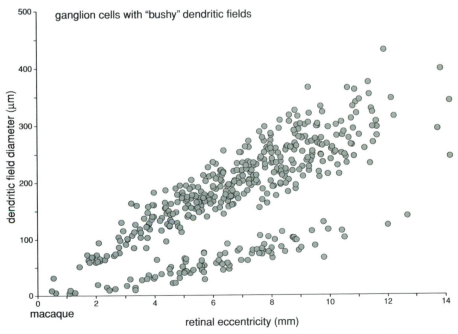

after Watanabe and Rodieck, 1989

The data points from this subset of cells form two distinct clusters. The gap between the clusters indicates an absence of intermediate forms. This difference provides a natural basis for distinguishing two groups of ganglion

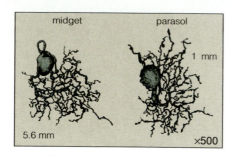

midget and parasol ganglion cells
at different retinal eccentricities

after Watanabe and Rodieck, 1989

cells within the "bushy" population. Stephen Polyak (1889–1957) named the cells of the upper cluster *parasol ganglion cells* and those of the lower cluster *midget ganglion cells.*

As seen in the scatter plot on the preceding page, the dendritic field sizes of parasol ganglion cells at small retinal eccentricities overlap those of midget ganglion cells at greater eccentricities, so dendritic field size in itself does not distinguish midget and parasol ganglion cells. The diagram at left shows the same midget ganglion cell illustrated on the top of page 227 next to a parasol ganglion cell with a similar dendritic field size, which was nearer the fovea. The dendritic field sizes of these two cells prove to be quite similar. Over the range of overlap in their dendritic field sizes, it would be difficult to distinguish midget ganglion cells from parasol ganglion cells on the basis of morphology alone. It is the additional parameter of retinal eccentricity that allows the two clusters to be made evident.

Midget ganglion cells do not constitute a type, however, nor do parasol ganglion cells, because the cells that compose either the "midget" or the "parasol" cluster show other properties that allow them to be further distinguished. This diagram shows additional properties of a population of "bushy" ganglion cells, in which the midget/parasol distinction is indicated by the size of the symbol. Here, the depth of dendritic stratification in the inner synaptic layer is plotted against the size of the cell body:

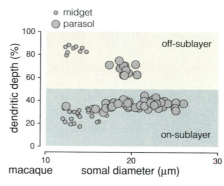

stratification of ganglion cell dendrites

after Watanabe and Rodieck, 1989

The dendritic fields of midget and parasol ganglion cells stratify either in the outer portion of the inner synaptic layer or in the inner portion. Again, there is an absence of intermediate forms, since no cells stratify in the middle. The additional parameter of somal diameter is not necessary to distinguish these two clusters, because depth of stratification alone provides an analytical knife that divides both the parasol group and the midget group into two additional groupings (imagine shadow cast of the data points onto the vertical axis). This property is, of course, an anatomical correlate of the functional difference between on and off ganglion cells.

One might be concerned that this process of splitting could go on indefinitely, with additional parameters slicing the population into ever finer divisions. But for retinal cells, this doesn't happen. Additional parameters either fail to produce distinct clusters, as in the lower cluster in the scatter diagram above, or repeat previously established clusters, as somal diameter does for the upper pair of clusters above. The data in the above two scatter diagrams thus provide one means of distinguishing four different types within the population of "bushy" ganglion cells, shown at left.

So, distinctions such as these are discovered and demonstrated rather than defined. In practice, when it does not appear possible to further distinguish the cells within a group by the absence of intermediate forms, that

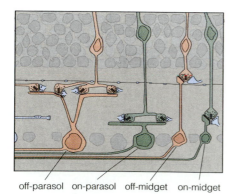

off-parasol on-parasol off-midget on-midget

four types of ganglion cells

group is referred to as a **cell type.** This designation remains a working hypothesis, however, because one can't exclude the possibility that some new property will come to light that further distinguishes what were formally considered to be members of the same cell type. Indeed, Polyak considered parasol and midget ganglion cells to be single types, and decades were to pass before depth of stratification and functional differences were used to further subdivide them.

There are many other means of distinguishing cells. Labeling by means of antibodies has been particularly useful in revealing cell populations that are composed of only a single cell type, or a few. Again, there must be an absence of intermediate forms (that is, cells in the sample must be either labeled or unlabeled or separable in some other way). In addition to the properties of *cells* of the same type, there are also properties of the *population as a whole* that can be considered, such as their spatial density, as we have already seen for rods, cones, and ganglion cells.

Given a number of cell types, there is a natural tendency to group them according to some particular criterion. If your concerns lie mainly with the functional difference between on- and off-ganglion cells, or with stratification in the inner synaptic layer, then you might be tempted to view "on-ganglion cells" as a **genus** that includes a number of types, distinguished by other criteria:

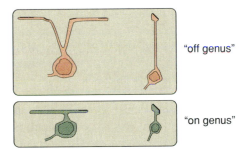

"off genus"

"on genus"

If, however, your concerns lie more with other anatomical aspects, such as where the axons of these cells go to in the brain, or with response properties other than the on/off distinction, then you might be tempted to believe that midget and parasol ganglion cells each constitute a genus, composed of two types that are distinguished by the sign of their response:

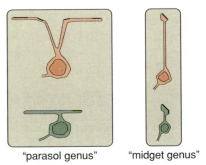

"parasol genus"   "midget genus"

Since they are created for different purposes, one should not expect such different schemes to agree with each other, and in general they do not. It is easy to see why this must be the case: every pair of cell types must differ in one or more ways, or they would not be distinguishable. And if the factors that distinguished them were included in the set of criteria used to establish the classification scheme, then the pair would not be grouped together in this scheme. Thus for every scheme that lumps two or more types, there are others that split them.

The close relation between the process of classification and human psychology was recognized by William Whewell (rhymes with "yule") in 1847. He noted that we can hardly think without categorizing and classifying the rich variety of phenomena we experience, and that we do so incessantly. Yet this very process acts upon our perception of these phenomena by focusing our attention on those features that form the basis for the classification. This focusing reinforces the classification that generated it, and produces a recursive situation, made all the more difficult to untangle because it is the words used that are themselves at stake. There appears to be a natural tendency to develop classification schemes that allow one to order phenomena as well as, to some degree at least, a natural tendency to believe in them once they have been established, whatever their objective basis.

Given these predilections, Whewell recognized that a distinction needed to be drawn between "artificial" classification schemes, which are man-made and organized for the benefit of human psychology and communication, and "natural" classification schemes, which he presumed to have an independent and objective reality (see the Box *ARTIFICIAL CELL TYPES*). Whewell's discussion of the distinction between artificial and natural schemes is clear-headed, and continues to be worthwhile reading. He summarized the criterion that a natural system of classification must satisfy in the following maxim: "The arrangement obtained from one set of characters coincides with the arrangement obtained from another set."

Applied to genera of retinal cell types, this maxim reduces to an analysis of clusters of clusters. The on/off genera scheme is based upon a single correlation of two parameters (depth of stratification and response polarity), but on- and off-parasol ganglion cells share so many other properties, as discussed later, that they can usefully be viewed as two closely related types. The same can be said for on- and off-midget ganglion cells, inner and outer starburst amacrine cells, and certain direction-selective ganglion cells, which are also discussed later. But caution is still needed, since, nominal or otherwise, hierarchical classification schemes more often dull thinking than sharpen it. There is much to be said for a lighter touch that is sensitive to all correlations within a set of types.

The term **group** is used here to refer to a collection of cell types. Sometimes it is implicit, as when we speak of *cones, parasol ganglion cells, on-ganglion cells*, or *ganglion cells*. These are groupings of convenience, imply no particular hierarchy, and are arbitrary in the sense that they are not falsifiable. But there is a particular use of *group* that has a limited epistemological content, and comes about when the number of types within a population of cells is uncertain, but is clearly more than one. For example, it is not yet clear how many different ganglion cell types project to the superior collicu-

Artificial cell types

In attempting to draw distinctions within a population of cells, it is often useful to divide them into two or more groups based upon arbitrary criteria. For example, one might separate a group of ganglion cells according to whether the diameter of their dendritic field is larger or smaller than 200 μm. Such distinctions are often made in scientific papers to test some hypothesis (e.g., do more large-field cells than small-field cells take up a certain chemical?), and are not intended to outlast the conclusions of the paper. To refer to them as the "small-field type" and the "large-field type" would be to draw an artificial distinction between these cells.

Natural types are discovered and demonstrated. Artificial types are defined; but the power of words in shaping our thoughts is such that the terminology attached to artificial distinctions sometimes takes on a life of its own.

lus (see INFORMING THE BRAIN). What does seem to be true is that those that do can be separated into three *groups,* termed M, S, and T (page 276), on the basis of their dendritic size and morphology. Although the nature and number of cell types within the S group is uncertain, this grouping would be falsified if any cell within it belonged to the same cell type as any cell in any other group. This usage has utility in that it allows tentative empirical distinctions to be drawn even when the types that compose a group remain uncertain.

The various properties of the individual cells within a type, or of their population, form a theme that continues through the rest of this chapter as we take a closer look at a few of the large variety of cell types that compose the retina. Since the properties of photoreceptors were discussed in detail in a previous chapter, we begin with horizontal cells.

Horizontal cells

As discussed in RETINAS (page 46), the primate retina contains two types of horizontal cells. HI cells have a dendritic arbor that receives from cones and an axonal arbor that receives from rods. In other mammals, HI cells are termed Type B. Just as the dendrites of Type B cells are coupled together via gap junctions, so too are their axonal arbors coupled together, and this may be true of HI cells as well.

HII cells have dendrites that receive from cones and a short axon that gives rise to a few processes that also receive from cones. They too also couple with one another. In other mammals, HII cells are termed Type A.

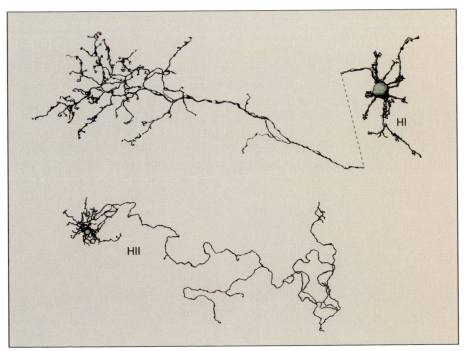

macaque   ×300

from Rodieck, 1988

So far as we know, the contacts between different cone types and different horizontal cell types are the same throughout the retina. As described earlier (page 48), the dendritic processes of HI cells contact M and L cones, but virtually no S cones; whereas HII cells make extensive contacts with S cones, but only sparse contacts with M and L cones. HI cells are also electrically connected with one another by means of gap junctions, and HII cells are likewise interconnected. Thus the transmembrane potential of any horizontal cell dendritic arbor results from a mixture of the activation of that cell by the cones it receives from and the potential of the adjacent horizontal cells of the same type. These connections have some interesting consequences which we will now consider.

From the perspective of the cones, the lateral processes within the synaptic invaginations of either an M cone or an L cone belong almost exclusively to HI horizontal cells, which are activated by the summed contributions of these two cone types over the local area. By some means still not understood, horizontal cells act back upon the cones they contact so as to attenuate their signals. *If* the action of the HI cells is simply to subtract from the cone transmembrane potential, or from its effect, then they will subtract equally for both M and L cones. They will thus not affect the *difference* between the photic stimulation of the M and the L cones. As discussed later, it is this difference between the stimulation of the M and the L cones that forms the basis for red–green color vision.

The lateral processes connected to S cones, on the other hand, all come from HII horizontal cells. Although HII cells make only sparse contacts with M and L cones, there are many more of these cones than there are S cones. Consequently, HII cells are activated by the summed contributions of both S cones and a mixture of M and L cones. If HII cells act in the manner suggested above for HI cells, then their effect on S cones will be to attenuate their signals in such a manner so as not to alter the difference between the photic stimulation of S cones and that of a mixture of M and L cones; it is this difference that forms the basis for blue–yellow color vision. To summarize, horizontal cells simply sum the stimulations they receive from cones. Thus they do not create differences between cone types, but the manner in which they contact cones suggests that they may be able to preserve those differences in cone stimulation that are critical for color vision.

Although the qualitative aspects of horizontal cell connections and functions appear to be about the same throughout the retina, the great change in the spatial density of cones from fovea to periphery produces a number of quantitative differences. Both HI and HII cells contain calcium-binding proteins that can be labeled by means of antibodies, and this allows their collective spatial density to be determined, as shown in the following diagram:

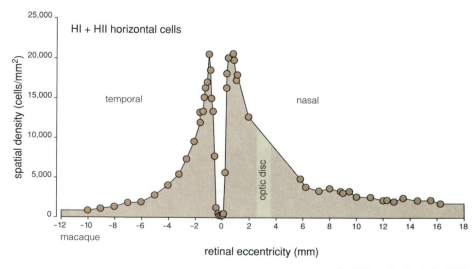

after Röhrenbeck et al., 1989

The dip at the center of the fovea is a consequence of the pedicle-free zone (page 206). Nevertheless, the spatial density of horizontal cell bodies does not drop to zero.

The foveal distribution of horizontal cells is shown in this drawing:

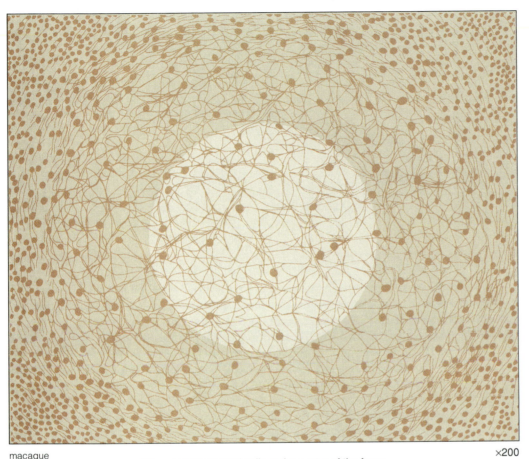

macaque   HI and HII horizontal cells at the center of the fovea   ×200

S cones

percentage of all cones

retinal eccentricity (mm)

Only the cell bodies were well labeled; the lines suggest the directions of the larger processes. The radius of the dip in horizontal cell density is about 250 μm in the macaque retina. As shown by the shaded zone in the inset diagram, the percentage of S cones reaches only about 4% at this retinal eccentricity, or about half the value found at greater eccentricities. Thus most of the labeled cells within this zone are presumably HI cells. The pedicle-free zone in macaques has a radius of about 150 μm, as indicated by the lighter zone at the center of this illustration. The dendrites of the horizontal cells found within this zone presumably span it to reach cone pedicles on the opposite sides.

The dendritic field sizes of both types of horizontal cells, plotted as a function of retinal eccentricity, are shown in the diagram at the top of the next page. The dendritic fields of HI horizontal cells are relatively small near the fovea, and at an eccentricity of 2 mm, there are about twice as many of them as there are HII cells. However, the diameters of the HII dendritic fields are about 1.5 times larger, and thus cover about twice the area of the HI fields. Consequently, the number of cones covered by either group is about the same. In this region there are about two M or L cones per HI horizontal cell, and about 1.6 S cones per HII cell.

At greater retinal eccentricities, HI cells show a large increase in dendritic field size; the scatter in the diagram is probably due mainly to the inclusion of cells within the nasal quadrant. The dendritic fields of HII cells,

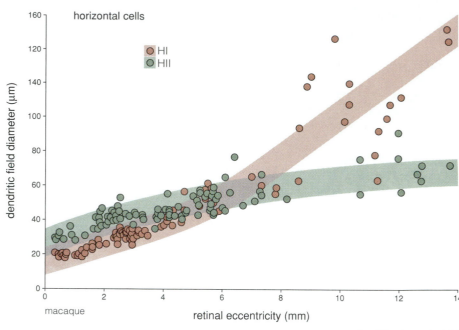

after Wässle et al., 1989

coverage factor
see page 200

which are larger near the fovea, show a much smaller increase in size with retinal eccentricity, so that at large eccentricities they are considerably smaller than the average fields of HI cells. This smaller increase may be because an HII cell need contact only one S cone and make a few contacts with L and M cones. Since more than one HII terminal process can contact the same M or L cone pedicle, the dendritic field need not be large. By comparison, for HI cells to show about the same coverage factor for M and L cones, their dendritic fields must increase as the spacing between these cone types increases. At any retinal eccentricity, each M or L cone receives the processes of three or four different HI cells. Near the fovea, where the spatial density of cones is high, the dendritic fields of HI cells are small and compact; but in the retinal periphery, the drop in cone density results in a more extended dendritic field:

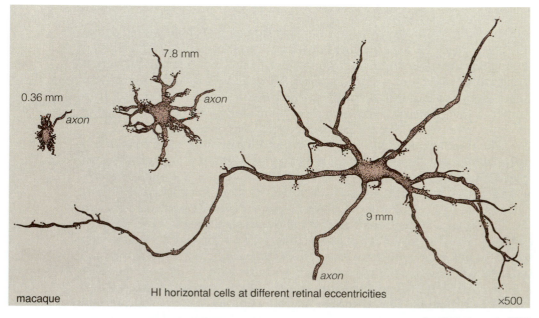

macaque   HI horizontal cells at different retinal eccentricities   ×500

after Wässle et al., 1989

Bipolar cells

All bipolar cells have a dendritic arbor in the outer synaptic layer and an axonal arbor in the inner synaptic layer. The scatter diagram at right plots the dendritic versus axonal field areas of all the Golgi-stained bipolar cells (360) observed in a localized region of the retina. The sample lay in a strip 6.2–8.0 mm from the fovea in a flat-mounted macaque retina. The data points can be seen to form two thick clusters, labeled *midget* and *diffuse*. In addition, 4 cells lie to the upper right of the midget group, forming a sparse cluster labeled *S cone*, and 15 lie to the upper right of the diffuse group, forming a sparse cluster labeled *giant*. There are other means of segregating the various types of bipolar cells into different groupings, but the following discussion is organized according to these clusters, as well as whether an increase in light intensity causes the cells to depolarize (on) or hyperpolarize (off).

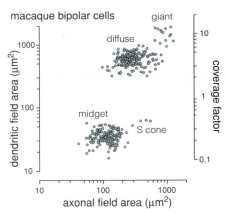

after Rodieck, 1988

Bipolar cells

    on-bipolar cells   *off-bipolar cells*

Midget cluster

    on-midget bipolar cells   *off-midget bipolar cells*

    L cone on-midget bipolar   L cone off-midget bipolar

    M cone on-midget bipolar   M cone off-midget bipolar

                                  S cone off-midget bipolar

S cone cluster

    S cone on-bipolar

Diffuse cluster

    on-diffuse bipolar cells   *off-diffuse bipolar cells*

    rod bipolar

    DB4 bipolar   DB1 bipolar

    DB5 bipolar   DB2 bipolar

    DB6 bipolar   DB3 bipolar

Giant cluster

    giant inner monostratified (on?)

    (there may be more cell types in this cluster)

Some of these names are a bit of a mouthful, such as *L cone on-midget bipolar cell*, but at least they are clear. Resist the temptation to think of any of them as *subtypes*; a cell type is a cell type, and a subtype is an implicit, arbitrary, and unnecessary mental construct.

In general, the anatomical features that best distinguish bipolar cells have to do with the size, morphology, and level of stratification of the axonal arbor within the inner synaptic layer. Therefore, the term "on" is often replaced by "inner" (e.g., "L cone inner midget bipolar cell") and "off" by "outer," particularly when the emphasis is on anatomical correlates.

Several bipolar cell processes receive from each cone pedicle. Before discussing the different bipolar cell types, it is worth reviewing the different bipolar cell processes that receive from each cone pedicle (right). The most distinctive of these are the **invaginating,** or **central,** processes that abut the pedicle directly below the synaptic ribbon. There may be three or four such processes in an invagination, which are aligned along the length of the ribbon. **Triad-associated** or **semi-invaginating** processes branch on either side of the invaginating processes and effectively surround them. The remaining

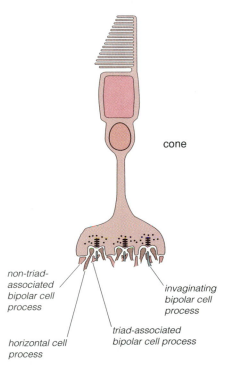

cone

non-triad-associated bipolar cell process

invaginating bipolar cell process

triad-associated bipolar cell process

horizontal cell process

synaptic contacts at cone pedicle

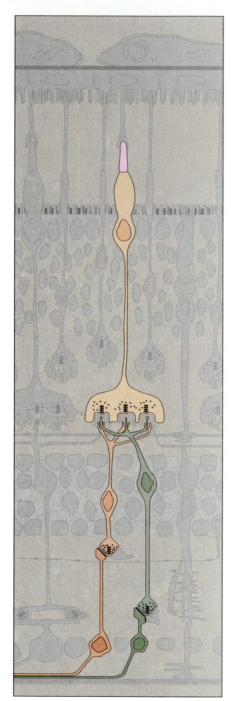

off- and on- midget pathways

bipolar cell processes abut the base of the pedicle, and are termed **non-triad-associated** or **flat** processes.

Bipolar cells that receive from photoreceptors via invaginating processes all appear to have axonal arbors that stratify in the on-sublayer of the inner synaptic layer, and *depolarize* in response to an increase in light intensity. Conversely, bipolar cells that make flat contacts with cone pedicles all appear to have axonal arbors that stratify in the off-sublayer and *hyperpolarize* in response to an increase in light intensity. Bipolar cells that make triad-associated (semi-invaginating) contacts constitute a heterogeneous group in this respect. Some, such as off-midget bipolar cells, hyperpolarize in response to light; others, observed in other species, depolarize in response to light.

Midget bipolar cells

Midget bipolar cells, first described by Stephen Polyak in 1941, are readily recognized by their small and compact dendritic arbors, which generally receive from only one cone, although in the peripheral retina a few receive from two cones. Furthermore, their axonal arbors always contact a single midget ganglion cell, without even a single synapse to a neighboring ganglion cell. Thus the pathways from cones to midget bipolar cells and hence to midget ganglion cells generally show neither convergence nor divergence.

Midget bipolar cells can be further distinguished in terms of whether they receive from cones via invaginating contacts (on) or via triad-associated contacts (off in this case; see figure at left). The three cone types and two midget bipolar types thus far distinguished create six combinatorial possibilities, but only five of these have been observed.

Cone	Invaginating (on)	Triad-associated (off)
L	+	+
M	+	+
S	−	+

The invaginating bipolar cell that receives from S cones is not a midget, but rather the S cone on-bipolar, discussed below. Each M or L cone contacts both an on- and an off-midget bipolar cell, and each S cone contacts an off-midget bipolar cell. Except for the occasional peripheral midget bipolar cell that contacts two cones, the spatial density of off-midget bipolar cells in any region of the retina should thus match that of cones, and the spatial density of on-midget bipolar cells should be about 90% of that value.

L and M cones are distinguished by the nature of the rhodopsin molecules contained in their outer segments, but there appear to be no anatomical features by which they can be distinguished. Surprisingly, it appears that L and M cones can nevertheless be distinguished by certain anatomical features of the midget bipolar cells that they contact. These differences are summarized in the schematic diagram at the top of the next page. Each cone in the diagram contacts both an on- and an off-midget bipolar cell. Both of the bipolar cells that contact the cone on the left have small terminals in the inner synaptic layer, and both have relatively few synaptic ribbons. But both midget bipolar cells that contact the cone on the right have larger terminals that contain a larger number of synaptic ribbons.

The following scatter diagram plots the number of synaptic ribbons in the terminals of an on-midget bipolar cell against the number in the off-midget bipolar cell that contacts the same cone. Ignoring the vertical axis for

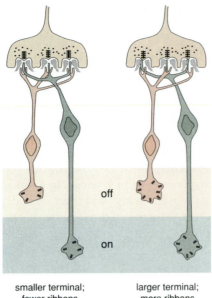

smaller terminal;
fewer ribbons

larger terminal;
more ribbons

off

on

the moment, we see that for the on-midget bipolar cells, there is no overlap between the cluster containing the smaller number of ribbons (32 ± 3 in macaques, ~50 in humans) and the cluster containing about 50% more (49 ± 3 in macaques, ~76 in humans):

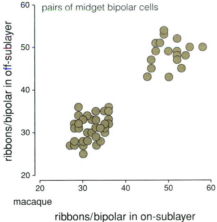

after Calkins et al., 1994

It is also clear that if an on-midget bipolar that contacts a cone has relatively few synaptic ribbons in the inner portion of the inner synaptic layer, then it is guaranteed that the off-midget bipolar cell that contacts this cone will also have relatively few synaptic ribbons within its terminals in the outer portion of the inner synaptic layer. In effect, the cone appears to determine the properties of both the on- and the off-bipolar cell it contacts, and two distinct cone types can be distinguished on this basis. It seems almost certain that one of these types corresponds to the L cones and the other to the M cones, but at the present it is not known which is which.

It is intriguing to speculate as to how this relation between the cone type and the number of ribbons in the two midget bipolar cells it contacts comes about. One possibility is that the two cone types are born at different times, and thus under different conditions for differentiation. Another is that developing midget bipolar cells are somehow able to recognize the cone types they are destined to receive from, just as S cone bipolar cells can somehow recognize S cones. As discussed in PHOTORECEPTOR ATTRIBUTES, the only difference thus far detected between M and L cones involves the amino acid sequences of the rhodopsins they contain. Could a small amount of the rhodopsin in the plasma membrane of the outer segment diffuse to the synaptic terminal to provide a means of identifying the cone, or is a second marker involved? Or is this an unproductive way of looking at the situation?

Whether they receive from M cones or from L cones, off-midget bipolar cells can be selectively labeled by means of an antibody to a protein named recoverin, which is also found in photoreceptor outer segments. The spatial density of the labeled cells matches that of cones in the same area, indicating that the antibody labels either all three types of off-midget bipolar cells, or the 90% that receive from either M or L cones. In a flat-mounted retina, their cell bodies form a quasi-regular array, and their axonal arbors show a coverage factor of about 58% of the zone of the inner synaptic layer in which they ramify. The general pattern of their axonal arbors is similar to that of rod bipolar cells (page 129):

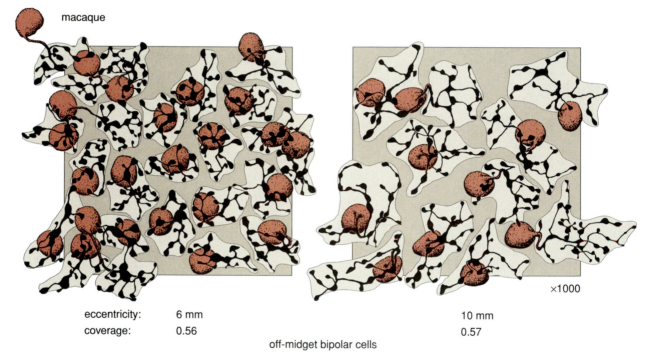

macaque

| eccentricity: | 6 mm | 10 mm |
| coverage: | 0.56 | 0.57 |

off-midget bipolar cells

×1000

after Milam et al., 1993

It is interesting to note that this population of two or three different types of cone bipolar cells shows features that are generally associated with cells belonging to the same type: stratification at the same level of the inner synaptic layer, and a similar territorial domain size. In effect, they are distinguished by type only in terms of the difference in the cone type they receive from. This is a good example of a feature of cell types not thus far discussed, namely the "importance" of certain distinctions. The criterion for distinguishing cells by type is the absence of intermediate forms. One does not need to make the case that the particular distinction is important; indeed, to do so would undermine the whole approach, because "importance" is subjective. Put another way, cell types are distinguished by objective criteria; the importance one attaches to any particular distinction is a separate matter. Some researchers may believe that the difference between L and M cone off-midget bipolar cells plays no significant role in vision other than the weighting produced by the different number of synaptic ribbons at the bipolar–ganglion cell synapse. Other researchers may hold that this difference is vital for red–green color discrimination, but all can agree as to the cell types.

Returning to the cells in the above illustration, since the vertical processes of the midget bipolar cells do not cross one another, and since every cone contacts an off-midget bipolar cell, the array of their axonal arbors more or less matches the cone array. Allowing for the connections with S cones and the occasional midget bipolar cell that receives from two cones, the total number of midget bipolar cells is thus slightly less than twice the number of cones, or about 8.5 million. The total number of macaque ganglion cells is about 1.6 million; thus most of the midget bipolar cells must contact midget ganglion cells that receive from more than one midget bipolar cell. These midget ganglion cells, located in the peripheral retina, do not appear to distinguish between L and M cone midget bipolar cells (page 260). Midget bipolar cells are exceptional in that even at large retinal eccentricities, most continue to receive from only a single cone, and consequently almost all of the convergence of cone signals takes place at the ganglion cell. One senses that there is a reason for this arrangement, but because the signals of L and M cones become mixed, it is hard to come up with good possibilities.

S cone bipolar cells

S cone bipolar cells have invaginating dendritic processes that receive exclusively from S cones (right). Their axonal arbors ramify in the innermost portion of the inner synaptic layer, and are presynaptic to a ganglion cell type termed **small bistratified**, discussed below. They contain a neuropeptide named cholecystokinin (CCK), and can be identified by an antibody to this peptide.

Near the fovea, most S cone bipolar cells have dendritic arbors that are so small and compact that the they are able to receive from only a single S cone:

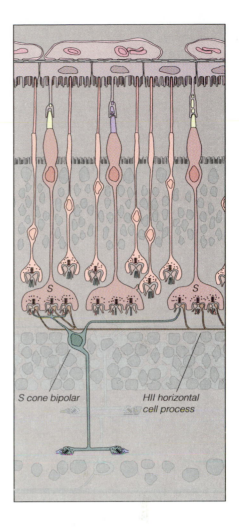

S cone bipolar   HII horizontal
                                  cell process

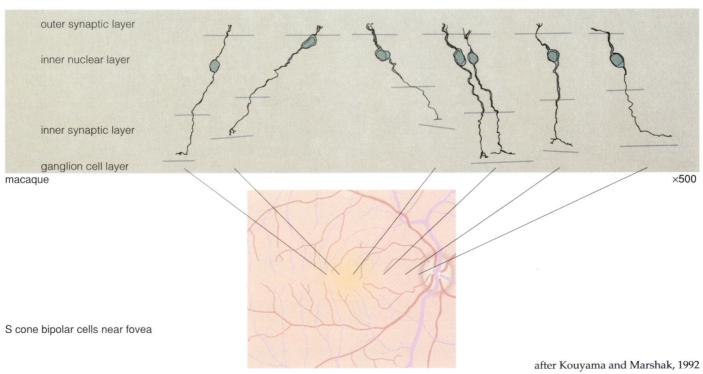

outer synaptic layer

inner nuclear layer

inner synaptic layer

ganglion cell layer

macaque   ×500

S cone bipolar cells near fovea

after Kouyama and Marshak, 1992

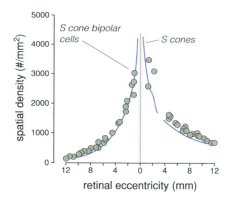

after Kouyama and Marshak, 1992 (bipolar cells);
after De Monasterio et al., 1985 (cones)

As shown at left, the spatial density of S cone bipolar cells across the retina more or less follows that of S cones, but is about 1.4 times greater. Because of this difference in spatial density, many S cones are necessarily presynaptic to more than one S cone bipolar cell. In the peripheral retina, an S cone bipolar cell can receive from two or three S cones, and each S cone can contact a few of these bipolar cells, as seen in the flat-mounted view below. In this diagram, each S cone, represented by a blue circle, contacts at least one S cone bipolar cell; however, not every S cone bipolar cell contacts an S cone. It may be that not all of the S cones were labeled; alternatively, S cones are more fragile than M and L cones, and some may have died earlier. But it is also possible that the antibody to CCK also labeled some of the on-midget bipolar cells, which have a morphology similar to that of some S cone on-

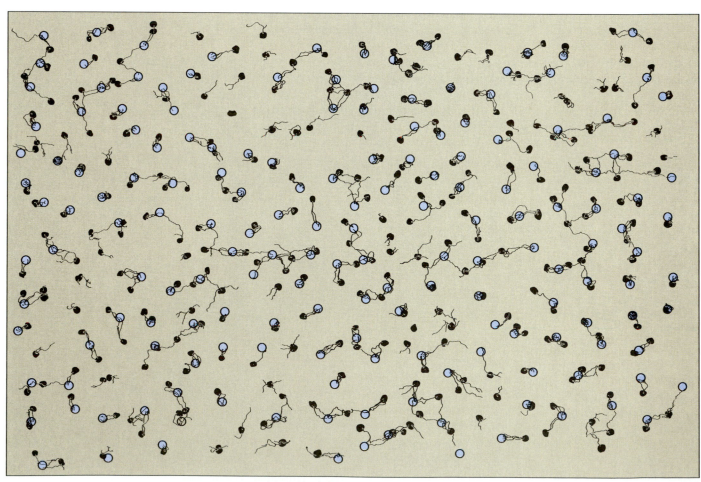

macaque

S cone bipolar cells contacting S cones

×200

source: Kouyama and Marshak, 1992

bipolar cells. Had more samples been added to the clusters of bipolar cells labeled "midget" and "S cone" in the earlier scatter diagram (page 235), the cluster of S cone bipolar cells would be seen to merge with that of the midget bipolar cells.

Not all of the invaginating processes at an S cone pedicle arise from S cone bipolar cells; the remainder presumably come from diffuse or giant bipolar cells, which we consider next.

Diffuse cone bipolar cells

The term "diffuse bipolar" was coined by Stephen Polyak to mean a bipolar cell with dendritic processes that—unlike those of midget bipolar cells— spread out in the outer synaptic layer so as to receive from a number of photoreceptors. The dendrites of diffuse cone bipolar cells receive from between five and ten cones. Six types are currently recognized, distinguished by their size, morphology, and level of stratification, as summarized in the schematic diagram below. The top panels show the appearance of the axonal arbor of each bipolar cell in flat view, and the lower panels in transverse view. The manner in which any of these bipolar cell types responds to visual stimulation is not known.

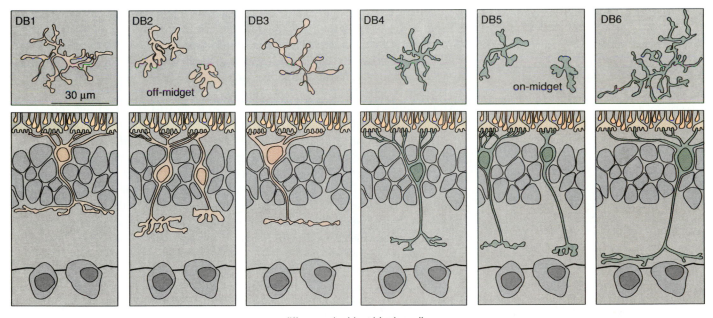

diffuse and midget bipolar cells

after Boycott and Wässle, 1991

Based upon their level of stratification in the outer portion of the inner synaptic layer, DB1–DB3 are presumptive off-bipolar cells. So far as is known, each of these types receives from cones in an indiscriminate manner. All three types make either non-triad-associated or semi-invaginating contacts with the cone pedicles that they receive from. However, there is a report that DB1 bipolar cells make non-triad-associated contacts with those cones whose midget bipolar cells have relatively few synaptic ribbons, and triad-associated contacts with those whose midget bipolar cells have more ribbons. If so, this creates the possibility that DB1 cells are hyperpolarized by M cones and depolarized by L cones (or vice versa), thereby producing a response that depends upon the difference between the stimulation of these two cone types. Within the inner synaptic layer, the axonal terminals of DB1

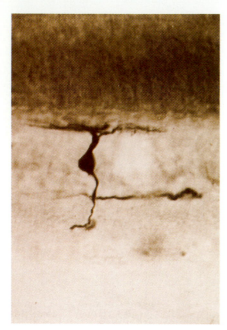

macaque   ×1000

giant bistratified bipolar cell

source: Mariani, 1983

bipolar cells lie beyond the reach of the processes of parasol and midget ganglion cells, and thus presumably contact some other group of ganglion cells. Off-parasol cells receive from DB2 and DB3 cells, as well as a few off-midget bipolar cells.

DB4, DB5, and DB6 are presumptive on-cone bipolar cells, but nothing is known of their response properties or their synapses with ganglion cells.

Giant bipolar cells

Giant bipolar cells have dendritic and axonal fields that are about three times wider than those of diffuse bipolar cells in the same locale (left). Thus their dendritic fields extend over an area that includes about nine times more cones. Little else is known about them.

Amacrine cells

Near the end of the nineteenth century, Ramón y Cajal discovered a group of neurons in the retina that were neither bipolar cells nor ganglion cells. He believed that all of these cells lacked axons, and so termed them **amacrine cells** (Greek a- = lacking + *makros* = long, + *inos* = fiber). But some of the cell types within this group have subsequently been found to have *many* axons. The current distinction between amacrine cells and ganglion cells is whether the cell has an axon that passes out of the eye via the optic nerve. This redefinition illustrates a critical distinction between cell *types* and most cell *groups*. As discussed at the beginning of this chapter, cell types have an objective reality. Large cell groups, on the other hand, such as the different classes of retinal cells, exist in name only, and are defined and redefined to satisfy some vague feeling that these cells should be grouped together. William Whewell termed this procedure the *method of blind faith*. Such groupings are both useful and necessary, but it is worthwhile to keep in mind that they are arbitrary, since there is a natural tendency to give greater weight to larger groupings, whatever their objective basis.

Amacrine cells constitute the most diverse group of cell types within the retina with respect to morphology, size, and retinal coverage. There appear to be between 30 and 40 distinct types, but the functions of only one type, AII amacrine cells, are understood in any detail. Some ganglion cells show certain response properties, such as *directional selectivity* or *local edge detection,* that cannot be readily explained in terms of the summation of photoreceptor signals onto bipolar cells and those of bipolar signals onto ganglion cells. It seems almost certain that the neural circuits that generate these response properties are based upon specialized amacrine cell types.

Cell bodies of amacrine cells are found in the inner nuclear layer, in the middle of the inner synaptic layer, and in the ganglion cell layer. In the inner nuclear layer, they comprise the innermost layer of cell bodies, which is termed the **amacrine cell layer**. The amacrine cells in the middle of the inner synaptic layer all belong to the same cell type, A1, which is discussed below. The amacrine cells in the ganglion cell layer are found throughout the retina, and in the peripheral portion of the temporal retina their spatial density exceeds that of ganglion cells. Such is the tyranny of language that amacrine cell bodies within the ganglion cell layer are sometimes termed *displaced*. This usage appears to be based upon the idea that amacrine cells belong in the amacrine cell layer and ganglion cells belong in the ganglion cell layer—a presumption that the investigator, rather than the retina, knows best. In his paper on the human retina, published in 1891, Alexander Dogiel referred to the outer nuclear layer, the middle nuclear layer, and the inner nuclear layer (ganglion cell layer), and it is regrettable that this terminology didn't catch on. In any case, this usage of *displaced* is confusing and unfortunate. Likewise, in other vertebrates, the cell bodies of some ganglion cell types normally lie at the inner border of the inner nuclear layer; these have also been referred to as displaced, again converting a terminological confusion into a conceptual one.

This section discusses four different amacrine cell types, on-starburst, off-starburst, dopaminergic, and A1, since these types illustrate many of the diverse properties possessed by amacrine cells.

Starburst amacrine cells

Starburst amacrine cells are found in every vertebrate class, and are readily recognized by their distinctive morphology. Radiate processes extend from the cell body, branch, thicken, and branch again near their endings. Most of the synaptic contacts occur away from the cell body, at the thickenings:

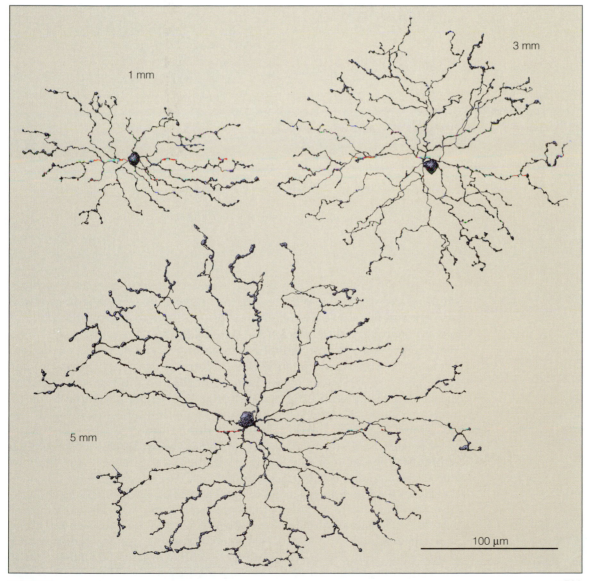

macaque   starburst amacrine cells at different retinal eccentricities   ×500

after Rodieck, 1989

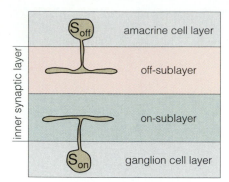

starburst amacrine cells

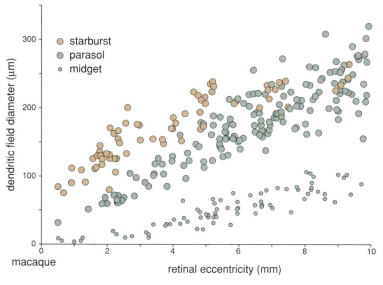

macaque

after Rodieck, 1989

There are two types: those with processes in the middle of the off-sublayer of the inner synaptic layer are termed **off-starburst amacrine cells** (S_{off}), and those with processes in the on-sublayer are termed **on-starburst amacrine cells** (S_{on}). The cell bodies of each type are located in the nearest nuclear layer: the cell bodies of S_{off} cells lie in the amacrine cell layer. Likewise, the S_{on} cell bodies lie in the ganglion cell layer, where they constitute about 40% of the amacrine cell population within that layer at all retinal eccentricities (left).

The dendritic field size of starburst amacrine cells increases with retinal eccentricity, and exceeds that of parasol ganglion cells, except at large retinal eccentricities. The dendritic fields of those in the nasal quadrant are smaller than in the other quadrants, and are excluded from this scatter plot:

acetylcholine

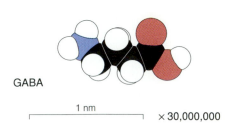

GABA

1 nm

× 30,000,000

Starburst amacrine cells release a neurotransmitter termed **acetylcholine**, and in most vertebrates are the only retinal cells that do so. They also contain metabolic machinery for the synthesis and accumulation of a second neurotransmitter named **GABA**, which they presumably release as well (left). Whereas acetylcholine is generally associated with excitatory synapses, GABA is associated with inhibitory synapses. It is possible that these cells are excitatory to one group of cells and inhibitory to another group. It is also possible that their effect is both excitatory and inhibitory with respect to the same cell, but following stimulation of the cell, the delays and durations of their release may differ.

Because only starburst amacrine cells appear to synthesize acetylcholine, it is possible to label their cell bodies by means of an antibody to one of the enzymes (choline acetyltransferase) used to synthesize this neurotransmitter. The upper portion of the diagram on the facing page shows a human retina in which they were labeled in this manner. The positions of all labeled cells in both the amacrine cell layer and the ganglion cell layer were determined for a vertical strip located in the upper portion of this retina. Strips from each layer are shown ten times enlarged on either side of the retina. Each labeled cell is represented by a dot. There were fewer labeled cells within the amacrine cell layer (ACL), so a wider strip was used to compensate for their lower density.

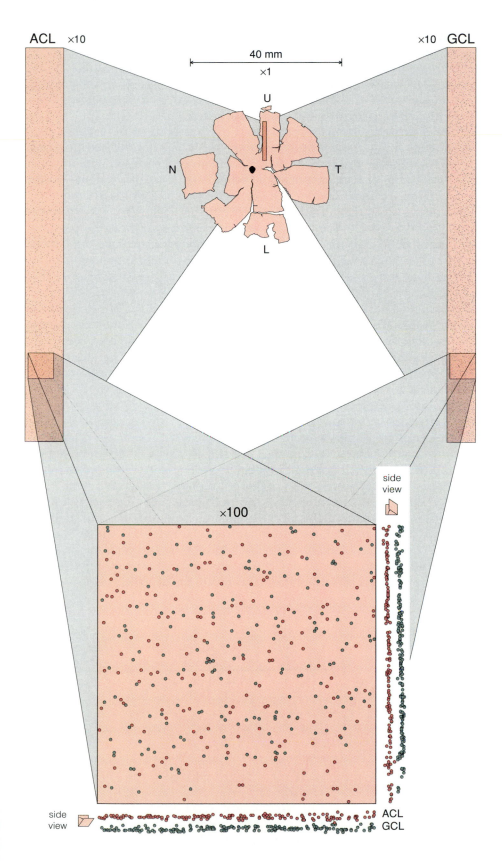

ACL ×10

×10 GCL

40 mm
×1

U

N   T

L

×100

side
view

side
view

ACL
GCL

distribution of cell bodies of starburst amacrine cells along a vertical strip of retina

after Rodieck and Marshak, 1992

A 1 mm² square from the lower portion of each strip is shown one hundred times enlarged at the bottom. Cell bodies in the ganglion cell layer are shown as green circles, and those in the amacrine cell layer as red circles. Because the vertical position of each cell was also recorded, it was possible to plot their positions in transverse section as well, as shown below and to the right of the enlarged 1 mm² portion of retina.

At first sight, it might appear that the positions of the labeled cells within either layer are entirely random, but this is not the case. Instead, there is a zone with a radius of about 30 μm around each cell within which the probability of finding other cell bodies is lower than what one would predict from a purely random (Poisson) distribution. This "dead" zone may have been formed when these cells were born and before retinal expansion occurred. In order to see how this might come about, imagine partially inflating a balloon so that it just acquires a rounded form. Take some small paper discs, such as those that collect in a paper punch, and attach a number of them to the surface of the balloon, by means of a point contact, so that (1) their density is roughly equal throughout and (2) no two discs overlap. Blow up the balloon to a much larger size and record the positions of the centers of the discs. Discs that almost touched have been pulled away from one another by the expansion of the balloon, but because no discs originally overlapped, there is a zone around each disc that is free of neighbors. It is not known whether this quasi-ordering has any functional significance.

One of the striking features of starburst amacrine cells is the large coverage factor of their dendritic fields: about 10 in primates, 20 in cats, and up to 70 in rabbits. The spatial densities of starburst amacrine cells in these three species are about the same, so the lower coverage factor in primates is mainly a consequence of the smaller size of their dendritic fields. What possible functional role this extensive degree of dendritic field overlap might serve is another of the mysteries of this cell group.

In rabbits, cats, and probably other species as well, the processes that compose the dendritic fields of starburst amacrine cells do not randomly cover the retina. Instead, they form an irregular net, with "cords" of processes following the same path (below). In rabbits, and probably in other species, each starburst amacrine cell receives from both cone bipolar cells and other amacrine cell types at all locations in the dendritic field.

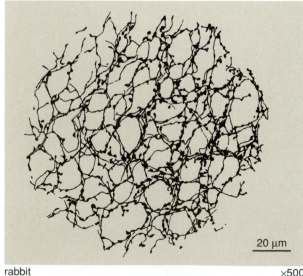

rabbit   ×500
dendritic processes of five starburst amacrine cells

from Tauchi and Masland, 1985

In response to small spots of light, starburst amacrine cells show a receptive field that is coextensive with their dendritic field. On-starburst amacrine cells respond to a stepwise increase in light (i.e., sudden and maintained) with a transient depolarization that can initiate action potentials. As the step change in light intensity is maintained, the depolarization drops to a lower maintained level, which continues for the duration of the increase. Off-starburst amacrine cells respond in a similar manner to a stepwise decrease in light intensity. Both types respond well to moving borders, but do not discriminate between different directions of movement. They also respond well to any rapid changes in light intensity.

Starburst amacrine cells do not appear to be coupled to other retinal cells via gap junctions, nor do they appear to make any form of synaptic contact with one another. Their presynaptic output occurs via the distal portions of their dendrites, and appears to go mainly to two groups of ganglion cells—parasol and on-off direction-selective—although they may provide input to other ganglion cell types as well.

The dendrites of on- and off-*parasol* ganglion cells stratify with those of the corresponding starburst type, and tend to follow the irregular network of starburst processes illustrated above. The time course of the change in firing rate of a parasol ganglion cell is similar to the time course of the graded response of starburst amacrine cells, which suggests that these amacrine cells may play a primary role in shaping the time course of the responses of these ganglion cells to changes in light intensity. It is also possible that action potentials generated by a starburst amacrine cell may initiate corresponding action potentials in the parasol cell.

On-off direction-selective ganglion cells, illustrated earlier (page 202), have bistratified dendritic fields, and the processes in each retinal layer costratify with those of the corresponding type of starburst amacrine cell. Like parasol ganglion cells, they respond well to moving light or dark borders, and both types are excited by input from starburst amacrine cells. As their name suggests, on-off direction-selective ganglion cells respond to movement in a preferred direction, whereas parasol ganglion cells do not. As previously noted, recordings from starburst amacrine cells indicate that they show no preference for direction of movement. There has been much speculation as to how direction-selective ganglion cells might acquire their directional preference via connections to starburst amacrine cells, but no model has yet gained wide acceptance, and recent work suggests that the directional selectivity of these ganglion cells persists following destruction of the starburst amacrine cells in the local vicinity.

To summarize, although many aspects of the spatial distribution, morphology, connections, and response properties of starburst amacrine cells are now known, the specific roles of these cells remain unappreciated.

Dopaminergic amacrine cells

Like starburst amacrine cells, dopaminergic amacrine cells are common to all vertebrates. Within any one species, there appears to be only a single type, whose cell body lies in the amacrine cell layer and whose processes stratify in the outer portion of the inner synaptic layer, where they contact the cell bodies and lobular appendages of AII amacrine cells. As discussed below, dopaminergic amacrine cells control the degree to which AII amacrine cells are interconnected via gap junctions.

The following drawing shows a dopaminergic amacrine cell that had been injected with a label (HRP) so as to reveal its morphology. Two sets of processes arise from the cell body. One set consists of a thick dendritic arbor

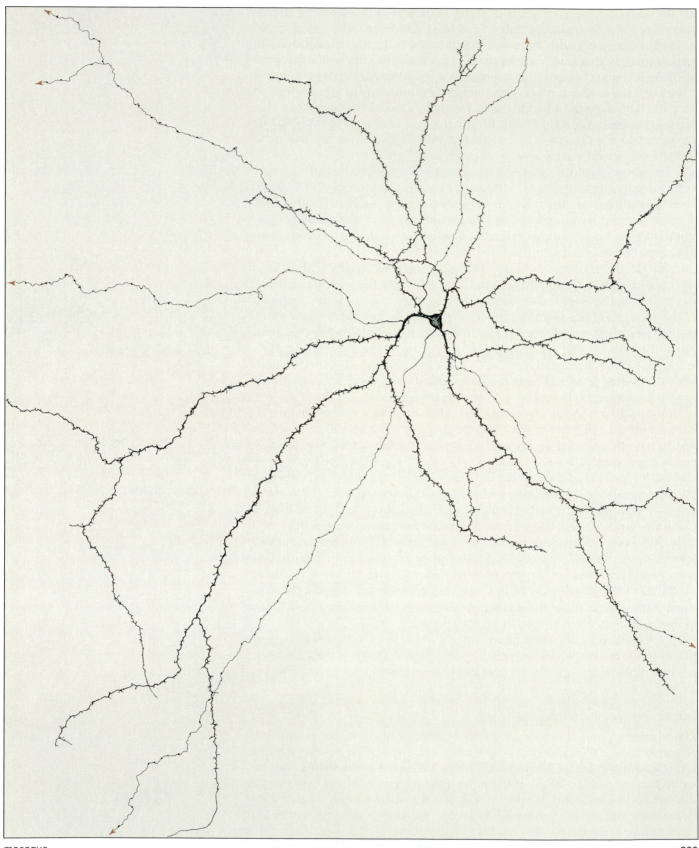

macaque   dendritic field of dopaminergic amacrine cell   ×200

source: Dacey, 1990

that possesses numerous small spiny processes. This dendritic field receives from cone bipolar cells, and has a diameter of about 400 μm near the fovea, rising to about 600 μm in the periphery. The spatial density of dopaminergic amacrine cells has a peak of about 50 cells/mm^2 in the foveal region and declines to about 10 cells/mm^2 in the far periphery, giving these dendritic fields an average coverage factor of about 2.7. The second set is composed of thin axonlike processes that also arise from the cell body, or from the nearby primary dendrites. These thin processes are studded with small varicosities (swellings) that are packed with synaptic vesicles. This drawing shows the same cell, redrawn at a lower magnification, so as to reveal more of the axonal arbor:

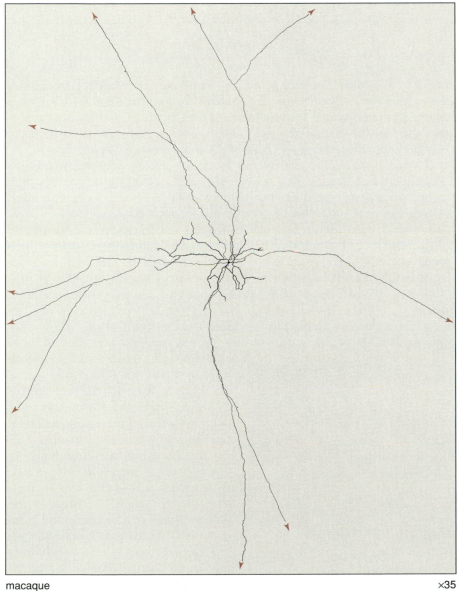

macaque   ×35
axonal and dendritic field of dopaminergic amacrine cell

source: Dacey, 1990

The following scatter diagram plots the field diameters for both sets of processes. Note the logarithmic scale for these diameters. The upper cluster underestimates the true size of the axonal field, because individual axons

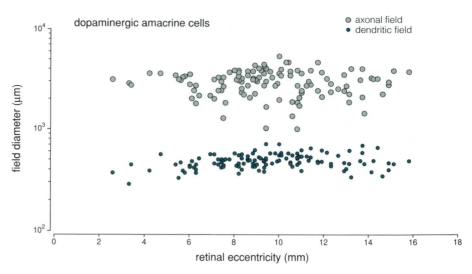

source: Dacey, 1990

cannot be traced farther than about 2 to 3 millimeters before the label fades away. Indirect estimates suggest that the average axon is 4 to 5 mm in length, giving an axonal field diameter of 8 to 10 mm. The calculated coverage factor for the axonal arbor is thus quite large, but it is also difficult to correlate with other factors because of the sparseness of this arbor.

The great majority of the axonal processes stratify at the same level as the dendritic processes. In a few of the cells, occasional processes pass inward either to the middle of the inner synaptic layer or to its inner border. A few other cells send processes outward, through the inner nuclear layer to the outer synaptic layer. Such processes are common in nonprimate species, and their dopamine-containing amacrine cells are termed **interplexiform** cells. Although the issue is not entirely settled, the weight of evidence suggests that there is but one type of dopaminergic amacrine cell in all vertebrates, with a variable predilection for outward-directed processes among species.

Whereas the dendritic field receives the main, if not the entire, synaptic input to dopaminergic amacrine cells, via cone bipolar cells and other amacrine cells, the axonal field constitutes the main, if not the entire, output of these cells, via the release of dopamine from the varicosities. The diagram at left summarizes these relations in a semi-schematic manner.

In assessing the functions of dopaminergic amacrine cells in primate retinas, it is worthwhile to take a step or two back to consider the broader issues of how dopamine influences neurons generally, and the various roles it plays in other vertebrate retinas. Dopamine belongs to a group of chemical messengers known as neuromodulators (page 198). Packaged in vesicles and released by depolarization, dopamine molecules influence other cells, either directly at a presynaptic contact or indirectly via diffusion through tissue. There are

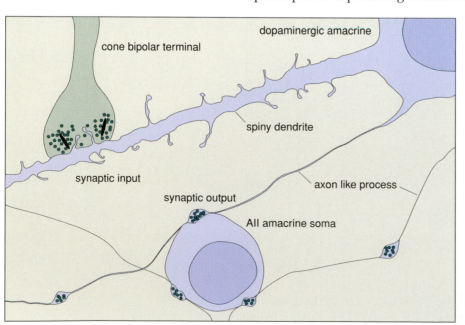

after Dacey, 1990

two types of receptors for dopamine, named D_1 and D_2. Both receptors are metabotropic, and both act to alter the concentration of cAMP within a cell by activating or inhibiting the enzyme (adenylyl cyclase) that synthesizes it. Dopamine applied to D_1 receptors increases the concentration of cAMP; conversely, its effect on D_2 receptors decreases cAMP. The role this second messenger plays within a cell depends upon its type.

In the retina, dopamine concentration is high during the day and low at night. In fishes, amphibians, and birds, the release of dopamine by dopaminergic amacrine cells is inhibited by melatonin. Conversely, the synthesis of melatonin by photoreceptors is inhibited by dopamine via D_2 receptors on the plasma membrane of the photoreceptors. These mutual inhibitions, possibly aided by other amacrine cells, produce a "flip-flop" effect, so that during the day the concentration of dopamine is high and the concentration of melatonin is low, and at night they reverse.

In fishes and amphibians, the lengths of the photoreceptors change. During the day the cones are short, and the rods elongate so that their outer segments are shielded from most of the light by pigment granules contained in the processes of the retinal epithelium. During the night, rods and cones change position. As previously noted (page 212), disc shedding and rhodopsin synthesis in rods and cones are likewise synchronized to the circadian cycle of night and day. In fishes and turtles, dopamine acts to decouple horizontal cells, and also appears to alter the manner in which horizontal cells interact with photoreceptors in a manner that enhances signals from cones and inhibits those from rods. It is not clear whether this occurs in mammals. The one thing that mammalian dopaminergic amacrine cells are known to do is to decouple AII amacrine cells. This is illustrated in the following pair of photographs, which compare the spread of a tracer (Neurobiotin) in a control rabbit retina and in one in which the extracellular concentration of dopamine had been increased to 10 μM. In the dark, the strong intercoupling of AII amacrine cells spreads the signals of rod bipolar cells over a greater region of cone bipolar cells than in brighter conditions, when cone bipolar cells mainly convey the signals of the cones they receive from. Dopaminergic amacrine cells probably produce other changes in primate retinas, but they have not yet been demonstrated.

metabotropic receptor
see NEURONS, page 98

cAMP
see *NUCLEOTIDES*, page 164

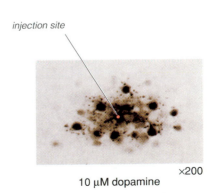

injection site

×200

10 μM dopamine

rabbit   control   ×200

from Hampson et al., 1992

A1 amacrine cells

A1 amacrine cells constitute a single cell type, which is characterized by two components: a dense dendritic field, and a more sparsely branched tree of axonlike processes that extends for a number of millimeters beyond the dendritic arbor. In this photograph, only a portion of the axonal arbor is shown:

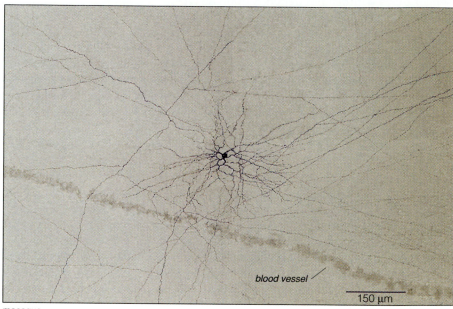

macaque   *blood vessel*   150 µm   x100

dendritic field of A1 amacrine cell

source: Stafford and Dacey, 1997

More of this arbor is shown in this drawing of the same cell at a lower magnification:

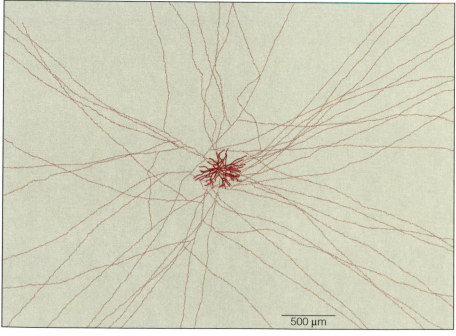

500 µm

x280

axonal arbor of A1 amacrine cell

source: Stafford and Dacey, 1997

Even so, 43 of the 44 axonlike processes extend beyond the frame of the last drawing. This diagram shows the same drawing superimposed upon the human fundus in order to better convey the extent of the axonal arbor:

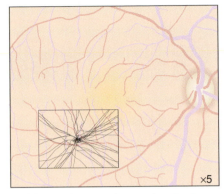

A1 amacrine superimposed on fundus

Unlike most other neurons within the inner retina, A1 amacrine cells show only a relatively small change in dendritic field diameter with retinal eccentricity, as shown in the lower cluster of this scatter diagram:

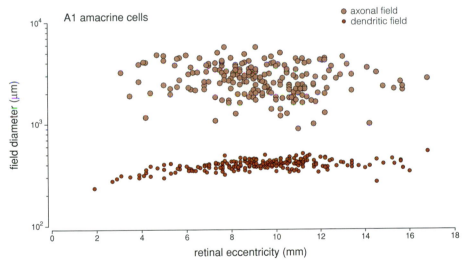

after Stafford and Dacey, 1997

The average spatial density of these cells is $21/mm^2$ (range = 30–13 cells/mm^2 in moving from the foveal region to the periphery). As indicated in the above diagram, the dendritic field has a diameter of about 420 µm. Combining these values gives an average coverage factor for the dendritic arbor of about 3. The cell bodies form a single and regular array across the retina; nevertheless, cell bodies can be found within the amacrine cell layer, the middle of the inner synaptic layer, or the ganglion cell layer. Their dendritic fields, symmetrical about the cell body, tile the retina in an overlapping manner and stratify together at the border between the on- and off-sublayers of the inner synaptic layer. Thus, even though the cell bodies can stratify at three different levels, all of these amacrine cells appear to constitute a single cell type, despite the rule for distinguishing cell types.

The axonal processes arise from the dendritic field, and after extending beyond it, become studded with small boutons (swellings). The axonal arbors have an observed diameter of about 4.5 mm, and on this basis, their calculated coverage factor is 720. But it has not yet been possible to trace any of these long processes all the way to their terminations, so the actual coverage may be considerably larger.

A1 amacrine cells are coupled together, as shown in this photograph:

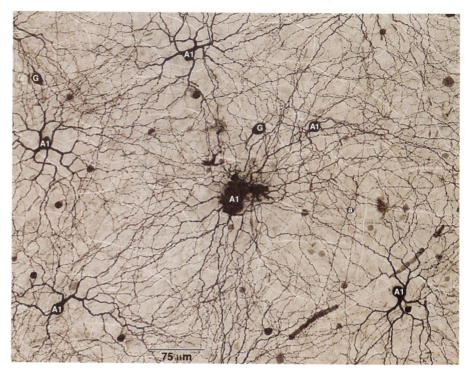

coupling between A1 amacrine cell, other A1s, other amacrine cells (a) and ganglion cells (G)

source: Stafford and Dacey, 1997

The cell labeled A1 in the center was injected with Neurobiotin, which spread to the other cells shown, revealing a regular array of A1 cells, as well as other amacrine cells (A) and a single ganglion cell type (G), neither of which had been previously described.

A1 amacrine cells respond to either an increase or a decrease in light intensity. This on/off response is, of course, consistent with the stratification of the dendrites at the border between the on- and off-sublayers. The response consists of a depolarization upon which is superimposed a burst of 3–10 action potentials that have an amplitude of about 60 mV. These responses can be elicited well above rod saturation levels, and must therefore come from cones. When tested with small spots of light, the cells respond over a region about 50% larger than the dendritic field, and thus a region that is very much smaller than the axonal field. All of these findings suggest that the dendritic field receives directly or indirectly from both on- and off-cone bipolar cells. The action potentials, generated by the summed contributions of these synaptic inputs, propagate down all of the axons.

There are many types of amacrine cells with large fields in addition to A1 amacrine cells, although descriptions of the others are not as extensive. The functional roles of all of them remain unappreciated.

Aspects of vision that have a global character are generally presumed to arise in the visual cortex, or beyond. One example is the observation that large changes in the spectral composition of the illuminant produce only small changes in the color appearance of objects, a phenomenon known as "color constancy." The possibility that color constancy arises in the retina does not appear to have been tested. But because the long processes of amacrine cells provide potential mechanisms for extensive interaction throughout the entire extent of the retina, there appears to be no reason to reject the idea that such phenomena have a retinal origin.

Whatever the different types of amacrine cells do, their ultimate role is to influence the response properties of ganglion cells, to which we now turn.

Ganglion cells

The focus of this section is on three groups of ganglion cells: midget, parasol, and small bistratified, all of which send their axons along the optic nerve to the lateral geniculate nucleus of the brain.

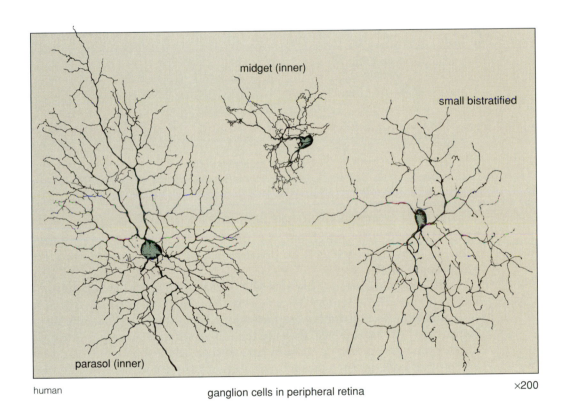

midget (inner)

small bistratified

parasol (inner)

human   ganglion cells in peripheral retina   ×200

source: Dacey, 1993

This section discusses the morphology, connections, and spatial distributions of these ganglion cells; their functional properties are described in the last chapter SEEING. The following chapter (INFORMING THE BRAIN) describes some additional cell types that project to the lateral geniculate nucleus, as well as what is known about the ganglion cells that project to the superior colliculus and to the other regions of the brain that receive direct retinal input. This section also describes an exceptional type of ganglion cell that receives directly from rods, but whose destination in the brain is not known.

The dendritic field size increases with eccentricity within all three groups, as shown on the next page. At large eccentricities, the cluster of parasol cells begins to overlap that of midget ganglion cells, presumably because of the inclusion of cells from the nasal quadrant. In humans, small bistratified cells have about the same dendritic field size as parasol cells at all eccentricities.

Away from the fovea, the increase in dendritic field size with retinal eccentricity is more or less matched by a decrease in spatial density, keeping the coverage factor approximately constant over most of the retina:

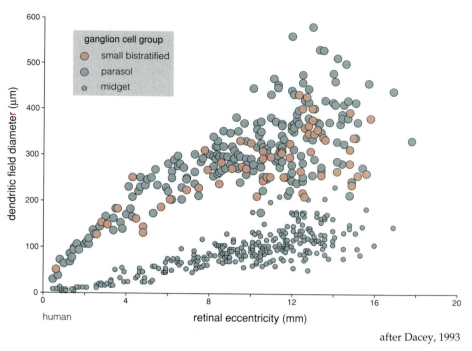

after Dacey, 1993

Midget and parasol ganglion cells dominate the primate retina

More than any other ganglion cell groups, midget and parasol ganglion cells are the ones we see with, so it is worthwhile to consider their properties in some detail.

Midget ganglion cells constitute 45% of the total ganglion cell population in the peripheral retina. This value rises at retinal eccentricities of 4 mm or less; the highest percentage reported is 95%, although this has not been confirmed. Within the fovea, they are the cell group that subserves fine spatial discriminations, such as reading an eye chart, since the message sent by each foveal cone is conveyed by two midget ganglion cells. Collectively, midget ganglion cells constitute about 70% of the 1.25 million ganglion cells in the human retina (1.6 million in the macaque). Parasol ganglion cells compose an additional 8–10% of the ganglion cell population.

These values are much higher than those for similar cell groups in other mammalian species, primarily as a consequence of the small dendritic fields of midget and parasol ganglion cells (see the Box *CELLS SIMILAR TO MIDGET AND PARASOL GANGLION CELLS ARE FOUND IN OTHER SPECIES*, on page 258). If coverage is to be maintained, then a reduction in dendritic field size by a factor of 3 implies an increase in spatial density by a factor of 9. Thus evolutionary pressure for higher spatial acuity can result in a great increase in the number of cells that subserve this aspect of vision. The very high spatial density of these two cell groups is the most distinctive feature of the primate retina.

Because of their great number, it is easy to gain the impression that midget ganglion cells are the most important ganglion cells in the retina. But if I had to give up one ganglion cell group, then I would probably choose the midgets, since their loss would only reduce my spatial acuity to that of a cat, and hopefully would not disturb the neural circuitry of my visual system that deals with more important aspects of seeing, such as object recognition.

The midget and parasol groups in the human retina are similar to those in other Old World primates, as suggested in the following logarithmic plots of dendritic field diameter and retinal eccentricity. Away from the fovea, the dendritic fields of human ganglion cells are somewhat larger than those of the macaque, when the eccentricity is expressed as distance on the retina. Human eyes are about 40% larger than those of macaques, however, and most of this difference disappears when the horizontal axis is expressed as visual angle. Put another way, projections of these measurements onto the visual world show about the same spatial densities. This approximate relation holds for a number of other primates, including New World marmosets, which have even smaller eyes than macaques. This constancy is essentially a feature of the peripheral retina, and its significance is unclear.

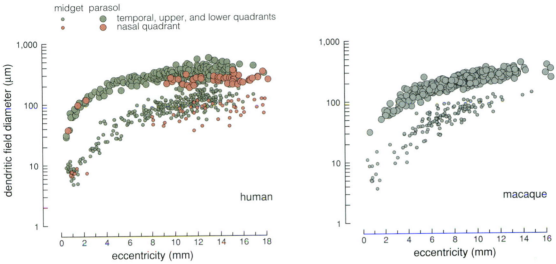

after Dacey and Peterson, 1992 (human); after Watanabe and Rodieck, 1989 (macaque)

Midget ganglion cells

At retinal eccentricities of 2 mm or less, each midget ganglion cell receives from only a single midget bipolar cell, and thus has a very small and compact dendritic field. But toward the periphery, these ganglion cells show a great increase in dendritic field area:

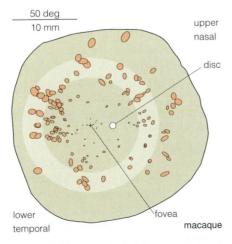

dendritic fields of midget ganglion cells (×10)

after Watanabe and Rodieck, 1989

Cells similar to midget and parasol ganglion cells are found in other species

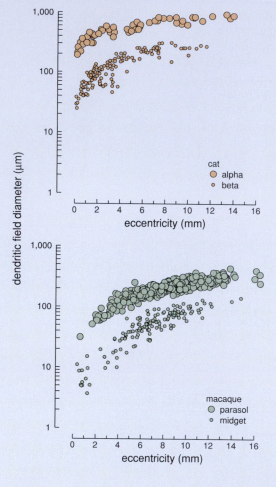

after Boycott and Wässle, 1973 (cat data);
after Watanabe and Rodieck, 1989 (macaque data)

The scatter diagrams at left compare primate midget and parasol ganglion cells with two groups of cat ganglion cells that also have "bushy" dendritic fields. The cluster of cat **alpha** ganglion cells consists of two types, *on-alpha* and *off-alpha*, that stratify at the appropriate levels of the inner synaptic layer. Likewise, the cluster of cat **beta** ganglion cells consists of *on-beta* and *off-beta* ganglion cells, also with appropriate dendritic stratification. The beta and alpha clusters are separated on the vertical axis by a factor of about 3 in dendritic field diameter, which corresponds to a factor of 9 in area. The ratio of the number of beta cells to alpha cells is about 9, suggesting that their coverage factors are similar.

In addition to the similarities between these pairs of clusters, and thus between the populations, there are also qualitative similarities between the properties of the individual cells. Cat beta cells, like midget ganglion cells, do not appear to be coupled to any other cell. Cat alpha cells, on the other hand, show coupling to other alpha cells and amacrine cells in apparently the same way as primate parasol ganglion cells are intercoupled via amacrine cells.

In all of these properties, the alpha and beta groups parallel primate parasol and midget ganglion cells. But the pair of macaque clusters is shifted downward with respect to the cat pair. An attempt to bring the monkey pair into alignment with the cat pair by means of a vertical shift (i.e., scaling of dendritic field diameter) is shown in the diagram at left on the next page.

The vertical shift between species for best fit at large eccentricities requires a scaling factor of 3.0 (this value happens to be the vertical scaling factor for the two clusters within each species, but this appears to be fortuitous).

The diagram on page 257 shows the dendritic fields of several sample midget ganglion cells at different retinal eccentricities. The dendritic field of each cell is represented by a best-fitting oval, shown 10 times enlarged. Those in the nasal quadrant are smaller than others at the same eccentricity, as indicated by the light annulus that marks a retinal eccentricity of 9 mm. This decrease in size is accounted for by the increase in the spatial density of ganglion cells in the nasal quadrant, since the majority of them are midget ganglion cells.

The two types of midget ganglion cells are termed *on-midget ganglion cells* and *off-midget ganglion cells*, or alternatively, *inner midget ganglion cells* and *outer midget ganglion cells*. The dendritic fields of both types form tight territorial domains, as shown in this diagram (right) of a portion of the mosaic of inner (on-) midget ganglion cells in the peripheral retina. Each cell was injected with Neurobiotin, and those whose dendrites were completely filled by the reaction product were drawn. Behind each drawing is a tracing of the extent of the dendritic field. These outlines are seen to interlock, giving a coverage of slightly less that 1 (the calculated coverage factor was greater than 1, for reasons discussed earlier). The average dendritic field

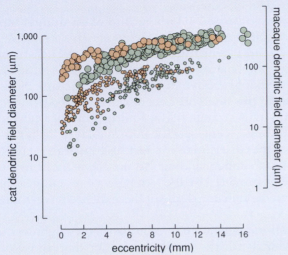

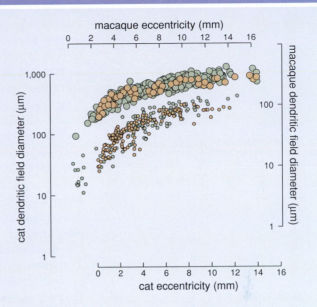

Although this alignment is satisfactory for large eccentricities, it clearly fails near the central area. However, this first approximation suggests that an additional horizontal shift to the right could bring the cell clusters of the cat into alignment with those of the macaque. The result is shown in the diagram at right. The horizontal shift for best fit is 2.5 mm, and this yields a good alignment at all but the smallest eccentricities. Put another way, as a rule of thumb, given a cat alpha cell of a given dendritic field diameter and eccentricity, a parasol cell at a temporal eccentricity 2.5 mm greater will have a dendritic field diameter approximately one-third that of the alpha cell. The same rule converts the parameters for cat beta cells to the parameters for macaque midget ganglion cells.

The total number of beta and alpha cells in the cat retina is about 90,000. The macaque retina contains about 1,600,000 ganglion cells, of which 600,000 lie within 2.5 mm of the foveal center, leaving 1,000,000 for the rest of the retina. Of this group, about 800,000 are midget and parasol cells, or about 9 times more than the total number of cat beta and alpha cells.

Thus the major differences between the ganglion cell populations in cats and macaques appear, at a first approximation, to be quantitative rather than qualitative, with the major differences being their dendritic field sizes and consequent spatial densities. Because of these and other similarities, I believe that midget ganglion cells are homologous at the level of cell type with cat beta cells, and likewise for parasol and alpha cells. But others disagree, and the question remains open.

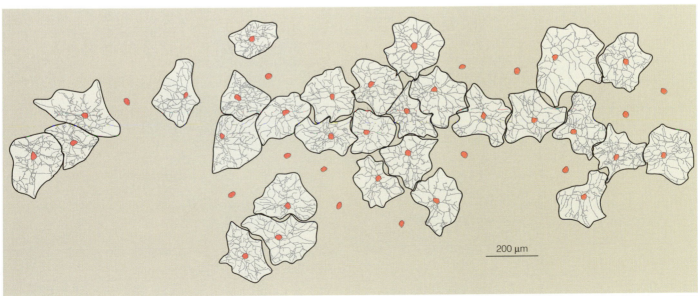

human   on-midget ganglion cells   *after Dacey, 1993* area in this patch was 0.027 mm^2. At this retinal eccentricity, the spatial density of cones is about 3500/mm^2; thus the dendritic field of each of these ganglion cells covers an area containing about 100 cones and a slightly smaller number of on-midget bipolar cells.

As previously discussed (page 235), the group of on-midget bipolar cells is composed of two cell types, *L cone on-midget bipolar cells* and *M cone on-midget bipolar cells*. M and L cones appear to be randomly distributed, and thus each on-midget ganglion cell in the retinal periphery, with its coverage factor of 100 or so, should receive from a variable mixture of M or L cones. As discussed below, this inference is confirmed by electrical recordings from these cells. It seems strange that on-midget bipolar cells in the peripheral retina would convey cone-specific information to the inner synaptic layer, only to have that discrimination lost by convergence onto the same ganglion cells. A key to understanding this puzzle might lie in the different synaptic weightings provided by the two types of on-midget bipolar cells (page 236), although the functional role of these different weightings is itself unclear.

The population of off-midget ganglion cells also shows tight territorial domains. However, their dendritic fields are smaller than those of on-midget ganglion cells, and their spatial density is about 70% higher; why the two types should differ in this manner is not understood. Midget ganglion cells do not appear to be coupled—via gap junctions—to themselves, or to any other retinal cell type.

Parasol ganglion cells

Whereas midget ganglion cells receive from midget bipolar cells, parasol cells receive mainly from diffuse bipolar cells, have larger dendritic fields, and collect from many more cones. The diagram below shows the dendritic fields of a sample of parasol ganglion cells at different locations in the retina, plotted in the same manner as in the previous diagram for midget ganglion cells (page 257). Just as for midget ganglion cells, the dendritic fields of parasol cells in the nasal quadrant are considerably smaller than those elsewhere in the retina, as seen at the circle that marks a retinal eccentricity of 8 mm. This difference is reflected in their increased spatial density as shown in the left panel of the graph at the top of the next page. In macaques, parasol cells constitute about 6–10% of all ganglion cells over

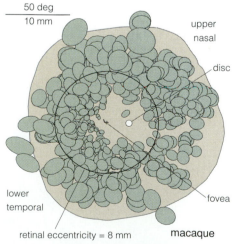

dendritic fields of parasol ganglion cells (×10)

after Watanabe and Rodieck, 1989

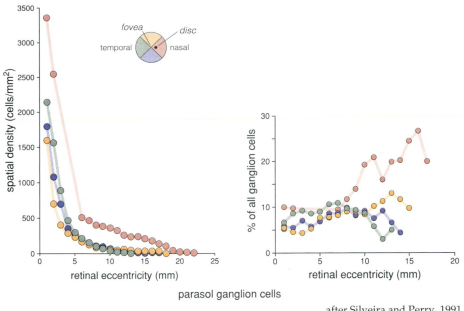

parasol ganglion cells

after Silveira and Perry, 1991

most of the retina, but in the nasal quadrant this percentage rises with increasing eccentricity (above right panel). Since midget ganglion cells dominate the total ganglion cell population, the nasal quadrant must contain a higher fraction of parasol cells relative to midget ganglion cells; it is not understood why this is so.

On-parasol ganglion cells show tight territorial domains, as do off-parasol cells. Dogiel illustrated this pattern over one hundred years ago (page 199). Just as in midget ganglion cells, on-parasol ganglion cells have dendritic fields that are larger than those of off-parasol cells; this difference is compensated by a higher spatial density for the off-parasol type. Again, the reason for this difference is unclear.

Parasol ganglion cells are coupled to two types of amacrine cells

In striking contrast to midget ganglion cells, injection of Neurobiotin into a parasol ganglion cell reveals extensive coupling among parasol cells and at least two distinct types of amacrine cells, as seen in this photograph:

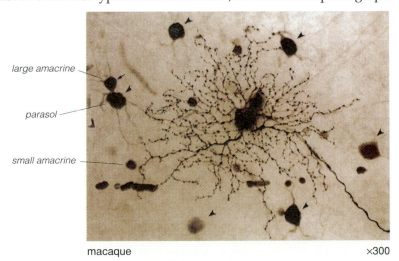

macaque   ×300

coupling of parasol ganglion cell to other neurons

after Dacey and Brace, 1992

The tracer was injected into the parasol ganglion cell at the center of this photograph. The arrowheads point to the cell bodies of other parasol ganglion cells of the same type. They can be seen to form a regular array, again illustrating the strong territorial domains shown by the array of parasol cells of the same type. The small arrow at the upper left points to a coupled amacrine cell, some of whose processes can be seen; the smaller cell bodies belong to a different group of amacrine cells. The parasol cells are probably not coupled directly to one another, but indirectly via the amacrine cells.

Two coupled amacrine cells, one with a relatively large cell body and another with a small cell body, are shown in this drawing:

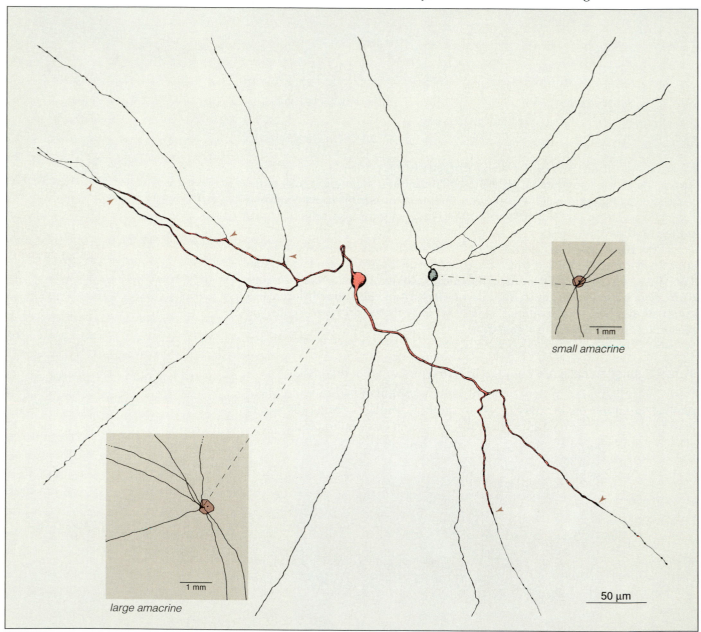

small amacrine

large amacrine

macaque

amacrine cells coupled to parasol cells

after Dacey and Brace, 1992

The larger amacrine cell has thick processes that suddenly taper (arrowheads) and give rise to a beaded axonlike process that continues across the retina for a number of millimeters (inset at left). Both the thick processes and the thin axonlike processes stratify at the same level as the dendritic fields of the coupled parasol cells. Other amacrine cells have been described that show a similar overall morphology, but none of them costratify with the dendritic fields of parasol cells; thus these amacrine cells appear to represent a distinct type.

The amacrine cells with the smaller cell bodies appear to correspond to an amacrine cell type in the cat retina known to accumulate the neuromodulator **serotonin**. Their processes are very thin, extend for a few millimeters across the retina, and stratify in the middle third of the inner synaptic layer.

All of the processes extending from amacrine cells coupled to a single injected parasol cell are shown in this drawing:

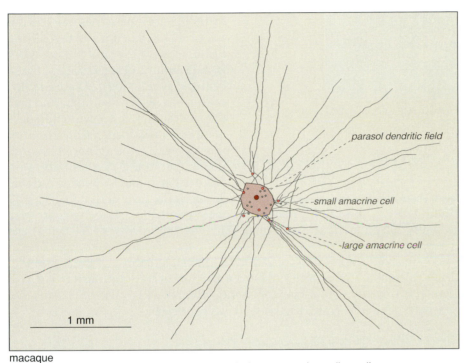

parasol dendritic field

small amacrine cell

large amacrine cell

1 mm

macaque

amacrine cell processes coupled to a parasol ganglion cell

after Dacey and Brace, 1992

Over 30 long amacrine cell processes extend away from this one ganglion cell. Why parasol cells are coupled to these amacrine cells, and what roles these amacrine cells play in retinal function, remain a complete mystery.

Small bistratified ganglion cells
compare S cones with M and L cones

The dendrites of small bistratified ganglion cells arborize in both the on- and off-sublayers of the inner synaptic layer (right). The outer dendritic arbor receives from two types of off-diffuse bipolar cells, DB2 and DB3, each of which in turn receives from about 20 M and L cones. The inner arbor receives from two or three S cone bipolar cells, but most of its synaptic contacts are with only one of them. As discussed in the chapter SEEING, these ganglion cells respond to the difference between the degree of stimulation of the S cones and of the M and L cones, and thereby provide a neural correlate for the perception of yellows and blues.

The two dendritic arbors of these ganglion cells tend to lie at the opposite margins of the inner synaptic layer, where the dendritic fields of on-

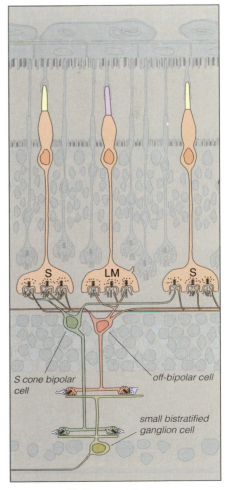

S cone bipolar cell

off-bipolar cell

small bistratified ganglion cell

S cone on pathway

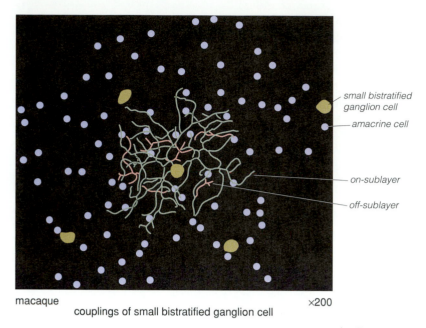

small bistratified
ganglion cell

amacrine cell

on-sublayer

off-sublayer

macaque

couplings of small bistratified ganglion cell

×200

after Dacey, 1993

and off-midget ganglion cells are also found. Their dendritic fields are about the same size as those of parasol ganglion cells. Just as off-parasol cells tend to have a smaller dendritic field than on-parasol cells at the same location, small bistratified cells have a smaller dendritic arbor in the off-sublayer than in the on-sublayer. Both arbors are smaller in the nasal quadrant.

The spatial density of human small bistratified ganglion cells ranges from about 400 cells/mm^2 in the central retina (coverage about 1.8) to about 20 cells/mm^2 in the periphery. Small bistratified ganglion cells are coupled with a single type of amacrine cell. (top left). The cell bodies of these amacrine cells form a quasi-regular mosaic across the retina. Although not shown in this diagram, the dendritic fields of these amacrine cells are also bistratified, and ramify at the same levels as do those of the small bistratified cells. In the retinal periphery, their dendritic arbors are compact, roughly 100 μm in diameter, with a spatial density of about 1700 cells/mm^2 (coverage factor of about 13).

Could our impressions of reds and greens, like those of blues and yellows, also come from a minority population of ganglion cells? We will return to this issue in the chapter SEEING, where the neural mechanisms that underlie color vision are discussed in greater depth.

Biplexiform ganglion cells receive directly from rods

As their name suggests, biplexiform ganglion cells have processes in both the inner and the outer synaptic layers. In primates, their outer processes receive only from rods (left). Viewed in a whole-mounted retina, these outer processes appear to meander about, unlike the compact dendritic fields of rod bipolar cells:

biplexiform ganglion cell

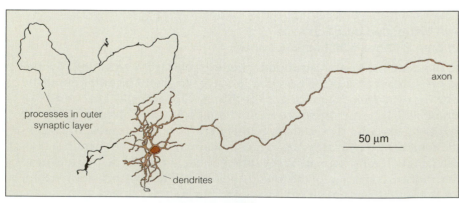

processes in outer
synaptic layer

axon

50 μm

dendrites

macaque

biplexiform ganglion cell

after Mariani, 1982

Biplexiform ganglion cells depolarize in response to light, and their response shows contributions from both rods and cones. The cone contribution could arise from the interphotoreceptor contacts between cones and rods, or via the dendritic processes in the inner synaptic layer, which can be best seen in transverse view:

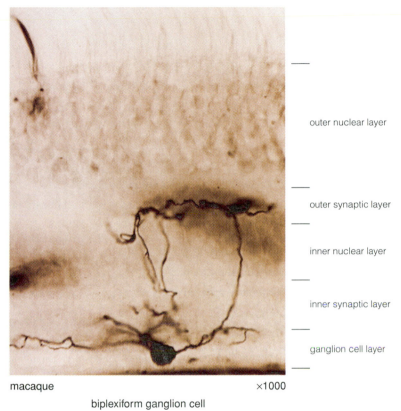

outer nuclear layer

outer synaptic layer

inner nuclear layer

inner synaptic layer

ganglion cell layer

macaque   ×1000

biplexiform ganglion cell

source: Mariani, 1984

These are the only ganglion cells known to receive directly from photoreceptors. By doing so, they bypass the interactions between bipolar and amacrine cells that serve to emphasize contrast at the expense of light intensity per se. Thus their response properties may depend more upon light intensity than upon anything particular in their receptive field. There appear to be only two aspects of vision that depend directly upon ambient light intensity and thus might possibly be subserved by these cells. One is the change in average pupil size, discussed earlier (page 153). The other is the synchronization of the internal rhythm of the body with the daily rhythm of night and day, which is discussed in the next chapter.

Biplexiform cells have also been observed in mice, frogs, and fishes, suggesting that they may be a common feature of the vertebrate retina. There are some differences between species, which are difficult to interpret because the functional role of these cells is so uncertain.

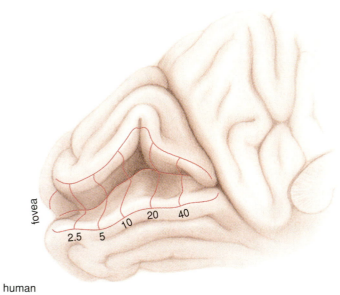

fovea

2.5 5 10 20 40

human

calcarine fissure opened so as to expose the striate cortex

source: Horton and Hoyt, 1991

12

Informing the brain

There are many different types of ganglion cells, and many sites in the brain to which their axons project. In primates, with one minor exception, the axons of each ganglion cell type appear to go to only a single site on each side of the brain. Conversely, most of these brain sites receive from only a few ganglion cell types. This chapter describes how different types of ganglion cells project to different brain structures. The pathway from the lateral geniculate nucleus to the visual cortex is also described so as to provide an introduction to the functional properties of the different cell types along it, which are discussed in the chapter SEEING.

Brain evolution guides retinal evolution

The visual system works as an integrated whole, and the functions of the retina need to be understood within a broader context that includes rapid eye and body movements, immediate comprehension of objects, and other aspects that contribute to survival. Evolution modifies the properties of every cell type involved in vision, and each type has an evolutionary history. Evolutionary change, however, hinges only upon the survival and reproduction of the organism as a whole, not of any particular cell type. Put simply, *cooperation* among cell types within an organism acts to enhance the successful *competition* of that organism with others in the struggle for survival.

When we think in functional terms, we think of the action of one neuron preceding that of those to which it sends its message. But evolution ignores the temporal sequence of events in a neural pathway, for its action depends only on the performance of the organism as a whole. Thus a random variation that results in a minor improvement in some cortical function could, from generation to generation, also modify one or more ganglion cell types to further improve this function, just as useful variations in a property of some ganglion cell type could act to modify the central visual circuitry. Throughout this process, there is never the opportunity to redesign and rebuild the system from scratch, and the result seems closer to a breadboard circuit than a printed one. As François Jacob said, "this process resembles not engineering but tinkering, *bricolage* as we would say in French."

Ganglion cell axons terminate in many different sites in the brain

Just as the eyes and retinas of vertebrates are based upon a common structural plan, so too are their brains. In every vertebrate, ganglion cell axons pass to the same six regions of the brain. The schematic illustration at the top of the next page shows the neural pathways from the two eyes to the left side of a primate brain. The brain regions shown lie within the interior of the brain; their relative positions are roughly correct, but they are greatly enlarged in this illustration. Most of these regions consist of **nuclei** (aggregations of neuronal cell bodies with related functions) or single layers within a nucleus. The nuclei within each region are represented by the same color. There are some 23 anatomically distinguishable sites within these regions (each LGN layer shown consists of two sublayers). Each site receives from a subset of ganglion cell types from one eye, or, in some cases, both eyes. In primates, at least to a first approximation, the axons of a particular ganglion cell type from one eye go to only one site. In other species, the axons of some ganglion cells branch within the brain to go to more than one region. Some sites receive from only a single type of ganglion cell, but most receive from a number of types.

Ganglion cell types and their central projections are fundamental

On leaving the eye and entering the brain, we encounter a new country in which different methods and languages are used. In the absence of relevant neurobiological information, psychologists and psychophysicists needed to describe their findings by means of a terminology that was not tied to any particular assumptions as to the neural substrate involved. Many of these terms have been around for a long time and are familiar to anyone who has

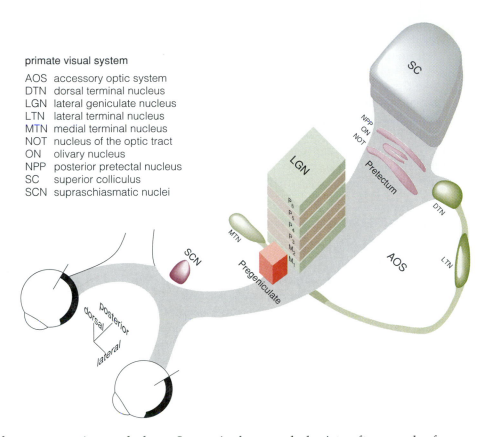

primate visual system

AOS   accessory optic system
DTN   dorsal terminal nucleus
LGN   lateral geniculate nucleus
LTN   lateral terminal nucleus
MTN   medial terminal nucleus
NOT   nucleus of the optic tract
ON   olivary nucleus
NPP   posterior pretectal nucleus
SC   superior colliculus
SCN   suprachiasmatic nuclei

taken a course in psychology. In particular, psychologists often speak of **channels** for *form*, for *motion*, or for *color*, as if each of these aspects of vision flowed through a separate pathway. Words have power, because they organize the mind into particular ways of seeing things. The channel construct readily leads to a paradigm built from *the* channel for form, *the* channel for motion, and *the* channel for color.

However plausible, and however useful at some stages, the notion of channels has proved to be a poor descriptor of how the visual system works. For example, a number of ganglion cell types respond well to motion. As discussed in the next chapter, on-off direction-selective ganglion cells respond best to fast image motion (~10°/s), on-direction-selective ganglion cells respond only to slow motion (~0.1°/s), parasol and midget ganglion cells respond over a middle range, and so on. Each of these groups projects to a different region of the brain, and subserves a different functional role: parasol ganglion cells also play an important role in the perception of form, and midget ganglion cells may play a role in the perception of color. Ironically, the activities of the two groups of ganglion cells specialized to signal the direction of motion appear to make no direct contribution to conscious visual perception.

Within the paradigm of channels, then, one is naturally led to think that the signals from, say, parasol cells pass through more than one channel, and that the channel for, say, motion includes axons of more than one group of ganglion cells. At this point, the utility of continuing to think in terms of channels has all but disappeared, since reality has to be rearranged to fit the model, instead of the other way around. Rather than the abstract notion of channels, what is important and fundamental to the first steps in seeing is the set of ganglion cell types that send their messages to each of the different sites in the brain, and the degree to which the signals of the different types interact, and thus mix, along subsequent pathways.

This perspective also influences how one views the anatomical substrate of the visual system. The *layering* of the lateral geniculate nucleus or the visual cortex may reflect an efficient layout for the neural circuitry, either for interconnections or for modulation by diffusible substances; but, like the layers of the retina, it is an *epiphenomenon*, of no particular importance in itself, and best viewed as *permanent scaffolding*, or alternatively as a breadboard that supports a collection of components and their interconnections.

The map of the projection of ganglion cell types to central nervous system regions is incomplete—in part because the list of ganglion cell types is incomplete—but the following survey summarizes what is known.

Suprachiasmatic nucleus

The suprachiasmatic nuclei (SCN) are found in all vertebrates. As their name suggests, they lie above the optic chiasm. These paired nuclei lie together at the midline of the brain, where they receive ganglion cell axons that emerge from the optic chiasm. In humans, each nucleus has a diameter of about 0.5 mm. Together, and in synchrony, they generate the circadian rhythm of the body. This rhythm influences a number of global aspects of our physiology,

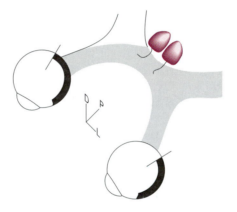

suprachiasmatic nuclei

including daily variations in temperature, hormonal secretion, and sleep and wakefulness. The direct retinal input presumably acts to synchronize the circadian rhythm to the diurnal cycle of night and day. A shift in the phase of the diurnal cycle due to air travel can produce jet lag, which persists until the circadian rhythm can get back into phase with the diurnal rhythm.

Most ganglion cell types ignore the general level of light intensity in the environment because presynaptic horizontal cells and certain amacrine cells act to emphasize contrast at the expense of light intensity per se. This is obviously a useful property for vision, since the daily cycle of night and day produces large changes in light levels. But the ganglion cells that go to the suprachiasmatic nuclei need to respond in some way to these changes in light intensity.

Although it is easy to demonstrate that ganglion cell axons project to the suprachiasmatic nuclei, the specific ganglion cell type or types involved are not known. In any case, the most likely possibility is biplexiform ganglion cells, which receive directly from rods (page 264) and thus bypass the interactions between bipolar and amacrine cells that emphasize differences in light intensity at the expense of intensity per se.

circadian, diurnal
These two terms were introduced in PHOTORECEPTOR ATTRIBUTES (page 214). The cycle of night and day, which is produced by the rotation of Earth, is termed the *diurnal rhythm*. A rhythm generated within the body that has a period similar to that of diurnal rhythm, can be synchronized with it, and can persist in the absence of influences from the diurnal rhythm is termed a *circadian rhythm*.

Identification of ganglion cell destinations by means of retrograde transport

The standard method for determining the types of retinal ganglion cells that project to some region of the brain consists of two steps. In the first step, an experimental animal is anaesthetized, and a minute amount of a tracer substance is injected into some small region of the brain known to receive the axons of retinal ganglion cells. As described below, the tracer substance enters the axons, and over a day or so, travels down them to accumulate in the ganglion cell bodies. In the second step, the animal is killed, its eyes removed, and the retina laid flat and placed in a chamber. The chamber is placed on a microscope stage, and the retina is nourished by an oxygenated bathing medium that flows across it. The ganglion cell bodies that contain the tracer are identified and injected with a stain, which fills the dendrites. The retina is then flat-mounted on a microscope slide, and the stained cells are photographed or drawn.

Axons are thin, but they are also long, and can constitute most of the volume of a neuron. Some 97% of the volume of a parasol cell, for example, lies in its axon. The terminals of an axon are active sites for the release of neurotransmitters, and possibly other substances, but the proteins that accomplish this are manufactured in the cell body, which contains the nucleus. For this and other reasons, neurons have developed mechanisms for moving synaptic vesicles as well as other small organelles along axons.

One mechanism moves material from the cell body to the axon terminals; this process is termed **anterograde transport** (Latin *ante* = before, but in this case, forward + Latin *-gradus* = stepping). Unidirectional protein motors, termed *kinesins*, move the organelles down microtubules from the cell body to the terminals. Anterograde transport has been used to identify the sites in the brain to which retinal ganglion cells project. A tracer, such as a radioactive amino acid, is injected into the vitreous of the eye, where it is taken up by retinal ganglion cells, incorporated into proteins, and anterogradely transported to the axon terminals in the brain. This method was used to identify the projection of the ipsilateral and contralateral eyes to the superior colliculus, shown in the illustration on page 275.

A second neuronal mechanism transports material from the axon terminal back to the cell body, via unidirectional protein motors termed *dyneins*, which step along the same microtubules in the opposite direction. This process is termed **retrograde transport** (Latin *retro* = backward). The returning vesicles normally contain debris destined to be digested in the cell body, as well as molecules taken up at the axon terminal by a common cellular process termed *endocytosis*. In the experimental situation described above, some of the tracer is taken up by this means and retrogradely transported to the cell body. But axons that are damaged by the injection electrode can also retrogradely transport the tracer, which can complicate the situation if retinal axons destined for other sites pass through the region of the injection site.

The tracer used is usually a fluorescent dye, often packaged within latex microspheres. Different fluorescent dyes, each injected into a different brain region, can be used to identify ganglion cells whose axons branch to terminate in more than one region.

A variety of substances are now available for intracellularly injecting a fluorescent-labeled cell body, which can be used to reveal even the finest dendritic arbors of ganglion cells. Although I have termed them "stains" in order to suggest the role they serve, these substances are usually not dyes, but precursors of dyes. Of particular note is a naturally occurring molecule named *biotin*, and a modified derivative of it named *Neurobiotin*, which have been used to investigate a number of different retinal cell types (see page 44).

Accessory optic system

The accessory optic system (AOS) consists of one or more bundles of axons that branch away from the optic tract. The term "accessory" is old and is based upon the inconsequential fact that these bundles leave the main pathway. Within the main branching bundle, there are usually three concentrations of neuronal cell bodies. These nuclei are small, about 0.5 mm in diameter. An unusual feature of the accessory optic systems of all vertebrates is that the direct retinal input comes entirely from the contralateral eye, as indicated at right. This ancient pathway helps to stabilize the retinal image during head movement; its functional aspects are discussed in LOOKING (page 322).

Early vertebrates had laterally directed eyes, and the axons of their ganglion cells projected contralaterally. In the accessory optic system, this pat-

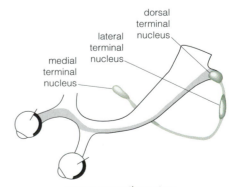

accessory optic system

tern persisted even in species whose eyes became directed forward, so that the temporal retina of each eye now viewed the contralateral visual hemifield. In almost all mammals, the axons of some of the ganglion cells in the temporal retina continue to pass to the contralateral optic tract along with those from the nasal retina. The cell types within this group include those that project to the accessory optic system, which is thus able to receive from ganglion cells throughout the entire retina on the contralateral side. But in primates, essentially no ganglion cells in the temporal retina project contralaterally. Thus the primate accessory optic system does not appear to receive a direct input from the temporal retina of either eye, although it may be influenced indirectly via other pathways from the temporal retina.

The accessory optic system receives from a group of ganglion cells termed **on-direction-selective**. Like the *on-off direction-selective* ganglion cells mentioned previously, these ganglion cells respond preferentially to movement in a specific direction, and give no response to movement in the opposite direction. The group contains three cell types, each with a different preferred direction. As you might guess, the axons of each type preferentially go to one of the three nuclei of the accessory optic system. As discussed in LOOKING, these ganglion cells help us to maintain the direction of gaze in the presence of head movements.

The morphology of the ganglion cells that project to these nuclei in *primates* is not known; however, those in several other mammal species show similar morphologies, suggesting that those of the primates are also similar. The drawing below is an example of a ganglion cell that projects to the cat medial terminal nucleus. The dendritic arbor is thin, lies in the inner portion

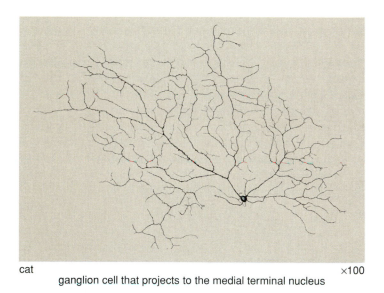

cat   ×100
ganglion cell that projects to the medial terminal nucleus

from Rodieck et al., 1993

of the inner synaptic layer, and has a mazelike appearance, consisting of processes that rarely cross.

During the chase, each time either the gazelle or the cheetah turned its head in some direction, its eyes turned in the opposite direction by about the same amount, so as to stabilize the image of the visual world on the retina. These ganglion cells and their pathways play a critical role in such stabilization, and the fascinating way in which they do so is described in detail in the next chapter.

Superior colliculus

The superior colliculus (SC) integrates visual and auditory information, together with head motions, and directs the eyes to regions of interest in the external world. In nonmammalian vertebrates, most of the ganglion cell axons go to this nucleus, which in these species is termed the **tectum** (Latin *tectum* = roof, in this case the roof of the midbrain). It is the most important

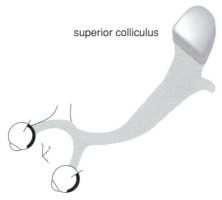

superior colliculus

colliculus

The term *colliculus* (Latin mound or hill) comes from mammalian anatomy, in which the relatively large tectal region of other vertebrates is reduced to a few bumps on the roof of the midbrain. This region, seen on the back surface of the midbrain, is divided into four "bumps," two on each side of the midline. The upper bumps are the superior colliculi, and the lower bumps, which contain an auditory map of the external world, are the inferior colliculi.

visual region in the brains of fishes, amphibians, and reptiles, and is a major and large region in the brains of birds. In mammals, some or most visual processing has been taken over by the neocortex, but the superior colliculus retains the important function of directing the eyes to points of interest.

The superior colliculi are a pair of nuclei that lie close to one another on the top of the midbrain. Each nucleus is only about 6 mm wide; they are shown below greatly enlarged relative to the retinas (compare the upper and lower scales). In this schematic representation, the view is from behind, looking forward at the backs of the two retinas. Both retinas send information about the right visual field to the left nucleus, and vice versa. Conversely, each nucleus receives from the portions of both retinas that receive the image of the contralateral visual field. The line that separates ganglion cells that project ipsilaterally from those that project contralaterally is termed the **nasotemporal division**; it divides the retina into two **hemifields** (see the Box *VIEWING DIFFERENT PORTIONS OF YOUR VISUAL FIELD*). The boundary of each hemi-

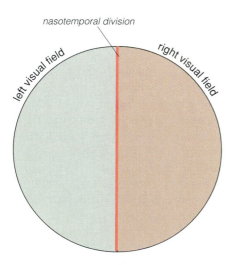

projection of nasotemporal division
onto visual field

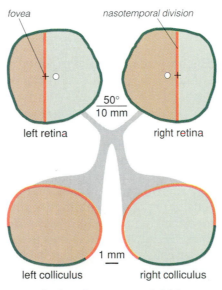

projection of nasotemporal division
onto superior colliculi

rostral, caudal

Rostral means toward the nose (Latin *rostrum* = beak). *Caudal* is the antonym of *rostral*, and thus is used to refer to the back portion of the primate brain; its inappropriate root (Latin *cauda* = tail) reflects the relation between brain and body in most mammals.

field consists of two parts, the nasotemporal division, shown in red, and the edge of the retina, shown in green.

The portion of each nucleus that receives ganglion cell axons consists of a thin sheet that lies at the surface of the midbrain. The axons terminate within this sheet in an ordered manner according to their retinal location. This ordering of incoming sensory messages is common to many regions of the brain; in vision it is termed a **retinotopic map** (-topic, eventually from Greek *topos* = place). In the superior colliculus, the nasotemporal division of each hemifield maps to the **rostral** border of one of the nuclei. The nasal hemifields are wider than the temporal hemifields, so it is the edge of the nasal retina that maps to the **caudal** border. Within the border of the temporal hemifield, ganglion cells from both eyes supply the retinotopic map. Within this region of **binocular overlap**, each point in the map corresponds to the small region in each eye that contains ganglion cells whose axons terminate about that point in the collicular map. The two points in each eye from which this convergence arises are termed **corresponding points**.

The **horizontal meridian** is an imaginary line that passes through the fovea and thereby distinguishes the upper retina from the lower retina:

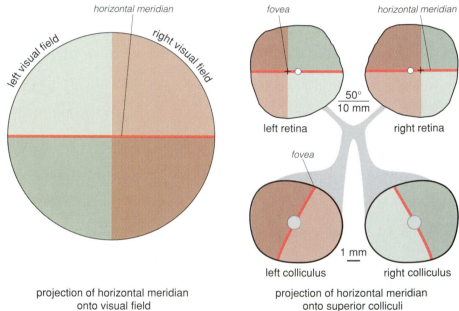

projection of horizontal meridian
onto visual field

projection of horizontal meridian
onto superior colliculi

By construction, the horizontal meridian passes through the fovea; in humans and macaques it also passes through the optic disc, which lies in the nasal hemifield. Unlike the nasotemporal division, which marks the vertical division between ganglion cells that project ipsilaterally and those that project contralaterally, the horizontal meridian is nothing more than a definition, which serves as a convenient benchmark in the retinotopic map. The retinotopic projection of the optic disc lies roughly at the center of the retinotopic map. Of course, the region of the disc in the contralateral eye contains no ganglion cells, so this region receives entirely from ganglion cells at the corresponding location in the ipsilateral eye. The horizontal meridian divides each collicular nucleus into two approximately equal portions. The lower retina maps to the medial portion of each nucleus and the upper retina maps to the lateral portion. This is the general pattern found in vertebrates.

A more detailed retinotopic map is shown in this diagram, in which half of the image of a radial coordinate system in the visual field is projected onto each nucleus by the ordered arrangement of ganglion cell axons arising from both retinas:

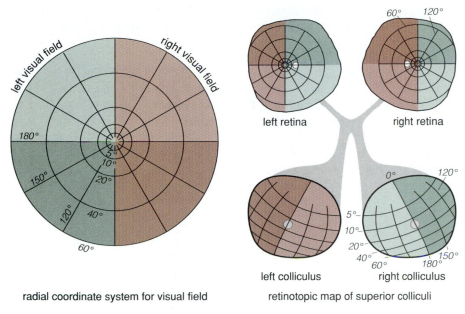

radial coordinate system for visual field   retinotopic map of superior colliculi

after Kaas and Huerta, 1988

Notice that the map of the region around the fovea (e.g., within 10°) occupies a greater fraction of the nucleus than the fraction of the retina occupied by this region. This **retinotopic magnification** occurs because more ganglion cells project to the colliculus from the central retina than from a similar area in peripheral retina.

The superior colliculus consists of a number of layers. As noted above, the more superficial layers receive direct retinal input, whereas the deeper layers initiate signals that lead to eye and head movement. The axons of ganglion cells from the contralateral eye terminate along a relatively dense band near the surface of the colliculus; those from the ipsilateral eye terminate a bit deeper and are less dense, as seen in this **coronal** section:

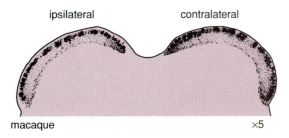

terminals of retinal axons in superior colliculi

after Kaas and Huerta, 1988

coronal section

This diagram plots dendritic field size, somal (cell body) size, and retinal eccentricity for four different groups of ganglion cells. The three scatter plots shown can be viewed as different shadow casts of a three-dimensional scatter plot (imagine cutting out the empty square at the lower left, folding the bottom plot upward at the horizontal axis, and the left plot inward at the vertical axis). As shown, the axes for somal size point downward in the lower plot, and leftward in the left plot.

The ganglion cells that project to the superior colliculus have large dendritic fields, as shown in the upper right quadrant of this diagram. The ganglion cells with the largest dendritic fields project to the pretectum (PT), as discussed below. Parasol and midget ganglion cells project to the lateral geniculate nucleus, and are included for comparison. The cells that project to the superior colliculus (SC) have dendritic fields that are generally larger than those of parasol cells at the same retinal eccentricity (upper right plot), but somal diameters that tend to be smaller (left and bottom plots).

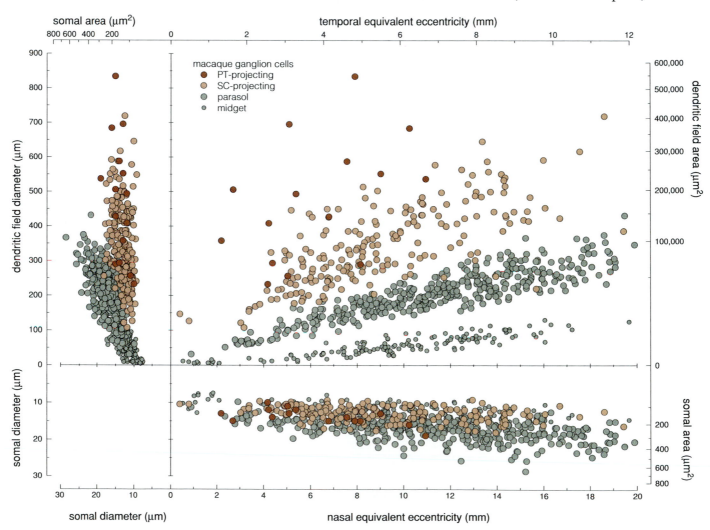

source: Rodieck and Watanabe, 1993

A variety of different ganglion cell types project to the superior colliculus, probably more than to any other region of the brain that receives direct retinal input. The number of types is not known because it has proved difficult to sharply distinguish between them on morphological grounds alone. Nevertheless, it is possible to distinguish three groups within this population, which have been termed the **S group**, **M group**, and **T group**. In this context, *group* means a collection of cells that are readily distinguishable from other cells, and thus appear to belong to different cell types than those other cells. However it has not yet been possible to distinguish the different cell types within a group (see page 230). Thus, for example, the ganglion cells in the S group are readily distinguishable from those in the T group, and almost certainly belong to different cell types than those in the T group. But the number of cell types within the S group remains obscure because no good means of cleanly distinguishing among them has yet been found.

The S group consists of cells with a sparse and sometimes bistratified dendritic field, like the one illustrated here:

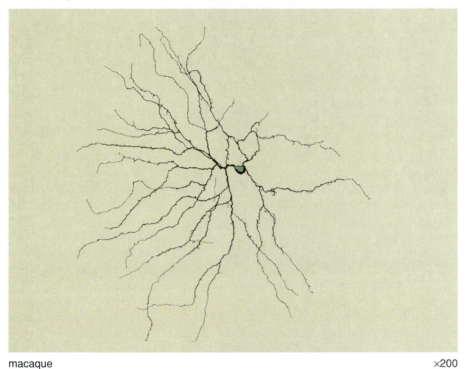

macaque   ×200

S-group ganglion cell

source: Rodieck and Watanabe, 1993

The S group includes cells with a great variety of morphological forms, suggesting that it encompasses a number of different ganglion cell types. Unlike the other two groups, S-group cells show little increase in dendritic field size with retinal eccentricity.

The T group consists of cells with a dense and usually bistratified dendritic field, like the one illustrated at right. The M group (shown on the following page) appears to consist of a single cell type, termed **maze** ganglion cells. These cells are always monostratified; their dendritic processes rarely cross and tend to be distributed uniformly across the dendritic field, giving the impression of a maze. Adjacent maze cells stratify at the same level and appear to form tight territorial domains, reinforcing the hypothesis that they constitute a single type.

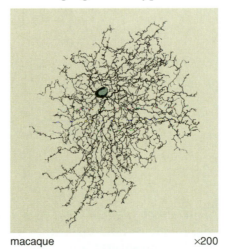

macaque   ×200

T-group ganglion cell

source: Rodieck and Watanabe, 1993

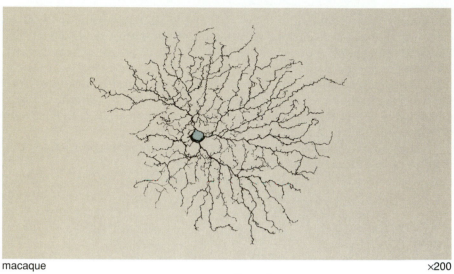

macaque   ×200

maze ganglion cell

source: Rodieck and Watanabe, 1993

The dendritic fields of cells in the M and the T groups are about the same size at any eccentricity, and both show a notable increase in size toward the peripheral retina. By contrast, the dendritic fields of cells in the S group show a relatively small change in size with eccentricity, suggesting that they may serve a different role than the other groups.

Ganglion cells that show a morphology and size similar to those that project to the colliculus have not been observed to project to any other region of the brain. Conversely, none of the other known ganglion cell types (e.g., midget, parasol, small bistratified) appears to project to the superior colliculus. The notion that in primates each type of ganglion cell goes to only one region of the brain is based primarily on this observation. However, a tiny fraction of the population of parasol ganglion cells appears to project to the pretectum, thereby ensuring that rules were meant to be broken.

Pretectum

In mammals, the vertebrate *tectum* is usually referred to as the *superior colliculus*, but the term *pretectum* is still used for all vertebrates. The pretectum lies among the ganglion cell axons passing to the superior colliculus. By this

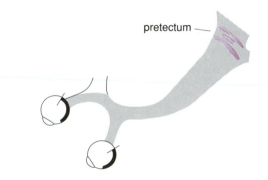

pretectum —

point in their journey, these axons have become ordered according to their retinotopic destination within the superior colliculus. The pretectum is divided into several zones, some of which are elongated so as to span the width of the bundle of axons destined for the superior colliculus and thus fall in the path of all the ganglion cell axons that project to it. The middle portion has a U shape, and appears to intercept axons from only the central portion of the retina; it may compose two distinct zones.

Retrograde tracers show that the ganglion cells that project to the pretectum include some with relatively large and sparse dendritic fields, like the one shown here:

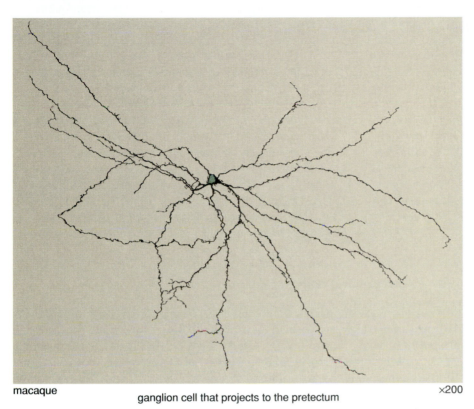

macaque   ×200
ganglion cell that projects to the pretectum

source: Rodieck and Watanabe, 1993

A variety of morphological forms have been observed, which suggests that a number of different ganglion cell types project to the pretectum, including, as noted above, occasional parasol cells. The previous scatter plot (page 276) includes ganglion cells that were retrogradely labeled by injection of tracers into the pretectal area. Some of these cells overlap the cluster of cells that project to the superior colliculus, and show a similar morphology. It is possible that the axons of these ganglion cells branch to terminate in both the pretectum and the superior colliculus, as has been observed in cats. If so, this would be an exception to the observation that in primates, each type of ganglion cell goes to only one region. But because the pretectum is surrounded by ganglion cell axons destined for the superior colliculus, it seems more likely that some of these axons that were broken by the injection electrode also took up the retrograde tracer.

The pretectum is known to play a role in adjusting the size of the pupil in response to changes in light intensity, and in the reflex tracking of large moving objects. But its full spectrum of functions remains poorly understood.

Pregeniculate

The ganglion cell type or types that project to the **pregeniculate** are not known, and the functional role of this region remains unappreciated. The term *pregeniculate* is used only in primates; its relation to visual nuclei of other species is described in the Box *PREGENICULATE HOMOLOGS*.

Pregeniculate homologs

In the schematic illustration at the beginning of this chapter, the pregeniculate is shown in front of the lateral geniculate nucleus (LGN), but it actually forms a rind over part of the upper portion of the LGN. It is probably homologous to either the **ventral lateral geniculate nucleus (LGN$_v$)** and/or the **intergeniculate leaflet (IL)** in other vertebrates, both of which also receive direct retinal input. Both are part of the ventral thalamus, and unlike the LGN, do not project to the striate cortex or, for that matter, any portion of the cerebral cortex. The LGN of nonprimate mammals is termed the dorsal lateral geniculate nucleus (LGN$_d$) to distinguish it from the LGN$_v$. The pathways to and from the LGN$_v$ and the IL are similar, as are some aspects of their neurochemistry, suggesting they may have similar functions. In other vertebrates, these regions lie below the dorsal LGN, but because of some quirks during development, the primate pregeniculate comes to lie above the LGN.

Every vertebrate has an LGN$_v$. In some species with well-developed vision, such as squirrels, it is about the same size as the LGN$_d$, but in most species it is small. An intergeniculate leaflet has been recognized in pigeons and frogs, so this may be another region common to all vertebrates.

The LGN$_v$/IL region is the least understood of any region of the brain that receives direct retinal input. Neurons within this region send axons to the suprachiasmatic nuclei (SCN). There is some suggestive evidence that, whereas the suprachiasmatic nuclei set the period of the circadian rhythm, the LGN$_v$/IL plays a role in determining its phase. Most of the neurons in the IL appear to be sensitive to the level of ambient light intensity, which is at least consistent with this idea. In effect, the direct projection from the retina to the SCN is not the only visual input that the SCN receives. Other evidence suggests that the LGN$_v$/IL somehow contributes to eye movements, but it is not clear in what way.

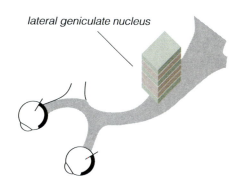

lateral geniculate nucleus

Lateral geniculate nucleus

Our conscious perception of the visual world comes from the ganglion cells that project to the lateral geniculate nucleus (LGN). The cells of this nucleus project in turn to a portion of the cerebral cortex that is termed the **striate cortex**, or **V1** (below). The LGN on each side of the brain receives from ganglion cells that view the contralateral visual hemifield. A roughly horizontal section of the brain shows all the components of this pathway, as shown at right on the next page. Here the eyes have been replaced by retinas, viewed from the back, and colored according to the visual hemifield each hemiretina receives from. The general features of the pathways from the retinas are almost identical to those of the pathways to the superior colliculus, and are presented here in greater detail. The left visual hemifield projects to the right striate cortex via both eyes. The *temporal* retina of the *right*

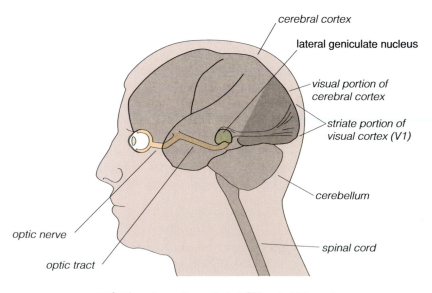

projection of ganglion cells to LGN and striate cortex

eye views the left visual hemifield, but its view is limited because of the nose. The *nasal* retina of the *left* eye has a more extensive view of the left visual field. The portion of the visual field that only this eye sees is termed the **monocular** portion of the left visual field, and is indicated by the darker green. The lighter green indicates the part of the left visual field seen by both eyes, and is termed the **binocular** portion.

The lateral geniculate nucleus is composed of twelve distinct sublayers

The lateral geniculate nucleus consists of six superimposed layers, each containing two sublayers. Each layer is about half a millimeter thick and receives from the retinal hemifield of only one eye. The photomicrograph at the top of the next page has been colorized to show the *eye* that each layer receives from: The lowest two layers contain large cell bodies, and are termed the **magnocellular layers** (Latin *magnus* = large); they are collectively referred to as the **magnocellular zone.** The upper four layers contain cells with smaller somata and are termed the **parvocellular layers** (Latin *parvus* = small), and collectively, the **parvocellular zone.** The terminals of the ganglion cell axons that project to each layer form an orderly retinotopic map. Furthermore, the maps of all of the layers are in register, so that a given *point* in the visual world that is seen by both eyes projects to a *line* within the LGN, which passes through all layers. One of these **projection lines** is shown in the photomicrograph.

Another feature, which you may have noticed, is that darkly staining cell bodies are confined to the upper portion of each layer. The lower portion also contains cell bodies, but there are fewer of them, and they don't take up standard stains as readily. Thus each layer is composed of two sub-

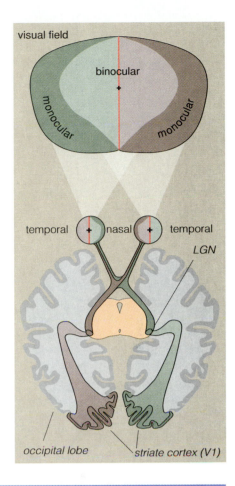

Viewing different portions of your visual field

- Look straight ahead at a distant object, and imagine a vertical line passing through it. Everything you see to the right of that line lies in your *right visual field*, and will be seen by your *left visual cortex*.
- Close your right eye, and place the tip of your index finger directly in front of your left eye at a convenient distance (e.g., the distance you use for reading). Without changing the direction of your gaze, move your finger to the left along an arc, keeping it about the same distance from your eye, until it disappears. Make a rough judgment of the angle over which it moved. While your finger was visible, its image was sweeping across the *nasal* portion of your left retina.
- Bring your finger back to your point of gaze, and then slowly swing it to the right until it just disappears behind your nose. The angle over which your finger remained visible was smaller. While your finger was visible, its image was sweeping across the *temporal* portion of your left retina, which is narrower than the nasal portion.

Angles 369

- Without changing the direction of your gaze, or the position of your finger, open your right eye. Your index finger can be seen by your right eye, but not by your left eye. Your finger, and everything to the right of it, lies in the *monocular portion of your right visual field*.
- Bring both of your index fingers together so that they touch directly in front of you. Close your right eye, and without altering your gaze, move your right index finger to the right until it just disappears from the view of your left eye. Now switch eyes, and do the same for your left index finger. Open both eyes; the region between your two fingers is your *binocular visual field*. Note the extent of the monocular visual fields on each side of the binocular visual field.

The above demonstrations were done with the tips of your index finders at the same height as your eyes, so that they were confined to the horizontal plane that included your direction of gaze. If you repeat them with your fingers well above or below this plane, you will find that the portions of the right or left visual fields that correspond to the monocular visual fields are much smaller.

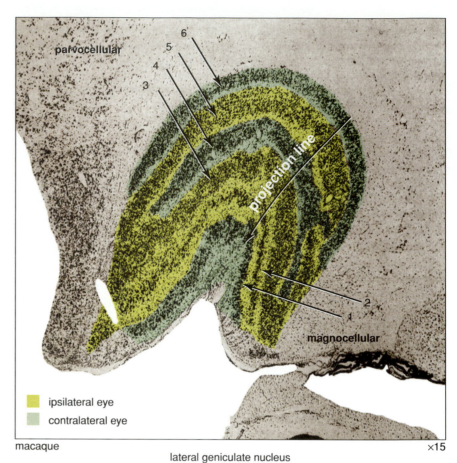

parvocellular

projection line

ipsilateral eye
contralateral eye

macaque   ×15

lateral geniculate nucleus

magnocellular

after Hubel and Wiesel, 1977

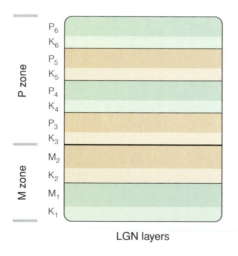

LGN layers

layers. The upper portion is termed the **principal sublayer**, and the lower portion, which contains cell bodies smaller than those of the upper portion, is termed the **koniocellular sublayer** (Greek *konis* = dust). Each sublayer is referred to by a letter that identifies its type (P or M for a principal sublayer of the parvo- or magnocellular zone, K for a koniocellular layer) followed by a numerical subscript that identifies the layer (left). The two sublayers in each layer are innervated by the same eye, but receive from a different set of ganglion cell types, as discussed below.

Three factors modify this simple picture. First, for retinal eccentricities greater than about 15° (e.g., the center of the optic disc), layers 6 and 4 come together, as do layers 5 and 3; this can be seen in the lower left portion of the photomicrograph above. Second, since the monocular portion of the visual field is viewed only by the contralateral eye, the merged ipsilateral layers do not extend as far as the merged contralateral layers. Third, because each retina has a hole in it at the optic disc, the contralateral layers also have a hole at this retinotopic location. When convenient, we can ignore all these variations by considering only the central portion of the retina, out to 15°, as in the illustration above.

The striate cortex contains a retinotopic map of the visual field

Only a small portion of the striate cortex can be seen when viewing the intact brain. Most of the striate cortex lies along the medial surfaces of the two cerebral hemispheres, which face each other along the midline of the body. If the right hemisphere is removed, the striate cortex can be seen to lie within an infolding of the cerebral cortex, termed the **calcarine fissure**:

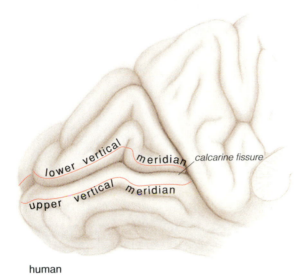

human

source: Horton and Hoyt, 1991

The nasotemporal division of the retina maps to the lines marked upper and lower vertical meridian. The upper and lower portions of the calcarine fissure can be spread apart so as to reveal the striate cortex within:

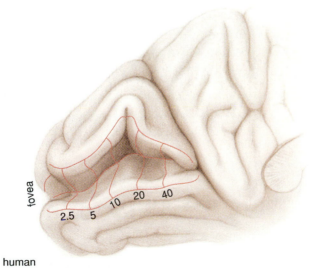

human

calcarine fissure opened so as to expose the striate cortex

source: Horton and Hoyt, 1991

The diagram at the top of the next page shows a flattened striate cortex from one hemisphere, together with its retinotopic map; the striate cortex is shown at its actual size, and contains a complete representation of the contralateral visual hemifield. The foveal portion is normally folded so as to lie along the back surface of the brain. Notice that about half the striate cortex

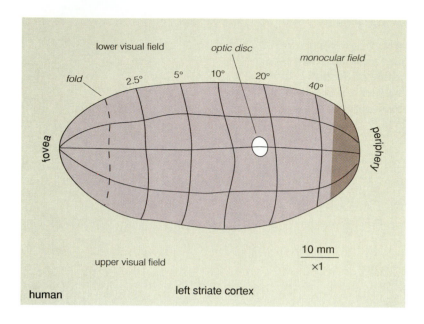

human   left striate cortex

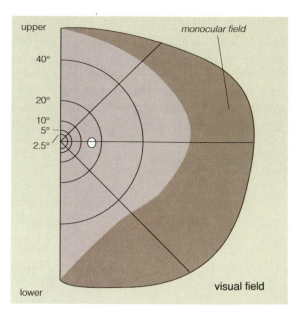

source: Horton and Hoyt, 1991

is devoted to the relatively small portion of the retina that lies within 7° of the fovea. The angular size of this portion is about the same as that of your fist, held at arm's length, and covers about 1% of the retina. Thus the other half of the striate cortex receives from the remaining 99% of the retina. Each portion contains about half of the ganglion cells.

The signals from the two eyes are segregated into ocular dominance bands

Although the striate cortex is retinotopically ordered overall, each point within it generally receives from only one eye. The inputs from the two eyes form **ocular dominance bands**. Each band is about 0.4 mm wide, and thus about twice as wide as the ridges of a fingerprint, shown here at a magnification of 2:

fingerprint

from Hubel and Wiesel, 1977

ocular dominance bands in flattened striate cortex

after Florence and Kaas, 1992

The diagram at left shows the complete projections of one eye onto the striate cortices of a monkey, as seen in a flattened view. The representation of the right eye is shown in color on each cortex; the interspersed gray portions reflect the innervation from the left eye. Near the foveal representation, the bands consist of short segments that branch, fuse, and terminate. In the midperipheral region, the bands are more nearly parallel and branch less. Because the optic disc lies in the nasal retina, which projects contralaterally, the contralateral cortical map has a "hole" in it at the corresponding position. Conversely, the ipsilateral cortex receives from the temporal retina of the right eye, and fills in the cortical representation of the region corresponding to the optic disc of the left eye. In the periphery, the bands break down into a pattern of dots for the ipsilateral eye; the representation of the far periphery (monocular field) is due entirely to the contralateral eye. Ocular dominance bands can be clearly seen in this flattened visual cortex of a man who was blind in his right eye:

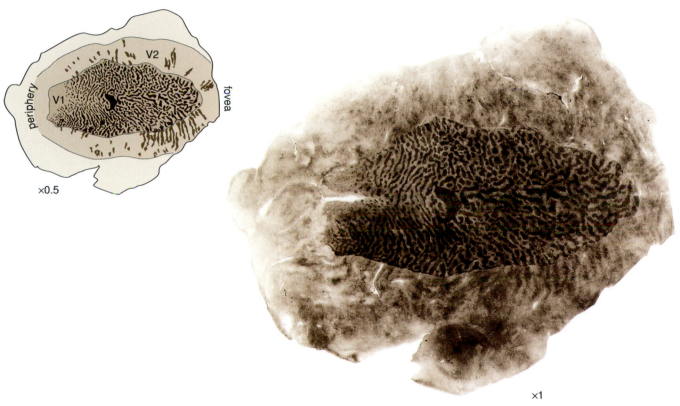

ocular dominance bands in right visual
cortex of a man blind in his right eye

courtesy of Jonathan C. Horton

The striate cortex is vertically layered

The striate cortex is about 1.5 mm thick, and like the rest of the cerebral cortex, consists of interconnected neurons whose cell bodies stratify at different levels. The semi-schematic diagram on the next page focuses on the portions that receive direct input from the LGN, which are shown colored. Most of the axons from the LGN terminate in layer 4, where they form the ocular dominance bands. Unique to the striate cortex is a two-dimensional array of **blobs**, found mainly in layer 3. The blobs can be revealed by histological stains that detect high metabolic activity. Each blob lies centered on an ocular dominance band, which in humans lie about 0.5 mm apart. Each blob also receives axons from LGN cells.

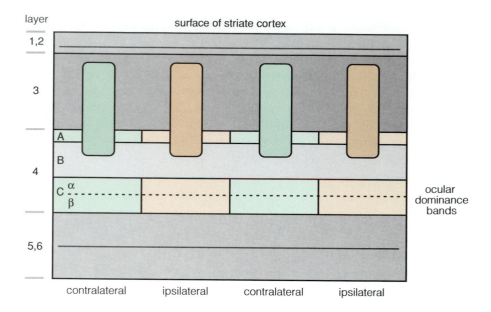

layer   surface of striate cortex

1,2

3

A
B

4

C α
   β   ocular
                                          dominance
                                          bands

5,6

contralateral   ipsilateral   contralateral   ipsilateral

We now have sufficient scaffolding to show the projections of different ganglion cell types to the LGN and the projection of LGN cells to the striate cortex.

Messages from different ganglion cell types go to different portions of the striate cortex

The LGN consists of six layers, but only three for each eye. As previously discussed, each layer consists of two sublayers: principal and koniocellular.

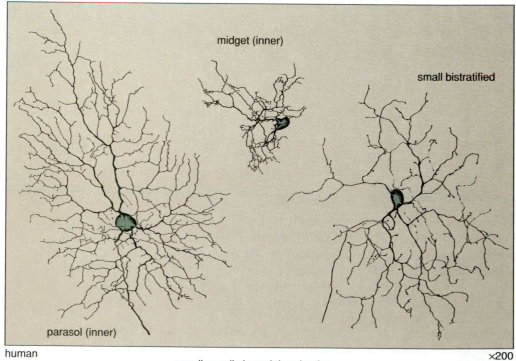

midget (inner)

small bistratified

parasol (inner)

human   ×200

ganglion cells in peripheral retina

after Dacey, 1993

The axons of all **midget ganglion cells** project only to the LGN, where they terminate in the principal portions of the parvocellular layers (P_3–P_6) (right). Each contacts a single LGN midget relay cell, which projects in turn to layer $4C_\beta$ of the appropriate ocular dominance band:

foveal midget ganglion cells

after Polyak, 1941

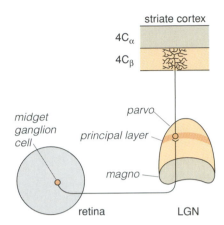

pathway of midget ganglion cells

The axonal terminals of the LGN midget relay cells form a tight cluster within layer $4C_\beta$, which extends throughout the entire thickness of this sublayer. Off-midget ganglion cells tend to terminate in LGN layers P_6 and P_5, and on-midgets in P_4 and P_3, but the axonal terminals of both on- and off-relay types costratify together within layer $4C_\beta$ of the striate cortex. There, each axonal arbor extends over a region that includes about 100 other midget relay axon terminals, or 50 of each type. Nevertheless, retinotopic order appears to be preserved in that the centers of the terminal fields are retinotopically ordered. At the retinal level, the receptive fields of on-midget ganglion cells do not overlap. But the axonal processes of their LGN relays overlap so that each small region within $4C_\beta$ is close to the processes of a cluster of about 50 on-midget ganglion cells. In the fovea, each midget ganglion cell receives from a single cone within a small region of the photoreceptor array:

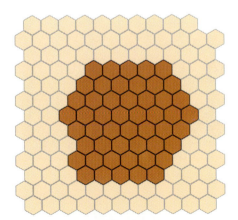

foveal region containing 50 cones

In SEEING, we will consider possible relations between this coverage and the ongoing movement of the image across the retina.

parasol ganglion cells   ×300

after Polyak, 1941

Near the edge of an ocular dominance band, the axon of an LGN midget relay cell may send a collateral branch across the band of the other eye to ramify near the edge of the next band for the same eye. Thus a precise retinotopic order appears to be preserved both within a band and between bands for the same eye, whatever the extent of the terminal arbors.

The pathway for **parasol** ganglion cells shows many of the features of the midget pathway. Their axons terminate in either of the two principal magnocellular sublayers (M_1 or M_2), depending upon the eye. Their LGN relay cells terminate in layer $4C_\alpha$ of the ocular dominance bands, just above the relay cells for the midget ganglion cells. Their axonal arbors are about three times wider than those of the LGN midget relay cells, but the coverage factor within $4C_\alpha$ is also about 100.

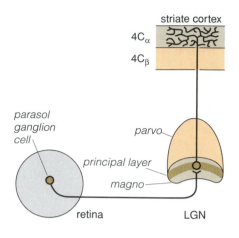

pathway of parasol ganglion cells

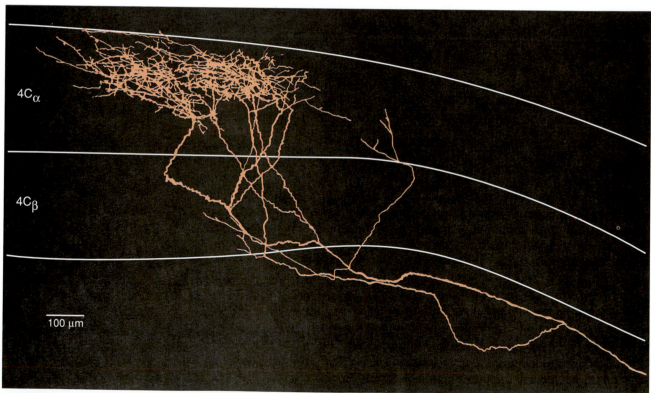

macaque

axonal arbor of LGN cell driven by an on-center parasol ganglion cell

after Blasdel and Lund, 1983

As discussed in CELL TYPES (page 258), primate midget and parasol ganglion cells appear to be homologous with cat beta and alpha cells, respectively. In the cat LGN, the axons of the beta ganglion cells likewise tend to stratify above those of the alpha cells, although their separation is not as sharp as is seen in primates.

The small bistratified ganglion cells project to sublayers K$_3$ or K$_4$ of the LGN, and the LGN relay cells they contact appear to terminate within a subset of the blobs. Other ganglion cell types also project to these sublayers, some of which can be labeled by antibodies to a protein called α **cam kinase**. They appear to connect to LGN cells that are also labeled by this antibody; these relay cells appear to terminate within a different subset of blobs than do the small bistratified cells. Both of these ganglion cell types are discussed in SEEING, in the context of their potential roles in color vision.

Some ganglion cells with very large dendritic fields, termed **P-giant** cells, also terminate somewhere within the parvocellular zone. This scatter diagram compares their properties with those of small bistratified ganglion cells, together with the reference set of parasol and midget ganglion cells from the scatter diagram on page 276. The cortical destinations of P-giant cells are not known. Some of them have the largest dendritic fields of any in the primate retina, yet their somal sizes are some of the smallest, as seen in the scatter plot below and in the drawing on the next page.

At least two other types of ganglion cells, **epsilon** and **gamma**, project to the LGN, although the layers in which they terminate have not yet been determined. Both types have small cell bodies and very large dendritic fields that are monostratified. Epsilon ganglion cells are found in other mammals. Their dendritic fields stratify in the innermost portion of the

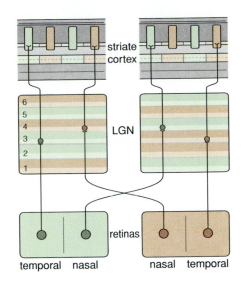

pathways of small bistratified ganglion cells

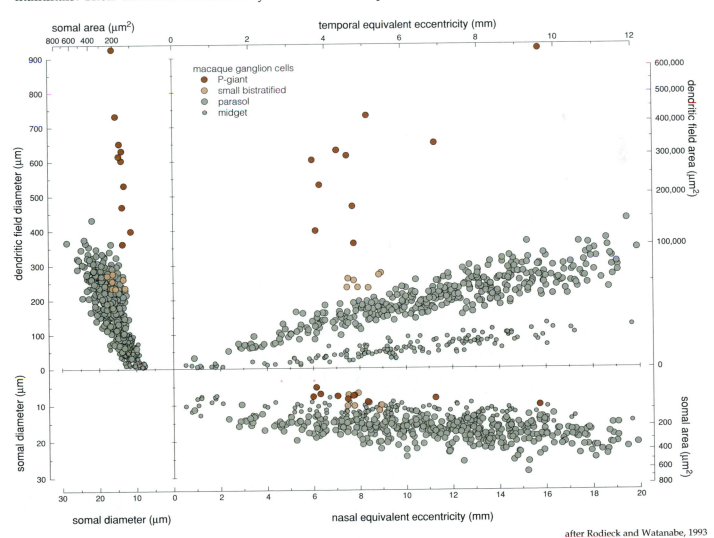

after Rodieck and Watanabe, 1993

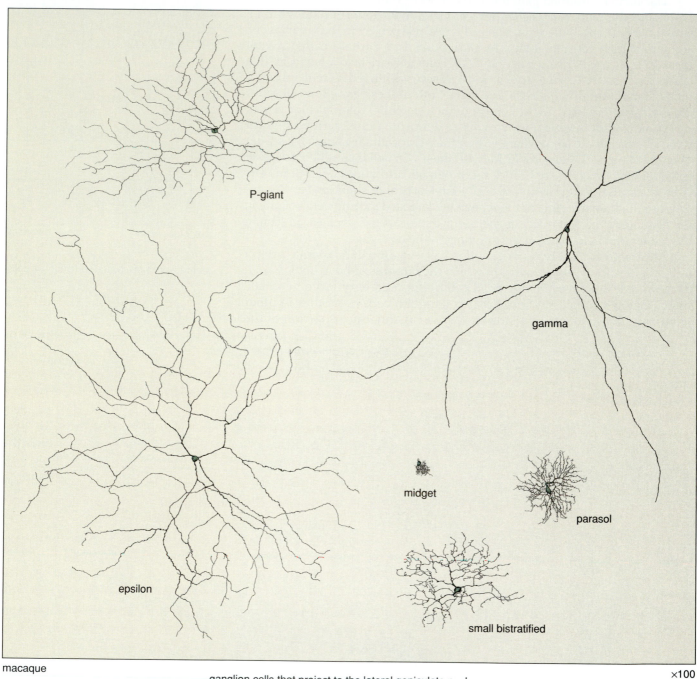

P-giant

gamma

epsilon

midget

parasol

small bistratified

macaque

ganglion cells that project to the lateral geniculate nucleus

×100

after Rodieck and Watanabe, 1993;
after Watanabe and Rodieck, 1989; after Dacey, 1993

inner synaptic layer, and their main dendrites emerge from the sides of the cell body, giving it a scalloped appearance. Gamma ganglion cells have about the same somal size and dendritic field size as epsilon cells, but their dendritic fields are quite sparse, with few branches. Both of these cell types are also found in the cat retina, and project to the lower portion of the cat LGN, which is also composed of small cells. This koniocellular zone is particularly noticeable in nocturnal animals, suggesting that these ganglion cells may play a special role in night vision by collecting from rods over a wide area.

To summarize, at least twelve different types of ganglion cells project to the lateral geniculate nucleus, and from there to the visual cortex. The functional roles of some of them will be discussed in SEEING.

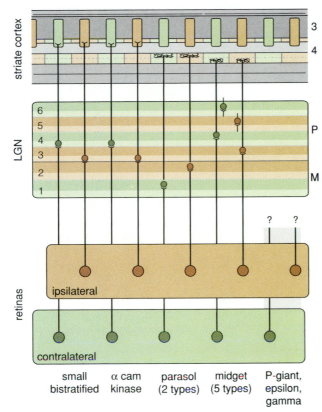

pathways of ganglion cells to LGN and striate cortex

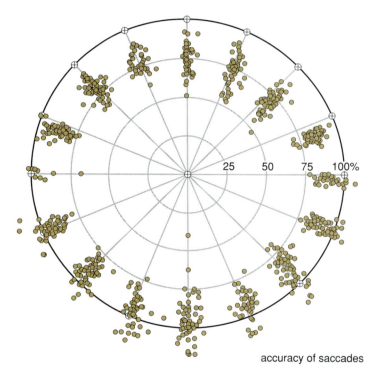

accuracy of saccades

13

Looking

This chapter takes a closer look at themes introduced in THE CHASE. *For vision to work, the retinal image must be stabilized for a period long enough that information about the visual world can be acquired and sent to the brain. We see best not when the image is perfectly stabilized, but when it moves with a velocity in the range of roughly 0.50°/s to 2.0°/s. As we go about our daily lives, most of our head movements are considerably greater than this; on average, eye movements compensate for about 97.5% of these head movements, and thereby bring image motion into the above range. The information needed to make such compensatory movements comes from a variety of sources, including the vestibular apparatus of the ear. But perhaps the most important information about image motion comes from the retina itself, since it contains a number of different ganglion cell types that are sensitive to different aspects of image motion.*

What does the visual system need?

. . . Both animals move at great speed, eyes darting, the machinery of the body reacting to what each sees before it. During the chase, each animal's view of the external world rapidly changes as it covers ground and turns its body, head, and eyes.

As discussed in THE CHASE (page 8), the visual behavior of a wide variety of creatures consists of holding gaze steady on a target, then suddenly shifting the gaze to a new target. The period of time during which gaze is held steady is essential, and it is the first thing that the visual system needs.

The visual system needs time

In order to better appreciate the various temporal factors at stake, consider a simple task in which you are asked to push a button as soon as you see a light come on. This is a more sedate version of the pattern of action and reaction that takes place during the chase of the gazelle and the cheetah. Most people can press the button within about 180–200 ms.

We can list a rough sequence of events between the light coming on and the button being pressed. The time it takes for the light to travel from the source to your eye is so small that we can ignore it.

Retina to optic nerve	20 ms
Optic nerve to striate cortex	10 ms
Processing time in brain	110–130 ms
Brain–spinal cord to finger muscles	20 ms
Activation of finger muscles	20 ms
Total	180–200 ms

The retinal contribution is the time between the absorption of photons and the change in the firing rates of the ganglion cells that respond to the light. Much of this time appears to be taken by the activation of G molecules in the photoreceptor outer segment. It takes time for neurons to propagate action potentials from one place to another; hence the delay from the optic nerve to the cortical surface of the brain, and from the brain to the finger muscles; the synaptic delay at the lateral geniculate nucleus is relatively small. The activation time of the finger muscles is primarily due to the time it takes to overcome the inertia of the finger after the forces generated by the muscles are applied to it. All of these times are more or less fixed, leaving 110–130 ms for the brain to receive the arriving messages from the eye and deal with them. This period is a mixture of the duration of the message from the eye and the brain activity attending its arrival. But even if we assume that the brain activity is instantaneous, so that the entire period is given to the message, the message itself is limited; for if a ganglion cell responds by increasing its firing rate by 100 action potentials per second, its message will consist of only an additional 7–9 action potentials in this 110–130 ms period. Thus the primary reason that we must stabilize our gaze for a certain period of time, even during a hectic chase, is that it takes time to reliably indicate a change in firing rate, quite apart from any delays encountered along the way.

As discussed later in this chapter, this minimum time interval is comparable to the pauses we make when reading, despite the fact that reading is a more sophisticated activity than detecting a light flash, suggesting that message duration may be the dominant factor in both situations.

The visual system needs retinal information to stabilize the image

The need for time implies a need for a period of relative image stability. The only part of the visual system that can detect whether an image is stable on the retina is the retina itself. As we will see in this chapter, a number of different ganglion cell types are adapted to detect different forms of image motion, and their messages are used to move the eyes so as to stabilize the image.

The visual system needs to map the image to the external world

This factor is so obvious that it requires explanation. As first discussed in THE CHASE (page 12), the fact that the visual world remains stationary as we move our eyes is a remarkable feature of vision. How this is accomplished is not well understood, but some of the factors involved can be readily demonstrated.

The critical question to be asked is not why the visual world does not move, but how we are able to determine the location of an object in the world around us based upon the location of the image of that object on the retina. Vision would be of limited usefulness in the absence of this ability; we would know something is in our visual field, but not where it is located with respect to ourselves. In order to answer this question, we need to start with the location of the image on the retina. That location is determined, first, by the location and orientation of the head and, second, by the orientation of the eyes with respect to the head.

Even in the absence of vision, you know the positions of your limbs and head, as you can easily demonstrate by closing your eyes, bringing an arm up, and touching your nose with a finger. Although we are perceptually unaware of it, the information needed to accomplish this task is provided by specialized receptors in the muscles and joints that inform the brain about muscle and tendon tension, muscle stretch, and the angle between two bones connected by a joint. These receptors are collectively termed **proprioceptors** (Latin: *proprius* = one's own; in this context, knowledge of one's body). The task of touching your nose depends upon the combined activities of proprioceptors in your neck and arm. It is by means of these proprioceptors that we know the position of the head relative to the rest of the body.

The remaining piece of information necessary to locate an object in space is the position of the eyes relative to the head. Eye muscles have rudimentary proprioceptors in the form of stretch receptors and tendon organs, but they are anatomically degenerate, and their use by the brain to infer eye position is minor at best. The main, and possibly the only, information about eye position comes not from eye position per se, but from the neural activity that is necessary to hold the eyes at some orientation relative to the head. The portion of this neural activity used by the brain to infer eye position is termed the **efference copy** (Latin *efferens* = to carry away).

Some of the factors considered thus far are shown in this diagram, which summarizes the flow of information between the eye and the brain:

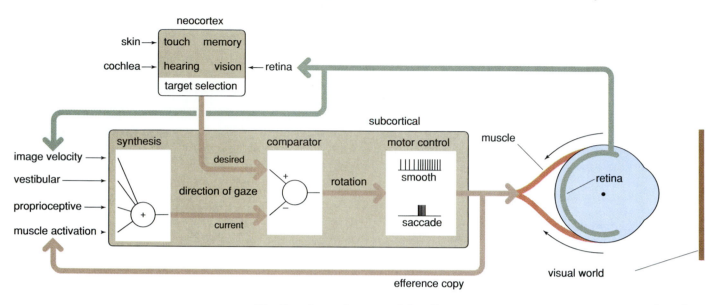

Starting from the top of the diagram, eye movements are initiated within the neocortex on the basis of a variety of factors. A noise, a touch, a sight, or a memory of the location of some object may attract our attention and cause us to direct our eyes to the target; alternatively, we may be attempting to track a target in a dynamic situation. A primary function of subcortical visual regions, shown in the lower portion of the diagram, is to determine the direction of current gaze with respect to the external world, using whatever information is available. For the static direction of gaze, this includes information from the vestibular apparatus about the orientation of the head with respect to gravity, as we will see below; from the proprioceptors about the orientation of the head with respect to the rest of the body; and from the efference copy about the orientation of the eyes with respect to the head. For the dynamic aspects of gaze, the retina provides information about the direction and velocity of image motion, as well as other things, and the vestibular apparatus supplies information about the rotation of the head. All of this information is available to infer the current direction of gaze, as indicated by the box labeled "synthesis." The eye movement required is simply the difference between the desired direction and the (inferred) current direction of gaze, as indicated by the box labeled "comparator." The shift in gaze may be accomplished by either smooth or saccadic eye movements, as indicated by the box labeled "motor control." The output is the neural activation of six eye muscles for each eye.

As discussed in INFORMING THE BRAIN, the striate portion of the neocortex receives from a subset of retinal ganglion cells, via the lateral geniculate nucleus. A different set of retinal ganglion cells supplies the subcortical regions of the brain. Although there are neural pathways between the visual cortex and the subcortical regions, the roles of these two parts of the visual system are very different. We probably have no direct conscious visual awareness of any of the ganglion cell types that project only to the subcortical regions. Their primary task is to aid in image stabilization, and since there are different circumstances in which this needs to be done, there are different ganglion cell types adapted for each form of stabilization. An image can move in any direction across the retina, and so more than one type of ganglion cell is required to resolve the direction of movement. The message each type conveys to the subcortical neural mechanism that controls eye position acts as an error signal to reduce the form of image motion that this ganglion cell type is adapted to detect, quantify, and convey.

The schematic diagram just presented provides a unifying reference for the rest of this chapter. Since it is based upon changes in the direction of gaze under different circumstances, the first factor to be considered is the relation between gaze and the external world.

The geometry of gaze

Head movements come first

As we go about our daily lives, whether walking, stalking, or pursuing gazelles, what is presented to us changes in complex ways. Even when the external world is stationary, as in a quiet forest, what we see changes as we walk along. It also changes as we turn our heads to look about.

Although it seems obvious, it is worthwhile noting that because the eyes are in the head, it is motions of the head that determine what is presented to the eyes. There are two qualitatively different types of head motion we need to consider, **rotation** and **translation**:

Each type of motion has three components. *Head rotations* can be described as turning from left to right, as when we express "no" (axis vertical), nodding, as when we express "yes" (axis lateral), and tilting, as when we express "what . . .?" (axis forward). *Head translations* generally result from movements of the body, and likewise have three components, as when we squat (axis vertical), step to the side (axis lateral) or step forward (axis forward).

Consider viewing a gazelle that is about 100 m away (about the length of a football field). In this situation, *head translations* have almost no effect on your direction of view. For example, let's say that you move your head to

© A & M Shah / Animals Animals

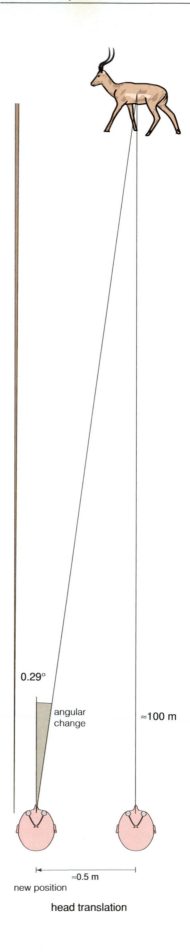

0.29°

angular change

≈100 m

≈0.5 m

new position

head translation

the left by the distance between your shoulders (about 0.5 m). The diagram on the left shows the situation as viewed from above, although it is not drawn to scale. The angular change produced by this head *translation* is about 0.29° (correctly drawn at the far left). It is thus equivalent to a head *rotation* of 0.29°, as is evident from the diagram. This angle is about the width of a wooden matchstick held at arm's length (about 2.6 mm). The effect of head translation on visual direction disappears for distant objects such as a mountain peak or a star. Conversely, head translations can have a large effect when viewing nearby objects, as you can readily verify.

Eye movements depend upon viewing distance

The motions of the human eye, *within the orbit of the skull,* are all rotational. How do all of the motions of the head and eyes combine?

Consider first looking at a point in the far distance, such as a mountain peak. We can ignore head translations, for the reasons discussed above. Thus we need consider only head rotations and eye rotations. If the *head* turns to the *left* by 10°, then the direction of gaze can be maintained if both *eyes* turns to the *right* by 10°:

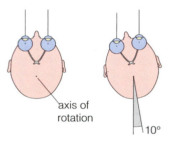

axis of rotation

10°

head rotation

The situation is a bit more complicated when you view a nearby object. Look at a letter on this page and turn your head to the *left* by 10°.

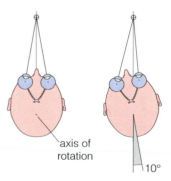

axis of rotation

10°

head and eye rotations for near target

Now the translation of the eyes, produced by the head rotation, becomes more important. In order to maintain fixation, your *left* eye must turn to the right by about 13.4°, whereas your *right* eye must also turn to the right, but by about 14.0°. Much of our visual experience is concerned with the space within our grasp, in which we eat, fight, and reproduce; it is termed *praxic* or *lifespace,* and these complications of the geometry of gaze are thus an aspect of everyday experience. These effects rapidly disappear with increasing distance, however. For example, when a target is just beyond your reach

(0.7 m), the same 10° head movement requires the left eye to turn by 11.2° and the right eye by 11.3°.

How the eyes are moved

Six muscles turn the eye

The vertebrate eye is rotated by means of six eye muscles. Each of these muscles is attached at one end to the eye and at the other end to the back of the bony orbit of the skull by connective tissue tendons:

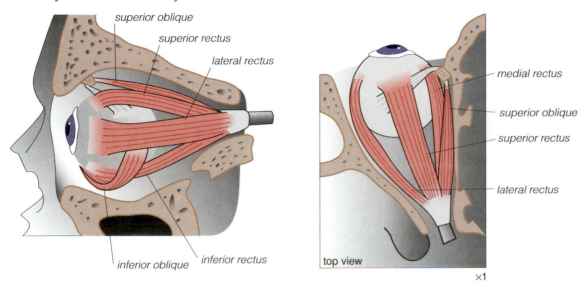

The paths of the **rectus muscles** (Latin: *rectus* = straight) run straight to the eye, whereas the paths of the **oblique muscles** run obliquely.

Eye muscle pairs are reciprocally innervated

Contraction of the **medial rectus** muscle rotates the eye toward the midline of the head, so that the left eye rotates to the right. The **lateral rectus** muscle rotates the eye in the opposite direction. Together these two muscles form a **complementary pair**. Both members of the pair rotate the eye about the same axis, which in this case is vertical.

The tension, or pull, generated by each eye muscle depends upon the collective rate of firing of nerve fibers that arise in the brain, pass through nerves, and innervate the muscle. In the state of rest, both muscles in a pair are receiving a steady rate of activation:

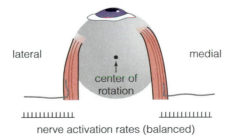

This diagram is greatly simplified in that the activation is represented in terms of the firing rate of a single nerve axon, whereas each muscle receives from a number of them.

The neural activation of a complementary pair of muscles is always **reciprocal**, meaning that when there is an *increase* in the rate of activation of one muscle, there is always a *decrease* in the activation of the other muscle. For example, an *increase* in the stimulation of the medial rectus is coupled to a *decrease* in the stimulation of the lateral rectus, causing the left eye to rotate to the right:

nerve activation rates (unbalanced)

The total retraction into the orbit remains about the same, so the mechanical effect approximates a pure torsion about the *center of rotation* of the eye. The greater the difference between the neural activation of the muscles in the pair, the greater will be the rotation of the eye from its position of rest. This is the general way in which the direction of gaze is determined by neural activation of the eye muscles.

Turning the eye by means of a pair of eye muscles is similar to turning a doorknob. Within the mechanism of the door latch, there are one or more springs attached to the knob that both give it a resting position and resist its displacement from that position. As you increase the torque on the knob with your hand, you turn the knob more and more away from this resting position. In order to keep the knob displaced by some angle, you must continue to apply the torque necessary to hold it at that position. In the same way, the tissue of the orbit and the stretch of the relaxed muscles resist the displacement of the eye from its position of rest. In order for the eye to be directed away from this position, there must be a continuing difference in the rates of activation of reciprocally innervated eye muscle pairs. The amount of rotation is proportional to the difference in activation, so the relation between the efference copy and eye position is simple.

The situation for the remaining four muscles is more complicated, primarily because our eyes are directed forward. The earliest vertebrates had laterally directed eyes. In order to understand our situation, it is useful to take a step back and look at the geometry of eye movements in a modern animal with laterally directed eyes, such as a rabbit (see the Box *RABBIT VISION*).

When the eyes are laterally directed, the **superior rectus** and **inferior rectus** form a complementary pair that are reciprocally innervated so as to *move the eye vertically*. Likewise, the **superior oblique** and **inferior oblique** form a third complementary pair, also reciprocally innervated, that *rotate the eye about its direction of gaze*. Each axis of rotation is thus perpendicular to each of the other axes, and thus independent of them (left). When a rabbit *nods* its head up and down, the axis of rotation is lateral, and thus parallel to the optical axes of the two eyes. Consequently, the eyes are rotated about their optic axes. The *oblique* complementary pair can produce a counter-rotation so as to stabilize the image of the visual world on the retina. Thus a *downward* rotation of the head can be compensated for by a *counterclockwise* rotation of the left eye and a *clockwise* rotation of the right eye.

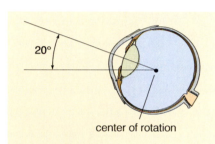

20°

center of rotation

center of rotation
When the eye rotates, its center of rotation varies only slightly. This relative constancy is due mainly to the fact that the surrounding connective tissue and fat create a socket in which the eye rotates.

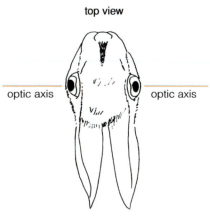

top view

optic axis   optic axis

after Hughes, 1971

Rabbit vision

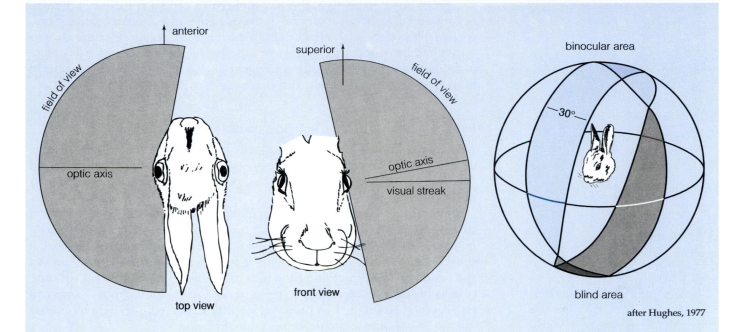

top view

front view

binocular area

blind area

after Hughes, 1977

FIELD OF VIEW

Laterally directed eyes provide rabbits with a panoramic view, allowing them to see almost the entire horizon (left diagram). Like gazelles and cheetahs (page 32), rabbits have a visual streak that is directed toward the horizon. The optic axis of the eye is directed slightly upward, allowing anything directly overhead to be seen (center).

A perspective view, combining the fields of view in the previous diagrams, shows an almost complete view of the entire visual sphere, with a binocular portion above and in front of the head (right). The blind area is relatively small and is limited to the portion of the sphere occupied mainly by the rest of the rabbit.

EYE MUSCLES

Rabbits have three complementary pairs of eye muscles that are arranged in a simpler manner than those in human eyes. Two muscles retract the eye, and the remaining four rotate it. The direction of the eye is entirely determined by the rectus muscles: the anterior/posterior pair produces slightly tilted horizontal movements and the superior/inferior pair produces slightly tilted vertical movements (below). The oblique muscles produce a pure torsion, meaning a rotation about the optic axis. These three axes are perpendicular to one another, but only one of them is aligned with a semicircular canal: the vertical axis of the anterior/posterior pair is aligned with that of the horizontal semicircular canals.

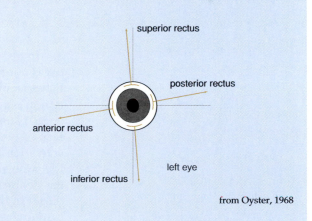

from Oyster, 1968

But when evolution altered the skull of our ancestors so that the eyes were directed forward, the eyes became rotated vertically by 90° and the geometry of gaze thereby altered. When we nod our heads, the compensatory movement to a *downward* rotation of the head is an *upward* rotation of *both* eyes. In humans and other species with forward-directed eyes, this change in geometry resulted in changes in the muscle attachments and directions of pull that mixed the mechanical contributions of the superior/inferior rectus and oblique muscle pairs, which thereby lost their independence.

From our perspective, these complexities can be considered details, because all directional rotations of the eye are still possible. Furthermore, these evolutionary adaptations of both the mechanical aspects of the musculature and its neural activation yield a performance on tasks such as image stabilization that is essentially equivalent to that of the simpler mechanical plan of animals with laterally directed eyes.

Eye orientation is aligned with the visual horizon

However accomplished, all eye movements can be reduced to two aspects. The first is the **direction of gaze** in visual space, also termed the **point of fixation**. Normally, it corresponds to a point in visual space that is imaged at the center of the fovea.

The second aspect is the rotation of the eye with respect to the direction of gaze, which is termed **torsion**. Common to all vertebrates is this fact: Insofar as mechanically possible, torsional eye movements keep the visual horizon at the same orientation on the retina, whatever the orientation of the head and the direction of the gaze. This fact is important for locating objects in space, as discussed in the next section. Torsional movements can be observed when the head is tilted slightly to one side, in which case the eyes can be seen to rotate in the opposite direction.

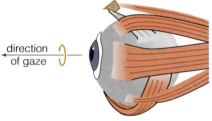

direction of gaze

torsional movement

In human eyes, torsional movements are somewhat limited, but then so too is our normal variation in head tilt. The range of torsional movements in fishes is much larger, as one might expect in an environment in which gravitation plays a smaller role in the range of possible body orientations.

To summarize, the eyes are oriented with respect to the skull by a pattern of neural activation of the eye muscles. The relation between neural activation and eye orientation is lawful (follows fixed rules), and this allows the subcortical regions of the brain to infer eye orientation from a copy of the neural pattern. So as we examine the task of inferring the location of an object in the visual world from the location of its image on the retina, we can now say something about the direction of the eyes with respect to the skull.

In order to specify the direction of the eyes with respect to the external world, we need to know the orientation of the head. Part of the information about head position comes from proprioceptors in the muscles and joints of the neck, as previously mentioned. But additional information, particularly about head motions, comes from the vestibular part of the ear, which we consider next.

Viewed in geometrical terms, the problem of inferring the location of an object with respect to ourselves, based upon the location of its image on the retina, is quite complex, since it involves the lengths and tensions of muscles spread throughout the body. But we can easily look about, close our eyes, and point to or grasp some object in the external world. Indeed, correlating one's grasp with the location of the image of an object on the retina is one of the most fundamental aspects of vision—as any cheetah will readily attest.

The vestibular apparatus provides information about head position and motion

The inner ear of all vertebrates contains both a detector of sound, termed the **cochlea**, and a detector of acceleration (changes in movement), called the **vestibular apparatus** (below). The cochlea is so named because it contains a spiral chamber (Greek *kokhlos* = land snail). The vestibular apparatus appears as if hollowed out from the bone of the skull and resembles a chamber, or *vestibule*. It plays an important role in both balance and the stabilization of gaze.

The vestibular apparatus consists of a large chamber that contains a pair of connected bags, termed the **saccule** and the **utricle**, from which arise three fluid-filled tunnels, termed the **semicircular canals**. The saccule and utricle contain small stones **(otoliths)** that lie in a jellylike material above a layer of sensory cells, which are sensitive to any distortion of the overlying gel. The stones are heavier than the gel and are thus pulled down by gravity. They are also deflected by any linear acceleration of the head (in effect, *translational* movements), just as you are pulled backward as a car acceler-

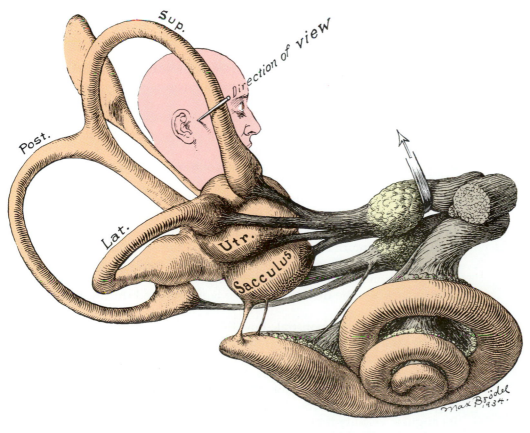

vestibular apparatus   cochlea

after Hardy, 1934

ates. The resulting deflection of the gel is detected by the sensory cells. The information provided to the brain by these cells is used both for balance and for eye orientation in response to postural changes.

The semicircular canals lie approximately at right angles to one another, as in a corner of a cube. They are adapted to detect *rotational* movements of the head. Each canal is filled with fluid; free movement of this fluid is blocked by a jellylike material that overlies sensory cells similar to those in the saccule and utricle. As noted, the canals are contained in the skull, so that when the head rotates, so too must the canals. As the canals begin to turn, the inertia of the fluid within them exerts a force on the gel, and its deflection stimulates the sensory cells. The physical stimulus is angular acceleration, but the mechanical system is highly damped, and this causes the initial deflection of the gel to be proportional to the angular velocity of the head.

Imagine holding a pail of water by the handle. If you rotate the pail by turning the handle, the pail will turn, but the water will lag behind, due to its inertia. The greatest effect will occur for the water nearest the side of the pail. If you were sitting on the edge of the pail, the water would seem to be moving in the direction opposite to your own movement. In this situation, the axis of rotation is vertical, and the inertial forces lie perpendicular to it, in the horizontal plane:

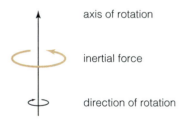

axis of rotation

inertial force

direction of rotation

The sensory cells associated with the *horizontal* semicircular canals on each side of the head are stimulated in a similar manner by rotations of the head to the left or right. Note that the rotational axis of the superior canal on one side of the body is aligned with that of the posterior canal on the other side. Each of these pairs responds to the component of head rotation along their rotational axis. In effect, the three pairs of semicircular canals determine the three independent components of head rotation along any axis.

The responses of the sensory cells in the horizontal canals are conveyed to the brain via other neurons, as shown schematically on the next page. The brain can then make use of this information to control the pair of eye muscles (medial and lateral) that rotate the eye horizontally in the opposite direction. The information provided by these sensory cells can also be used to assist saccadic eye movements, as when both eyes and head turn in the same direction to gaze at a peripheral target, or to assist smooth eye movements, as when the direction of gaze is maintained during head movements.

You can easily demonstrate how the vestibular apparatus assists in stabilizing your gaze during head movements. Look directly at some object in front of you and, while continuing to look at it, rapidly turn your head. Your gaze will not appear to have left the object. During the brief period when your head was in motion, the vestibular apparatus responded to the angular acceleration of your head, and produced a response proportional to its angular velocity that was sent to your brain. Your brain, in turn, activated each of your 12 eye muscles so that your two eyes turned as one. This is a natural task for us, so much so that it might seem automatic, and thus

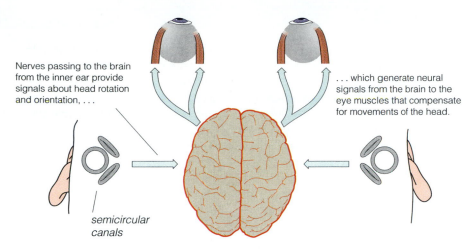

Nerves passing to the brain from the inner ear provide signals about head rotation and orientation, . . .

. . . which generate neural signals from the brain to the eye muscles that compensate for movements of the head.

semicircular canals

beyond our control. But this is not the case; choice remains important, as you can easily demonstrate. Look directly in front of you, and become aware of some object off to the side, without turning your eyes to look directly at it. Now quickly turn your head so as to look directly at that object. The movement of your head may have been exactly the same as before, but this time your gaze has shifted to the new target.

The cheetah and the gazelle are faced with the same situation. Since each has a limited field of view, they must move their heads in order to redirect their gaze to objects in their peripheral field. The information about head motion that is provided by the vestibular apparatus is thus there to be used; how it will be used depends upon the intent of the cheetah or gazelle to either continue their gaze or to redirect it.

You can get a feeling for how fast images can be roughly stabilized during head movements by means of the following experiment. Hold one of your hands about a foot in front of your face and, while looking at it, turn your head back and forth (or, up and down). Start slowly, and gradually increase the rate at which you are shaking your head, which you can check with a metronome. You will find that even back-and-forth movement of three to four times a second still keeps the eyes pointed in about the same direction. Instead of looking at your hand, you could also try reading this section, and find the rate at which you can still read. We don't spend much time shaking our heads. But we do walk and run, which changes the direction of rotation of our heads with every footfall. The importance of the information provided by the vestibular system is made clear by its absence, as discussed in the Box *LIVING WITHOUT A BALANCING MECHANISM*.

We have seen that the vestibular apparatus provides information about both the orientation of the head and its movement. In the process of looking, summarized in the schematic diagram above (page 296), we first direct our eyes to a target (auditory, tactile, visual, or remembered), and then hold the target steady on the retina. Information about the direction of the eyes with respect to the external world is provided by a number of factors, including the efference copy, neck proprioceptors, and a portion of the vestibular apparatus. All of these factors have limited accuracy, but may be critical in certain situations. When the target is visual, its location on the retina with respect to the fovea provides the best information about target location. To use a baseball analogy, a pitcher may not be perfectly accurate, but he does much better than he would trying to hit the catcher's mitt in the dark. However we infer the location of the target, our only means of directing our eyes to it involves a saccadic eye movement, which we now consider.

Living without a balancing mechanism

About 46 years ago, a physician named John Crawford permanently lost the function of his vestibular apparatus as a result of overdoses of streptomycin (6 gm/day intramuscularly). The aim of the medication was to treat a form of tuberculosis located in his knee. One morning during this treatment, he brought a hot washcloth up to his face, and with the visual world obscured, suddenly and unexpectedly fell over. He describes what happened next:

> During that first day symptoms increased rapidly. Every movement in bed now caused vertigo and nausea, even when I kept my eyes open. If I shut my eyes the symptoms were intensified. At first, I found that by lying on my back and steadying myself by gripping the bars at the head of the bed I could be reasonably comfortable. Later, even in this position the pulse beat in my head became a perceptible motion, disturbing my equilibrium.

Most of us have experimented with motion pictures at home. This experience can be used to illustrate the sensations of the patient with damage to the vestibular apparatus. Imagine the results of a sequence taken by pointing the camera straight ahead, holding it against the chest and walking at a normal pace down a city street. In a sequence thus taken and viewed on the screen, the street seems to career crazily in all directions, faces of approaching persons become blurred and unrecognizable, and the viewer may even experience a feeling of dizziness or nausea. Our vestibular apparatus normally acts like the tripod and the smoothly moving carriage on which the professional's motion picture camera is mounted. Without these steadying influences, the moving picture is joggled and blurred. Similarly, when the vestibular influence is removed from the biological cinema system, the projection on the visual cortex becomes unsteady.

Dr. Crawford gradually discovered ways of compensating for his disability, but the elaborate measures he had to take to perform ordinary activities demonstrate what a normally functioning vestibular system does for us.

> . . . At that point my courage began to return, and there began the slow process of learning to live with a handicap. The subsequent period was one of consuming interest to me. In it I saw demonstrated how effectively the loss of one of the sensory systems of the body can be compensated for by the other systems. My first efforts were devoted to overcoming my difficulty in reading. I found that by bracing my head between two metal bars at the head of the bed I could minimize the effect of the pulse beat, which made the letters on the page jump and blur. I gradually learned to keep my place by using a finger or pencil on the page.
>
> Once I was again able to read, time began to pass more and more quickly. I soon persuaded myself, nevertheless, that I must try to walk. Already I had discovered, as I lay in bed, that if I turned my head from side to side while looking forward I had the sensation that the room turned around me, rather than that I was turning around

Saccades

As discussed in THE CHASE (page 10), a saccade is a quick movement of the eyes brought about by a brief but powerful activation of the eye muscles. The eye is *flung* to a new position according to the magnitude of this brief activation. The diagram shows the change in position of an eye with time as a result of a saccade that changed the angular position of the eye by 5°:

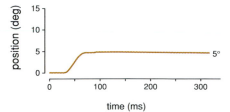

from Becker, 1991

The change took about 30 ms, so the average velocity was about 5°/0.03 s, or 170°/s. This period is so brief that there is no opportunity to make adjustments to a saccade while it is in progress. A 5° saccade is fairly typical, the sort you might make while reading this text, or scanning the diagram above .

5°

when viewed at normal reading distance (≈ 30 cm)

in the room. This was less disturbing, however, if I focused on a distant object rather than on one but a few feet from my eyes. I had also learned that less vertigo was associated with moving about or turning over in bed if I kept my eyes closed. This maneuver had its drawback, however, in that with my eyes closed I had the giddy feeling that the bed was no longer horizontal but had been tipped up on end or on its side. On my first attempt at walking, I found that it helped to close my eyes and steady myself with both hands on the bed. Thus oriented by tactile sense, I groped my way around the bed, telling myself, despite sensations indicating the contrary, that both the floor and the surface of the bed were stationary and in a horizontal plane. Later, I learned to open my eyes, fix on a distant object to add visual to tactile orientation and move around the bed.

. . . I began to take excursions around the ward, and later along the endless corridors of the hospital. In these corridors I had the peculiar sensation of being inside a flexible tube, fixed at the end nearest me but swaying free at the far end. In various places the corridors led up or down gentle inclines. On these ramps I had to learn to appreciate that I was going downhill through the sensation of strain on the extensors of my legs or that I was climbing a grade through the strain on the flexor muscles. Of course, if there was a window nearby I could corroborate the proprioceptor signals by comparing the plane of the floor with that of the horizon outside.

I learned not to do certain things. One of these was not to look at a newspaper or letter in my hand while walking. In those early days proprioceptive orientation was insufficiently developed to permit even momentary withdrawal of visual orientation. When I was allowed to go outside, I quickly found that it was imperative to restrain the impulse to look up when an airplane passed overhead until I could brace myself against a railing or tree. I discovered, when beginning to walk in open places without a nearby wall available for hasty support, that it was a mistake to slow down or stop. It was as if I were riding a bicycle; the faster I walked, the more easily could I keep a stable upright position. Indeed, I soon noticed that unconsciously I had begun to walk the same type of course that is steered by a ship's gyroscopic compass, veering first slightly to the left and then overcompensating and veering equally to the right.

During a walk I found too much motion in my visual picture of the surroundings to permit recognition of fine detail. I learned that I must stand still in order to read the lettering on a sign. These early excursions taught me a habit foreign to one of my New England background—that of greeting anyone who happened to pass in the opposite direction. Since I was unable to distinguish the familiar from the unfamiliar faces when walking, the obvious solution was to pretend to recognize everyone.

(1952)

From the perspective of the retina, a saccade results in a sudden shift of the image of the visual world. This shift presumably activates many ganglion cells, although there is no perceptual correlate of this activation, and we are generally unaware of the saccades that we make.

movement of image on retina

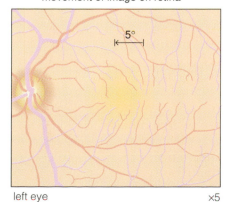

5°

left eye   ×5

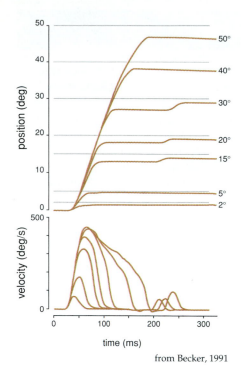

from Becker, 1991

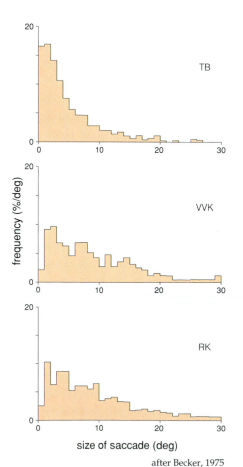

after Becker, 1975

Saccades of any magnitude are rather stylized. The upper part of the diagram to the left shows the change in the *position* of an eye resulting from saccades of different amplitudes. These records are superimposed upon one another; the 5° record is the one we considered earlier. It is apparent that larger saccades take longer. The 2° saccade took only about 20 ms, whereas the 50° saccade took about 150 ms. This is because there is a *maximum rate of rotation*. This maximum angular velocity is indicated by the alignment of the rising slopes of the superimposed records in this diagram.

The lower graph shows the change in the *angular velocity* of the eye during the course of the saccade for the same set of eye movements. Again, the records are shown superimposed. The maximum velocity is about 500°/s. Note also that there is a maximum *rate of change of velocity*, as indicated by the alignment of the rising slopes of the superimposed records. This peak acceleration results from the maximum physiological activation of the eye muscles. For large eye movements, the amount by which a saccade rotates the eye depends upon the *duration* of this maximum activation.

At large amplitudes, there is often a second saccade, which occurs a minimum of 120 ms after the first. This can be seen in the 15°, 20°, and 30° saccades. These secondary movements are termed **corrective saccades**; however, they often occur even when the original saccade is on target. The minimum time of 120 ms is sufficiently brief that it remains unclear whether these secondary saccades depend upon retinal input when viewing the image at the end of the initial saccade. Even if the second saccade is corrective, retinal input may not be required, since the visual system may monitor the neural activity sent to the eye muscles and use this information to initiate the second saccade. In any case, we rarely, if ever, make large saccadic eye movements under ordinary circumstances, as discussed below.

Both eyes move during a saccade. When gaze is directed to a distant scene, the two eyes move as one. But for nearby objects the geometry is different, as discussed earlier, and the saccadic eye movements of the two eyes differ, so as to enable both of them to be quickly directed toward the target.

Saccades are typically small

We can make saccadic eye movements as large as 100°, but we rarely, if ever, do so under natural conditions. The diagrams to the left show the amplitudes of saccadic eye movements recorded under natural conditions from three subjects; and their average is shown below:

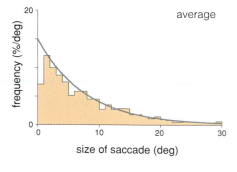

after Becker, 1975

The subjects showed some individual variation, but their saccades were typically small, the average being 7.6°. The histogram of the average for the three subjects can be approximated by an *exponential* curve, as shown by the gray curve in the diagram.

Saccades have limited positional accuracy

The manner in which a saccade flings the eyes to a new position can be likened to a pitcher throwing a baseball. Consider a task in which a subject was asked to look at a target some distance to the right of the direction of gaze. This diagram represents a series of attempts to make a saccade so as to shift the direction of gaze to the target:

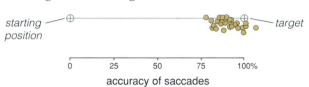

Each dot shows the position of the eye at the end of a saccade. The horizontal distance between the starting position and the destination target was varied between 6° and 12°. The final eye position was plotted as a percentage of the distance between the start and target; thus a perfect eye movement would plot as a dot falling on the target. Most saccades failed to reach the target. The cluster of dots is wider than it is high, indicating that the accuracy in direction of the saccade exceeded that of its amplitude.

These trials were a portion of a more complex experiment in which the target could appear along any of 12 directions that radiated from the starting position (right). For this subject, there was a bias toward a lower position in the visual field, whatever the location of the target.

Exponentials *439*

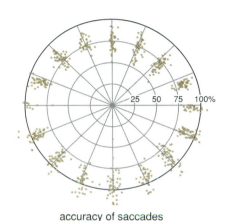

accuracy of saccades

after Deubel, 1987

Intersaccadic intervals are often brief

There is little data available on the pattern of saccades during normal activities in the natural world. From the perspective of visual function, perhaps the most interesting issue is the minimum time needed to "visually comprehend" one retinal image before the next saccade presents the retina with another image. Eye movements during reading are useful in this context because reading provides a practical meaning to "visual comprehension."

The horizontal path of the eyes when reading five lines of text appears as a sequence of ramps, each consisting of a sequence of steps.

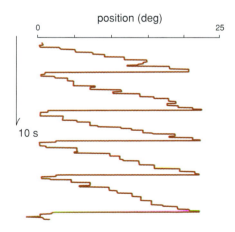

horizontal eye movements while reading

after Epelboim et al., 1994

Each horizontal step corresponds to a saccade that rapidly turns the eye to the right. These saccades have amplitudes of about 2°, and are termed **pro-**

2.
Direct your eyes
to this target:

1.
Center your head with
respect to this line:

gressive saccades. There are also occasional **regressive** saccades that move the eye leftward, and thus over text already passed:

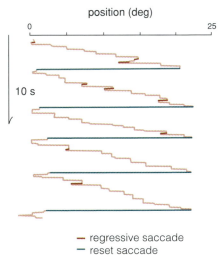

—— regressive saccade
—— reset saccade

after Epelboim et al., 1994

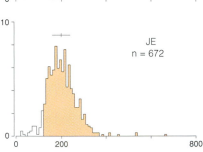

frequency (%/bin)

time interval between saccades (ms)

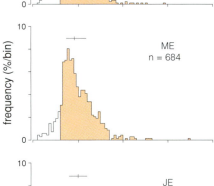

median & quartiles

ME   ◄— subject
n = 684   ◄— samples

after Epelboim et al., 1994;
primary data supplied by Julie Epelboim

Each ramp is terminated by a large leftward movement, termed a **reset** saccade, when the eyes jump from the end of one line to the beginning of the next.

It is said that an engineer once remarked to a convention of toolmakers that customers were not so much interested in drill bits as they were in holes. In that spirit, our concern lies not so much with saccades, but with the time intervals between them—during which we see.

Looking at the graphs above from this new perspective, the *vertical* portion of each step corresponds to a period during which eye position remains unchanged. During this period the rapid movement of the eye is checked by the cessation of strong activation of the eye muscles, and the stabilized image is made available to the visual system. It is this fixation period, or at least the beginning of it, that was originally termed a *saccade* by Javal (page 10).

Frequency distributions of many fixation periods show that they are typically brief, as shown in the histograms of intersaccadic durations from three subjects at the left. The number of fixations during the trial period is shown below the initials of each subject. The bar above each distribution shows its first quartile, median, and third quartile as indicated by the smaller key at the bottom.

The median duration for all three subjects was 190 ms, and 70% of the time intervals lay between 135 ms and 265 ms. About 10% of the saccades had durations less than 120 ms. These short intervals were often preceded by, or followed by, a *regressive* saccade, or a very large *progressive* saccade, or some other special eye movement, such as a *reset* saccade. Thus the visual system appears to be able to operate normally with periods of image stabilization as short as 120–130 ms; how it copes with the occasional shorter times that occur remains uncertain.

3.
Quickly turn both eyes and
head to view this target:

Large changes in gaze combine eye and head movements

Thus far we have considered only saccades that occur when the head is not moved. This is the case in reading and other close work done while sitting still. But it does not characterize our eye movements when we stand, walk, run, chase, fight, or flee. Large changes in the direction of gaze are generally accomplished by means of a combination of eye and head movements. You can readily convince yourself of this by becoming conscious of your eye and head movements as you go about in the natural world.

Here is a task that serves to illustrate the general features of combined eye and head movements. Read the instructions in the diagram at the top of this pair of pages. The diagram should be viewed at a reading distance of about 25 cm in order for the visual angles to be correct. Now do the task.

The diagram to the right shows the initial and final positions of your head. Your shift in gaze of 60° to the right was accomplished by a 30° rotation of the eyes within the head, superimposed upon an additional 30° rotation of the head itself.

Here are records of the time courses of each of these movements as performed by a human subject. Consider first the change in the direction of gaze by 60°. This occurs within about 130 ms, which is comparable to the time taken for a saccade of this magnitude. Indeed, the rising phase of the eye movement record is effectively a saccade. The head cannot rotate as quickly, but as it turns toward the right, the eyes now turn toward the left by just the right amount to hold the gaze steady at the new position.

This brief survey of saccadic eye movements provides an orientation and perspective on the sequence of images presented to both retinas as a result of saccadic eye movements. The next chapter considers the ganglion cells that send messages about these images to the visual cortex via the lateral geniculate nucleus. Here we now consider a different set of ganglion cells that are adapted not to convey messages about the contents of an image, but rather about its movement during the period between saccades, and thereby to assist in stabilizing the image during this period.

To summarize, as we look about, we normally make a few saccades each second, each of which changes the direction of our gaze by a few degrees. In active vision, the intervals between saccades typically last about a fifth of a second, but may be as short as 120 ms. It is during these brief periods that we acquire information both about the content of the image and about its movement with respect to the retina. The content of the image, which is taken up in the next chapter, degrades rapidly when image motion exceeds about 3°/s. As discussed in the following section, head motions are typically greater than this, and image motion is brought within bounds by smooth compensatory eye movements.

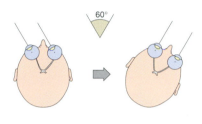

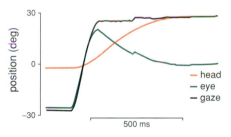

from Becker, 1991

Movements of the head, eyes, and image

The head is in constant motion

When we **fixate** on a target, we are attempting to hold it as steady as possible on the fovea, but that is not easy. Although we are generally unaware of it, our heads are in constant motion. In 1952, Horace Barlow attempted to study the ability of the *eye* to fixate on a target by means of a method that was sensitive to *head* translation. He had to go to extraordinary lengths to stabilize his head, as he described:

> The principle of the method used here is that a small droplet of mercury is placed on the cornea, and the image of a small light formed in the droplet is photographed through a microscope on a moving film. Movements of translation of the droplet in one direction are recorded; to calculate movement of the image over the retina it is necessary that the centre of rotation should be stationary, and this necessitates keeping the head as still as possible. This was done by having the subject lying supine with his head resting on a stone slab let into the wall. A rigid iron frame fitted round the head, and wedges were driven in on one side. The head was thus fixed between the wedges and the frame at the sides, and was resting on the stone slab. In addition the teeth were fixed by a dental impression in gutta percha which was clamped to a crossbar of the frame. This arrangement never stopped all movements of the head, but in the best cases there remained only a slight movement with each heart beat.

Barlow's reference to heartbeats recalls John Crawford's difficulties in stabilizing his gaze following the failure of his vestibular apparatus (see the Box *LIVING WITHOUT A BALANCING MECHANISM*).

Fortunately for the study of eye movements, less heroic methods are now available that allow *rotational* movements of both the head and the eyes to be recorded accurately and reliably, independently of translational movements—which can also be recorded. It is thus possible to determine how the head is moving about, and how the eyes move within the head to partially compensate for these head movements. Ignoring translations for the moment, there are three rotations that need to be considered: head movements with respect to the external world (head/space); eye movements with respect to the head (eye/head); and the resulting direction of gaze with respect to the external world (eye/space).

The diagram at the left is a tracing of *head rotations* recorded while a subject was sitting as still as possible and attempting to continuously fixate on a target 6 m away. The path of the tracing shows the angular position of the head over a 25 s period. It is as if a laser, clamped to the head, traced its path on a piece of photosensitive paper. Six meters is about the distance at which an eye chart is read, so the diagram includes the 20/20 line of the chart for comparison. Even from second to second, head rotations can exceed the size of the letters on the chart.

The next diagram shows the path of the subject's compensatory eye movements (rotations), and the resulting direction of gaze:

head/space

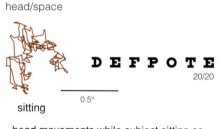

DEFPOTE
20/20

—————
0.5°

sitting

head movements while subject sitting as
still as possible

after Skavenski et al., 1979

head/space   eye/head   eye/space

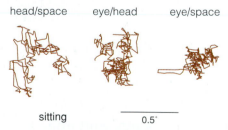

sitting

—————
0.5°

after Skavenski et al., 1979

The path on the left is the same as in the previous diagram. The path in the middle shows the compensatory eye movements made in an attempt to maintain fixation. The resulting direction of gaze is shown on the right. The compensatory eye movements partially stabilized the direction of gaze as the subject viewed a stationary visual world.

The significance of this variation is best seen in terms of the retinal image:

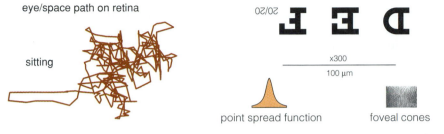

after Skavenski et al., 1979

Despite the subject's attempt to be as still as possible, the movement of the image is larger than the image of a letter of the eye chart, and considerably larger than the image of a star (point spread function). Furthermore, the image is constantly moving across the mosaic of foveal cones, shown at the same scale.

You can use this diagram to observe your own eye movements while sitting still. Close one eye and fix your gaze on the center of the white circle for about 20 s. It's OK to blink, but try to hold your fixation. Now shift your

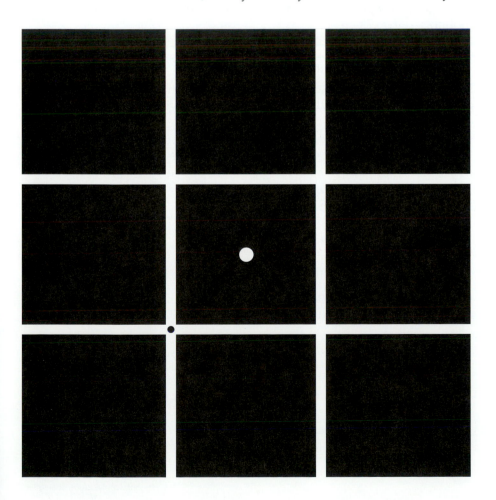

fixation to the black dot. While fixating, you will also see a black grid in your more peripheral vision that appears to move about slightly as this **afterimage** persists. The grid results from the effect of differential bleaching of visual pigment (page 156) during the time that you were viewing the white circle. It is imprinted on your retina and thus does not move with respect to the retina. The impression of movement that you do see while attempting to fixate upon the black dot is thus due to the eye and head movements you are making while doing so. You can get a rough quantitative measure of the extent of your eye movements by noting that the bars of the white grid are about 0.5° wide at a normal reading distance of about 30 cm.

Standing upright while fixating causes much greater head movements:

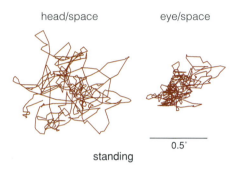

after Skavenski et al., 1979

But, again, compensatory eye movements eliminate much of this head motion.

The retinal image is in constant motion

If we ignore occasional excursions of gaze while sitting or standing still, we can say that gaze generally remains stabilized within a region having a diameter of about 0.25°:

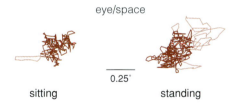

after Skavenski et al., 1979

Even when the head is held motionless by means of a biteboard, eye movements persist, and continue within a region about 0.25° across:

head/space   eye/head   eye/space

biteboard   0.25°

after Skavenski et al., 1979

biteboard
A device for holding the head steady by clenching a rigid object with one's teeth. The object is usually a hardened dental impression of the subject's teeth, which is clamped to a metal frame.

At the center of the fovea, a circular region 0.25° in diameter contains about 700 cones:

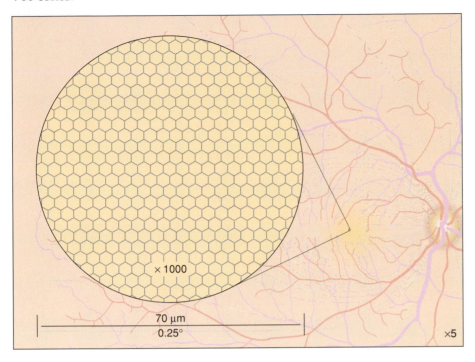

In each the above tasks, the subject attempted to remain as motionless as possible. This is useful in that it shows that even slight head movements can result in compensatory eye movements. But our heads are normally moving as we go about our daily activities. Here is what happens when we *walk:*

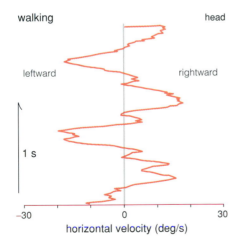

after Grossman et al., 1989

This diagram shows the angular velocity of horizontal head movements for a sequence of four to five steps over a period of 2 s, which is an ordinary walking pace. At the start of the trace, the right foot moves forward, turning the body, and thus the head, leftward. The maximum horizontal angular velocity of head movements is about 15°/s; in the absence of eye movements, this would also be the maximum velocity of the image.

When viewing objects far away, the velocity of the direction of gaze is simply the sum of the velocity of the head and the velocity of the eye *with respect to the head*. The horizontal movements of the eyes with respect to the head in the walking subject, measured at the same time, had about the same velocity as the head movements, but were in the opposite direction, as shown to the left.

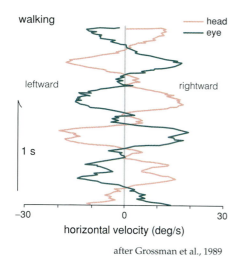

after Grossman et al., 1989

Consequently, the horizontal component of gaze showed much smaller velocities:

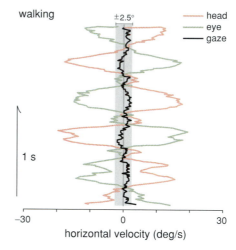

after Grossman et al., 1989

The shaded area delimits leftward and rightward velocities of 2.5°/s, and the gaze velocity lay mainly within these bounds.

One way of interpreting these data is that eye movements are able to compensate for almost all of the subject's head movements. From the perspective of retinal function, however, eye movements fail to fully compensate for head movements, and image velocities of 2.5°/s or so are common as we walk about. Interestingly, image velocities of this magnitude are not particularly noticeable to us.

The situation changes dramatically for people with impaired vestibular function:

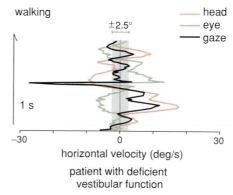

after Grossman and Leigh, 1990

One patient, tested in about 1989, had a long-standing loss in vestibular function following a bout of meningitis in 1946. The head rotations were normal, if cautious, but the patient's eye movements with respect to the head were no longer a near mirror image of the head movements. Consequently, the patient's velocity of gaze was larger than normal. It often exceeded 2.5°/s, and the patient reported blurred vision while walking, as well as an apparent movement of the visual world (*oscillopsia*). This situation appears to parallel that of John Crawford. Over a period of time, both he and this patient were able to compensate partially, but not completely, for their loss of vestibular function.

Returning to normal function, it is sometimes necessary to *run*, as cheetahs and gazelles will attest. Here is what happens to a normal running subject attempting to keep fixation on a distant target:

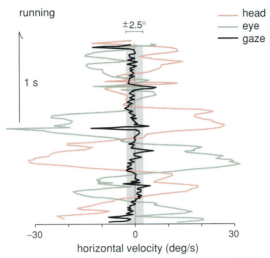

after Grossman and Leigh, 1990

Head movement velocities are much larger, but they are followed closely by eye movements. Remarkably, the resulting gaze movements remain mainly with the 2.5°/s bounds, except for brief shifts of gaze.

To summarize, rotational and translational head movements are a constant feature of our daily lives. In the absence of compensatory eye movements, these head movements would produce corresponding movement of the image on the retina. Compensatory eye movements come into play even for slight head movements, at least when we are attempting to fixate on some object. With the exception of occasional and brief excursions, they act to hold the *direction of gaze* to within about 0.25°, and the *velocity of gaze* to within about 2.5°/s.

Smooth eye movements track stationary targets

The previous section described the degree to which the gaze is stabilized under various conditions. Except for a few occasional saccades, this stabilization is produced by smooth eye movements, even when we attempt to gaze at a *stationary* target.

As discussed in THE CHASE (page 10), smooth eye movements correct for errors in image *velocity*, and it is these eye movements that are used as we attempt to maintain fixation on a stationary object. At first glance, this might appear paradoxical, since the fovea has a specific location on the retina. But it is necessary to distinguish the act of directing one's gaze to some location, which involves a voluntary saccade, from the act of maintaining the direction of gaze, which involves more automatic smooth eye movements with respect to an already fixated target.

Assume for the moment that there are no head movements and that the image is not moving on the retina. There is thus no stimulus to initiate eye movements. The eye starts to drift away from the target as a result of slight differences in the tensions of the eye muscles. But as soon as it starts to drift, a compensatory eye movement attempts to correct the drift. These are the eye movements seen with the biteboard. This situation can be likened to balancing an upright cane or long stick on your hand. There is no defined location of the cane with respect to a point on the floor, but if you are good at making compensatory movements, the upper portion of the cane won't move much, and you won't need to move your feet.

Stabilized images disappear

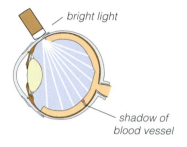
bright light

shadow of
blood vessel

As first discussed in THE CHASE (page 12), if an image is held perfectly stationary on the retinal surface, what we see of it disappears in a fraction of a second. It was noted there that special procedures are required to demonstrate this. One of the best means of generating a fully stabilized image on the retina is to place a strong light to the side of the eye, so that it shines through the translucent sclera. This light casts a shadow of the blood vessels found in the inner portion of the retina onto the photoreceptor outer segments, as shown at left. It is thus possible to observe the pattern of one's own blood vessels. The effect is striking, but continues only so long as the light source is jiggled back and forth so as to keep the shadow moving on the outer segment. As soon as the movement stops, the pattern disappears. The visual system thus *requires* movement of the image in order to work.

Of course, no special eye movements are needed to create this image movement, since involuntary head and eye movements are sufficient to keep the image in motion. On the other hand, it is possible that these residual image motions may serve a useful purpose in the detection of borders by ganglion cells near the fovea.

To summarize, we have seen that smooth eye movements mainly compensate for a variety of factors that cause the position and orientation of the head to change. In part, these compensatory eye movements are the result of messages from proprioceptors, the vestibular apparatus, and the efference copy. But although each of these messages may aid in reducing image motion, none of them contains any direct information about the actual motion of the image on the retina. Only the cells of the retina have that information; so it comes as no surprise that messages from the retina play a critical role in the manner in which smooth eye movements stabilize the image.

Retinal circuitry assists eye movements

Vertebrate retinas have a number of ganglion cell types that appear to be adapted to assist in eye movements. Every vertebrate has an accessory optic system that receives direct input from a subset of retinal ganglion cells. This pathway assists in maintaining the direction of gaze in the presence of head movements.

Some, if not all, *mammals* have at least two groups of ganglion cells that are involved in eye movements. These groups have been best investigated in the rabbit retina; consequently, much of what is said here will be based upon these studies. Squirrels have very similar cells, indicating that these particular cell groups are not exclusive to rabbits (see the Box RABBIT VISION on page 301).

Very little is known about ganglion cell contributions to *primate* eye movements. Consequently, it has been difficult to sort out the roles different ganglion cell types play in these movements. Here it is not really necessary to confront this issue. The primate visual cortex may have taken over a portion, most, or possibly all of the functions of the ganglion cell types described here; but in evolutionary terms, the retinal pathways came first, and it is useful to understand what they do.

Some retinal ganglion cell types are specialized to detect image motion

Any ganglion cell will respond to the movement of the visual world across its receptive field. For most of them, the change in response depends upon the *nature of the contrast* in a pattern. Consider, for example, two bars, one lighter than the background and the other darker, as shown on the right. These two patterns can be said to differ only in the **sign** of the contrast. The response of on- and off-ganglion cells, first discussed in A CONE PATHWAY (page 115), depends critically upon the sign of the contrast. Reversing the sign changes an increase in firing rate to a decrease, and vice versa. Other features of the pattern are generally ignored, including the direction of movement of the pattern.

But the response of other ganglion cells depends critically upon the *direction of movement*. These cells are said to be **direction-selective**. The rabbit retina contains two quite distinct groups of direction-selective ganglion cells, which for historical reasons are termed **on-off direction-selective** and **on-direction-selective**. These terms reflect the response of the ganglion cell to a small spot of light flashed within the center of the cell's receptive field. Flashing a small spot of light helps to identify to which group a direction-selective ganglion cell belongs, but it otherwise has little to do with the more striking functional properties of these cells. Briefly, on-off direction-selective ganglion cells appear to be involved in the smooth tracking movements of the eyes, whereas on-direction-selective ganglion cells indirectly assist in the stabilization of gaze during head movements.

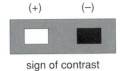

sign of contrast

Rabbit on-off direction-selective cells are aligned with the eye muscles

The on-off direction-selective ganglion cells respond when a small spot of light is turned either on or off within its receptive field. The diagram to the right represents the receptive field of one such cell, where the symbol "±" is used to represent this on-off response, and the symbol "●" is used to indicate no response, indicating that these locations lie outside the receptive field. Mapping with small spots of light showed a roughly circular receptive field with a diameter of about 2°, and little more. But when *moving* spots of light were used, this cell showed a well-defined preference for the upward movement of a spot of light, and no response to a downward movement:

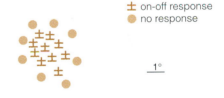

± on-off response
● no response

1°

receptive field of on-off direction-selective cell

from Barlow et al., 1964

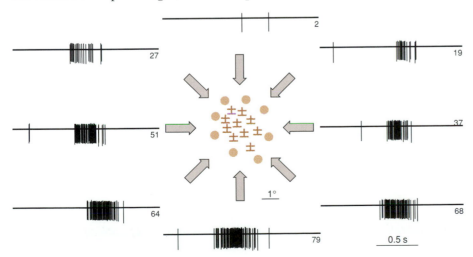

response of on-off direction-selective cell to movement of spot in different directions

from Barlow et al., 1964

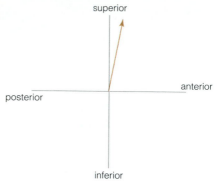

preferred direction of one
on-off direction-selective cell

after Oyster, 1968

The preferred direction is the same within any portion of the cell's receptive field, and is independent of the contrast of the spot. The response properties of this cell can be represented by an arrow that is pointing toward the superior portion of the visual field, so as to represent the direction of movement within the visual field that produced the largest response. Here is a representation of one such cell, from another study, which also showed a preference for upward movement, as shown in the diagram at left.

Each on-off direction-selective cell always has the same preferred direction. If the preferred directions of many cells are superimposed, a pattern emerges in which the preferred directions form four clusters:

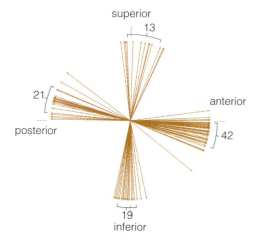

preferred directions of on-off direction-selective cells

after Oyster, 1968

Each cluster consists of ganglion cells of the same *type*; thus on-off direction-selective cells comprise four types, distinguished by their preferred direction.

The significance of these types becomes clear when their directions are compared with the directions in which the eye is rotated by each of the four rectus muscles:

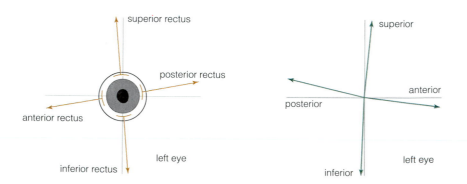

directions in which each of the rectus muscles move the left eye of the rabbit

average preferred directions in the visual field for each type of on-off direction-selective cell in the left eye of the rabbit

after Oyster, 1968

The diagram on the left shows the lines of action (directions of pull) of the four rectus muscles of the left eye as one would view it. The diagram on the right shows the average directions of the four clusters, referenced to the visual field of the left eye. These different perspectives produce a mirror reversal between the two diagrams.

Consider an anterior movement of the visual field of the left eye. This movement will stimulate the on-off direction-selective cells whose preferred direction is anterior. If these cells activate the anterior rectus muscle, then the eye will rotate forward, and thereby track the forward movement. The same applies to other directions of movement in the visual field. Here, then, is a simple feedback mechanism for stabilizing the image of a moving visual environment.

On-off direction-selective cells respond best to movement velocities of 10°/s or greater:

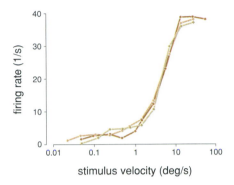

response of on-off direction-selective
cells as a function of stimulus velocity

from Oyster et al., 1972

Rabbits get chased, just as gazelles do, and their ability to briefly hold the image of their surroundings as they flee and dart about is no less critical to their existence.

On-off direction-selective ganglion cells have a bistratified dendritic field that ramifies in both the on- and off-sublayers of the inner synaptic layer:

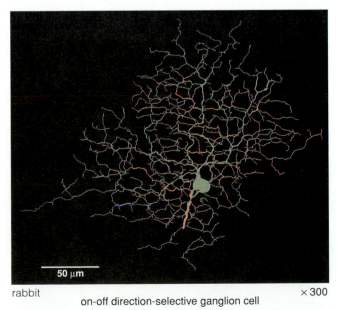

rabbit   × 300
on-off direction-selective ganglion cell

after Amthor et al., 1989

Stratification in both sublayers is consistent with a direction selectivity that is independent of the contrast of the moving image. No feature of the dendritic field has yet been found by which it is possible to predict the preferred direction of movement. Although a number of possibilities have been put forward, the nature of the retinal circuitry that generates the direction selectivity is unknown. It may be that these cells simply make connections with direction-selective amacrine cells, and the ganglion cells do little more than collect information from them.

As discussed in RETINAL ORGANIZATION (page 199), cells of certain types are interconnected by means of gap junctions. These interconnections can be demonstrated by injecting one of the cells with Neurobiotin, a substance that can pass through gap junctions. Neurobiotin injected into one cell can thereby spread to fill the dendrites of the nearby ganglion cells to which it is connected.

The diagram on the facing page is a graphic reconstruction of seven cells so labeled; the injected cell is shown in red and the remaining six cells have been assigned different colors, so as to distinguish them from one another. Within the patch of labeled cells, there is more or less uniform coverage of the retina within each sublayer. By comparison, the morphologies of the individual cells are quite variable. If there is some movement of the image in the preferred direction, then no matter where that movement is, and no matter what its contrast, some cell in the array of ganglion cells of this type is there to respond to it.

On-off direction-selective ganglion cells send their axons to both the superior colliculus and the lateral geniculate nucleus (LGN). The stabilization of gaze during head movements could involve both pathways. The fact that there is a pathway to the visual cortex, via the LGN, suggests that these cells may also play a role in tracking moving objects in the external world.

Rabbit on-direction-selective cells are aligned with the semicircular canals

On-direction-selective ganglion cells show direction selectivity for advancing bright borders, but not advancing dark borders. A plot of the preferred directions of a number of these cells shows that they fall into three clusters, rather than four, as shown at the left. There are thus three types of on-direction-selective cells, distinguished by the cluster to which each belongs.

The critical feature of this group of ganglion cells is that each of these preferred directions corresponds to a component of head rotation that selectively activates one pair of semicircular canals:

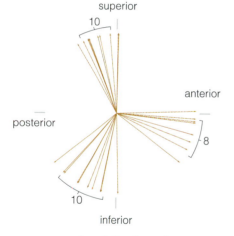

preferred directions of
on-direction-selective cells

after Oyster, 1968

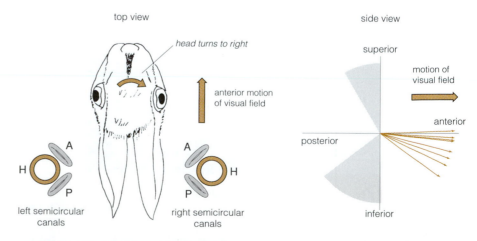

top view   side view

activation of horizontal semicircular canals

activation of on-direction-selective
ganglion cells

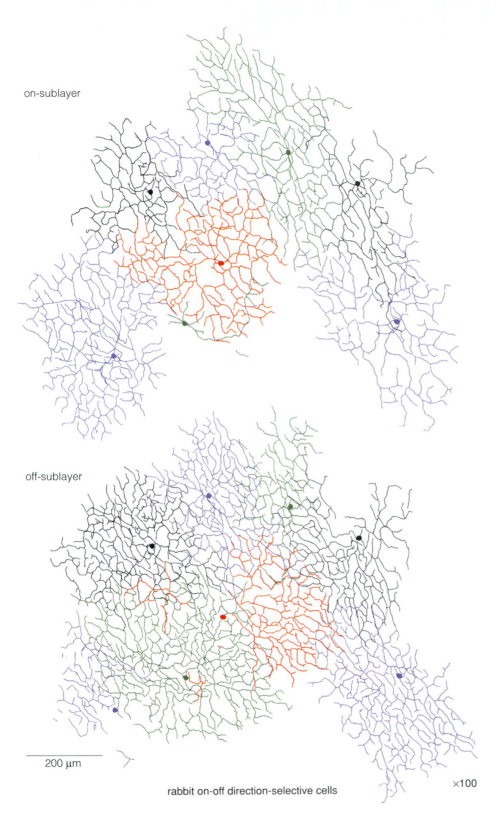

on-sublayer

off-sublayer

200 µm

×100

rabbit on-off direction-selective cells

after Vaney, 1994

Consider, for example, head rotations about a vertical axis, as when the head turns to the right. This type of rotation selectively activates the horizontal semicircular canals of the two ears. *In the absence of compensatory eye movements*, this head rotation also causes the image of the external world to shift horizontally across the retina, thereby activating the type of on-direction-selective ganglion cells that prefer motion of bright edges in the *anterior* direction. But if compensatory eye movements occur, as a result of information received by the brain from the semicircular canals, then there will be little or no image displacement, and the on-direction-selective ganglion cells will not respond.

This reasoning applies only if the eye movements *perfectly* compensate for the head movements about the rotational axis of the semicircular canals. If there is too little compensation, then the image will slip backward on the right retina, which is equivalent to a forward movement of the visual field. Thus, for example, if the head turns in one direction by 10°/s, but the eyes turn in the opposite direction by only 9.7°/s, there will be a slippage of the retinal image of 0.3°/s. In effect, the on-direction-selective ganglion cells respond to this slippage of the retinal image during head movements resulting from errors in compensatory eye movements.

Whereas on-off direction-selective cells respond best to fast movements of 10°/s or greater, on-direction-selective cells respond best to very slow motions; those in the visual streak respond best to velocities of about 0.3°/s as shown to the left. These ganglion cells are thus well adapted to respond to image slippage during head movements.

This image slippage is not necessarily a result of some malfunction of either the semicircular canals or the eye muscles. Instead, the issue lies with the neural circuitry in between that couples the neural receptors in the semicircular canals with the neurons in the brain whose axons innervate the corresponding complementary pair of eye muscles. A head movement stimulates a pair of semicircular canals, and this results in some particular stimulation of the muscles of each eye. It is useful to define a **gain** for this overall pathway:

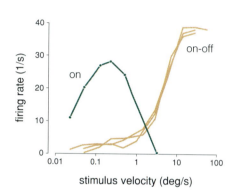

response of an on-direction-selective cell as a function of stimulus velocity

from Oyster et al., 1972

$$gain = -\frac{\text{rotation of eyes}}{\text{rotation of head}}$$

where the rotations are in degrees and the minus sign allows the gain to be positive. Perfect compensation thus corresponds to a gain of 1. If the gain is too small, then the compensatory eye movement is also too small.

The primary function of on-direction-selective ganglion cells is to adjust the gain of the neural pathway between canal rotation and eye rotation. They do so by producing long-term modifications of certain synapses along this pathway. These modifications are referred to as **plastic changes** (from Greek: *plassein* = to mold) in order to distinguish them from the moment-to-moment activity of the nervous system.

These long-term changes can be demonstrated by means of spectacles equipped with optics that produce a mirror reversal of the field of view. Thus objects to the left appear to lie to the right, and vice versa. Human subjects initially find that wearing these spectacles is quite disconcerting. But if they continue to wear them night and day for about a month, the gain gets smaller until it reverses. Their eye movements are again compensatory, and the subjects are able to perform complex tasks, such as skiing downhill.

On-direction-selective ganglion cells have a monostratified dendritic field that lies within the on-sublayer of the inner synaptic layer, as shown in the diagram at the top of the next page. The axons of all on-direction-selective ganglion cells cross the optic chiasm to go to the contralateral accessory optic system (AOS). This crossing is common to all vertebrates, and sug-

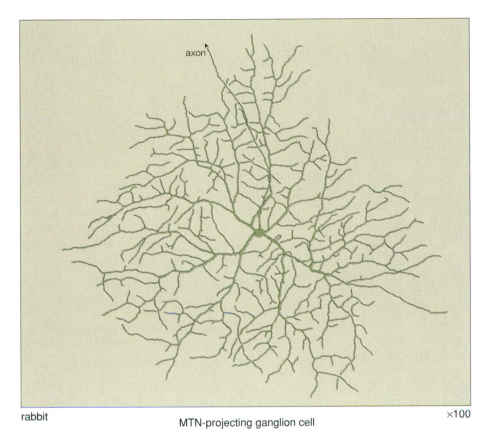

rabbit   ×100

MTN-projecting ganglion cell

from Buhl and Peichl, 1986

gests that this pathway is ancient. The ganglion cells in the cat that project to the AOS are indistinguishable in form from those in the rabbit, which suggests that these rabbit ganglion cells are representative of those of other mammals.

The vertebrate accessory optic system contains three nuclei, termed the dorsal terminal nucleus (DTN), lateral terminal nucleus (LTN), and medial terminal nucleus (MTN). To a first approximation, the response properties of most of the neurons in each nucleus correspond to one of the three ganglion cell types within the on-direction-selective group:

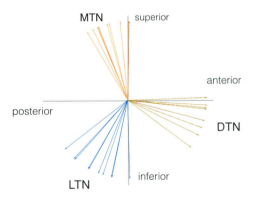

But there are complications, not considered here, that indicate that this is only part of the story.

Ernst Mach's view of his study

from Mach, 1914

14

Seeing

This chapter describes the functional properties of the ganglion cells we see with—those whose messages pass, via the lateral geniculate nucleus, to the striate cortex. Seeing is so immediate and so powerful, that it is useful to lay down a few links that can help bridge the conceptual gap between the responses of the different ganglion cell types and our perceptual world. One link that can readily be formed is that between the reduction in the spatial density of ganglion cells with increasing retinal eccentricity and our loss of various spatial acuities with a corresponding increase in visual eccentricity. The first portion of this chapter offers some exercises intended to develop this link. The general manner in which some of the different ganglion cell types acquire their response characteristics is then described, followed by a discussion of additional links, some speculative, between the response properties of specific ganglion cell types and certain aspects of our visual perception.

Exercises in seeing

We become so accustomed to vision that we often ignore some of its fundamental features. The engraving at the start of this chapter was published in 1886 by Ernst Mach (1838–1916) and is intended to show what he saw of his study with (from) his left eye. It appears to have been made by a professional artist, based upon Mach's sketches, one of which is also shown here.

Both illustrations emphasize the bounds of the visual field, which we generally ignore as we concentrate on what we see. They correctly reflect our subjective *impression* of a visual world that shows no marked changes in appearance away from our center of gaze. But whatever our impression, however arrived at, our visual acuities rapidly decline with visual eccentricity. These losses are a direct result of decreases in the spatial densities of different ganglion cell types with increasing visual eccentricity.

Before discussing these relations, two exercises are presented. The first is devised to familiarize you with different aspects of the extent of the visual field when the eye is free to rotate. The second deals with the losses in vision that occur with increasing visual eccentricity. Please take a few minutes to perform these exercises, as they provide the best means of both appreciating these aspects of seeing, and distinguishing between them.

Warm-up exercise: The extent of the visual world

- Remove your spectacles if you wear them; sharp vision will not be necessary. Close one of your eyes and keep it closed while performing each of the steps described.
- Turn your opened eye to view your nose. Slowly direct your eye downward as far as you can. If you cannot see your upper lip, then puckering your mouth may help, although high cheekbones may still block the view.
- Slowly continue moving your opened eye around, step by step, and attempt to view the edges of your face. A grin may reveal your cheek, and a frown, your eyebrow.
- After completing the circle, so that your eye is again directed at your nose, continue for a second rotation of your eye, again slowly and step by step. This time, attempt to attend to the portion of your face that is *away* from your direction of gaze. Thus, with your eyes directed downward, attempt to view your eyebrow. With the possible exception of the tip of your nose, the facial features opposite to your direction of gaze will probably be just out of view. You can test this by placing a finger on the portion of your face opposite to your direction of gaze, and noting whether your finger is visible.

The bones of the cheek and brow partially protect the eye from a direct blow. Depending upon how deeply the eyes are inset, the field of view at any eye position is roughly limited by the general form of the skull and of the cartilage and skin that overlie it. Rotating the eye within its orbit reveals the portion of the back of the eye that can ever receive an image of the external visual world that lies beyond the rim of the orbit. The boundary of this portion corresponds to the border of the retina. There is thus a balance, or evolutionary interplay, between the extent to which the anatomy of the bony orbits of the skull limits the field of view, the extent to which each eye can move within its orbit, and the extent of the retina across the back of the eye. The edge of the retina is sharp, with the distribution of rods, cones, and ganglion cells ending abruptly as the sensory retina suddenly thins to a single layer of epithelial cells; this boundary is termed the **ora serrata**.

Exercise: Seeing out of the corner of your eye

Spatial acuity:

- Look directly ahead with one eye closed. Contemplate the *border* of your field of view without changing your direction of gaze. *Border* means the transition between what is visible and what is not. Thus, whether or not a portion of your nose is visible is irrelevant. Take your time and occasionally move your eye.

The ora serrata is a sharp anatomical border, but the border of your visual field is anything but sharp. Rather, it seems vague and difficult to define.

- Direct your gaze to some object directly before you, and extend your arm horizontally away from the side of your body and far enough behind you that it is not visible. Extend either two or three fingers, and slowly swing your arm forward until these fingers can just be seen. Be careful not to change your gaze when your fingers come into view.

You will not be able to determine whether there are two or three fingers raised.

- In the following line of text, direct your gaze at the bullet symbol ("•") and determine how many letters to the left or the right of it you can discern without shifting your gaze:

xquperbiaghe•thqfsawlbghzp

You could probably distinguish only a few of the letters on either side.

- Fix your gaze on the center of the following chart, and judge how readable each of the letters is:

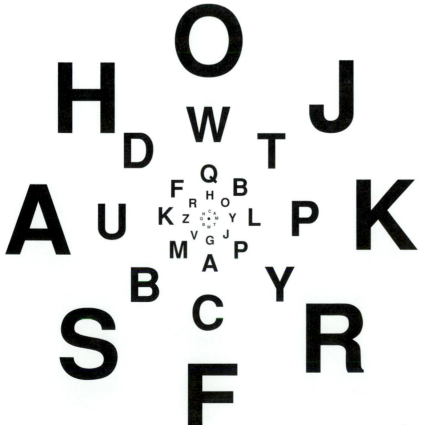

after Anstis, 1974

You probably found that they were all about equally readable.

Movement:

- Position your index finger in your far peripheral field, and hold it as steady as possible.

If you have a steady hand, you will be not be able to detect any movement of your finger.

- Hold your hand in front of you and directly view the tip of your index finger.

No matter how steady your hand, you will have no difficulty in observing the movement of your fingertip. Lore has it that we are particularly good at detecting movement in the periphery of our visual field. But compared with foveal viewing, or anywhere in between, the reverse is true.

Color:

- Gaze at the bullet at the center of the line of colored discs, and determine how many discs to the left or the right of it you can distinguish by color without shifting your gaze:

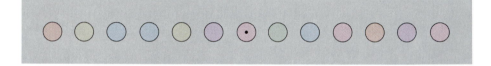

You probably could distinguish only a few discs on either side of the bullet.

- Gaze at the bullet in this diagram, and attempt to judge the colors of the different-sized discs:

You probably found that your ability to judge the color was roughly the same for all the discs.

These exercises are, in themselves, informative about the loss of visual performance at large retinal eccentricities. They are also exercises in using your visual system to look *inward* rather that *outward*—in effect, they encourage you to contemplate, and thereby experience, the nature of your own visual processes. There is no particular gain in doing so, other than increasing your awareness of the difference between the external world on the one hand and your visual representation of it on the other.

The visual world is so immediate, so informative, and so compelling that it has a powerful impact upon our mental state—so powerful that the message tends to overwhelm the messenger, whatever our intent. Evolution, in forging the neural substrate of our mental processes, has not deliberately hidden the underlying mechanisms of visual perception from our conscious awareness; it has simply ignored them with a grand nonchalance, leaving us with neither a user's manual nor a circuit diagram.

Minimum angular resolution

Visual acuities that vary with visual eccentricity can be measured as the smallest visual angle ($\Delta\theta$) that allows some property to be resolved, termed the **minimum angular resolution** (right; see also ANGLES).

To measure spatial resolution, you might be asked to determine the orientation of the gaps in these "C" symbols:

C Ɔ U C ∩ ∩ U Ɔ C Ɔ U Ɔ

If you view this diagram from a distance of 2.3 meters (7.6 feet), each gap will subtend a visual angle of 1 minute. If you can just detect the gaps at this distance, then your minimum angular resolution for spatial acuity when directly viewing the symbols is 1 minute. Otherwise, stand closer or farther away until you determine this threshold. You can go on to plot your minimum angular spatial resolution as a function of visual eccentricity (i.e., the angle away from the direction of gaze) in a similar manner.

For color resolution, the minimum angular resolution at each visual eccentricity is the smallest disc whose color can be distinguished from that of other discs, and for movement, it is the minimum angular movement of a bar or border that can be resolved. Both of these measurements can also be plotted as a function of visual eccentricity.

An old convention is to plot the *reciprocal* of the minimum angular resolution as a function of visual eccentricity. This yields a curve that peaks at the fovea and declines gradually with increasing visual eccentricity (diagram to the upper right). Notice that spatial acuity is higher in the nasal retina than in the temporal retina, reflecting the higher density of ganglion cells in the nasal retina.

You may have seen graphs of visual acuity plotted in this way. There is no theoretical reason for plotting the reciprocal of the minimum angular resolution; it is just a device for placing better spatial acuity higher on the vertical scale. But a cleaner and more informative graph can be obtained by plotting the minimum angular resolution itself as a function of visual eccentricity. For both spatial acuity and motion acuity, the values for minimum angular resolution increase with visual eccentricity along a straight line (right).

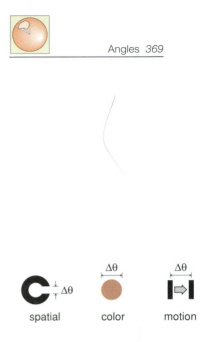

Angles *369*

acuities as minimum angular resolutions

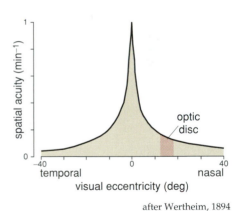

after Wertheim, 1894

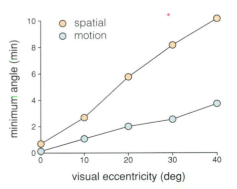

after Weymouth 1958;
after McKee and Nakayama, 1984

For color, the results are not so easily summarized, but the minimum angular resolution still shows a rise with visual eccentricity, as shown in this diagram, in which the color of the data symbol suggests the hue of the colored stimulus viewed:

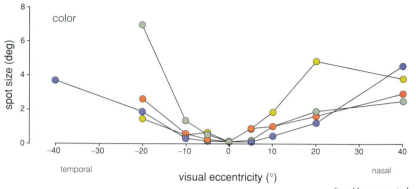

after Abramov et al., 1991

The dendritic field diameters of retinal ganglion cells also increase linearly with visual eccentricity:

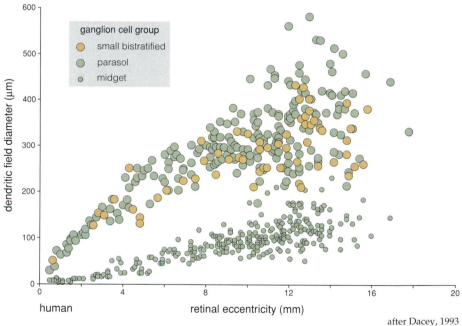

after Dacey, 1993

The data in this diagram were not corrected for variations in ganglion cell density at the same visual eccentricity. In macaques, when that correction is included, the slight curve in the upper data points disappears (see the scatter diagram on page 204). To the degree that retinal coverage is constant, the spacing between ganglion cells of the same type also increases in a linear manner with eccentricity.

In order to put all of this information together in a quantitative way, it is necessary to devise a model based upon the experimental methods used to obtain the psychophysical data, together with a quantitative model of the spatial distributions and response properties of each of the ganglion cell types. In some situations, visual acuity appears to be based upon the sequential activation of cells of the same type. For example, as discussed in LOOKING, some ganglion cell types respond only to specific directions of motion. In primates, however, none of the ganglion cell types that project to the visual cortex via the lateral geniculate nucleus appear to do so. Instead, the visual cortex makes use of the sequential activation of some group of ganglion cells as a border moves across their array; the firing rate of an individual cell says nothing about the rate or direction of movement. By contrast, blue–yellow color vision is based upon ganglion cells whose firing rates reflect the relative activation of the different cones types, as discussed below. Despite these differences, the simplest models consistent with the data for any of these discriminations all assume that minimum angular resolution is proportional to the local spacing between the cells of the ganglion cell type or types that set the threshold. A more detailed consideration would include any variation with eccentricity in the response properties of those ganglion cells.

To summarize, although the details have not yet been worked out, there appears to be a strong correlation between our various perceptual acuities and the spacing between the ganglion cells that subserve them. What variations there are in this relation may be due mainly to intratype differences in response properties that correlate with the coverage of the dendritic fields at different eccentricities. But all of this depends upon how the different ganglion cell types respond to the moving image, which we now consider.

Midget and parasol ganglion cells

Center–surround receptive field organization

Both midget and parasol ganglion cells respond well to a spot of light that falls only upon the photoreceptors that directly activate them via bipolar cells. On-ganglion cells are so named because they respond by increasing their firing rate well above the maintained level; off-ganglion cells may stop generating action potentials altogether. The magnitude of a ganglion cell's change in firing rate in either direction in response to a light stimulus is termed its **response amplitude**. Up to a point, increasing the diameter of the spot of light increases the response amplitude, as more photoreceptors that drive the ganglion cell are stimulated. However, when the spot of light is made larger than the area covered by these photoreceptors, the response amplitude decreases. Furthermore, when an **annulus** of light is presented that falls *only* on the surrounding region, the response of the ganglion cell is reversed from that produced by light stimulation of the central region: the firing rate of an on-ganglion cell decreases below the maintained level, and that of an off-ganglion cell increases above the maintained level.

Thus, for either on- or off-ganglion cells, the effect of stimulating the surrounding region is opposite to that produced by stimulating the center region. Stimulation of either region affects the firing rate of the ganglion cells, and they are collectively termed the **receptive field** of the cell. Both midget and parasol ganglion cells show this form of **center–surround organization**, and we can refine our terminology by referring to what have up to now been termed, say, "on-parasol cells" as "on-*center* parasol cells."

annulus
The area bounded by two concentric circles.

Camping

The hours pass, and the sky to the east begins to lighten, obliterating first the 6th magnitude stars, then the 5th magnitude stars, and so on, until they are gone.

When you last looked at Polaris in the early dawn, the rain of photons from the dawn sky fell over a wide region of your retina, but the rain of photons from this star fell mainly on only a few cones as its image moved across the retina. At any instant, this image—a point spread function—can be represented as a hill, with photon flux density plotted perpendicular to the retinal surface:

image of Polaris
(point spread function)

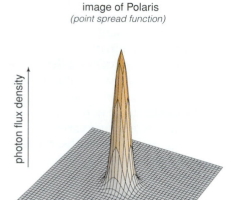

The cones will be activated to varying degrees, depending upon the rate at which they are catching photons. Their degree of hyperpolarization can be represented by means of a similar diagram:

cone array
(L+M)

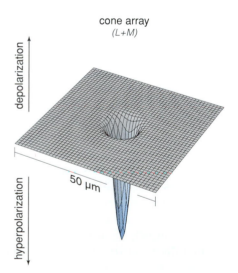

Because cones are discrete, the hyperpolarization of each cone could be individually represented by a vertical column. But that level of detail is unnecessary here, where our focus is on the overall pattern of retinal activity.

The foveal center contains only M and L cones, and their decrease in glutamate release hyperpolarizes the horizontal cells. The activation of all cones by the light of the dawn sky provides a steady and uniform activation of the array of HI horizontal cells. Superimposed upon this background is the effect of the cones activated by the image of Polaris. Because the horizontal cells are electrically interconnected via gap junctions, the hyperpolarization of the array of HI horizontal cells spreads over a larger retinal area than the zone of activated cones within the image of Polaris (top diagram, next page):

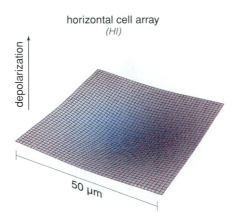

horizontal cell array
(HI)

This hyperpolarization of the horizontal cell array feeds back on the cone array so as to partially suppress the influence of the activated cones on all the bipolar cells they contact. When you looked at Polaris, you saw it with your parasol cells, which receive mainly from diffuse bipolar cells. Here is a representation of the activity within the array of on-diffuse bipolar cells:

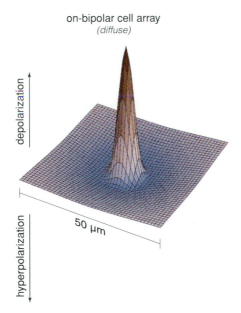

on-bipolar cell array
(diffuse)

Depolarization is shown in brown, and hyperpolarization in blue. The depolarization results from the sign-inverting synapses between the cones and the bipolar cells, which contain metabotropic glutamate receptors (page 110). The region of depolarization is wider than that of the hyperpolarization of the cone array because each diffuse bipolar cell receives from a number of cones. The cones outside the point spread function have a low photon catch rate from the sky, and they provide a weak activation of the array of on-bipolar cells outside of the image of Polaris. But this weak activation is suppressed by the effect of Polaris on the array of horizontal cells, resulting in a slight hyperpolarization of the bipolar cells in the surrounding region.

These on-bipolar cells make presynaptic contacts with on-center parasol ganglion cells. Because each parasol cell receives from a number of on-diffuse bipolar cells, the region over which their array collects from photoreceptors is larger than that of the array of on-diffuse bipolar cells (see the diagram on the next page).

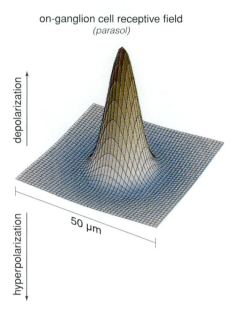

on-ganglion cell receptive field
(parasol)

Diagrams of this sort can be viewed in two different ways. The view presented thus far reflects the variation in the activity of an *array* of cells across the retina in response to a small spot of light located at the center of the array. This perspective works well for the array of cones or bipolar cells, whose spatial densities are high, and whose receptive fields are small and comparable in size to the point spread function. For the same reasons, it can also work well for midget ganglion cells near the fovea. But for parasol cells in the peripheral retina, where receptive fields are large and the spacing between cells is comparable to the diameters of their dendritic fields, the representation of the array as a smooth surface breaks down.

Another way of viewing such diagrams, which applies to all cell types, is to consider the activity of a single cell, located at the center of the array, in response to different locations of the small spot of light. This is the sort of result obtained when recording the change in firing rate of a single ganglion cell in response to the presentation of a spot of light in different portions of its receptive field. It can also be the change in the transmembrane potential of a single photoreceptor, horizontal cell, or bipolar cell in response to different positions of the spot. In these cases, it is termed the **receptive field profile** of the cell. For parasol and midget ganglion cells, this surface has a sombrero-like shape with a shallow brim; however, when detailed plots are made of receptive fields, none of them show such perfect symmetry. Thus this receptive field profile is only a convenient idealization, and its exact shape is not important. Earlier, we saw the same sort of idealization with respect to the point spread function (page 81). Either recalls the remark "This is a typical day, but it doesn't occur very often." The key concept to keep in mind is that a system adapted to emphasize *spatial* differences in light intensity at the expense of the ambient light level needs to make *spatial* comparisons.

A small spot of light can also be used as a test probe to determine other response characteristics of retinal cells. Using an on-center ganglion cell as an example, movement of the spot toward the center of the receptive field (centripetal movement) causes an increase in the firing rate of the ganglion cell, as you might expect. Likewise, centrifugal movement of the spot causes a decrease in firing rate. But a tangential movement of the spot around the center of the receptive field generally does not cause a change in firing rate. The response to any possible small movement of the spot depends only on whether it is moving up or down on the receptive field profile. This is the expected result if there is a simple and static relation between the position of the spot and the firing rate of the cells.

It is conceptually useful to spatially decompose the receptive field profile of a ganglion cell into a **center component** and a **surround component**:

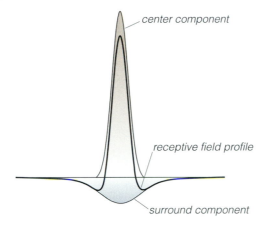

The receptive field profile of a bipolar cell can be decomposed in the same way. In either case, the center component results from the summed contributions of the photoreceptors in the absence of the influence of the horizontal cells, and the surround component results from the action of the horizontal cells on *the same group* of photoreceptors. Photoreceptors that lie outside the center region of the receptive field of a ganglion cell are not directly connected to it via bipolar cells, but they indirectly influence the response properties of the bipolar cells and the ganglion cell by acting on the horizontal cells, which act in turn on the photoreceptors within the center region. Whereas the width of the center component is determined by the group of cones that drives the bipolar cell or ganglion cell, the width of the surround component is determined by the electrical coupling between horizontal cells. There may also be an amacrine cell contribution to the surround component, but not much is known about this, so it is not considered further here.

The observed properties of ganglion cell receptive fields are entirely consistent with what is known about the properties of photoreceptors, horizontal cells, and bipolar cells, as discussed above. However, there are probably other mechanisms, as yet unappreciated, that contribute to response properties of ganglion cells, so the above description is likely to be incomplete. What is useful to keep in mind is that the firing rate of ganglion cells with center–surround organization, however realized, reflects a difference between the opposing tendencies of the center and surround components of the receptive field profile. The center component is tall and thin, the surround wide and shallow, but their summed contributions (i.e., their volumes) are approximately equal. It is this approximate balance between opposing influences that provides the ganglion cells with their insensitivity to the ambient light level. In primates, more often than not, the total center contribution exceeds that of the surround, so the cell responds to a large flashing spot with the same polarity (on or off) as the center component, but more gradual changes in ambient light intensity have little effect.

This diagram shows the response of a cat off-center ganglion cell to the presentation of black or white paper discs before a gray paper background:

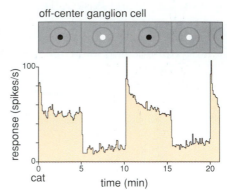

off-center ganglion cell

after Bishop and Rodieck, 1965

The size of the center region was first determined by plotting it with small spots of light, and the paper discs were cut to the same size. The gray circle that surrounds each disc shows the measurable extent of the surround region. Every 5 minutes the color of the disc was changed. The presentation of the black disc caused a transient increase in firing rate. Under natural conditions, this transient increase would be the only response, as eye movements always keep the image in motion. In this experiment, the firing rate settled down to a steady level until the white disc was suddenly substituted for the black one. The firing rate immediately dropped because the off-bipolar cells that drove this ganglion cell were hyperpolarized by this stimulus, and remained hyperpolarized during its presentation.

If paper annuli were used instead of discs, the changes in firing rate were reversed:

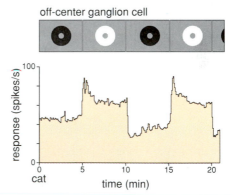

off-center ganglion cell

after Bishop and Rodieck, 1965

The change from the black annulus to the white annulus caused the firing rate of the ganglion cell to increase. Both annuli lay outside the group of cones that composed the center region that activated the ganglion cell via bipolar cells. The change from black to white increased the hyperpolarization of the horizontal cell array. This reduced the response of the cones at the center to the gray background, thereby causing a depolarization of the off-center bipolar cells, and an increase in the firing rate of the ganglion cell.

Finally, large sheets of white or black paper were used to cover the entire receptive field:

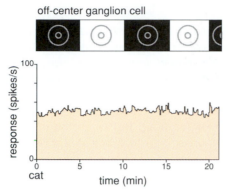

off-center ganglion cell

after Bishop and Rodieck, 1965

These overall changes in light intensity produced no change in firing rate. When the paper was changed from black to white, the direct effect of the central cones was to hyperpolarize the off-bipolar cells they contacted. But this effect was antagonized by the increased influence of the horizontal cells, so that the two influences canceled.

As the experiment with annuli shows, the surround component of a receptive field can have a direct effect on the firing rate of a ganglion cell, in which case it is termed an **antagonistic surround**. Others types of receptive field organization show a different type of surround; the differences between them are discussed in the Box *ANTAGONISTIC AND SUPPRESSIVE SURROUNDS*.

The response of an on-center ganglion cell to a white paper stimulus before a gray background is the same as that of an off-center cell to a black paper stimulus before the same gray background. Indeed, without knowing the contrast of the stimulus, it is not possible to tell from a response whether the ganglion cell is of the on- or the off-center type.

The spatial organizations of the receptive fields of parasol and midget ganglion cells appear to be basically similar. But at any visual eccentricity outside the fovea, the diameters of the dendritic fields of parasol cells are about three times larger than those of midget ganglion cells. Since parasol cells receive from diffuse bipolar cells, which have a lateral spread of their own, the center component of the receptive field of a parasol cell should be slightly larger than its dendritic field. The diameter of the center component of the receptive field of a midget ganglion cell within about 2 mm of the center of the fovea should be that of a single cone, and thus the diameter of the cone's inner segment, which funnels the light into the outer segment.

Transient and maintained response components

A second difference between parasol and midget ganglion cells involves the time course of their response to a step change in light intensity over the center of the receptive field, as shown in the diagram to the right. Parasol cells respond mainly to the *change* in light intensity; within about 200 ms, their firing rate drops to a value close to the maintained rate. Parasol cells also respond strongly, but briefly, to the movement of a bar or border. Midget

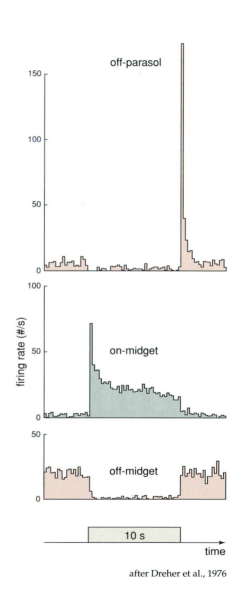

after Dreher et al., 1976

Antagonistic and suppressive surrounds

Thus far we have considered a surround region that can actively drive the response of a ganglion cell. The nature of the surround of a cell with an antagonistic center–surround form of organization can be illustrated by choosing stimuli restricted to either the surround or the center region, as described in the main text.

The are many types of ganglion cells that have forms of receptive field organization other than the center–surround form, some of which are described later in this chapter. Many of these have a surround region that is termed **suppressive** rather than antagonistic. As its name suggests, a suppressive surround reduces or eliminates the center response, but is ineffective in changing the firing rate of the ganglion cell when it alone is stimulated.

A nice example is a type of ganglion cell known as a local edge detector, which is found in the rabbit retina. Cells of this type respond well to edges moving across the center region of the receptive field. The more edges that pass across the center region and can still be resolved, the more action spikes are generated. Here is an example of a local edge detector responding to a black and white grating that was slowly passed through the receptive field. The grating was moved behind a mask matched to the size of the center region (top). But when the mask was removed, the response of this cell was almost entirely suppressed (bottom). Movement of edges confined to the surround region was without effect.

Other cell types appear to have little or no surround. Examples are the ganglion cells that code for color, discussed in this chapter, and those that detect slippage of the image of the visual world on the retina, which are described in LOOKING.

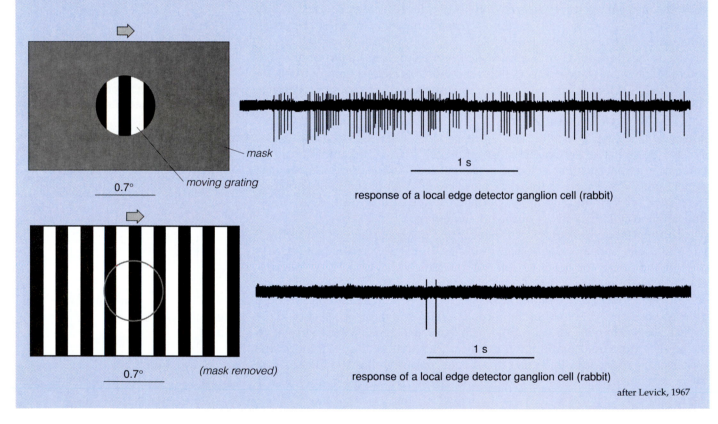

mask

moving grating

0.7°

response of a local edge detector ganglion cell (rabbit)

1 s

0.7°   (mask removed)

response of a local edge detector ganglion cell (rabbit)

1 s

after Levick, 1967

ganglion cells may also respond with a transient change in firing rate, but their response always includes a significant *sustained* change in firing rate in response to the new light intensity.

Just as the spatial characteristics of receptive fields can be decomposed into two components (center–surround), so too can their temporal characteristics be decomposed into two components (sustained–transient) as shown at the top of the next page. The symmetry shown in this schematic diagram is not always observed; for example, in the previous diagram, the on-midget ganglion cell had a transient increase in firing rate following the

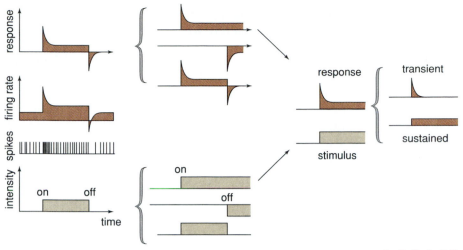

after Rodieck, 1965

step increase in light intensity that was not matched by a transient suppression of firing following the step decrease.

There is an interesting and quite striking aspect of seeing that appears to be based upon this difference in the temporal response characteristics of parasol and midget ganglion cells, which is termed the **Cheshire Cat effect.** The apparatus needed to demonstrate it is simple; here is the setup used at the San Francisco Exploratorium, where this effect was discovered:

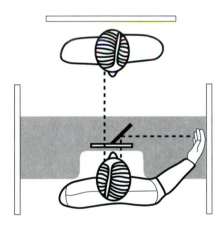

after Duensing and Miller, 1979

The observer looks through a mask that contains two holes, one for each eye. One eye views someone's face. The other eye looks through a mirror at a white wall in front of which the observer can move his hand. When the observer moves his hand, the portion of the face over which it appears to pass is erased, except for the portion that falls on his fovea. Thus, if he directs his gaze toward one of the eyes of the person he is looking at, the eye will remain. Likewise, if his gaze is directed toward the mouth, only that will remain (right).

This effect is quite striking, and I encourage you to demonstrate it for yourself. For best results, move your hand slowly before a bright white wall, and be careful not to move your eyes as you do so.

Consider the responses of the midget and parasol cells in the eye that is viewing the face before the hand moves. When the observer first directs his gaze to the person's mouth, both parasol and midget ganglion cells respond to the movement of the image across the retina. But the activity of the para-

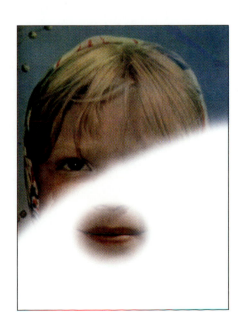

sol cells, which respond mainly to changes in light intensity, soon subsides, leaving only the sustained component of the response of the midget ganglion cells.

The movement of the hand, seen by the other eye, has no effect upon the responses of these parasol and midget ganglion cells, yet it erases the perception of most of the face. Thus the sustained component of the response of the midget ganglion cells need not produce a sustained perceptual correlate. The brain seems somehow able to sample the image and hold it in our minds until a shift of gaze replaces it with another.

Why does the grin persist? As you know, even when we attempt to gaze steadily at something, the eyes are in constant motion as a result of residual head movements. This causes a slight movement of the entire image over the retina. In the retinal periphery, the receptive fields of both midget and parasol cells are much larger than in the fovea, and the thresholds for detection of movement there are much higher (see the figure on page 331). But in the foveal region, where the receptive fields are small and movement detection is best, this slight image motion appears to be sufficient to preserve vision during steady gaze as the ganglion cells respond to the borders that move over them.

The Cheshire Cat effect undercuts the notion that all of the information contained in neural representations is available at the perceptual level; conversely, perceptual constancy need not necessarily be maintained by means of peripheral—or possibly even central—firing rates.

Midget and parasol cell responses to more complex stimuli are predictable

The previous sections have shown how the receptive field profile and the temporal response of a ganglion cell can be characterized by means of a single small spot of light presented over different portions of the receptive field. If the receptive field is tested with two spots of light, the response of the ganglion cell, expressed as a change in firing rate, is approximately the sum of its responses to each of the two spots presented separately. The same additive property also holds for three or more spots. If these small stimuli are superimposed, then the response varies according to the summed responses to each of the stimuli. This property is termed **superposition**, or **linearity**. It appears to hold for much of ordinary viewing in the natural world, where responses to visual stimuli lie well within the operating ranges of the retinal cells.

To the degree that superposition holds, it is possible to use the spatial and temporal properties of ganglion cells to predict their responses to more complex stimuli. Consider the movement of an arbitrary figure through the receptive field of a retinal ganglion cell as shown at the top of the next page. The dark triangular figure is moving to the right and, at different times, covers different parts of the receptive field shown. Imagine that a fine-meshed grid lies between the stimulus and the receptive field. It tessellates the image in much the same way that an image on a computer screen is composed of an array of pixels. Light passing through each hole in the grid can be considered an individual stimulus acting on a discrete region of the receptive field. As the leading edge of the dark triangle passes behind a certain hole in the grid, the light through that hole is reduced, and remains so until the trailing edge of the figure passes across the hole and the background light intensity is restored. Each individual stimulus is thus equivalent to a small light turned off and on in a small region of the visual field, like one light in the array of lights in a sports stadium.

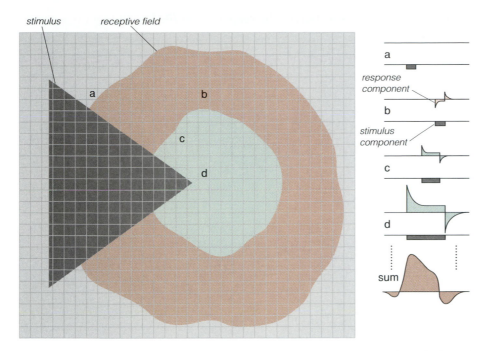

stimulus   receptive field

a

response component

b

stimulus component

c

d

sum

after Rodieck, 1965

The contributions of four small regions of the visual field (the squares of the grid labeled a–d) are shown on the right. In each graph, the upper line is the response component, while the lower line is the stimulus component. The response of the ganglion cell is the sum of all of the response components over the grid.

This type of analysis correctly predicts the responses of ganglion cells with center–surround receptive field organization to a wide variety of stimuli. A typical response profile for a spot moving across the receptive field is shown at the lower right. This response profile can be viewed in two different ways, just like the response profile for a stationary spot. If we view it as the response of an array of ganglion cells of a given type, then the spot and the response profile itself can both be seen as moving from right to left. The left–right asymmetry of the response is due to the transient component of the response. In the absence of a transient component, the receptive field profile would look like one plotted with small stationary spots of light. But the presence of the transient component gives a direction to the receptive field profile, and thus a direction within the array of ganglion cells.

If the spot is lighter than the background, then this response profile characterizes the response of an array of some type of on-center ganglion cell. Its off-center counterpart would show the same profile, but reversed in sign, so that the increase in firing rate would follow the movement of the spot. In either case, the actual pattern of response for the negative component will be truncated when the firing rate of each ganglion cell is driven to zero. If we imagine the activity of the on-center ganglion cells controlling the intensity of green lights in a stadium array and off-center ganglion cells controlling orange lights, we return to the image of the arrays of parasol ganglion cells introduced in A CONE PATHWAY (page 118).

We can also view this profile as the response of a single ganglion cell to different transits of the moving spot across the receptive field, with time progressing from *left to right*.

From the response to a moving spot, one can readily calculate the response to a moving edge or bar, in the manner described previously. For

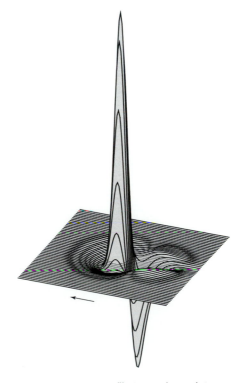

response profile to moving point

a moving bar, a cross section of the response profile has the following general form:

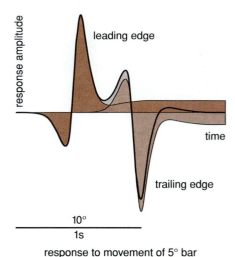

response to movement of 5° bar

after Rodieck, 1965

The response to the leading edge—and thus the response to the movement of any border—dips as the border encroaches on the surround, swings high as it passes over the center, is pulled down as the transient component of the center response dies away and the surround component continues to exert its influence, and finally goes to a maintained level that reflects any difference between the surround and center components. The same sequence of events occurs for the trailing edge of the bar, but is delayed by the width of the bar, and is opposite in sign. Here again, for a light bar, an increasing in firing in the array of on-center cells marks the leading edge and an increasing in firing in the array of off-center cells marks the trailing edge; for a dark bar their roles are reversed.

All of these examples are based upon sharp borders, but the principles apply to gradual changes in light intensity as well. In particular, if a sinusoidal spatial variation in light intensity is passed over a receptive field, then all cells produce a sinusoidal variation in their firing rate with time. The fact that sinusoidal stimuli always produce sinusoidal responses for all cell types—at least at low enough contrasts—can be viewed as either an advantage or a disadvantage, depending upon one's perspective. Some investigators like it because it provides common ground for comparing how different cell types respond to a limited set of stimulus parameters, such as the speed or spatial frequency of the sinusoidal pattern. Other investigators dislike it for the same reason, in that the limited stimulus set makes the differences between the responses of different cell types less evident, and they prefer to search for visual stimuli that sharpen these differences.

Summing cone inputs

Current findings are consistent with the hypothesis that the center regions of the receptive fields of both midget and parasol ganglion cells are driven by a random mixture of M and L cones. To the degree that this is true, the differences in cone inputs to these ganglion cells appear to be more quantitative than qualitative. S cones are a special case, discussed below.

In the mid-periphery of the retina (10 mm eccentricity), cone density is about 5000/mm². At this eccentricity, the dendritic field of the average midget ganglion cell covers about 40 cones, and that of the average parasol ganglion cell covers about 360 cones. Assuming that M and L cones occur in about equal numbers, and are randomly distributed, the fractions of M cones in the dendritic fields of these ganglion cell types shows these probability distributions:

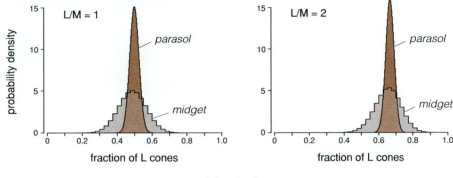

peripheral retina

For parasol cells, the variation in the fraction of M cones is relatively small (0.5 ± 0.05); for midget ganglion cells, it is about three times larger. This is true whether an equal number of L and M cones is assumed (L/M = 1), or whether their ratio is 2:1.

But if we move to the fovea, there is a dramatic change: there, each midget ganglion cell receives from only a single cone, and each parasol cell receives from about 20 cones:

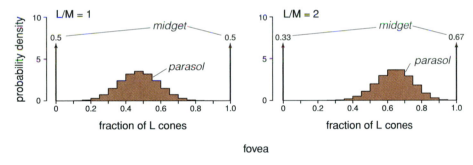

fovea

Again ignoring S cones, and assuming equal numbers of L and M cones, there is a probability of one-half that a particular midget ganglion cell receives from an L cone (0 on the horizontal axis) or from an M cone (1 on the axis). The fraction of M cones that a foveal parasol cell can receive from shows a larger variation than for parasol cells in the peripheral retina, but the probability that a parasol cell will be strongly biased toward either M or L cones remains small.

It is possible that parasol cells narrow the above distributions, either by receiving from a subset of cones or by weighting the contributions of the cones they receive from via bipolar cells. Likewise, it is possible that midget ganglion cells in the peripheral retina are biased toward one cone type or the other within the domain of their dendritic field. However, there is no strong evidence for either possibility. But even in the absence of some selection mechanism, midget ganglion cells can, by chance, show relatively large variations in their cone inputs compared with parasol cells. This larger variation may or may not have something to do with color vision, as discussed below.

Comparing cone inputs

The principle of univariance (page 86) states that all caught photons have the same effect upon the photoreceptor that absorbs them. This is equivalent to saying that a photoreceptor cannot distinguish caught photons

according to their frequencies. But a limited amount of information can be gained from comparisons of the responses of photoreceptors with different spectral sensitivities; this is the basis of all color vision.

A few amphibians have two types of rods with different spectral sensitivities, and appear to possess a limited form of color vision based upon a comparison of their responses. In mammals, however, color vision is based upon comparisons of different cone types. The number of independent comparisons that can be made is one less than the number of spectrally distinct cone types in the retina. In neural terms, there must be some site in the circuitry at which this comparison is made; this site is termed the **critical locus**.

Most mammals have only two cone types, S cones and "LM" cones (see page 217), and thus can make only one comparison. The spectral sensitivities of these two cone types lie at opposite ends of the visible spectrum:

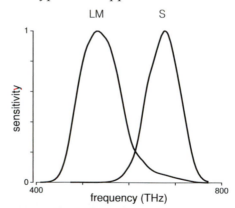

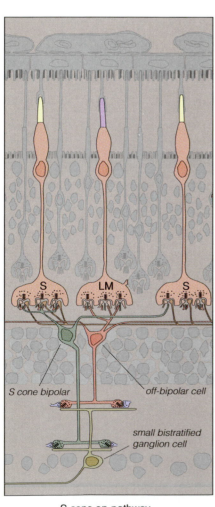

S cone on-pathway

In primates—and probably in mammals generally—this comparison is made by the small bistratified ganglion cells, whose anatomical properties were previously described (page 263). These ganglion cells receive from *on*-S cone bipolar cells and from *off*-bipolar cells that receive from both M and L (or from "LM") cones, as shown schematically at the left. It is the convergence of both on- and off-bipolar cells onto the same ganglion cell that provides the neural mechanism for comparison, and it is this convergence that constitutes the critical locus for blue–yellow color vision.

As we have seen, the response of a midget or parasol ganglion cell to a spot of light decreases when the size of the spot is larger than the center of the receptive field—the region over which the ganglion cell is driven by cones, via bipolar cells. In striking contrast, small bistratified ganglion cells show little or no decrease in the amplitude of their response as the spot size increases; in effect, they lack an antagonistic surround. As we will see, the absence of an antagonistic surround is absolutely necessary in order for the activity of these ganglion cells to consistently reflect the difference between the activation of S cones and that of "LM" cones.

Why don't the receptive fields of these ganglion cells show an antagonistic surround? After all, the effects of the horizontal cells appear to be exerted on the cones themselves, not directly on the bipolar cells. Thus all bipolar cells will be influenced by horizontal cells.

Consider the situation in which the spot just covers the cones that drive a ganglion cell one way or the other. Assume that the spectral composition of the spot is such that it activates the S cone pathway onto the ganglion cell more than it does the "LM" pathway. This situation is shown schematically in the left portion of this diagram:

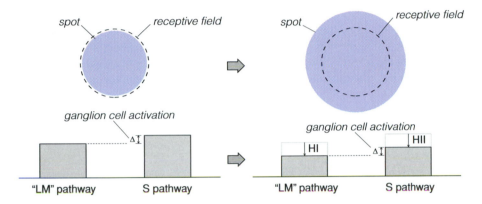

The activations of both cone pathways are shown upward; and the response of the ganglion cell depends upon the difference between them. The response of each pathway to a larger spot is shown in the right portion of the diagram.

Consider first the response of the "LM" pathway. Remember that these cones are influenced almost entirely by HI horizontal cells, which receive only from M and L cones (page 48). Thus increased activation of HI cells will reduce the activation of this pathway by some amount, as shown. Now consider the S pathway. If its activation is reduced by about the same amount, then the response of the ganglion cell will be the same as before, and the increase in the size of the spot will be without effect.

How might this come about? Remember that S cones are influenced almost entirely by HII horizontal cells, which themselves are activated by all three cone types (page 49); they make fewer contacts with M and L cones, but there are many more of these cones, so the combined effect of all the cone types nevertheless has a strong effect on HII cells. To the degree that the effect of HII cells on the S cone pathway reflects the combined activation of M and L cones, there need be no change in the response amplitude of the ganglion cell. So the issue boils down to the relative contribution of the S cones to the mix received by HII cells: if it is small, then the increase in the spot size will have little influence on the ganglion cell.

There are two reasons to believe that the S cone contribution has little effect. First, if the S cones had the same spectral sensitivity as a mix of L and M cones, there would be no problem. So we are not so much concerned with the stimulation of the S cones per se as with the difference between their stimulation and that of M and L cones due to spectral variations. In the case of spectral light (i.e., photons of a single frequency) such differences

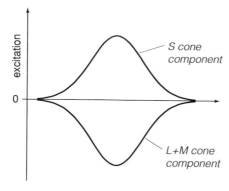

excitation

0

S cone component

L+M cone component

small bistratified ganglion cell receptive field

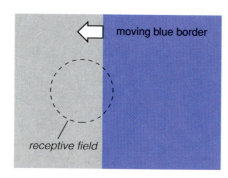

moving blue border

receptive field

can be quite large, but as discussed in PHOTON CATCH RATE, in the natural world, these differences are generally small. Second, in the natural world, M and L cones catch about nine times more photons than S cones do, because sunlight contains relatively few photons in the high-frequency portion of the spectrum to which S cones are most sensitive (see PHOTON CATCH RATE).

In any case, the small bistratified ganglion cells don't show a significant surround component, and would not work well if they did. Their receptive fields can thus be viewed as consisting of two center components: an *on*-center driven by S cones, and an *off*-center driven by L and M cones, which has about the same shape but is opposite in sign (left). This is because depolarization of the on-bipolar cells results from an *increase* in the photon catch of the S cones, whereas depolarization of the off-bipolar cells results from a *decrease* in the photon catch of the M and L cones.

Consider, for example, the movement of a blue paper border crossing a gray background. We assume that the gray background is producing about the same stimulation of all three cone types, and that the on- and off-bipolar cells are activated to the same degree (left). The blue paper is assumed to reflect more high-frequency photons and fewer low-frequency photons than the gray background. When the blue border passes over the receptive field, it increases the photon catch of the S cones and decreases the photon catch of the M and L cones. The increase in the photon catch of the S cones depolarizes the on-bipolar cells, and thereby excites the ganglion cell. The decrease in the photon catch of the M and L cones depolarizes the off-bipolar cells, which also excites the ganglion cell:

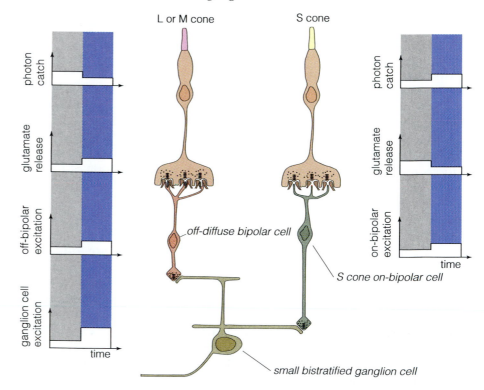

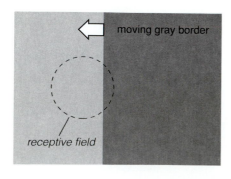

moving gray border

receptive field

We now replace the blue paper with a piece of darker gray paper, and move it over the receptive field (left). This darker paper, of course, decreases the photon catches of all three cone types. The decrease in the photon catch of the S cones hyperpolarizes the on-bipolar cells and thus *decreases* the excitation of the ganglion cell. But the decrease in the photon catch of the M and L cones depolarizes the off-bipolar cells and thus *increases* the excitation of the ganglion cell. Thus movement of the darker border produces little or no change in the net excitation of the ganglion cell, because the opposite effects of the on- and off-bipolar cells cancel each other:

Photon catch rate *471*

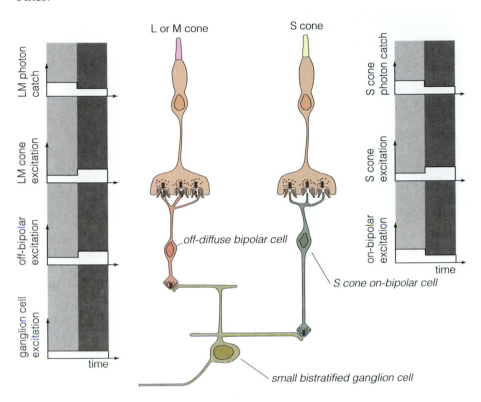

Work out for yourself the response to a gray piece of paper that is lighter than the background and to a piece of paper that reflects fewer high-frequency photons and more low-frequency photons than the background. The general conclusion from these four examples is that small bistratified ganglion cells do not respond well to light or dark borders, unlike parasol ganglion cells and many midget ganglion cells. But they do respond well to stimuli that alter the relative contributions of S cones compared with the combined contributions of M and L cones.

An interesting feature of HII cells is that they do not respond to a spectral change in light—say, from red to green—that does not alter the combined contributions of the L and M cones. This is also mainly true of HI cells; put another way, spectral changes in the red–green direction have little or no effect on the pathway we are considering. Thus the small bistratified ganglion cells will be insensitive to increases in the photon catches of M cones that are balanced by decreases in the photon catches of L cones—or vice versa.

As you might expect, a grating composed of blue and yellow paper strips moved through the receptive field is particularly effective at stimulating a small bistratified ganglion cell, but a black/white grating is not. Interestingly, this absence of a response to a black/white grating is preserved even when the ambient light in the room is changed from fluorescent to incandescent. This suggests that the cone comparison mechanisms of the retina are somehow able to adjust for spectral variations in ambient light, although this effect has not been much studied.

However achieved, the absence of an antagonistic surround is a critical feature of this form of receptive field organization. Consider, for example, how a ganglion cell with a center–surround organization would respond to a blue paper spot on either a white or a black background:

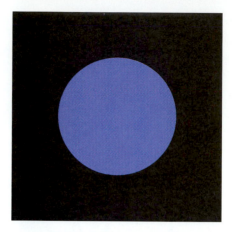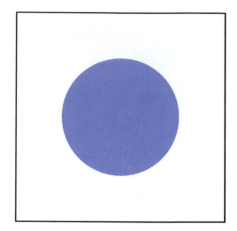

For simplicity, we will assume that the black background reflects none of the incident light and the white background reflects all of it. Thus, every photoreceptor, regardless of type, will capture *more photons* from the blue spot than from the black background, and *fewer photons* from the blue spot than from the white background.

In particular, consider how a ganglion cell with an on-center and an off-surround would respond to the leading edge of a blue paper spot as it entered the center region of the receptive field. Regardless of the cone types that composed the center region, or those that composed the surround region, this on-center ganglion cell would *increase* its firing rate when the blue spot was in front of the *black* background. Likewise, this ganglion cell would *decrease* its firing rate when this spot was in front of the *white* background. Now replace the blue spot with a yellow spot:

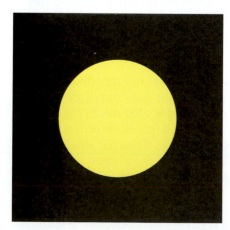

This ganglion cell would again produce an on-response when the spot was in front of the black background and an off-response when it was in front of the white background. Thus the sign of the response would depend entirely upon the nature of the background, and not at all upon the spectral reflectance of the spot. Demonstrate for yourself that this generalization applies as well to ganglion cells with off-centers and on-surrounds. Thus the response polarity of all center–surround ganglion cells depends only upon whether the background is black or white.

To summarize, other than foveal midgets, ganglion cells that respond well to spatial differences in light intensity do so by comparing the responses of what is typically a *similar* set of cones in *different* spatial locations, whereas ganglion cells that respond well to differences in spectral composition do so by comparing the responses of *different* cone types in about the *same* spatial location.

Each S cone, in addition to contacting one or more on-S cone bipolar cells, also contacts an off-midget bipolar cell that is presynaptic to an off-center midget ganglion cell. Objects that reflect poorly over the high-frequency portion of the visible spectrum, such as a red, orange, or yellow piece of paper, cause these off-center midget ganglion cells to increase their firing rate by activation of the *off*-bipolar cells they receive from (right). These ganglion cells, although about as numerous as the small bistratified type, have not been well studied, and it is not clear whether they show an on-center–off-center receptive field organization like the small bistratified cells, or an antagonistic center–surround organization, like that of other off-midget ganglion cells.

What do we see when the relative contribution of S cones is altered? A few human males have one normal eye and one that lacks either functional M cones or functional L cones. For them, the hues seen by the abnormal eye are restricted to yellows and blues. Although the sensations of blue and yellow appear to depend in some manner upon the small bistratified and S cone off-midget ganglion cells, it is not clear which components of their responses are important, or even relevant, to these sensations. For example, does the sensation of blue arise wholly from an increase in the firing rates of the small bistratified cells, or does it involve the difference between their firing rate and that of the S cone off-midget ganglion cells? Likewise, to what degree does the sensation of yellow depend upon an *increase* in the firing rate of the S cone off-midget ganglion cells, or a *decrease* in the firing rate of the small bistratified cells? The observation that we never see a color that appears to be both blue and yellow suggests that these color sensations ultimately depend upon either the firing rate of a single cell type, or more likely, upon the firing rates of two cell types coupled by means of mutual inhibition.

Whatever the neural mechanism for blue–yellow color discrimination, it depends upon a comparison between the stimulation of S cones and that of the other cones, and this comparison can conveniently be represented as a balance:

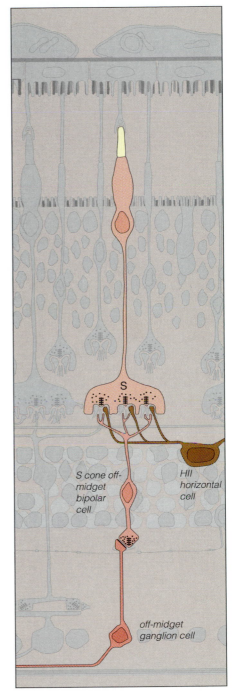

S cone off-pathway

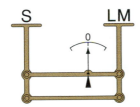

The light that comes to our eyes from objects depends in part on the light that falls on it—typically daylight—and the manner in which the object reflects light of different frequencies, which is termed its **spectral reflectance.**

Flat spectral reflectances—same reflectance at all frequencies—in daylight produce contributions of equal weight from the cones on each side of the balance, resulting in the sensation of white, gray, or black, depending upon the amount of reflectance:

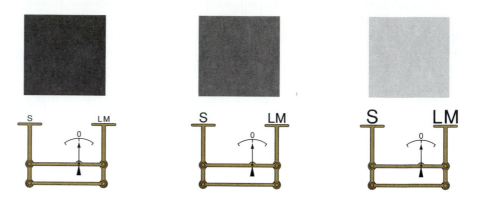

But other spectral reflectances tip the balance one way or the other, resulting in the sensation of yellow or blue:

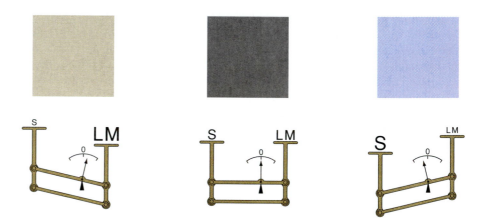

This scheme probably applies to mammals generally, although the spectral sensitivities of the cone types on either side of the balance can vary with species.

A special feature of primate vision is the emergence of two cone types, L and M, from the ancestral mammalian LM cone type, together with a neural mechanism by which their activities can be compared. This new dimension of color vision can also be represented by means of a balance, which weighs the responses of M cones and L cones:

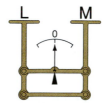

Grays reflect a balance between the contributions of the cones on each side, whereas other spectral reflectances tip the balance one way or the other, resulting in the sensation of red or green:

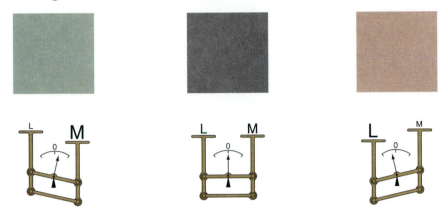

Just as we never perceive a yellowish blue, we never perceive a reddish green. Light from an object acts on both balances in a manner that depends upon the spectral reflectance of the object.

We can quantify these observations by determining the relative sensitivities of the different cone types to spectral light of different frequencies, and thereby establish a scale for each balance:

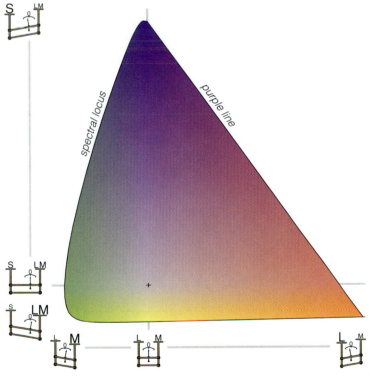

Each scale is adjusted to the same total length. All spectral lights (lights composed of photons of a single frequency) lie on the curved dark line, which is termed the **spectral locus**. All other lights are composed of various mixtures of spectral lights and lie within the interior of the spectral locus.

Color and language

What we perceive is reflected in our language. The English words *yellow*, *blue*, *red*, and *green* are pure in the sense that they are derived from earlier words that referred only to color. By comparison, *orange* is derived from the Sanskrit word *naranga*, meaning an orange or an orange tree. We can perceive both yellow and red in orange, whereas yellow and red themselves are perceived as pure. These perceptions depend neither upon culture nor upon language.

The colors represented in the diagram on the previous page are not accurate, because it is not possible to reproduce them with printer's ink. A true representation about a middle gray occupies only a small portion of the domain defined by the spectral locus:

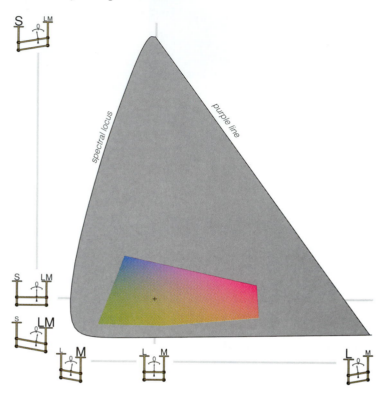

The problem lies not with the spectral reflectances of the inks themselves, but rather with the very nature of reflected light. Put simply, an object reflects some fraction of the incident light, depending upon its spectral reflectance. The narrower the spectral range over which the object reflects light, the dimmer that reflected light, because only a small portion of the incident light is reflected:

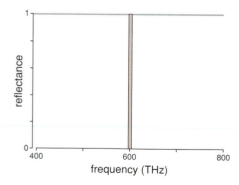

Optimal colors *447*

The trade-off between lightness and saturation is discussed in OPTIMAL COLORS.

Color perception depends upon differences in the photon catches of different cones, which in turn depend upon the differences in their spectral sensitivities. With reference to the light that enters the eye, the peak spectral sensitivity of S cones differs from that of M or L cones by about 130 THz, which is comparable to the effective spectral width of any visual pigment. By comparison, the difference between the peak sensitivities of L and M cones is only about 24 THz, and their spectral sensitivities strongly overlap:

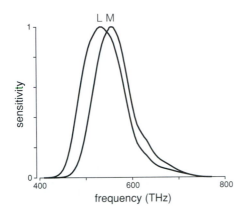

S cones are insensitive to photons with frequencies over the low end of the visible range; consequently, differences between their photon catches and those of M and L cones are often large. However, the photon catches of M and L cones for naturally viewed objects tend to differ by only a few percent, partly because their spectral sensitivities are so similar, and partly because the spectral reflectance curves of most natural objects are broad. These issues are considered in greater detail in PHOTON CATCH RATE. Nevertheless, psychophysical experiments demonstrate that we can detect a red–green modulation in color that causes a variation in the photon catch rate of L cones of as little as 0.2%.

Photon catch rate *471*

At present, it is not clear which ganglion cell types subserve red–green color vision. There are cells in both the retina and the lateral geniculate nucleus whose receptive fields consist of two antagonistic center regions, one receiving from L cones and the other from M cones, which lack a surround. As discussed in INFORMING THE BRAIN (page 285), the striate cortex contains anatomically identified regions known as blobs. Recordings from cells within the blobs show that some respond to color changes along the blue–yellow axis, while others respond to changes along the red–green axis. These two types of blobs receive their inputs from different populations of koniocellular neurons. The cells responsive to blue–yellow color changes appear to be part of a pathway that originates from the small bistratified ganglion cells, as previously discussed. The pathway to the blobs responsive to red–green color changes is not known.

The hypothesis currently held by most investigators is that red–green color vision is based upon the midget ganglion cells, and that the critical locus for red–green color vision lies in the striate cortex, where the patterns of action potentials arising from different midget ganglion cells are compared, and the problem of their surrounds is somehow dealt with. But some blobs receive from LGN relay cells that contain α cam kinase (see INFORMING THE BRAIN, page 288), and these relay cells appear to receive from ganglion cells that contain the same enzyme; this recently described pathway provides an alternative hypothesis.

Seeing with our visual pathways

Neural snapshots

As we've seen, voluntary movements of the eyes consist of a sequence of saccades that rapidly change the direction of gaze. Here is a photograph of a girl on the left, with the eye movements of an observer superimposed on the photograph at the right:

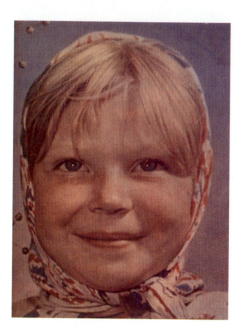

after Yarbus, 1967

Look at the image of the girl's face, first her left eye, then her right eye, and finally her mouth; take a bit less than a second to complete the whole path (i.e., the typical rate of 3 to 4 saccades/s that you normally use for inspecting larger objects or scenes). The next diagram attempts to represent the retinotopic map of the image of your right visual field on your left striate cortex as you viewed parts of her face:

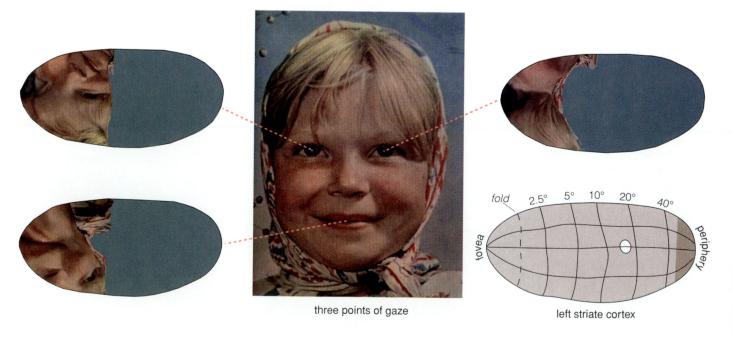

three points of gaze

left striate cortex

fold 2.5° 5° 10° 20° 40°

fovea *periphery*

Assume that you viewed each image for 0.2 second, the remaining time being taken by the two saccades. During the 0.2 s duration of each view, a ganglion cell that increased its firing rate from 30 to 50 action potentials per second as a result of what it saw would have contributed, on average, an additional 6 action potentials. There are a lot of other ganglion cells in your retinas, some of which increased their firing rate by more or less than 6 action potentials, others that decreased it. Their collective activity, received by your striate cortex, constitutes a **neural snapshot.** This snapshot is immediately processed by the visual areas working in concert so as to allow you to rapidly see and inspect objects in the visual world.

I end this chapter with two sections that are somewhat speculative. They lay out my best guesses as to the trails and bridges that lie between the pathways of the different ganglion cell types and seeing.

Camping

Take yourself camping; go beyond city lights. Toward the end of the day, you walk through the forest and gather fallen branches while there is still enough light to do so. Earlier in the day, sharp rays of sunlight pierced the canopy, creating a rich world of sharp contrasts. Now, as dusk gathers, you are surrounded by a soft luster of subdued colors and forms. As you return to your campsite and prepare the branches for a fire, you are aware of how much darker it has become. Color has now disappeared, or almost so, yet there is still plenty of light to see by.

As dusk approaches, the silencing of midgets gives luster to the world

Of the different groups of ganglion cells we have been considering, the midgets are the ones that require the most light to function. The midget ganglion cells are silenced when the photon catch rate for cones falls below about 1200 photon/cone/s, but we can continue to distinguish colors until it falls below about 3 photon/cone/s. This is an intensity range of about 400. During this period of dusk the midget ganglion cells are silent, but the parasol cells and those that convey color information are not. The world doesn't appear that different, although finer detail is lost.

Although not much has changed, some 70–80% of the ganglion cells in your retina are now unresponsive. (A few presumptive midget ganglion cells are reported to receive rod input; they have not been studied much and are not further considered here.) This unresponsiveness may seem paradoxical, but as discussed in CELL TYPES (page 256), the perception of detail comes at great cost. For every time spatial acuity is doubled, the number of neurons dealing with this task must increase by a factor of four. With nine times more midgets than parasol cells, our acuity is improved by a factor of about 3:

Viewed from the perspective of evolution, the large number of midget ganglion cells found in primates reflects selective pressure for increased spatial acuity; it is not clear what additional roles they may play, if any.

As dusk progresses, the ganglion cells responsible for the perception of color are silenced, but the parasol cells remain active, now driven by the rods, as described in THE RAIN OF PHOTONS ONTO RODS. Among the ganglion cell groups we have been considering, they are now the only ones still functioning. A few days ago, when you stayed up all night and you could just make out the border between the trees and the overcast sky, the photon catch rate of your rods was reduced to one every 85 minutes. Which ganglion cell types were active then? The answer to that question isn't known, but, as discussed in INFORMING THE BRAIN, the LGN receives from some ganglion cells with very large dendritic fields, such as the P-giant cells whose dendritic fields cover an area about 15 times greater than parasol cells at the same visual eccentricity:

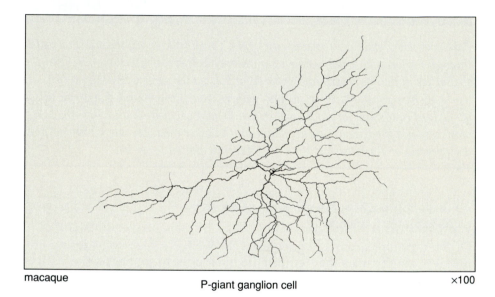

macaque

P-giant ganglion cell

×100

from Rodieck et al., 1993

The ganglion cell types that operate at the lowest light levels do so in a photon-sparse environment. It is this sparsity of photons that limits our sharpness of view. An increase in the numbers of these ganglion cell types should have little or no effect under these conditions. There are strong evolutionary pressures to make the best use of photons at any light level. When photons are very plentiful, the midgets contribute to an increase in acuity; when photons are very sparse, other cell types come into play. Although their numbers are far smaller, their contribution to survival may be no less than that of the midget ganglion cells.

Parasol cells are important for perceiving form and movement

As discussed in the previous section, parasol cells operate over a wide range of light intensities, from daylight to dark. When dusk reaches the point at which both the midget and color pathways are silenced, seeing comes to depend mainly, if not exclusively, upon our parasol cells. With this night vision we see various things, and we see them move.

During the day, when all of the cell types we have been considering are active, one might think that all of them would contribute to our sense of form and motion to the degree that they respond to moving borders. Surprisingly, this does not appear to be the case, as the role of parasol cells remains the most important. This can be demonstrated by means of a trick by which the stimulation of the parasol cells is greatly reduced compared with that of the midgets or the cells of the color pathway, most of which continue to respond strongly. Under these conditions our perception of form and motion is much impaired.

The trick is based on the fact that parasol cells receive a summed contribution from a number of M and L cones. As we have seen, when the number of cones that drive a parasol cell is large, the relative numbers of M and L cones will be about the same from parasol to parasol, even if the parasol cells make indiscriminate connections onto randomly distributed M and L cones. Earlier, the L/M pathway for color was represented by a *balance* that *compared* the outputs of the L and M cones. We can also represent the parasol pathway by a weighing device, but in this case, one that *combines* the contributions of the L and M cones:

comparison   combination

The only information the parasol cell receives is the combined contributions of the L and M cones.

Consider three spectrally different lights that have different effects upon the L/M pathway for color, but have the same effect upon the parasol pathway:

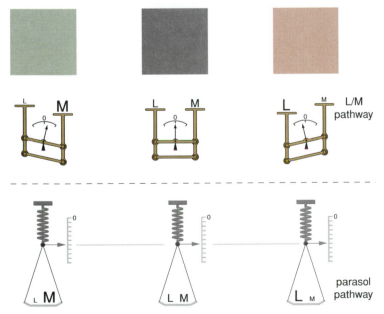

Photometry *453*

Each of these lights has a different effect upon the L/M pathway for color, whatever its intensity. But suppose we adjust the intensities of the three lights so that the combined contributions of the L and M cones are the same in response to each one. This condition is termed **equiluminance**, meaning equal **luminance**. Luminance, discussed in PHOTOMETRY, is a quantitative measure of light intensity, which we have just discussed in qualitative terms.

Consider how the array of parasols would view these two squares:

The square on the left contains a moving colored border; the one on the right is uniformly gray. Each of the three surfaces is equiluminant. The array of parasol cells thus responds to the moving border only to the degree that the L and M cone contributions to each cell differ from equiluminance. The difference in color across the border remains evident and obvious. We would expect it to be obvious, as there will be a big difference in the activities of the retinal cells that underlie color perception. However, it becomes difficult to locate the border itself. Furthermore, although one is aware of the passage of the border from right to left, the sensation of movement is almost entirely gone.

It is difficult, as a practical matter, to set up an entirely equiluminant pattern. The main problem is that parasol cells are very sensitive to small changes in the combined activities of M and L cones. There are also differences among individuals, so it is necessary for each person to adjust the apparatus that generates the pattern in order to find the point at which the border becomes least distinct. But this experiment shows that when the stimulus to the parasol cells is reduced, the perception of both form and movement is greatly reduced. What remains of these perceptions appears to be due to a combination of differences among parasols in the relative numbers of M and L cones they receive from and a residual ability of the midget and color pathways to contribute to these perceptions. Put another way, parasol ganglion cells play a critical role in the perception of both form and movement.

Ignorance

"Just look along the road, and tell me if you can see either of them."
"I see nobody on the road," said Alice.
"I only wish I had such eyes," the King remarked in a fretful tone. "To be able to see Nobody! And at that distance too! Why, it's as much as I can do to see real people, by this light!"

Lewis Carroll (1902)

My aim in writing this book was to provide a common introduction to a vast and multifaceted topic. There is enough known about seeing to fill many books the size of this one. The literature and the rich matrix of findings it contains is an astonishing human accomplishment, constructed and refined with care and dedication by many investigators over generations.

The result of all this effort is, in part, an appreciation of what is known; but at a deeper level, it is also an appreciation of what is not known. Indeed, the strength of an active empirical field of study lies in its ability to clearly express the state of its ignorance. In this context, an appreciation of ignorance can be as valuable as an appreciation of knowledge. Here are four of the many things we don't know about seeing; they have no particular order.

We do not know how ganglion cells respond under natural conditions

On this photograph three small regions have been marked, each having a different color, brightness, and texture:

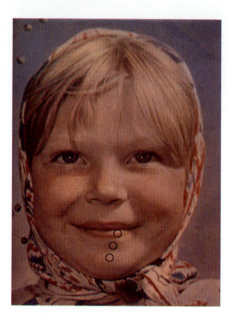

Consider three ganglion cells of the same type, each with a receptive field within one of these regions. If your gaze remains fixed, then from what you know of receptive fields, each of these ganglion cells should be responding in different ways.

When you surveyed the girl's face on page 356, your eyes jumped to some feature, remained roughly steady for a brief period (about 200 ms), and then jumped to the next feature. Suppose you do the same now, shifting your gaze from the girl's mouth to her forehead.

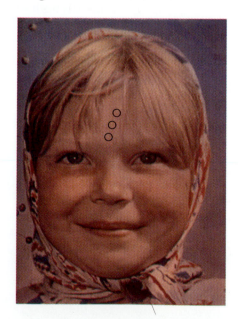

We know that most ganglion cells are particularly sensitive to changes in the light falling on their receptive fields. But each of the three ganglion cells experiences a *different* change following the sudden displacement of the image caused by the saccade. Does this mean that the responses of the three ganglion cells are different? We do not know. It is possible that a sudden change over a wide area of retina somehow activates some array of amacrine cells that effectively resets the retina to some reference state. The ganglion cells would then respond in the same way to similar small regions of the face. There are a number of other possible hypotheses, which involve the LGN or the striate cortex, or both. Because we do not know enough to choose between these hypotheses, we remain ignorant of a critical factor in the manner in which ganglion cell responses are used.

We do not know how ganglion cell action potentials are used

As discussed earlier (page 286), each LGN cell receives its excitatory input from a single retinal ganglion cell. To a first approximation, the LGN cell simply relays each action potential received from the ganglion cell to the striate cortex. In effect, the sequence of action potentials from each ganglion cell goes directly to the striate cortex, without modification. A more detailed discussion involves the potential role of the LGN as a gate that may block some of the action potentials, but that is not directly relevant here. Each small area of the striate cortex thus effectively receives action potentials from a number of nearby ganglion cells within the retina. The successive action potentials from each ganglion cell are essentially identical, so that only their time of occurrence is important. Furthermore, the responses of a given ganglion cell to repeated presentations of exactly the same stimulus produce a slightly different pattern of action potentials from response to response.

What do the cells in the striate cortex do with all these action potentials? Two quite different hypotheses come to mind, whose consequences are profoundly different.

The **rate hypothesis** holds that it is the *rate of occurrence of the action potentials from an individual ganglion cell* that is important. Individual action potentials are important only insofar as they contribute to the *rate*, however this term may be defined. If the cells of the striate cortex compare the inputs of different ganglion cells, it is their rates that are compared. This is the implicit hypothesis of much current work. The weakness of this hypothesis is best seen when we consider the shorter intersaccadic time intervals over which we catch an image (about 200 ms). Much of the natural world does not produce the strongest possible activation of ganglion cells of any type. But whatever a response of 30 action potentials per second might mean (absolute rate or change in rate), it boils down to a rate derived from just 5 or 6 action potentials during the brief period between saccades. One action potential more or less thus has a big effect on the "rate."

The **synchrony hypothesis** holds that it is the *synchrony of individual action potentials between nearby ganglion cells* that is important. This hypothesis is thus not directly concerned with *rate* per se. Nearby ganglion cells in the cat retina show a correlated discharge with a time resolution of only a few milliseconds, even in the absence of visual stimulation. This correlation occurs only for nearby cells, and its extent is about equal to that of the ganglion cells that have the smallest receptive field. If there was a similar and significant correlation of this form in primates, then a neural mechanism based upon synchrony could serve some useful functions. For example, parasol cells are quite sensitive to low contrasts, but lack the spatial resolution of midget ganglion cells. The receptive field of each parasol cell overlaps that of a number of midgets, and synchrony between some of the action potentials from the parasol and those of one or two midget ganglion cells could potentially provide improved spatial resolution:

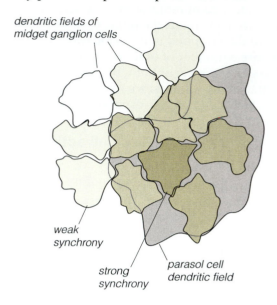

These two hypotheses are not mutually exclusive, nor do they exhaust the possibilities. But they allow us to appreciate that we remain ignorant of how ganglion cell action potentials are used.

We do not know how cortical action potentials are used

Brain waves are small fluctuations in voltage that can be recorded from the surface of the brain, or even from the scalp. During periods of active visual experience, regions of the visual cortex show rhythmic oscillations that have frequencies between 35 Hz and 80 Hz. These brain waves reflect the massed neural activity of many neurons (field potentials), like the roar of a crowd. The action potentials of individual neurons occur in synchrony with the phase of these rhythms:

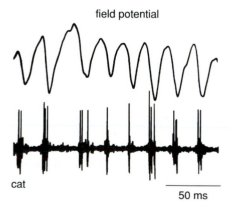

synchronized firing by a local group of
cortical neurons in response to a visual stimulus

These particular oscillations, and the synchrony they imply, are absent during sleep, or when a subject is anesthetized. Does this rhythm reflect the tempo of visual consciousness? We do not know. Does visual awareness require such rhythms over local regions of the visual cortex? We do not know.

We do not know how the striate cortex deals with image movement

The previous chapters described how eye movements compensate for the movement of the image of the visual world on the retina. This compensation is only partial, and the image is usually in constant motion as we go about our daily lives. Surprisingly, image velocities on the retina of 1–2°/s generally improve visual performance. Yet we are able to detect small movements within the external visual world, and thus small movements that are superimposed upon the movement of the image as a whole.

Consider this array of dots:

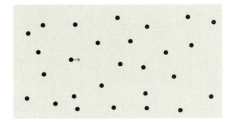

One of these dots, shown at the middle left, moves to the right, as indicated by the gray arrow; you would immediately detect the movement of this dot, even if there were many more dots than the ones shown here. You thus correctly saw what happened: one dot moved, and the rest didn't. But while you were doing so, the entire image, and thus all the dots, were moving across the retina in some direction. For simplicity, assume that the image motion was in the opposite direction; then the motion of all the dots with respect to the retina might look something like this:

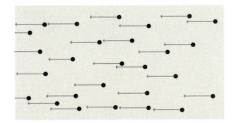

Every dot is moving across the retina, as indicated by the arrows; the arrows are of equal length—except for the one from the dot that is moving in the external world, which is slightly shorter.

How do we distinguish between image motion and motion within the image? For a long time, evolution has had to confront the problem of distinguishing image motion from motion in the external world. Does this mean that subcortical regions are involved, or has our visual cortex wholly or partially taken over? Does the first stage of visual processing in the striate cortex involve a neural mechanism whose purpose is to remove image motions, so as to reveal motions in the external world? A number of lines of evidence suggest that something like this may be going on, but we don't know what it is.

Topics

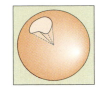

Angles

Angles come up in vision in two related contexts. One is the visual angle subtended at the eye by viewed objects; the other is photometry and radiometry, and involves the amount of light coming from a point, or a small area. This topic summarizes the definitions and terms used to describe plane and solid angles.

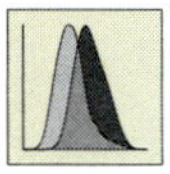

Photometry *453*

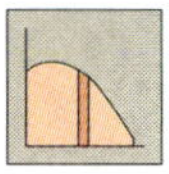

Radiometry *499*

Plane angles

Everyone is familiar with angles expressed in **degrees;** here they are related to finer divisions and to another measure occasionally used here, termed **radians**.

Degrees

The Babylonians (ca. 3000 B.C.) divided the circle into 360 equal portions, which we term **degrees.** This unit is abbreviated as **deg,** and symbolized by a ° following the number:

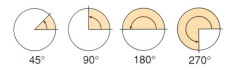

45°   90°   180°   270°

The term *degree* refers to one of a series of steps in a progression, and is also used in other contexts, such as temperature, academic rank, and severity of burns.

1°

The Babylonians further divided 1° into 60 equal parts that we term **minutes;** both *min*-ute and mi-*nute* come from Latin *minutus* (= small). The abbreviation for minute is **min,** and its symbol is ', as in 1'. Each minute is further divided into 60 finer parts termed **seconds,** which refers to the *second* division by 60, just as for time. The symbol for seconds is ", as in 1".

Radians

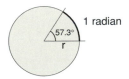

Another unit used as a measure for angles is the **radian**, which is the distance along the perimeter of a circle divided by the radius of the circle. This term is based upon *radius* and is abbreviated **rad,** which is also its symbol. Since the perimeter of a circle is equal to its radius multiplied by 2π, there are 2π radians in a circle, and 1 radian is thus equal to 57.3°.

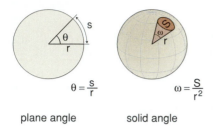

$$\theta = \frac{s}{r}$$

plane angle

$$\omega = \frac{S}{r^2}$$

solid angle

Solid angles

Just as a plane angle can be viewed as a portion of the circumference of a circle, a **solid angle** can be viewed as a portion of the surface of a sphere. The length of the circumference of a circle is equal to $2\pi r$, so there are 2π radians in a circle. The surface area of a sphere is equal to $4\pi r^2$, so there are 4π **steradians** in a sphere. Steradians are considered a "dimensionless unit" in the SI system of units, and are abbreviated **sr**.

We can ask, for example, what solid angle Australia subtends from the center of Earth. Including Tasmania, Australia has an area of 7,632,969 m^2, and the mean radius of Earth is 6370 km; hence Australia subtends a solid angle of about 0.188 sr.

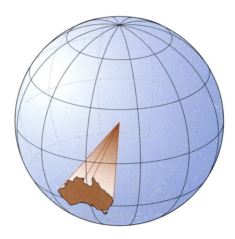

solid angle of Australia

You may also find solid angles expressed in **square degrees**, based upon multiples of a $1° \times 1°$ "square" on the surface. By definition,

$$1 \text{ square degree} = (\pi/180)^2 \text{ steradians}$$

This is something of a bastard term, and makes sense only with respect to small and thus approximately flat portions of the sphere.

Biochemical cascade

HOW PHOTORECEPTORS WORK *provided an overview of the biochemical cascade that concentrated on the initial sequence of events from the capture of a photon to the closing of the cG-gated channels. The molecular and ionic characters in this story were introduced, and the sequence of events that unfolded was described in a qualitative way. This topic retells portions of this sequence at a deeper level and describes the subsequent processes by which the previous conditions are restored.*

Rod response to a single photon

The arena of activation lies between two discs

About 50% of the outer segment consists of discs, and the remainder consists of cytoplasm; thus the cytoplasmic space between the two discs has a thickness equal to that of a disc:

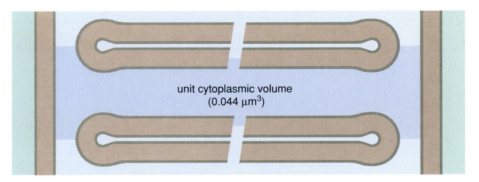

unit cytoplasmic volume
(0.044 μm^3)

The cytoplasmic volume between the two discs will be referred to as the **unit cytoplasmic volume.**

Most of the molecules we are interested in exist in micromolar (μM) concentrations. A useful conversion factor in going back and forth between concentrations and numbers is that, within the unit cytoplasmic volume, a concentration of 1 μM corresponds to about 25 molecules, ions, or subunits.

Both concentrations and numbers are important

The thing to keep an eye on during phototransduction is the number of, or the concentration of, *free* and *lightly bound* cG molecules, since this is what links the activity on the disk to the activity on the plasma membrane. If we view the photon as the **first messenger**, whose absorption activates the disc surface, then the message from the disc to the cG-gated channels is conveyed within the outer segment via a fall in the concentration of cG molecules, which thus acts as a **second messenger**.

Icons and abbreviations

This alphabetical list presents all the icons and abbreviations used here to represent the molecules, channels, exchangers, and pumps involved in phototransduction.

ADP	ADP	adenosine diphosphate
ATP	ATP	adenosine triphosphate
cG	cG	guanosine 3′,5′-cyclic monophosphate (cyclic GMP)
		cG-gated channel, closed state
		cG-gated channel, open state
GMP	GMP	guanosine monophosphate
GDP	GDP	guanosine diphosphate
GTP	GTP	guanosine triphosphate
G	G	G molecule
G_α^*	G_α^*	activated G_α subunit of G molecule
GC	GC	inactivated guanylate cyclase

GC*	GC*	activated guanylate cyclase
		K-selective ionic channel
PDE	PDE	cG phosphodiesterase subunit
PDE*	PDE*	activated PDE subunit
Pi	Pi	inorganic phosphate group
		Na/Ca,K exchanger
		Na/K pump
R	R	rhodopsin
R*	R*	activated rhodopsin

When considering **sites** to which cG molecules can bind, such as the catalytic sites on a PDE molecule or the binding sites on a cG-gated channel, the relevant factor is the rate at which cG molecules *encounter* the site as they diffuse about within the cytoplasm; this rate depends upon the *concentration* of cG molecules within the cytoplasm. But when considering the activated PDE subunits, or the rate at which each catalyzes the degradation of cG molecules, it is necessary to think in terms of the *number* of subunits, or the number of cG molecules degraded per second.

The biochemical cascade disturbs the dark equilibrium

The first telling concentrated on the *activation phase* of the response to a single photon. This sequence of steps that leads to the reduction in cG concentration and the closing of channels can be viewed as a *disturbance of the equilibrium conditions found in the dark*. The *inactivation phase* of the response represents a

tightly bound cG

Most molecules tend to associate in some way with one another as a result of electrical attractions between certain portions of the surfaces of each molecule. Most of these attractions are weak, and the association is momentary; *lightly bound* cG molecules belong to this group. But if the attraction is strong, then the two molecules will associate for a long time—possibly indefinitely—and they are said to be *tightly bound* together. In this topic we are concerned only with cG molecules that are sufficiently weakly bound that they are exchanging with the free cG at a rate faster than the time course of the response to a single photon.

The concentration of free cG in the cytoplasm of the outer segment is about 4 µM, and another 4 µM is lightly bound to cG-gated channels; but by chemical means, it is possible to extract the equivalent of about 60 µM of cG from an outer segment. As noted in the diagram, this difference is due to the presence of two strong binding sites for cG on the PDE molecule; they play no apparent role in mammalian rods, and are not further discussed or illustrated.

Each PDE molecule contains two sites that tightly bind a cG molecule. These sites are not catalytic and thus do not convert cG to GMP. In mammalian rods the binding is so tight that they are effectively fixed in place, and thus do not exchange with the free cG in the cytoplasm.

restoration of this equilibrium. Disturbed or restored, the notion of equilibrium is central to understanding how photoreceptors work. There are a number of components that contribute to this equilibrium. Here only the factors that directly relate to the response of a rod to a photon are discussed. When the response of cones to photons is considered, other factors become important, particularly those that depend upon the concentration of calcium ions.

cG is continuously being synthesized and destroyed

The response to a photon depends upon a decrease in the concentration of free cG molecules. These molecules are continuously being synthesized from high-energy GTP molecules by means of a membrane-associated enzyme termed **guanylate cyclase** (GC), which lies in the disc membrane (right). Associated with each GC molecule is another molecule termed GCAP, which is able to control the rate by which guanylate cyclase synthesizes cG. In the dark or at low light levels, rod guanylate cyclase is in an "inactive" state, in which it synthesizes only a few cG molecules from GTP molecules every second. Following a convention introduced in HOW PHOTORECEPTORS WORK, the icons that represent an inactive state as well the other molecules associated with it are shown in a paler color (see the Box ICONS AND ABBREVIATIONS). The activated state, which comes into play at higher light levels, will be described later.

Surprisingly, cG molecules are not only being continually synthesized, but are also being continually *removed* by conversion to GMP at catalytic sites on the PDE molecules, which are active at a very slow rate in the absence of G_α^*:

guanosine triphosphate

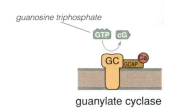

guanylate cyclase

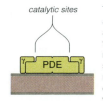

catalytic sites

The sites at which cG molecules are converted to GMP molecules are active at a very slow rate in the absence of a bound G_α^* molecule. This slow rate, at two sites on every PDE molecule, removes the cG molecules continually being produced within the outer segment.

At each PDE catalytic site, cG molecules are **hydrolyzed** to form GMP molecules. Chemically, this means that one of the two bonds between the phosphate group and the rest of the molecule is broken:

cyclic guanosine monophosphate (cG)   guanosine monophosphate (GMP)

The term *hydrolyzed* refers to the fact that a water molecule is taken up during the reaction. The bond broken is termed an *ester* bond. The abbreviation PDE stands for *cG phosphodiesterase*, meaning that this enzyme (*-ase*) recognizes two (*-di-*) ester bonds between the phosphate group and the rest of the molecule, and breaks one of them. As discussed in HOW PHOTORECEPTORS WORK (page 167), each PDE molecule consists of two independent subunits, and most of the following diagrams will show only one of them:

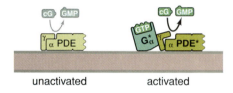

unactivated   activated

For every guanylate cyclase molecule, there are about 10 to 20 PDE subunits. In the dark, the total rates of synthesis and degradation of cG are necessarily equal. Thus the rate at which each PDE subunit hydrolyzes a molecule of cG is about 10 to 20 times slower than the rate of synthesis of cG molecules by a guanylate cyclase molecule.

The continual creation and removal of cG is combined in this diagram:

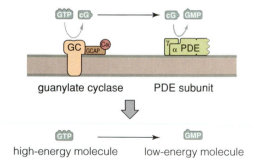

guanylate cyclase   PDE subunit

high-energy molecule   low-energy molecule

In the dark, the concentration of free cG molecules is about $4\,\mu M$. The rate of synthesis and degradation of cG is probably about $40\,\mu M/s$. In effect, the outer segment gets a new batch of cG molecules every 100 ms or so. This spontaneous sequence of reactions thus converts high-energy GTP molecules to lower-energy GMP molecules at a high rate. Since the concentration of free cG in the cytoplasm remains unchanged, this might seem like a futile expenditure of energy. It is as if you kept hot water in a basin by keeping both the tap and drain open. However, it does allow fast changes in the concentration of cG to occur by modulating the rates of either its synthesis or its degradation. To the degree that the turnover rate of cG in this cycle is high, a small change in either rate can produce large and rapid changes in the concentration of cG. Our interest lies in the amount of free cG; this amount, whether viewed in terms of concentration or number, can usefully be represented as a "pool," fed by the guanylate cyclase "spring" and emptied by the PDE "drain":

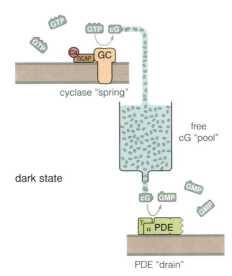

There is another pool of cG molecules that needs to be considered: the molecules bound to the cG-gated channels. In primate rods, the number of cG molecules bound to these sites at any instant is about equal to the total number of free cG molecules in the cytoplasm. The cG molecules move rapidly between the cytoplasm and the channels, so that the two pools are strongly connected. These sites can be incorporated into our pool diagram:

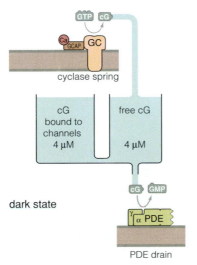

When considering the response of a primate rod to a single photon, we can probably assume that the GC spring flows steadily at a constant rate. The depth of the pool represents the concentration of free cG. In the dark, the rate at which the PDE subunits hydrolyze cG is approximately proportional to the concentration of free cG, and thus to the depth of the pool, because the rate at which a catalytic site on a PDE subunit encounters cG depends upon the free concentration of cG. This relation between the catalytic rate of PDE and cG concentration provides a rough regulation. For example, if there were an increase or decrease in the rate of *synthesis* of cG, then the concentration would rise or fall until the rate of degradation again equaled that of synthesis:

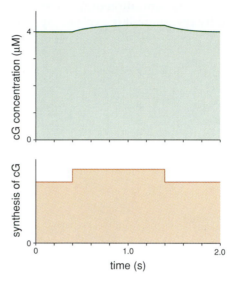

The turnover period of free cG is about 100 ms; but the cG spring has to charge both the free pool and the pool of cG bound to the channels, so the time constant for returning to equilibrium is about 200 ms.

When the PDE subunits become activated, their rate of degradation of cG molecules increases by a factor of about 100, but the rate of synthesis probably remains unchanged in primate rods, as noted above. This imbalance in the equilibrium causes a fall in the concentration of free cG in the cytoplasm, and thus a fall in the number of cG molecules bound to the cG-gated channels as well:

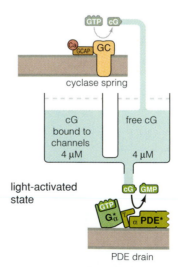

The fraction of open channels is thus reduced, and the current flowing into the plasma membrane is likewise reduced, thereby hyperpolarizing the outer segment membrane. As discussed in HOW PHOTORECEPTORS WORK (page 169), the fall in cG concentration amounts to less than 1% of its concentration in the dark; hence the values listed in the pools remain unchanged, and the change in their depths is exaggerated.

When the PDE subunit is inactivated, its catalytic activity returns to the previous rate in the dark. The concentration of cG then returns to the equilibrium level with a time constant of about 200 ms, as discussed with reference to the diagram at the top of page 376.

This inactivation phase depends upon—indeed, requires—the constant synthesis of new cG molecules and thus the continual two-step conversion of high-energy GTP molecules to low-energy GMP molecules. What seemed like "futile cycling" is now seen to play a critical role in reestablishing the dark equilibrium. Channels that had closed reopen, and the transmembrane potential returns to its previous value, as does the rate of glutamate molecules released from the synaptic terminal. Could energy be saved by eliminating the dark activities of both GC and PDE molecules, by turning on the guanylate cyclase only when needed? In principle, perhaps, but things can get rather complicated and unstable if the mechanism that shapes the falling phase of the response to a single photon must first detect that response, since it is the reliability of the detection itself that is at stake.

This description of cG springs, pools, and drains provides a *qualitative* description of the interplay of some of the main factors involved in the response to a single photon. There are a number of other aspects of this process that are best understood from a more quantitative perspective, which we now consider. In order to do so, I've used what I consider to be the best current estimates for the values of certain parameters. Subsequent work is bound to provide more accurate values, so you should view these numbers with a bit of caution.

About 700 **PDE*** molecules are created by **R***

Within about 2 ms, an absorbed photon has converted one of the many rhodopsin molecules in an outer segment to its activated form, **R***. This activated molecule immediately starts converting G molecules to their activated form, G_α^*:

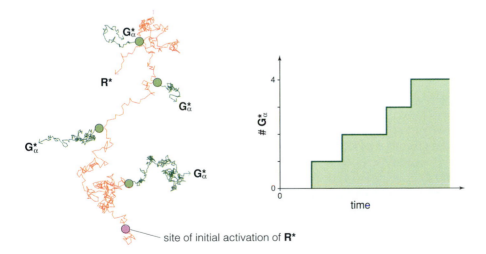

site of initial activation of **R***

As **R*** encounters and activates G molecules, the number of G_α^* molecules rises. Over time, so long as **R*** maintains its full catalytic power, the rise in the concentration of G_α^* molecules will approximate a ramp. For reasons necessary for a reliable response, but not yet understood mechanistically, **R*** appears to gradually lose its catalytic power, so that the rate of increase of G_α^* molecules begins to decline. Although the time course of the decrease in the rate of creation of G_α^* has not been directly measured, the subsequent events are consistent with a decaying **exponential** with a time constant of about 50 ms:

$$G_\alpha^*(t) = R_g \times e^{-t/\tau_g}$$

where

$G_\alpha^*(t)$ is the time course of the *rate* of creation of G_α^* molecules by the photoisomerized molecule R^*, which occurred at $t = 0$

R_g is the *initial* rate of creation of G_α^* (this value has not been measured directly, but indirect evidence suggests that it is about 16,000 molecules per second)

τ_g is the time constant of the decay in the rate of creation of G_α^* estimated here to be about 50 ms.

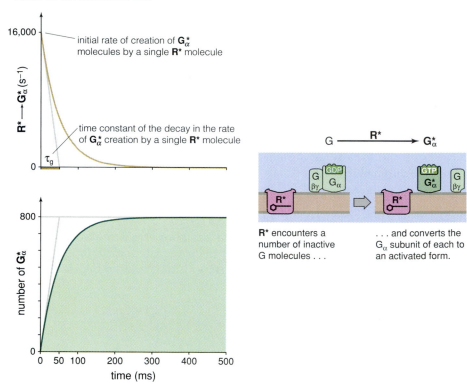

R* encounters a number of inactive G molecules . . .

. . . and converts the G_α subunit of each to an activated form.

The gradual inactivation of R^* ensures that each activated rhodopsin molecule will generate a reliable response. For more information, see the Box *WHY R^* SLOWLY TURNS OFF, AND HOW IT MIGHT DO SO*.

The number of G_α^* molecules created rises to a value of about 800 by the time the catalytic power of R^* is exhausted. This represents about 8% of the 10,000 G molecules on the disc membrane. Activation of G_α^* means that it is primed to bind to an unactivated PDE molecule. Each disc membrane also contains about 1600 PDE subunits, so there are enough present to enable each G_α^* molecule to bind to one of the PDE subunits and convert it to **PDE***. The G_α^* molecules appear to be reasonably stable up to the time of binding to a **PDE*** subunit. Thus each G_α^* will diffuse about on the surface of the disc membrane until it encounters an unactivated PDE subunit, at which time it will bind to it, and thereby activate it.

We will first have a look at the events that surround *one* of the 800 **PDE*** subunits, and then consider the effect of their combined activities. The activation of a PDE subunit increases its rate of hydrolysis of cG molecules by a factor of about 100, and this increase remains in effect as long as G_α^* remains bound to the PDE subunit. Assuming a dark concentration of cG of about 4.2 µM, the initial rate of conversion of cG to GMP increases from about 0.7 to 80 molecule/s:

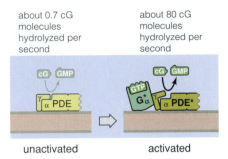

about 0.7 cG molecules hydrolyzed per second

about 80 cG molecules hydrolyzed per second

unactivated   activated

In order to simplify the discussion, we will assume that this rate remains constant during the lifetime of the **PDE*** subunit. In fact, the rate will be less than this when many **PDE*** subunits are active, because they reduce the concentration of cG in the cytoplasm adjacent to the disc membrane, and thus lower the rate at which cG molecules encounter the catalytic site. This is a complicated case of diffusion that causes the rate to vary with both time and the location of the **PDE*** subunit, but for a single photon, the fall in rate appears to be relatively small, and is ignored here.

We have reached the point at which the PDE subunit is activated, and is hydrolyzing cG molecules at a certain rate; the final step is to inactivate this subunit so as to terminate the response. What happens next is related to how G_α^* was originally formed, by replacement of the GDP molecule in the pocket of the G_α subunit with a GTP molecule:

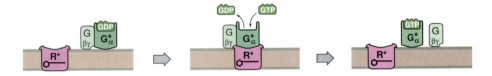

The G_α subunit is itself an enzyme, able to remove the terminal phosphate group from the GTP molecule, converting it to GDP. However, its catalytic power is normally inactivated, so G_α^* is stable as it diffuses about on the membrane. But after G_α^* binds to and activates **PDE***, this complex is recognized by another membrane protein, dubbed **GAP**, which binds to it:

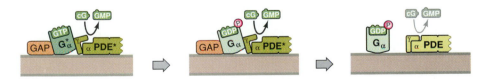

with the assistance of GAP, the enzyme activity of G_α^* deactivates **PDE***

GAP activates the catalytic power of G_α^*, which converts the GTP in its pocket to GDP by the removal of a phosphate group. The binding between G_α^* and **PDE*** is lost, and **PDE*** is thereby deactivated. Interestingly, the phosphate group probably remains attached to the G_α subunit; it is not yet clear how it is eventually removed, but while it is present, the G_α subunit cannot be a part of a G protein that can be activated by the next **R*** molecule.

Why R* slowly turns off, and how it might do so

The following discussion is a bit speculative in that it attempts to draw inferences based upon the properties of the various reactions of phototransduction that are currently known. Nevertheless, it highlights some of the factors, such as a minimum activation period for R*, that need to be accounted for, whatever additional pathways turn up.

Phototransduction can be viewed as a very large amplification of a single molecular change. A photoisomerization of one visual pigment molecule results in a decrease in the dark current that rarely, if ever, is smaller than a certain minimum value. This allows a rod to reliably convey each photoisomerization to its bipolar cells. If one attempts to explain this process in terms of conventional molecular machinery, a number of problems arise.

Take, for example, the manner in which a molecule, or a molecular configuration such as an ionic channel, goes between its normal and its activated form. This is almost always a transition between two quasi-stable states. The conversion of a rhodopsin molecule to its activated form provides an example. This transition results from the photoisomerization of the rhodopsin chromophore from one stable form (11-*cis*) to another stable form (all-*trans*). In either form, the rhodopsin molecule is being knocked about as a result of incessant collisions with other molecules. Thus both forms must be sufficiently stable to survive the wild chaos of the microscopic world.

The same reasoning applies to the deactivation of a rhodopsin molecule by the addition of a phosphate group by a rhodopsin kinase molecule and the binding of an arrestin molecule (see VISUAL PIGMENT REGENERATION). Each of these steps is quasi-stable in the sense that random motions will not cause the rhodopsin molecule to be converted back to its activated form. But each of these steps creates a problem in that each involves a random encounter of the rhodopsin molecule with some other molecule.

Visual pigment regeneration *509*

Molecular machinery can be quite elegant, as phototransduction demonstrates. But molecules have no internal clock, and cannot "decide" to wait for a sufficient time, say, to activate a certain number of G proteins and then allow kinase and arrestin binding to occur. The time of the

Exponentials *439*

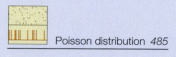
Poisson distribution *485*

first encounter with some other molecule depends upon a number of factors—diffusion coefficients, concentrations, and so forth. But each is a Poisson process, and thus the distribution of time intervals always has the same form, that of a decaying exponential:

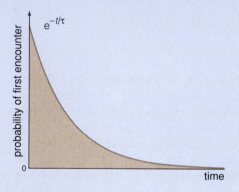

The average time to the first encounter is equal to the time constant of the exponential, which depends upon a number of factors, as noted above.

It may go against intuition, but the most probable time to the first encounter is zero. Of course, an R* molecule that is immediately deactivated will not activate any G molecules, and thus will not be detected by the cell—the absorption of the photon will have been in vain. Put another way, if we assume that some minimum number of G proteins need to be activated to generate a threshold response, and that the rate at which R* activates them is limited only by diffusion, then there is a minimum time that R* must exist in order to generate a threshold response:

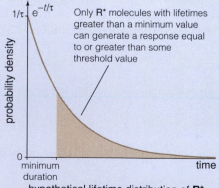

Only R* molecules with lifetimes greater than a minimum value can generate a response equal to or greater than some threshold value

hypothetical lifetime distribution of R*

The chances are improved to the degree that inactivation involves two successive steps—phosphorylation and arrestin binding—each with its own decay curve for first encounter. But the general problem, illustrated schematically above, remains. In terms of the factors we have considered thus far, some fraction of the responses will have amplitudes smaller than others to varying degrees, going down toward zero.

We know, however, that this problem does not actually exist in rods. As discussed in the Box THE RESPONSE TO A SINGLE PHOTON IS STEREOTYPED (page 382), every response to a photon has a minimum response amplitude that is almost certainly above threshold. It seems inescapable that any succession of two or three steps based upon first-encounter probabilities could not accomplish this. But, in the absence of feedback, that is about all that molecular machinery can provide. However, if there is feedback, then whatever is fed back cannot not bind to R^* in a stable manner, otherwise the first-encounter problem would remain.

All of this suggests that the catalytic activity of a single R^* molecule might depend upon a change in the concentration of some factor produced by the biochemical cascade that it generates. This factor is hypothesized to be able to rapidly interact with a binding site on R^* and thereby influence its catalytic ability to activate G molecules. It is the multiple and sequential nature of the interactions of this factor with R^* that avoids the difficulty discussed above.

The change in the concentration of this factor could potentially be a decrease or an increase. If it were a decrease, then the factor would have to be present in order for R^* to activate G proteins at its maximum rate. But no such additional factor has yet been identified. The other possibility is a factor that would increase in concentration, and would inactivate R^* during the time that it would be bound to R^*. This "inactivation" doesn't need to be anything more than temporarily binding in such a manner as to prevent the epitopes on R^* and inactivated G protein molecules from coming into contact.

The issue at stake involves a single R^* and the biochemical cascade that it generates. Any cytoplasmic factor that builds up has the difficulty of rapid dilution by diffusion throughout the entire outer segment. Not so for any protein on the disc surface containing R^*. Four such proteins come to mind: G_α^*, $G_{\beta\gamma}$, phosphorylated G_α (G_α with a phosphate group bound to it), and the **PDE*** subunit.

In order to be specific, assume that G_α^* is the factor we are looking for. The concentration of G_α^* starts at 0 and builds up at an approximately linear rate in the 50 ms period following photoisomerization. Thus, as R^* diffuses about on the disc membrane, the probability that it will encounter G_α^* molecules increases with time. The initial rate at which R^* activates G molecules is about 16,000/s (page 378), so that about 16 are activated in the first millisecond. Assume that R^* has a binding affinity for G_α^* so as to cause it to bind to each G_α^* molecule it encounters for an average of about 2 ms. This would have no effect upon the G_α^* molecule, which is already activated. But this one "time out" would decrease the maximum catalytic rate by 4% over the 50 ms period. By 50 ms, some 7% of the G molecules on the disc surface have been activated, so that about 1 in 14 of the encounters will be with a G_α^*, reducing the catalytic rate of R^* to about one-third of its initial value.

The following diagram shows a simulation of this possibility:

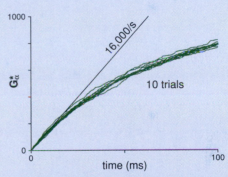

simulation of R^*–G_α^* binding hypothesis

The ramp shows the accumulation of G_α^* molecules if R^* were to continue at its peak rate of catalytic activity. The other curves shows what happens for an average binding time of R^* to G_α^* of 2 ms. They all start out at the maximum rate, but become progressively slowed as the concentration of G_α^*s increases. This is a simple model that assumes a "well stirred" distribution of G_α^* molecules on the disc surface. In fact, the concentration of G_α^* will be somewhat higher near R^*, where they were generated. In an attempt to compensate for this effect, the total number of G molecules on the disc surface was reduced from about 10,000 to 2500.

This is only a hypothesis as to how rods are able to generate reliable responses to single photons; it is not the only one there is, but it does serve to highlight the factors that are at stake.

The response to a single photon is stereotyped

In a rod, every photon that photoisomerizes a visual pigment molecule produces a stereotyped response of about the same amplitude and duration. It is for this reason that a rod can reliably signal single photoisomerizations. The fact that a single molecular change becomes a reliable response at the cellular level is perhaps the most remarkable feature of the entire phototransduction process. The manner by which it appears to be achieved is discussed in the Box *WHY R* SLOWLY TURNS OFF, AND HOW IT MIGHT DO SO* (page 380); the experimental evidence that underlies the claim for this stereotyped response is presented here.

One can detect the response to a single photon by recording from a rod outer segment and flashing a very dim light. The intensity of the light is adjusted so that, on average, less than one photoisomerization takes place per flash. Because the absorption of a photon is a matter of probability, as is the photoisomerization produced by the absorbed photon, this is as far as the intensity of a light can be controlled in an experimental situation. Most flashes will not produce any photoisomerizations, some flashes will produce one, and occasionally two or more photoisomerizations will occur.

This diagram shows the response of the entire cell, shown as a series of records of the current flowing through an outer segment following the presentation of flashes:

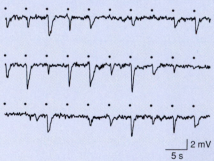

| 2 mV
5 s

after Schneeweis and Schnapf, 1995

The dots mark the time of the flashes. For some flashes, only the random electrical noise of the recording situation is evident; others show a response whose amplitude is either about 1.5 mV or 3 mV.

Here is a histogram of the amplitudes of the peak responses, which includes recordings in addition to those shown in the above illustration:

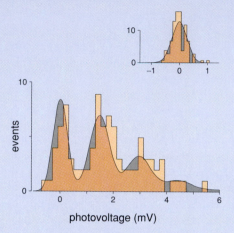

after Schneeweis and Schnapf, 1995

As expected from the previous diagram, the histogram shows three peaks, consistent with 0, 1, or 2 photoisomerizations. The widths of these peaks are a combination of the variation in the amplitude of the response to the flash and the random fluctuations in the transmembrane potential in the dark. These fluctuations are probably due to a number of factors, but can be estimated by measuring the observed fluctuation in the dark, as shown in the inset, which is fitted by a Gaussian distribution with a standard deviation of 0.27 mV. The smooth curve in the main diagram takes this factor into account, and is the best fit when (1) a Poisson distribution of photoisomerizations per flash is assumed, (2) the average response amplitude to a photoisomerization is 1.5 mV, and (3) the standard deviation of the response itself is 0.26 mV. On this basis, it appears that the variation in the amplitude of the peak response is only some 17% of the average amplitude of the peak response. It is the smallness of this variation that needs to be accounted for.

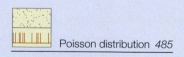

Poisson distribution *485*

In the normal function of rods, where the photon catch rate is low, the delay in the reconstitution of the G molecule is probably of little significance, since the fraction of G molecules in this state will be small. But in cones, where the photon catch rate can be high, it is possible that it serves as a means of allowing the cones to operate at higher light intensities by reducing the effect of each caught photon. But our focus remains on the effect of G_α^* on PDE: G_α^* converts PDE to **PDE***, and in the process of doing so, sets up the conditions that will eventually cause **PDE*** to revert to PDE.

The lifetime of a PDE* subunit is variable

This diagram summarizes the sequence of events we have been considering:

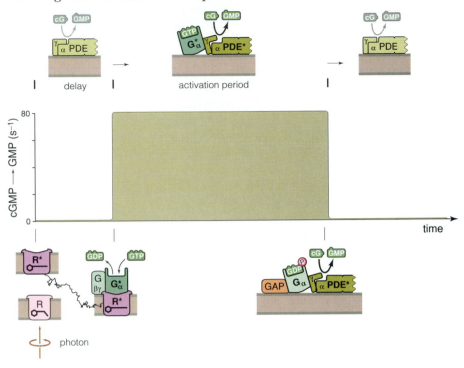

The *delay* between the creation of the **R*** molecule and the activation of a G molecule is variable in that it depends upon the moment during the lifetime of **R*** that it encounters this particular G molecule. Since **R***'s greatest catalytic rate occurs at the beginning of its lifetime, most of the G_α^*s it creates are generated within this period. The *average delay* corresponds to the time constant of decay of **R***'s catalytic action, or about 50 ms. The time taken for the G_α^* molecule to bind to a PDE subunit and activate it is probably quite short compared with this time, on the order of 1 ms. Thus the time to activate the PDE subunit is only slightly greater than that of the creation of the G_α^* molecule. Likewise, the *variability* in the time to create the activated PDE subunit is essentially the same as that of the creation of G_α^*.

The time during which **PDE*** subunits remain activated, the **activation period**, is also variable. It has been difficult to directly measure this average period. The time course of the current flowing into the outer segment (see the diagram on page 382) has been measured by a number of investigators, and is well established, so it is possible to calculate what average period of activation of a single PDE subunit is consistent with the observed time course of this photocurrent. This calculation leads to an estimated value of 100 ms, which will be used here to illustrate the general features of the response to a single photon. It is worth keeping in mind, however, that this is a calculated value, based upon a somewhat simplified model of what is going on (e.g., the catalytic rate of guanylate cyclase is assumed to remain constant). Nevertheless, it provides a plausible value that allows the major factors at play to be portrayed in broad outline.

If the **PDE*** subunit catalyzes cG molecules at a rate of about 80 molecules per second, then each subunit will hydrolyze about 8 cG molecules during its average lifetime of 100 ms. The value for any particular subunit is the product of its catalytic rate (80/s) times its activation period, and thus corresponds to the shaded area in the diagram above.

Poisson distribution *485*

The end of the activation period occurs when the $\mathbf{G}_\alpha^*$ molecule binds to GAP and catalytically converts the GTP molecule it holds to a GDP molecule. As in most molecular interactions, the *probability* that this event will occur at any particular moment is probably constant. This is another example of a **Poisson process,** in which the distribution of lifetimes is a decaying exponential probability density function with a time constant equal to the average period of 100 ms:

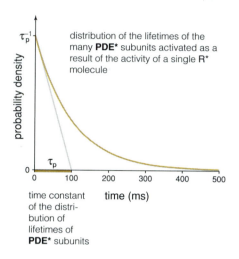

distribution of the lifetimes of the many **PDE*** subunits activated as a result of the activity of a single R* molecule

time constant of the distribution of lifetimes of **PDE*** subunits

This is a **density function**, and in this sense similar to that of the spectral distribution of a light source (see page 74). Thus it shows the probability that some *particular* lifetime will occur within some *range* of lifetimes. For example, the probability that the lifetime will be in the range from 0 to 100 ms is 63%:

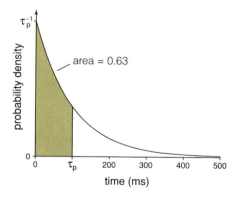

area = 0.63

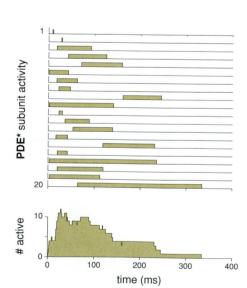

It is characteristic of such random processes that the most likely intervals are the shortest. This is the inevitable result of a process of decay that has no memory (see POISSON DISTRIBUTION, page 486).

In summary, there is a randomness to both the time at which the PDE subunit is activated and the subsequent time at which it becomes inactivated. The consequences of this can be illustrated by simulating what happens to 20 randomly selected PDE subunits that become activated during the response to the absorbed photon, as shown in the diagram to the left. The top portion of this diagram shows the activation period of each PDE subunit; the bottom portion shows the number of PDE subunits that are activated at any moment.

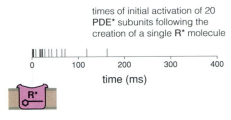

Consider first the times when the different PDE subunits became activated in this simulation, as indicated by the short vertical lines:

times of initial activation of 20
PDE* subunits following the
creation of a single R* molecule

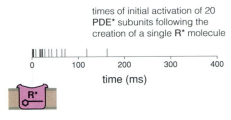

These are effectively the times of creation of the 20 G_α^* molecules that activate these PDE subunits. Thirteen of the 20 occurred within the first 50 ms, which is about what one would predict (65% vs. 63%).

Now consider the *lifetimes* of the different **PDE*** subunits. So that we can visualize them as a group, they have been aligned at their activation times, and ordered according to their lifetimes:

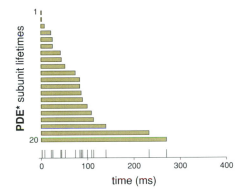

The short vertical lines now indicate the ends of the lifetimes. Again, short lifetimes are most common, characteristic of a Poisson distribution of events in time. Because the time constant of the lifetime (~100 ms) is twice as long as that of the rate of creation of G_α^* molecules (~50 ms), the average lifetime is about twice the average duration of the activation time.

The number of **PDE*** subunits active at any time can be found by simply counting the active ones at each time:

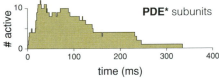

The overall curve shows a relatively rapid rise up to a peak at about 60 ms, followed by a more gradual decline. This curve is fundamental, for in describing the *number of activated* **PDE*** *subunits* with time, it also describes the *potential rate at which cG molecules can be hydrolyzed by these subunits*. That, after all, is the function of the **PDE*** subunits: to rapidly hydrolyze cG molecules. Because the number of **PDE*** subunits in the simulation is relatively small, the curve reflects the random nature of the events to a significant degree. A simulation based upon 700 subunits activated as a result of the activation of the single **R*** molecule gives a smoother curve (right). Even when 700 subunits are activated, some variation from the average is seen. This diagram also shows the average curve for the time course of **PDE***, which is discussed in the next section.

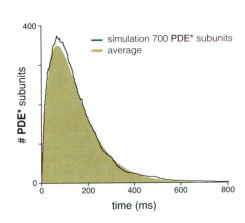

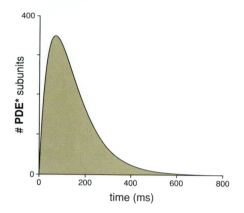

The time course of PDE activation is fundamental

The time course of the activation of PDE subunits provides an excellent vantage point for understanding HOW PHOTORECEPTORS WORK, for it occupies the central position in the biochemical cascade, between the activated disc and cG-gated channels. This diagram shows the average time course for the rise and decline in the number of **PDE*** molecules, also shown in the previous diagram (left). As discussed in the previous section, this curve is defined by only three parameters, R_g, τ_g, and τ_p; it is summarized by the following equation, which is derived in the notes:

$$PDE^*(t)\frac{R_g\tau_p\tau_g}{\tau_p-\tau_g}\left(e^{-t/\tau_g}-e^{-t/\tau_p}\right)$$

where

R_g = the initial rate at which a single **R*** activates G molecules; here it is assumed to have a value of 16,000 G_α^* subunits per second

τ_g = time constant of the decline in the rate of creation of the G_α^* by **R***, which approximates the rate of creation of **PDE***, and is assumed here to have a value of 50 ms

τ_p = time constant for the lifetime of **PDE***, assumed here to have a value of 100 ms.

There are a number of interesting relations between these three numbers and the curve that describes the average time course of the number of activated PDE subunits. Consider first the *area* of the time course, of *PDE**(*t*), which is simply the product of the three parameters:

$$area = R_g \times \tau_g \times \tau_p$$

The area is an effective measure of the **catalytic power** of the activated **PDE*** subunits to hydrolyze cG. This equation is derived in the notes, but it is easy to see intuitively. The product of the first two factors is simply the number of G_α^* molecules created, and thus the number of PDE subunits activated. The last factor, τ_p, is the average period of activation of a subunit. So you have how many there are times how long each lasts, and that is the common understanding of power. For the values assumed, we have

$$area = 16{,}000 \text{ molecules/s} \times 0.05 \text{ s} \times 0.1 \text{ s} = 80 \text{ molecules} \times s$$

where "molecules" is either the number of G_α^* molecules created or PDE subunits activated.

The catalytic power is thus equivalent to 80 activated PDE subunits acting over a period of one second. Assuming a catalytic rate for each subunit of 80 cG molecules/s, the maximum number of converted cG molecules is 80 s × 80/s = 6400. As noted earlier (page 379), the actual number is smaller because the simultaneous activation of many **PDE*** subunits lowers the concentration of cG in the cytoplasm above the disc, and thus reduces the rate at which cG molecules encounter the catalytic sites on the subunits.

In any case, it is reasonable to make the following definition:

$$PDE^* \text{ potential} = R_g \times \tau_g \times \tau_p$$

The ability of a photoreceptor to respond to a single photon depends upon developing a sufficiently large value of the **PDE*** potential, which can be brought about by increasing the value of any of the three parameters.

Consider first R_g, the rate at which **R*** catalyzes G molecules. In this regard it is worthwhile to step back and consider the entire surface membrane of the disc. Two general comments can be made about the disc membrane. First, the concentration of protein molecules in or on the membrane is exceptionally high. Second, the lipid matrix of the membrane contains a high fraction of lipid species that have a high fluidity, meaning that the protein molecules can readily diffuse about. The number of the different protein molecules is also worth considering:

	Concentration (μM)	#/Outer segment	#/Disc membrane	#/Rhodopsin
Rhodopsin	3000	1.42×10^8	80,000	—
G	375	1.77×10^7	10,000	0.125
PDE subunit	80	2.84×10^6	1,600	0.020
Guanylate cyclase	3	1.42×10^5	(?) 80	0.001

As shown at right, about 85–90% of the protein molecules on a disc in a rod are rhodopsin molecules. Vision starts with the capture of a photon, and in the competition for survival, a high concentration of visual pigment molecules is obviously useful.

The second most common protein is G. This is where the value of R_g comes in, because the rate at which **R*** can activate G molecules is limited to the rate at which it can encounter them. The **R*** molecule activates only about 8% of the G molecules on the disk surface, but the rate at which it encounters them depends upon the total number on the membrane.

The third most common protein molecules are the PDEs. There are about twice as many PDE subunits as are required by the **G$_\alpha^*$**s. Thus each **G$_\alpha^*$** won't have much trouble finding a mate. To summarize the discussion thus far in qualitative terms, a high concentration of rhodopsin molecules maximizes photon catch, and a relatively high concentration of G molecules maximizes the value of R_g.

The last two factors of the **PDE*** potential, τ_g and τ_p, are usefully considered as a pair. The average time after the activation of **R*** that a **PDE*** subunit is active is simply the sum of these two time constants, or 150 ms:

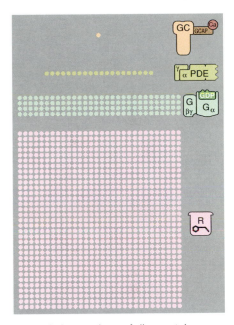

relative numbers of disc proteins

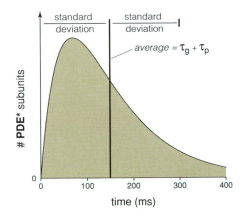

This relation is also derived in the notes, but is also easy to see intuitively, since τ_g is the average time for a **G$_\alpha^*$** to be created and activate a PDE subunit, and τ_p is the average lifetime of the subunit. As it happens, the *temporal spread* of the distribution, as measured by the standard deviation, is also equal to this sum. Here another definition is useful:

$$\text{PDE* spread} = \tau_g + \tau_p$$

There is an obvious advantage to a short response time, and a good case can be made for minimizing spread as well. Thus performance should be enhanced if **PDE*** spread is *minimized*. But this creates a conflict, because increasing the time constants to improve **PDE*** potential necessarily *increases* **PDE*** spread. Thus it is not possible to vary either one of the time constants so as to improve both measures.

One way of framing the issue is to consider the ratio of these two measures:

$$\frac{\text{PDE* potential}}{\text{PDE* spread}} = \frac{R_g \tau_p \tau_p}{\tau_g + \tau_p} = R_g \frac{\tau_g \tau_p}{\tau_g + \tau_p}$$

Since performance improves as the potential increases and the spread decreases, it improves as this ratio increases. So we are interested in values of the two time constants that maximize this ratio. One means of doing so is to search for a combination of τ_g and τ_p that *minimizes* the denominator—and thus the spread—while holding the product in the numerator—and thus the potential—constant. It is easy to show that this minimum occurs when the two time constants are equal. The current best estimates of these two time constants that are used here differ by a factor of 2. Nevertheless, the spread produced by this ratio is only 15% larger than the minimum value:

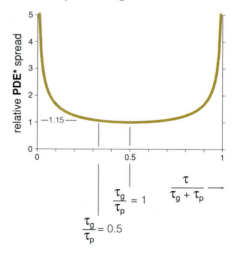

In effect, a significant increase in **PDE*** spread would occur only if the ratio of time constants were somewhat higher than this.

To summarize this section, the fluidity of the disc membrane, the relatively high concentration of G molecules, and two brief time constants with roughly similar values allow this portion of the biological cascade to generate a brief but powerful removal of cG molecules from the interior of the outer segment.

Diffusion of cG during the response to a photon is efficient

As described in HOW PHOTORECEPTORS WORK (page 170), when the disc surface becomes a significant drain for cG molecules, they are drawn from a region of the outer segment that extends well beyond the region immediately around the disk that contains the **R*** molecule. It is the diffusion of these cG molecules, resulting from the random bombardments of other molecules, that happens to bring some of them to the catalytic sites on the disc. The situation is thus similar to that of a G molecule encountering the **R*** molecule, except that the diffusion occurs in three dimensions rather than two. cG molecules diffuse rapidly within the cytoplasm of the outer segment, but are impeded by the presence of the discs, which reduces their effective rate of diffusion, and by the presence of the binding sites on the cG-gated channels, which also slows them down.

In any case, enough of them reach the activated disc surface and are hydrolyzed there, via the **PDE*** subunits, to lower the concentration of cG over some portion of the outer segment. At the peak of the electrical response, the inward dark current is reduced by about 0.7 pA: This reduction represents about 2% of the total dark current due to the cG-gated channels. Put another way, it represents a 2% decrease in the number of *open* channels.

In the physiological range of cG concentrations, the fraction of cG-gated channels that are open varies as the *power* of the cG concentration:

$$\frac{\text{Ch}_{\text{open}}}{\text{Ch}_{\text{total}}} = \left(\frac{[\text{cG}]}{K}\right)^{n}$$

where

Ch$_{\text{open}}$ = number of cG-gated channels that are open at any moment

Ch$_{\text{total}}$ = total number of cG-gated channels

[cG] = concentration of free cG molecules within the cytoplasm

n = a constant, termed the **Hill coefficient**, equal to about 2.8

K = another constant, characteristic of the channel, equal to about 18 μM.

In the dark, the concentration of cG is about 4 μM, so that the fraction of channels open in the dark is about $(4/18)^{2.8}$ or 1.5%.

$$\frac{\text{Ch}_{\text{open-in-dark}}}{\text{Ch}_{\text{total}}} = \left(\frac{[\text{cG}_{\text{dark}}]}{K}\right)^{n}$$

It is useful to take the ratio of this pair of equations, so as to eliminate the total number of cG-gated channels, as well as the constant K:

$$F = \frac{\text{Ch}_{\text{open}}}{\text{Ch}_{\text{open-in-dark}}} = \left(\frac{[\text{cG}]}{[\text{cG}]_{\text{dark}}}\right)^{n}$$

where F, the ratio of the number of channels open at some time during the light response to the number open in the dark, provides a useful means of keeping track of what happens when the concentration of free cG molecules, [cG], is changed. The change in F, ΔF, produced by a small change in [cG], Δ[cG], is the *channel amplification* introduced in HOW PHOTORECEPTORS WORK (page 169), and is readily calculated from the above equation:

$$\text{channel amplification} = \frac{\Delta F}{\Delta[\text{cG}]} = n\left(\frac{[\text{cG}]}{[\text{cG}]_{\text{dark}}}\right)^{n-1}$$

This equation tells us two things. First, notice that where the *difference* between the concentration of cG and the dark concentration is small, the last factor is approximately equal to 1, so that

$$\text{channel amplification} \cong n$$

The reason why the value of the Hill coefficient, n, is about 3 is discussed in cG-GATED CHANNELS (page 407).

cG-gated channels *405*

The second thing that this equation tells us is the most efficient means of distributing the reduction in the cG concentration along the length of the outer segment so as to maximize channel amplification. In order to understand the factors at stake, it is useful to pose this issue as a problem. Imagine that you could remove a fixed number of cG molecules along the length of the outer segment in any manner you choose, and you are trying to maximize channel amplification. For example, you could remove all of them from a local region, say, just around the activated disc. This "all eggs in one basket" strategy, shown in this figure, would produce the largest possible change in cG concentration in the outer segment membrane nearest the activated disc. However, the decrease would occur over only a short length of the outer segment, and thus the number of open cG channels available to be closed by this large drop in cG would be small.

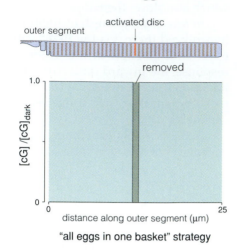

"all eggs in one basket" strategy

At the opposite extreme, you could remove the cG molecules uniformly along the length of the outer segment:

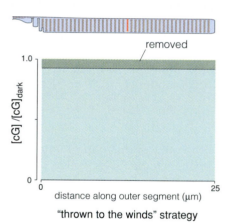

"thrown to the winds" strategy

With this "thrown to the winds" strategy, the decrease in cG would be made available to all of the channels, but the change in concentration throughout the outer segment membrane would very small.

A third possibility would be to remove the cG over a wider region than in the first strategy, so as to include more channels, but not so wide a region as to obtain as small a change in concentration as in the second strategy:

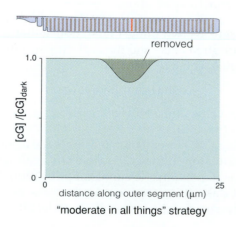

"moderate in all things" strategy

Which of these strategies would produce the largest decrease in the dark current?

Hmm . . .

Going back to the equation we have been considering,

$$\text{channel amplification} = n \left(\frac{[cG]}{[cG]_{dark}} \right)^{n-1}$$

The channel amplification depends upon two factors: n, which is a constant; and the ratio of $[cG]$ to $[cG]_{dark}$. Now the effect of photons is to reduce the concentration of cG below the dark value, and thus to reduce this ratio. The channel amplification can thus never be greater than n, and can have this value only if the change in cG is as small as possible. Somewhat paradoxically, the highest gain occurs when the change in the concentration is smallest. Thus the "thrown to the winds" strategy—uniform distribution—produces the largest gain at each point along the length of the outer segment, and thus the largest decrease in the dark current.

This fact allows us to calculate the *minimum* decrease in the number of cG molecules necessary to produce the observed decrease in dark current. The result, calculated from the above equations, is about 1600 cG molecules. This is the number at the peak of the decrease in the dark current, which occurs at about 200 ms following the absorption of the photon.

Earlier we saw that the **PDE*** subunits, operating at their full potential, could hydrolyze a total of about 6000 cG molecules over the entire time course of the PDE activation. Seventy-five percent of this activity occurs within the first 200 ms of the activation, resulting in a maximum of about 4500 cG molecules by the time of the peak. This value is only about three times that of the minimum number required to account for the peak response. Thus without going any further, we see that *the operation of this step in the biochemical cascade is remarkably efficient*.

Consider the factors that can potentially reduce the *maximum* number of 4500 to the *actual* number:

- We have already seen that there is a rapid turnover of cG produced by the combined actions of the guanylate cyclase and the slow catalytic rates of the unactivated PDE subunits. The turnover rate is about 10/s, or a period of about 100 ms. This process resists any change in the concentration of cG, and accounts for the falling phase of the response. By the peak of the response at 200 ms, it is well under way.
- Any decrease in the cG in the cytoplasm immediately above the PDE subunits will lower the catalytic rate by reducing the rate at which cG molecules encounter the catalytic site.

Other factors could also be mentioned, but these two may be the most significant. Each depends upon the spatial distribution of the concentration of cG throughout the outer segment, so that the magnitude of the effect of each is not readily calculated. But even in combination, they cannot readily exceed a factor of much more than about three.

This step is the link between the activity on the disc membrane and the activity on the outer segment membrane, which is taken up at a deeper level in cG-GATED CHANNELS.

cG-gated channels *405*

The rod response to a single photon summarized

As noted above, the vast majority of the protein molecules on a disc membrane are rhodopsin molecules; this enhances the ability of the outer segment to catch photons. An absorbed photon photoisomerizes the chromophore of the rhodopsin molecule, thereby activating it. The **R*** molecule probably activates a few hundred G molecules within about 50 ms. G molecules are the next most common protein on the disc membrane, and their relatively high concentration allows **R*** to rapidly encounter them. Each G_α^* molecule binds to a PDE subunit, thereby activating it.

Deactivation of **PDE*** occurs when the G_α^* molecule bound to **PDE*** enzymatically converts the GTP molecule it contains to GDP. In order to do this, G_α^* must be bound to **PDE***, and this process appears to be aided by another disc protein named GAP.

This sequence of events is oversimplified. Other processes, some of which are described when the biochemical cascade of cones is discussed below, may also influence the response of primate rods, but there is not much evidence for them when a rod responds to a single photon. Here, the only events considered are those that start with the photoisomerized rhodopsin molecule and end with the change in the concentration of cG at the cG-gated channels. The properties of the channels themselves are described at a deeper level in cG-GATED CHANNELS, and the renewal of the deactivated rhodopsin molecule is described in VISUAL PIGMENT REGENERATION.

Here we will also take a deeper look at how cones work, but the responses of cones show aspects of outer segment physiology that thus far I have dealt with only in passing. In particular, the concentration of **free calcium ions** within the cytoplasm plays a major role in the deactivation of the cone response, as well as a number of other aspects of photoreceptor function. This is an interesting story, which rounds out the biochemical aspects of how photoreceptors work. But in order to understand the role of calcium ions, it is necessary to place them within the milieu of ionic species both within and without the outer segment. As usual, there is no better way to start than to consider the nature of their various and interrelated equilibria.

Ionic equilibria

As you now know from HOW PHOTORECEPTORS WORK (page 164), in the dark, a small fraction of the cG-gated channels are open, allowing both sodium and calcium ions to pass from the extracellular fluid into the outer segment:

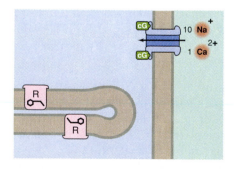

These ions can pass in either direction through the channel. However, both ions are found in higher concentration in the extracellular fluid than in the cytoplasm. Furthermore, as in all cells, there is an electrical voltage across the membrane, inside negative, that acts to draw positively charged ions into the cell. Thus, in the dark, both the gradient in concentration and the gradient in electrical potential act to produce a net inward movement of sodium and calcium ions. On average, about 10 Na ions enter the cell with

cG-gated channels *405*

Visual pigment regeneration *509*

pump, exchanger
see Interlude: NEURONS, page 96

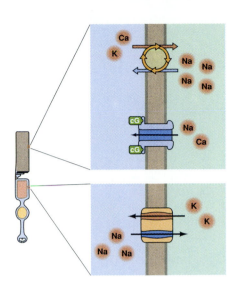

each Ca ion that enters (about 5% of the current is carried by magnesium ions [Mg^{2+}], but no function is known for this component of the dark current, which will be ignored here). If the photoreceptor is to maintain long-term equilibrium, the entry of Na and Ca ions must be balanced by mechanisms that remove them from the cytoplasm. This is achieved by the combined actions of a **pump** and an **exchanger**.

Whereas the outer segment contains all of the components necessary for phototransduction, the inner segment contains all of the components necessary for cellular metabolism (right). A major portion of this metabolism involves the **sodium/potassium pump.** This pump is a molecular machine found in the plasma membrane of all cells, which pumps Na ions out of the cell and K ions into it. Energy is required for both movements, and is supplied by the conversion of high-energy ATP molecules to low-energy ADP molecules:

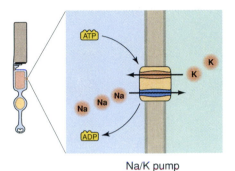

Na/K pump

ATP molecules are synthesized by the metabolic machinery of the cell, which breaks down high-energy glucose molecules to obtain the necessary energy:

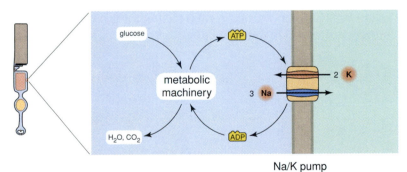

Na/K pump

All cells generate ATP, and it is used in a wide variety of ways. When we are at rest, about 30% of our metabolic activity goes into creating the ATP molecules that drive our Na/K pumps. The energy supplied by the conversion of one molecule of ATP to ADP is used to move three Na ions out of the cell and two K ions into it. Na and K ions diffuse rapidly though the cell. Thus the Na ions that enter the cG-gated channels located in the *outer* segment of a photoreceptor are removed by the pumps located in the *inner* segment.

The **Na/Ca,K exchanger**, located in the outer segment, is a molecular machine that acts to move calcium ions out of the cell (right). The exchanger does not require ATP or other high-energy molecules to move a calcium ion *up* its energy gradient. Instead, it couples this movement to the movements of four sodium ions and one potassium ion *down* their energy gradients. The exchanger can operate in either direction, as can be demonstrated experi-

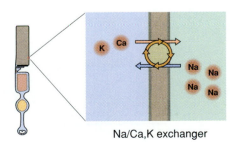

Na/Ca,K exchanger

mentally by reducing the concentration of external sodium ions in the fluid surrounding the outer segment. But in the normal environment of the cell, the exchanger is always removing calcium ions from the interior of the cell. Notice that the energy supplied by the movement of Na and K ions is ultimately derived from the Na/K pump located in the inner segment.

To summarize, in the dark, the transmembrane potential is held at a relatively depolarized value by the open cG-gated channels in the outer segment, which allow calcium and sodium ions to enter the cell. The calcium ions that enter are pumped out of the cell by the Na/Ca,K exchanger, at the expense of more sodium ions entering. The sodium ions that enter the cell via the cG-gated channels and the exchanger are removed via the Na/K pump.

Before putting all of this together, it is necessary to briefly discuss potassium ions. In addition to Na/K pumps, the inner segment also contains channels selective for potassium ions:

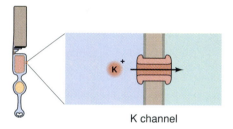

K channel

The internal concentration of K ions is high compared with the extracellular fluid as a result of the Na/K pump: the ratio of internal to external concentration is about 20. In order to balance the tendency of K ions to move out of the cell down this concentration gradient, the transmembrane potential would have to have a value of about –80 mV. This value is termed the **equilibrium potential** for potassium ions. It is the transmembrane potential that would just balance the concentration ratio so that there would be no net tendency for potassium ions to move in either direction:

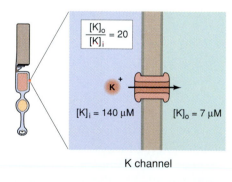

K channel

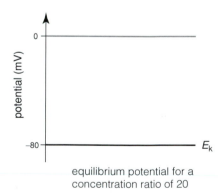

equilibrium potential for a concentration ratio of 20

The equilibrium potential is a useful way to express a concentration ratio, because it allows the tendency of ions to move down a concentration gradient to be compared directly with the effect of the electrical gradient on those ions. The transmembrane potential of a photoreceptor in the dark is about –35 mV. But it would have to be –80 mV to balance a concentration ratio of 20. The difference between the transmembrane potential and the equilibrium potential is 45 mV, which represents the net tendency of K ions to move *out* of the cell (left). Thus K ions have a net energy gradient that tends to move them out of the cell, and thereby pull the transmembrane potential, E_m, down toward their equilibrium potential, E_k. Potassium ions thus make a significant contribution to the balance of influences that set the transmembrane potential. Their energy gradient is also used by the Na/Ca,K exchanger to assist in the outward movement of Ca ions. Ignored until now is the fact that the cG-gated channels are permeable to all cations, so that there is also a small movement of K ions out of the outer segment through those channels:

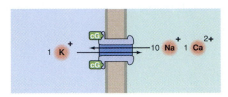

The diagram at right attempts to account for all the ions considered thus far, referenced to a single calcium ion, which enters the outer segment via a cG-gated channel and later leaves it via an exchanger. In the process of the Ca^{2+} ion moving in and out, some 14 Na^+ ions enter the outer segment via the cG-gated channels and the exchanger. They must be pumped out by about 5 cycles of the Na/K pump, which means that about 9 K ions are carried inward by this pump. With one K ion passing outward via the exchanger and one via the cG-gated channels, there is a net movement of 7 K ions into the cell, which pass out of the inner segment via K channels so as to balance the books.

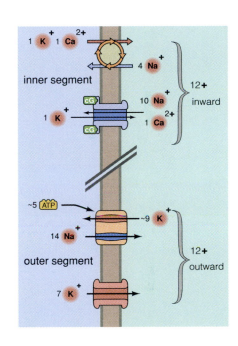

Viewed in terms of charge, in the outer segment there is a net inward movement of 12 positive charges, which is balanced by a net outward movement of the same amount of charge from the inner segment. Thus the books for both ions and charge are in balance. At a transmembrane potential of −35 mV, the net influx of each of these ions is zero, and thus so too is the net influx of charge.

A balance is a requirement for an equilibrium, but the test of an equilibrium is what happens when it is disturbed. If only the components shown in the diagram at right were present, then there would be a rough equilibrium. For example, a brief decrease in the inward current carried by the cG-gated channels would produce a slight decrease in the transmembrane potential. This hyperpolarization would reduce the outward movement of K ions via their channels, thereby restoring the transmembrane potential to its previous level. On a longer time scale, the slight reduction in the internal concentration of Na ions would be made up by a slight reduction in the rate of activity of the Na/K pump. This rough ionic equilibrium provides a foundation for a more dynamic and finely tuned equilibrium for the concentration of cG in the dark. We thus turn to the interior of the outer segment for a closer look at this internal messenger.

Calcium ions are a second messenger

The concentration of free Ca ions in every cell is always low, typically 1 μM or less. Their concentration in mammalian rod outer segments is not certain; here we assume a value of 0.5 μM, which is the value observed in the outer segments of rods in amphibians. This value is about 5000 times less than the concentration of calcium ions in the extracellular fluid (right). A concentration of 0.5 μM corresponds to a total of about 12,000 free Ca ions in the outer segment, or an average of about 13 free Ca ions in the cytoplasmic volume between two discs. But it would be a mistake to visualize the dark state in terms of just 13 or so Ca ions moving about within this space. The reason

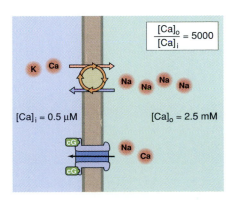

has to do with the dark current flowing inward through the cG-gated channels. For rods, about 15% of this 34 pA current is carried by Ca ions, and by this means about 18,000 Ca ions per second enter the space between two discs. These ions are removed by the Na/Ca,K exchanger as fast as they come in, but the turnover rate (18,000/13) is one of the highest known in cell biology. Cones have not been studied as extensively as rods, but about 30% of the dark current through their cG-gated channels appears to be carried by Ca ions.

The concentration of Ca ions is about 12% of the dark concentration of cG molecules. Just as free cG molecules can be graphically represented in terms of a pool, so too can free Ca ions:

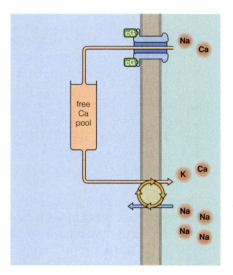

As noted in the previous section, the energy cost of this seemingly futile cycling of Ca ions into and out of the cell is about 5 ATP molecules per Ca ion, or some 90,000 ATP molecules per second in the dark. This is about the highest continuous rate of energy expenditure found in any cell.

In addition to the free calcium ions diffusing within the cytoplasm, a large number of them are bound to different protein molecules within the outer segment. The amount of this bound calcium greatly exceeds that of free calcium:

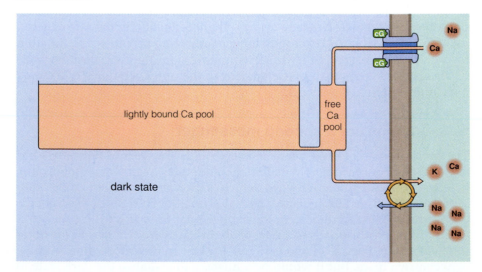

This diagram includes only the pool of bound Ca that is sufficiently lightly bound to be able to act as a buffer for the pool of free Ca^{2+} on the time scale of the response to a single photon or a brief flash. The size of this pool in primate rods or cones is not known, but it is undoubtedly larger than the free pool of calcium. In amphibian rods, the lightly bound pool is about 10 times larger than the free pool, and the size of the lightly bound pool in above diagram is based on this value.

Consider, now, what happens if all of the cG-gated channels are briefly shut by a flash of light:

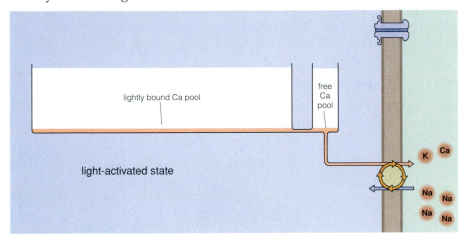

Prior to the flash, the cG-gated channels were carrying Ca ions into the cell at the rate of 16 million per second, and the Na/Ca,K exchanger was carrying them out of the cell at the same rate. Immediately after the channels close, the rate at which Ca ions are entering the cell goes to zero, but the rate of removal by the exchanger continues unabated. Assuming that the lightly bound pool is 10 times larger than the pool of free Ca ions, the rate of removal is sufficient to exhaust both the free pool and the lightly bound pool in only 8 ms.

In effect, closing the cG-gated channels has a profound effect upon the concentration of Ca ions. Put another way, the concentration of Ca ions is a sensitive measure of the number of cG-gated channels that are open at any moment, for even a small change in the number of open channels is sufficient to cause a significant and rapid change in both the pool of free Ca ions and the pool of lightly bound Ca.

It is worth recalling that the primary role of **PDE*** molecules is not to reduce the pool of free cG molecules per se, but rather to reduce the coupled pool of cG molecules bound mainly to the cG-gated channels:

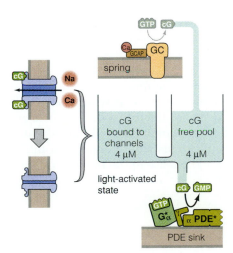

The channels close as the lightly bound cG molecules are pulled into the depleted pool of free cG molecules. Of course, cG molecules still go back and forth between the free state and the bound state, but since their number is reduced and so too is the average number in the bound state at any moment.

In the same way, the primary effect of the net outward movement of Ca ions is not so much to reduce the concentration of free Ca ions per se as it is to remove Ca from binding sites on certain protein molecules within the outer segment. The message about the fraction of open channels conveyed by the concentration of free Ca ions is used in a number of different ways.

Calcium ions regulate cG synthesis

First, and perhaps most important, Ca *regulates the concentration of cG within the cytoplasm by controlling its rate of synthesis.* This brings us back to guanylate cyclase:

Attached to each guanylate cyclase (GC) molecule is a "guanylate cyclase activating protein" (GCAP), which has its own site of attachment to the disc membrane and has three binding sites for Ca ions, two of which are important to this description. If the guanylate cyclase molecule does not have a GCAP molecule attached to it, it is either incapable of synthesizing cG molecules, or does so only at a low rate. The function of the GCAP molecule is thus to *activate* the GC molecule by increasing its rate of synthesis of cG molecules. But in the dark, at a Ca concentration of about 0.5 μM, it is prevented from fully doing so by the presence of Ca ions at two binding sites. This condition gives the dark rate of synthesis of cG, which, as noted earlier, is sufficient to open enough cG-gated channels to produce a steady dark current of about 34 pA. Closure of the cG-gated channels, and the resulting fall in the concentration of Ca ions, removes those bound to the GCAP; this provides full activation of the guanylate cyclase, now **GC***, increasing its rate of synthesis of cG by a factor of 5–10:

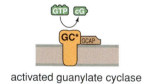

activated guanylate cyclase

Consider now what would happen *in the dark* if the concentration of cG were to *fall* slightly for some reason. This would reduce the fraction of open channels, and thereby decrease the influx of Ca ions through the channels. The pools of free and lightly bound Ca would fall slightly, including the Ca bound to the GC molecules. This would activate some of the GCAP molecules and thereby cause an increase in the rate of synthesis of cG molecules, thus raising their concentration. Conversely, if the concentration of cG molecules were to rise slightly, more Ca ions would enter the outer segment via the channels, increasing their concentration and thereby decreasing the rate of synthesis of cG, which would fall.

If you trace the consequences of a change in calcium rather than cG, you will see how cG acts to regulate the concentration of calcium ions. Thus these two second messengers are tightly coupled so as to maintain the dark concentrations of both. This is a good example of what is termed negative feedback. Any change in the situation produces other effects that tend to reduce or eliminate that change.

An important consequence of the interactions of cG and Ca in the dark is that the dark current is held at a constant and stable level. This interaction thereby allows the transmembrane potential to remain poised at a level to which the voltage-sensitive channels at the synaptic terminal are presumably most responsive.

The same mechanism applies to *steady background light intensities* as well. For *rods*, it presumably helps to maintain the amplitude of the flash response when the steady rate of photoisomerizations/s rises into the hundreds and approaches saturation (page 182, HOW PHOTORECEPTORS WORK). Thus far, however, this has not been demonstrated. It is likely that this mechanism plays a vital role in the ability of cones to operate at any steady light level (page 185, HOW PHOTORECEPTORS WORK), but again, this has not yet been demonstrated. An additional role of this mechanism is to sharpen the time course of the inactivation phase of the cone photocurrent, as discussed below.

Calcium ions regulate other aspects of phototransduction

Although they have not been studied in as much detail, there are a number of other calcium-binding proteins in the outer segment that appear to play a regulatory role:

- **Na/Ca,K exchanger**   If all of the cG channels are closed, as when rods saturate, the Na/Ca,K exchanger could potentially reduce the concentration of Ca ions to a level of about 0.2 nM, given the energy made available by the exchange of 4 Na and 1 K ions for 1 Ca ion. But the actual concentration does not appear to drop below 50–100 nM. This appears to be due to a sensor on the cytoplasmic portion of the exchanger that is sensitive to the intracellular concentrations of Ca, Na, and K.

- **Calmodulin and cG-gated channels**   High concentrations of Ca ions activate a ubiquitous calcium-binding protein named *calmodulin*. The Ca–calmodulin complex binds to the cG-gated channels, thereby lowering their affinity for cG. This negative feedback mechanism is discussed in greater detail in cG-GATED CHANNELS.

cG-gated channels *371*

- **Recoverin**   Another calcium-binding protein, termed *recoverin*, has been identified in mammalian outer segments, but its role in phototransduction remains unclear.

- **Activated rhodopsin**   Finally, an as yet unidentified calcium-binding protein appears to alter the properties of activated rhodopsin, **R***, either directly or indirectly.

The inactivation phase is speeded by guanylate cyclase

As discussed in HOW PHOTORECEPTORS WORK (page 179), the response of a cone to a weak flash of light consists of a fast-rising phase of the photocurrent followed about 100 ms later by an undershoot:

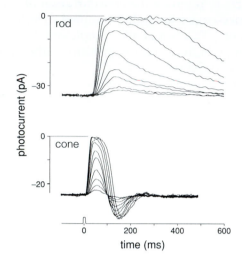

This diagram shows the current responses of a rod and a cone to flashes of increasing intensity. The undershoot in the cone photocurrent at any flash intensity implies that the current at this time *exceeds* the dark current. The primary reason for the undershoot appears to be an *increase* in the concentration of cG within the outer segment. This increase proves to be brought about by a large and rapid increase in the rate of synthesis of cG by guanylate cyclase, caused by the fall in calcium concentration.

Blackbody radiation

Every heated body emits photons, and in this book we are mainly concerned with two heated bodies—the Sun and ourselves. Our interest in sunlight is obvious; it lights our world. The photons we emit, either to the external world or onto our own retinas, have lower average frequencies than those emitted by the Sun; nevertheless they act as a limit on our ability to detect low-frequency photons in the environment.

Qualitative description

Except near a temperature of absolute zero (0K or –273°C), every object radiates photons. The higher the temperature, the greater the *rate* at which photons are given off, and the higher the average *energy* of the photons. Because the frequency of a photon is proportional to its energy, hotter bodies emit photons of a higher average *frequency*.

All of this can be demonstrated by placing a poker in a wood fire so as to raise its temperature, and pulling it out at different times to inspect it. Early on, you can detect the warmth of the withdrawn poker by placing your hand nearby. This warmth results from the radiation of photons in the infrared region of the spectrum; the poker feels hot, but doesn't look hot. Later the poker will appear dull red, as its increased temperature causes the spectral distribution of the photons it radiates to encroach into the visible spectrum. The radiant warmth you can feel also increases. Eventually the poker glows orange or yellow, and the heat felt by your nearby hand becomes intense.

If you have ever had a chance to look, via the peephole, into a potter's kiln during firing, you will probably have been struck by the fact that you cannot see the pots it contains, only a uniform glow. Potters monitor the temperature within the kiln by placing small cones of clay so that they can be seen through the peephole. The cones are placed upright and are designed to bend over at a certain temperature. But because the cones are at the same temperature as everything else in the chamber, they cannot be seen. In order to see the cones, the potter usually needs to blow through the peephole so as to reduce their temperature, and thereby visualize them against the hotter backdrop of everything else.

Within a kiln whose sides are all at the same temperature, the spectral distribution of photons depends only upon the temperature. It doesn't matter whether the walls are white, black, or have some other surface reflectance. It also doesn't matter what the sides are made of. The situation in which spectral distribution is determined entirely by temperature is termed

Radiometry *499*

blackbody radiation. The key feature of this situation is that the radiation within the interior is in equilibrium with the walls; this means that there is no net transfer of energy from the walls to the interior over any small range of photon frequencies. The nature of the spectral distribution of such radiation lies at the heart of physics, and at the turn of the twentieth century led to the prediction that the energy had to be quantized into particles, which were later termed photons. The surfaces of heated bodies emit photons in a manner that approximates the blackbody radiation coming out of the peephole of the kiln.

Quantitative description

The **spectral emittance** (see RADIOMETRY) of a blackbody radiator, using standard *physical constants*, is

$$M_n(\nu) = \frac{2\pi \nu^2}{c^2 \left(e^{h\nu/kT} - 1\right)} \left(\text{photon/s/m}^2/\text{Hz}\right)$$

where ν is the frequency and T is the absolute temperature (K). This spectral distribution describes the number of photons per second that are emitted by a unit area of the radiator for each frequency interval.

The only variables in this equation are the frequency, ν, and the temperature, T; all of the other factors are constants. The term $h\nu/kT$ in the denominator is a ratio of a radiant energy to a mechanical energy and is the key to this equation. The radiant energy, $h\nu$, is simply the energy of a photon in the frequency interval considered. The mechanical energy, kT, is the average energy of some particular form of motion of a particle at this temperature.

At low frequencies, where $(h\nu/kT) \ll 1$, the energy of a photon is small compared with that of the motions of particles due to the temperature. Under these conditions, $(e^{h\nu/kT} - 1)$ is approximately equal to $h\nu/kT$, and the spectral emittance, $M_n(\nu)$, increases in proportion to the frequency, ν. But at high frequencies such that $(h\nu/kT) \gg 1$, the energy of the photon dominates, and the spectral emittance decreases as $\nu^2 \times e^{-h\nu/kT}$. In between the emittance reaches a maximum when $(h\nu/kT) = 1.59$.

The peak rate of emission, M_{np} is

$$M_{np} = 1.966 \times 10^4 T^2 \ (\text{photon/s/m}^2/\text{Hz})$$

The rate of photon emission thus increases as the square of the temperature. The frequency that corresponds to peak emittance occurs at

$$\nu_p = 1.59 \frac{kT}{h} = 3.32 \times 10^{10} T \ (\text{Hz})$$

and thus increases linearly with temperature. This is a restatement of Wien's law (1894), which was originally expressed in terms of wavelength rather than frequency.

The spectral density function has a fixed shape when plotted on log–log axes:

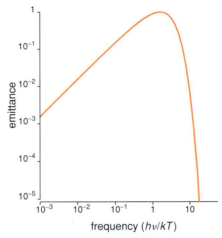

For example, if the temperature is increased by a factor of 10, then the curve is shifted to the right by a factor of 10 (1 log unit) and upward by a factor of 100 (2 log units).

The fact that the spectral density function has a fixed shape on log–log axes implies that it also has a fixed shape when plotted on linear axes, provided that both the abscissa and ordinate are scaled appropriately (right).

The distribution of photons as a function of frequency is best represented using linear coordinates, because the frequency intervals are equispaced, rather than compressed toward higher frequencies, as in the log plot. The area under this curve, found by integrating over all frequency intervals, gives the total rate of emission:

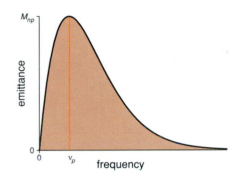

$$N_\nu = \int_0^\infty N_\nu d\nu = 4.81\frac{kT^3}{c^2 h} = 1.52 \times 10^{15} T^3 \; (\text{photons/s/m}^2)$$

Thus the number of photons emitted increases as the cube of the temperature, as expected from the dependence of $N_{\nu p}$ and ν_p on T. This is a restatement of Stefan's law (1879), which was originally expressed in terms of energy density, rather than photon emission.

Historically, it was the failure of classical physics to account for the observed spectral emittance of a blackbody radiator that led to the first suggestion that light was composed of particles. This slightly advanced topic is taken up in the Box *PHOTONS AND BLACKBODY RADIATION* on the following page.

Photons and blackbody radiation

Blackbody radiation came to haunt nineteenth-century physics, which had no way of accounting for it. In a complex world governed by many factors, here was a phenomenon that depended only upon temperature. The size and shape of the kiln and the nature of its walls made no difference. By the beginning of the twentieth century, the theory of electromagnetic radiation was well developed, and correctly predicted a variety of phenomena. Its successful application might have suggested that electromagnetic theory was not only correct, but complete. Yet this theory predicted that the spectral emittance of a blackbody radiator, expressed in energy units, $M_e(\nu)$, should be:

$$M_e(\nu) = \frac{2\pi kT\nu^2}{c^2}$$

This is known as the **Rayleigh–Jeans law**, although it can hardly be called a law, as it predicts that the energy density of the radiation should continue to grow as the square of the frequency. If the energy per frequency interval continued to grow in this manner, the total amount of energy radiated per second would have to be infinite, an absurdity dubbed the *ultraviolet catastrophe*. Worse, it did not agree with experimental results:

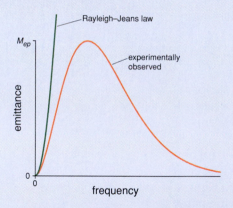

Max Planck (1895) realized that the experimental results could be accounted for by making what was for the time a rather strange pair of assumptions. The first was that, at any frequency, the energy could not take on just any value, but was limited to discrete values. The second was that the increment from one value to the next was proportional to the frequency:

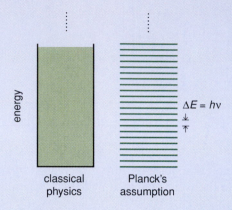

classical physics   Planck's assumption

Einstein (1905) proposed the modern interpretation of Planck's assumptions. The energy of light at some frequency is not continuous; instead, it is composed of discrete *packets*, or *quanta*. The energy of each packet is proportional to the frequency of the light.

Given Planck's assumption, it can be readily seen why the ultraviolet catastrophe is avoided. Consider some particular frequency—say, 750 THz, which appears violet to our eyes. The classical theory says that the relative propensity of the walls of a chamber to contribute energy to this frequency is much higher than at lower frequencies; furthermore, it is possible for any amount of energy resulting from thermal agitation to be emitted, no matter how small the amount.

With Planck's assumption, the relative propensity of the walls to contribute to this frequency is also much higher than at lower frequencies, just as for the classical case. However, the energy can be added only in packets whose size is proportional to the frequency. The thermal agitation of the molecules of the wall may create a lot of potential for radiating at this frequency, but only if this mechanical energy becomes equal to or greater than $h\nu$ can it be thrown off in the form of a photon.

cG-gated channels

The plasma membrane of the outer segment of both rods and cones contains ionic pores, termed cG-gated channels. The opening of these channels is regulated by the concentration of cG molecules within the outer segment. These channels were introduced in HOW PHOTORECEPTORS WORK *(page 158), and their functional role was discussed in a bit more detail in* BIOCHEMICAL CASCADE. *This topic takes a closer look at the structure and function of these channels.*

Biochemical cascade *371*

cG-Gated channels have four subunits

As discussed in HOW PHOTORECEPTORS WORK, page 168, a cG-gated channel appears to be composed of four subunits. The channels are shown here in the open and closed states, as three-dimensional models and as icons.

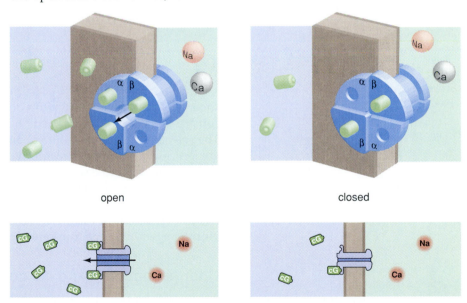

open   closed

cG-gated channel

Each subunit possesses a number of domains

There are two types of subunits, termed α and β, each of which consists of a single polypeptide chain, and both of which have been cloned and sequenced. The diagram on the next page shows the inferred membrane topology of the α subunit, which has a molecular weight of about 80 k, or about twice that of rhodopsin. The β subunit is larger, with a molecular weight of about 155 k, or roughly twice that of the α subunit. A portion of its polypeptide chain is very similar to that of the α subunit, and probably con-

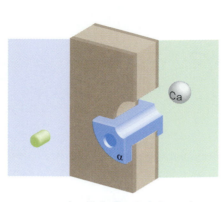

α subunit of cG-gated channel

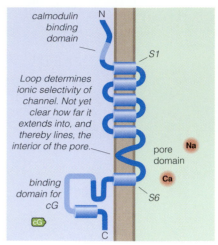

calmodulin binding domain

Loop determines ionic selectivity of channel. Not yet clear how far it extends into, and thereby lines, the interior of the pore.

binding domain for cG

S1

pore domain

Na

Ca

S6

domains of α subunit

tributes to the channel in the same way. The role of the remaining portion is unclear, and the following discussion considers only the "α-like" portion of the β subunit. Although not yet demonstrated, indirect evidence suggests that the pore is formed from the contributions of two α and two β subunits, whose pore domains are arranged alternately:

subunits of cG-gated channel

The α subunit appears to have six transmembrane helices, S1 to S6, as shown in the diagram at the top of the page. The pore region appears to be constructed from helices S5 and S6 and the polypeptide loop between them. The selectivity of the pore for Na and Ca ions depends critically on the presence of a glutamic acid residue at a certain point on this loop. It is not known how this ionic selectivity is accomplished.

The binding domain for cG lies on an intracellular portion of the polypeptide chain that lies near the C terminus. In β subunits, but apparently not α subunits, the intracellular portion near the N terminus contains a binding site for the calcium-binding protein *calmodulin*, as discussed below.

Biochemical cascade *371*

Channel opening and cG concentration

As discussed in BIOCHEMICAL CASCADE, in the physiological range of cG concentrations, the fraction of cG-gated channels that are open varies as the *power* of the cG concentration:

$$\frac{Ch_{open}}{Ch_{total}} = \left(\frac{[cG]}{K}\right)^{n}$$

where

Ch_{open} = number of cG-gated channels that are open at any moment
Ch_{total} = total number of cG-gated channels
$[cG]$ = intracellular concentration of free cG
n = a constant, termed the *Hill coefficient*, equal to about 2.8
K = another constant, characteristic of the channel

At high cG concentrations this relation breaks down, as shown by the data points in the following diagram:

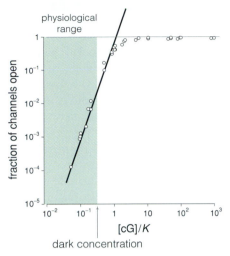

after Zimmerman and Baylor, 1986

In this diagram, logarithmic scales are used for both axes. The concentration of cG, plotted along the abscissa, is normalized by dividing it by the constant, K. The data come from salamander rod outer segments.

As the cG concentration approaches a value equal to that of K (i.e., as $[cG]/K$ approaches 1), the fraction of open channels rises toward a value of 1, as shown by the data points, and obviously cannot rise any higher. The straight line plots the above equation, which reflects the data points within the physiological range, but not outside it.

A slightly more complex equation,

$$\frac{Ch_{open}}{Ch_{total}} = \frac{[cG]^n}{[cG]^n + K_{0.5}^n}$$

correctly describes the fraction of open channels over the entire range of concentrations, as shown by the curve labeled **allosteric** in this diagram:

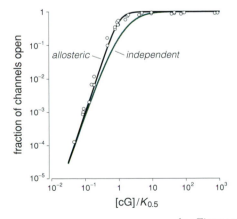

after Zimmerman and Baylor, 1986

The Hill coefficient, n, in this case is 3.0. $K_{0.5}$ is a constant that, for salamander rods, is equal to 9.6 μM. As can be seen from the preceding equation, half the channels will be open when $[cG] = K_{0.5}$; this is why this constant is symbolized in this way. Equations of this form that have a value of *n* that is greater than 1 are common in biochemistry. An example is the binding of oxygen molecules to the subunits of a hemoglobin molecule. Such interactions are termed **allosteric**, and the subunits are considered to be **strongly cooperative**.

The curve labeled **independent** also fits the data points within the physiological range as well as at high cG concentrations. But it is too low for cG concentrations at the "knee" of the curve, where $[cG]/K_{0.5}$ is close to 1. This curve, which is discussed below, shows the expected relation if the probability of binding of a cG molecule to a given site on a channel is independent of whether cG molecules are bound to the other sites.

In fact, the binding of cG molecules to the subunits probably *is* independent when binding to a closed channel. As discussed below, there does appear to be an advantage to the allosteric form of the equation, but it has little to do with the binding affinity of individual cG molecules in the closed state. Instead, it acts to effectively lower the buffering power of the cG molecules bound to these sites. In order to unravel what is going on, we need to take a closer look at the molecular interactions.

Channel subunits provide amplification

To a first approximation, a channel is open if at least three of the four binding sites on the channel have a cG molecule attached to them. Just why three or more are required is not yet clear, but it is not difficult to come up with hypothetical molecular machines that would work this way. Here we assume that this approximation is true and explore its consequences.

The observation that the fraction of open cG-gated channels varies approximately as the cube of the concentration of cG is a direct consequence of this assumption, and only it.

In order to understand why this is so, we start by ignoring the channels, and consider only the binding sites. Assume that the probability that a given site will have a cG molecule bound to it at any moment is a constant equal to 0.162. Thus the site will have a cG molecule bound to it about one-sixth of the time.

Now consider a large array of binding sites (top diagram on facing page). The probability that any subunit has a cG molecule bound to it is fixed at 0.162. Thus the probability that a subunit will be bound to a cG molecule is independent of whether any other subunit has a cG molecule bound to it. In this simulation, 286 of the 1600 binding sites, or 17.9% of the total, had a cG molecule bound to them.

Now let us arbitrarily arrange the subunits into groups of 4 so as to simulate 400 channels (bottom diagram on facing page). The underlying array of subunits in this simulation remains unchanged. If you search through this array, you will find, outlined in red, 5 channels that have three cG molecules bound to them and 1 channel that has four bound to it. Applying the rule for when a channel is open, a total of 6 of the 400 channels, or 1.5% of the total, are open. A number of such simulations yields an average value of 1.5%, which corresponds to the fraction of channels of the rod outer segment that are open in the dark.

What happens if we change the concentration of cG molecules? In the simulation, the probability that a given binding site will contain a cG molecule depends on this concentration. If the change in concentration is small, then the probability will be proportional to it.

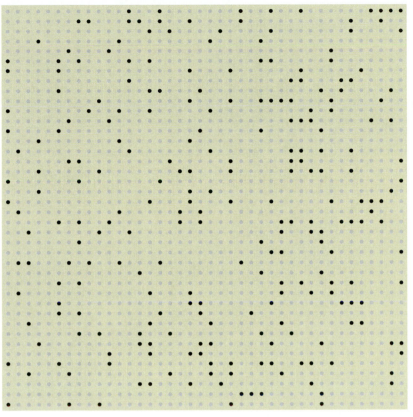

probability of site filled = 0.162

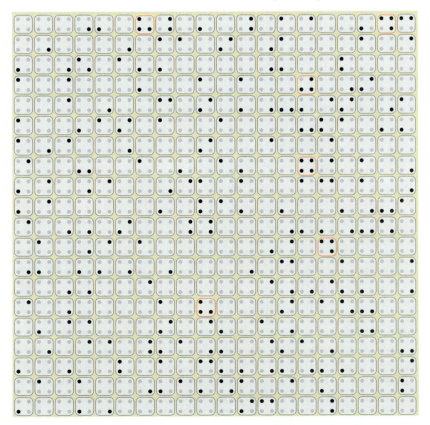

probability of site filled = 0.162

In order to get a rough feel for what is going on, let us simply halve the probability and see what happens:

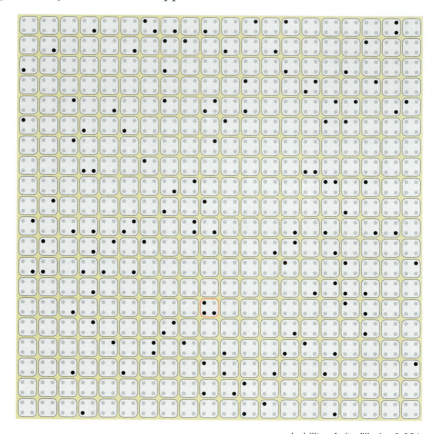

probability of site filled = 0.081

Now there is only one channel that has at least three cG molecules bound to it. Thus, halving the probability to simulate halving cG concentration leads to a much larger decrease in the number of open channels. The only factor at stake is the consequence of combinatorial probabilities:

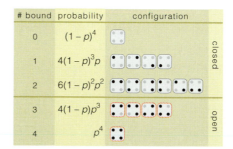

A probability, p, of binding to a *site* that has a value of 0.162 gives a probability that the *channel* will be open of $4(1 - p)p^3 + p^4 = 4p^3 - 3p^4 = 0.0171 - 0.0021 = 0.015$. This corresponds to the fraction of channels open in the dark. Notice that the second term contributes relatively little when p is small. Hence the fraction of open channels varies approximately as the cube of the probability of binding and thus as the cube of the cG concentration when the concentration is small. With this value for the probability, the ratio of the fractional change in open channels to the fractional change in concentration is 2.86, which is close to the observed Hill coefficient.

Over the full range of cG concentrations, the fraction of sites that have a cG molecule bound to them is governed by simple first-order chemical reaction kinetics:

$$\frac{\text{average number of sites with cG bound to it}}{\text{total number of sites}} = \frac{[cG]}{[cG] + K_{0.5}}$$

Since the number of sites is fixed, this is equal to the probability that a given site will have a cG molecule bound to it:

$$p = \frac{[cG]}{[cG] + K_{0.5}}$$

Thus the fraction of channels open is

$$\frac{Ch_{open}}{Ch_{total}} = 4p^3 - 3p^4 = \left(\frac{[cG]}{[cG] + K} \right)^n \left(\frac{[cG] + 4K_{0.5}}{[cG] + K_{0.5}} \right)$$

This is the equation for the curve labeled *independent* in the plot on page 407, using a value for $K_{0.5}$ of 15.2 μM. For low cG concentrations, it likewise reverts to the simpler equation used in BIOCHEMICAL CASCADE.

Biochemical cascade *371*

To summarize, the relation between the concentration of cG and the fraction of channels open can be accounted for in terms of four independent binding sites on the cG-gated channel, and the rule that the channel will be open if at least three of the four sites has a cG molecule bound to it. This model proves to be too simple to account for cG concentrations greater than those in the dark, but it is useful in identifying the origin of channel amplification.

Allosterism reduces the buffer power of the channels

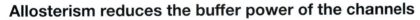

The observation that the data conform to an equation of the form

$$\frac{Ch_{open}}{Ch_{total}} = \frac{[cG]^n}{[cG]^n + K_{0.5}^n}$$

doesn't by itself imply any specific model for what is going on at the microscopic level.

When three or four cG molecules bind to the sites on the channel, their combined effect is to *change the three-dimensional shape of the cG-gated channel.* One of the consequences of this change in shape—and the only one considered thus far—is to convert the channel from the *closed* to the *open* state. We can refer to this combined effect as "opening cooperativity"; as three people might combine their physical strength to move a heavy rock, the binding sites act independently, but their combined effects accomplish a change that no one of them could achieve alone.

A specific model, termed the MWC model after its formulators (Monod, Wyman, and Changeux), contains a critical additional hypothesis: *the conformational change in the channel from the closed to the open state alters the binding affinity.* This is termed an **allosteric effect,** for reasons that do not immediately concern us. For the cG-gated channels, the affinity of a binding site for cG *is greater in the open state than in the closed state.* The effect of this difference is complicated in its detail; but its overall effect is *to reduce the amount of cG bound to these channels.*

Biochemical cascade *371*

As discussed in BIOCHEMICAL CASCADE (page 375), the pool of free cG is in rapid equilibrium with the pool of cG attached to the binding sites of the channels. Thus the activated **PDE*** subunits must lower both pools:

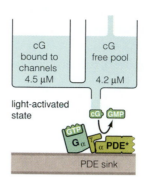

If cG molecules bound to the cG-gated channels were released into the cytoplasm, they would increase the concentration by about 4.5 µM. This bound cG thus effectively acts as a *buffer* for cG. In order to decrease the concentration of free cG, the **PDE*** subunits must deplete both pools. The **buffer power** is the ratio of both pools to the pool of free cG:

$$\text{buffer power} = \frac{[\text{cGMP}]_{\text{free}} + [\text{cGMP}]_{\text{bound}}}{[\text{cGMP}]_{\text{free}}} = \frac{4.2\ \mu M + 4.5\ \mu M}{4.2\ \mu M} = 2.1$$

In effect, the **PDE*** subunits must degrade 2.1 times the number of cG molecules they would have to if all of the cG were in the free state. Of course, we can hardly object to the **PDE*** subunits having to deplete the bound pool as well, since that is the ultimate function of this mechanism.

This is where the allosteric effect comes in, for it acts to lower the bound pool. In the absence of this effect, the bound pool would have an effective concentration of 15.4 µM as noted earlier, and a buffer power of about 5 rather than 2.1. Put another way, the **PDE*** subunits would have to degrade 2.5 times more cG in order to close the same number of channels.

Just why the MWC model leads to an equation of the above form, and thus to a reduced buffering power, is difficult to explain without going into issues that lie beyond the scope of this book. Briefly, and perhaps too simplistically, once channels open, they tend to be held open a bit longer by the increased binding affinity for cG. By extending the fraction of time in the open state, the probability of reaching it from the closed state, and thus the binding affinity of the closed state, can be correspondingly reduced.

Calcium and calmodulin alter the binding affinity of cG

High concentrations of Ca ions activate a ubiquitous calcium-binding protein named calmodulin. The Ca–calmodulin complex binds to the cG-gated channels, thereby lowering their affinity for cG. Calmodulin is a small (17 k) protein molecule that acts as a *sensor for Ca ions* in virtually all cells. It has four binding sites for Ca ions, and becomes *activated* when three or four Ca ions become bound to it. The activated form, Ca–calmodulin, can bind to other proteins so as to modify their properties. It does so by wrapping around a specific portion of a protein termed a "docking structure," which consists of a positively charged α helix. By this means the properties of other proteins can become modified by the concentration of Ca, without their having to contain a calcium sensor of their own.

The β subunits of cG-gated channels contain a docking site for Ca–calmodulin. The binding of Ca–calmodulin to these sites lowers the binding affinity of the channels for cG. This represents another negative feedback pathway, since the effect of an increase in Ca ions is to lower the binding affinity of cG, thereby closing channels and thus reducing the rate of entry of Ca ions. The particular functional role played by calmodulin in mammalian photoreceptors will become clearer when better estimates of the physiological range of calcium concentrations within them become available.

In the open state, cG-gated channels flicker between open and closed

Most ionic channels that have been studied pass currents of about 2000 fA, and the current is relatively steady when the channel is open. By comparison, the current passing through a cG-gated channel has an average value of about 3 fA and rapidly fluctuates. This lower current appears to be due to the pore being blocked at one site by a Ca or Mg ion, since removal of these divalent cations from solution increases the current to about 2000 fA. Under these conditions, the current passing through a single channel within a small patch of membrane can be measured; the diagram below shows such recordings from a patch of outer segment membrane from a salamander rod. Each panel shows a continuous recording at the indicated concentration of cG. The continuous lines through the traces indicate the baseline or closed channel level.

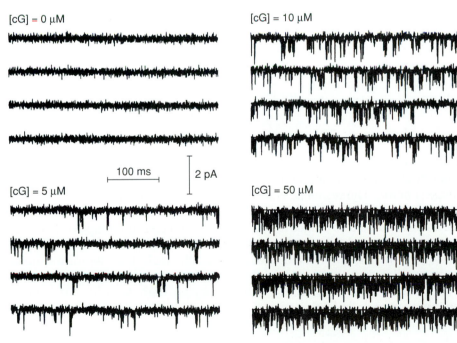

[cG] = 0 μM   [cG] = 10 μM

100 ms   2 pA

[cG] = 5 μM   [cG] = 50 μM

source: Taylor and Baylor, 1995

In the absence of cG, the channel is closed; the irregular trace is due mainly to electrical noise in the recording configuration, which contributes to all traces. At 5 μM, the channel opens occasionally, as indicated by the brief bursts of fluctuating current. Since this is an inward current, it is shown downward. At a concentration of 50 μM, there is an almost continuous rapid fluctuation in the current, indicating that the channel was almost exclusively in the open state. This concentration is much higher than ever occurs in a photoreceptor, but well illustrates the rapid and continuous movement of cG molecules onto and off of the binding sites.

This "fluttering" of the ionic current appears to be due to "traffic congestion" within the pore. The ions apparently pass through the channel one by one; Na ions pass readily through, but Ca and Mg ions can be temporarily stuck within the channel, thereby briefly reducing the conductance.

Many channels, each with a small current, reduce noise

The dark current of a primate rod is about –34 pA. Assuming that each open channel carries an average current of 3 fA (0.003 pA), there are about 11,000 channels open at any instant.

As noted in the previous section, other types of ionic channels pass currents of the order of 2 pA. Thus only about 17 cG-gated channels would be required to carry the dark current. Consider, however, a rod that adopted an alternative strategy of having fewer channels, each carrying a larger current. Since the channels open and close independently, there would be a statistical fluctuation in the number of channels open at any instant. The result would be a Poisson distribution:

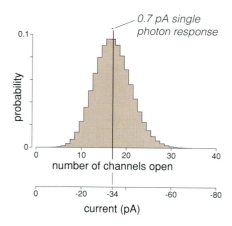

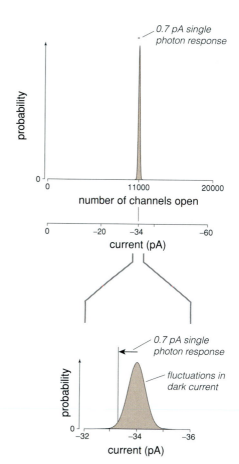

Poisson distribution 485

Clearly, this wouldn't work, as the fluctuations in the number of channels open from moment to moment would be much larger than the response to a single photon. The response would thus be lost in the "noise" produced by these fluctuations. By comparison, the statistical fluctuation in 11,000 independent channels averages about 1%, or about half the amplitude of the response to a single photon (diagram at left). In effect, *noise* is produced by statistical fluctuations in the number of open channels. In order for this noise to be smaller than the fractional decrease in the number of open channels produced by a single photon, it is necessary for there to be 10,000 or more channels open in the dark.

Opened channels do not reduce membrane resistance

A feature of cG-gated channels not previously discussed is that the opening of the channel varies as a function of the transmembrane potential. Briefly, depolarization increases channel opening and hyperpolarization decreases it. In effect, hyperpolarization, however produced, *decreases* the transmembrane conductance. In the absence of this effect, the opening of a number of channels in response to light would *increase* the transmembrane conductance. As a result of these two factors, the current produced by a given light

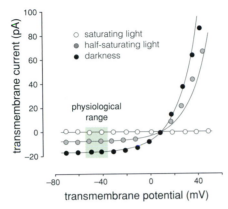

source: Baylor and Nunn, 1986

intensity is largely independent of the transmembrane potential, as shown in the above diagram. In effect, the current passing inward through one open channel will not be "shunted" outward through any other channels that happen to be open. This allows the effects of the different channels on the transmembrane potential to be independent of one another.

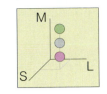

Cone input space

This topic discusses a useful geometrical way of representing the stimulation of the different cone types. Any light maps to a single point in a three-dimensional space defined by the photon catch rates of the three cone types. The effects of spectrally distinct lights can be readily inferred from the points to which they map. For example, two spectrally distinct lights that map to the same point produce the same catch rate for each of the different cone types and thus cannot be distinguished by the cones.

catch, capture
As discussed in THE RAIN OF PHOTONS ONTO CONES (page 86), the terms *catch* and *capture* are used here to refer to photons that are absorbed by a visual pigment molecule and photoisomerize its chromophore, thereby activating the molecule.

Cone inputs

We would like to know how light falling on each of the three cone types influences the bipolar and horizontal cell types they contact. This big step is, however, the consequence of a sequence of small steps, not all of which are fully understood. But even if all of these smaller steps were known, it would still be useful to have an effective measure of the inputs to the three cone types that gets beyond considerations of spectral sensitivity.

As first discussed in THE RAIN OF PHOTONS ONTO CONES, the initial step in vision occurs when a visual pigment molecule catches a photon:

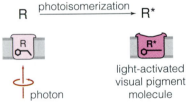

The probability that a particular photon will be caught by a particular molecule depends upon the frequency of the photon and the sensitivity of the molecule to photons of that frequency. But once a rhodopsin molecule catches a photon, it acts exactly like a rhodopsin molecule that has caught a photon of a different frequency. In effect, the response of the photoreceptor depends only upon the number or rate at which its visual pigment molecules are catching photons, whatever the spectral composition of the light. This important simplification, termed **univariance,** captures the essence of what it is about light that is important for some particular photoreceptor type. This notion is summarized in the diagram at left but is sufficiently important that it is worth restating in a bit more detail.

The *physical stimulus* presented to a photoreceptor is the rain of photons of different frequencies. From a *radiometric* perspective, this is termed the **spectral irradiance,** which consists of a spectral density *curve* in which the rate of photons per unit area per frequency interval is plotted as a function of frequency. This stimulus, presented to a cone, causes some of these photons to be absorbed by its visual pigment molecules, with a probability that

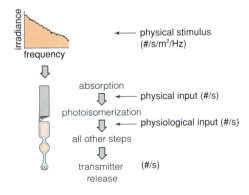

Radiometry *499*

depends upon the frequency of each photon; this is the effective *physical input* to the cone. From a physiological perspective, it is not absorbed photons per se that are important, but only those absorbed photons that produce a photoisomerization of the chromophore. By this stage, if not before, the frequency of the photon that produced a given photoisomerization has become totally irrelevant. Put another way, a photoisomerization is a change in the shape of the chromophore, and because this change is always the same (11-*cis* → all-*trans*), there is no way of determining the frequency of the photon that produced it. Thus the effective *cone input* is the rate of photoisomerization, which is a number or rate (photoisomerizations/s) rather than a measure that depends upon other factors, such as the frequency or state of polarization of the arriving photons. This is the **principle of univariance,** discussed earlier (page 86).

Here the effective cone input will be referred to simply as the *cone input*. Since the cone input is simply a value, we can represent it as a point on a line that represents all possible rates of photoisomerization for some cone:

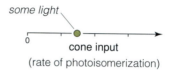

(rate of photoisomerization)

It is worthwhile to immediately broaden this definition to refer to all of the cones of the same type within a given region of retina.

We assume ordinary viewing of the natural world, in which the fraction of visual pigment molecules available to catch photons is high and relatively constant. We also assume that the size of the pupil doesn't change much, and thus that the intensity of the light falling on the retina doesn't change much, which is also true in ordinary circumstances. These assumptions allow us to associate a given light with a given point on this axis. In effect, a given light **maps** to a given point on this axis. Furthermore, so long as the fraction of rhodopsin molecules remains high and relatively constant, as is usually the case, the cone input will be proportional to the intensity of the light. This proportionality has nothing to do with how a cone responds to this input; it refers only to how this input is produced.

If the intensity of some particular light suddenly doubles, so too will the rate of photoisomerization. Our mapped point will thus move to the right so that its distance from the origin has doubled:

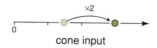

Consider two spectrally different lights, A and B; they will, in general, map to two different points along the line that represents the cone input:

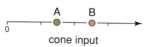

Light B provides the greater input to this cone, and will thus stimulate the cone to a greater degree than will light A. But we can reduce the intensity of light B until its input to this cone is equal to that of light A:

Since both of these spectrally distinct lights produce the same input to this cone, they are now indistinguishable in terms of all subsequent steps. Thus a neat exchange of light A with light B would not alter the response of the cone, although there may have been a large change in the spectral composition of the light received by the cone.

Cone input space

Consider now the inputs to both the M and L cones in some region of the retina, each represented with its own axis:

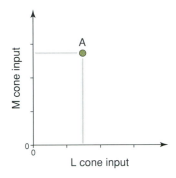

Any light produces some particular input to the L cones and some other input to the M cones. The light can be located at a single point in the diagram by adjusting the horizontal position of the point so that it corresponds to the input to the L cones, and its vertical position so that it corresponds to the input to the M cones. As the intensity of the light is varied, the point at which it maps moves along a straight line, its **intensity locus**, that passes through the origin:

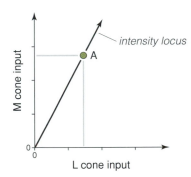

Just as before, the distance of the point from the origin is proportional to the intensity of the light it represents.

This diagram shows the same two spectrally distinct lights that were previously considered:

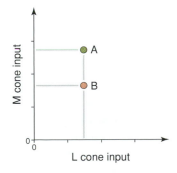

The L cones receive the same input from the two lights, but the M cones receive a greater input from light A. If we vary the intensity of either light, then each point can be shifted along its intensity axis:

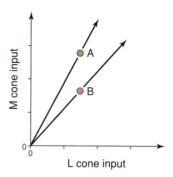

No adjustment of the intensities of the two lights can bring the two points to the same location except at the origin, where both disappear.

We can include S cones in such diagrams by adding a third axis that is perpendicular to both the M and the L cone axes:

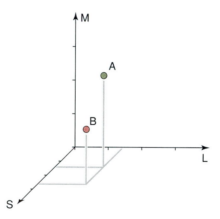

Every possible light maps to some point in this space, just as before. Such three-dimensional diagrams are harder to represent on a two-dimensional page, and a few additional lines and tick marks have been added to help visualize the positions of the two lights in three-dimensional space. Both lights result in the same photon catch rate for the L cones. Light A produces a larger photon catch than light B for the M cones, but a smaller catch for the S cones.

Sometimes it helps to view such three-dimensional diagrams by directing one's gaze parallel to one of the axes, so that the points are shadowcast onto the plane formed by the remaining pair of axes. The resulting three two-dimensional diagrams look like this:

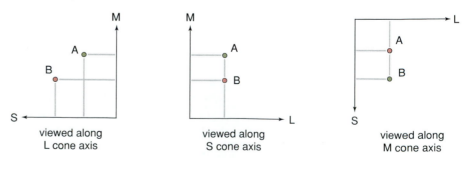

viewed along   viewed along   viewed along
L cone axis   S cone axis   M cone axis

These diagrams can be rearranged to form a two-dimensional representation that draftsmen term a *plan view:*

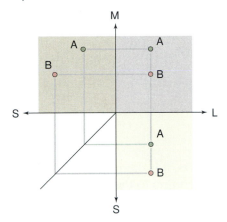

The lower left quadrant can be viewed as plotting the S cone photon catch on both axes, so that all points must necessarily fall on the diagonal line. When the risers are extended into this quadrant, the result is three points representing each light, which form three corners of a rectangle; the rectangle is completed by the point along the diagonal in the lower left quadrant.

A way of thinking about the plan view is to imagine that the corner of the three-dimensional representation had been cut along the S axis, and the two portions folded outward into the plane formed by the M and L cone axes:

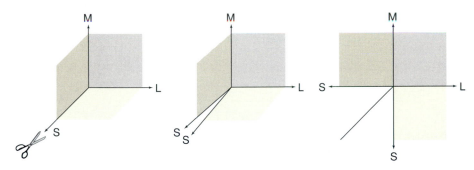

Each of these geometric representations, whether based upon one, two, or three cone types, is termed a **cone input space**.

Combining lights

One of the most useful features of cone input space is that it shows in a simple geometric manner the effect of combining lights of different spectral composition. An example from the natural world would be an object initially illuminated only by daylight; then there is a change in the cloud pattern so that the object becomes partially illuminated by daylight and partially by direct sunlight. The image of some portion of the object falls on the retina and stimulates the cones.

Consider the effect on the M and L cones of adding together two lights, d and s (left). For L cones, light d produces a photoisomerization rate of 5, and light s

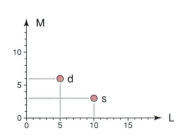

produces a rate of 10. When both lights illuminate the object, their photoisomerization rates add for the L cones to produce a rate of 15. Likewise, for the M cones, the combination of the two lights produces a photoisomerization rate of 9:

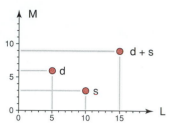

When combining lights, it is often useful to represent them by means of an arrow drawn from the origin to the point:

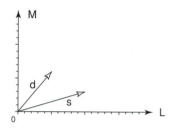

Addition then consists of linking the arrows head to tail:

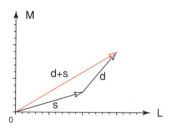

The order in which the arrows are linked is not important, as you can easily verify. The arrows are termed **vectors**, and their linking is termed **vector addition**. The M and L values for a vector to any point are termed the **components** of the vector.

Mixing

Any light that can be formed by the combination of two lights lies in the space defined by the intensity loci of the two lights:

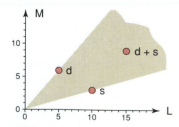

Any point in this space can be reached by adjusting the intensities of the two lights:

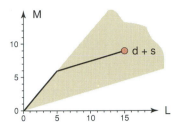

The component vectors are readily found by drawing a line from the point that is parallel to one of the intensity loci. You can readily verify that no point outside of the region can be reached by a mixture of the two lights. Another way of expressing this is to say that the region represents the *domain* of all possible **mixtures** of the lights. In such mixtures, we presume that the light can be adjusted to any intensity along its intensity locus.

In the three-dimensional cone input space, the two lights again define a planar region:

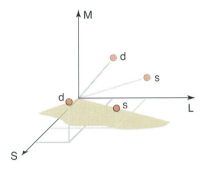

But mixtures of three or more spectrally distinct lights realize a **solid** whose extent is defined by the convex region that lies within the domain defined by any three of them:

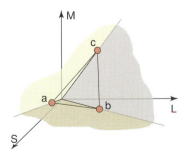

This is an important deduction, for it provides the basis of determining the domain of all lights within cone input space, as discussed in the next two sections.

Metrics of cone input space

How should the axes of cone input space be scaled?

A seemingly obvious answer is to express each of the axes in terms of the rate of photoisomerizations per cone. But there are a number of difficulties with this approach. For example, the rate at which a photoreceptor catches photons depends upon the cross-sectional area of its inner segment. With increasing retinal eccentricity, there is a considerable increase in this area as the cone inner segments grow fatter. In terms of the cone input space, this inflation in the photon catches of the three cone types drives each of the points away from the origin as if the corresponding light had increased in intensity.

Conversely, the macular pigment decreases with retinal eccentricity, and this can change the *relative* photon catches of the three cone types, since the reduction in photon catch is greater for the S cones.

For these and other reasons, any particular scaling of the three axes is to some extent arbitrary. But whatever the scaling, some relationships remain the same. Consider, for example, two lights, one of which stimulates the L cones slightly more than the other. No matter how the L cone axis is scaled, the two points will continue to lie close together, and the dimmer one will continue to lie closer to the origin. Furthermore, any plane in cone input space remains a plane, whatever the scalings.

In general, any plane or curved surface that divides cone input space into two regions is invariant to a scaling of any axis or any combination of them. These invariant relationships prove to be the most useful aspects of cone input space. Consequently, we are free to adjust the scales in a manner that is convenient from some other point of view.

Spectral locus

Just as for any other light, the intensity locus for a light composed of photons of the same frequency is a straight line that passes through the origin. The S cones are insensitive to spectral lights below about 550 THz, so the intensity locus of a light at 500 THz lies within the LM plane. A spectral light at 700 THz mainly stimulates the S cones, so its intensity locus lies close to the S axis:

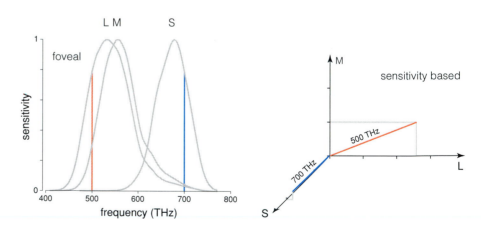

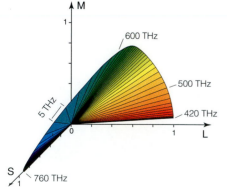

A plot of the intensity loci of the spectral lights that span the visible range looks as shown at left. The spectral locus forms a surface that spreads out from the origin, resembling a bent fan. In order to help visualize the shape of this surface, the intensity loci for each spectral light have been truncated to the same length, and a line has been drawn to connect their tips. At the low end of the spectrum, one edge of the surface approaches the L cone axis, and at the high end, the other edge approaches the S cone axis. In between it rises toward the M cone axis, but stays well away from it.

In order to make this diagram, it was necessary to choose scaling factors for the axes. They have been scaled so that an object that reflects all the light

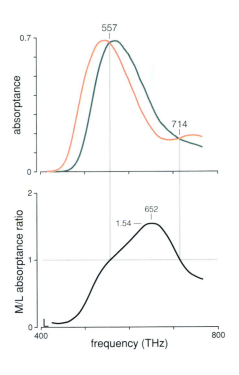

falling on it (i.e., white) that is viewed in daylight produces the same input for each cone; the resulting cone input space is said to be **daylight based**.

The manner in which the spectral locus approaches the M cone axis can be seen more clearly if the spectral locus is projected onto the plane formed by the M and L cone axes, as if the above diagram were viewed along the S axis:

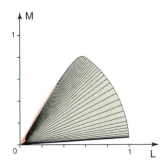

The M cone axis is not approached more closely because any spectral light to which M cones are sensitive is one to which L cones are also sensitive, a situation best seen by comparing the spectral absorptances of the two cone types (right). The ratio of M to L cone stimulation is never greater than about 1.5.

Cone solid

As discussed earlier, three or more spectrally distinct lights yield a conical solid in cone input space. The curved surface of the spectral locus likewise encompasses a three-dimensional conical solid. This solid is bounded along its lower portion by the intensity loci that define the edges of the surface of the spectral locus—essentially the low and high ends of the visible spectrum.

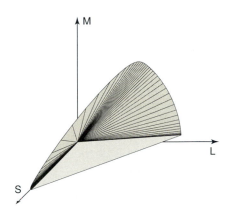

Because the surface of the cone solid is everywhere convex, any *mixture* of spectral lights must lie on or within the cone solid. But *every* light can be viewed as composed of a mixture of spectral lights. Consequently, the cone solid formed by the spectral locus is also the domain of all lights.

Neural surfaces

Cone input space is built from little more than the spectral sensitivities of the three cone types. The axes of this space reflect the effective inputs to the three cone types, and there is nothing within it that gives any hint as to *how* the different cone types respond to the input each receives. But the retinal circuitry makes use of cone *outputs*, and the issue considered here is how to relate cone input space to the different neural cell types that make use of these cone outputs. For simplicity of discussion, we will consider cone outputs to reflect only the photon catch of the cone itself. A fuller discussion would include the effect of interphotoreceptor contacts and horizontal cells, but would not change the broader points considered here.

We have seen that many spectrally different lights can map to the same location in cone input space, and are thus indistinguishable from one another. This means that knowing the location of a light in cone input space tells one only a limited amount about the spectral composition of the light. In the same way, a given neuron may receive many inputs. Its output, however, is singular, for it consists of some rate of transmitter release onto some other neuron, or some current passed via a gap junction. The output of the neuron can thus be represented by a single number. A thermometer is another example of something that provides only a single number at any one time. The output of neurons and thermometers is said to be **scalar**, a word that comes from Latin *scalae* = stairs.

When we attempt to map a scalar quantity onto cone input space, we are attempting to map a one-dimensional quantity onto a three-dimensional space. In general, a given value of the scalar quantity must map to some **surface** in the cone input space. This surface necessarily lies within the cone solid, *and describes the loci of cone inputs that are equivalent to one another in terms of the response of some neural type*. This neural surface has nothing to do with how some neural type responds to some stimulus; rather, it specifies a domain within which any light that maps to a point on this neural surface has the same effect as any other light that maps to the same surface.

This is a key concept, and one that we will use repeatedly. In order to avoid complexities that do not add much at this level of consideration, we assume that a given light stimulus produces a fixed response from a neuron, and thus ignore various adaptations and the time course of the response itself.

Cone outputs

Photoreceptors are neurons, and a good place to begin investigating the properties of a neural surface is to consider that of L cones. Since the output of L cones is assumed to depend only upon the inputs to those cones, it might seem at first sight that the neural surface for some light corresponds to a plane in cone input space that is perpendicular to the L cone axis and intersects it at the value for the cone input:

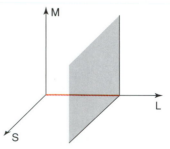

But neural surfaces are based upon outputs, and we have implicitly assumed that the output of L cones always increases as the photon catch rate rises, and is thus **monotonic**. It is at least possible that the output rises initially, and then falls with a further increase in the photon catch rate, so that the relation between output and input is **non-monotonic:**

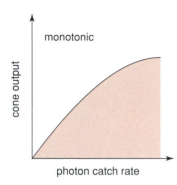

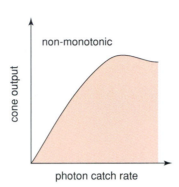

Since all of the lights that map to this plane are equivalent in terms of input to the L cones, they must also be equivalent in terms of their outputs. For the non-monotonic case, however, there would exist two different photon catch rates that produce the same output for the L cones. The neural surface for this cone output would then consist of two such planes:

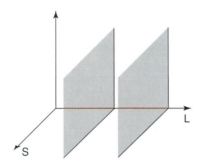

non-monotonic neural surface

Were this the neural surface for this cone type, then, starting from the portion due to the lower catch rate, a sufficient increase in the photon catch of the L cones would return to the second portion of the same neural surface and thus become indistinguishable in terms of L cone outputs. This is never observed for any cone type, since an additional increase in photon catch is never perceived as a fall in intensity. We can thus conclude that the output of a cone is monotonically related to its input. Of course, we know this already from the physiological properties of the cones; the purpose of this example is to illustrate the factors involved in thinking in terms of cone outputs.

Luminance plane

The photopic luminous efficiency function, $V_n(v)$, of *photometry* proves to be a mixture of the spectral sensitivities of the M and L cones, via the equation

Photometry *453*

$$V_n(v) = 0.669 \, L(v) + 0.366 \, M(v)$$

For any particular light, the resulting luminance, V_n, is thus linearly related to a fixed combination of catch rates of these two cone types. Consequently, a given luminance maps to a **plane** in cone input space. In particular, the plane of **unit luminance** ($V_n(v) = 1$) has this form:

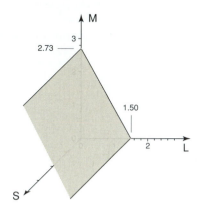

plane of unit luminance

This plane is parallel to the S cone axis, because the experiments upon which luminance is based were designed to exclude the contributions of the S cones.

Not much should be concluded from the fact the luminance surface is a plane; that follows from the above equation, which presumes a fixed relation between the relative outputs of the M and L cones. At high light levels, photometric additivity fails, the surface of constant luminance is no longer a plane, and luminance as a photometric measure is thereby compromised.

The intersection of this plane with the surface of the spectral locus shows the domain of realizable lights of unit luminance:

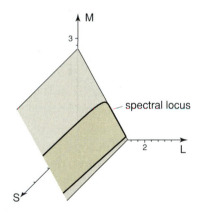

plane of unit luminance

Photometry *453*

The lights that map to any particular value of luminance are said to be **isoluminant**. Thus there is a sequence of such planes, corresponding to different luminances, all parallel to one another.

The equation that characterizes the photopic luminous efficiency function as a mixture of the spectral sensitivities of the M and L cones also defines an axis in cone input space. This axis is perpendicular to the isoluminant planes, as shown in the diagram at the top of the next page.

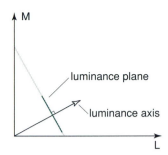

As discussed in PHOTOMETRY, the neural basis for the notion of luminance involves the summed contributions of cone signals onto *parasol* ganglion cells, via diffuse bipolar cells. The isoluminant plane describes the *neural surface* in cone input space for which discrimination by the parasol cells is at a minimum. One example is a border between two lights that minimizes their response. It is, in effect, the neural surface of the array of both on- and off-parasol cells *for some particular form of discrimination.*

This qualification is important; parasol cells receive from diffuse bipolar cells, some of which may receive a contribution from S cones. However, the various discrimination tasks that support luminance as a scalar quantity were devised in such a manner as to reduce or eliminate the contributions of the S cones to the discrimination. Other tasks, devised to emphasize the contribution of the S cones, could produce a different neural surface for these parasol cells to the degree that they are influenced by these cones.

Properly, we should distinguish the neural surface of the on-parasol cells from that of the off-parasols. But these two cell types appear to produce neural surfaces that are parallel to one another, which allows us to usefully speak of parasol cells as a group.

Color solid

Color vision depends upon two distinct comparisons made between the outputs of the three cone types. As discussed in SEEING, the S/LM neural pathway compares the output of the S cones with a mixture of the outputs of the L and M cones, and the LM pathway compares the outputs of the M and L cones.

For the **LM pathway**, the output depends in some way on the *difference* between the outputs of the M and L cones. The conditions under which this difference is zero provide a starting point. The photon catch by M cones required to cancel some photon catch by L cones appears to be about the same for the daylight-based cone input space. Hence, in the LM plane, the locus for cancellation is a straight line with a slope of approximately 1:

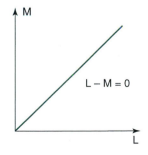

The S cones do not contribute to this pathway, so the plane for which $L - M = 0$ contains the S axis:

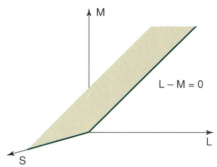

This is the neural surface for an *absence* of stimulation of the LM pathway. Differences in M and L stimulation produce other neural surfaces that may lie above or below this surface, but cannot intersect it.

The LM pathway is composite in that it appears to be based upon two antagonistic ganglion cell types: on-L–off-M/off-L–on-M. Each type has a null plane in cone input space. Just as for the two types of parasol cells, we assume that the two null planes of the LM pathway are coincident; in effect, that the ratio of the cone weightings is the same for both types. The frequency of the spectral light that gives a null response for one of these ganglion cell types is the same as that for the other, so this appears to be the case.

The responses of the cells of the **S/LM pathway** depend upon the difference between the output of the S cones and some combination of the sum of the M and L cone outputs. The plane for which the difference is zero looks like this:

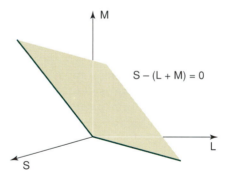

This is the neural surface for an absence of stimulation of the S/LM pathway.

The intersection of these two planes defines an intensity locus along which neither the cells of the LM pathway nor those of the S/LM pathway are stimulated:

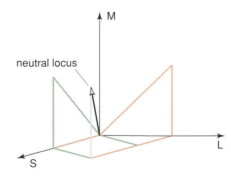

Objects that map to points along this **neutral locus** appear black, gray, or white according to their reflectivity.

We can now determine axes for each of the two pathways, but in order to do so, we must take a closer look at a convention that underlies a simple two-dimensional diagram:

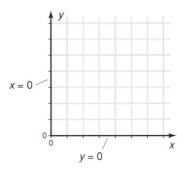

Although the y axis marks off the magnitudes of different y values, it also serves as the locus of all points for which $x = 0$. This holds true even when the two axes are not perpendicular to one another:

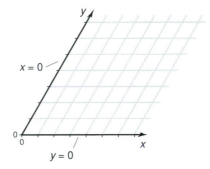

In effect, the direction of the y axis corresponds to the line for which the x value does not change. The key idea is that the direction of the y axis says nothing about variations in the y value; rather, it indicates the particular direction of change that leaves the x value unchanged. By contrast, the direction in which y values change most rapidly, termed the *gradient*, is perpendicular to the lines for which the y value remains unchanged.

If we extend this notion to the three dimensions of cone input space, then the direction of the neutral axis is seen to be determined by the intersection of the null planes of the LM and S/LM pathways. Whatever change takes place along the neutral axis is essentially unrelated to the direction in which it points, which defines what will not change.

Likewise, the axis for the LM pathway must lie in the plane for which the S/LM pathway remains unstimulated, and vice versa:

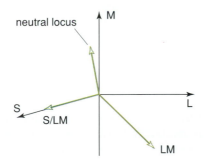

Although hard to visualize from the diagram on page 431, the three axes are roughly perpendicular to once another. This fact is not a product of these geometrical manipulations; instead, it is a result of the relative contributions of the three cone types to each of these mechanisms. As a consequence, each mechanism extracts a different aspect of the spectral composition of objects in the natural world.

Other solids, planes, and lines

A cone input space provides a common framework for expressing a variety of phenomena that involve the stimulation of the different cone types, as we will see below; but first it is worth reviewing what this space is, and what it is not.

Cone input space locates every possible light in a three-dimensional space. The coordinates of this space are the L, M, and S cone inputs. Each component is proportional to the photoisomerization rate of the light for the corresponding cone type. This photoisomerization rate depends upon the spectral distribution of the light, the spectral transmittance of the ocular media, and the spectral absorbance of the visual pigment of some cone type; but finally it is just a rate. Any two lights that produce the same photoisomerization rate for a given cone type cannot be distinguished by that cone type.

Cone input space does not in any way reflect the manner in which a cone responds to some particular rate of photoisomerization, nor does it reflect any neural interactions that may combine these cone contributions. These limitations are not a weakness of this model, but rather a strength. By separating the physical factors from the physiological ones at this critical chemical step, one can focus on either aspect without muddling it with the other.

Other solids

- **Illuminated scenes**   Much of what we see in the natural world consists of different things illuminated by daylight: grass, trees, cheetahs, and so on. The brightest object under these conditions would be a white surface, which reflects all of the light that is incident on it. All other surfaces reflect a smaller portion of the incident light, according to their spectral reflectance. The domain of all possible cone inputs is thus a cube in some cone input space:

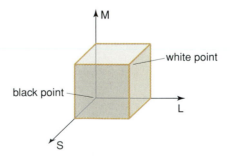

The intersection of the color solid with this cube further restricts the range of potentially realizable lights. But there is an even more severe restriction, which can be traced to the limited ability of spectral

reflectance to produce variations in the relative photon catches of the three cone types, even in theory. This restriction proves to be severe, reducing the volume of the possible daylight cone input space by about 80%; this issue is explored in OPTIMAL COLORS. Finally, dyes and pigments produce spectral reflectances that generally lie well within this theoretical boundary, and thus the domain of the colors of objects is even further constrained.

- **Color monitors** The colors produced on most TV and computer screens currently in use are based upon a cathode ray tube that contains three electron beams, each of which selectively activates one of three phosphors deposited upon the inner surface of the screen: R (red), G (green), and B (blue). The greater the electrical current in each beam, the more intense the light that comes from the phosphor it excites. The individual lights from the three phosphors are smeared (mixed) by the optics of the eye:

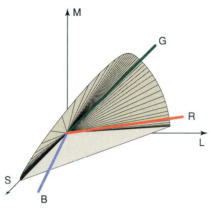

The diagram shows the three intensity loci of one particular set of phosphors. Any light that lies in the solid they define can be realized, at least up to the maximum intensities of the phosphors. Manufacturers have attempted to develop phosphors that encompass as large a fraction of the cone solid as possible, and it is evident from the diagram that they have largely succeeded; but because the spectral surface is curved, no set of three phosphors can include all of its domain.

- **CIE system** For mainly historical reasons, much useful data is expressed in an arbitrary transformation of cone input space. This system was developed by a standards group known as the CIE (Commission Internationale de l'Eclairage). Instead of plotting the photon catch rates of the three cone types directly, it uses three other axes, termed X, Y, and Z:

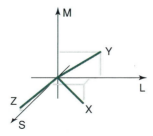

The Z axis lies close to the axis for the photon catch of the S cones and thus approximates some scaling of the S cone photon catch. The Y axis was set to correspond to the luminance axis, discussed above, and thus equal Y values map to isoluminant planes. The X axis is directed below the plane formed by the S and L axes; it is roughly parallel to the L–M axis of the color solid, discussed earlier.

The X, Y, and Z axes are not perpendicular to one another in cone input space, and cannot all be made perpendicular by any scaling of the L, M, and S axes. Nevertheless, it is straightforward to determine the X, Y, and Z components of any point in cone input space. All that is necessary is to construct a plane parallel to the remaining axes, and determine where this plane intersects the axis considered. For example, in order to determine the Z component of some point, we would construct a plane through it that is parallel to the plane defined by the X and Y axes. This construction can also be applied to the L, M, or S axis as well. Because the X, Y, and Z axes lie outside the conical color solid of spectral lights, any point within this solid has X, Y, and Z components that are either positive or zero.

Other planes

- **Cone triangle**   Any plane that intersects each of the axes in cone input space defines a triangle bounded by the domain of positive cone inputs:

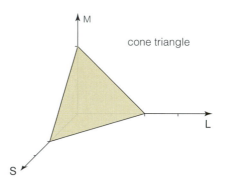

The intensity locus of any light must pass through this plane at some point, which must also lie within the conical solid of the spectral locus:

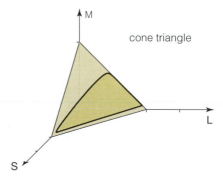

By effectively removing intensity from consideration, we achieve a two-dimensional surface within which all lights can be represented, which is termed a cone triangle.

Other lines

The most interesting lines in cone input space are those that are parallel to one of the axes:

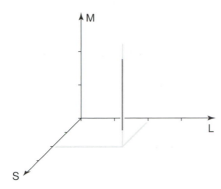

In this diagram, the line parallel to the M cone axis has been darkened over the portion that passes through the cone solid; any point on this darkened portion can thus by realized by some light. Over this portion, the rate of photoisomerization of the M cones varies by a factor of about five. Because the L component remains unchanged along the entire line, the lights that lie along it all produce the same rate of photoisomerization for the L cones. In the same manner, along this line there is no change in the stimulation of the S cones. Thus along this line the only change in stimulation that takes place is for the M cones. This feature has two useful applications: exchange stimulation and tests for color blindness.

- **Exchange stimulation**   When analyzing the properties of the visual system, it is useful to present stimuli that change the stimulation of only one of the photoreceptor types. Typically one light is neatly exchanged for another. We can realize this type of stimulation by means of two lights, g and p, that differ only in their stimulation of the M cones:

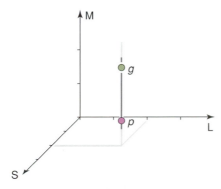

There are many possible stimuli that can be based upon these two lights; here, we simply move a paper border that has a reflected light of g across a paper background that has a reflected light of p:

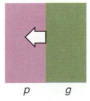

Plots of the photon catch rates of the three cone types would then look something like this:

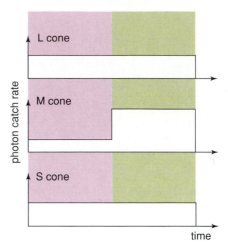

As the border crosses the array of cones, the light of the image suddenly changes from p to g. The photon catches of the L and S cones remain unchanged, rendering them unable to detect this change in the spectral composition of the light falling upon them. But the M cones receive a sudden increase in their photon catch. Their response, and the cone response of any other neuron in the visual system, is based entirely upon this stimulation of the M cones.

• **Tests for color blindness**   About 1% of human males lack functional M cones, and are termed deuteranopes. They are thus unable to distinguish the three lights shown here at three different intensities:

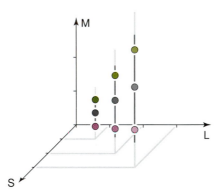

People with normal color vision can make out a green X and a purple O in the diagram below, which is based upon these lights:

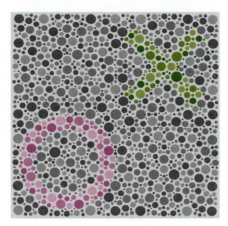

But to a deuteranope, all the circles appear to have the same hue, as suggested in the diagram below:

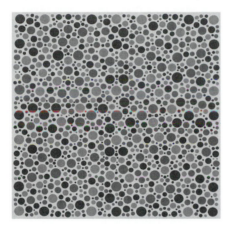

There are a variety of different variations and abnormalities in color perception, particularly among males, and each can be usefully related to cone input space.

Exponentials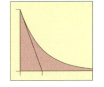

Exponential relations are common in the natural world because they reflect a change in the amount of something that is proportional to the amount itself. Biology is filled with examples of exponential growth, but all of the exponential relations in this book involve decays, and this section reviews their properties.

Qualitative description

Many of the processes discussed in this book decay with time or distance:

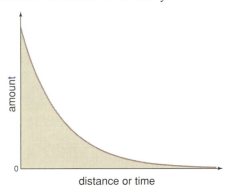

With each small step along the horizontal axis, the amount drops by a constant fraction of itself; this pattern is termed **exponential decay**. For example, if you start with a certain amount of money in a bank account, and each day spend 1% of the amount that remains in the account, that amount will decay in an exponential manner.

A measure of the rate of decay can be found by extending the slope of the curve at some point until it intersects the horizontal axis:

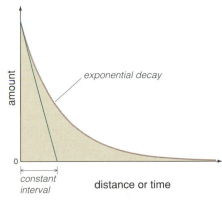

This interval is termed a **space constant** or a **time constant**, depending upon the dimension used for the horizontal axis. Over this interval, the amount has dropped to 37% of the initial amount. It doesn't make any difference where you start plotting the slope of the exponential curve; you get the same interval, which is why it is termed a constant.

If the logarithm of the amount is plotted, the exponential curve plots as a straight line:

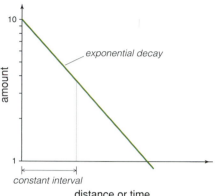

There is no real start or end to the curve of exponential decay; it rises forever toward the left and falls forever toward the right. It is thus entirely characterized by its space or time constant, and the value of the amount at any particular point in time or space. These quantities are determined by the physical situation that is modeled.

Exponential decays also appear in probability density distributions. One example has to do with random events in time. As discussed in POISSON DISTRIBUTION, the intervals between adjacent events are distributed in an exponential manner:

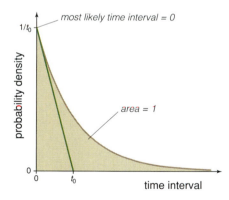

distribution of time intervals
of a Poisson event process

A second example has to do with the free exchange of some conserved quantity, such as energy. At the microscopic level, atoms and molecules are in continuous motion, trading energy with one another as they interact, as shown at the top of the next page.

density distributions
See THE RAIN OF PHOTONS ONTO CONES: *LOOKING AT SPECTRAL DENSITY CURVES*, page 74, for a general discussion of density curves.

Poisson distribution *485*

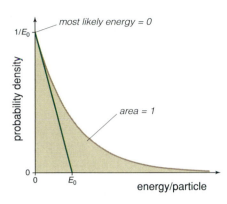

distribution of energy among
interacting particles

The fact that the probability density function for energy is an exponential has less to do with the physical nature of this quantity than with the rules that govern its conservation.

Quantitative description

The general algebraic form of a decaying exponential is

$$y = y_0 n^{-x}$$

where n is any positive real number and y_0 is a scaling factor that y becomes equal to when $x = 0$. The term *exponential* comes from the fact that the variable x enters the equation as an exponent. For algebraic convenience, n is almost always set to the mathematical constant e:

$$e = 2.71828\ldots$$

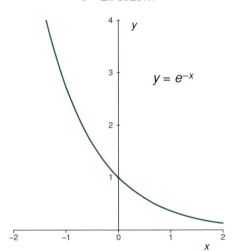

This choice yields the following expansion:

$$e^{-x} = 1 - x + \frac{x^2}{2!} - \frac{x^3}{3!} + \frac{x^4}{4!} \cdots$$

When x is small, the higher terms can be ignored, yielding the following approximation:

$$e^{-x} \cong 1-x$$

when $x \ll 1$, or

$$1 - e^{-x} \cong x$$

Blackbody radiation *401*

This is the approximation used in BLACKBODY RADIATION (page 402), to show that at low frequencies, the number of photons radiated by a heated body per frequency interval is proportional to the frequency.

Because x is an exponent, it must be a dimensionless number. When describing physical situations in which variables have dimensions, it is replaced by the ratio of a dimensional variable to a constant that is assigned the same dimensions, and in a time constant,

$$e^{-t/t_0}$$

and in a space constant,

$$e^{-x/x_0}$$

The equation for the spectral emittance of a heated body (BLACKBODY RADIATION, page 402) includes a term in which the exponent is the ratio of two energy terms, the energy of a photon at a particular frequency ($h\nu$) and the average energy of each form of motion of a particle at some temperature (kT).

$$M_n(\nu) = \frac{2\pi\nu^2}{c^2(e^{h\nu/kT} - 1)} \text{ (photon/s/m}^2\text{/Hz)}$$

As noted above, when a large number of particles interact, their conserved quantities are exponentially distributed. This gives us further insight into the above equation, where the numerator of the exponent ($h\nu$) can be interpreted as the probability density of *mechanical* energy at some temperature that is in equilibrium with a corresponding amount of radiant energy.

Light absorption

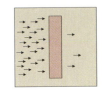

Here we look at the absorption of light from a macroscopic perspective. This topic surveys the quantitative bookkeeping involved when photons are absorbed under various circumstances. This bookkeeping involves three related measures, each associated with some fate of a photon. The relationships are simple, and this section mainly involves the definition of terms.

For simplicity, the light described in this section is assumed to be spectral (i.e., at a single frequency). In order to apply the measures discussed here to a spectral distribution, it is necessary to break the distribution up into small spectral intervals and apply the following considerations to each interval.

Light that encounters some medium can be transmitted, reflected, or absorbed. **Transmittance** (T) refers to the fraction of light that passes *through* some absorbing material. **Reflectance** (R) refers to the fraction that is *reflected* or *scattered backward* by the material. **Absorptance** (A) refers to the remaining fraction of the light that is *absorbed* by the material. Since all of these are fractional values, each can vary between 0 and 1. Since they are mutually exclusive, and cover all possible fates for a photon, they sum to 1:

$$T + R + A = 1$$

Consider a beam of light having a flux, ϕ_1, that is incident on a transparent chamber containing a light-absorbing substance. Examples of interest here include a solution of visual pigment molecules, some portion of the retina, or the lens of the eye. We assume that the absorbing substance is not fluorescent:

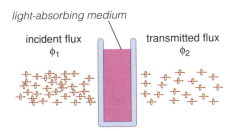

light-absorbing medium

incident flux
ϕ_1

transmitted flux
ϕ_2

A standard convention is to distinguish the lights by means of a numbered subscript, as shown. The same convention gives the transmittance a subscript that combines those of the incident and transmitted light, which is thus written as

$$T_{12} = \phi_2/\phi_1$$

The absorptance cannot be measured directly, but when the reflectance is zero or insignificant, it can be readily calculated:

$$A_{12} = 1 - T_{12} = 1 - \phi_2/\phi_1$$

We saw in THE RAIN OF PHOTONS ONTO CONES (page 84) that the peak absorptance of a foveal cone outer segment was about 0.68. Because the light reflected back from the photoreceptor was insignificant, the transmittance at this frequency was $1 - 0.68 = 0.32$.

It is often necessary to keep track of light as it passes through a series of optical media, such as cornea, aqueous, lens, and vitreous. Consider two chambers in sequence:

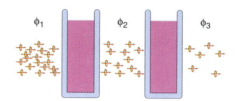

The transmittance for the first medium is calculated as already discussed. For the second medium, where ϕ_2 is the flux of the incident light, we have

$$T_{23} = \phi_3/\phi_2$$

The total transmittance of the two chambers in series is, by definition,

$$T_{13} = \phi_3/\phi_1$$

But note that this equation can be expanded to

$$T_{13} = \phi_3/\phi_1 = \phi_2/\phi_1 \times \phi_3/\phi_2$$

or

$$T_{13} = T_{12} \times T_{23}$$

To generalize: When light passes through a series of optical media, the total transmittance is equal to the *products* of the transmittances of the individual media.

This sequence of products suggests another measure, which is termed **optical density**, D:

$$D = -\log_{10}(T)$$

Since T is less than or equal to 1, its logarithm is less than or equal to 0, and the minus sign in the definition ensures that the optical density will always be a positive number. This measure is also termed the **extinction** or the **absorbance** (note the small difference between the terms *absorbance* and *absorptance*).

Continuing from the previous example, the peak absorbance of a foveal cone is $-\log_{10}(0.32) = 0.50$. The optical density of the pair of media above is

$$D_{13} = -\log(T_{13})$$

This expands to

$$D_{13} = -\log(T_{13}) = -\log(T_{12} \times T_{23}) = -\log(T_{12}) - \log(T_{23})$$

or

$$D_{13} = D_{12} + D_{23}$$

To generalize: When light passes through a series of optical media, their total *optical density* is equal to the *sum* of the optical densities of the individual media. This is what makes optical density such a useful measure.

If the light path is doubled by placing two identical chambers in series, then the optical density is also doubled, *as is the effective length of the light path*. To generalize: The optical density of some homogenous medium will be proportional to the length of the light path through it:

$$\text{optical density} = \text{some constant} \times \text{length of the light path in the direction of the light}$$

or

$$D = a \times l \qquad\qquad \text{(Lambert's law, 1760)}$$

where l is the length of the light path in the direction of the light, and a, the **absorptivity**, is an intrinsic factor characteristic of the medium. (Johann Lambert had more than one relation named after him; see page 508.) Again, it is necessary to distinguish between three similar words: *absorptivity*, *absorptance*, and *absorbance*. Since the optical density is dimensionless, and the path length has units of meters (m), absorptivity has units of m^{-1}. Continuing the above example, the length of the outer segment of a foveal cone is about 33 μm, hence the absorptivity of the outer segment is

$$a = \frac{D}{l} = \frac{0.5}{0.033 \text{ m}} = 15 \text{ m}^{-1}$$

If the medium consists of a transparent solvent and a light-absorbing solute, then a similar consideration leads one to expect the absorbance to be proportional to the concentration of the solute (Beer's law, 1852). Combining these two laws gives:

$$D = \varepsilon \times c \times l$$

where c is the molar concentration of the solute and ε is an intensive factor, termed the **molar absorptivity**, which depends upon the light-absorbing properties of the solute molecules. We can thus speak about the molar absorptivity of a rhodopsin molecule, or some other light-absorbing molecule. The concentration of rhodopsin molecules in an outer segment is about 3 mM, so from the above, the molar absorptivity of a rhodopsin molecule in an outer segment is

$$\varepsilon = \frac{D}{c \times l} = \frac{0.5}{0.003 \text{ M} \times 0.033 \text{ m}} = 50{,}000 \text{ M}^{-1} \text{ m}^{-1}$$

This value is somewhat higher than that of rhodopsin molecules in solution, because the chromophores in the outer segment are oriented so as to best catch the incident light.

Optimal colors

The colors of objects depend upon their spectral reflectances, and this constrains the degree to which they can be saturated. Optimal colors are those that show the maximum amount of saturation for some value of lightness. In general, the greater the lightness, the smaller the maximum possible saturation for any particular hue. This section discusses why this is so. In color vision based upon two cone types, the spectral reflectances that produce optimal colors are the same for all species, despite the fact that species differ in terms of the spectral sensitivities of their photoreceptors. As a consequence, a tropical fish that appears highly colored to members of its own species will usually appear highly colored to us as well.

Cone differences

As discussed in SEEING (page 345), color vision is based upon differences in the photon catch rates of the different cone types. The largest differences occur when spectral lights are used (left).

Consider a light composed entirely of photons with frequencies at 600 THz. The M cones are most sensitive to this light, followed by the L cones, and then the S cones. Relative to the spectral sensitivity of the M cones, that of the L cones is 69% as large, whereas that of the S cones is about 23%. Such a light appears to us as a saturated (strongly colored) blue-green. How might this color be realized by reflected light from objects in the natural world?

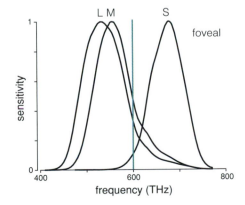

When we view an object in the natural world, the light from it depends in part upon the spectral composition of the illuminant, and in part upon the spectral reflectance of the object. For simplicity, we will ignore glossy surfaces and other complexities that cause the light coming from the object to depend upon the direction from which it is viewed. Assume that an object is diffusely lit by sunlight:

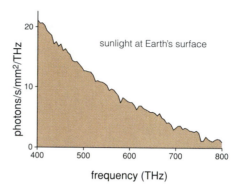

The spectral reflectance of the object can vary between 0 and 1 over the visible spectrum:

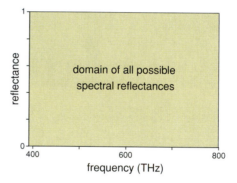

Assume that we can sculpt this domain so as to yield any possible spectral reflectance. Which spectral reflectance, then, will yield the best match to the saturated blue-green?

An obvious answer to this puzzle is to set the spectral reflectance to 1 near 600 THz and to zero elsewhere:

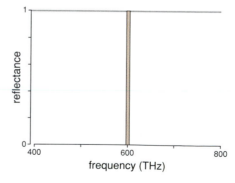

The light from the object now consists entirely of photons with frequencies near 600 THz, all of which are reflected from its surface. Thus the saturation of the blue-green hue will be almost the same as that for a light consisting of photons with frequencies at exactly 600 THz. However, an object with this spectral reflectance will be very dark, because all but the photons near 600 THz will be absorbed by it.

If the object is to appear lighter, then it is necessary to reflect more photons from the object. The best thing we can do to accomplish this is to increase the width of the spectral region at which all of the photons are reflected:

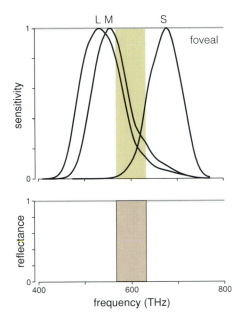

This broadening of the reflectance band greatly increases the amount of light coming from the object, and thus its *lightness*. But it also reduces the difference in photon catch between the three cone types, thereby reducing the *color saturation* of the object. As the width of the reflectance band continues to broaden, the lightness continues to increase, and the saturation continues to decrease. At the limit of full reflectance, the surface would become a perfect white that reflected all of the light, and the saturation would disappear.

A moment's consideration is sufficient to show that step changes in reflectance are always better at increasing saturation than more gradual changes:

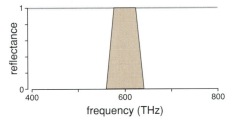

This diagram shows a spectral reflectance whose sides are sloped rather than vertical. It has the same area as the rectangle we have been considering, and thus reflects about the same number of photons, and produces a similar lightness. But this change is equivalent to replacing photons with frequencies nearer 600 THz with photons farther away:

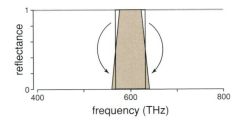

That substitution can only make matters worse by reducing the differences between the different cone types. Thus the spectral transmittance that provides a color with the most saturation for any given lightness is one that, for any frequency, either reflects all of the photons or none of them.

Thus far we have considered only the hues of the spectrum. Purples and deep reds are realized by lights composed of a mixture of photons at both the high and the low ends of the spectrum, with relatively few in between. Maximum saturation for these colors is realized by spectral reflectances that are equal to 1 at both the high and low ends of the spectrum and zero for some range in between:

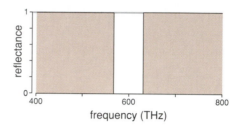

A spectral reflectance that provides the greatest saturation for any given lightness is termed an **optimal spectral reflectance**, or somewhat less precisely, an **optimal color**. Either form can be characterized in terms of two frequencies:

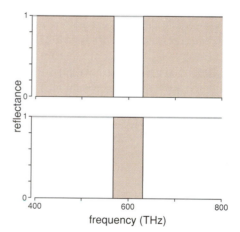

We will refer to them as **transition frequencies**, as they mark a transition between a reflectance of zero and a reflectance of one. Given the desired ratios of cone photon catches, it is possible to specify two transition frequencies, f_1 and f_2, that characterize the optimal spectral reflectance for a given lightness.

The theory of optimal colors is independent of the nature of the neural mechanisms engaged in comparing the outputs of the different cone types. Instead, it speaks only to the types of spectral reflectance able to generate the largest differences in the relative stimulation of the three cone types.

Comparative aspects

The theory of optimal colors was developed with reference to human color vision. But its ideas are more general, and could have been developed equally well with regard to the vision of bees or some other species. We can continue to speak of spectral reflectances that produce maximum differences in photoreceptor stimulation without concerning ourselves with the neural correlates that result in perceptions such as hue or saturation.

If a species compares the outputs of n spectrally distinct photoreceptor types, then the number of transition frequencies required to realize an optimal spectral reflectance is $n - 1$. For humans, if we include the rods, there are four distinct photoreceptor types, but comparisons are made between the three cone types, so only two transition frequencies are required. Most mammals appear to possess only two spectrally distinct cone types; for them, only a single transition frequency is required.

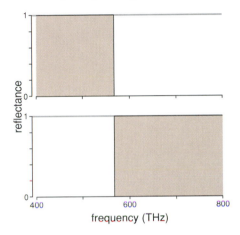

In human vision, only the M and L cones are sensitive to frequencies below about 550 THz, and only one transition is required over this portion of the spectrum. Notice that when only one transition frequency is required, all species have the same set of optimal spectral reflectances. Hence spectral reflectances that produce large differences in the relative stimulation of the different photoreceptor types in one species often do so as well for other species.

Photometry

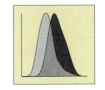

Photometry is a measurement system that attempts to quantify light intensity in a manner that is relevant to human vision. On a sunny day your body is warmed by an intense rain of photons, whose energy is turned to heat as they are absorbed. Most of this heat comes from photons of low frequency that lie in the infrared portion of the spectrum, and are thus invisible to us. The focus of photometry is thus not the rain of photons per se, but the rate at which that rain stimulates human photoreceptors. There are two forms of photometry, termed scotopic and photopic. Scotopic photometry deals with dim conditions, in which our vision is dominated by the rods; photopic photometry deals with bright conditions and foveal viewing, in which our vision is dominated by the cones.

Scotopic and photopic photometry are qualitatively different

Quantifying light intensity in terms of rod vision is straightforward, and boils down to comparing the relative abilities of spectral lights of different frequencies to photoisomerize the visual pigment molecules contained in the rods. When the photoisomerization rates are the same for two lights, even when they are of different frequencies, then all subsequent events in the visual system will be the same, and hence the two lights will be indistinguishable.

The situation is more complex in photopic photometry, in which there are three cone types with different spectral sensitivities—and thus three rates of photoisomerization—to keep track of, rather than one. If the intensity of a light is changed without altering its spectral composition, then all the photoisomerization rates change proportionally, and the situation is effectively equivalent to scotopic photometry. Likewise, when one light produces a greater rate of photoisomerization for all three cone types than a second light, then the notion that the first light is more intense is unambiguous. The problem arises in the middle range, where one light produces the highest rate of photoisomerization in one cone type, and a second light produces the highest rate in another cone type. In a deep sense, comparing these lights in terms of intensity is either meaningless, definitional, or based upon some particular aspect of vision beyond the photoreceptors, such as the way in which the outputs of different cone types converge onto diffuse bipolar cells.

Photopic photometry was developed to meet a practical need, and is entirely justifiable in these terms, but it is relevant to vision only insofar as it concerns the restricted set of issues that it was devised to cope with. The aim of this topic is to develop an understanding of photometry and its measure, luminance, from this perspective.

Radiometry *499*

Qualitative description

A poorly lit factory floor can be a dangerous place; as a result, federal and state regulations specify minimum values for the amount of illumination in such settings. Architects, in consultation with lighting engineers, design workplaces so as to ensure that lighting is sufficient and standards are met. Indeed, their specifications generally exceed the legal minimum. We can readily understand the distinction between poorly lit and well lit, but in order to comply with regulations or meet specifications, it is necessary to quantify the amount of illumination. Photometry was developed to meet this need.

Few lights in our environment are **spectral** (i.e., consist of photons that all have about the same frequency). But for photometry to be of general usefulness, it must be able to determine for any spectral light how much radiometric intensity is required to match some particular reference light.

Here is a simple apparatus that could be used to develop a system of photometry:

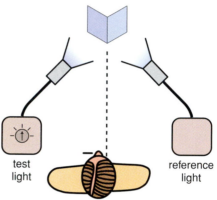

Each light source shines only on one-half of the piece of bent cardboard. The subject sees the bent cardboard edge-on, with the left side illuminated by the test light and the right side by the reference light:

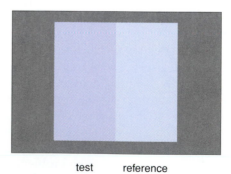

test   reference

The intensity and spectral composition of the reference light are fixed. The subject adjusts the intensity of the test light until he or she judges that a match between the two lights has been obtained. Just what *match* means proves to be the heart of the matter, but we will put that issue aside for the moment. Nevertheless, it is clear that the test light can be spectral, and that a match with a spectral light that lies toward either end of the visible spectrum will require higher intensity settings, simply because the sensitivities of all of the photoreceptors will be less. Put another way, these spectral lights produce a lower photoisomerization rate than spectral lights in the middle of the visible spectrum, and thus are less effective in illuminating the shop floor.

So the general idea behind a system of photometry is to determine the relative effectiveness of spectral lights over the visible spectrum. Although it has fewer practical applications, it is useful to first consider how one might develop a photometric system based upon rod vision, since only a single photoreceptor type is involved.

Scotopic photometry

If the reference light is so dim that only the rods can detect it, then the subject will adjust the intensity of each test light so that it produces the same rod photon catch as the reference light. At this point the border between the two sides of the bent cardboard disappears, since there is no change in rod photon catch across it. If the reference light were brighter, so that cones were active, the test lights, being spectral, would appear highly colored; but when only the rods are active, the test lights cannot be distinguished from the reference light, or from one another.

A plot of the intensity settings across the spectrum of test lights might look something like this:

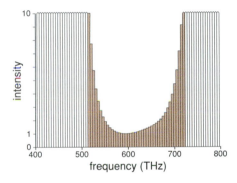

The vertical scale in this diagram has been normalized so that the minimum intensity ever required is equal to one. In order to match a spectral test light at either 548 or 667 THz to the reference light, its intensity must be doubled, reflecting the fact that the sensitivity of the rods in the eye has dropped to half of its peak value. Below about 520 THz and above about 740 THz, the intensity required is more than ten times greater, and thus the sensitivity has dropped to less than a tenth of its peak value. We can see this more directly simply by plotting the reciprocal of the intensity settings:

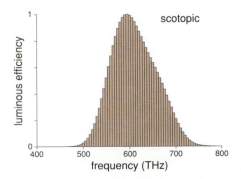

In photometry, this curve is termed the **scotopic luminous efficiency function,** but we recognize it as the spectral sensitivity curve of rods in the eye.

Light absorption *443*

Since it is based upon the intensities of lights entering the eye, it depends upon both the direct spectral transmittance of the ocular media and the spectral absorptance of the rod outer segments (see LIGHT ABSORPTION for a discussion of these terms).

As first discussed in THE RAIN OF PHOTONS ONTO CONES, with respect to L cones, single photoreceptor types respond only to the rate of photon catch, not the frequencies of the photons. The total photon catch rate is thus the sum of the photon catch rates over each spectral interval. This means that the scotopic luminous efficiency function can be used to determine a measure proportional to rod photon catch for any spectral distribution. Except for a scaling factor that carries with it the required photometric units, this is all there is to *scotopic photometry*.

Photopic photometry

The general idea behind photopic photometry is much the same: devise a **photopic luminous efficiency function** that combines the spectral sensitivities of the cone types, and can be used as a weighting function. Again, the subject is presented with a sequence of spectral test lights, and is asked to adjust the intensity of each so that it matches the reference light. Assume that the reference light is white. Since each of the spectral lights appears colored, it is obvious that no adjustment of the intensity knob is going to make the border between the test and reference lights disappear. Thus the issue of what constitutes a "match" becomes important.

At first sight, it might seem that the subject should adjust the intensity until both sides of the cardboard appear "equally bright." Despite the fact that a color difference remains, subjects can use spectral lights to make brightness judgments in a consistent and reproducible manner. If two spectral lights, A and B, are each adjusted to be as bright as the reference light, they will also appear to be as bright as each other. Furthermore, if the intensities of A and B are each doubled, they continue to appear equally bright.

But there is one test of consistency that fails. If half of spectral light A is added to half of light B, the mixture generally does not appear to have the same brightness as the reference light. In photometry, this is termed a *failure of additivity*. Because of this failure, it is not possible to take an arbitrary spectral distribution, divide it into spectral intervals, weight each according to some brightness measure, add them together, and get a consistent result. Whatever the neural mechanism that underlies the perception of brightness, it is more complex than any weighted sum of the photon catches of the different cone types.

Of course, there would be no problem if we had only a single cone type, rather than three. Getting rid of the contribution of any one cone type would help, and finding some measure that depended upon the summed contributions of the remaining two cone types would solve the problem. Historically, this is the implicit tack taken by photometry. There are a number of experimental ways of doing this by means of a match, but each is based upon a different type of match. All of them prove to be equivalent in that they minimize the contribution of the S cones, and all produce a weighting function based upon the same additive combination of the spectral sensitivities of the M and L cones. Only one method will be described here, known as the match that produces a *minimally distinct border*.

Minimally distinct borders

This means of establishing a match does not attempt to compare the two lights in any way. Instead, it is entirely concerned with the distinctness of the vertical border between them. The observer adjusts the intensity of the test light so that this border appears *minimally distinct*. Because of limitations in color printing, it is difficult to show a printed version of what a minimally distinct border looks like. The following illustration attempts to simulate its appearance, by blending:

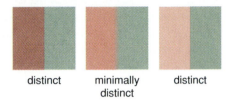

distinct   minimally   distinct
             distinct

A minimally distinct border is perfectly visible; it just appears "fuzzy" compared with other settings of the intensity knob. It turns out that if border distinctness is the criterion, then additivity holds, so that all spectral test lights can be matched against the reference light in a self-consistent manner.

The positions of the intensity knob that produce a minimally distinct border for different spectral lights prove to be different from those that produce equal brightness. But for natural lights, the difference between the two settings is not very great. Hence the minimally distinct border criterion, although a seemingly odd measure, has two useful attributes: its matches are usually not greatly different from brightness matches, and it is additive. The resulting sensitivity curve for the spectral lights, termed the **photopic luminous efficiency function,** looks like this:

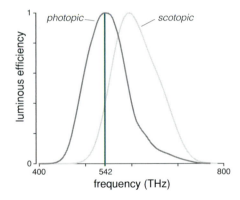

This curve happens to be based on a different experimental arrangement, described in the Box OTHER MEASURES LEAD TO THE SAME PHOTOPIC LUMINOUS EFFICIENCY FUNCTION.

Physiological correlates

Photoreceptors

The above description is based upon photometric judgments made by human observers, but says nothing specific about the underlying neural mechanisms. One of the first questions that can be asked is which photore-

Other measures lead to the same photopic luminous efficiency function

There are a number of other methods of determining a photopic luminous efficiency function that also display additivity. One such method is to rapidly alternate the test light with the reference light at a rate of about 10 Hz. This produces a flickering sensation, and the subject's task is to adjust the intensity of the test light so as to minimize this *flicker*. This match is also additive, and the approach is termed **heterochromatic flicker photometry** (Greek *heteros* = other, here in the context of "different"). The standard photopic luminous efficiency function is derived from measurements based upon this technique. What is remarkable is that two spectral lights adjusted to minimize flicker also form a minimally distinct border when placed side by side. Thus the luminous efficiency function based upon minimal flicker is indistinguishable from that based upon minimally distinct borders.

Another method is to move the border back and forth and ask the subject to minimize the sensation of *movement*. Again, lights adjusted in this way prove to be additive in terms of minimal movement. Furthermore, the luminous efficiency function obtained by this method is indistinguishable from that obtained by the other two methods. It is as if each of these methods were measuring different aspects of the same thing.

ceptors are involved in photopic photometry. Since the judgments are usually made by direct fixation, and thus by the rod-free area of the fovea, we need consider only the cones. Luminous efficiency is measured in the same way as the spectral sensitivity of a cone in that both depend upon the reciprocal of the light intensity necessary to match a reference light. By convention, sensitivity functions are normalized to have a peak value of 1:

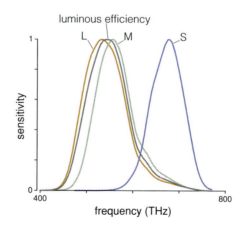

The luminous efficiency function does not show the spectral sensitivity of any cone type. Instead, its peak lies between the spectral sensitivity curves of the L and M cones. The shape of this function can be approximated by an additive mixture of the spectral sensitivities of the L and M cones in the ratio of about 1.83:1, based upon an average of the spectral sensitivity functions of a number of *observers*. The shapes of the M and L cone spectral sensitivity functions are due in part to the spectral sensitivity of the cones themselves, and in part to the spectral transmittance of the ocular media, and possibly to other factors.

Nothing much can be directly inferred from the particular ratio of L and M cone spectral sensitivities needed to fit the luminous efficiency function. There are at least three factors that make such inferences difficult.

First, the curve fitting depends upon the spectral sensitivity curves assumed for the standard observer. The values used in this book for foveal viewing are based upon calculations of Stockman et al. (1993) from a photometric standard known as the CIE_{1964} 10° Color Matching Functions. An alternative standard, based upon the measurements of Stiles and Burch (1959), also proposed by Stockman et al., yields an L/M ratio of 1.2.

Second, the ratio depends critically upon the values assumed for the peak frequencies of the M and L cones, and these vary among individuals, particularly L cones in males (see PHOTORECEPTOR ATTRIBUTES, pages 218.

Third, the ratio depends upon the relative numbers of L and M cones that contribute to the luminous efficiency function, as well as the strength of the synaptic contributions made by each. These factors are qualitatively different, but they are not readily untangled. In Old World monkeys, the ratio of L to M cones appears to be close to 1. Evidence in chimpanzees suggests that their photopic luminous efficiency function, obtained by behavioral testing, also has an L/M ratio close to 1. There is as yet no firm evidence for the average L/M *cone ratio* in humans, or the variation among individuals (see the Box below), but a value of 3.8 has been measured in one subject (David R. Williams, personal communication).

The finding that the luminous efficiency function is based upon adding together some mixture of the spectral sensitivities of L and M cones suggests that their signals are neurally combined at some level. As discussed below, most diffuse cone bipolar cells connect indiscriminately to any M and L cones that lie within their dendritic fields. The collective activity of these bipolars probably corresponds to the first point at which neural signals can show a spectral sensitivity that approximates the luminous efficiency function under the conditions in which this function is determined.

There is no measurable contribution from the S cones to the photopic luminous efficiency function that can be distinguished from experimental error. This absence appears to be partly a matter of the relative sparsity of S cones, and partly an outcome of choosing parameters for the judgments of luminous efficiency that minimize the contributions of the S cones so as to achieve additivity. For example, in a method based upon rapidly alternating two lights, the frequency of alternation is set at about 10 to 20 Hz (see the Box *OTHER MEASURES LEAD TO THE SAME PHOTOPIC LUMINOUS EFFICIENCY FUNCTION*). At this rate there is essentially no sensation of flicker when the stimulus is arranged so as to activate only the S cones; the reason for this is not entirely clear. Likewise, chromatic aberration and the sparsity of S cones combine to minimize the contributions of S cones to the distinctiveness of borders. This is a useful perspective to keep in mind when considering the neural pathways

Variation among individuals

The different methods for determining the luminous efficiency function appear to be equivalent when measured for the same individual. Different individuals, however, make slightly different average judgments. There are two general reasons for this individual variation: differences in the structure of the visual pigment molecules that result in differences in their spectral sensitivities, and differences in macular and lens pigmentation. It is also possible that individuals differ in the relative numbers of cones of each type, particularly the M and L cones, but this has not yet been demonstrated. Consequently, photometry, as a system of measurement that best reflects the population at large, needs to average over a number of individuals.

The variation among individuals is sufficiently small that it has little effect upon the primary aim of photometry, namely, to specify general levels of light intensity in a manner that takes into account the spectral sensitivity of the human eye. But if a subject's photometric judgments are to be used for psychophysical studies of visual performance for lights of different spectral composition, then it is usually necessary to determine the subject's own photopic luminous efficiency function.

that detect differences in luminance, since the absence of a measurable contribution from S cones need not imply that S cones fail to contribute to these pathways.

Horizontal cells

HI horizontal cells receive only from M and L cones, and act upon both of them according to their summed contributions. The full spectral sensitivity function of HI cells has yet to be determined, but what measurements have been made are consistent with the photopic luminous efficiency function. Let us assume this to be the case, and investigate the consequences.

Consider a minimally distinct border:

minimally distinct

Whenever we view a border, it is not held stationary on the retina, but moves about as a result of residual eye movements. As the border moves across the array of photoreceptors, the photon catch rate of L cones will fall and that of M cones will rise. But to the degree that the summed contributions of the M and L cones to the array of HI horizontal cells are weighted in the same manner as for their relative contributions to the photopic luminous efficiency function, the HI cells will be minimally stimulated by the movement of this border:

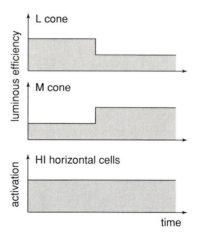

The question of whether the array of HI cells produces a residual response to the movement of this border hinges upon whether the time courses of the responses of M and L cones to increments and decrements in their photon catch rates are similar and symmetrical. Any variation resulting from random distributions of M and L cones should be relatively small because of the relatively large summation area of the HI array.

To the degree that the HI array produces little or no response to a minimally distinct border between spectrally distinct lights, it will also fail to respond to the other types of matches described in the Box OTHER MEASURES LEAD TO THE SAME PHOTOPIC LUMINOUS EFFICIENCY FUNCTION. All of these measures are based upon some minimization procedure, and thus characterize what one or more neural pathways *fail to respond to*. This leads to the notion of neural surfaces within CONE INPUT SPACE (page 425) .

 Cone input space *417*

The properties of HI horizontal cells are consistent with their being part of a neural pathway that fails to distinguish between equiluminant stimuli. By contrast, the dendrites of HII horizontal cells make sparse and occasional contacts with M and L cones, but provide all or almost all of the lateral elements in the pedicles of S cones. Thus HII horizontal cells can be expected to respond strongly to equiluminant stimuli, particularly those that vary according to the stimulation of the S cones.

Bipolar cells

Based upon the cones that they receive from, the bipolar cells that could potentially contribute to the photopic luminous efficiency function are those of the *midget* and the *diffuse* groups.

The foveal midget ganglion cells, which receive from individual midget bipolars, do not have a peak spectral sensitivity that corresponds to the photopic luminous efficiency function for the simple reason that each is dominated by the input from a single cone. These spectral sensitivities remain essentially unchanged up to the visual cortex. Because of their large number, it is at least theoretically possible that the photometric discriminations that observers make could be based upon an average of many midget ganglion cells. But selective destruction of the parvocellular laminae of the lateral geniculate nucleus leaves intensity discriminations unchanged, making this hypothesis unlikely.

The more likely candidates are a subset of the diffuse bipolar cells that appear to receive from both M and L cones. They receive from 5–10 L or M cones in an unselective manner; thus each diffuse bipolar cell has a variable ratio in the numbers of L and M cones they receive from. This variation may be reduced when a number of diffuse bipolar cells converge onto a ganglion cell.

Ganglion cells

Of the ganglion cells that send their messages to the visual cortex via the lateral geniculate nucleus, only the *parasol cells* appear to show a spectral sensitivity that approximates the luminous efficiency function. They appear to connect to all cone types in an indiscriminate manner via diffuse bipolars. The judgment of a minimally distinct border presumably occurs when the test and the reference light stimulate M and L cones so that their summed contributions onto parasol cells via diffuse bipolar cells are roughly equal. Thus as the image of the border passes across the receptive field of a parasol cell during eye movements, there is little or no change in the summed contributions of the L and M cones, and consequently little or no change in the output of the parasol cells. Similar comments apply to the other methods of determining the luminous efficiency function.

As discussed in THE CHASE (page 18), parasol cells in the central retina collect from about 20 L or M cones. They appear to do so indiscriminately, and in roughly equal numbers. Some receive from a few more L cones than M cones, and vice versa. When studied functionally, the test light intensity for a minimally distinct border varies slightly from parasol cell to parasol cell in terms of the response to, say, a moving border. Thus when observers minimize the distinctness or movement sensation of a border, they appear to be minimizing the responses of the population of parasol cells involved.

There may well be other ganglion cell types whose cone inputs are essentially the same as those of parasol cells. Indeed, as discussed in SEEING (page 344), the luminous efficiency function may be nothing more than an indiscriminate mixture of cone inputs. The issue at stake in photometry, however, is the particular mix, random or otherwise, that contributes to the judgments of luminance differences made by observers, and this necessarily focuses attention upon the ganglion cell types that contribute to the pathways from the retina to the visual cortex via the lateral geniculate nucleus.

Parasol cells respond to differences in luminance, not to luminance

All of the measurements discussed in this section are based upon attempts to equate two lights in terms of some criterion. Parasol cells, like most other types of ganglion cells, are generally insensitive to the *level* of light intensity. Instead, they respond to *differences* in the combined stimulation of the L and M cones. Although different light levels are expressed in terms of some photometric measure that is based upon the properties of the visual system, this does not imply that there exist neural mechanisms whose output depends upon luminance per se.

To summarize, in order to compare lights of different spectral composition in a physiologically meaningful way, photometry seeks judgments that are consistent in terms of additivity. This property allows the efficacy of photons of different frequencies to be computed and summarized in a luminous efficiency function. As it turns out, different methods lead to the same luminous efficiency function. That function, together with a radiometric measure of some light, such as spectral radiance, allows a corresponding photometric measure to be calculated that does not correspond to a measure based upon brightness differences, but in ordinary situations is not greatly different from it.

This description of photometry is qualitative in the sense that it deals with the nature of photometric measures, but is not directly concerned with the units in which these measures can be quantified. We now shift gears and present a more formal and quantitative description of photometry, which follows the corresponding quantitative development of RADIOMETRY.

Radiometry *499*

Quantitative description

Photometry began as an attempt to compare and scale the subjective brightness of different radiant sources. Originally experimental, it has evolved into a set of rules and definitions able to support government regulations and contract law. As discussed in the previous section, its intent is to combine some standard luminous efficiency function with a spectral distribution of light, as specified in radiometric terms, so as to yield a single number that reflects some physiological feature of the visual system with respect to spectrally different lights.

Mesopic photometry

Away from the fovea, there is a range of light intensities over which both rods and cones simultaneously contribute to photometric judgments. This is termed the **mesopic range.** Additivity can still be made to hold so that photometric measures can still be defined. The resulting luminous efficiency function approaches the scotopic curve at the lower end of the mesopic intensity range and the photopic curve at the higher end.

Parasol ganglion cells are capable of doing this, and there is no evidence to suggest that mesopic photometry requires additional cell types. Assuming that mesopic photometry is entirely based upon the activities of parasol cells, the shift in luminous efficiency function over the mesopic range provides an indirect description of the relative contributions of rod and cone inputs to these cells as a function of light intensity.

Lumens

A **lumen (lm)** is defined as a *radiant flux* of 4.09×10^{15} photons/s at a frequency of 540 THz. There is no particular significance to either of these values; they were chosen to be consistent with earlier definitions and systems of units that date back to the use of a candle as a standard in the nineteenth century. This physical standard is termed the **reference lumen**, in order to distinguish it from the measurements made by human observers that allow other spectral lights to be converted to lumens.

Units

The basic measure upon which photometry is conventionally based uses a unit of lumens/steradian (i.e., per *solid angle*; see ANGLES), which is termed the **candela.** Here, photometry is developed in terms of lumens rather than candelas because of the simple relation between photons and lumens and the tangible nature of the measures derived from it. Consistent with the rest of this book, spectral distributions are based upon the rate of photons as a function of their frequencies. The historical convention has been to use units of energy instead of photons and to express their spectral distribution in terms of defined wavelength rather than frequency. Conversions between photon/frequency and energy/wavelength units are described in WAVE-LENGTH AND ENERGY.

Angles *368*

Wavelength & Energy *513*

Photometric measures

For each of the measures of *radiometry,* there is a corresponding measure in photometry:

Spectral radiometric measure			**Spectral photometric measure**		
Radiant flux	$\phi_n(v)$	photon/s/Hz	Luminous flux	ϕ_v	lm
Irradiance	$E_n(v)$	photon/s/m²/Hz	Illuminance	E_v	lm/m²
Emittance	$M_n(v)$	photon/s/m²/Hz	Luminous emittance	M_v	lm/m²
Radiant intensity	$I_n(v)$	photon/s/sr/Hz	Luminous intensity	I_v	lm/sr
Radiance	$L_n(v)$	photon/s/m²/sr/Hz	Luminance	L_v	lm/m²/sr

By convention, each of the photometric measures is given the subscript v (vision) to distinguish it from the corresponding photon (n) and energy (e) measures of radiometry. Photometry also defines two spectral sensitivity functions, the **scotopic luminous efficiency function,** $V'_n(v)$ and the **photopic luminous efficiency function,** $V_n(v)$.

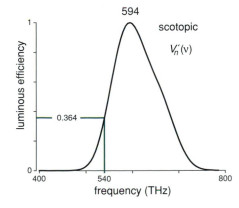

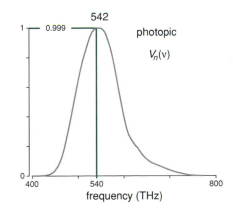

The convention in photometry is to use the prime symbol (') to distinguish the scotopic function from the photopic one. As in the radiometric measures, the subscript n is used to indicate that these curves are based upon the sensitivity of photoreceptors to a certain rate of photons. The manner in which these luminous efficiency functions were arrived at is described in the previous section. The photopic function is for foveal vision and thus includes the effect of the macular pigment.

The convention in photometry is to set the peak value of each luminous efficiency function to 1. This means that an additional conversion factor is needed to convert a radiometric measure, based upon photons per second, into a photometric one based upon lumens. The photopic factor in photon units is given the symbol K_n and the scotopic factor K_n'. Thus, for a spectral light at any particular frequency:

$$\text{photopic photometric measure} = K_n \times \text{radiometric measure} \\ \times \text{photopic luminous efficiency}$$

and

$$\text{scotopic photometric measure} = K_n' \times \text{radiometric measure} \\ \times \text{scotopic luminous efficiency}$$

These two factors can be determined in terms of the reference lumen and the corresponding luminous efficiency function. The physical specification of the reference lumen is 4.09×10^{15} photon/s at 540 THz, and is thus independent of photopic or scotopic measures. The luminous efficiencies at this frequency are shown in the diagram on page 463. Hence,

$$1 \text{ lm} = K_n \times 4.09 \times 10^{15} \text{ photon/s} \times 0.999$$

$$1 \text{ lm} = K_n' \times 4.09 \times 10^{15} \text{ photon/s} \times 0.364$$

or

$$K_n = 2.45 \times 10^{-16} \text{ lm s/photon}$$

$$K_n' = 6.72 \times 10^{-16} \text{ lm s/photon}$$

The relation between the incremental photopic luminance, ΔL_v, and the radiance, $L_n(v)$, for photons over some narrow frequency interval Δv is:

$$\Delta L_v = K_n V_n(v) L_n(v) \Delta v$$

The total photopic luminance is found by summing all of the incremental values:

$$L_v = \Sigma \Delta L_v(v) \\ = K_n \Sigma V_n(v) L_n(v) \Delta v$$

Similar relations associate each radiometric measure with the corresponding photometric one:

Luminous flux: $\qquad \phi_v = K_n \Sigma V_n(v)\phi_n(v)\Delta v$

Illuminance: $\qquad E_v = K_n \Sigma V_n(v) E_n(v)\Delta v$

Luminous emittance: $\qquad M_v = K_n \Sigma V_n(v) M_n(v)\Delta v$

Luminous intensity: $\qquad I_v = K_n \Sigma V_n(v) I_n(v)\Delta v$

with similar relations for the scotopic luminance:

$$L_v' = K_n' \sum V_n'(v) L_n(v) \Delta v$$

and so forth.

These relations are sometimes expressed in terms of an integration operation, $\int$, rather than an incremental summation, Σ. This formalistic refinement has no practical meaning, as the luminous efficiency functions are based upon judgments by observers that were made at a limited number of frequencies and exist only in tabulated form.

Intensity of the retinal image

In one way or the other, we are finally interested in the rate at which the visual pigment molecules within photoreceptors are being photoisomerized by the photons that fall upon them. This section describes how to convert radiometric and photometric quantities into the rain of photons onto photoreceptors in the eye. The rate of photoisomerizations produced by this rain is discussed in PHOTON CATCH RATE. The radiometric measure is discussed first, since the photometric measure follows from it.

Photon catch rate *471*

Radiometric intensity of the retinal image

As you might expect, the intensity of some small portion of the retinal image depends upon both the intensity of the light coming from the corresponding portion of an object and the size of the pupil. Further, it must be the area of the pupil, rather than its diameter, that governs how much light will be able to enter the eye. Doubling either the light intensity from the object or the area of the pupil should double the intensity of the image, so image intensity must be proportional to the product of these two factors.

The irradiance of the retinal image can be calculated from the following equation, which is derived below:

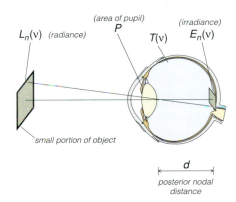

$$E_n(v) = \frac{T(v)PL_n(v)}{d^2} \text{ (photon/s/m}^2\text{/Hz)}$$

where:

$L_n(v)$ is the spectral radiance of the object (photon/s/m^2/sr/Hz)

$E_n(v)$ is the spectral irradiance of the retinal image of the object (photon/s/m^2/Hz)

$T(v)$ is the direct spectral transmittance of the ocular media of the eye (this factor includes light losses due to absorption and to scattering, and is dimensionless)

P is the area of the pupil (m^2)

d is the distance from the nodal point of the eye to the photoreceptors, termed the posterior nodal distance (m).

In the absence of light losses in the atmosphere, the retinal irradiance does not depend upon the distance of the object from the eye. This is in accord with common observation: If mountains do get dimmer with increasing distance, it is because of intervening haze or other factors that attenuate the light passing through the atmosphere. The direct spectral transmittance of the ocular media is discussed in THE RAIN OF PHOTONS ONTO CONES (page 73). In general, both light scattering and light absorption increase with increasing photon frequency. Scattering is due mainly to the cornea, lens, and vitreous humor; absorption is due mainly to the lens and the macula lutea. The posterior nodal distance, *d,* is equivalent to the focal length of a camera, and determines the size of the image. For the standard observer described in Appendix B, viewing a distant object, it is 16.1 mm. This value changes slightly with viewing distance for any particular eye. Furthermore, it increases with age during childhood, and varies from person to person. Photometry ignores these differences, in part because it seeks to characterize the light coming from objects in the external world. The "retinal illuminance" is thus considered to depend only on the product of the luminance of the object and the area of the pupil; all other aspects of a real eye are based upon standard values. The pupil size refers to the entrance pupil, meaning the size of the pupil observed when looking into an eye. The entrance pupil is slightly larger than the true diameter of the pupil because of the magnifying effect of the cornea.

Photometric intensity of the retinal image

The photometric specification of the intensity of the retinal image is

$$E_{\mathrm{v}} = \frac{PL_{\mathrm{v}}}{d^2} \ (\mathrm{lm/m^2})$$

where

L_{v} is the luminance of the object ($\mathrm{lm/m^2/sr}$)

E_{v} is the intensity of the retinal image of the object ($\mathrm{lm/m^2}$):

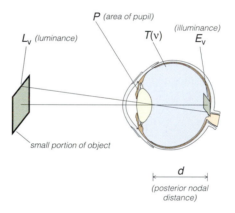

The photometric equation is similar to the radiometric one, but does not include the spectral transmittance term because this term has already been included in the specification of the luminance term, L_{v}. This is a subtle point, best explained by naively attempting to convert the radiometric specification on the previous page to a photometric one:

$$E_{\mathrm{v}} = K_n \sum E_{\mathrm{v}}(v)\Delta v = \frac{P}{d^2} K_n \sum T(v) V_n(v) L_{\mathrm{v}}(v)\Delta v \ \ (\mathrm{Invalid})$$

The problem lies with $[T(v)V_n(v)]$, because $V_n(v)$ is the sensitivity of the *eye* to photons of different frequencies, and thus already includes the transmittance of the ocular media, $T(v)$. This equation implies that *another eye*, with its own

Derivation of retinal irradiance

This derivation consists of two steps. The first expresses the size of the retinal image of a small portion of the viewed object; the second expresses the amount of light from that small portion that enters the eye and reaches the photoreceptors. In the ratio of these two expressions, the area of the small portion of the object disappears, leaving the retinal irradiance.

Step 1: Image size

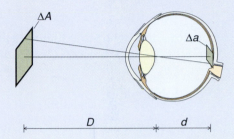

where:

ΔA is the area of some small portion of an object; for simplicity, this portion is assumed to be viewed face on, as shown

D is the distance from this portion of the object to the nodal point of the eye

Δa is the area of the retinal image of ΔA

d is the posterior nodal distance, as above

By a simple consideration of proportions, as applied to areas, we have

$$\frac{\Delta a}{\Delta A} = \left(\frac{d}{D}\right)^2$$

which can be rearranged as

$$\frac{\Delta a}{d^2} = \frac{\Delta A}{D^2}$$

In words, the solid angle to the small area of the object is equal to the solid angle of its image on the retina.

Step 2: Amount of light entering the eye

Light from the small portion of the object, ΔA, radiates in all directions; our concern lies with the cone of light that

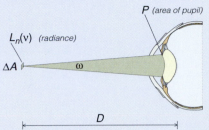

encounters the eye and enters the pupil. The **spectral radiance**, $L_n(\nu)$, is the radiometric measure of light intensity defined by this situation. It can be expressed as the spectral radiant flux $\phi_n(\nu)$ per unit of area per steradian. The area refers to the source, and the steradian to the solid angle of the receiver from a point on the source. In this situation, the area is ΔA, and the solid angle is effectively equal to P/D^2. Hence the **spectral radiant flux, $\phi_n(\nu)$**, entering the eye is

$$\phi_n(\nu) = L_n(\nu)\Delta A \frac{P}{D^2} \text{ (photon/s/Hz)}$$

As noted above, from the nodal point, the solid angle to the portion of the object, $\Delta A/D^2$, is equal to the solid angle to its image, $\Delta a/d^2$. Substituting,

$$\phi_n(\nu) = L_n(\nu)\Delta a \frac{P}{d^2} \text{ (photon/s/Hz)}$$

This equation expresses the light flux *entering the eye* in terms of the spectral radiance of the object, $L_n(\nu)$, and three terms associated with the eye itself. The light flux reaching the photoreceptors within the image of the small portion of the object is found by multiplying this flux by the spectral transmittance of the ocular media, $T(\nu)$:

$$\phi_n(\nu) = \Delta a \frac{T(\nu)L_n(\nu)P}{d^2} \text{ (photon/s/Hz)}$$

This is the light flux falling upon the retinal image, whose area is Δa. Dividing both sides of this equation by Δa gives the **spectral irradiance** of the retinal image:

$$E_n(\nu) = \frac{T(\nu)PL_n(\nu)}{d^2} \text{ (photon/s/m}^2\text{/Hz)}$$

ocular losses, would have to be placed at the retinal surface. In effect, *there is no photometric specification for light once it has entered the eye.* For this reason, E_v is characterized as the *intensity* of the retinal image (lm/m^2) with reference to light *incident upon the eye* from an object of luminance L_v:

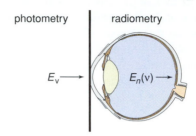

photometry　　　　radiometry

$E_v \longrightarrow$　　　$E_n(v) \longrightarrow$

Trolands

A **troland (td)** captures the two factors that determine the intensity of the retinal image: the intensity of the light from the object (L_v), and the size of the pupil (P). By definition,

$$T_v = 10^6 P L_v \text{ (photopic td)}$$

$$T'_v = 10^6 P L'_v \text{ (scotopic td)}$$

An equivalent definition is the product of the luminance and the pupil area, as measured in mm^2 rather than m^2, which gets rid of the 10^6 factor. For example, a pupil with a diameter of 3 mm has an area of about 7 mm^2; for this pupil size, the value in trolands is equal to 7 times the luminance of the object.

When the pupil is large, cones are less sensitive to light entering the eye from the edge of the pupil than to light entering the center. This factor, termed the Stiles–Crawford effect (page 155), is not included in the definition of the photopic troland since it is not significant in daylight conditions in which the pupil is small.

Comparative photometry

Standard photometry is wedded to human vision via the spectral sensitivities of human cones, the transmittance of human ocular media—including a yellowish lens—and a particular weighting of the spectral sensitivities of the human M and L cones. Attempts to use our photometric system to characterize intensity differences or lighting conditions for other animals are fraught with pitfalls. For example, only in the last few years has it been recognized that many vertebrate species, including some rodents, have photoreceptors able to detect ultraviolet light that we cannot see.

It is probably advantageous to avoid photometric quantities altogether when describing visual stimuli presented to animals. If the stimulus is a spectral light, then a radiometric quantity (e.g., radiance) plus its frequency are sufficient. If the stimulus has a known spectral distribution, then this distribution, or the nature of the light source, can be specified. Then, even if light intensities are specified in photometric units, it is still possible to work backward to the spectral radiometric distribution.

---

troland

This measure is named after Leonard Thompson Troland (1889–1932), who devised it; its abbreviation is *td*. Troland (1916) had originally named this measure a *photon*, a word later used by Lewis (1918) to mean a particle of light. Both meanings persisted for a while, but Lewis's usage became more common, and in 1944 a committee that Troland had previously chaired renamed this unit in his honor.

It is nevertheless instructive to consider how a photometric measure might be devised for a given species. A *scotopic* specification is straightforward, provided that there is only one spectrally distinct rod type. A knowledge of the spectral absorbance of the rod visual pigment, together with the spectral transmittance of the ocular media, is all that is required. The K'_n value can then be determined from the calculated spectral sensitivity curve, just as for humans.

A *photopic* specification is more complicated only if, as usual, the retina contains more than one spectrally distinct type of cone. Three possible approaches to this situation come to mind.

The first, and most fundamental, is to determine by means of behavioral testing how the animal discriminates for minimally distinct borders, minimal flicker, and so on, just as for human observers. Provided additivity can be shown to hold, this approach would lead to a spectral luminous efficiency function for the species. Whether that would ever be worth doing is another issue.

Second, the retinas of most mammals contain two cone types, S cones and LM cones (page 217). Most mammals probably make photometric-like discriminations on the basis of their LM cones, which are in the majority. To the degree that this is true, a photometric system based upon the spectral sensitivity of these cones might be adequate, and might not be that different from the human system, at least over the lower portion of the frequency spectrum.

Third, a photopic photometric system for each cone type is also possible, yielding troland measures from which photon catch rates could be calculated, given the pupil size.

Photon catch rate

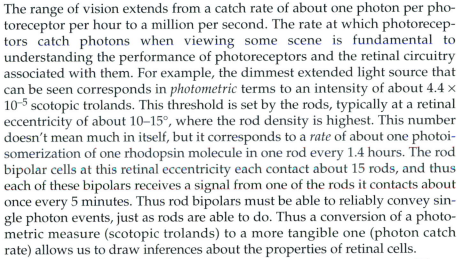

This topic discusses how to convert light intensities that are expressed in radiometric or photometric units into the rate at which a single rod or cone catches a photon that photoisomerizes a visual rhodopsin molecule.

Overview

The range of vision extends from a catch rate of about one photon per photoreceptor per hour to a million per second. The rate at which photoreceptors catch photons when viewing some scene is fundamental to understanding the performance of photoreceptors and the retinal circuitry associated with them. For example, the dimmest extended light source that can be seen corresponds in *photometric* terms to an intensity of about 4.4×10^{-5} scotopic trolands. This threshold is set by the rods, typically at a retinal eccentricity of about 10–15°, where the rod density is highest. This number doesn't mean much in itself, but it corresponds to a *rate* of about one photoisomerization of one rhodopsin molecule in one rod every 1.4 hours. The rod bipolar cells at this retinal eccentricity each contact about 15 rods, and thus each of these bipolars receives a signal from one of the rods it contacts about once every 5 minutes. Thus rod bipolars must be able to reliably convey single photon events, just as rods are able to do. Thus a conversion of a photometric measure (scotopic trolands) to a more tangible one (photon catch rate) allows us to draw inferences about the properties of retinal cells.

As previously explained (THE RAIN OF PHOTONS ONTO CONES, page 85), we are not concerned with the *absorption* of photons by rhodopsin molecules per se, but only with those absorbed photons that successfully *photoisomerize* the chromophore of a rhodopsin molecule from the 11-*cis* to the all-*trans* form. This happens to two-thirds of the photons absorbed by rhodopsin molecules, apparently independent of their frequency. Once photoisomerization occurs, we can ignore what produced it and concentrate on its consequences. Thus the rate of photoisomerizations ("catch rate") forms a natural boundary between the *physical events* that lead up to them and the *physiological events* that follow from them.

We will first consider the fraction of photons entering the outer segment that are absorbed when the frequency of the photons corresponds to the peak sensitivity of the rhodopsin molecules contained in the outer segment. This value is converted to photoisomerizations. Next the transmittance of the ocular media and of the macula are used to determine the fraction of photons caught that enter the eye. The size of the pupil is taken into account by converting to troland units. Finally, the area of the photoreceptor inner segment is used to calculate the photon catch rate per photoreceptor.

Peak absorptance and photoisomerizations by outer segments

The values of peak absorptance in the table at the top of the next page refer to the fraction of photons *entering the outer segment* that are absorbed.

Photometry *453*

---

transmittance, absorptance, absorbance, absorptivity
These terms are defined and discussed in LIGHT ABSORPTION. Each is a value that varies as a function of frequency. Briefly:

Transmittance is the fraction of light that is not absorbed when passing through some absorbing material.

Absorptance is the fraction of the light absorbed when passing through some absorbing material.

Absorbance, also termed *optical density*, is an intrinsic factor that characterizes the light-absorbing properties of some absorbing material.

Absorptivity is the absorbance per unit length.

Light absorption *443*

Peak absorptance of photoreceptors

Photoreceptor	Frequency (THz)	Outer segment length (mm)	Absorptance (%)	Eccentricity (deg)
Rod	601	31	66	~10
L cone	550	33	68	0
M cone	570	33	68	0
S cone	719	33	68	0

Each photoreceptor thus absorbs approximately two-thirds of the photons to which it is most sensitive. This table is based upon the assumption that the peak absorptivity of each of these photoreceptors is 0.015/μm, which agrees with measurements to within experimental error. However, certain theoretical considerations lead to the prediction that peak absorbance should vary inversely with peak frequency, and thus give L cones the highest peak absorptivity. S cone *inner* segments are slightly longer than those of M and L cones (page 217), suggesting that their *outer* segments may be smaller than those of the M or L cones; quantitative data is lacking, however, and this factor is ignored here.

Only about two-thirds of the photons caught by a visual pigment molecule result in the photoisomerization of its chromophore (*catch*). Combining this figure with the peak absorptance yields a peak catch of about 45%:

Peak photoisomerization of photoreceptors

Photoreceptor	Frequency (THz)	Photoisomerizations (%)	Eccentricity (deg)
Rod	601	44	~10
L cone	550	46	0
M cone	570	46	0
S cone	719	46	0

Peak absorptance and photoisomerizations for photoreceptors in the eye

As described in THE RAIN OF PHOTONS ONTO CONES (page 77), when we view a natural scene, only a fraction of the photons that encounter the cornea reach the retinal surface. The transmittance of the ocular media falls as the frequency of the photons rises, so that the photoreceptors that are sensitive to higher-frequency photons receive a smaller fraction of the incident photons at those frequencies, as shown below. This curve shows the *direct* ocular transmittance, which does not include scattered light. At their peak sensitivi-

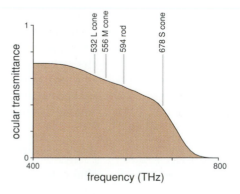

ties for light entering the eye, the L cones receive about 62% of the incident photons, whereas the S cones receive only 38%. The losses at low frequencies are due mainly to light scattering, particularly by the cornea, whereas those at high frequencies are due mainly to light absorption, mainly by the lens. These ocular losses apply to all retinal regions.

In the fovea, the macular pigment within the retina absorbs photons in the blue region of the spectrum:

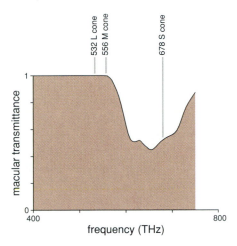

This pigment is concentrated in the fovea, but is found at lower concentrations throughout the retina. Combining these factors gives the following figures:

Peak absorbance with reference to light entering the eye

Photoreceptor	Frequency (THz)	Ocular transmission (%)	Macular transmission (%)	Photoisomerizations (%)	Eccentricity (deg)
Rod	594	54	—	23	~10
L cone	532	62	100	27	0
M cone	556	59	100	26	0
S cone	678	38	52	7	0

The spectral transmittance of the ocular media and macular pigment exerts two effects. First, and most directly, it reduces the number of photons that reach the photoreceptors, as indicated in the table. The second effect involves the *variation* in transmittance with frequency, which shifts the peak sensitivity for photons entering the eye with respect to the peak sensitivity for photons entering the outer segment. Because the ocular media absorb more photons at higher frequencies, the peak sensitivity shifts to a lower frequency. For example, the L cone peak shifts from 550 THz to a rather broad peak at 532 THz, a change of 18 THz. The magnitude of the shift depends upon the rate of the change and thus upon the slope of the curve of ocular transmittance. For S cones, the shift is from 719 THz to 678 THz, a change of 41 THz. Because of this change, the peak frequency of light entering the eye lies at a lower frequency than the absorptance peak of the outer segments. This effect is minor for rods, M cones, and L cones, but reduces the S cone catch by an additional factor of 73% of the uncorrected value. The combination of these factors reduces the photon catch of S cones to about 28% of the average of the L and M cones.

The values in these tables give the percentage of photons caught at the frequency to which each photoreceptor type is most sensitive. This is interesting to know, but the light presented to any small portion of the retina has the same spectral distribution for all the photoreceptors. The question thus arises as to how the different photoreceptor types perform under more natural conditions.

Relative photon catch rates in the natural world

Let us consider a white surface viewed in average daylight:

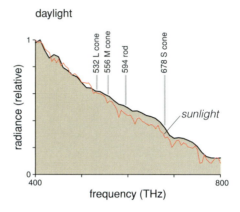

Daylight is a combination of direct sunlight and scattered light, primarily from the sky. Direct sunlight, represented by a red line, is included for reference, but there is not much difference between the two curves, except at high frequencies, where the radiance of daylight is made larger by the contribution of the blue sky. The intensity is not important, provided that it is not so bright as to reduce the concentration of visual pigment in the outer segment (see page 155). Setting the L cone catch to 100% gives:

Photoreceptor	Frequency (THz)	Photon catch in daylight (%)	Eccentricity (deg)
L cone	532	100	0
M cone	556	76	0
Rod	594	65	~10
S cone	678	10	~0

In order to make these calculations, it is necessary to include the effective cross-sectional area over which photons will be channeled through the outer segments. This factor, discussed later, is approximately the same for each of the photoreceptor types at the retinal eccentricities specified. The differences between the photoreceptor types are accounted for mainly by the decreases in both ocular transmittance and spectral radiance with increasing frequency. The S cone catch is thereby reduced to only 10% of the L cone catch.

Photon catch rates per troland

The following values are based upon the reference lumen of PHOTOMETRY, which consists of photons at a frequency of 540 THz. Since all of the photoreceptors are receiving photons at 540 THz, the effect of ocular transmit-

Photometry *453*

troland

A troland (td) is a photometric measure that characterizes the intensity of the retinal image of some portion of the external world. It is equal to the product of the luminance of an object times the area of the pupil, in square millimeters (see page 468).

tance is the same for all. Further, at this frequency, the macular pigmentation does not absorb photons:

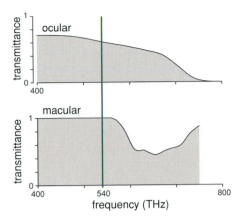

The resulting table is similar in some respects to the previous one, except that the radiant source is not daylight, but photons of a single frequency, and the scale is absolute rather than relative. For reasons discussed later in this section, the effective catchment region of a photoreceptor is approximated by the cross-sectional area of its inner segment:

Photoreceptor	Frequency (THz)	IS area (μm^2)	Catch rate (photon/s/td)	Eccentricity (deg)
L cone	532	4.15	18.3	0
M cone	556	4.15	15.9	0
Rod	594	3.64	4.6	~10
S cone	678	4.15	0.005	~0

The variation among cones is due entirely to their different spectral sensitivities to photons at 540 THz:

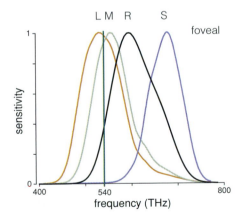

The photon catch for the rods is reduced mainly by their lower sensitivity at 540 THz, but includes an additional factor of 0.88 because of their smaller catchment area relative to the cones.

Many observations of visual performance are based upon photometric measures. Thus the conversion of a photometric measure to photoreceptor catch rates has practical importance, despite the fact that it has little direct relevance to retinal function per se.

Photometry is internally consistent, but the rates at which photoreceptors catch photons are not reflected in this system. Photometry favors photopic over scotopic vision by choosing photons to which the L and M cones are most sensitive to define its reference physical source. Both photopic and scotopic photometry must agree when viewing this physical source. But at 540 THz, rods catch fewer photons than do cones, mainly because of their lower spectral sensitivity at this frequency. Had photometry been based upon photons at 600 Hz, the photon catch per troland for rods would then exceed that for L or M cones. Likewise, had the physical source been composed of photons at a frequency of 680 Hz, then S cones would have shown the highest rate of photon catch rate per troland.

To summarize, the choice of the reference physical source in photometry has a strong effect upon the relative rates at which the different photoreceptor types catch photons per troland. Thus a photometric comparison of catch rates *between* photoreceptor types other than the L and M cones is essentially meaningless.

Within photometry it is further necessary to distinguish three groups: rods, M and L cones, and S cones.

For rods, the scotopic luminous efficiency function is simply the rod absorptance curve for light presented to the eye, normalized to give a peak value of 1. Consequently, two spectrally distinct lights that are equivalent in terms of *scotopic* trolands necessarily produce the same photon catch rate for rods, and thus cannot be distinguished from one another when viewing only with the rods.

The photopic luminous efficiency function differs from the spectral sensitivity curve of either the M or the L cones. Because of this, two spectrally distinct lights that are equivalent in terms of *photopic* trolands will not, in general, produce the same photon catch rate for either the M or the L cones. Indeed, the perception of color is based upon exploiting just this difference. Nevertheless, as discussed below, most spectral radiances in nature are rather broad, and the values listed in the table can generally serve as useful approximations of the photon catch rates of these cone types. When retinal illumination is specified only in terms of photopic trolands, we have no other choice.

S cones operate at photopic levels, but their spectral sensitivity varies greatly from the photopic luminous efficiency function. The fact that two spectrally distinct lights are equivalent in terms of photopic trolands says virtually nothing about the photon catch rates of S cones. Consequently, the value given in the table on page 475 has no practical application.

We now change pace and provide some quantitative examples of how the values in the above tables were obtained.

Maximum fraction of photons caught by rods

In terms of light entering the eye, rods show a peak sensitivity at 594 THz (left). At this frequency, about 46% of the photons entering the eye are either scattered or absorbed before reaching the retina, leaving 54% to enter the retina, as shown in the diagram at the top of the facing page. The spectral absorptance of the rods is expressed in terms of the light presented to their outer segments, rather than to the eye, as in the diagram at left, and has a peak of 601 THz. The slight difference of this peak from the peak sensitivity for light entering the eye comes about because of the fall in ocular transmittance with increasing frequency, as previously described. The absorptance at 594 THz is 98% of the peak value for rod absorptance.

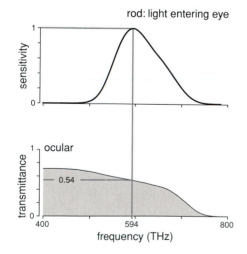

The maximum fraction of the photons entering the eye and passing through the outer segment that are *absorbed* is thus the product of the ocular transmittance and the absorptance of the rods at 594 THz:

$$\text{fraction absorbed} = 0.54 \times 0.66 \times 0.98 = 0.35$$

But, as noted above, only about two-thirds of the absorbed photos photoisomerize the rhodopsin molecule, and thereby initiate the phototransduction cascade. Thus, the fraction that photoisomerize a visual pigment molecule is:

$$0.35 \times 0.67 = 0.235$$

The fractions for the other photoreceptor types listed in the table on page 473 were calculated in the same manner, using the values in Appendix B.

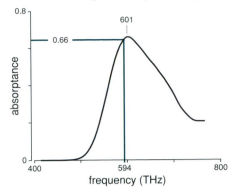

rod: light entering outer segment

Photoisomerization rate of rods per troland

Were it not for the fact that much useful data on vision is expressed in photometric terms, this section would be an empty exercise. The situation for rods is the simplest, as the scotopic luminous efficiency function is simply the spectral sensitivity of rods in the eye. This means that the value calculated for rods is independent of the spectral distribution of the light.

Since any spectral distribution of light will serve, we have the opportunity of choosing one that is convenient on other grounds. The most convenient one proves to be the radiometric definition of a lumen, which is a radiant flux of 4.09×10^{15} photon/s at a frequency of 540 THz. For this light source, the distinction between photopic and scotopic photometric quantities is abolished. As an added benefit, at this frequency, the absorptance of macular pigment is effectively zero, which removes regional variation prior to the light encountering the photoreceptors. Finally, using the reference lumen allows the catch rate to be calculated by means of either radiometry or photometry. Here we do it both ways.

Radiometric approach to photon catch rate

A troland (td) is defined in PHOTOMETRY as:

$$T_v = 10^6 P L_v$$

Photometry *453*

where
L_v is the *luminance* of the object (lm/m²/sr)
P is the area of the pupil (m²).
For the reference lumen, at 540 THz, there are 4.09×10^{15} photon/s for each lumen. Hence the radiance of the object must be

$$L_n = 4.09 \times 10^{15} L_v \ (\text{photon/s/m}^2/\text{sr})$$

The irradiance of the retinal image is described by the following equation, which is derived in PHOTOMETRY on page 467:

$$E_n = \frac{t P L_n}{d^2} \ (\text{photon/s/m}^2)$$

where
L_n is the spectral radiance of the object (photon/s/m²/sr)
E_n is the spectral irradiance of its retinal image (photon/s/m²)
t is the direct spectral transmittance of the ocular media
P is the area of the pupil (m²)
d is the posterior nodal distance of the eye (m).

Dividing the irradiance by the magnitude of a troland gives the retinal irradiance per troland:

$$\frac{E_n}{T_v} = \frac{tPL_n}{10^6 d^2 PL_v} = \frac{4.09 \times 10^{15} tL_v}{10^6 d^2 L_v} = 4.09 \times 10^9 \frac{t}{d^2}$$

The ocular transmittance, t, at 540 THz is 0.61, and the posterior nodal distance, d, is 0.161 m:

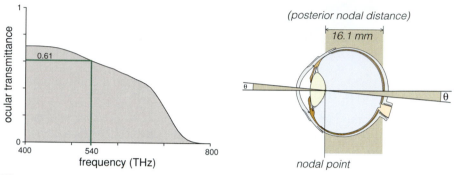

Hence,

retinal irradiance per troland = 9.67×10^{12} (photon/s/m²/td)

This is a useful reference value, which, except for definitions, depends only on the estimates of the direct ocular transmittance at the reference frequency and the posterior nodal distance of the eye. It is thus applicable to all photoreceptor types.

The next step is to consider the rate at which the photons that reach the retina pass through a rod outer segment. This is a somewhat tricky optical issue because of the differences in the refractive indices of the components of the rod, the extracellular space, and the adjacent cells, as well as the small size of some of these components. Because of the refractive difference, light passing through the rod inner segment tends to be funneled into the outer segment. Thus the *effective catchment area* of the *outer* segment is probably approximated by the cross-sectional area of the *inner* segment. Rods at an eccentricity of 10° have an inner segment diameter of about 2.15 μm, and thus a cross-sectional area of 3.64×10^{-12} m². Multiplying this value by the retinal irradiance gives:

rate of photons entering outer segment = 35.1 (photon/s/td/rod)

The rate at which these photons will be absorbed depends upon the spectral absorptance of the rods for light passing through their outer segments:

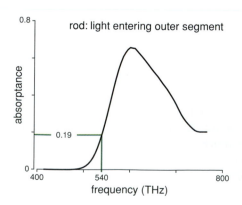

About 19.4% of the photons at this frequency will be absorbed. Consequently,

$$\text{rate of absorption} = 0.194 \times 35.1 = 6.83 \text{ (photon/s/td/rod)}$$

Finally, quantum efficiency for photoisomerization is 0.67.

$$\text{rate of photoisomerization} = 6.83 \times 0.67 = 4.57 \text{ (photon/s/td/rod)}$$

Three critical factors that are specific to rods enter into this calculation. One is the cross-sectional area of the inner segment; a change in this value of about 10% is sufficient to change this value by 1 photon/s. Second and third, the rod spectral absorptance is set by the peak absorptance of the outer segments, and by the frequency of this peak. It would take a 22% change in the peak absorptance, or a 28 THz decrease in the peak frequency, to produce a change of 1 photon/s/td.

Photometric approach to photon catch rate

The scotopic photometric intensity of the retinal image, as derived in PHOTOMETRY, is:

$$E'_v = \frac{PL'_v}{d^2} \text{ (lm/m}^2)$$

Photometry 453

where

L'_v is the scotopic luminance of the object (lm/m^2/sr)
E'_v is the scotopic intensity of the retinal image of the object (lm/m^2).
Dividing by the scotopic troland:

$$\frac{E'_n}{T'_v} = \frac{PL'_v}{10^6 d^2 PL'_v} = \frac{1}{10^6 d^2} = 3.87 \times 10^{-3} \text{ (lm/m}^2\text{/td)}$$

This is the scotopic retinal intensity, and it is about as far as one can go within photometry. For reasons discussed in PHOTOMETRY (page 466), in order to get into the eye, it is necessary to step outside of photometry by converting from the unit of scotopic luminous flux, ϕ'_v (lm), to that of radiant flux, ϕ'_n (photon/s), at some frequency v. By definition,

$$\phi'_v = K'_v \phi'_n(v) V'_n(v) \text{ (lm)}$$

where K'_v is the scotopic conversion factor (6.72 × 10^{-16} lm s/photon), hence the ratio of radiant flux to scotopic luminous flux is:

$$\frac{\phi'_n(v)}{\phi'_v} = \frac{1}{K'_v V'_n(v)} \text{ (photon/s/lm)}$$

which yields:

$$\frac{E'_n(v)}{T'_v} = \frac{3.89 \times 10^{-3}}{K'_v V'_n(v)} = \frac{5.79 \times 10^{12}}{V'_n(v)} \text{ (photon/s/m}^2\text{/td)}$$

This is the value of the retinal irradiance at frequency v for each troland. Within scotopic photometry, one can choose any frequency and determine the value of the irradiance necessary to produce the same photon catch. Because the direct transmittance of the ocular media is already factored into the scotopic luminous efficiency function, $V'_n(v)$, it does not appear directly in this equation. The smallest value of the irradiance occurs at the frequency to which rods are most sensitive, 594 THz, where $V'_n(594) = 1$. At any other frequency, more photons are required to produce the same photon catch.

For the reference lumen at 540 THz, $V'_n(540) = 0.364$, so that:

$$\frac{E'_n(v)}{T'_v} = \frac{5.74 \times 10^{12}}{0.364} = 15.7 \times 10^{12} \text{ (photon/s/m}^2\text{/td)}$$

This is the retinal intensity *as presented to the eye*, which, as noted above, is as far as photometry can go. In order to obtain the intensity at the level of the retina itself, it is necessary to include the ocular transmittance at 540 THz, which is 0.61, as described in the previous section. Hence,

$$\text{retinal intensity} = 0.61 \times 15.7 \times 10^{12} = 9.67 \times 10^{12} \text{ photon/s/m}^2/\text{td}$$

This is the same value as obtained via the radiometric approach, and the remaining calculations are thus identical. The photometric approach introduces nothing new, at least at 540 THz, but it does serve to illustrate the relationships between the two approaches.

Photoisomerization rate of cones per troland

Here we consider only foveal cones. With increasing eccentricity there is a considerable increase in the cross-sectional area of the cone inner segments, which increases their photon catch rates by a factor of ten or more compared with the values for foveal cones discussed here. A complication for foveal cones is that their outer segments may be as small as 1 μm across. This is about the size at which photons can undergo a complex resonance with their surroundings, which in classic optics is termed a "wave-guide mode." The magnitude of this effect is difficult to estimate, and it is ignored here. Otherwise, the calculations of these rates for the three cone types are identical to those listed in the table on page 475, part of which is reproduced here for convenience.

Photoreceptor	Frequency (THz)	Catch rate (photon/s/td)	Eccentricity (deg)
Rod	594	4.6	~10
L cone	532	18.3	0
M cone	556	15.9	0

The S cones are not included because, as noted earlier, their spectral sensitivity is so low at the frequency of the reference lumen as to make such a measure meaningless.

We change pace once again and consider quantitatively two issues discussed in a qualitative way at the beginning of this topic. The first is the lower photon catch rate per troland for rods than for L or M cones. Earlier it was stated that this is primarily a consequence of the lower absorptance of rods compared with cones for photons at 540 THz. But it might be proposed that photometry should have already taken this difference into account. It has, but in the form of developing what is essentially a separate measure for scotopic photometry. The other issue concerns variations in the photon catch of M and L cones when retinal illuminance, expressed in photopic trolands, remains constant.

Comparison of scotopic and photopic catch rates

One means of disentangling photometry from photon catch rates is to consider a light consisting of photons at a frequency of 571 THz, for which the photopic and scotopic sensitivities are equal (left). The ratio of scotopic to photopic trolands is then easy to calculate. By definition,

$$T_v' = 10^6 P L_v' \text{ (scotopic td)}$$

$$T_v = 10^6 P L_v \text{ (photopic td)}$$

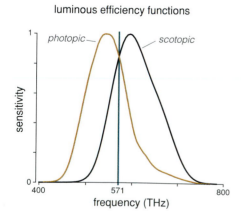

luminous efficiency functions

photopic   scotopic

sensitivity

400   571   800
frequency (THz)

hence,

$$\frac{T'_v}{T_v} = \frac{10^6 P L'_v}{10^6 P L_v} = \frac{L'_v}{L_v} = \frac{K'_n L_n(v) V'(v)}{K_n L_n(v) V(v)} = \frac{K'_n V'(v)}{K_n V(v)}$$

But since we have chosen a frequency such that

$$V'(v) = V(v)$$

we have

$$T'_v = T_v \frac{K'_n}{K_n} = 2.48 T_v$$

When the spectral composition of a light source shows the same luminous efficiency for both photopic and scotopic vision, the number of scotopic trolands is about two and a half times greater than the number of photopic trolands. For this light source, the calculated photon catch rate for rods should be increased by this factor, which makes the rod photon catch rate roughly the same as that of the M and L cones.

From a broader perspective, the role of the reference lumen is to define the scaling factors K'_n and K_n, as suggested in the following diagram:

$$L_v = K_n \sum L_n(v) \, V(v) \, \Delta v$$

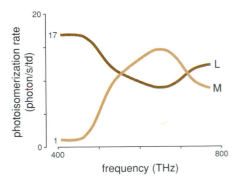

photometry | reference lumen | radiometry | observer

Interpreting M and L cone catch rates

Because the spectral sensitivity curves of the L and M cones within the eye do not match the photopic luminous efficiency function, spectrally distinct lights that have the same intensity in terms of photopic trolands will produce different photon catch rates for each of these cone types. The largest variations that can occur come from lights composed of photons of the same frequency. The variation in photon catch rate as a function of frequency is shown in this diagram:

There is considerable variation in the red-to-green region of the spectrum between 400 and 550 THz, and somewhat less at higher frequencies, where the differences between M and L cone spectral sensitivities are smaller. The curve for L cones is inverted with respect to the curve for M cones, and shows a smaller variation. This is a consequence of the fact that the photopic luminous efficiency curve reflects a mixture of the spectral sensitivities of the M and L cones, with L cones contributing more to the mixture than M cones. To the extent that the photopic luminous efficiency curve approximates the L cones, their photon catch would become flat in this diagram.

The diagram at the bottom of the last page shows extreme values; considerably smaller variations occur in the natural world. The following diagram shows the variation for natural objects, based upon standard daylight and the spectral reflectances of 338 different portions of the natural world, as recorded by Krinov (1947):

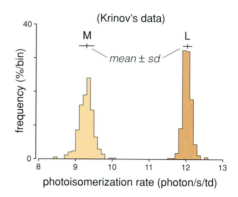

Just as for the previous diagram, a higher catch by the L cones implies a lower catch by the M cones. Ignoring the outliers, the range in photon catch for the L cones is only about 0.7 photon/s/td, or some 6%. The effective range for M cones is 2 times larger at 1.1 photon/s/td, or about 12%. The standard deviations are 0.12 (L) and 0.20 (M) photon/s/td, or variations on the order of about 1% for L cones and 2% for M cones. Considered as stimuli equated for luminance, these are the variations in photon catch produced by typical variations in the spectral composition of the natural world that the neural mechanisms for color must contend with.

We can find larger variations in the natural world if we go looking for them:

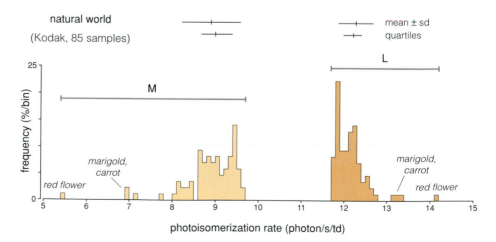

None of Krinov's samples of the natural world included animals, and the number of flowers was limited. Since many species of tropical fish, birds, and flowers are highly colored, the total range found in the natural world is greater than indicated by this diagram.

The synthetic dye industry extends the range even further for manufactured products:

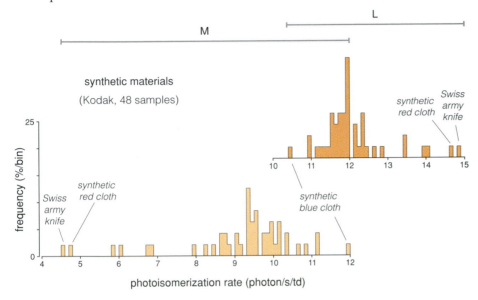

The largest difference in photon catch rates between L and M cones observed is 10.3 photon/s/td, for a dark red Swiss army knife. The maximum possible difference between these two cone types is about 16 photon/s/td, which is achieved with low-frequency photons, as shown in the earlier diagram of photon catch versus frequency (page 481). The fact that this largest difference corresponds to a *dark* color is a consequence of the notion of OPTIMAL COLORS. For either cone type, the mean photon catch in terms of photon/s/td cone for the above three diagrams remains virtually unchanged, but the standard deviation increases by a factor of 7.5. As noted above, this need not imply that the dye industry has bested nature in this regard.

Finally, we have been speaking only about objects viewed in standard daylight. Rainbows, sunsets, and other atmospheric phenomena can show L and M cone differences more like the earlier diagram (page 481) that plotted their photon catches per troland as a function of frequency.

Optimal colors *447*

Poisson distribution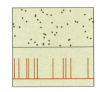

There are many seemingly random events in nature—the spatial pattern formed by raindrops on a flat surface, the arrival of photons at a photoreceptor outer segment, the opening and closing of an ionic channel in the membrane of a cell, or the emission of particles from a radioactive source. It is entirely unpredictable where or when each drop, photon, opening, or particle will occur. There is a predictability to the behavior of the group, however, which increases in accuracy as the number of drops, photons, openings, or particles increases. The boundary between total uncertainty and total certainty is thus soft. Although the objects considered are different, the underlying regularities in their group behavior are essentially identical. Random events come up frequently when considering how the retina works, and this topic provides the rudiments of a quantitative understanding of their collective properties.

Photons arrive randomly at the cornea of the eye, at the inner surface of the retina, or at the base of a photoreceptor outer segment. cG molecules also arrive randomly at the binding sites of cG-gated channels. It is no exaggeration to say that such random encounters typify the microscopic milieu that underlies much of the world and all of biology. Here we are mainly interested in random occurrences in either two-dimensional space or in the single dimension of time:

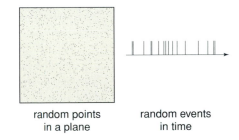

random points   random events
in a plane   in time

These situations were first analyzed by Siméon Poisson (1781–1840), based upon an analysis of games of chance by Jakob Bernoulli (1654–1705). Whether the events are located in time or in space, their analysis proves to be much the same. Random events in time provide a convenient place to start; they well illustrate the general features of the analysis, and have a few special features of their own. A sequence of random events is termed a **Poisson process**.

Poisson processes

The classic physical example of a Poisson process is the emission of alpha particles (ionized helium atoms) by a radioactive source. These events can be detected by a Geiger counter, which produces a click each time it detects an alpha particle. Here is a graphical representation of a pattern of clicks, each represented by a vertical bar on a time line, from a Geiger counter that is detecting alpha particles at an average rate of 1 per second:

average rate = 1/s   10 s

detection of α particles by Geiger counter

An event occurs when a radioactive atom within the source spontaneously emits an alpha particle. The time at which this event occurs is independent of the activity of other atoms, and it is this independence that characterizes this type of random activity. Thus, the only property that we can ascribe to this process is its **average rate**; this rate is proportional to the number of radioactive atoms in the source, and also depends upon the placement of the detector.

The natural world contains a good deal of structure, and civilization adds more. As a result, purely random events in time, although ever present at the microscopic level, are infrequently encountered at the macroscopic level of our sense impressions. To the untrained ear or eye, random events appear to cluster, whether heard from a Geiger counter or seen from a plot of its output, as in the above diagram. There are a number of other aspects of randomness that are less than intuitive, which are discussed below.

A Poisson process is a mathematical idealization of physical processes such as this. Each event is presumed to occur at a certain point in time, and thus to lack duration. The critical feature of a Poisson process is that *an event has no aftereffect on subsequent events*. Thus, at a given instant in time, there is no telling when the next event is going to occur. A Poisson process is thus said to lack *memory*, and it is the only type of event process that has this property. For this reason it is sometimes referred to as a *purely* random process.

We are accustomed to cause and effect—one thing leads to another; effect follows cause. The fact that a Poisson process has no memory implies that cause and effect play no role. Put another way, a recording of the output of a Geiger counter played backward could not be distinguished from the output itself.

A Poisson process can be informally characterized in mathematical terms by saying that over some small interval of time, Δt, the probability that an event will occur is proportional to Δt:

$$\text{probability of an event between time } t \text{ and time } t + \Delta t = \alpha \Delta t$$

where the proportionality constant, α, proves to be equal to the average rate of the events. This definition has an intuitive appeal, for if we halve the time interval over which we look, we would expect to halve the chance of an event occurring during the interval. If we move the detector on the Geiger counter a bit closer to the radioactive source, it continues to produce a Poisson process, but at a higher rate because the detector now intercepts more alpha particles. It is now responding to the alpha particles it would have detected at the previous position, plus the additional particles that became detectable due to its closer position. We can infer from this that when two or more Poisson processes sum in time, the result is another Poisson process, whose rate is equal to the sum of the original processes.

Our interests fall into two broad groups:

- The distribution of the total number of events that occur over some fixed time interval. This is termed a **Poisson distribution**, and readily extends to spatial distributions as well, in which the number of points over some fixed domain of space is considered.
- The distribution of the time intervals between successive events, or from a given instant to the next event. For historical reasons, these intervals are termed **waiting times**.

In a variety of circumstances, there are reasonable grounds to expect that some physical system will behave like a Poisson process. An example is the number of cG-GATED CHANNELS in the plasma membrane of an outer segment that are open in the dark at any instant (page 414). Given the mean value, one can calculate the expected variation in the number of channels open, and thus the variation in the dark current.

cG-gated channels *405*

In other situations, we are concerned with distributions in space or time that have some uncertainty associated with them, but are not purely random. Examples include the ongoing rate at which ganglion cells generate action potentials in the dark, and the distribution of some cell type across the retina. The manner in which such distributions *deviate* from a purely random distribution focuses our attention on those aspects of the process that cannot be accounted for in terms of "pure randomness" alone.

Poisson distributions

Distribution in time

This diagram presents the sample of a Poisson process shown in the previous diagram, divided into a sequence of one-second time intervals:

average rate = 1/s

10 s

Poisson process

Some intervals contain no events, about an equal number contain one event, and a few contain multiple events, as shown in this histogram:

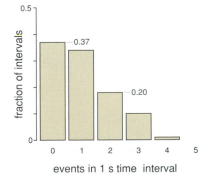

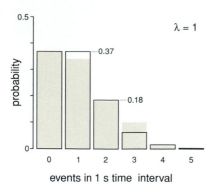

events in 1 s time interval

Exponentials *439*

Of course, the particular values vary somewhat from sample to sample. This variation is gradually reduced as the duration of the sample is increased and each sample thus includes more events.

Based upon the definition of a Poisson process, discussed above, Siméon Poisson derived an equation that gave the probability that some particular number of events would occur within a given time interval, given the average rate. The diagram at left shows the *probability distribution* of there being 0, 1, 2 … events for the sample. Here is the general equation upon which this distribution is based:

$$P(n) = \frac{\lambda^n e^{-\lambda}}{n!}$$

where

n is the number of events

$P(n)$ is the probability that there are n events

λ is the average number of events in the interval

and

e is a mathematical constant = 2.718… (discussed in EXPONENTIALS)

$n!$ is termed *factorial n* and is equal to the product of all of the integers from 1 to n (e.g., $3! = 3 \times 2 \times 1 = 6$). For the special case of $n = 0$, $0! = 1$.

The average number of events, λ, is simply the rate at which the events are occurring, α, times the time interval considered, τ:

$$\lambda = \alpha \times \tau$$

For simplicity, the examples use integer values for the rate and the time interval, but either can be any positive real number, which thus applies to λ as well. In this example, the average rate is 1/s, and the time interval is 1 s, so that:

$$\lambda = 1/s \times 1\,s = 1$$

and $P(n)$ simplifies to:

$$P(n) = \frac{e^{-1}}{n!} = \frac{0.3679}{n!}$$

from which the values shown in the above diagram are readily derived.

If the time interval is expanded to 10 seconds, then the average number of events, λ, is 10, and the Poisson distribution becomes:

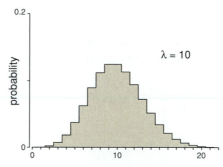

Distribution in space

The diagram at left shows 100 points randomly distributed within a region composed of 100 unit areas (e.g., 1 cm²). The spatial density is thus 1 point per unit area. The average number of points, λ, is simply the spatial density, σ, times the area considered, A:

$$\lambda = \sigma \times A$$

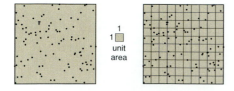

100 random points within a 10 × 10 area

The average number of points, λ, is thus equal to 1, and the probability distribution of the number of points within a unit square is exactly the same as shown previously for λ = 1.

The unit rows and/or columns in the diagram are composed of 10 unit area, so that for them, λ = 10. The Poisson distribution for the number of points in a row or column thus corresponds to the one shown previously for this value of λ. Just as two or more Poisson processes in time combine to produce another Poisson process, two or more random distributions of points in space sum to produce another random distribution, whose average spatial density is equal to the sum of those of its components.

The notion of random points in a plane readily extends to random points in three-dimensional space, where λ becomes the product of the density (number per unit volume) times the volume considered. It also reduces to random points along a line (number per unit length), and thereby becomes formally identical to events in time.

In a more abstract sense, we can dispose of time, space, rates, and densities and consider only λ, the average number of events in any sample or trial. Consider, for example, the current flowing into an outer segment in the dark. At any instant, that current is carried by a certain *number* of cG-gated channels that are open. Only a small fraction of the channels are open, and each channel operates independently of the rest. This situation can be characterized to a good approximation by a Poisson distribution with the value of λ set to the average number of channels open. This average number may be equal to the total number of channels in the outer segment times the fraction of time that a given channel is open. But we don't need to know these two values, as only their product is important; in fact, neither is currently known with much accuracy.

Variance and standard deviation

More often than not, our concern lies not so much with the value of λ—which is usually the starting point—as with the expected variation from instant to instant, or from sample to sample—in effect, the typical amount by which the actual number in a sample deviates from λ. For example, the possibility that the dark current of a rod outer segment could be carried by only 17 open channels is discussed in cG-GATED CHANNELS (page 414). This hypothesis is rejected there because the expected variation in this number from instant to instant would result in a variation in current that well exceeds the change in current produced by a single photon, and we know that rods can reliably detect single photons.

cG-gated channels *405*

The standard measure of variation is termed **variance**. It is found by multiplying the probability of an outcome by the square of the difference between that outcome and the average value, and summing over all outcomes. In the case of the Poisson distribution, this yields a remarkably simple result:

$$\text{variance} = \sum_{n=0}^{\infty} P(n)(n-\lambda)^2 = \lambda$$

The variance of a Poisson distribution has a number of uses. Here we are concerned with its use in characterizing the *width* of the distribution—in effect, the typical deviation from the mean. Notice that the variance is calculated by summing the product of two factors, $P(n)$ and $(n-\lambda)^2$. The second factor gives the *square* of the deviation we are concerned with, and is always positive. The first should be viewed as a weighting factor, which scales this squared deviation according to the probability of its occurrence. In effect, the variance is the typical, or average, squared deviation. Thus, a reasonable measure of the width of the distribution is the square root of the variance, which is termed the **standard deviation**, and abbreviated as σ:

$$\sigma = \sqrt{\text{variance}} = \sqrt{\lambda}$$

The deviation can be on either side of the average value, so it is typically represented as extending on both sides of the average value.

    This diagram shows the mean and standard deviation for the probability distribution we have been considering:

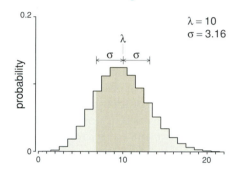

The probabilities of the shaded events sum to 0.64, so that about two-thirds of the samples lie within the bounds set by the standard deviation. On either side of it lie two "tails" as the probability drops toward zero for either very few events or very many events. Notice that this Poisson distribution is not symmetrical about the average value, as the tail on the right is broader than that on the left. Quantitatively, the average deviation on the right is 3.29, whereas that on the left is only 3.03. This difference is relatively small, and can usually be ignored when λ equals 10 or more. The distribution can be characterized as the mean plus or minus the standard deviation: 10 ± 3.16.

    NIGHT AND DAY (page 139) described viewing a star, when the average number of photoisomerizations in 0.1 s was about 28. This was also the value of the variance; the expected variation was found by arranging 28 dots in rows and columns to approximate a square:

The number of dots along the side of the square provided an estimate of the expected variation. This is, of course, a simple geometric visualization of taking a square root,

$$\sigma = \sqrt{\lambda} = \sqrt{28} = \pm 5.3$$

which comes in handy when trying to get a feel for the expected variation.

    Often the **fractional variation**—the ratio of the standard deviation to the mean—is the factor at stake:

$$\text{fractional variation} = \frac{\sigma}{\lambda} = \frac{\sqrt{\lambda}}{\lambda} = \frac{1}{\sqrt{\lambda}}$$

For example, if $\lambda = 10$, then the fractional variation is 31.6%. Because the variation decreases only with the square root of the average number, the value of λ needed to limit the fractional variation to some particular value rises rapidly.

Variation	λ
31.6%	10
10%	100
1%	10,000
0.1%	1,000,000

This is why the boundary between total uncertainty and total certainty is soft, for it takes a large value of λ to finally pin things down, and bring order and regularity out of chaos.

Limiting case of the Poisson distribution

As λ, the average number in the sample, increases, the Poisson distribution assumes an increasingly symmetrical form:

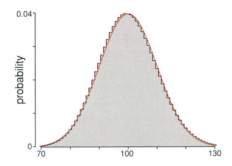

It also approximates a **normal** or **Gaussian distribution**, shown as a red curve. The approximation continues to improve as λ increases. A normal distribution is a *continuous* probability density function, which provides the limiting case of many *discrete* distributions, and has the analytic form

$$p(x) = \frac{1}{\sqrt{2\pi}\sigma} e^{-(x-\lambda)^2 / 2\sigma^2}$$

where $\sigma = \sqrt{\lambda}$ as before.

The manner in which the Poisson distribution approaches the normal distribution is elegant in that it involves only the single parameter λ.

Waiting times

Sensory systems operate at the border between chaos and certainty

The Poisson distribution can be said to characterize the *macrostructure* of a Poisson process, in that it focuses on the number of events over some time interval. We now shift the focus to the underlying *microstructure*, quantified in terms of the time interval between successive events:

When will the next photon be absorbed? When will the next cG molecule encounter the catalytic site on an activated PDE molecule? When will the next synaptic vesicle release its contents into the synaptic cleft? When will a ganglion cell generate the next action potential? We have no means of predicting the occurrence of any particular microevent, and physicists agree that we never will be able to do so with any accuracy. Nevertheless, macroscopic regularity emerges from microscopic chaos. For example, if we return to the macroscopic perspective, then the average rate at which cG molecules encounter a particular catalytic site on an activated PDE molecule is approximately proportional to their concentration. If we draw back further, by looking over longer times and more PDE molecules, then the approximation becomes as good or better than the accuracy of the measuring apparatus.

The purposeless chaos of the microscopic world, which causes the universe to slowly unwind, is simply an annoyance in most fields of investigation. For example, in order to obtain reliable parameters that characterize certain processes, it is often necessary to average a lot of data, or to use a lot of some substance. In certain fields this is all that is necessary. For example, only concentrations and the equations based upon them are required for an understanding of metabolic pathways. But when we consider sensory systems, the situation changes, since most of our concerns lie at the soft region between chaos and certainty. The reason is simple: evolution made it so. For example, adaptations that allowed the detection of dimmer and dimmer light pushed photoreceptors, synapses, and neural pathways toward—and ultimately well into—this region.

We first look at time intervals, in order to illustrate the underlying probability function, and then go on to explore the properties of the variability itself.

Time between successive events

A histogram of the time intervals in our simulated Geiger counter output shows the preference for shorter intervals, discussed previously:

average rate = 1/s   10 s

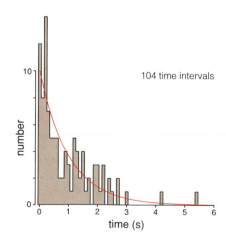

104 time intervals

Increasing the number of intervals to 1000 is sufficient to demonstrate that the times between successive events are distributed in an *exponential* manner:

Exponentials *439*

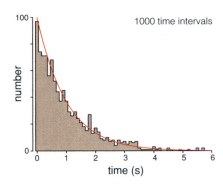

As discussed in the Box LOOKING AT SPECTRAL DENSITY CURVES (page 74), as the number of samples increases and the bin width decreases, the normalized histogram of a distribution becomes a probability density function:

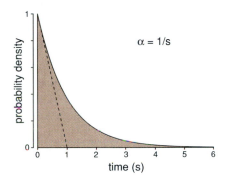

The general form, for an arbitrary rate constant, α, looks like this:

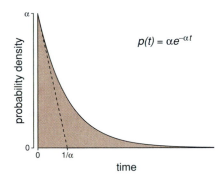

Since this is a probability density function, and the next event is certain to occur eventually, the area under the curve is equal to 1.

There are a number of features of a Poisson process that are not at all intuitive, and one means of coming to terms with this process is to confront some of its paradoxical aspects.

Time interval from arbitrary point to next event

Consider the *average time interval* from an *arbitrary* point in time to the next event. Since events are presumed to lack duration, this arbitrary point will lie somewhere between the last event and the next event:

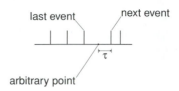

What is the average time interval to the next event? There are two different ways of analyzing the situation that lead to different conclusions.

You might reason as follows: The time to the next event can take on a value approaching zero if the arbitrary point falls immediately before the next event, or a value approaching the interval between the last and the next event if the arbitrary point falls just after the last event:

The arbitrary point can lie anywhere within the time interval with equal probability, since it was chosen without regard to the sequence of events. Thus the average time interval to the next event is the average of these equal probabilities, or half the time interval to the next event. Since, as previously discussed, the *average* time interval between events is $1/\alpha$, the average time interval from an arbitrary point to the next event must be one-half this interval, or $1/(2\alpha)$.

Or you might reason as follows: A Poisson process lacks memory, and so the time of the occurrence of the last event doesn't make any difference. Thus the average time to the next event is simply $1/\alpha$, just as it is for the time between successive events.

Which line of reasoning is *incorrect*? Hmm . . .

It turns out to be the first possibility that is incorrect: *the average time to the next event is always $1/\alpha$.* The nature of the error is subtle, but can be seen in a qualitative manner by simply looking at a Poisson event process and recognizing that longer intervals contain more time in which points can fall than do shorter intervals. Thus an arbitrary point tends to fall within longer intervals. Quantitatively, the average interval containing an arbitrary point proves to have an average value of $2/\alpha$, and with this value the discrepancy is resolved.

This is why the term *waiting time* can be used to describe both intervals that start from an event and those that start from an arbitrary time—it does not make any difference (see the Box WAITING FOR A BUS).

Most likely time interval

The *most likely* time interval is, of course, the interval that has the highest probability density (diagram at left). But the duration of that interval is always zero, whatever the average rate of the process! This is true of any process in which the probability of an event is constant over any small time interval.

Consider an activated rhodopsin molecule, **R***, diffusing about on a disc surface. The *average* time it takes to encounter the next G molecule is a com-

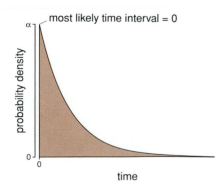

Waiting for a bus

The Poisson Bus Company operated for some time until growing frustration among its patrons forced the company into financial difficulties and resulted in a takeover by Metronome, Inc. The organizers of PBC had convinced their investors that since patrons arrive at bus stops at random times throughout the day, their needs could best be satisfied by arranging for the buses to arrive at random times as well. The average rate of bus arrivals would be once every half hour. Someone—investigators later had trouble determining just who—pointed out that because patrons arrived between bus arrivals, the average wait would be half the average period, or 15 minutes. Buses left the depot whenever the master Geiger counter generated a click. It was driven by a weak radioactive source that was carefully positioned so that the average rate of clicks was once every half-hour. Extensive testing showed that the system worked accurately and flawlessly.

Customers gradually became dissatisfied, however. This feeling simmered for a while at various stops and later developed into collective outrage. If other patrons were waiting at the bus stop, it did no good to ask them how long they had been waiting. Furthermore, the average wait proved to be about half an hour, rather than the 15 minutes claimed by the Poisson Bus Company. Most disheartening was the fact that you could wait and wait, only to see a convoy of two or three buses approaching at about the same time!

Riders were relieved when Metronome took over, although that company did have one peculiar eccentricity: even though a bus appeared regularly every half hour, there was no schedule. Nevertheless, the average waiting time was only 15 minutes, and you never needed to wait more than half an hour.

Metronome's operation resulted in satisfied patrons. But when the weather turned bad, and traffic jams ensued, one of the patrons huddled at a stop was heard to remark, "Seems like that damn Poisson Bus Company is back in operation again!"

---

plicated matter of diffusion theory, which leads to an estimated value of about 60 μs. But the *most likely* time to encounter the next G molecule is *immediately*. This fact has consequences for vision. For example, if the deactivation of **R*** occurred at the time when it first encountered an arrestin molecule, then some fraction of the **R*** molecules would be inactivated before they had the opportunity to activate sufficient G molecules to generate a reliable photocurrent. This potential difficulty is discussed in BIOCHEMICAL CASCADE: *WHY **R*** SLOWLY TURNS OFF, AND HOW IT MIGHT DO SO* (page 380).

Biochemical cascade *371*

If you have not had the opportunity to deal with random processes in a quantitative way, this conclusion might seem to be counterintuitive—something more true in the idealized world of mathematics than in the real world. But, properly viewed, it is part of our common experience.

Consider a beam of light of some particular frequency that enters an absorbing material such as a photoreceptor outer segment:

Exponentials *439*

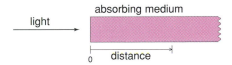

This situation is described in EXPONENTIALS. As the light passes through the absorbing material, its intensity decreases exponentially with a space constant determined by the concentration of pigment molecules within the absorbing material (right). In exponential decay, a small fraction of the remaining amount of stuff is removed over each small step. This is straightforward and intuitive.

Now reconsider this situation from the perspective of individual photons. Each photon enters the absorbing material and passes through it until

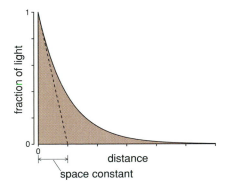

the photon is absorbed by a pigment molecule:

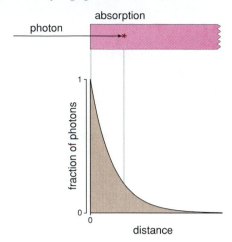

This curve shows the behavior of an ensemble of photons. If we consider only one photon, then the graph becomes a probability density function representing the probability that the photon will be absorbed:

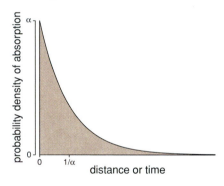

Since photons travel at a constant velocity, the abscissa can be expressed in terms of either distance or time. This curve has all the characteristics of the waiting time of a Poisson process, and thereby leads to the heart of the matter.

If we start our consideration at some given instant, such as the moment the photon enters the absorbing material, then the photon has some small probability of being absorbed in the first small distance. This event would *eliminate* the possibility of the photon being absorbed in the next small distance, and its small probability thereby *decreases* the probability that the photon will be absorbed in subsequent small distances.

Sequential events

Visual pigment regeneration *509*

It often takes a sequence of events to accomplish some task. For example, as discussed in VISUAL PIGMENT REGENERATION, a number of steps are required to deactivate the activated rhodopsin molecule, **R***. First, **R*** must encounter a molecule of **rhodopsin kinase** (RK) in the right way, so as to bind to it:

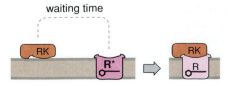

Then the RK molecule must use an ATP molecule to phosphorylate the rhodopsin molecule:

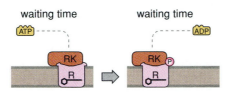

Finally, an **arrestin** molecule replaces RK:

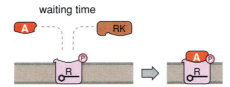

These diagrams identify a number of waiting times between the successive steps, each of which is random in nature and has the character of a Poisson process, at least approximately. Often one of the waiting times is considerably longer than any of the other intervals between successive steps. When this is the case, it is this slowest rate that sets both the rate of the process and its random character. The waiting time to accomplish some task then approximates the intervals between successive events in a Poisson process:

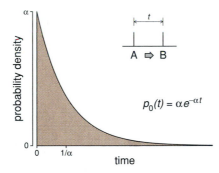

$$p_0(t) = \alpha e^{-\alpha t}$$

A likely example is the regeneration of rhodopsin, which appears to be dominated by the time taken for the all-*trans* retinal group of photoisomerized rhodopsin to break its attachment from the opsin and become a free molecule of all-*trans* retinol, as described in VISUAL PIGMENT REGENERATION (page 510).

But when waiting times between different successive steps are comparable, the shape of the probability density function changes. For example, consider a two-step process in which the duration of each step is characterized by a Poisson process having the same average rate (α). The time taken to complete the task is then the sum of the time taken for each of the steps. The resulting distribution of time intervals then looks quite different (right). This shape is similar to the time course of PDE activation, as described in BIO-CHEMICAL CASCADE. This time course was dominated by two Poisson-like steps: the generation of G_α^* molecules (as modeled) and the lifetime of **PDE***, which had roughly similar rates (20/s and 10/s).

The equation for n steps, each with the same rate constant, is

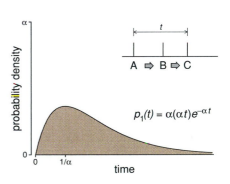

$$p_1(t) = \alpha(\alpha t)e^{-\alpha t}$$

Biochemical cascade *371*

$$P_n(t) = \frac{\alpha(\alpha t)^n e^{-\alpha t}}{n!}$$

where n is the number of events between the initial event and the final event. This is the probability distribution in time for *a fixed number of events* (steps) to occur. Except for the scaling factor, α, this is the same equation as the Poisson distribution of the number of events within *a fixed time interval*, which was discussed earlier (page 488). Both distributions approximate the Gaussian distribution for large values of n. In effect, when a large number of successive events are expected, the distribution of times needed to collect that number is about the same as the distribution of events that occur in the expected time interval needed to collect that number.

Radiometry

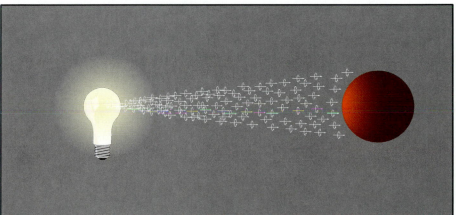

Radiometry is based upon a set of measures that allow photons of different frequencies to be kept track of as they are created, emitted, scattered, reflected, and absorbed. These measures are described twice, first in the form of an overview that is primarily qualitative, and then in a more formal manner that provides a basis for calculation.

Radiometry provides the primary methods by which one can calculate the rate at which photons are captured by the different types of photoreceptors in the eye in terms of the spectral distribution of light in the environment. Once this spectral distribution is converted to the photon catch rate of some photoreceptor type, the distribution itself becomes irrelevant. PHOTOMETRY *is a closely related set of measures that is based upon photon catch rates.*

Photometry *453*

Qualitative description

As its name suggests, **radiometry** is concerned with the measurement of radiation. This diagram illustrates the sorts of things it deals with:

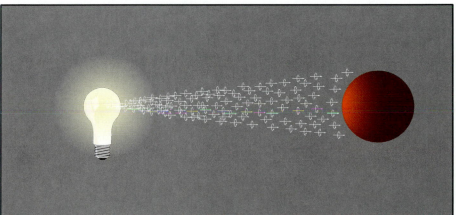

The heated filament of the light bulb radiates photons to the frosted surface of the bulb, which then scatters those photons in different directions. Some photons fall on part of the red ball, and a portion of them are scattered or reflected from the ball, thereby illuminating a portion of it. The fraction of photons scattered or reflected from the surface of the ball depends upon its spectral reflectance. Consequently, the spectral distribution of the photons coming from the ball has a different shape than that of the photons falling upon it. This diagram provides an informal introduction to the different measures described in this topic:

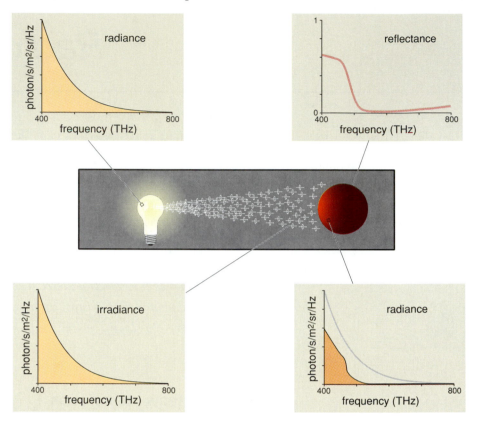

Wavelength & Energy *513*

The surface of the bulb gives off light in all directions. The amount of light that a small portion of it gives off in a certain direction is termed *radiance* (upper left diagram). Radiance is a spectral density function (see page 74) that specifies the amount of light given off per frequency interval. Imagine that you are looking at the ball under these conditions. The direction of the light coming from the ball to your eye depends upon a number of factors. First, and most obviously, the light from the bulb can directly illuminate only about half of the ball's surface. The light that comes to your eye from the illuminated half also varies from portion to portion. There are two components to this variation: (1) the manner in which each small portion of the ball is illuminated, and (2) the manner in which this incident light is scattered or reflected from the surface.

A ball that is uniformly illuminated by a single light source approximates the situation we are considering, particularly when the distance between the light bulb and the ball is large:

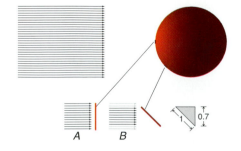

Consider two portions of the surface of the ball, *A* and *B*, that are in the path of the beam of light. We assume that these portions are sufficiently small that they can be considered flat. At *A*, the surface is perpendicular to the incident light. Portion *B* lies below *A*, and the incident light makes an angle of 45° with respect to this surface. Both portions are the same size, but because *B* is tilted, it receives only about 70% of the amount of light that *A* receives. Since *B* receives less light, it will also scatter or reflect less light, and will thus appear darker than *A*, as observed. This variation in the amount of uniform light falling upon different portions of a solid provides us with physical cues that can be used to infer the three-dimensional properties of the solid from its two-dimensional image.

The amount of light falling upon different portions of the ball depends entirely upon the geometry of the situation. But the light that is scattered or reflected from the ball depends upon its surface properties. Two factors are at stake. The first is the degree to which the surface of the ball absorbs incident photons as a function of their frequency. The second is the way in which the photons that are not absorbed come off of the surface. A **mirror surface**, such as a polished piece of metal or a quiet pond, *reflects* photons in a direction that depends in a simple way upon their angle of incidence, as shown in the left portion of this diagram:

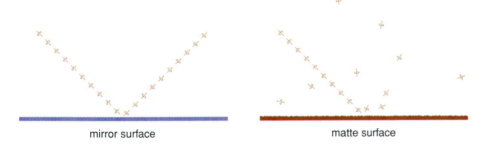

mirror surface   matte surface

A ray of light is represented as a regular line of photons. In contrast, a photon that falls on a **matte surface**, shown to the right, penetrates into the interior of the surface and is reflected a few times before leaving it. Because of these multiple reflections, the photons are *scattered* from the surface in all directions.

Many surfaces in nature partially reflect and partially scatter photons:

The bright spot on each pearl shows the reflective component, which will move to a different portion of the surface if you move your head to the side.

Put another way, two observers will see the bright spot at different locations, depending upon their vantage points.

The radiometric measure that quantifies the spectral distribution of photons that come from any small portion of a surface to reach your eye, whether by reflection or scatter, is its radiance, just as for a luminous object. The radiance of the red ball thus varies across its surface, and in a manner that depends upon the direction of the illuminant with respect to some portion of the surface, the reflective properties of the surface, and the direction from which it is viewed.

Radiometry deals with spectral distributions of photons by dividing the spectrum into a sequence of small spectral intervals. It then applies a form of bookkeeping to each spectral interval. This bookkeeping needs to deal with different quantitative measures of the spectral distribution, such as radiance and irradiance, that take into account the different things that can happen to the photons within each interval:

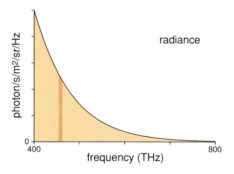

Doing this for each small interval, over the visible range of the spectrum, allows the spectral radiance from some small portion of an object in some particular direction to be calculated.

There are five basic measures in radiometry, each based upon geometric considerations. For each measure we will need to consider the rate of photons in each small frequency interval. But for the moment we will consider only spectral lights (i.e., lights composed of photons of about the same frequency), in order to simplify the discussion.

• **Flux** refers to the number of photons per second under any circumstance that can be specified in this way. For example, a 100 W light bulb gives off a total flux of about 8.5×10^{20} photon/s:

flux (photon/s)

In THE RAIN OF PHOTONS ONTO CONES, when you looked at Polaris with a 40 mm^2 pupil, a *flux* of 94,000 photon/s in the visible range entered your eye.

- **Irradiance** is the *flux density*, meaning the flux per unit area, of photons *falling upon* some surface, as shown in the left portion of this diagram:

irradiance (photon/s/m^2) emittance (photon/s/m^2)

When you looked at Polaris, the irradiance onto your pupil was 2350 photon/s/mm^2 over the visible range. As suggested by the illustration, irradiance characterizes the rate at which photons are arriving at some surface, but says nothing about the directions from which they are arriving. In radiometry, the unit area used is a square meter (m^2) instead of a square millimeter. Since one square meter is equal to 10^6 square millimeters, the irradiance of Polaris is about 2.4×10^9 photon/s/m^2.

- **Emittance** is the flux density of photons *emitted by* some surface, as shown in the right portion of the above diagram. As suggested by the illustration, emittance characterizes the rate at which photons are being emitted, but says nothing about the directions in which they are heading. The source of the photons could be a *luminous* object, such as the surface of the light bulb (a 100 W light bulb has a total emittance of about 7.5×10^{22} photon/s/m^2), or an *illuminated* object that gives off photons as a result of scattering and reflection, such as a small portion of the red ball.
- **Radiant intensity** is a measure used to describe photons given off from a point source of light or from a very small surface area. Just as irradiance and emittance refer to the *flux per unit area*, radiant intensity refers to the flux per unit *solid angle*, and has units of photon/s/steradian.

Angles *369*

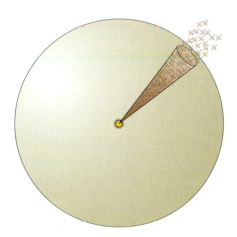

As noted above, the total flux of a 100 W light bulb is about 8.5×10^{20} photon/s. The radiant intensity of the bulb, viewed at a far distance, can be readily calculated, provided we neglect its base. Since there are 4π steradians in a sphere, the radiant intensity of the bulb is everywhere equal to 8.5×10^{20} photon/s divided by 4π steradians, or 6.8×10^{19} photon/s/sr.

Objects don't need to be spherically symmetrical in order to specify radiant intensity. Just as it is possible to specify a sufficiently small surface area over which the irradiance or the emittance of a surface is reasonably uniform, it is possible to specify a sufficiently small solid angle over which the radiant intensity is reasonably uniform. As the solid angle becomes smaller, the direction from which the photons are emitted or are received becomes more accurate. Neither irradiance nor emittance are concerned with the direction of photons, and thus neither is of much use in keeping track of where photons go. The key idea behind radiant intensity is that it captures the direction of arrival of the photons, without concerning itself with the spatial extent of the region from which they are arriving. The primary use of this measure is not with true point sources, such as a star, but in keeping track of photons emitted by a small area or volume into a cone of light in some particular direction.

One example, which serves as a prelude to discussing radiance, occurs when you view a small surface area of the red ball that was discussed above:

When you view the ball, that small portion will be imaged somewhere on your retina. The photons emitted by the small portion of the ball go off in all directions, but a fraction of this total flux encounters your eye and passes through your pupil, to fall upon a small portion of your retina. The larger the area of the pupil, the larger will be the solid angle subtended by the small portion of the ball, and thus the larger will be the number of photons that fall on the retinal image of this small portion.

It is unfortunate that the term *radiant intensity* conveys little of the nature of this measure, and nothing of how it differs from the other radiometric measures.

- **Radiance** was the radiometric measure we began with. It is the measure that describes the amount of light, *the radiant flux*, that comes to your eye from some small portion of an object that you view. Radiance is a combination of *emittance*, which captures the notion of the flux per unit of surface area given off by the small portion of the object, and *radiant intensity*, which refers to the fraction of that flux that goes off in some particular cone of light. This is best understood in terms of the diagram above. The light entering the eye from the small portion of the ball depends upon both the solid angle and the area of the small portion. Doubling the area of either the source (the small portion) or the receiver of the light (the pupil size)—and hence the solid angle—will double the number of photons entering the eye per second. Total radiance is thus a measure of flux per unit area of the emitting surface per solid angle, and has units of photon/s/m^2/sr. That is a lot of units, but it is the number necessary to specify a radiometric measure that reflects the bookkeeping of photons in their interaction with matter. Radiance, or some derivative of it, is the radiometric measure that is needed to calculate the *photon catch rate* of the different photoreceptor types of the eye when viewing some small portion of an object.

Photon catch rate *471*

Quantitative description

This section is more formal in the sense that it presents photon-based radiometry in mathematical terms. On the other hand, it is more practical in that each of the numbers presented in the previous section is derived.

Radiation in the natural world exhibits a rich variety of phenomena. Radiometry deals with a subset of these phenomena, in which photons are given off by some *surfaces* and received by other *surfaces*. For example, in order to deal with the spectral radiance of a clear blue sky, radiometry posits an imaginary surface that shows the same spectral radiance, and an absence of scattering or absorption between this surface and some receiving surface. By such tricks, radiometry is able to partially extend into the fuller range of phenomena associated with light.

Symbols and definitions

The standard symbol for **radiant flux** is the Greek lowercase phi: ϕ. In energy-based radiometry the subscript *e* is used: ϕ_e. PHOTOMETRY makes use of the related measure of luminous flux, for which the symbol ϕ_v is used in order to distinguish it from ϕ_e. In this spirit, ϕ_n is used here to represent flux, the subscript *n* denoting photon-based radiometry. The Greek lowercase nu, ν, is used to represent frequency, which is a convention of physics.

Photometry 453

A spectral distribution of radiant flux is represented by $\phi_n(\nu)$, and, like other radiometric quantities, is a measure of the amount per frequency interval (Hz). Such distributions were introduced in THE RAIN OF PHOTONS ONTO CONES (see *LOOKING AT SPECTRAL DENSITY CURVES*, page 74). A spectral light of some frequency is represented as ϕ_n. The measures, symbols, and units used in radiometry are as follows.

Measure	Spectral distribution		Spectral light	
Radiant flux	$\phi_n(\nu)$	photon/s/Hz	ϕ_n	photon/s
Irradiance	$E_n(\nu)$	photon/s/m^2/Hz	E_n	photon/s/m^2
Emittance	$M_n(\nu)$	photon/s/m^2/Hz	M_n	photon/s/m^2
Radiant intensity	$I_n(\nu)$	photon/s/sr/Hz	I_n	photon/s/sr
Radiance	$L_n(\nu)$	photon/s/m^2/sr/Hz	L_n	photon/s/m^2/sr

The values of these radiometric measures vary from point to point, as illustrated by the illuminated surface of the red ball. No matter how much spatial and directional detail is associated with the source, one can ignore variations in radiant flux over an incremental area, ΔA, or solid angle, $\Delta \omega$, whose geometrical image on the retina is smaller than the *point spread function* of the eye—optics thereby blurs details. An incremental surface area or incremental solid angle implies an incremental radiant flux, $\Delta \phi_n(\nu)$, whose magnitude is proportional to the incremental area or angle.

Radiometric equations are easier to read when incremental areas that *receive* photons, ΔA_r, are distinguished from those that act as *sources* for photons, ΔA_s. A source may be luminous, such as a frosted bulb, or illuminated, such as a ball or other object that reflects and scatters photons from its surface.

This terminology and symbolism allow **spectral irradiance** to be expressed as

$$E_n(\nu) = \frac{\Delta \phi_n(\nu)}{\Delta A_r} \ (\text{photon/s/m}^2/\text{Hz})$$

In words, over any small spectral interval about frequency ν, irradiance is equal to the incremental spectral flux (photon/s/Hz) divided by the incremental area (m²) over which it was received. For uniform conditions, this simplifies to

$$E_n(\nu) = \frac{\phi_n(\nu)}{A_r} \text{ (photon/s/m}^2\text{/Hz)}$$

In either case, $E_n(\nu)$ refers to the amount of irradiance over a small spectral interval, $\Delta\nu$, that is centered about some frequency ν. The incremental irradiance is thus

$$E_n(\nu)\Delta\nu \text{ (photon/s/m}^2\text{)}$$

In principle, it would be possible to sum the incremental irradiances over the spectrum and thereby obtain the total irradiance, E_n:

$$E_n = \Sigma \, E_n(\nu)\Delta\nu \text{ (photon/s/m}^2\text{)}$$

THE RAIN OF PHOTONS ONTO CONES began with the rain of photons from Polaris expressed in this way. But because the fate of photons depends upon their frequencies, such summations can do little more than give an indication of overall values (e.g., the fraction of photons from Polaris that lie within the visible range). The calculation of the photon catch for L cones, described in that chapter, required frequency intervals to be dealt with one by one, as the photons within each interval were absorbed, reflected, or scattered by the intervening media. Only the photons that reach the photoreceptors are important. The fraction that do so at a given frequency, $T(\nu)$, is termed the *direct transmittance*. Thus, over some frequency interval, the incremental irradiance at the level of the photoreceptors is

$$T(\nu)E_n(\nu)\Delta\nu \text{ (photon/s/m}^2\text{)}$$

Again, we could sum the incremental irradiances, but there is no gain in doing so, because the irradiance within each frequency interval is still required to calculate the photon catch rate. In effect, the basic measure in radiometry is a spectral density function, rather than a number.

The **spectral emittance** is similar to the spectral irradiance, except that it deals with sources rather than receivers:

$$M_n(\nu) = \frac{\Delta\phi_n(\nu)}{\Delta A_s} \text{ (photon/s/m}^2\text{/Hz)}$$

The **spectral radiant intensity** is the flux over some solid angle:

$$I_n(\nu) = \frac{\Delta\phi_n(\nu)}{\Delta\omega} \text{ (photon/s/sr/Hz)}$$

This quantity generally varies with the *direction* of the solid angle. Photons are almost always emitted by *surfaces,* and the direction of the solid angle is naturally expressed in terms of the direction perpendicular to the surface:

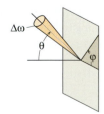

In order to provide a full specification of the direction of the incremental cone, we also need an additional angle, φ, within the plane of the surface, with respect to some arbitrary axis.

The **spectral radiance** is the measure that characterizes the light coming to the eye from some small surface area:

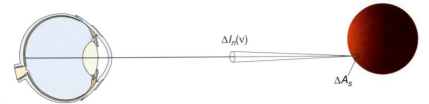

Radiance is defined without reference to an observer, but since this measure was devised to characterize the light captured by eyes, it is useful to keep the observer in mind. The incremental radiant intensity, $\Delta I_n(\nu)$, specifies the radiant flux in the direction of the eye that is emitted from the incremental area of the source, ΔA_s. At first sight, it might seem that radiance is simply the ratio of these quantities: $\Delta I_n / \Delta A_s$. But it is necessary to take into account that this surface area is not viewed straight on, but from some angle. From the perspective of the eye, the surface area is *foreshortened*. The area we see is ΔA_s times the cosine of the angle to the normal:

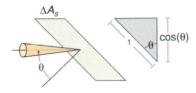

The effective area, $\Delta A_s'$, is

$$\Delta A_s' = \Delta A_s \times \cos(\theta)$$

The radiance coming to the eye from the surface is thus

$$L_n(\nu) = \frac{\Delta I_n(\nu)}{\Delta A_s'} = \frac{\Delta I_n(\nu)}{\Delta A_s \cos(\theta)} \quad (\text{photon/s/m}^2/\text{sr/Hz})$$

Among radiometric measures, radiance is the most complicated because so many factors need to be included. The various radiometric measures are expressed in their most general form, which makes no assumptions about the surfaces involved. The following section describes some simplifications that occur when photons leave a surface in all directions.

Lambert surface

A Lambert surface is one from which photons emerge in all directions, without preference. This describes not only heated surfaces, but also diffuse ones that reflect light, such as chalk or blotting paper. Because of foreshortening, such surfaces have a radiant intensity in some direction that is proportional to the cosine of the angle the direction makes with respect to a line normal to its surface:

$$I = I_o \cos \theta$$

where I_o is the radiant intensity in the direction normal to the surface ($\theta = 0$). The radiant intensity is greatest when the surface is viewed straight on ($\theta = $

0), and drops to zero when the surface is viewed from it side ($\theta = 90°$). This relation is termed **Lambert's law,** after Johann Heinrich Lambert (1728–1777), a German physicist also known for the development of a variety of graphical means of expressing data, some of which are used in this book. A surface that obeys this relation is termed a **Lambert surface.** The radiance of a Lambert surface is thus independent of the angle of the surface with respect to the eye:

$$L_n(v) = \frac{\Delta I_n(v)}{\Delta A_s \cos(\theta)} = \frac{\Delta I_{on}(v)}{\Delta A_s} \;\; (\text{photon/s/m}^2/\text{sr/Hz})$$

Although it is roughly spherical, the Sun appears to us as a flat disc because its luminous surface approximates a Lambert surface. A red ball with a matte surface also approximates a Lambert surface. It will appear as a flat disc if illuminated diffusely from all directions, as when viewed in a fog. But irradiance almost always has some directional component to it, and it is the unequal distribution of irradiance over the surface of the ball that allows us to infer its shape.

Examples

The following examples derive values given in the qualitative description of radiometric measures. The light bulb in our examples is assumed to have a spectral distribution that corresponds to that of a *blackbody radiator* at a temperature of 2850 K and a transmittance of the glass envelope of 0.9 (Wyszecki and Stiles 1982, 18–19). Because the intensity of the bulb is expressed in units of energy, it is necessary to convert from units of energy flux to units of photon flux.

Blackbody radiation *401*

Total photon flux of 100 W bulb

The total emittance of a blackbody radiator is

$$M_n = 1.52 \times 10^{15} T^3 \;\; (\text{photon/s/m}^2)$$

This is the photon version of Stefan's law (1879); in energy units, this law is expressed as

$$M_e = 5.67 \times 10^{-8} T^4 \;\; (\text{W/m}^2)$$

Their ratio provides a measure independent of the area of the radiator:

$$\frac{M_n}{M_e} = \frac{2.68 \times 10^{22}}{T} \;\; (\text{photon/s/W/K})$$

The factor T in the denominator reflects the fact that the average frequency of photons in a blackbody radiator is proportional to the temperature. Substituting a temperature of 2850 K and multiplying by a wattage of 100 W and a transmittance of 0.9 gives 8.47×10^{20} photon/s.

Total emittance of 100 W light bulb

The spherical portion of a conventional light bulb has a diameter of 6 cm. Assuming that the light bulb consists of a sphere of that size, its area is 0.011 m^2. Dividing the total flux from the previous example by this area gives 7.5 $\times 10^{22}$ photon/s/m^2.

Visual pigment regeneration

When a rhodopsin molecule captures a photon, its light-catching chromophore is converted from the bent form of 11-cis retinal to the straightened form of all-trans retinal. Regeneration of the rhodopsin molecule occurs in two steps. First, the activated rhodopsin molecule is recognized by an enzyme, and a sequence of steps brings its ability to activate G protein molecules to a complete halt. Second, the deactivated rhodopsin molecule loses its all-trans chromophore, which leaves the outer segment and enters the retinal epithelium, where it is converted to 11-cis retinal. The 11-cis chromophore then leaves the retinal epithelium and enters an outer segment, where it combines with the protein portion of a rhodopsin molecule; the rhodopsin molecule is thereby reconstituted to its original form, where it awaits the next photon.

Renewal of rhodopsin involves a number of steps

Once a rhodopsin molecule catches a photon, it changes its shape. An enzyme attached to the surface of the disc membrane, termed **rhodopsin**

rhodopsin kinase

kinase (RK), can recognize an activated rhodopsin molecule, **R***, and bind to it:

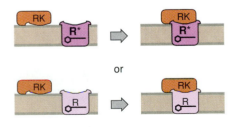

or

binding of rhodopsin kinase to
photoisomerized rhodopsin

It is not clear whether the photoisomerized rhodopsin is still catalytically able to activate G proteins after binding to rhodopsin kinase, so two alternative diagrams are shown. After binding, the rhodopsin kinase uses ATP to add a phosphate group to one of the amino acids of the rhodopsin molecule.

Icons and abbreviations

A	A	arrestin
ADP	ADP	adenosine diphosphate
ATP	ATP	adenosine triphosphate
O		opsin
O (P)		phosphorylated opsin
P	P_i	inorganic phosphate group
R	R	rhodopsin
R*	**R***	activated rhodopsin
R		photoisomerized rhodopsin
R (P)	R_p	phosphorylated rhodopsin
RK	RK	rhodopsin kinase

Biochemical cascade *371*

The rhodopsin molecule is then said to be **phosphorylated** (Rp), and is represented by the icon in the right panel:

phosphorylation of
photoisomerized rhodopsin

Phosphorylation does not appear to change the properties of the photoisomerized rhodopsin molecule, but it does cause it to be recognized by a protein in the cytoplasm, named **arrestin**, which tightly binds to it, replacing the rhodopsin kinase:

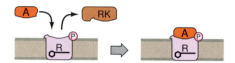

arrestin binds to phosphorylated rhodopsin

Every biochemical reaction has the potential to go in either direction. The tight binding of arrestin to R_p *strongly reduces* the probability that the sequence of events will be reversed. As discussed in BIOCHEMICAL CASCADE (page 377), the time course of the photocurrent suggests that the catalytic activity of **R*** falls to a low level during the rising phase of the photocurrent. In the absence of complete quenching, the accumulation of many partially quenched rhodopsin molecules would produce a low level of photoreceptor activation in the dark that would prevent the rods from detecting a single photon. Thus this action of arrestin is critically important to rod function.

The arrestin molecule remains on a phosphorylated rhodopsin molecule until the all-*trans* chromophore is removed, however long that takes. This removal is initiated in a break in the bond between the all-*trans* chromophore and the protein portion of the molecule, **opsin.** As a result, the chromophore becomes **all-*trans* retinal,** which is converted by a membrane protein, termed **retinal dehydrogenase**, into **all-*trans* retinol:**

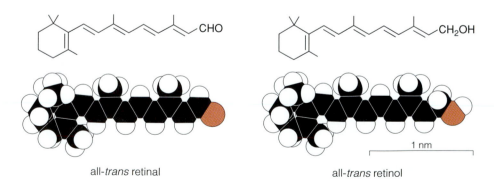

all-*trans* retinal   all-*trans* retinol

All of this probably happens within the membrane, but the details remain uncertain. The result is that the chromophore is removed from the interior of the rhodopsin molecule. This removal produces a conformational change in the opsin that breaks the bond with the arrestin, leaving phosphorylated opsin:

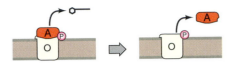

rhodopsin loses chromophore and arrestin
detatches from phosphorylated opsin

There are two remaining steps, which happen at about the same time. The phosphate group is removed from the opsin by yet another protein, termed a **phosphatase**, and **11-*cis* retinal** enters the opsin, probably from within the membrane, to re-form a rhodopsin molecule that is again able to absorb a photon and activate G proteins:

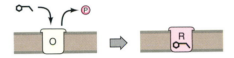

11-*cis* retinal binds to phosphorylated
opsin so as to reconstitute rhodopsin

The time it takes to regenerate a rhodopsin molecule is on the order of minutes, rather than the fraction of a second taken by events that produce the rise and fall of the photocurrent. We now turn to the fate of the all-*trans* retinol that was released, and the source of the 11-*cis* retinal that replaces it.

11-*cis* retinal is regenerated within the retinal epithelium

The retinal epithelium obtains all-*trans* retinol from the photoreceptors—or from the blood, as discussed below—and converts it to 11-*cis* retinal. An enzyme, **retinyl-ester isomerase**, converts all-*trans* retinol to 11-*cis* retinol; and another enzyme, **11-*cis* retinol dehydrogenase**, uses metabolic energy to convert 11-*cis* retinol to 11-*cis* retinal.

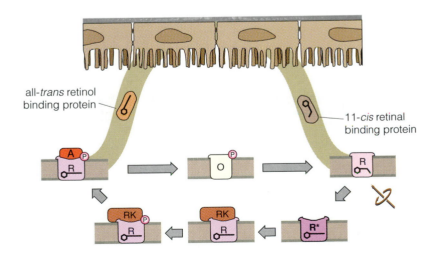

all-*trans* retinol
binding protein

11-*cis* retinal
binding protein

carotenoid, xanthophylls

These pigments are synthesized by plants, and absorb the high-energy photons found in the blue–violet portion of the spectrum. Like chlorophyll, carotenoids harvest photons for photosynthesis; they also protect the plant against the damaging effects of high-energy photons. In a leaf there is about one carotenoid molecule for every three chlorophyll molecules. The orange-yellow color of carotenoids is normally masked by the green chlorophyll, but in the fall, when the chlorophyll of deciduous trees disappears, they come into their own glory. We can obtain carotenoids from many sources, including the fat of plant-eating animals.

Xanthophylls have the same general structures as carotenoids, but have one or two oxygen atoms attached to the two ring structures at each end. They are the main pigments of the macula lutea, where they serve a protective role similar to that of carotenoids in plants. The pigments found in the outer rind of a carrot are mainly carotenoids, whereas those in the core of a carrot are mainly xanthophylls.

1 nm

×30,000,000

β-carotene

The chromophore is highly insoluble in any form, and can pass from one cell to another only in the company of specific binding proteins, adapted for this purpose. These binding proteins probably envelop the chromophore, and this complex is then free to diffuse within the extracellular space. These proteins are highly specific, so all-*trans* retinol is recognized and conveyed by an **all-*trans* retinol binding protein**, whereas 11-*cis* retinal is conveyed via an **11-*cis* retinal binding protein**. Although the overall pathway for the conversion of all-*trans* retinol to 11-*cis* retinal is well understood, certain steps remain unclear. In particular, retinol-binding proteins have not been found within outer segments. Thus, when a rhodopsin molecule releases its chromophore, the all-*trans* retinol, being insoluble, presumably remains within the disc membrane. There it is free to migrate, via diffusion, to the edge of the disc. But how it gets from there to the all-*trans* retinol binding protein in the extracellular space outside the outer segment is not known.

All-*trans* retinol, also known as vitamin A, is ultimately obtained from dietary sources, generally in the form of **carotenoids** such as β-carotene. These molecules are taken up by the small intestine and enzymatically cleaved to form two molecules of all-*trans* retinal, which are converted to all-*trans* retinol. Retinol is stored in the liver, and circulates in the blood bound to a retinol-binding protein that is distinct from the one found between the outer segments and the retinal epithelium. Lack of retinol precursors in the diet can eventually lead to a depletion of both retinols and retinals, producing a condition known as night blindness. In many mammals the retinal epithelium acts as a secondary store for all-*trans* retinol, but in rodents this store is relatively weak, and they are more sensitive to dietary deficiencies.

Wavelength and energy

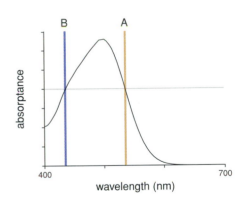

This book describes light in terms of photons at different frequencies, but for reasons that are mainly historical, much of the literature continues to describe light in terms of energy at different wavelengths. This topic discusses the differences between curves based upon these two pairs of units, and describes how to convert from one pair to the other.

Photons or energy?

When light produces a *chemical* change, it is always necessary to express the intensity of the light in photon units. In order to see why, consider a thought experiment in which our task is to compare the effects of two lights on a solution of rod rhodopsin molecules. For this experiment, it doesn't make any difference whether the horizontal axis is plotted in units of frequency or wavelength, and to help make that point, I've plotted the data both ways.

wavelength
The wavelength of a photon, discussed in greater detail below, is defined as the speed of light in a vacuum divided by the frequency of the photon.

absorptance
As discussed in LIGHT ABSORPTION, *absorptance* refers to the fraction of a spectral light that is absorbed by a solution. This is a dimensionless number that can be determined for each spectral light across the spectrum; thus the units along the horizontal axis that are used to plot the spectrum are irrelevant.

Light absorption *443*

The first step in the experiment is to measure the absorptance of the solution over the visible spectrum. Two spectral lights, A and B, are then chosen so that their absorptances are equal; in this case, 40% of either light is absorbed. The diagram shows their positions in the spectrum. We'll use these letters to distinguish the two lights, their positions in the spectrum, and the vials of rhodopsin that each shines on. Each light is presented to a different vial of the same solution for a fixed period of time. At the end of that period, two measurements are made on each vial: (1) the rise in temperature, and (2) the number of rhodopsin molecules that were photoisomerized.

If we adjust the two lights so that they emit the same *energy,* then for the two vials, we find that

1. The rise in temperature is the same for both vials.

2. The number of photoisomerized rhodopsin molecules in vial A is about 23% greater than the number in vial B.

The first finding is a direct consequence of the conservation of energy: if the two lights have the same energy, and 40% of each is absorbed, then the rise in temperature will be the same. The second finding cannot be explained in terms of energy, and this is the crux of the problem.

If we adjust the two lights so that they emit the same *number of photons,* then for the two vials, we find that

1. The rise in temperature is greater in vial B than in vial A.

2. The number of photoisomerized rhodopsin molecules in both vials is the same.

The first finding is explained by the fact that the photons of light B have a higher frequency, and thus more energy, by the relation

$$E_{photon} = h \times \nu$$

where h is the Planck constant and ν is the frequency. The second finding is explained by the fact that the photon flux was the same for the two lights, and 40% of each was absorbed, together with the fact that quantum efficiency is constant over the visible range.

Thus one can't get away from using photon units in vision, or in other areas of photobiology. When a spectral distribution of light is expressed in energy units, it must be sliced up into small spectral increments, and each of these must be converted to photon units in order for any meaningful number to be calculated.

Consider, for example, the scotopic luminous efficiency function, which, as described in PHOTOMETRY, reflects the spectral sensitivity of rods in the eye, and thus the effect of ocular transmittance:

Photometry *453*

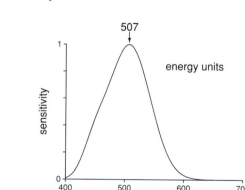
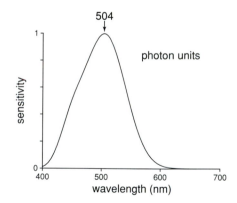

scotopic luminous efficiency function

The horizontal axis is plotted in wavelength units, but this is irrelevant to the point to be made. When the efficiency function is plotted in the conventional way, with the vertical scale plotted in energy units, the maximum value of the curve occurs at 507 nm, as seen in the diagram on the left. But when it is plotted in photon units, the peak occurs at 504 nm, as shown on the right.

What is the wavelength to which rods are most sensitive? The answer to this question depends upon what you want to do. If you want to *heat* the photoreceptors, then light at 507 nm is the most efficient means of doing so, in the sense that it requires the least energy. But if your orientation is toward vision, and you want to minimize the number of photons necessary to activate a certain number of rhodopsin molecules, then you should use a light of 504 nm.

Frequency or wavelength?

Whereas the frequency of a photon is essentially fixed, its wavelength depends upon the refractive index of the material through which it passes. The equation for wavelength is

$$\lambda = \frac{c}{vn}$$

where λ is the wavelength, c is the velocity of light, v is the frequency, and n is the refractive index. A vacuum has an index of refraction of 1, and that of air is close to 1; water and the interior of the eye have refractive indices close to 4/3. Thus when a photon enters the eye, its wavelength is reduced to about three-fourths of its wavelength in air. Outer segments of photoreceptors have an even higher refractive index (1.41), and the wavelength of a spectral light in them is even shorter than that in water.

Do we ever need a correction factor that takes into account the change in wavelength that occurs when rhodopsin molecules are placed in media with different refractive indices? No, because the absorbance spectrum of rhodopsin, as well as other pigments, depends upon the frequencies of the photons rather than their wavelengths. This is a deep result in physics in that it involves the general means by which photons interact with matter, so there is nothing special about rhodopsin in this regard. In fact, when speaking about the interactions of light with matter, *actual* wavelengths are never used. Instead, a *defined* wavelength is used, equal to the wavelength that light would have if it were in a vacuum. In effect, n is set to 1, and the defined wavelength becomes c/v, which is simply a constant (c) divided by the frequency. Thus, just as a mathematical transformation is required to convert energy units to a measure that reflects the photon nature of light, so too must the actual wavelength be transformed to a measure that depends only upon the frequency of the photon.

Since defined wavelength depends upon frequency, no conflict in experimental results arises when it is used, and in this limited sense, wavelength and frequency are formally equivalent. But the use of a measure that is proportional to the reciprocal of a photon's energy can produce some peculiar effects. Here are some examples:

1. When spectral distributions are plotted as a function of frequency, the values along the horizontal axis are proportional to the energy of the photon; when plotted as a function of wavelength, the energy of a photon goes to infinity as the origin is approached.

2. The intensity of an absorption band is proportional to the area of its spectrum when plotted against frequency. Since the spectral widths of visual pigments are about the same when plotted against frequency, so too should be their peak spectral absorptivities. Plots against wavelength reflect none of these underlying relations.

3. The current physical reference light for PHOTOMETRY is defined in terms of frequency, rather than wavelength.

Photometry *453*

Radiometry *499*

George Wald (1965), who won the Nobel prize for his work on visual pigments, argued for the use of frequency over wavelength, but he never developed a consistent scheme for doing so.

Photons or energy?

As the previous sections make clear, photons and frequencies are the basic units in vision, and in all practical cases it is necessary to convert energy and wavelength measures to them, either explicitly or implicitly. But every book on PHOTOMETRY, RADIOMETRY, or photochemistry is based upon energy and wavelength. With the exception of some of the papers by W. S. Stiles (1978), so too is just about every spectral diagram in the visual literature. This convention is so well rooted that it would appear quixotic to tilt against it. But since this book seeks an understanding of how we see, it seems appropriate to present this understanding at its most basic level. To do otherwise would create misleading impressions.

Consider, for example, the spectral irradiance of the Sun as measured outside the atmosphere:

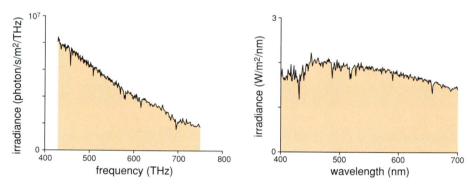

sunlight above Earth's atmosphere

The same data is used in both curves; only the units in which they are expressed have changed. Over the visible range, the energy–wavelength curve on the right has a broad peak at about 450 nm, and if you were familiar only with spectral distributions plotted in this way, then you might gain the impression that evolution arranged the peak sensitivities of the visual pigments so as to make use of this apparent peak in the solar spectrum. But this peak is absent when the natural units of photons and frequency units are used.

The remainder of this topic describes the changes that take place when converting between units; these changes are first described in a qualitative manner and then redescribed quantitatively.

Conversions between units

Conversions between frequency–photon units and wavelength–energy units are straightforward, but can produce some nonintuitive consequences. We consider three types of conversion, each built in part upon the previous one.

Spectral reflectance, transmittance, and absorptance

The diagram at the top of the facing page shows the surface reflectance of a red flower, plotted as a function of both frequency and wavelength. The

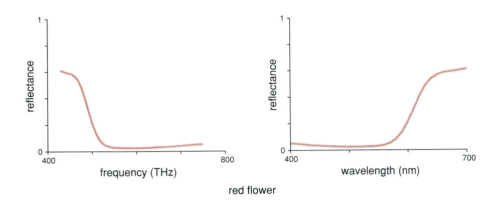

red flower

fraction of light reflected at some particular frequency is the same whether that light is expressed in terms of a photon flux or an energy flux. Thus the only factor we need to consider in this situation is the conversion between frequency and wavelength. The conversion of one measure to the other is readily calculated from the following equation:

$$\text{frequency} \times \text{wavelength} = \text{velocity of light} = 3 \times 10^8 \text{ m/s}$$

A handy conversion rule is

$$\text{frequency} \times \text{wavelength} = 300{,}000 \text{ nm THz}$$

For example, a frequency of 600 THz corresponds to

$$\text{wavelength} = \frac{300{,}000 \text{ nm THz}}{600 \text{ THz}} = 500 \text{ nm}$$

Applying this rule to every point in the curve for spectral reflectance in terms of frequency yields a point in the curve in the diagram to the right above, in which wavelength is plotted along the horizontal axis. The relation between frequency and wavelength plots as a hyperbola:

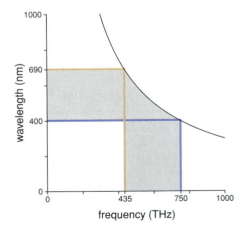

The gray zone indicates the approximate extent of the visible range. The fact that higher frequencies correspond to lower wavelengths, and vice versa, indicates that the conversion "flips" the spectral reflectance curve horizontally.

An additional factor comes in when we consider equal steps in frequency (right). The same step in frequency produces a larger change in wavelength when it is at the low end of the visible range than when it is at

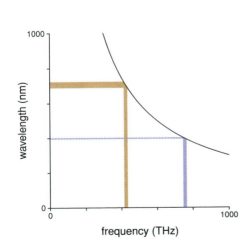

the high end of the range. Thus conversion involves not only a horizontal flip of the curve, but also a relative stretching toward the higher end of the wavelength spectrum and a compression toward the lower end. For example, a spectral reflectance curve that is symmetrical on a frequency axis is not symmetrical on a wavelength axis:

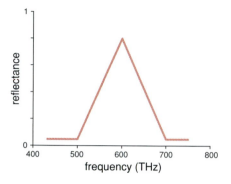
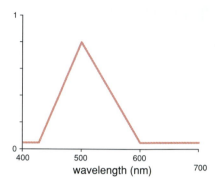

All of the above considerations are equally applicable to spectral transmittance and spectral absorptance.

Spectral sensitivity

This illustration shows the spectral sensitivity of rods within the human eye, plotted in terms of both photon–frequency and energy–wavelength units. By convention, the peak sensitivity is assigned a value of 1. These sensitivity

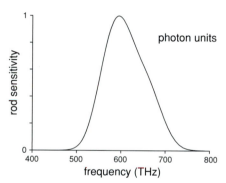
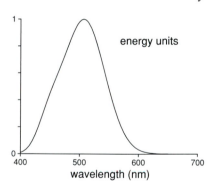

curves are equivalent to the scotopic luminous efficiency function, discussed earlier, and the diagram on the right appeared in the illustration that dealt with peak sensitivity. The two sensitivity curves in this illustration differ in two respects. The first, and most obvious, is that the horizontal scales are different. Less evident is that the sensitivity values that are plotted also depend upon which units are used. This is because these values refer to the intensity of the light at some frequency required to produce some criterion rate of photoreceptor activation. The greater the intensity required to reach the criterion, the lower the sensitivity. Thus the vertical scale in a spectral sensitivity curve is the ratio of the intensity required at the frequency of the peak of the curve to the intensity at a given frequency. At any one frequency, this ratio is a dimensionless number, so there are no dimensional units associated with the vertical scale. But as we saw earlier, two spectrally distinct lights equalized in terms of their energy flux are not equal in terms of their photon flux. So the vertical scale in a spectral sensitivity curve *does* depend upon whether energy or photon units are used, and it is the normalizing step that masks them.

Conversion to energy–wavelength units involves two steps. The first is the conversion of the abscissa from frequency to wavelength; this step is exactly the same as for spectral reflectance or transmittance, as described above. The energy–wavelength curve will be stretched at the high end and compressed at the low end, relative to the photon–frequency curve, just as before. The second step is the conversion of the vertical scale from (reciprocal) photon units to (reciprocal) energy units, for each point on the spectrum, and the renormalization of the resulting curve to give a peak value of 1.

The following describes spectral-sensitivity conversions in quantitative terms, using the symbols of RADIOMETRY.

Let the sensitivity in photon–frequency units be $S_n(v)$, and in energy–wavelength units be $S_e(\lambda)$. Since both curves are normalized to one, we are concerned only with relative amplitudes, and thus need to deal with proportional relations.

Radiometry *499*

$S_n(v)$ is proportional to the reciprocal of the radiometric flux of photons, $\phi_n(v)$, at some frequency required to detect or match the stimulus:

$$S_n(v) \sim \frac{1}{\phi_n(v)}$$

Likewise, $S_e(\lambda)$ is proportional to the reciprocal of the energy flux, $\phi_e(\lambda)$, at the corresponding wavelength:

$$S_e(\lambda) \sim \frac{1}{\phi_e(\lambda)}$$

Two equations are needed: (1) the relation between defined wavelength and frequency, termed the *wave equation*:

$$\lambda = \frac{c}{v}$$

where c, the velocity of light, is a *physical constant*, and (2) the relation between the frequency of a photon and its energy,

$$E_{\text{photon}} = hv \ (\text{J})$$

where h is Planck's constant.

The energy of the photons at this frequency is proportional to the frequency,

$$\phi_e(\lambda) \sim v\phi_n(v)$$

Hence,

$$S_e(\lambda) \sim \frac{1}{v\phi_n(v)} \sim \frac{S_n(v)}{v}$$

Using the wave equation, this can be expressed as

$$S_e(\lambda) \sim \lambda S_n(v)$$

Thus a flat spectral sensitivity in photon–frequency units yields a ramp in energy–wavelength units. Conversely,

$$S_n(v) \sim v S_e(\lambda)$$

So a flat spectral sensitivity curve in energy–wavelength units also yields a ramp in photon–frequency units.

Photometry *453*

Luminous efficiency

The photopic luminous efficiency function, used in PHOTOMETRY, is similar to a spectral sensitivity curve in that it plots the reciprocal of the amount of light necessary to match some reference light. It arises physiologically from the combined stimulation of the M and L cones. When plotted in photon–frequency units, this luminous efficiency function is well matched by a combination of the spectral sensitivities of the L and M cones, such that the ratio of the amplitude of the L cone spectral sensitivity to that of the M cones is about 1.8 (see page 458). This is one of the few situations in which the same result (1.8) is obtained when energy–wavelength units are used. This can be understood by considering the L/M ratio at some particular frequency. Converting from frequency to wavelength has no influence on this ratio, and converting to energy consists of multiplying each factor by the same scaling value, which again does not change this ratio.

Spectral density

An earlier illustration compared the spectral irradiance of light from the sun above the earth's atmosphere using the two sets of units. Conversion of photon–frequency units to energy–wavelength units involves the same two steps employed in the previous two conversions. The first is the conversion of the abscissa from frequency to wavelength; this step is exactly the same as for surface properties and spectral sensitivities, as described above. The energy–wavelength curve will be stretched at the high end and compressed at the low end, relative to the photon–frequency curve, just as before. This horizontal distortion alone cannot account for the fact that the spectral density plotted in units of energy–wavelength units shows a peak in the visible range.

The second step involves the conversion of the vertical axis from photon units to energy units. Since both curves are density plots, the basis of the conversion needs to deal with equating some frequency interval in the photon–frequency plot with the corresponding wavelength interval in the energy-wavelength plot:

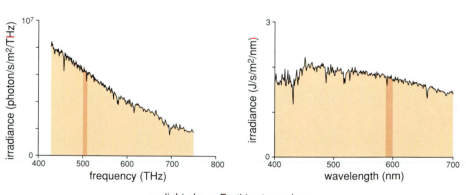

sunlight above Earth's atmosphere

In these diagrams I have used relatively large steps along the abscissa in order to show how the wavelength step is related to the frequency step. In practice, to convert in either direction, much smaller steps are used in order to preserve the irregularities in the density curve.

The *area* above the frequency step in the diagram to the left is the product of the frequency step, measured in THz, and the amplitude of the spectral irradiance at the frequency of the step. This area has units of photon/s/m^2. The area above the corresponding wavelength step in the diagram to the right is likewise seen to have units of J/s/m^2. The only difference is between photons and energy as measured in joules. The energy of a photon is proportional to its frequency, and is thus readily calculated. Equating the two areas on this basis allows the amplitude of the spectral irradiance in energy–wavelength units to be calculated.

Radiometry 499

Using the symbols of RADIOMETRY, $E_n(\nu)$ is the spectral irradiance in photon–frequency units at a frequency of ν. $E_e(\lambda)$ is then the spectral irradiance in energy–wavelength units at a wavelength of λ. The problem at hand is to calculate $E_e(\lambda)$ given $E_n(\nu)$.

Let $\Delta\nu$ be an incremental frequency step, and $\Delta\lambda$ the corresponding wavelength step. The incremental area for photon–frequency units is thus

$$E_n(\nu)\Delta\nu \ \ (\text{photon/s/m}^2)$$

Expressed in energy units, this becomes

$$E_n(\nu)h\nu\Delta\nu \ \ (\text{J/s/m}^2)$$

The corresponding area for energy photon units is

$$E_e(\lambda)\Delta\lambda \ \ (\text{J/s/m}^2)$$

The conversion requires that these two areas be the same:

$$E_n(\nu)h\nu\Delta\nu = E_e(\lambda)\Delta\lambda$$

Incrementally differentiating the wave equation,

$$\Delta\lambda = -\frac{c}{\nu^2}\Delta\nu$$

Substituting the magnitudes in this relation in the above equation, and simplifying,

$$E_e(\lambda) = E_n(\nu)\frac{h\nu^3}{c} \ \ (\text{J/s/m}^2/\text{m})$$

or

$$E_n(\nu) = E_e(\lambda)\frac{\lambda^3}{hc^2} \ \ (\text{photon/s/m}^2/\text{Hz})$$

It is the cubic relation between the radiometric measure and the spectral parameter that produces such a severe change in the shape of the curve when converting between these two sets of units.

Notes

For the most part, these notes provide references for further reading. I've also added summaries of how certain values were obtained, a few of which presume a knowledge of matters or techniques not otherwise discussed in this book.

PROLOGUE: *The watch*

The letters between Newton and Bentley can be found in Brewster (1965). Newton's *Opticks* remains in print (1952), and the full version of the query cited here can be found on page 369. Paley's general line of argument goes back to John Ray (1628–1705), who was in turn influenced by Newton (Gillespie, 1987). Paley's philosophy is discussed by LeMahieu (1976), and the difficulties with it, which go back to Hume, are emphasized by Hurlbutt (1985). Bowlby (1990) describes Paley's influence on Darwin, and some of the conflicts Darwin had to face when he brought his book on evolution to press. Barrow and Tipler (1986) provide a recent summary of the design argument.

Calvin (1986) has written an excellent introduction to modern evolutionary theory, cast in the form of a raft journey through the Grand Canyon. Partridge (1982) discusses the distinctions between evolution and engineering. Dawkins (1990, 1996) argues the case that evolution can produce an eye. Behe (1996) argues the opposite at the biochemical level, but, as Coyne (1996) points out, his theory of "irreducible complexity" has a few problems. Natural selection is not design, but the critical aspects of this process that allow it to emulate design remain poorly understood.

 The chase   *6–19*

Cheetahs appear to have the highest recorded running speed of any animal (29 m/s or 65 miles/hr; Sharp, 1997), yet are able to maintain the height of their eyes within a narrow range, as shown in one of the illustrations in this chapter. Cheetahs and gazelles appear frequently on the "Discovery" channel on cable television, where it can be seen that both animals successfully use body reflexes to stabilize eye position during the chase.

Image stabilization

As mentioned in this chapter, image stabilization need not involve eye movement, as long-necked birds may use head movements, and insects generally orient their entire body. In addition, insects and some flying birds make sudden rotations of their body that are, effectively, saccades. All of this and more is reviewed and discussed by Kirschfeld (1994). Catch-and-hold proves to be a universal theme for active animals, although the mechanisms to accomplish this pattern of seeing vary across species. Eye movements are discussed in greater depth in LOOKING, which begins with a reconsideration of the catch-and-hold pattern, and the notes to that chapter provide a pathway into the literature of eye movements.

The other aspects of vision discussed in this chapter are taken up in greater depth in the next few chapters.

 Eyes   *20–34*

The eyes of invertebrates, mentioned here only in passing, are reviewed by Bullock and Horridge (1965), Land (1981, 1988), Land and Fernald (1992), and papers in Cronly-Dillon and Gregory (1991). Kirschfeld (1976) discusses optical reasons why bug-eyed monsters are unlikely to exist and provides some amusing illustrations of what we would have to look like if we possessed compound eyes with a spatial acuity similar to what we now have with cameralike eyes. Walls (1942) and Polyak (1957) present a broad picture of the different forms of eyes found in vertebrates.

For reviews of the optics of the human eye, see LeGrand (1957), Levi (1980), and Wyszecki and Stiles (1982). The detailed structure of the human eye is described in depth by Hogan, Alvarado, and Weddell (1971), and most recently by Oyster (in press).

Pagon (1988) provides a broad and well-written survey of retinitis pigmentosa.

Macular pigment

In 1886, Max Schultze presciently proposed two functions for the macular pigment of the retina: reduction in chromatic aberration and protection from the harmful effects of light, and there is now support for both of these possibilities (Reading and Weale, 1974; Kirschfeld, 1982). The distribution of this pigment in the retina is described by Snodderly, Auran, and Delori (1984b) and Snodderly, Handelman, and Adler (1991). For the absorbance spectrum of this pigment, see Wyszecki and Stiles (1982), Snodderly et al. (1984a), and Bone, Landrum, and Cains (1992). Chemically, it consists of the carotenoid lutein and two stereoisomers of the xanthophyll zeaxanthin (Bone et al., 1993). The amount of macular pigment in an eye varies among individuals, and also depends to a limited degree upon diet (Landrum et al., 1997). Nussbaum, Pruett, and Delori (1981) provide a nice historical review.

Tapetum

The upper fundus of many nocturnal species contains a reflecting layer, and evolution has found many ways to accomplish this. For reviews see Walls (1942), Pirie (1966), and Rodieck (1973).

Retinas   *36–55*

For general reviews on retinal anatomy and physiology, see Cajál (1893), Rodieck (1973), Dowling (1987), Sterling, (1990), and Wässle and Boycott (1991). The primate retina is described by Polyak (1941) and Rodieck (1988) and the human retina by Hogan et al. (1971) and Duke-Elder (1961). The development of the foveal region is described by Yuodelis and Hendrickson (1986) and Kirby and Steineke (1992); the distribution of cones about the adult fovea is described by Østerberg (1935) and Curcio et al. (1990).

 Interlude: Size   *57–67*

For the chaos of the microscopic world, and its implications, see Feynman, Leighton, and Sands (1964) and Atkins (1993). Some philosophical implications are discussed by Atkins (1996). For a broader spectrum of sizes, see Morrison (1982); Packard (1994) provides some inventive means of developing a perspective on large differences in scale.

 The rain of photons onto cones   *68–87*

The photon images of Polaris are simulations based upon the point spread function of Vos, Walraven, and van Meeteren (1976). The solar spectral irradiance is from the World Meteorological Organization report number 590 (1982), and the transmittance of the atmosphere is from Jeske (1988). For the spectral transmittance of the lens I used the values given in Table 1(2.4.6) of Wyszecki and Stiles (1982), as modified by Stockman, MacLeod, and Johnson (1993), and added an additional absorbance of 0.15 (70.8% transmittance) at all wavelengths, which is based upon Norren and Vos (1974). The values for macular transmittance are taken from Table II(2.4.6), page 719, of Wyszecki and Stiles (1982).

Photons are particles of light

The model of light adopted here, based upon photons that travel along the rays of geometrical optics, is sufficient for the purposes of this book, but it necessarily leaves out a great deal that is relevant to vision. From a physical perspective, Feynman (1985) has written an excellent popular account of the nature of photons and how they *really* travel from place to place. Atkins (1983) develops blackbody radiation from the perspective of photons. The nature of photons is still not settled, and Gribbin (1995) provides an update.

Polarized light

Little is said in the text about the polarization of light, because we have not developed mechanisms for distinguishing photons on that basis. But polarization vision is critical to the survival of other species, and this aspect of vision is discussed by Werner (1989), Lythgoe (1979), Land (1981), and Dusenbery (1992). The parallels between polarization vision and color vision are discussed by Bernard and Wehner (1977).

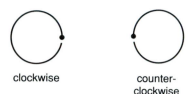

clockwise   counter-
                   clockwise

the two states of circular polarization

I'm not aware of any photon-based description of polarized light; here is a brief summary. When an electron emits a photon, the photon takes from the electron a variable amount of energy, depending on its frequency, and a fixed amount of angular momentum, which can be either clockwise or counterclockwise. I'll represent these two states as small round heads attached to circular tails (left).

Photons in either of these states are said to be **circularly polarized**. If the photon *does not* interact with matter until it is absorbed by an electron, then the absorbing electron acquires both the energy and the unit amount of angular momentum—clockwise or counterclockwise—that was conveyed by the photon at the time it was emitted. But if the photon *does* interact with matter prior to its absorption, then its state of polarization becomes uncertain in a very fundamental way. The electron that absorbs the photon will still acquire a fixed amount of angular momentum, but whether it will be clockwise or counterclockwise becomes a matter of probability. The transitional states can be represented as a graded series of ellipses:

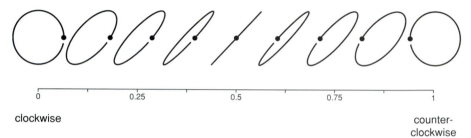

clockwise   counter-
                                                                             clockwise

probability that angular momentum will be counterclockwise

All of these possibilities are conveniently represented on the surface of a unit sphere, termed a Poincaré sphere:

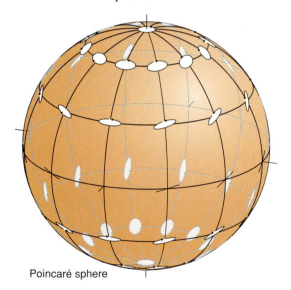

Poincaré sphere

The polarization state of any photon maps to some point on the Poincaré sphere; conversely, every point on the sphere represents a potential polarization state for a photon. All counterclockwise polarization states lie in the northern hemisphere, and those with clockwise states lie in the southern hemisphere. The two circular states lie at either pole, and the linear polarized states lie along the equator; the axis of the probability that the angular momentum will be counterclockwise extends from the south to the north pole. Between the equator and the poles, the photons are elliptically polarized for all of the possible orientations of the ellipses shown in the previous diagram.

Unpolarized light

Within classical optics the definition of unpolarized light is somewhat complex (e.g., Hurwitz, 1945; Born and Wolf, 1964; Shurcliff and Ballard, 1964). But within photon optics the definition is quite simple: *Unpolarized light consists of photons that are uniformly distributed over the Poincaré sphere.* Note that every photon is "fully" polarized, but light can be polarized to different degrees, depending upon the distribution on the Poincaré sphere of the photons that compose it. This distribution, in turn, depends upon the interaction of the light with matter. Consider an unpolarized light, like that from the Sun, that is reflected from the surface of a pond. The arriving photons are randomly, and thus uniformly, distributed on the Poincaré sphere. Those that are reflected shift symmetrically toward or past the point on the sphere that represents horizontal linear polarization, each point moving along a great circle, by an amount that depends only on the difference between the angle of incidence and Brewster's angle. The photons of the refracted light go the other way toward (but not past) the point of vertical polarization. In either case, the polarization states of the photons are no longer uniformly distributed, but have become concentrated toward a certain portion of the sphere, and we say the light has become polarized. Animals that have polarization vision can detect this concentration of polarization states over the Poincaré sphere, just as animals with color vision can detect concentrations of energies (frequencies) of photons over the spectrum.

Viewing polarization geometrically in terms of the distribution of photons on the surface of the Poincaré sphere provides a simpler and more intuitive understanding of polarization than does the mathematical approach of classical optics. For example, in unpolarized light, what is the typical polarization state of a photon over the range from linear polarization to circular polarization? Put slightly more formally, what is the average ratio of the width to the length of the ellipse (ratio of minor to major axes)? This problem was first solved by Hurwitz (1945) using calculus and Fourier analysis. He calculated a value of 0.268.

Here is a simpler solution, based upon the geometrical properties of the Poincaré sphere. The top half of this sphere contains all of the counterclockwise polarization states. The median is the horizontal cut that divides the upper hemisphere into two portions that have the same number of polarization states and thus equal surface areas on the sphere. So the problem reduces itself to determining the height of the horizontal cut that does so. The answer comes from one of the beautiful simplicities of geometry, which I'll introduce as a puzzle. Imagine placing a sphere in an egg slicer so as to produce a series of slices of equal thickness:

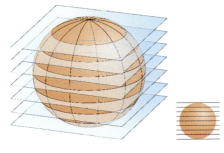

Which slice has the greatest area on the surface of the sphere? Hmm . . .

The surface area of a slice of a sphere formed by two parallel cuts can be shown to depend only on the distance between the cuts and not on their locations on the sphere. Thus all the slices have the same area. The height of the median thus lies halfway between the center of the sphere and the pole. In the earlier diagram that showed the probability axis for counterclockwise polarization, this is the ellipse that lies above the value of 0.75. Simple algebraic analysis of probability amplitudes (i.e., square root of probability) yields:

$$\frac{\text{minor axis}}{\text{major axis}} = \frac{\sqrt{p} - \sqrt{1-p}}{\sqrt{p} + \sqrt{1-p}}$$

where p is the probability for clockwise rotation. For $p = 0.75$ (or 0.25) this evaluates to 0.2679. . . and thus the same value determined by Hurwitz using classical optics.

Interlude: Neurons *89–101*

There are many introductory textbooks in neurobiology, including Kandel, Schwartz, and Jessell (1995) and Purves et al. (1997).

The rain of photons onto rods *122–133*

The increase in the point spread function with retinal eccentricity is described by Navarro, Artal, and Williams (1993).

Night and day *134–148*

Rods reliably signal the capture of single photons

This fact was established by Hecht, Schlaer, and Pirenne (1942), using psychophysical methods. From a historical perspective it is interesting that the stimulus used—a small spot, briefly presented—made the demonstration of this fact unnecessarily difficult. This may have led to the mistaken notion, still occasionally found in the literature, that rods respond to single photons only under exceptional circumstances, and always near the threshold of vision.

One photon per rod every eighty-five minutes

The overcast sky is an exemplar of the dimmest extended source that can be detected. Experimental determinations of the dimmest photometric luminance that can be detected are typically based upon a large test stimulus, presented for a long time, with natural pupils, and freely moving eyes. The stimulus is centered at a retinal eccentricity of about 10°, where the threshold for rod vision is lowest. The results are generally expressed in terms of the photopic luminance of the stimulus, despite the fact that this threshold is determined entirely by the rods. The reason for this is technical; luminance is determined by comparison to a reference source, and is most accurate at high light levels.

Pirenne (1962) tested a number of subjects and found a mean photopic luminance for 50% seeing of 0.75×10^{-6} cd m^{-2}. Based upon the incandescent light source he used (color temperature of 2400 K), this corresponds to a scotopic luminance of 0.88×10^{-6} cd m^{-2}, and with a natural pupil, to an illuminance of 4.4×10^{-5} scotopic trolands. The lowest individual threshold was 2.3×10^{-5} scotopic trolands and the highest was 11.7×10^{-5} scotopic trolands. Pirenne cites Luria (1958), who gave a value with a 2040 K source equivalent to 3.5×10^{-5} scotopic trolands. He also cites Weinstein and Arnulf (1946), who had a subject able to see an 8° field with a threshold value of 0.28×10^{-6} cd/m^2 for a 2390 K source; this corresponds to 1.6×10^{-5} scotopic trolands. See also Wyszecki and Stiles (1982, page 523).

The values thus range from 1.6 to 11.7×10^{-5} scotopic trolands. Pirenne's mean value of 4.4×10^{-5} scotopic trolands lies midway in this range, and is here assumed to be the threshold. Combining this value with the conversion factor of 4.5 photoisomerizations/s/td from the topic PHOTON CATCH RATE yields one caught photon per rod every 85 minutes. Pirenne (1962, page 126), using the values for different parameters current at the time, calculated a value of one caught photon per rod every 100 minutes, which is close to the value used here.

Overcast sky

Why was the sky overcast when you went camping and could just make out the border between the tops of the trees and the sky? Briefly, because the light of the clear night sky is much brighter than the dimmest we can detect. Roach and Gordon (1973) have written a fascinating book about the light of the night sky.

How photoreceptors work *158–186*

Biochemical cascade

This area has been extensively reviewed. Stryer's textbook (1995) provides a clear presentation of phototransduction from the perspective of biochemistry. Hofmann and Heck (1996) have written a detailed review of protein–protein interactions on the disc membrane.

Electrotonic spread

The general pattern of the currents produced by photoreceptors was described by Hagins, Penn, and Yoshikami (1970). They underestimated the resulting change in the transmembrane potential at the synaptic terminal, probably because the recording electrodes used created low-resistance paths.

Transmitter release and reuptake

Rao-Mirotznik et al. (1995) discuss a number of anatomical aspects of the rod synaptic terminal. See Attwell (1990) for a review of the functional aspects of the photoreceptor synapse; Attwell, Barbour, and Szatkowski (1993) for a discussion of non-vesicular release; and Attwell and Mobbs (1994) for a discussion of transporters.

Photon absorption time

I have not found in the literature a value for the photon absorption time; the value of 3 fs is my own estimate. There are a number of ways of obtaining a value of this magnitude from first principles, but all require some knowledge of higher mathematics, which is assumed in the following discussion. The spectral sensitivity curve of a visual pigment molecule has a certain width, and this implies an uncertainty in the frequency of an absorbed photon. But an uncertainty in frequency implies an uncertainty in time, which can be found by going from the frequency domain to the time domain via the Laplace transform. In the limiting case of Gaussian distributions in both domains:

$$\Delta f \Delta t = \frac{1}{2\pi}$$

where Δf and Δt are the width factors. The Lamb template for the spectral absorbance of rhodopsin (Lamb, 1995) best fits a Gaussian curve when $f/f_{max} = 0.086$. Assuming the peak sensitivity is at 600 THz for rod rhodopsin, solving for Δt yields 3 fs. This is a matter of mathematics applied to signal analysis, rather than physics. Multiplying both sides of the above equation by the Planck constant, so as to convert the uncertainty in frequency to an uncertainty in energy yields:

$$\Delta E \Delta t = h$$

which is the corresponding limiting case of a familiar equation of quantum mechanics (e.g., Feynman et al., 1964, volume 3). A physical insight now comes in: namely, that the uncertainty in the time of absorption of the photon is equivalent to the time of absorption, which, of course, is again 3 fs.

Photoisomerization time

This time has been experimentally measured by Schoenlein et al. (1991). A series of events occurs during this period, which is reviewed by Birge et al. (1988) and Birge (1990a,b).

Contribution of photon energy

This was first demonstrated by Cooper (1979); some of the implications are discussed by Rodieck (1973, page 290) and Birge (1990a). Diffusion of rhodopsin and other molecules within the disc surface is discussed in detail by Pugh and Lamb (1993).

The psychophysical sensitivity of rod vision is much lower than for rods

Baylor (1987) has an excellent discussion of this issue.

Rods saturate at bright light levels but cones do not

Aguilar and Stiles (1954) used psychophysical methods to demonstrate saturation of the rod pathway. Baylor, Nunn, and Schnapf (1984) showed that individual primate rods saturate at about the same light intensity as for the psychophysical studies; see also Baylor (1987).

Photoreceptors spontaneously generate photon-like events

This was discovered by Baylor, Matthews, and Yau (1980) in recordings of the current passing through toad outer segments. These outer segments are large, and individual photon-like events could be readily distinguished from the noise associated with the recording apparatus. Such events have also been demonstrated in the currents of primate rod outer segments (Baylor, Nunn, and Schnapf, 1984), but the analysis of the data is more complex.

Rhodopsins

Following an old convention (Dartnall, 1962; Rodieck, 1973; Knowles and Dartnall, 1977), all retinal-based visual pigments, whether from rods or cones, are here termed "rhodopsin." Currently, most authors restrict this term to the rod pigment, and have devised a variety of other terms for the cone pigments. The reason for drawing such a distinction between rod and cone pigments is unclear. Rod rhodopsin appears to have originated from the ancestral LM cone pigment (Okano et al., 1992), and the amino acid sequences of these two pigments are closer to one another than they are to that of the S cone pigment. Primate cone pigments regenerate faster than do primate rod pigments, but the rate of regeneration of alligator rod pigment is 25 times faster than bovine rod pigment (Wald, Brown, and Kennedy, 1957; Smith et al., 1995). Thus there appears to be no clear criterion for distinguishing rod and cone visual pigments, and for the first steps in seeing, that's the first thing to know.

For recent reviews of rhodopsin structure and function, see Hargrave (1995) and Hamm (1998).

The manner in which the rhodopsin polypeptide chain threads through the disc membrane shown in the illustrations in this section of HOW PHOTORECEPTORS WORK follows Hargrave (1995). The amino acid sequence of bovine rod rhodopsin was determined by Ovchinnikov et al. (1982), and the gene sequence by Nathans and Hogness (1983). The identity of the counter ion to the protonated Schiff base was established by Zhukovsky and Oprian (1989). The genes for cone rhodopsins were sequenced by Nathans, Thomas, and Hogness (1986).

Rhodopsins are ancient

The sequence of the *Drosophila* rhodopsin is from Zuker, Cowman, and Rubin (1985). The alignments of amino acid sequences from different species follow Applebury and Hargrave (1986).

There are virtually no animal fossils older than the Cambrian period, but many such fossils appeared shortly thereafter. Darwin recognized that this "Cambrian explosion" posed a problem for his theory of evolution, but had no ready answer for it. However, the recent "explosion" in gene sequences from many species, together with the known geological periods in which certain species diverged, makes it clear that complex animals diverged long before the Cambrian period, and our last common ancestor with insects appears to have existed about a billion years ago (Wray, Levinton, and Shapiro, 1996).

Point mutations in rod rhodopsin
can lead to retinitis pigmentosa

The point mutations shown in the illustration on page 193 are based upon Table 1 of Gal et al. (1997). Mutation Arg135Leu (although included in my diagram) results from a change of two nucleotides in the codon sequence rather than one, as indicated in this table. This paper provides an excellent review of what is known in this area as of March, 1996; it also discusses the somewhat complex relations between each amino acid substitution and its phenotypic expression, as well as genetic correlates of other genetically based retinal diseases, including congenital night blindness. Table 2 of the paper lists the deletions/insertions mentioned in the text. For possible relations between point mutations of *Drosophila* rhodopsin and corresponding mutations in human rhodopsin that lead to retinitis pigmentosa, see Colley et al. (1995) and Kurada and O'Tousa (1995).

 Retinal organization *194–209*

Cell coupling is reviewed by Vaney (1994b; 1995). Many other aspects are reviewed in the references listed in the notes for the chapter RETINAS.

 Photoreceptor attributes *210–223*

For reviews of circadian clocks, see Green and Besharse (1996), Barinaga (1996), and Reppert and Weaver (1997). The genes that encode the three cone pigments in humans were determined by Nathans, Thomas, and Hogness (1986) and discussed by Nathans et al. (1992a), while Nathans et al. (1992b) review inherited variations in these genes. Jacobs (1993) surveys the distribution of color vision among mammals, including the variations seen among New and Old World primates.

 Cell types *224–265*

See Rodieck and Brening (1983) for a fuller discussion of the notion of cell types. You might be concerned that this notion is based upon distinctions between cell groups that are themselves undefined, and that my appeal to our ability to distinguish between cherry and dogwood trees leaves something to be desired. But as William Whewell pointed out, beyond a certain point, attempts to define real things face insurmountable difficulties:

> If we define a tree to be "a living thing without the power of voluntary motion," we shall be called upon to define "a living thing"; and it is manifest that this renewal of the demand for definition might be repeated indefinitely; and, therefore, we cannot in this way come to a final principle. And . . . most of those who use language, even with great precision and consistency, would find it difficult or impossible to give good definitions even of a few of the general names which they use; and therefore their practice cannot be regulated by any tacit reference to such definitions. (1847, page 471)

For specific cell types, the papers referenced in the figure citations in this chapter provide a good place to start. For an overview of mammalian horizontal cells, see Boycott (1988), Mariani (1985), and Sandmann, Boycott, and Peichl (1996a,b). Midget bipolar cells were first described by Polyak (1941), and the difference between invaginating and semi-invaginating by Kolb, Boycott, and Dowling (1969). The different types of diffuse bipolars are described by Boycott and Hopkins (1991) and Boycott and Wässle (1991). Giant bipolar cells have been described by Mariani (1983), Rodieck (1988), and Kolb, Linberg, and Fisher (1992). Polyak (1941, fig. 55, cell 'g') showed a bipolar cell with a dendritic arbor about the same size of a giant bipolar, but the size of the telodendritic arbor was more like that of a diffuse bipolar.

For a description of the variety of amacrine cells found in the primate retina, see Rodieck (1988) and Mariani (1990). For an estimate of the number of unidentified amacrine cells, see Strettoi and Masland (1996).

 Informing the brain *266–291*

Rodieck, Brening, and Watanabe (1993) survey the ganglion cell types that project to different regions of the brain. The papers referenced in the figure citations provide information about specific brain regions. For the pregeniculate see Harrington (1997).

 Looking *292–325*

Steinman and Levinson (1990) have written an excellent review of the role of eye movements in the detection of contrast and spatial detail. Kowler (1990) provides a broad review that emphasizes smooth eye movements. Becker (1991) reviews saccadic eye movements. Sparks and Mays (1990) review the role of the retinotopic map in the colliculus in determining the direction and magnitude of saccades. Freedman and Sparks (1997) describe new findings of the role of the superior colliculus in the coordination of eye and head movements. Robinson (1981) reviews the operations of the neurons that move the eye muscles.

 Seeing *326–360*

Calkins (1998) reviews the anatomical connections of the ganglion cell types discussed in this chapter.

The manner in which the responses of center–surround ganglion cells to complex stimuli can be predicted from their response to simpler stimuli is described by Rodieck (1965), and tested by Linsenmeier et al. (1982).

Buchsbaum and Gottschalk (1983) point out that the spectral sensitivity curves for luminance, red–green color vision, and blue–yellow color vision are approximately orthogonal to one another—meaning that the information each conveys is independent of the information conveyed by the other two. This leads to the perspective that in terms of contrast, the three pathways can usefully be viewed as a group, although for other aspects of visual perception (e.g., motion), the ganglion cell types that unselectively sum cone inputs (i.e., the presumed basis here for luminance) play special roles.

Color names and perceptions

For many years, linguists and cultural anthropologists claimed that the division of the spectrum into named categories such as "red" and "green" was a matter of culture, not biology. For example, in a widely read textbook on linguistics, Gleason (1961) states:

> There is a continuous gradation of color from one end of the spectrum
> to the other. Yet an American describing it will list the hues as red,

orange, yellow, green, blue, purple, or something of the kind. There is nothing inherent either in the spectrum or the human perception of it which would compel its division in this way

This claim, as well as those of others, was based not on evidence but upon the then-common assumption in the social sciences that semantic universals did not exist. But experiments by Berlin and Kay (1969), Heider (1971a,b), Heider and Olivier (1972), as well as others, demonstrate that the gamut of colors is not a perceptual continuum. Instead there are focal zones within this gamut that include not only red, green, yellow, and blue—for which we have some neural correlates—but also brown, purple, pink, and orange—whose neural correlates are unknown.

Rodieck (1991) discusses difficulties with the hypothesis that red–green color vision is conveyed mainly by midget ganglion cells. The status of black, white, and gray is also unresolved, in the sense that the perceptions of these colors may depend upon one or more ganglion cell types not yet identified. Although they lack language, pigeons also appear to categorize the spectrum (Wright and Cumming, 1971).

TOPICS

Biochemical cascade *371–400*

Time course of PDE* activation

The equation for the time course of **PDE*** used here was devised by Edward N. Pugh, Jr. (personal communication). It correctly predicts the time course of the photocurrent, and is based upon two assumptions:

1. Following the creation of **R***, the rate of generation of G_α^* declines exponentially.

2. The lifetimes of individual **PDE*** molecules follow simple first order reaction kinetics and are thus Poisson distributed.

In the tables below, the parameters Pugh used to fit the observed photocurrent are referenced as "Pugh inactivation model" in the "Source" column.

The time course of **PDE*** concentration, developed from a graphical perspective in this topic, is mathematically equivalent to a *convolution* of the time course of the rate of creation of **PDE*** (assumed here to be equivalent to the rate for creation of G_α^*) with the time course of **PDE*** decline. Using the symbols defined in this topic:

$$PDE*(t) = \int_0^\infty R_g e^{-(t-\tau)/\tau_g} e^{-\tau/\tau_p} d\tau = \frac{R_g \tau_p \tau_g}{\tau_p - \tau_g}\left(e^{-t/\tau_p} - e^{-t/\tau_g}\right)$$

and it follows that:

$$\text{area} = \int_0^\infty PDE*(t)\, dt \frac{R_g \tau_p \tau_g}{\tau_p - \tau_g} \int_0^\infty \left(e^{-t/\tau_g} - e^{-\tau/\tau_p}\right) dt = \frac{R_g \tau_p \tau_g}{\tau_p - \tau_g}(\tau_p - \tau_g) = R_g \tau_p \tau_g$$

and:

$$\text{spread} = \frac{\int_0^\infty t\, PDE*(t)\, dt}{\int_0^\infty PDE*(t)\, dt} = \frac{R_g \tau_p \tau_g (\tau_g + \tau_p)}{R_g \tau_p \tau_g} = \tau_g + \tau_p$$

Channel amplification

The equation for channel amplification was derived by Edward N. Pugh, Jr. (personal communication), who also pointed out the fact that this equation implies that channel amplification is maximized by a uniform decrease in concentration of cG throughout the outer segment.

Parametric values

All of the values I have used in this topic come either from the tables in Appendix B, or from the following tables, for which the comments at the beginning of that appendix also apply. As discussed in this topic, some of these values are well established, whereas others are tentative and likely to change as further investigation refines our understanding, and thus need to be viewed with caution. Perhaps the greatest uncertainty comes from the fact that a number of values needed to calculate the assumed behavior of primate outer segments are thus far known only in cold-blooded vertebrates. This difficulty is discussed in detail by Pugh and Lamb (1993). There currently is no firm value for the concentration of cG, which plays a critical role in these calculations, and the value assumed here was calculated by working back from estimates of channel density, the fraction of channels open in the dark, and the allosteric relation between channel opening and cG concentration (Karpen et al., 1992).

   All calculated values work back to the literature referenced within these tables. Each parameter is given an arbitrary symbol, shown at the left of each row (e.g., os1, os2, etc.), and the parameters used in each calculation are listed under the column "Source." The abbreviations for some of the parameters follow Pugh and Lamb (1993), which should be consulted for a discussion of what they represent, and under what conditions.

Rod outer segment (OS)

	Parameter	Value/measure		Source	Species
os1	OS length, perifoveal	25	μm	Appendix B	macaque
os2	OS diameter	2	μm	Appendix B	macaque
os3	Disc linear density	35.7	/μm	Appendix B	macaque
os4	OS fractional cytoplasm volume	50	%	Pugh & Lamb, 1990, p. 1927	macaque
os5	OS discs	893		*Calculated:* os1, os3	macaque
os6	OS surface area	157	μm^2	*Calculated:* os1, os2	macaque
os7	OS disc area	3.14	μm^2	*Calculated:* os2	macaque
os8	OS volume	79	μm^3	*Calculated:* os1, os7	macaque
os9	OS surface membrane/disc	0.18	μm^2	*Calculated:* os2, os3	macaque
os10	OS unit height	0.028	μm	*Calculated:* os1, os5	macaque
os11	OS unit area	0.176	μm^2	*Calculated:* os5, os6	macaque
os12	OS unit volume	0.088	fl	*Calculated:* os5, os8	macaque
os13	OS cytoplasm volume	39.3	fl	*Calculated:* os4, os8	macaque
os14	Molecules/cytoplasmic vol/μM	2.36×10^4	molecules/μM	*Calculated:* os13	macaque
os15	OS unit cytoplasmic volume	0.044	fl	*Calculated:* os5, os13	macaque
os16	Molecules/unit cytoplasmic vol/μM	26.5	molecules/μM	*Calculated:* os15	macaque

Photoactivation and R*

	Parameter	Value/measure		Source	Species
p1	Absorption time	3	fs	This book	any
p2	Photoisomerization	200	ps	Schoenlein et al., 1991	any
p3	Formation of **R***	0.25–0.5	ms	Pugh & Lamb, 1993, p. 120	mammal
p4	**R*** lifetime (time constant)	0.05	s	Pugh inactivation model	macaque
p5	Fraction of total activation in 0.1 s	86.5	%	*Calculated*: p4	macaque

Rhodopsin

	Parameter	Value/measure		Source	Species
r1	Concentration	3000	μM	Appendix B	mammal
r2	Outer segment volume	78.5	μm^3	Appendix B	mammal
r3	Molecules/outer segment	1.42×10^8	molecules	*Calculated*: r1, r2	macaque
r4	Dark photoisomerization rate/OS	6.3×10^{-3}	/s	Baylor, Nunn, and Schnapf, 1984	macaque
r5	Dark period/OS	160	s	*Calculated*: r4	macaque
r6	Dark rate/molecule	4.44×10^{-11}	/s	*Calculated*: r3, r4	macaque
r7	Dark period/molecule	2.25×10^{10}	s	*Calculated*: r6	macaque
r8	Dark period/molecule	714	years	*Calculated*: r6	macaque
r9	#/disc membrane	7.95×10^4	molecules	*Calculated*: os5, r3	macaque
r10	Spatial density on membrane	2.53×10^4	/μm^2	*Calculated*: os7, r9	macaque
r11	Diffusion coefficient	1.5	μm^2/s	Pugh & Lamb, 1993, Table 1	mammal
r12	RMS displacement in 0.1 s	0.77	μm	*Calculated*: r11	mammal
r13	Collision period	4×10^{-13}	s	Hille, 1992, p. 264	any
r14	# collisions in 0.1 s	2.5×10^{11}	/s	*Calculated*: r14	any

G proteins

	Parameter	Value/measure		Source	Species
g1	G/R molar ratio in OS	0.125		Sitaramayya et al., 1986	mammal
g2	G concentration	375	μM	*Calculated*: r1, g1	mammal
g3	G number	1.77×10^7	molecules	*Calculated*: os8, g2	macaque
g4	#/disc membrane	9932	molecules	*Calculated*: os5, g3	macaque
g5	Spatial density on membrane	3162	/μm^2	*Calculated*: os7, g4	macaque
g6	G diffusion coefficient	1.8	μm^2/s	Pugh & Lamb, 1993, Table 1	mammal
g7	R–G encounter rate	1.77×10^4	1/s	Pugh & Lamb, 1993 (recalculated)	mammal
g8	Encounter period	56.57	μs	*Calculated*: g7	mammal
g9	Max # encountered in 0.1 s	1768		*Calculated*: g7	mammal
g10	Peak activation rate	1.57×10^4	1/s	*Calculated*: d18	mammal
g11	Encounter + activation	64	μs	*Calculated*: g10	mammal
g12	Binding period	7	μs/molecule	*Calculated*: g8, g11	mammal
g13	Fraction of time bound	0.11		*Calculated*: g11, g12	mammal
g14	Fraction of time diffusing	0.89		*Calculated*: g13	mammal
g15	Total $\mathbf{G}_\alpha^*$	786	molecules	*Calculated*: p4, g10	mammal
g16	$\mathbf{G}_\alpha^*$/G total on disc membrane	8	%	*Calculated*: g4, g15	mammal
g17	Total # $\mathbf{G}_\alpha^*$ in period	679	molecules	*Calculated*: p4, g15	mammal

PDE

	Parameter	Value/measure		Source	Species
d1	PDE subunit/R molar ratio in OS	0.02		Sitaramayya et al., 1986	mammal
d2	PDE subunit concentration	60	μM	*Calculated:* r1, d1	mammal
d3	PDE subunit number	2.84×10^6	molecules	*Calculated:* os8, r1, d1, d2	mammal
d4	PDE subunit/disc membrane	1589	molecules	*Calculated:* os5, d3	mammal
d5	Spatial density on membrane	506	μm²/s	*Calculated:* os7, d4	mammal
d6	PDE hydrolysis of cG in dark	42.5	μM/s	*Calculated:* cg5, ch16	toad
d7	PDE subunit hydrolysis rate	0.708	/s	*Calculated:* d3, d6	
d8	PDE subunit hydrolysis period	1.41	s	*Calculated:* d7	
d9	k_{cat} subunit turnover	2000	/s	Pugh & Lamb, 1993, Table 2	mammal
d10	K_m cG binding constant	100	μM	Pugh & Lamb, 1993, Table 2	mammal
d11	PDE buffering power	1.0		(because its cG is tightly bound)	mammal
d12	β_{sub} (rate constant of cG hydrolysis)	4.09×10^{-4}	/s	*Calculated:* os13, d9, d10, ch23	mammal
d13	**PDE*** subunit hydrolysis rate	1.74×10^{-3}	μM/s	*Calculated:* d12, ch16	mammal
d14	**PDE*** subunit hydrolysis rate	81.5	molecules/s	*Calculated:* d9, d10, ch16	mammal
d15	Activated/dark rates	115		*Calculated:* d7, d14	mammal
d16	Amplification constant (A)	18.0	/s²	Pugh inactivation model	mammal
d17	V_{rp} rate of production **PDE*/R***	1.57×10^4	/s	*Calculated:* d12, d16, ch1	mammal
d18	Total **PDE*** subunits activated	786	subunits	*Calculated:* g15	mammal
d19	Average activation period of PDE	0.1	s	Pugh inactivation model	mammal
d20	Maximum cGs hydrolyzed	6404	molecules	*Calculated:* d14, d18, d19	mammal
d21	Fraction PDE subunits on disc	49.4	%	*Calculated:* d4, d18	mammal
d22	PDE saturation rate/disc	40.5	photon/s	*Calculated:* d19, d21	mammal
d23	PDE saturation rate	3.61×10^4	photon/s	Calculated: os5, d22	mammal

cG

	Parameter	Value/measure		Source	Species
cg1	cG number in OS	1.00×10^5	molecules	*Calculated:* os13, ch16	mammal
cg2	Turnover rate in dark	10	/s	Pugh inactivation model	mammal
cg3	Rate of synthesis in dark (a)	42.5	μM/s	*Calculated:* cg2, ch16	various
cg4	Rate of synthesis in dark (a)	1.00×10^6	molecules/s	*Calculated:* cg1, cg2	mammal
cg5	Rate of hydrolysis in dark (b)	10.00	/s	*Calculated:* cg3, ch16	various
cg6	Free diffusion coefficient 20°C	400	μm²/s	Koutalos et al., 1995	frog
cg7	Longitudinal diffusion coefficient 20°C	70	μm²/s	Koutalos et al., 1995	frog
cg8	D37°/D22°	1.5		Pugh & Lamb, 1993, p. 119	
cg9	Free diffusion 37°C	600	μm²/s	*Calculated:* cg6, cg8	mammal
cg10	Longitudinal diffusion 37°C	105	μm²/s	*Calculated:* cg7, cg8	mammal
cg11	Free RMS displacement in 0.1 s	19.0	μm	*Calculated:* cg9	mammal
cg12	Longitudinal RMS displacement in 0.1 s	6.5	μm	*Calculated:* ch10	mammal
cg13	Free diffusion period, middle to edge	2.78×10^{-4}	s	*Calculated:* os2, cg9	mammal
cg14	# cG/unit volume	113	molecules	*Calculated:* os16, ch16	mammal

cG-Gated channels

	Parameter	Value/measure		Source	Species
ch1	Hill coefficient	2.8		Taylor & Baylor, 1995	salamander
ch2	K_d	17.0	μM	Pugh inactivation model	macaque
ch3	Salamander channel density	650	$\mu m^2/s$	Karpen et al., 1992	salamander
ch4	Salamander OS diameter	11.0	μm	Pugh & Lamb, 1993, Fig. 1	salamander
ch5	Macaque/salamander OS diameter	5.5		*Calculated:* os2, ch4	various
ch6	Channel density	3575	$\mu m^2/s$	*Calculated:* ch3, ch5	macaque
ch7	Channel/unit OS area	629	channels	*Calculated:* os9, ch6	various
ch8	Channel current	−3.0	fA	Yau & Baylor, 1989	amphibian, reptile
ch9	Total # channels	5.62×10^5	channels	*Calculated:* os6, ch6	macaque
ch10	Channel concentrations/cytoplasm	23.7	μM	*Calculated:* os13, ch9	macaque
ch11	Channel/dark current	1.13×10^4	channels	*Calculated:* ch8, cv1	various
ch12	Channel/photon	−233	channels	*Calculated:* ch8, cv3	various
ch13	#PDE/#channels	5		*Calculated:* d3, ch9	various
ch14	Fraction open in dark	2.02	%	*Calculated:* ch9, ch11	various
ch16	Fraction open 1 photon peak	1.98	%	*Calculated:* ch14, cv3	various
ch16	Free cG in dark	4.25	μM	*Calculated:* ch1, ch2, ch14	various
ch17	cG at 1 photon peak	4.22	μM	*Calculated:* ch1, ch2, ch16	various
ch18	Change in cG at 1 photon peak	−0.0321	μM	*Calculated:* ch16, ch17	various
ch19	Change in cG at 1 photon peak	−1569	molecules	*Calculated:* os13, ch18, ch23	various
ch20	Change in cG at 1 photon peak	−0.76	%	*Calculated:* ch16, ch18	various
ch21	Microscopic K_d	18.0	μM	Karpen et al., 1988, p. 1290	salamander
ch22	Bound cG in dark	4.5	μM	*Calculated:* ch10, ch16, ch21	various
ch23	Channel buffer power	2.1		*Calculated:* ch16, ch22	various
	Fraction open in dark	1	%	Yau & Nakatani, 1985	toad
	Fraction open in dark	1	%	Nakatani & Yau, 1988	toad
	Fraction open in dark	1–2	%	Yau and Baylor, 1989	toad
	Fraction open in dark	0.7–3	%	Pugh & Lamb, 1990	salamander

Channel density

Channels/μm^2	Channel/unit OS area	Source	Species
500	88.0	Zimmerman & Baylor, 1986	salamander
1000	175.9	Haynes et al., 1986	toad
400	70.4	Zimmerman & Baylor, 1986	salamander
650	114.4	Karpen, Loney, & Baylor, 1992	salamander

Currents and voltages

	Parameter	Value/measure		Source	Species
cv1	Dark current	−34	pA	Baylor, Nunn, & Schnapf, 1984	macaque
cv2	Dark current	−20	pA (max)	Kraft et al., 1993	human
cv3	Single photon current	0.7	pA	Baylor et al., 1984, p. 586	macaque
cv4	Dark current/single current	48.6		*Calculated: cv1, cv3*	macaque
cv5	Saturating flash	200	photons	Baylor et al., 1984, p. 580	macaque
cv6	Time to peak	0.2	s	Baylor et al., 1984, p. 581	macaque
cv7	Integral of normalized time course	1.14		*Calculated from above reference*	macaque
cv8	Single photon charge	0.160	pC	*Calculated: cv3, cv6, cv7*	macaque
cv9	Single photon charge	9.96×10^5	charges	*Calculated: cv8*	macaque
cv10	Current saturation	213	photon/s	*Calculated: cv1, cv8*	macaque
cv11	Single photon voltage	−1.2	mV	Schneeweis & Schnapf, 1995	macaque
cv12	Input resistance	1.2	GΩ	Schneeweis & Schnapf, 1995	macaque
cv13	Dark voltage	−37	mV	Schneeweis & Schnapf, 1995	macaque
cv14	Fractional current	−2.1	%	*Calculated: cv1, cv3*	macaque
cv15	Fractional voltage	3.2	%	*Calculated: cv11, cv13*	macaque
cv16	Dark current as charge	2.12×10^8	charge/s	*Calculated: cv1*	macaque
cv17	Current/unit volume	2.38×10^5	charge/s	*Calculated: os5, cv16*	macaque
cv18	Dark current by Na ions	80	%	Yau, 1994	toad
cv19	Dark current by Ca ions	15	%	Yau, 1994	toad
cv19	Dark current by Mg ions	5	%	Yau, 1994	toad
cv20	Na ions/Ca ions	10.7		*Calculated: cv18, cv19*	
cv21	Ca ion entry/exit for OS	1.59×10^7	Ca/s	*Calculated: cv16, cv19*	
cv22	Ca ion entry/unit volume	1.78×10^4	Ca ion/s	*Calculated: cv17, cv19*	various
cv23	Free Ca in dark	0.5	μM	*Based on free Ca table below*	primate
cv24	# free Ca in dark	1.18×10^4	ions	*Calculated: os14, cv23*	primate
cv25	Ca/unit volume	13.2	ions	*Calculated: os16, cv25*	primate

Free calcium in the dark

Method	Value/measure	Source	Species
Indo-dextran	554 nM	Gray-Keller & Detwiler, 1994	gecko
Aequorin	500 nM	McNaughton et al., 1986, page 263	salamander
Fura-2	220 nM	Ratto et al., 1988	frog
Aequorin	410 nM	Lagnado et al., 1992	salamander

Blackbody radiation *401–404*

Blackbody radiation is a fundamental topic in physics, and the derivation of the relevant formulas are covered in most textbooks (e.g., Feynman et al., 1964; Atkins, 1983). A derivation is a plausibility argument that traces the logic from a set of assumptions to a result that agrees with the experimental observations. Kuhn (1978) provides historical treatment of this topic that, by discussing the missteps, provides a deeper understanding.

 cG-gated channels *405–415*

These channels were discovered by Fesenko et al. (1985). The gene that codes for these channels in rods was cloned by Kaupp et al. (1989). Surprisingly, these channels prove to be homologous to voltage-gated channels (Jan and Jan, 1990). Finn, Grunwald, and Yau (1996) review the roles of cG-gated channels in a number of different cell types.

Zagotta and Siegelbaum (1996) review the molecular structure of these protein channels. Yau and Baylor (1989) review the properties of these channels and point out how a large number of channels, each carrying a small current, serve to reduce noise, and thereby improve the reliability of the response to a single photon. Stryer (1987) proposed an allosteric model for the relation between cG concentration and channel opening (Zimmerman and Baylor, 1986), which appears to be consistent with current findings (Taylor and Baylor, 1995).

 Exponentials *439–442*

Every book on calculus discusses exponential relations. Eli Maor (1994) has written a book about the historical origins of *e*, developed mainly from an algebraic approach. D'Arcy Thompson (1992) describes a rich variety of exponential relations that can be observed in the natural world.

 Optimal colors *447–451*

The theory of optimal colors was developed by the physicist Erwin Schrödinger (1920), and is discussed in greater detail by Wyszecki and Stiles (1982).

Photometry *453–469*

Kaiser (1981) describes the historical background to the development of current photometric standards. Kaiser (1981) and Lennie, Pokorny, and Smith (1993) review the psychophysical measures that yield photometric additivity. Wyszecki and Stiles (1982) provide a formal and detailed description of photometry that is based upon units of wavelength and energy. The photopic luminous efficiency function used in this topic is based upon the L and M cone fundamentals in the right-hand columns of Table 8 of Stockman, MacLeod, and Johnson (1993), combined by coefficients obtained by inverting the CIE_{1964} transformation matrix on page 2515 of that paper, after converting from energy/wavelength to photon/frequency units (Y = 0.669 L + 0.366 M).

The identification of parasol cells as the ganglion cells responsible for distinguishing photopic luminance differences was made by Lee, Martin, and Valberg (1988). Calkins (1998) describes the anatomical convergence of cones onto parasol ganglion cells via diffuse bipolar cells.

The scotopic luminous efficiency function, found in Table I(4.3.2) of Wyszecki and Stiles (1982, page 789) is based upon interpolations of threshold measurements at 10 points in the spectrum by 22 observers in a study by Wald (1945), and brightness matches at 21 points in the spectrum by 50 observers under 30 years of age in a study by Crawford (1949).

 Poisson distribution *485–498*

Feller's two-volume set (1968, 1971) provides an excellent introduction to Poisson distributions. The first volume deals with discrete events, and the second volume begins by considering waiting times.

SI units

Basic SI units

Physical quantity	Name of unit	Symbol
length	meter	m
mass	kilogram	kg
time	second	s
electric current	ampere	A
thermodynamic temperature	degrees kelvin	K
luminous intensity	candela	cd
substance	mole	mol

Dimensionless units

plane angle	radian	rad
solid angle	steradian	sr

Multipliers

Multiplier	Prefix	Symbol
10^{12}	tera	T
10^9	giga	G
10^6	mega	M
10^3	kilo	k
—	—	—
10^{-3}	milli	m
10^{-6}	micro	μ
10^{-9}	nano	n
10^{-12}	pico	p
10^{-15}	femto	f
10^{-18}	atto	a
10^{-2}	centi	c

When a prefix is attached to a basic unit a new unit is formed.

Derived units with special name

Physical quantity	Name	Symbol	Dimensions
energy	joule	J	$kg\ m^2\ s^{-2}$
force	newton	N	$kg\ m\ s^{-2}$
power	watt	W	$kg\ m^2\ s^{-3}$
electric charge	coulomb	C	$s\ A$
electric potential difference	volt	V	$kg\ m^2\ s^{-3}\ A^{-1}$
electric resistance	ohm	Ω	$kg\ m^2\ s^{-3}\ A^{-3}$
electric capacitance	farad	F	$kg^{-1}\ m^{-2}\ s^4\ A^2$
luminous flux	lumen	lm	$cd\ sr$
illumination	lux	lx	$cd\ sr\ m^{-2}$
frequency	hertz	Hz	s^{-1}
customary temperature	degree Celsius	°C	thermodynamic temperature −273.15
pressure	pascal	Pa	$kg\ m^{-1}\ s^{-2}$

Units allowed in conjunction with SI

volume	liter	l	$10^{-3}\ m^3$
energy	electron volt	eV	$1.6021 \times 10^{-19}\ J$

Physical Constants

Description	Symbol	Value	Units
Velocity of light in vacuum	c	3.000×10^8	$m\ s^{-1}$
Boltzmann	k	1.380×10^{-23}	$J\ K^{-1}$
Planck	h	6.626×10^{-34}	$J\ s$
Avogadro	N	6.023×10^{23}	mol^{-1}

Discussion and examples

There are seven basic units in the SI systems. Four of these are fundamental: mass, length, time, and charge (as current). The remainder were selected as a matter of convenience and compromise, rather than because they somehow reflect some fundamental underpinnings of the universe. For example, the inclusion of the **candela** is unnecessary from a physical perspective, as discussed in PHOTOMETRY. Likewise a **mole** is nothing more than 6.023×10^{23} *things* (molecules, ions, elephants). In any case, they provide us with a sufficient set to enable all of the other units to be based upon them.

Photometry *453*

Standard observer

In order to quantify some aspect of vision it is generally necessary to make some assumptions about the eye or retina. For example, the size of the retinal image depends upon the length of the eye. Since different human eyes have different lengths, it is necessary to choose a representative value. A "standard observer" is a collection of such values, chosen so that they are self-consistent.

In this appendix, measured values are shown in regular type. When there is more than one value for some measure, the one used for the standard observer is shown in boldfaced type. Values calculated from other values are shown in italic type. For example, in the first row of the first table ("Human optics") below, the posterior nodal distance is given as 16.7 mm. One degree is equal to $\pi/180$ radians, hence:

$$\text{magnification} = 16.7 \text{ mm} \times \frac{\pi}{180 \text{ deg}} = 0.291 \text{ mm/deg}$$

The values throughout this appendix are arranged so that calculated values are always based upon preceding values. They were rounded to two significant figures after all the calculated values had been determined. For internal consistency, calculated values are used whenever possible, even when these values have been measured directly. In general, there are no important and unresolved differences between measured and calculated values.

Human optics

Posterior nodal distance	Magnification	Reference	Comments
16.7 mm	*0.291 mm/deg*	Wyszecki & Stiles, 1982	LeGrand's *Theoretical Eye*, p. 99
15.7 mm	*0.274 mm/deg*	Drasdo & Fowler, 1974	Table, p. 710
	0.276 mm/deg	Holden et al., 1987	
16.1 mm	**0.280 mm/deg**	Standard observer	Average magnification

Photoreceptor inner and outer segments

Rod outer segments

	Diameter (μm)	Length (μm)	Reference/comments
salamander	11	22	Pugh & Lamb, 1993
toad	6	60	Pugh & Lamb, 1993
human	2	25	Pugh & Lamb, 1993
human parafoveal	2	35.2	Young, 1971; ecc: 0.75–1.25 mm (2.6°–4.3°)
human perifoveal	2	**31.2**	Young, 1971; ecc: 1.25–2.75 mm (4.3°–9.4°)
human periphery	2	23.9	Young, 1971
macaque		28	Polyak, 1941, p. 237
macaque		25	Baylor, Nunn, & Schnapf, 1984

Note the large size of the amphibian rods, compared with those of mammals. For example, the volume of a salamander rod outer segment is about 20 times greater than that of a human's. Small outer segments give mammalian rods a faster response time simply because there are fewer cG molecules to be removed. See Pugh and Lamb (1993) for a more detailed discussion of this point.

Rod inner segments

Eccentricity (mm)	Young (μm)	Old (μm)	Species
1.0	2.05	2.32	human
2.0	2.11	2.38	human
2.9	2.16	2.43	human
3.0	2.16	2.44	human
4.1	**2.22**	2.50	human
5.0	2.27	2.56	human

Because the inner segments funnel the photons into the outer segment, these values are important in determining the photon catch, given the flux density of the incident photons. From: Curcio et al., 1993

Rod discs and peak absorption

Parameter	Value/measure	Reference/comments
Disc spacing	28 nm	Pugh & Lamb, 1993
Disc packing density	36 μm^{-1}	Reciprocal of disc spacing
Discs/rod outer segment	1100	Parafoveal, 31.2 × 36
Peak specific optical density	0.015 μm^{-1}	Hárosi & MacNichol, 1974; Hárosi, 1975
Peak absorbance of rod	0.47	Parafoveal, 31.2 × 0.015
Peak absorptance of rod	0.66	$1 - 10^{-0.47}$

Photoreceptor inner and outer segments (continued)

Human foveal cone outer segments

Reference	Length (μm)	Peak absorbance	Peak absorptance	Comments
Polyak, 1941, p. 448	35	0.53	0.70	
Polyak, 1941, Fig. 38	43	0.65	0.77	(Diagram is partly schematic)
M. Schultze	36	0.54	0.71	Cited by Polyak, 1941, p. 448
R. Greeff	38	0.57	0.73	Cited by Polyak, 1941, p. 448
Stockman et al., 1993	27	0.40	0.60	
Standard observer	**33**	**0.50**	**0.68**	Based in part on Stockman et al., 1993, p. 2509

Macaque foveal cone outer segments

Reference	Length (μm)	Peak absorbance	Peak absorptance	Comments
Polyak, 1941, p. 200	67	1.01	0.90	
Polyak, 1941, p. 200	64	0.96	0.89	
Polyak, 1941, p. 200	46	0.69	0.80	
Dowling, 1965	40	0.60	0.75	
Borwein et al., 1980 (min)	30	0.45	0.65	
Borwein et al., 1980 (max)	40	0.60	0.75	
J. Neumann, *Rhesus*	45	0.68	0.79	Cited by Polyak, 1941, p. 448
J. Neumann, *Nemestrina*	54	0.81	0.85	Cited by Polyak, 1941, p. 448

Human cone inner segments

Eccentricity (mm)	Eccentricity (deg)	Diameter (mm)	Area (μm^2)	Area ratio	Reference
0	0	2.3	4.2	1.0	Curcio, 1987
1.40	5	3.3	8.6	2.1	Curcio, 1987
2.80	10	7.5	44.2	10.6	Curcio, 1987 (temporal retina)
4.21	15	7.9	49.0	11.8	Hecht & Mandelbaum, 1939
8.41	30	7.9	49.3	11.9	Hecht, Haig, & Chase, 1937 (nasal retina)

The large increase in the cross-sectional area of cone inner segments with eccentricity implies a corresponding increase in photon catch rate.

References

Abramov, I., Gordon, J. and Chan, H. 1991. Color appearance in the peripheral retina: Effects of stimulus size. *Journal of the Optical Society of America, Part A*, 8:404–414.

Aguilar, M. and Stiles, W. S. 1954. Saturation of the rod mechanism of the retina at high levels of stimulation. *Optica Acta*, 1:59–65.

Amthor, F. R., Takahashi, E. S. and Oyster, C. W. 1989. Morphologies of rabbit retinal ganglion cells with concentric receptive fields. *Journal of Comparative Neurology*, 280:72–96.

Anstis, S. M. 1974. A chart demonstrating variations in acuity with retinal position. *Vision Research*, 14:589–592.

Applebury, M. L. and Hargrave, P. A. 1986. Molecular biology of the visual pigments. *Vision Research*, 26:1881–1895.

Atkins, P. W. 1983. *Molecular Quantum Mechanics*. New York, Oxford.

Atkins, P. W. 1993. *Creation Revisited*. New York, W. H. Freeman.

Attwell, D. 1990. The photoreceptor output synapse. *Progress in Retinal Research*, 9:337–362.

Attwell, D., Barbour, B. and Szatkowski, M. 1993. Nonvesicular release of neurotransmitter. *Neuron*, 11:401–407.

Attwell, D. and Mobbs, P. 1994. Neurotransmitter transporters. *Current Opinion in Neurobiology*, 4:353–359.

Bahill, A. T., Adler, D. and Stark, L. 1975. Most naturally occurring human saccades have magnitudes of 15 degrees or less. *Investigative Ophthalmology*, 14:468–469.

Barinaga, M. 1996. Researchers find the reset button for the fruit fly clock. *Science*, 271:1671–1672.

Barlow, H. B. 1952. Eye movements during fixation. *Journal of Physiology*, 116:290–306.

Barlow, H. B., Hill, R. M. and Levick, W. R. 1964. Retinal ganglion cells responding selectively to direction and speed of image motion in the rabbit. *Journal of Physiology*, 173:377–407.

Barrow, J. D. and Tipler, F. J. 1986. *The Anthropic Cosmological Principle*. Oxford, Oxford University Press.

Baylor, D. A., Nunn, B. J. and Schnapf, J. L. 1984. The photocurrent, noise and spectral sensitivity of rods of the monkey *Macaca fascicularis*. *Journal of Physiology*, 357:575–607.

Baylor, D. A., Matthews, G. and Yau, K.-W. 1980. Two components of electrical dark noise in toad retinal rod outer segments. *Journal of Physiology*, 309:591–621.

Baylor, D. A. and Nunn, B. J. 1986. Electrical properties of the light-sensitive conductance of rods of the salamander *Ambystoma tigrinum*. *Journal of Physiology*, 371:115–145.

Baylor, D. A. 1987. Photoreceptor signals and vision. Proctor lecture. *Investigative Ophthalmology and Visual Science*, 28:34–49.

Becker, W. 1991. Saccades. In R. H. S. Carpenter (ed.), *Eye Movements*, Series: *Vision and Visual Dysfunction*, Vol. 8, J. Cronly-Dillon (series editor). Houndsmills and London, Macmillian Press. pp. 95–137.

Bedford, R. E. and Wyszecki, G. 1957. Axial chromatic aberration of the human eye. *Journals of the Optical Society of America*, 47:564–565.

Behe, M. J. 1996. *Darwin's Black Box: The Biochemical Challenge to Evolution*. New York, Free Press/Simon and Schuster.

Berlin, B. and Kay, P. 1969. *Basic Color Terms: Their Universality and Evolution*. Berkeley, University of California Press.

Bernard, G. D. and Wehner, R. 1977. Functional similarities between polarization vision and color vision. *Vision Research*, 17:1019–1028.

Birge, R. R., Einterz, C. M., Knapp, H. M. and Murray, L. P. 1988. The nature of the primary photochemical events in rhodopsin and isorhodopsin. *Biophysical Journal*, 53:367–385.

Birge, R. R. 1990a. Nature of the primary photochemical events in rhodopsin and bacteriorhodopsin. *Biochimica et Biophysica Acta*, 1016:293–327.

Birge, R. R. 1990b. Photophysics and molecular electronic applications of the rhodopsins. *Annual Review of Physical Chemistry*, 41:683–733.

Bishop, P. O. and Rodieck, R. W. 1965. Discharge patterns of cat retinal ganglion cells. In P. W. Nye (ed.), *Proceedings of the Symposium on Information Processing in Sight Sensory Systems*. Pasadena, CA, California Institute of Technology. pp. 116–127.

Blasdel, G. G. and Lund, J. S. 1983. Termination of afferent axons in macaque striate cortex. *Journal of Neuroscience*, 3:1389–1413.

Bone, R. A., Landrum, J. T. and Cains, A. 1992. Optical density spectra of the macular pigment in vivo and in vitro. *Vision Research*, 32:105–110.

Bone, R. A., Landrum, J. T., Hime, G. W., Cains, A. and Zamor, J. 1993. Stereochemistry of the human macular carotenoids. *Investigative Ophthalmology and Visual Science*, 34:2033–2040.

Born, M. and Wolf, E. 1964. *Principles of Optics*. Oxford, Pergamon Press.

Borwein, B., Borwein, D., Medeiros, J. and McGowan, J. W. 1980. The ultrastructure of monkey foveal photoreceptors with special reference to the structure, shape, size, and spacing of the foveal cones. *American Journal of Anatomy*, 159:125–146.

Bowlby, J. 1990. *Charles Darwin: A New Life*. New York, W. W. Norton.

Boycott, B. B. 1988. Horizontal cells of mammalian retinae. *Neuroscience Research Supplement*, 8:597-5111.

Boycott, B. B. and Dowling, J. E. 1969. Organization of the primate retina: Light microscopy. *Philosophical Transactions of the Royal Society of London, B*, 255:109–184.

Boycott, B. B. and Wässle, H. 1974. The morphological types of ganglion cells of the domestic cat's retina. *Journal of Physiology*, 240:397–419.

Boycott, B. B. and Hopkins, J. M. 1991. Cone bipolar cells and cone synapses in the primate retina. *Visual Neuroscience*, 7:49–60.

Boycott, B. B. and Wässle, H. 1991. Morphological classification of bipolar cells of the primate retina. *European Journal of Neuroscience*, 3:1069–1088.

Brewster, D. 1965. *Memoirs of the Life, Writings, and Discoveries of Sir Issac Newton*, Volume 2, reprinted from the Edinburgh Edition of 1855. New York, Johnson Reprint Corporation.

Brown, K. T. 1969. A linear area centralis extending across the turtle retina and stabilized to the horizon by non-visual cues. *Vision Research*, 9:1053–1062.

Buchsbaum, G. and Gottschalk, A. 1983. Trichromacy, opponent colours coding and optimum colour information transmission in the retina. *Proceedings of the Royal Society of London B*, 220:89–113.

Buhl, E. H. and Peichl, L. 1986. Morphology of rabbit retinal ganglion cells projecting to the medial terminal nucleus of the accessory optic system. *Journal of Comparative Neurology*, 253:163–174.

Bullock, T. H. and Horridge, G. A. 1965. *Structure and Function in the Nervous Systems of Invertebrates* (2 volumes). San Francisco, W. H. Freeman.

Cajál, S. R. 1893. La rétine des vertébrés. *La Cellule*, 9:17–257. (English translation in Rodieck, 1973.)

Calkins, D. J., Schein, S. J., Tsukamoto, Y. and Sterling, P. 1994. M and L cones in macaque fovea connect to midget ganglion cells by different numbers of excitatory synapses. *Nature*, 371:70–72.

Calkins, D. J., Tsukamoto, Y. and Sterling, P. In press. Microcircuitry and mosaic of a blue/yellow ganglion cell in the primate retina. *Journal of Neuroscience* 18.

Calkins, D. J. (1998) Synaptic organization of cone pathways in the primate retina. In K. Gegenfurtner and L. Sharpe (eds.), *Color Vision: from Molecular Genetics to Perception*. Cambridge, Cambridge University Press.

Calvin, W. H. 1986. *The River that Flows Uphill: A Journey from the Big Bang to the Big Brain*. New York, MacMillian.

Carroll, L. 1872. *Alice's Adventures in Wonderland*. Boston, Lee and Sheppard.

Carroll, L. 1902. *Through the Looking Glass*. New York, Harper & Brothers.

Chun, M.-H., Grünert, U., Martin, P. R., et al. 1996. The synaptic complex of cones in the fovea and in the periphery of the macaque monkey retina. *Vision Research*, 36:3383–3395.

Churchland, P. 1986. *Neurophilosophy*. Cambridge, MA, MIT Press.

Colley, N. J., Cassill, J. A., Baker, E. K. and Zuker, C. S. 1995. Defective intracellular transport is the molecular basis of rhodopsin-dependent dominant retinal degeneration. *Proceedings of the National Academy of Science, USA*, 92:3070–3074.

Cooper, A. 1979. Energy uptake in the first step of visual excitation. *Nature*, 282:531–533.

Coyne, J. A. 1996. God in the details. *Nature*, 383:227–228.

Crawford, B. H. 1949. The scotopic visibility function. *Proceedings of the Physical Society, Section B*, 62:321–334.

Crawford, J. 1952. Living without a balancing mechanism. *New England Journal of Medicine*, 246:458–460.

Cronly-Dillon, J. R. and Gregory, R. L. 1991. *Evolution of the Eye and Visual System. Vision and Visual Dysfunction*, Vol. 2, Basingstoke, UK, Macmillan.

Curcio, C. A. 1987. Diameters of presumed cone apertures in human retina. *Journal of the Optical Society of America, Part A*, 4:70.

Curcio, C. A., Sloan, K. R., Kalina, R. E., et al. 1990. Human photoreceptor topography. *Journal of Comparative Neurology*, 292:497–523.

Curcio, C. A., Allen, K. A., Sloan, K. R., et al. 1991. Distribution and morphology of human cone photoreceptors stained with anti-blue opsin. *Journal of Comparative Neurology*, 312:610–624.

Curcio, C. A., Millican, C. L., Allen, K. A. and Kalina, R. E. 1993. Aging of the human photoreceptor mosaic: Evidence for selective vulnerability of rods in central retina. *Investigative Ophthalmology and Visual Science*, 34:3278–3296.

Curtis, H. D. 1901. On the limits of unaided vision. *Lick Observatory Bulletin*, 2:67–69.

Dacey, D. M. 1990. The dopaminergic amacrine cell. *Journal of Comparative Neurology*, 301:461–489.

Dacey, D. M. and Brace, S. 1992. A coupled network for parasol but not midget ganglion cells in the primate retina. *Visual Neuroscience*, 9:279–290.

Dacey, D. M. and Petersen, M. R. 1992. Dendritic field size and morphology of midget and parasol ganglion cells of the human retina. *Proceedings of the National Academy of Science, USA*, 89:9666–9670.

Dacey, D. M. 1993. The mosaic of midget ganglion cells in the human retina. *Journal of Neuroscience*, 13:5334–5355.

Dacey, D. M., Lee, B. B., Stafford, D. K., et al. 1996. Horizontal cells of the primate retina: Cone specificity without spectral opponency. *Science*, 271:656–659.

Dartnall, H. J. A. 1962. *The Photobiology of Visual Processes*. (Vol. 2 of *The Eye*, H. Davson, series ed.) New York, Academic Press. pp. 323–533.

Dawkins, R. 1990. *The Selfish Gene*. Oxford, Oxford University Press.

Dawkins, R. 1996. *The Blind Watchmaker: Why the Evidence of Evolution Reveals a Universe Without Design*. New York, W. W. Norton.

De Monasterio, F. M., McCrane, E. P., Newlander, J. K. and Schein, S. J. 1985. Density profile of blue-sensitive cones along the horizontal meridian of macaque retina. *Investigative Ophthalmology and Visual Science*, 26:289–302.

Deubel, H. 1987. Adaptivity of gain and direction in oblique saccades. In J. K. O'Regan and A. Lévy-Schoen (eds.), *Eye Movements: From Physiology to Ccognition*. New York, Elsevier. pp. 181–190.

Dogiel, A. S. 1891. Ueber die nervösen Elemente in der Retina des Menschen. *Archiv für Mikroskopische Anatomie*, 38:317–344.

Dowling, J. E. 1965. Foveal receptors of the monkey retina: Fine structure. *Science*, 147:57–59.

Dowling, J. 1987. *The Retina: An Approchable Part of the Brain*. Cambridge, MA, The Belknap Press of Harvard University Press.

Drasdo, N. and Fowler, C. W. 1974. Non-linear projection of the retinal image in a wide-angle schematic eye. *British Journal of Ophthalmology*, 58:709–714.

Dreher, B., Fukada, Y. and Rodieck, R. W. 1976. Identification, classification and anatomical segregation of cells with X-like and Y-like properties in the lateral geniculate nucleus of Old World primates. *Journal of Physiology*, 258:433–452.

Duensing, S. and Miller, B. 1979. The Cheshire Cat effect. *Perception*, 8:269–273.

Duke-Elder, S. 1961. *System of Ophthalmology: The Anatomy of the Visual System*. London, Kimpton.

Dusenbery, D. B. 1992. *Sensory Ecolory*. New York, W. H. Freeman.

Einstein, A. 1905. Über einen die Erzeugung und Verwandlung des Lichtes betreffenden heuristische Gesichtspunkt. *Annalen der Physik*, 17:132–148.

Epelboim, J., Booth, J. R. and Steinman, R. M. 1994. Reading unspaced text: Implications for theories of reading eye movements. *Vision Research*, 34:1735–1766.

Euler, L. 1736. *Mechanica, sive, Motus scientia analytice exposita*. Petropoli, Academiae Scientiarum.

Feller, W. 1968. *An Introduction to Probability Theory and Its Applications*, Vol. 1. New York, Wiley.

Feller, W. 1971. *An Introduction to Probability Theory and Its Applications*, Vol. 2. New York, Wiley.

Fesenko, E. E., Kolesnikov, S. S. and Lyubarsky, A. L. 1985. Induction by cyclic GMP of cationic conductance in plasma membrane of retinal rod outer segment. *Nature*, 313:310–313.

Feynman, R. P., Leighton, R. B. and Sands, M. 1964. *The Feynman Lectures on Physics*. Reading, MA, Addison-Wesley.

Feynman, R. P. 1985. *QED: The Strange Theory of Light and Matter*. Princeton, Princeton University Press.

Finn, J. T., Grunwald, M. E. and Yau, K.-W. 1996. Cyclic nucleotide-gated ion channels: An extended family with diverse functions. *Annual Review of Physiology*, 58:395–426.

Florence, S. L. and Kaas, J. H. 1992. Ocular dominance columns in area 17 of Old World macaque and talapoin monkeys: Complete reconstructions and quantitative analyses. *Visual Neuroscience*, 8:449–462.

Freedman, E. G. and Sparks, D. L. 1997. Eye-head coordination during head-unrestrained gaze shifts in rhesus monkey. *Journal of Neurophysiology*, 77:2328–2348.

Gal, A., Apfelstedt-Sylla, E., Janecke, A. R. and Zrenner, E. 1997. Rhodopsin mutations in inherited retinal dystrophies and dysfunctions. *Progress in Retinal and Eye Research*, 16:1:51–79.

Gillespie, N. C. 1987. Natural history, natural theology, and social order: John Ray and the "Newtonian ideology." *Journal of the History of Biology*, 20:1–49.

Gleason, H. A. 1961. *An Introduction to Descriptive Linguistics*. New York, Holt, Rinehart, and Winson.

Goodsell, D. S. 1993. *The Machinery of Life*. New York, Springer-Verlag.

Gray-Keller, M. P. and Detwiler, P. B. 1994. The calcium feedback signal in the phototransduction cascade of vertebrate rods. *Neuron*, 13: 849–861.

Green, C. B. and Besharse, J. C. 1996. Identification of a novel vertebrate circadian clock-regulated gene encoding the protein nocturnin. *Proceedings of the National Academy of Science, USA*, 93:14884–14888.

Gribbin, J. 1995. *Schrodinger's Kittens and the Search for Reality: Solving the Quantum Mysteries*. New York, Little Brown.

Grossman, G. E., Leigh, R. J., Bruce, E. N., Huebner, W. P., et al. 1989. Performance of the human vestibuloocular reflex during locomotion. *Journal of Neurophysiology*, 62:264–272.

Grossman, G. E. and Leigh, R. J. 1990. Instability of gaze during locomotion in patients with deficient vestibular function. *Annals of Neurology*, 27:528–532.

Grünert, U. and Martin, P. R. 1991. Rod bipolar cells in the macaque monkey retina: immunoreactivity and connectivity. *Journal of Neuroscience*, 11:2742–2758.

Hagins, W. A., Penn, R. D. and Yoshikami, S. 1970. Dark current and photocurrent in retinal rods. *Biophysical Journal*, 10:380–412.

Hamm, H. E. 1998. The many faces of G protein signaling. *Journal of Biological Chemistry*, 273:669–672.

Hampson, E. C. G. M., Vaney, D. I. and Weiler, R. 1992. Dopaminergic modulation of gap junction permeability between amacrine cells in mammalian retina. *Journal of Neuroscience*, 12:4911–4922.

Hardy, M. 1934. Observations on the innervation of the macula sacculi in man. *Anatomical Record*, 59:403–418.

Hargrave, P. A. 1995. Further directions for rhodopsin structure and function studies. *Behavioral and Brain Sciences*, 18:403–414.

Hárosi, F. I. and MacNichol, E. F. J. 1974. Visual pigments of goldfish cones: Spectral properties and dichroism. *Journal of General Physiology*, 63:279–304.

Hárosi, F. I. 1975. Absorption spectra and linear dichroism of some amphibian photoreceptors. *Journal of General Physiology*, 66:357–382.

Harrington, M.E. 1977. The ventral lateral geniculate nucleus and the intergeniculate leaflet: Interrelated structures in the visual and circadian systems. *Neuroscience and Biobehavioral Reviews*, 21:705–727.

Haynes, L. W., Kay, A. R. and Yau, K. W. 1986. Single cyclic GMP-activated channel activity in excised patches of rod outer segment membrane. *Nature*, 321: 66–70.

Hecht, S., Haig, C. and Chase, A. M. 1937. The influence of light adaptation on subsequent dark adaptation of the eye. *Journal of General Physiology*, 20:831–850.

Hecht, S. and Mandelbaum, J. 1939. The relation between vitamin A and dark adaptation. *Journal of the American Medical Association*, 112:1910–1916.

Hecht, S., Shlaer, S. and Pirenne, M. H. 1942. Energy, quanta, and vision. *Journal of General Physiology*, 25:819–840.

Heider, E. R. 1971. "Focal" color areas and the development of color names. *Developmental Psychology*, 4:447–455.

Heider, E. R. 1972a. Universals in color naming and memory. *Journal of Experimental Psychology*, 93:10–20.

Heider, E. R. 1972b. Probabilities, sampling, and ethnographic method: The case for Dani colour names. *Man*, 7:448–466.

Heider, E. R. and Olivier, D. C. 1972. The structure of the color space in naming and memory for two languages. *Cognitive Psychology*, 3:337–354.

Hildebrand, M. 1959. Motions of the running cheetah and horse. *Journal of Mammalogy*, 40:481–495.

Hildebrand, M. 1961. Further studies of the locomotion of the cheetah. *Journal of Mammalogy*. 42:84–91.

Hille, B. 1992. *Ionic Channels of Excitable Membranes*. Sunderland, MA, Sinauer.

Hofmann, K. P. and Heck, M. 1996. Light-induced protein-protein interactions on the rod photoreceptor disc membrane. *Biomembranes*, 11:141–198.

Hogan, M. J., Alvarado, J. A. and Weddell, J. E. 1971. *Histology of the Human Eye: An Atlas and Textbook*. Philadelphia, W. B. Saunders.

Holden, A. L., Hayes, B. P. and Fitzke, F. W. 1987. Retinal magnification factor at the ora terminals: A structural study of human and animal eyes. *Vision Research*, 27:1229–1235.

Horton, J. C. and Hoyt, W. F. 1991. The representation of the visual field in human striate cortex: A revision of the classic Holmes map. *Archives of Ophthalmology*, 109:816–824.

Horton, J. C. and Hocking, D. R. 1996. An adult-like pattern of ocular dominance columns in striate cortex of newborn monkeys prior to visual experience. *Journal of Neuroscience*, 16:1971–1807.

Hubel, D. H. and Wiesel, T. N. 1977. Ferrier lecture. Functional architecture of macaque monkey visual cortex. *Proceedings of the Royal Society of London [Biol]*, 198:1–59.

Hughes, A. 1971. Topographical relationships between the anatomy and physiology of the rabbit visual system. *Documenta Ophthalmologica*, 30:33–159.

Hughes, A. 1977. The topography of vision in mammals of contrasting life style: Comparative optics and retinal organisation. In F. Crescitelli (ed.), *Handbook of Sensory Physiology*, VII/5, Berlin, Springer-Verlag. pp. 613–756.

Hurlbutt, R. H. 1985. *Hume, Newton, and the Design Argument*. Lincoln, University of Nebraska Press.

Hurwitz, H. J. 1945. The statistical properties of polarized light. *Journal of the Optical Society of America*, 35:525–531.

Jacobs, G. H. 1993. The distribution and nature of colour vision among the mammals. *Biological Reviews*, 68:413–471.

Jan, L. Y. and Jan, Y. N. 1990. A superfamily of ion channels. *Nature*, 345:672.

Jeske, J. H. 1988. Meterological optics and radiometerology. In G. Fischer (ed.), *Physical and Chemical Properties of the Air*, 4, New York, Springer-Verlag. New Series, pp. 187–348.

Johnson, G. L. 1968. Ophthalmoscopic studies on the eyes of mammals. *Philosophical Transactions of the Royal Society of London, Series B*, 254:207–220.

Kaas, J. H. and Huerta, M. F. 1988. The subcortical visual system of primates. In H. D. Steklis and J. Erwin (eds.) *Comparative Primate Biology*, Vol. 4. New York, Alan R. Liss, Inc. pp. 327–391.

Kaiser, P. K. 1981. Photopic and mesopic photometry: Yesterday, today and tommorow. *Golden Jubilee of Colour in the CIE.*, Society of Dyers and Colourists, Bradford, England.

Kandel, E. R., Schwartz, J. H. and Jessell, T. M. 1995. *Essentials of Neural Science and Behavior*. Norwalk, CT, Appleton & Lange.

Karpen, J. W., Zimmerman, A. L., Stryer, L. and Baylor, D. A. 1988. Gating kinetics of the cyclic-GMP-activated channel of retinal rods: flash photolysis and voltage-jump studies. *Proceedings of the National Academy of Science, USA*, 85:1287–1291.

Karpen, J. W., Loney, D. A. and Baylor, D. A. 1992. Cyclic GMP-activated channels of salamander retinal rods: Spatial distribution and variation of responsiveness. *Journal of Physiology*, 448:257–274.

Kaupp, U. B., Niidome, T., Tanabe, T., Terada, S., 1989. Primary structure and functional expression from complementary DNA of the rod photoreceptor cyclic GMP-gated channel. *Nature*, 342:762–766.

Koutalos, Y., Nakatani, K. and Yau, K.-W. 1995. Cyclic GMP diffusion coefficient in rod photoreceptor outer segments. *Biophysical Journal*, 68:373–382.

Kirby, M. A. and Steineke, T. C. 1992. Morphogenesis of retinal ganglion cells during formation of the fovea in the *Rhesus* macaque. *Visual Neuroscience*, 9:603–616.

Kirschfeld, K. 1976. The resolution of lens and compound eyes. In F. Zetter and R. Weiler (eds.), *Neural Principles in Vision*, Berlin, Springer–Verlag. pp. 354–370.

Kirschfeld, K. 1982. Carotenoid pigments: Their possible role in protecting against photooxidation in eyes and photoreceptor cells. *Proceedings of the Royal Society of London [Biol]*, 216:71–85.

Kirschfeld, K. 1994. Tracking of small objects in front of a textured background by insects and vertebrates: Phenomena and neuronal basis. *Biological Cybernetics*, 70:407–415.

Knowles, A. and Dartnall, H. J. A. 1977. *The Photobiology of Vision*. (Vol. 2B of *The Eye*, H. Davson, series ed.) New York, Academic Press.

Kolb, H., Linberg, K. A. and Fisher, S. K. 1992. Neurons of the human retina: A Golgi study. *Journal of Comparative Neurology*, 318:147–187.

Kolb, H., Boycott, B. B. and Dowling, J. E. 1969. A second type of midget bipolar cell in the primate retina. *Philosophic Transactions of the Royal Society, Part B*, 255:177–184.

Kouyama, N. and Marshak, D. W. 1992. Bipolar cells specific for blue cones in the macaque retina. *Journal of Neuroscience*, 12:1233–1252.

Kowler, E. 1990. The role of visual and cognitive processes in the control of eye movement. In E. Kowler (ed.), *Eye Movements and Their Role in Visual and Cognitive Processes.* New York, Elsevier Science. pp. 1–70.

Kraft, T. W., Schneeweis, D. M. and Schnapf, J. L. 1993. Visual transduction in human rod photoreceptors. *Journal of Physiology*, 464:747–765.

Krinov, E. L. 1947. *Spectral Reflectance Properties of Natural Formations.* Aero Methods Laboratory, Academy of Sciences, USSR. English translation published by the National Research Council of Canada, Technical Translation TT-439, 1953, Ottawa.

Kuhn, T. S. 1978. *Black-Body Theory and the Quantum Discontinuity, 1894–1912.* Chicago, University of Chicago Press.

Kurada, P. and O'Tousa, J. E. 1995. Retinal degeneration caused by dominant rhodopsin mutations in *Drosophila*. *Neuron*, 14:571–579.

Lagnado, L., Cervetto, L. and McNaughton, P. A. 1992. Calcium homeostasis in the outer segments of retinal rods from the tiger salamander. *Journal of Physiology*, 455:111–142.

Lamb, T. D. 1995. Photoreceptor spectral sensitivities: common shape in the long-wavelength region. *Vision Research*, 35:3038–3091.

Land, M. F. 1981. Optics and vision in invertebrates. In H. Autrum (ed.), *Handbook of Sensory Physiology.* Berlin, Springer-Verlag. pp. 471–593.

Land, M. F. 1988. The optics of animal eyes. *Contemporary Physics*, 29:5:435–455.

Land, M. F. and Fernald, R. D. 1992. The evolution of eyes. *Annual Review of Neuroscience*, 15:1–29.

Landrum, J. T., Bone, R. A., Joa, H., Kilburn, M. D., Moore, L. L. and Sprague, K. E. 1997. A one year study of the macular pigment: The effect of 140 days of a lutein supplement. *Experimental Eye Research*, 65:55–62.

Leber, T. 1865. Untersuchungen über den Verlauf und Zusammenhang der Gefässe im menschlichen Auge. *Archiv für Ophthalmologie. (Graefe)*, 2:1.

Lee, B. B., Martin, P. R. and Valberg, A. 1988. The physiological basis of heterochromatic flicker photometry demonstrated in the ganglion cells of the macaque retina. *Journal of Physiology*, 404:323–347.

LeGrand, Y. 1957. *Light, Colour and Vision.* London, Chapman & Hall.

LeMahieu, D. L. 1976. *The Mind of William Paley: A Philosopher and His Age.* Lincoln, University of Nebraska Press.

Lennie, P., Pokorny, J. and Smith, V. C. 1993. Luminance. *Journal of the Optical Society of America, A*, 10:1283–1293.

Levi, L. 1980. *Applied Optics: A Guide to Optical System Design.* New York, John Wiley.

Levick, W. R. 1967. Receptive fields and trigger features of ganglion cells in the visual streak of the rabbit's retina. *Journal of Physiology*, 188:285–307.

Lewis, G. N. 1926. The conservation of photons. *Nature*, 118:874–875.

Liang, J., Williams, D. R. and Miller, D. T. 1997. Supernormal vision and high-resolution retinal imaging through adaptive optics. *Journal of the Optical Society of America, Part A*, 14:2884–2892.

Linsenmeier, R. A., Frishman, L. J., Jakiela, H. G. and Enroth Cugell, C. 1982. Receptive field properties of x and y cells in the cat retina derived from contrast sensitivity measurements. *Vision Research*, 22:1173–1183.

Luria, S. M. 1958. Absolute threshold for extremely wide fields. *Journal of the Optical Society of America*, 48:884–886.

Lythgoe, J. N. 1979. *The Ecology of Vision.* Oxford, Clarendon Press.

Mach, E. 1914. *The Analysis of Sensations.* Trans. by C. M. Williams. Chicago, Open Court.

Maor, E. 1994. *E: The Story of a Number.* Princeton, Princeton University Press.

Mariani, A. P. 1982. Biplexiform cells: Ganglion cells of the primate retina that contact photoreceptors. *Science*, 216:1134–1136.

Mariani, A. P. 1983. Giant bistratified bipolar cells in monkey retina. *Anatomical Record*, 206:215–220.

Mariani, A. P. 1984. The neuronal organization of the outer plexiform layer of the primate retina. *International Review of Cytology*, 86:285–320.

Mariani, A. P. 1985. Multiaxonal horizontal cells in the retina of the tree shrew, *Tupaia glis*. *Journal of Comparative Neurology*, 233:553–563.

Mariani, A. P. 1990. Amacrine cells of the rhesus monkey retina. *Journal of Comparative Neurology*, 301:382–400.

McKee, S. P. and Nakayama, K. 1984. The detection of motion in the peripheral visual field. *Vision Research*, 24:25–32.

McNaughton, P. A., Cervetto, L. and Nunn, B. J. 1986. Measurement of the intracellular free calcium concentration in salamander rods. *Nature*, 322:261–263.

Milam, A. H., Dacey, D. M. and Dizhoor, A. M. 1993. Recoverin immunoreactivity in mammalian cone bipolar cells. *Visual Neuroscience*, 10:1–12.

Morrison, P. 1982. *Powers of Ten*. New York, W. H. Freeman.

Nakatani, K. and Yau, K. W. 1988. Guanosine 3′,5′-cyclic monophosphate-activated conductance studied in a truncated rod outer segment of the toad. *Journal of Physiology*, 395:731–753.

Nathans, J. and Hogness, D. S. 1983. Isolation, sequence analysis, and intron-exon arrangement of the gene encoding bovine rhodopsin. *Cell*, 34:807–814.

Nathans, J., Thomas, D. and Hogness, D. S. 1986. Molecular genetics of human color vision: The genes encoding blue, green, and red pigments. *Science*, 232:193–202.

Nathans, J., Merbs, S. L., Sung, C. H., Weitz, C. J. and Wang, Y. 1992a. Molecular genetics of human visual pigments. *Annual Review of Genetics*, 26: 403–424.

Nathans, J., Sung, C. H., Weitz, C. J., Davenport, C. M., Merbs, S. L. and Wang, Y. 1992b. Visual pigments and inherited variation in human vision. In *Sensory Transduction*, New York, Rockefeller University Press.

Navarro, R., Artal, P. and Williams, D. R. 1993. Modulation transfer of the human eye as a function of retinal eccentricity. *Journal of the Optical Society of America, Part A*, 10:201–212.

Newton, I. 1952. *Opticks*. New York, Dover.

Norren, D. V. and Vos, J. J. 1974. Spectral transmission of the human ocular media. *Vision Research*, 14:1237–1243.

Nussbaum, J. J., Pruett, R. C. and Delori, F. C. 1981. Macular yellow pigment: The first 200 years. *Retina*, 1:296–310.

Okano, T., Kojima, D., Fukada, Y., et al. 1992. Primary structures of chicken cone visual pigments: Vertebrate rhodopsins have evolved out of cone visual pigments. *Proceedings of the National Academy of Science, USA*, 89:5932–5936.

Østerberg, G. 1935. Topography of the layer of rods and cones in the human retina. *Acta Ophthalmologica*, 6:1–103.

Ovchinnikov, Y. A., Abdulaev, N. G., Feigina, M. Y., Artamonov, I. D., Zolotarev, A. S., Miroshnikov, A. I., Martynov, V. I., Kustina, M. B., Kudelin, A. B. and Bogachuk, A. S. 1982. The complete amino acid sequence of visual rhodopsin. *Bioorg. Khim.*, 8:1011–1104, 1424–1427.

Oyster, C. W. 1968. The analysis of image motion by the rabbit retina. *Journal of Physiology*, 199:613–635.

Oyster, C. W., Takahashi, E. and Collewijn, H. 1972. Direction-selective retinal ganglion cells and control of optokinetic nystagmus in the rabbit. *Vision Research*, 12:183–193.

Oyster, C. W. In press. *The Human Eye: its Structure and Function*. Sunderland, MA, Sinauer.

Packard, E. 1994. *Imagining the Universe: A Visual Journey*. New York, Perigee Books, Berkley Publishing Group.

Pagon, R. A. 1988. Retinitis pigmentosa. *Survey of Ophthalmology*, 33:137–177.

Paley, W. 1802. *Natural Theology: Evidences of the Existence and Attributes of the Deity. Collected from the Appearances of Nature*. Philadelphia, H. Maxwell. Reprinted 1986, Charlottesville, VA: Lincoln-Rembrant.

Partridge, L. D. 1982. The good enough calculi of evolving control systems: evolution is not engineering. *American Journal of Physiology*, 242:173–177.

Pirenne, M. H. 1962. Absolute threshold and quantum effect. In H. Davson (ed.), *The Eye*, Vol. 2. New York, Academic Press. pp. 123–140.

Pirie, A. 1966. The chemistry and structure of the tapetum lucidum in animals. In O. Graham-Jones (ed.), *Aspects of Comparative Ophthalmology*. Oxford, Pergamon Press. pp. 57–68.

Polyak, S. 1941. *The Retina*. Chicago, University of Chicago Press.

Polyak, S. 1957. *The Vertebrate Visual System*. Chicago, University of Chicago Press.

Pugh, E. N. J. and Lamb, T. D. 1990. Cyclic GMP and calcium: The internal messengers of excitation and adaptation in vertebrate photoreceptors. *Vision Research*, 30:1923–1948.

Pugh, E. N. Jr. and Lamb, T. D. 1993. Amplification and kinetics of the activation steps in phototransduction. *Biochimica et Biophysica Acta*, 1141:111–149.

Purves, D., Augustine, G. J., Fitzpatrick, D., Katz, L. C., et al. 1997. *Neuroscience*. Sunderland, MA, Sinauer.

Rao-Mirotznik, R., Harkins, A. B., Buchsbaum, G. and Sterling, P. 1995. Mammalian rod terminal: Architecture of a binary synapse. *Neuron*, 14:561–569.

Ratto, G. M., Payne, R., Owen, W. G. and Tsien, R. Y. 1988. The concentration of cytosolic free calcium in vertebrate rod outer segments measured with fura-2. *Journal of Neuroscience*, 8:3240–3246.

Reading, V. M. and Weale, R. A. 1974. Macular pigment and chromatic aberration. *Journal of the Optical Society of America*, 64:231–234.

Reppert, S. M. and Weaver, D. R. 1997. Forward genetic approach strikes gold: Cloning of a mammalian clock gene. *Cell*, 89:487–490.

Roach, F. E. and Gordon, J. L. 1973. *The Light of the Night Sky*. Boston, D. Reidel.

Robinson, D. 1981. Control of eye movements. In J. M. Brookhart and V. B. Mountcastle (eds.), *Handbook of Physiology*. Baltimore, Waverly Press. pp. 1275–1320.

Rodieck, R. W. 1965. Quantitative analysis of cat retinal ganglion cell response to visual stimuli. *Vision Research*, 5:583–601.

Rodieck, R. W. 1973. *The Vertebrate Retina: Principles of Structure and Function*. San Francisco, W. H. Freeman.

Rodieck, R. W. and Brening, R. K. 1983. Retinal ganglion cells: properties, types, genera, pathways and trans-species comparisons. *Brain Behaviour and Evolution*, 23:121–164.

Rodieck, R. W. 1988. The primate retina. In H. D. Steklis and J. Erwin (eds.), *Comparative Primate Biology*, Vol. 4. New York, Alan R. Liss, Inc. pp. 203–278.

Rodieck, R. W. 1989. Starburst amacrine cells of the primate retina. *Journal of Comparative Neurology*, 285:18–37.

Rodieck, R. W. 1991. Which cells code for color? In A. Valverg and B. B. Lee (eds.), *From Pigments to Perception: Advances in Understanding Visual Processes*. New York, Plenum Press. pp. 83–89.

Rodieck, R. W. and Marshak, D. W. 1992. Spatial density and distribution of choline acetyltransferase immunoreactive cells in human, macaque, and baboon retinas. *Journal of Comparative Neurology*, 321:46–64.

Rodieck, R. W. and Watanabe, M. 1993. Survey of the morphology of macaque retinal ganglion cells that project to the pretectum, superior colliculus, and parvicellular laminae of the lateral geniculate nucleus. *Journal of Comparative Neurology*, 338:289–303.

Rodieck, R. W., Brening, R. K. and Watanabe, M. 1993. The origin of parallel visual pathways. In R. Shapley and D. M. K. Lam (eds.), *Contrast Sensitivity: Proceedings of the Retina Research Foundation Symposia*, Vol. 5. Cambridge MA, The MIT Press. 117–144.

Röhrenbeck, J., Wässle, H. and Boycott, B. B. 1989. Horizontal cells in the monkey retina: Immunocytochemical staining with antibodies against calcium binding proteins. *European Journal of Neuroscience*, 1:407–420.

Rushton, W. A. H. (1962). The retinal organization of vision in vertebrates. *Symposia of the Society for Experimental Biology: Number XVI, Biological Receptor Mechanisms*, Society for Experimental Biology.

Sandmann, D., Boycott, B. B. and Peichl, L. 1996a. The horizontal cells of artiodactyl retinae: A comparison with Cajal's descriptions. *Visual Neuroscience*, 13:735–746.

Sandmann, E., Boycott, B. B. and Peichl, L. 1996b. Blue-cone horizontal cells in the retinae of horses and other *Equidae*. *Journal of Neuroscience*, 16:3381–3396.

Schein, S. J. 1988. Anatomy of macaque fovea and spatial densities of neurons in foveal representation. *Journal of Comparative Neurology*, 269:479–505.

Schnapf, J. L., Nunn, B. J., Meister, M. and Baylor, D.A. 1990. Visual transduction in cones of the monkey *Macaca fascicularis*. *Journal of Physiology*, 427:681–713.

Schneeweis, D. M. and Schnapf, J. L. 1995. Photovoltage of rods and cones in the macaque retina. *Science*, 268:1053–1056.

Schoenlein, R. W., Peteanu, L. A., Mathies, R. A. and Shank, C. V. 1991. The first step in vision: Femtosecond isomerization of rhodopsin. *Science*, 254:412–415.

Schrödinger, E. 1920. Grundlinien einer theorie der Farbenmetrik im Tagessehen. *Annalen der Physik*, 63:481–520.

Sharp, N. C. C. 1997. Timed running speed of a cheetah (*Acinonyx jubatus*). *Journal of Zoology*, 241:493–494.

Shurcliff, W. A. and Ballard, S. S. 1964. *Polarized Light*. Princeton NJ, Van Nostrand.

Silveira, L. C. and Perry, V. H. 1991. The topography of magnocellular projecting ganglion cells (M-ganglion cells) in the primate retina. *Neuroscience*, 40:217–237.

Singer, W. 1993. Neuronal representations, assemblies and temporal coherence. *Progress in Brain Research*, 95:461–474.

Sitaramayya, A., Harkness, J., Parkes, J. H., Gonzalez, O. C. and Liebman, P. A. 1986. Kinetic studies suggest that light-activated cyclic GMP phosphodiesterase is a complex with G-protein subunits. *Biochemistry*, 25:651–656.

Skavenski, A. A., Hansen, R. M., Steinman, R. M. and Winterson, B. J. 1979. Quality of retinal image stabilization during small natural and artificial body rotations in man. *Vision Research*, 19:675–683.

Smith, W. C., Adamus, G., Van Der Well, H., Timmers, A., Palczewski, K., Ulshafer, R., J., Hargrave, P. A. and McDowell, J. H. 1995. Alligator rhodopsin: Sequence and biochemical properties. *Experimental Eye Research*, 61:569–579.

Snodderly, D. M., Brown, P. K., Delori, F. C. and Auran, J. D. 1984a. The macular pigment. I. Absorbance spectra, localization, and discrimination from other yellow pigments in primate retinas. *Investigative Ophthalmology and Visual Science*, 25:660–673.

Snodderly, D. M., Auran, J. D. and Delori, F. C. 1984b. The macular pigment. II. Spatial distribution in primate retinas. *Investigative Ophthalmology and Visual Science*, 25:674–685.

Snodderly, D. M., Handelman, G. J. and Adler, A. J. 1991. Distribution of individual macular pigment carotenoids in central retina of macaque and squirrel monkeys. *Investigative Ophthalmology and Visual Science*, 32:268–279.

Snodderly, D. M., Weinhaus, R. S. and Choi, J. C. 1992. Neural-vascular relationships in central retina of macaque monkeys (*Macaca fascicularis*). *Journal of Neuroscience*, 12:1169–1193.

Soemmerring, S. T. 1818. *Abbildungen des menschlichen auges*. Frankfurt am Main, Varrentrapp und Wenner.

Sparks, D. L. and Mays, L. E. 1990. Signal transformations required for the generation of saccadic eye movements. *Annual Review Neuroscience*, 13:309–336.

Stafford, D. K. and Dacey, D. M. 1997. Physiology of the A1 amacrine: A spiking, axon-bearing interneuron of the macaque monkey retina. *Visual Neuroscience*, 14:507–522.

Steinberg, R. H., Fisher, S. K. and Anderson, D. H. 1980. Disc morphogenesis in vertebrate photoreceptors. *Journal of Comparative Neurology*, 190:501–508.

Steinman, R. M. and Levinson, J. Z. 1990. The role of eye movement in the detection of contrast and spatial detail. In E. Kowler (ed.), *Eye Movements and Their Role in Visual and Cognitive Processes*. New York, Elsevier. pp. 115–211.

Sterling, P. 1990. Retina. In G. M. Shepherd (ed.), *The Synaptic Organization of the Brain*. New York, Oxford University Press. pp. 170–213.

Stiles, W. S. and Burch, J. M. 1959. N.P.L. colour-matching investigation: Final report. *Optica Acta*, 6:1–26.

Stiles, W. S. 1978. *Mechanisms of Color Vision*. London, Academic Press.

Stockman, A., MacLeod, D. I. A. and Johnson, N. E. 1993. Spectral sensitivities of the human cones. *Journal of the Optical Society of America*, 10:2491–2521.

Strettoi, E. and Masland, R. H. 1996. The number of unidentified amacrine cells in the mammalian retina. *Proceedings of the National Academy of Science, USA*, 93:14906–14911.

Stryer, L. 1987. Visual transduction: Design and recurring motifs. *Chemica Scripta*, 27B:161–171.

Stryer, L. 1995. *Biochemistry*. New York, W. H. Freeman.

Tartuferi, F. 1887. Sull'anatomia della retina. *International Monatsschrift Anatomie Physiologie*, 4:421–441.

Tauchi, M. and Masland, R. H. 1985. Local order among the dendrites of an amacrine cell population. *Journal of Neuroscience*, 5:2494–2501.

Taylor, W. R. and Baylor, D. A. 1995. Conductance and kinetics of single cGMP-activated channels in salamander rod outer segments. *Journal of Physiology*, 483:567–582.

Thompson, D. W. 1992. *On Growth and Form: The Complete Revised Edition*. New York, Dover.

Vaney, D. I. 1994a. Territorial organization of direction-selective ganglion cells in rabbit retina. *Journal of Neuroscience*, 14:6301–6316.

Vaney, D. I. 1994b. Patterns of neuronal coupling in the retina. *Progress in Retinal and Eye Research*, 13:301–355.

Vaney, D. 1995. Cell coupling in the retina. In D. C. Spray and R. Dermietzel (eds.), *Gap Junctions in the Nervous System*. R. G. Landes Company. Austin, TX.

Vos, J. J., Walraven, J. and van Meeteren, A. 1976. Light profiles of the foveal image of a point source. *Vision Research*, 16:215–219.

Wald, G. 1945. Human vision and the spectrum. *Science*, 101:653–658.

Wald, G. and Griffin, D. R. 1947. The change in refractive power of the human eye in dim and bright light. *Journal of the Optical Society of America*, 37:321.

Wald, G., Brown, P. K. and Kennedy, D. 1957. The visual system of the alligator. *Journal of General Physiology*, 40:703–713.

Wald, G. 1965. Frequency or wavelength? *Science*, 150:1239–1240.

Walls, G. L. 1942. *The Vertebrate Eye and its Adaptive Radiation*. Michigan, Cranbrook Press.

Wandell, B. A. 1995. *Foundations of Vision*. Sunderland, MA, Sinauer Associates.

Wässle, H., Boycott, B. B. and Röhrenbeck, J. 1989. Horizontal cells in the monkey retina: Cone connections and dendritic network. *European Journal of Neuroscience*, 1:421–435.

Wässle, H. and Boycott, B. B. 1991. Functional architecture of the mammalian retina. *Physiological Reviews*, 71:447–480.

Watanabe, M. and Rodieck, R. W. 1989. Parasol and midget ganglion cells of the primate retina. *Journal of Comparative Neurology*, 289:434–454.

Wehner, R. 1989. Neurobiology of polarization vision. *Trends in Neuroscience*, 12:353–359.

Weinstein, C. and Arnulf, A. 1946. Contribution à l'étude des seuils de perception de l'oeil. *Communication des laboratoires de l'Institut d'optique* Tome 2, Fasc. 1, Communication No. 19:1–43.

Wertheim, T. 1894. Über die indirekte Sehschärfe. *Psychologie & Physiologie der Sinnesorgane*, 7:173–187.

Weymouth, F. W. 1958. Visual sensory units and the minimal angle of resolution. *American Journal of Ophthalmology*, 46:102–113.

Whewell, W. 1847. *The Philosophy of the Inductive Sciences*. Volume 1, Book VIII: *The Philosophy of the Classificatory Sciences*. London, John W. Parker. Reprinted 1967, New York, Johnson Reprint Corporation.

World Meteorological Organization. 1982. Commission for Instruments and Methods of Observation, Abridged Final Report No. 590.

Wray, G. A., Levinton, J. S. and Shapiro, L. H. 1996. Molecular evidence for deep precambrian divergences among metazoan phyla. *Science*, 274:568–573.

Wright, A. A. and Cumming, W. W. 1971. Color-naming functions for the pigeon. *Journal of Experimental Analysis of Behavior*, 15:7–17.

Wyszecki, G. and Stiles, W. S. 1982. *Color Science. Concepts and Methods, Quantitative Data and Formulas*, 2nd ed. New York, John Wiley.

Yarbus, 1967. *Eye movements and Vision*. New York, Plenum Press, 1967.

Yau, K.-W. 1994. Phototransduction mechanism in retinal rods and cones: The Friedenwald Lecture. *Investigative Ophthalmology and Visual Science*, 35:9–32.

Yau, K.-W. and Nakatani, K. 1985. Light-suppressible, cyclic GMP-sensitive conductance in the plasma membrane of a truncated rod outer segment. *Nature*, 317:252–255.

Yau, K.-W. and Baylor, D. A. 1989. Cyclic GMP-activated conductance of retinal photoreceptor cells. *Annual Review of Neuroscience*, 12:289–327.

Young, H. M. and Vaney, D. I. 1991. Rod-signal interneurons in the rabbit retina: 1. Rod bipolar cells. *Journal of Comparative Neurology*, 310:139–153.

Young, R. W. 1969. The organization of vertebrate photoreceptor cells. In . B. R. Straatsma, M. O. Hall, R. A. Allen and F. Crescitelli (eds.), *The Retina: Morphology, Function and Clinical Characteristics*. Berkeley, University of California Press. pp. 177–210.

Young, R. W. 1970. Visual cells. *Scientific American*, 223:81–91.

Young, R. W. 1971. Shedding of discs from rod outer segments in the rhesus monkey. *Journal of Ultrastructure Research*, 34:190–203.

Yuodelis, C. and Hendrickson, A. 1986. A qualitative and quantitative analysis of the human fovea during development. *Vision Research*, 26:847–855.

Zagotta, W. N. and Siegelbaum, S. A. 1996. Structure and function of cyclic nucleotide-gated channels. *Annual Review of Neuroscience*, 19:235–263.

Zhukovsky, E. A. and Oprian, D. D. 1989. Effect of carboxylic acid side chains on the absorption maximum of visual pigments. *Science*, 246:928–930.

Zimmerman, A. L., Yamanaka, G., Eckstein, F., Baylor, D. A. and Stryer, L. 1985. Interaction of hydrolysis-resistant analogs of cyclic GMP with the phosphodiesterase and light-sensitive channel of retinal rod outer segments. *Proceedings of the National Academy of Science, USA*, 82: 8813–8817.

Zimmerman, A. L. and Baylor, D. A. 1986. Cyclic GMP-sensitive conductance of retinal rods consists of aqueous pores. *Nature*, 321:70–72.

Zuker, C. S., Cowman, A. F. and Rubin, G. M. 1985. Isolation and structure of a rhodopsin gene from *D. melanogaster*. *Cell*, 40:851–858.

Index

ABOUT THE BOOK

Editor: **Peter Farley**
Project Editors: **Kerry L. Falvey, Paula Noonan**
Copy Editor: **Norma Roche**
Production Manager: **Christopher Small**
Book Production: **Janice M. Holabird, Wendy Beck**
Illustration Program: **R. W. Rodieck**
Book and Cover Design: **R. W. Rodieck**
Cover Manufacturer: **Henry N. Sawyer Company, Inc.**
Book Manufacturer: **Courier Companies, Inc.**